AMERICAN ARTISTS IN PARIS, 1918–1939

A TRANSATLANTIC AVANT-GARDE

AMERICAN ARTISTS IN PARIS, 1918–1939

A TRANSATLANTIC AVANT-GARDE

EDITED BY
SOPHIE LÉVY

ESSAYS BY
CHRISTIAN DEROUET
EMMANUELLE DE L'ÉCOTAIS
BRONWYN A. E. GRIFFITH
JANINE MILEAF
JOCELYNE ROTILY
KENNETH E. SILVER
GAIL STAVITSKY

university of california press
berkeley   los angeles

musée
d'art **américain** giverny
terra
foundation
for the arts

Published in conjunction
with the exhibition
**A Transatlantic Avant-Garde:
American Artists in Paris,
1918–1939**
organized by Sophie Lévy,
Musée d'Art Américain Giverny,
France.

EXHIBITION
VENUES

Musée d'Art Américain Giverny (MAAG),
France
August 31, 2003 – November 30, 2003

Tacoma Art Museum (TAM),
Tacoma, Washington
December 18, 2003 – March 28, 2004

Terra Museum of American Art
(TMAA), Chicago, Illinois
April 17, 2004 – June 27, 2004

The initials of the museums appear in
the captions of the plates in order to
indicate which works are exhibited at
each venue.

EXHIBITION

Curator
Sophie Lévy,
with the assistance of
Katherine Bourguignon and
Bronwyn A. E. Griffith

General coordination
Vanessa Lecomte

Loan coordination in New York
Megan Fox Kelly, Art Advisory

Registrar
Cathy Ricciardelli

Public relations
Géraldine Raulot and
Stacy Bolton Communications, in
New York

MUSÉE D'ART AMÉRICAIN GIVERNY, FRANCE

Registrar
Olivier Touren

Conservation
Véronique Roca

Exhibition design
Hugues Fontenas

Graphic design
Cyrille Fourmy (display panels) and
LD Publicité,
Guillaume Lesourd (production) and
Michel Lepetitdidier (invitation and
poster design)

Public relations
Catherine Dufayet Communication

Installation
Tom Skwerski, Didier Dauvel,
Didier Guiot

Education
Véréna Herrgott and
Veerle Thielemans, with the
assistance of Nathalie Aufort,
Anne Candau, Hélène Furminieux,
Marie-David Grégoire,
Renata Hernandez, Sophie Le Cam

Interns
Fanny Beaufrère,
Eran Guterman, Eliza Johnson,
Anne Rana, Adam Redwine,
Lia Wong

TACOMA ART MUSEUM, TACOMA, WASHINGTON

Curatorial coordination
Patricia McDonnell,
with Zoe Donnell and Rock Hushka

Registrar
Janae Huber

Exhibition and design installation
Vincent Warner

Public relations
Courtenay Chamberlin
with Chelsea Perry

Education
Anna Castillo
with Carri Campbell, Sarah Dillon,
Jason Sobottka, Sharon Winters,
Tara Young

Administrative coordination
Janeanne Upp
with Jessica Balsam, Rod Bigelow,
Kathe Frahm, Marge Gillies,
Kevin Guenzi, Al Haskins,
Sara Inveen, Jeanette Jones,
Elliott Kay, Leslie Martin Kinkade,
Maria Lautt, Arthur Navarro,
Leslie Patton, Nancy Thompson,
Katrina Townsley

TERRA MUSEUM OF AMERICAN ART, CHICAGO, ILLINOIS

Curatorial coordination
Elizabeth Kennedy,
with the assistance of Shelly Roman,
Laura Kalas and Leo Kelly

Registrar
Cathy Ricciardelli, with the
assistance of Kristina Bottomley

Conservation
Kristin Lister

Exhibition design and display panels
Tom Skwerski

Installation
Tom Skwerski and Tim Duncan

Marketing
Kiran Advani, Tom Wawzenek,
Caren Yusem

Education
Molly Carter, Dori Jacobsohn, Ann
Meehan, Miguel Pasqual, Stefanie
Shanebrook, Jenny Siegenthaler,
Elizabeth Whiting

CATALOGUE

Published by
**Musée d'Art Américain Giverny,
France**

in association with

University of California Press
Berkeley and Los Angeles, California

University of California Press, Ltd.
London, England

Edited and produced by
Francesca Rose
with the assistance of
Claire Guilloteau

Translation from French
Deke Dusinberre (p. 46–47,
55–62, 64–65, 81–90, 98–99,
139–150, 223–231, 239–250)

Copyedited by
Christine Schultz-Touge

Design by
Pascal Guth

Copyright © 2003 by Terra
Foundation for the Arts

Musée d'Art Américain Giverny
Terra Foundation for the Arts
99, rue Claude Monet,
27620 Giverny, France
www.maag.org

Cataloging-in-Publication Data is on
file with the Library of Congress

ISBN: 0-520-24207-6 Paperback

Manufactured in Italy

10 9 8 7 6 5 4 3 2 1

The paper used in this publication meets
the minimum requirements of ANSI/NISO
Z39 .48–1992 (R 1997) *(Permanence of Paper)*.

Cultural links have long been among the important
ties binding the United States and France. Indeed, French and American artists have influenced each other to such
an extent that it is impossible today to imagine the art of one country without the influence of the other.
The interwar period was one of the most fruitful times for artistic exchange, as Americans in Paris absorbed trends
in the French avant-garde and reshaped them through their own artistic lenses. American artists, in turn,
introduced new elements of modernism to their Parisian counterparts, contributing to a dynamic process of artistic
creativity and innovation. This outstanding exhibition is a wonderful opportunity for visitors to the Musée d'Art
Américain Giverny to see some of the masterpieces of the interwar period, including works by Alexander Calder,
Stuart Davis, Charles Demuth, Lee Miller, and Man Ray. The exhibition will subsequently travel to the United States,
underscoring the cross-cultural character of this American art inspired by France.

THE HONORABLE **HOWARD H. LEACH**
AMBASSADOR OF
THE UNITED STATES OF AMERICA
TO FRANCE

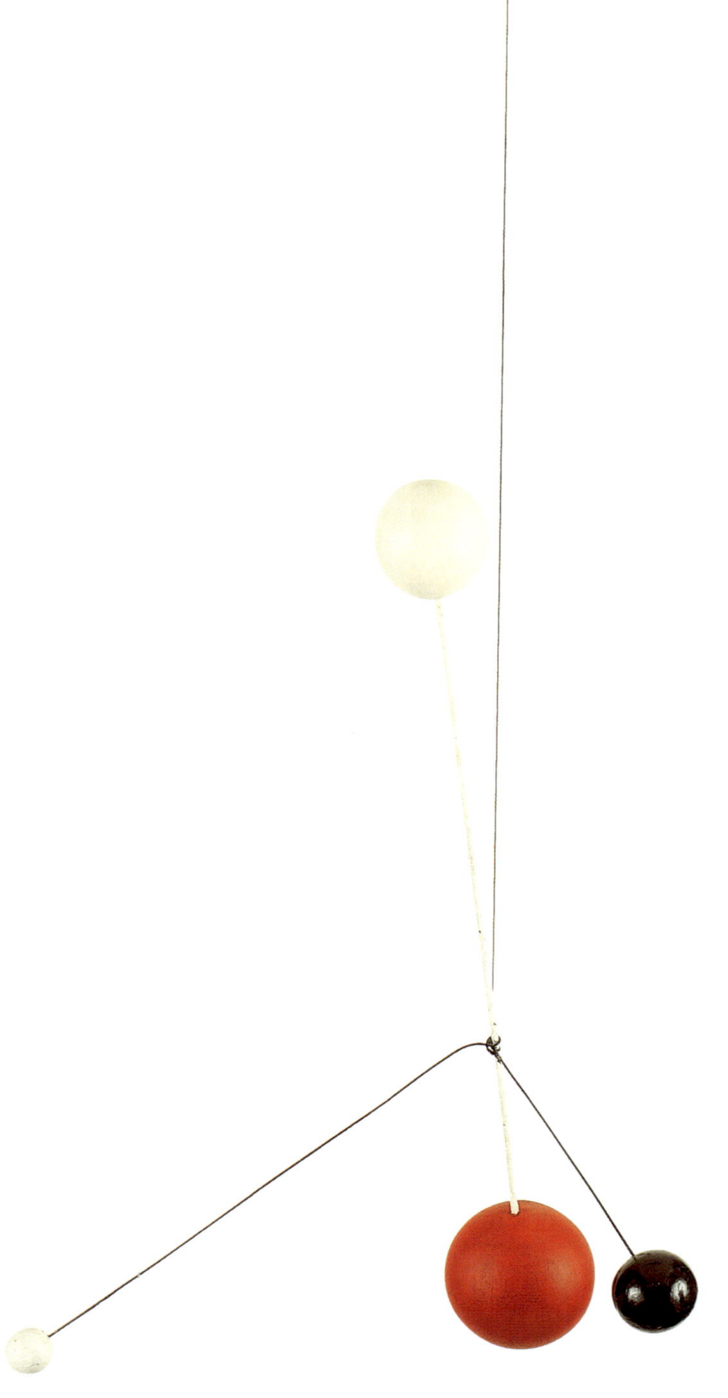

ALEXANDER CALDER
MOBILE, C. 1931
METAL AND PAINTED WOOD, 35 X 45 CM
PRIVATE COLLECTION
MAAG, TAM, TMAA

Paris has always been open to outside influences and foreign artists, welcoming diverse cultures from around the world.

The exhibition organized by the Musée d'Art Américain Giverny reveals that American artists significantly contributed to the burgeoning artistic production in Paris during the interwar period. At a time marked by international tensions and nationalist tendencies, Paris remained a forum opened to artists from both continents who, to the benefit of all, forged a resolutely modern path for art. It was largely due to this fertile exchange and intense dialogue that Paris emerged as the capital of new trends and avant-garde initiatives.

Reciprocal glances, shared inspiration, mutual fascination: the ties that bound Paris and America are apparent in the rarely seen artworks on display in *A Transatlantic Avant-Garde: American Artists in Paris, 1918–1939.* Each work testifies to the extraordinary artistic and cultural vitality that characterizes a period that hovered between hope and fear.

I therefore urge all art lovers to discover the boundless creativity of Americans who, from Man Ray and Stuart Davis to John Storrs, Lee Miller, Kay Sage, and Isamu Noguchi, helped to make Paris the artistic capital of the world. Furthermore, I would like to express the hope that artists of today and tomorrow, on both sides of the Atlantic, will continue to use their art to strengthen friendship and understanding between peoples.

BERTRAND DELANOË
MAYOR OF PARIS

ACKNOWLEDGMENTS

We would like to express our gratitude to both the Ambassador of the United States of America to France, the Honorable Howard H. Leach, and the Mayor of Paris, Bertrand Delanoë, for placing this exhibition under their patronage.

The exhibition and its related catalogue *A Transatlantic Avant-Garde: American Artists in Paris, 1918–1939* required the dedicated involvement of many participants. We are particularly indebted to the Tacoma Art Museum particularly Director, Janeanne Upp, as well as its Curator, Patricia McDonnell, and to the Terra Museum of American Art for supporting this initiative from start to finish. Staffs from both museums of the Terra Foundation for the Arts (Terra Museum of American Art and Musée d'Art Américain Giverny) provided their expertise in the many realms required for the success of this ambitious project. We are extremely grateful for their assistance.

Megan Fox Kelly deserves special mention for her decisive role in the final stages of the organization of the exhibition. Many loans were made possible thanks to her diplomatic negotiations with art collectors and American institutions.

Among the authors, we are particularly grateful to Christian Derouet, Chief Curator at the Musée National d'Art Moderne – Centre Georges Pompidou, and Emmanuelle de L'Écotais, Curatorial Officer at the Musée d'Art Moderne de la Ville de Paris, who patiently and generously shared their sources and information with us.

We are equally indebted to numerous museums, institutions, foundations and galleries for their generous loans and invaluable assistance throughout the preparation of the exhibition. We would particularly like to thank, in the United States:

Jeremy Adamson,
Prints and Photographs Division, Library of Congress, Washington D.C.;

Maxwell L. Anderson,
Whitney Museum of American Art, New York;

Anthony Bannon,
George Eastman House, Rochester;

Jim Wood,
Art Institute of Chicago;

Jeffrey B. Bergen,
ACA Galleries, New York;

David R. Goode,
Norfolk Southern Corporation;

Elizabeth Broun,
Smithsonian American Art Museum, Washington D.C.;

Thomas McCormick,
Thomas McCormick Gallery, Chicago;

Howard Creel Collinson,
University of Iowa Museum of Art;

Heike Kordish,
New York Public Library;

Keith Davis,
Fine Arts Program, Hallmark Cards, Inc., Kansas City;

Ned Rifkin,
Hirshhorn Museum and Sculpture Garden, Smithsonian Institution, Washington D.C.;

Marie Galbraith,
Mattatuck Museum, Waterbury;

Jay Gates,
Phillips Collection, Washington D.C.;

Adelheid M. Gealt,
Indiana University Art Museum, Bloomington;

Anne d'Harnoncourt,
Philadelphia Museum of Art, Philadelphia;

Eunice C. Hurd and Robert Klein,
Robert Klein Gallery, Boston;

Lyndel King,
Frederick R. Weisman Art Museum, University of Minnesota, Minneapolis;

Myron Kunin,
Curtis Galleries, Minneapolis;

Irwin Lippman,
Columbus Museum of Art;

Ann Mintz,
Berkshire Museum, Pittsfield;

James Mundy,
Frances Lehman Loeb Art Center, Poughkeepsie;

Francis M. Naumann,
Francis M. Naumann Fine Art, New York;

Jonathan O'Hara,
O'Hara Gallery, New York;

Katharina Rich Perlow,
Katharina Rich Perlow Gallery, New York;

Franklin Riehlman,
Franklin Riehlman Fine Art, New York;

Malcolm Rogers,
Museum of Fine Arts, Boston;

Michael Rosenfeld and hally k. harrisburg,
Michael Rosenfeld Gallery, New York;

Bonnie Rychlak,
Isamu Noguchi Foundation, Inc., Long Island City;

Lawrence Salander,
Salander O'Reilly Galleries, LLC, New York;

Gary Snyder and Elizabeth Moore,
Gary Snyder Fine Art, New York;

Ira Spanierman,
Spanierman Gallery, LLC, New York;

Jennifer Vorbach,
C&M Arts, New York;

and, in Europe:

Yves Chèvrefils-Desbiolles,
Institut Mémoires de l'Édition Contemporaine
(Fonds Jean Hélion), Paris;

Christian Derouet,
Musée Zervos, Vézelay;

Anne Dopffer,
Musée National de la Coopération
Franco-Américaine, Blérancourt;

Marcel and David Fleiss,
Galerie 1900-2000, Paris;

Fabrice Hergott,
Musées de Strasbourg;

Jean-Noël Jeanneney,
Bibliothèque Nationale de France, Paris;

Mark Jones,
Victoria & Albert Museum, London;

Annette and Rudolf Kicken,
Kicken Gallery, Berlin;

Kasper König,
Museum Ludwig, Köln;

Christine Laflorentie,
Musée Daniel Vannier, Beaugency;

Claire Legrand,
FRAC Bourgogne, Dijon;

Jean-Marc Léri,
Musée Carnavalet, Paris;

Marion Meyer,
Galerie Marion Meyer, Paris;

Alain and Françoise Paviot,
Galerie Françoise Paviot, Paris;

Alfred Pacquement,
Musée National d'Art Moderne – Centre de
Création Industrielle (Centre National d'Art et
de Culture Georges Pompidou), Paris;

Didier Schulmann,
Bibliothèque Kandinsky, Musée National d'Art
Moderne – Centre de Création Industrielle, Paris;

Julie Pellegrin-Gérard,
Musée de l'Ancien Évêché d'Évreux;

Anthony Penrose,
Lee Miller Archives, Chiddingly,
Great Britain;

Bénédicte Péré,
Musée de Mer;

Natalie Seroussi,
Galerie Natalie Seroussi, Paris;

Guy Tosatto,
Musée de Grenoble.

An exhibition of this magnitude would not
have been possible without the extremely
generous contributions of private art collectors,
who agreed to part with their works for several
months. Among them, we would like to
acknowledge John C. Donnelly from the Estate
of Honoria Murphy Donnelly, the Norma and
Myron H. Goldberg Art Trust, David and
Mary Winton Green, Georgia deHavenon,
the J. Donald Nichols Collection, the John and
Barb Wallace Collection, as well as all
the lenders who wish to remain anonymous.

This exhibition could never have happened
without the expert skills and support of a large
number of individuals. Special thanks
are extended also to those who contributed
in making this exhibition a success:
Bridget Alsdorf, Jean-Pierre Angremy,
Abigail Asher, Kelly Baker, Timothy Baum,
Barry R. Bauman, Eric W. Baumgartner,
Kathryn J. Beebe, Jennifer Belt, Neal Benezra,
Dorian Bergen, Adria Bernier, Evelyn Bertram-
Neunzig, James H. Billington, Claude Billot,
Michael D. Blakesle, Pascal Boissin, Stacy Bomento,
Catherine Bossis, Claire Both, Rod Bouc,
Jean-Michel Bouhours, Laure Bouvot,
Anita Bracalente, Thomas J. Branchick,
Rhonda S. Broom, Jack Perry Brown,
Margaret Brown, Frédéric Buisson, Jacklyn Burns,
John Moors Cabot, Isabelle Cailleteau,
Carole Callow, Valerie Carberry, Mikki Carpenter,
Sarah Cash, Estelle Cherfils, Caroline Cohen,
Jennifer Cole, Bonnie B. Coles, James A. Conlin,
Joanna Cook, Laurent Creuzet, Wanda Crew,
Devon Cummings, Verna P. Curtis,
Lisa D'Acquisto, Sylviane Dailleau, Lucia Daniel,
Elliot Bostwick Davis, James T. Demetrion,
Katherine Dehn, Lisa Dennison, Amy Densford,
Elizabeth Dion, Aimee Dolby, Kimberly M. Dorazewski,
Amy P. Dowe, Karen Fasano, Hélène Favard,
Alison H. Fenn, Sophie Fiblec, Michael J. Finnegan,
Erin K. Fitzpatrick, Lydie Fouilloux,
Kathleen A. Foster, Marina Fröhling, Pat Fundom,
Barbara P. Galasso, Marie Galbraith, Mrs. Galtier,
Yvonne Garborini, Richard Gault, Isabelle Geffrin,
Marie-Jeanne Geyer, Larry Giacoletti,
Mrs. Ginisty, Tom Gitterman, Arne Glimcher,
Catherine Goeres, Annick Gratton, Howard
Greenberg, Thierry Grilet, Raechel Guest,
Emmanuel Guigon, Barbara Haskell, Amy Hau,
Mark Haworth-Booth, Maura Heffner, Rebecca Herman,
Elizabeth Hines, Karen Casey Hines, Sanford Hirsch,
Joseph Holbach, Jessica Holmes, Elizabeth Hopkin,
Kelly Johannes, Jo Lavera Jones, Mrs. Joublin,
Katherine Kaplan, Brian G. Kavanagh,

Christopher Ketcham, Sophie Kimenau, Scott Knauer,
Frank Kolodny, Leslie A. Kott, Hildegard Küpper,
Ellery Howard Kurtz, Joelle LaFerrara,
Claude Lamouille, Eric T. Larsen, Brigitte Léal,
Kristen N. Leipert, Nathalie Leleu, Gaby Lewin,
Isabelle Lhoir, Patricia Loiko, Rose Mack,
Anne-Marie Mahé, Carol Mancusi-Ungaro,
Karen Marks, Donald Jeff Martin, Anne-Louise Marquis,
Jacqueline Matisse-Monnier, Rose May,
Patricia McDonald, Virginia M. Mecklenburg,
Anna Moritz, Laura Muessig, Amy Munger,
Charles Nichols, William Nichols, Caroline Nutley,
Roseann Panebianco, Eva Panek, Martha Parrish,
Kim Pashko, Diane Pelrine, Miranda Percival,
Courtney Rae Peterson, Elizabeth Phillips,
Arnauld Pierre, Joann Potter, Bruno Pouchin,
Yuki Puar, Robert Rainwater, James Reinish,
Françoise Reynaud, Isabelle Ribadeau Dumas,
Nora Riccio, Julie Richard, Franklin Riehlman,
Jennifer Robertson, Berenice Rose,
Melissa Rountree, Alexander S. C. Rower,
Phyllis Rosenzweig, Shira Rudavsky,
Stephen K. Saks, Anne Sanciaud, Margot Sands,
Alain Sayag, Saskia Scheffer, Daniel Schulman,
Jennifer Seeds, Karine Sérafin, Iain Slessor,
Joel Smith, Mary Solt, Richard H. Sorensen,
Christine Speroni, Barbi Spieler, Jenny Sponberg,
Amy Stack, Anne Steinberg, Parker Stephenson,
Elizabeth Stevens, Andrew Strauss,
Joseph R. Struble, Steven Tatum, Kathy A. Taylor,
Michael R. Taylor, Ann Temkin, Abigail Terrones,
Spencer Tomkins, Lucy B. Toole, Évelyne Tréhin,
Lucien Treillard, Jody Trowbridge, Paul Hayes Tucker,
Kathleen Tunney, Elizabeth Hutton Turner,
Karole Vail, Isabelle Varloteaux, Hélène Vincent,
Rachael Walker, Thomas Weski, Helen Whitcombe,
Pamela White Trimpe, Rony van de Velde,
Amy Wolf, Gabriele Woolever, Deborah Wythe,
Virginia Zabriskie, Xenia Zed and Judith Zilczer.

Finally, these acknowledgements, written
on behalf of the exhibition curators and
catalogue contributors, would be incomplete
without thanking the dozens of research
librarians and archivists, too numerous
to mention, who assisted with every stage
of this project and whose interest was
an on-going source of encouragement.

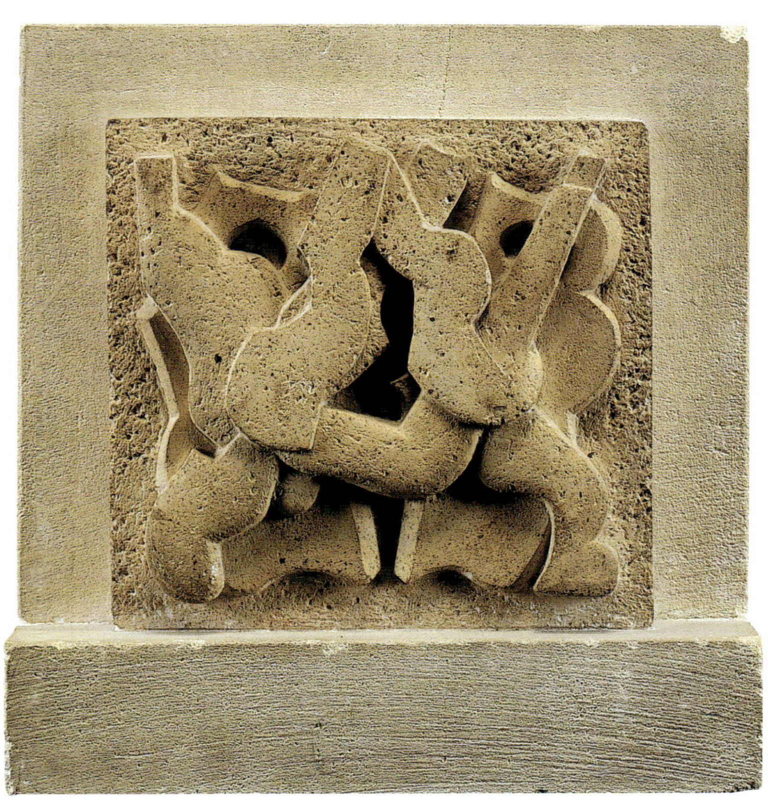

A *Transatlantic Avant-Garde: American Artists in Paris, 1918–1939* is an ambitious and original project focusing on the diverse and dynamic artistic exchanges between the United States and France during the interwar period. In Paris, the American artists encountered the international avant-garde, and seeing their own art in relationship to a new context, they were able to affirm or reaffirm their artistic identity that was simultaneously modern and American. This exhibition explores the development of several important aspects of modernism in American art through major trends of the Parisian avant-garde such as Purism, geometric abstraction, and surrealism, among others. It demonstrates that the American artists who travelled to and from France in the interwar period created works of art that contribute simultaneously to the history of the Parisian avant-garde and to the history of American art.

This in-depth study of an era rich in international relationships demonstrates that American artists were active in many different circles in Europe. It also illustrates the ongoing commitment of the Terra Foundation for the Arts to present innovative exhibitions that will further deepen our knowledge and awareness of American art. This event celebrating reciprocal artistic exchanges between France and the United States has received the generous patronage of the Honorable Howard H. Leach, Ambassador of the United States of America to France, and of Bertrand Delanoë, Mayor of Paris. We would especially like to thank them for their support to this transatlantic dialogue.

A Transatlantic Avant-Garde: American Artists in Paris, 1918–1939 is an endeavor that began four years ago with the former director of Musée d'Art Américain Giverny, Derrick R. Cartwright. The exhibition was conceived by Sophie Lévy, Chief Curator of the Musée d'Art Américain Giverny, with the collaboration of Assistant Curators Katherine Bourguignon and Bronwyn Griffith.

Assembled in this exhibition are approximately 150 works of art from public and private collections in the United States and Europe, by more than 35 artists, testifying both to the diversity of imagery and to the shared concerns of artists of the past century on both sides of the Atlantic in the interwar period. Lenders to this exhibition, listed in the acknowledgments in this book, have agreed to part with cherished works from their collections for the presentations in Giverny, Tacoma, and Chicago. The Musée d'Art Américain Giverny extends its deep appreciation to them for making this exhibition possible.

It is particularly appropriate and gratifying that this exhibition will travel to the United States and be seen at the Tacoma Art Museum and at the Terra Museum of American Art in Chicago. We are indebted to Janeanne Upp, Director, and Patricia McDonnell, Curator, at the Tacoma Art Musem, as well as to Elizabeth Kennedy, Curator, and Cathy Ricciardelli, Director of Exhibitions & Collection Services, at the Terra Museum of American Art, for their unwavering support of this project.

Artists of the interwar period explored with inspiration a variety of media including cinema. It is a pleasure to associate film to this exhibition through a collaboration with the Musée National d'Art Moderne — Centre Georges Pompidou in Paris for the important retrospective *En marge de Hollywood. La première avant-garde cinématographique américaine, 1893–1941* organized by Jean-Michel Bouhours, Bruce Posner, and Isabelle Ribadeau Dumas.

The exhibition catalogue also breaks new ground by juxtaposing essays by French and American scholars in each chapter in a transatlantic mode of exchange. We are especially grateful to these scholars — Christian Derouet, Emmanuelle de L'Écotais, Janine Mileaf, Jocelyne Rotily, Kenneth E. Silver, and Gail Stavitsky — for generously contributing their ideas in the eight essays in this volume.

We are pleased to have The University of California Press as our copublisher of the English language edition. Fine Arts Editor, Deborah Kirshman, has shown great enthusiasm for this project from its inception. Francesca Rose, Head of Publications of the Musée d'Art Américain Giverny, has directed this international collaboration with precision, sensitivity, and dedication.

An exhibition and publication of this magnitude could not have been realized without the unfailing support of the Board of Directors of the Terra Foundation for the Arts and its Chairman, Marshall Field, V. To them we express our deepest gratitude.

ELIZABETH GLASSMAN
DIRECTOR, TERRA MUSEUMS
EXECUTIVE VICE-PRESIDENT,
TERRA FOUNDATION FOR THE ARTS

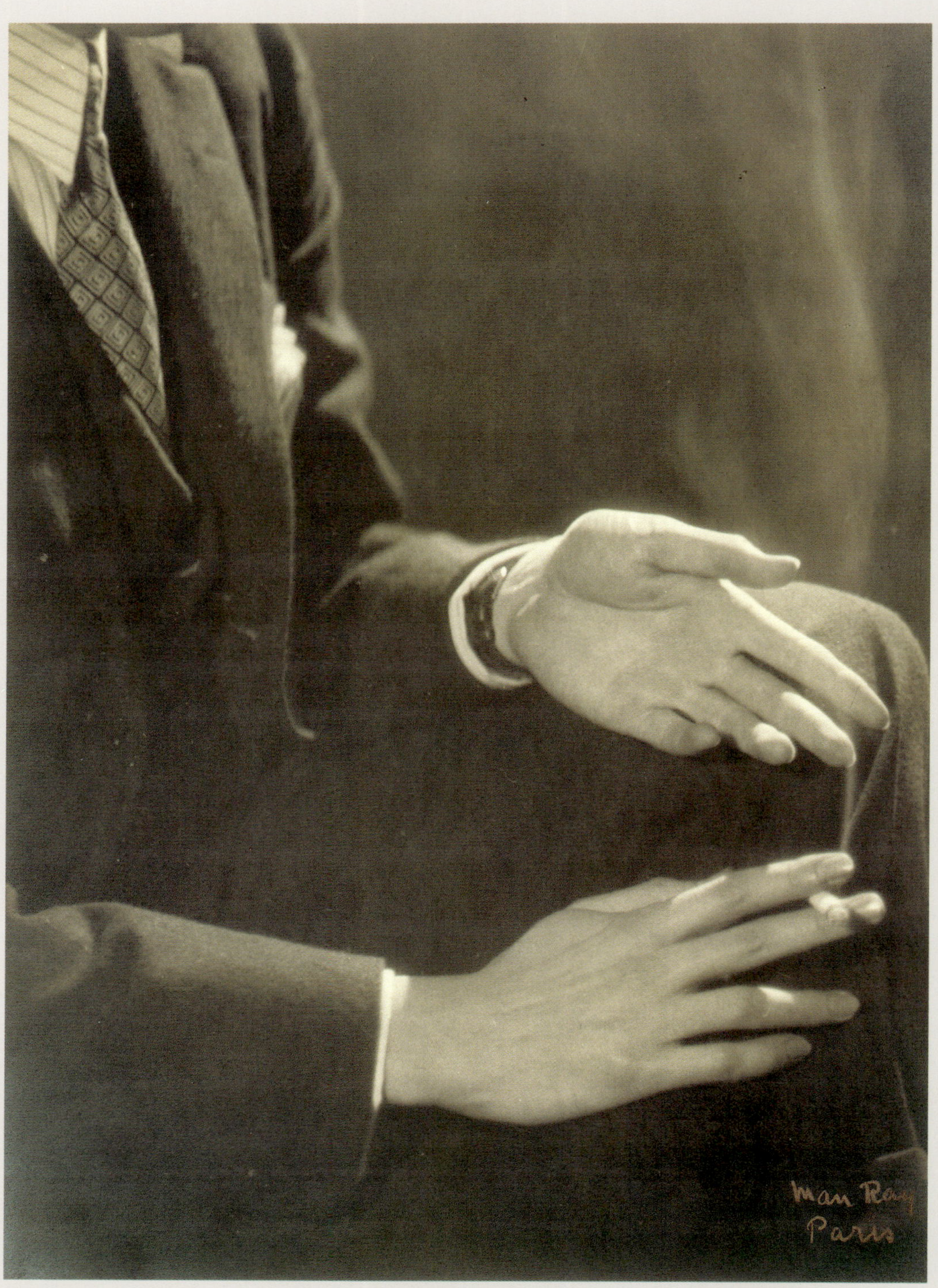

MAN RAY
HANDS OF CHARLES DEMUTH, C. 1921
GELATIN SILVER PRINT, 23.2 X 17.1 CM
[CAT. 150]

"SYMPATHETIC ORDER"

SOPHIE **LÉVY**

In recent years, art from the interwar period seems to fascinate and preoccupy art historians. Over sixty years after the start of World War II, several books and major exhibitions are now devoted to that era.[1] All provide a glimpse not only of its extreme melancholy, but also of its complexity and the difficulty of grasping it in an unequivocal manner.

The context of France—and of Paris in particular—during this era is subject to interpretations that appear contradictory. At times, Paris of the Roaring Twenties is presented as a haven, the only city able to absorb the world's cultures and religions without losing its own way, becoming fertile ground for international artistic production. In fact, census figures indicate that the foreign population in greater Paris initially increased significantly between 1921 and 1931 (rising from 5.3 percent to 9.2 percent of total inhabitants, including some 10,000 Americans), only to shrink subsequently due to the combined effects of economic depression and war (foreigners were only 4.1 percent of that population in 1946).[2]

In contrast, the Parisian art scene of the interwar period has also been described as the locus of a "return to order," of a quest for a French-style classicism that would transcend the ruptures provoked by the avant-garde, and even the xenophobia which would later give way to Vichy France.[3] Indeed, art magazines did seem to teem with articles rejecting foreign artists and avant-garde art en masse, often making no distinction between these two notions. The nationalist retrenchment, although basically aimed at everything that might seem Germanic in any way whatsoever, real or imagined, did not spare artists who came from a recent ally such as the United States. Louis Vauxcelles, in the February 8, 1923 issue of *Carnet de la semaine,* declared: "There are still people in Montparnasse who refuse to assimilate. . . . Just go to the [Salon des] Indépendants—entire rooms display a Slavicism, Bulgarianism, or Americanism that is a bit aggressive."[4] What recent authors seem to have overlooked is the ability of a large democratic capital to host, simultaneously, diametrically opposing artistic and political trends that manage to live together despite their conflicts—a situation that was of course particularly true of France during the interwar period, when a certain artistic and ideological confusion prevailed.

If we turn to the memoirs of key American figures, we see that many of them testify to a feeling of openness and freedom present in the French capital, or at least in its cosmopolitan neighborhoods. Marcel Duchamp described Montparnasse in 1934 in the following terms: "Montparnasse was the first really international colony of artists we ever had. Because of its internationalism it was superior to Montmartre, Greenwich Village or Chelsea [and] the colorful but non-productive characters of Montparnasse often contributed greatly to the success of the creative group. Liquor is an important factor in stimulating the exchange of ideas between artists."[5]

Even more striking are the observations made by Harold Rosenberg in 1940, because even though the period in question was barely coming to a close, he already seemed to adopt an historical perspective that corresponds to the one held today, insofar as his select list of artists includes only the most famous members of the avant-garde:

> [U]p to the day of the occupation, Paris had been the Holy Place of our time. The only one. Not because of its affirmative genius alone, but perhaps, on the contrary, through its passivity, which allowed it to be possessed by the searchers of every nation. By Picasso and Juan Gris, Spaniards; by Modigliani, Boccioni, and Severini, Italians; by Brancusi, Roumanian [*sic*]; by Joyce, Irishman; by Mondrian, Dutchman; by Lipchitz, Polish Lithuanian; by Archipenko, Kandinsky, Diaghilev, Larionov, Russians; by Calder, Pound, Gertrude Stein, Man Ray, Americans; by Kupka, Czechoslovak; Lehmbruck and Max Ernst, Germans; by Wyndham Lewis and T. E. Hulme, Englishmen . . . by all artists, students, refugees. . . .

> Thus Paris was the only spot where necessary blendings could be made and mellowed, where it was possible to shake up such "modern" doses as Viennese psychology, African

> sculpture, American detective stories, Russian music,
> neo-Catholicism, German technique, Italian desperation.
> Paris represented the International of culture.[6]

Studies of artistic relationships between the United States and France often follow the same meandering complexity. Paris is sometimes presented as the capital that attracted the most American artists—a stay in Paris became mandatory for all artists seeking respectability. Alexander Calder, for example, stated in his autobiography that, "Paris seemed the place to go, on all accounts of practically everyone who had been there, and I decided I would also like to go."[7]

According to data on foreigners who exhibited in Paris, American artists were allegedly the most heavily represented nationality in the various salons in Paris, at least up to 1914.[8] And while Paris also embodied a political and economic haven for many foreign artists, that was not the case for Americans—no political threat hung over them in the United States, and the wealth of their homeland already outstripped that of France. The gap between per capita gross domestic product in the United States and that in France steadily widened between 1900 and 1920, rising from a ratio of 1.44 to 1.74. Even at the height of the depression in America, this ratio never sank below 1.39.[9] France was therefore neither a political haven nor a potential market for their art.

Instead, testimony from artists and writers who left America for Paris reflects the general lack of interest in art back home, where the progressive intellectual and artistic milieu was still too limited to provide a real foundation for a career. A letter from John Storrs, dated 1913, points out the advantages of circulating back and forth between the two countries:

"I am only waiting and hoping for the moment when I shall receive enough real appreciation and material encouragement from America to make it possible for me to make my home here. In the meantime I shall continue to reside in France coming every year or so to America to bring over and show any new work and profit by the prestige which America gives to its artists coming from abroad."[10] In an article published in *The Little Review* in 1922, Storrs analyzed the American scene with the finesse of an artist familiar with both sides of the Atlantic. "Will New York be the world's art center? You have the money and a world in the building with something of a desire to understand. When will you give to your artists the opportunity that you have already given to scientists and engineers?"[11]

Occasionally, authors present Paris as an already weakened capital, rejected by the American avant-garde. Wanda Corn evokes a calculated rejection of the European tour by Alfred Stieglitz and his circle when she cites a passage from a review of a Georgia O'Keeffe exhibition in a 1927 issue of the *Nation*: "O'Keeffe is America's. Its own exclusive product. It is refreshing to realize that she has never been to Europe. More refreshing still that she has no ambition to go there."[12]

Although each of these viewpoints is based on documentary records, none of them really prevails over the others. We are therefore obliged to adopt a different, rather awkward, perspective that embraces oscillations that are inherent to the activities of the artists at the heart of this exhibition. Indeed, the movement between countries seems profoundly rooted in their state of mind. Apart from John Storrs and William Einstein, none of the artists in this exhibition died in France, each returned to the United States at one point or another, in striking contrast to other nationalities in Paris particularly artists from central Europe. There were undeniably American artists who remained in the United States—as well as French artists who strove to uphold a national tradition—who adopted and maintained a clear, deeply rooted, unambiguous position. Yet that was not the case with the likes of Stieglitz, who claimed in the 1920s to have been "trying to establish for myself an America in which I could breathe as a free man."[13] Stieglitz steeped at that time in the spiritualist culture of central Europe, did not seek to discover the essence of America through his art, but rather to to shape it to his own vision—a very significant distinction.

Material considerations alone do not explain the relationship American artists maintained between home and Paris. As Gladys Fabre adroitly points out in her essay on the school of Paris, exile, even temporary exile, imposes a sense of otherness, which she compares to an amorous relationship in terms of the energy and creativity that it engenders.[14] In this spirit, Storrs wrote to his French wife in a letter from New York: "I love America and all that—love it like one ordnairly [*sic*] loves one's mother—But France is my mistress & I am a lover of hers—a lover willing to sacrifice every thing to live in her heart—to rest his head in her peaceful lap of culture & age old beauty. It is not shame that I have for America but pitty [*sic*]—mixed with a sort of hopefulness."[15] To be abroad is to free oneself of the burden and constraints of a culture, a social milieu, a family history.

In fact, many authors have shown—through the testimony of numerous American artists—have shown that it was often the way these artists were perceived by their French counterparts that enabled them to affirm or reaffirm a pictorial identity that was both modern and specifically American. Long quotations from two letters written by Charles Demuth to Stieglitz help to shed light on various aspects of this concept. The first dates from 1921 during Demuth's final stay in Paris, the second just after his return to Lancaster that same year.

> All the French painters, the great ones, and the men interested
> in the two magazines—"L'Amour de l'Art" and "L'Esprit
> Nouveau," are very anxious to have the best of the Americans
> in with them. It is a thrill, really, to hear what they think of us,
> knowing us so slightly, mostly through the "Dial"—strange,
> isn't it?—but it is thought very well of in France & England.
> I am told either of the Rosenbergs will have our things—and

they have very impressive galleries. All the moderns are shown with great spirit, and there is no showing of the old masters as an excuse for their being—the spirit of often showing the younger men only to sell a Lawson is lacking entirely! . . . It would be so grand to be taken up, en masse, by the French, who know a "bit" about painting, after the way the mother country has treated us—wouldn't it? . . .

It is all very amazing, to me, to find this enthusiasm here—after knowing what we have always felt for the French, not thinking much of our own; and the great Frenchmen telling us that we are very good. It seems rather grand. It is like Baudelaire and Poe. I wish that you could be here to get the thrill of it, after the work and love you have given the painters French & American. It seems almost as though the dream were "coming true"—that after all, Art is not <u>only</u> pictures, books, etc.—but also the nearest we can get to—you can call it what you like—I'll write, Sympathetic Order!

Paris is as you see rather wonderful. It seems to shine. One feels, perhaps, it is the last grand flair. I don't know—it seems almost too grand.

I think that I will stay on for another month or two—and then come home. . . . I feel "In" America—even though its insides are empty. Maybe I can help fill them. . . .

Sometimes it seems almost impossible to come back—we are so out of it. Then one sees Marcel [Duchamp] or Gleizes, and they will say, " Oh! Paris. New York is the place—there are the modern ideas. Europe is finished. . . ."

Saw Gertrude Stein—she is fat & handsome and rides in the smallest "Ford" Henry ever turned out—also the most ugly. She is rather grand. But unlike the French thinks that we are all very dull. I do think that she should have a few months in the home land.[16]

First, Demuth indicates just how small the avant-garde milieu is in Paris as well as in New York. In the space of two sentences, he mentions the two principal avant-garde publications on either side of the Atlantic and the two most active galleries in the realm of modern art. The end of the letter confirms Gertrude Stein's central role in transatlantic relations—an undeniable hub for all expatriates, she retained an attitude of contempt vis-à-vis her compatriots, as she had since the turn of the century, notably buying no works from the many American artists who frequented her salon. The second element in this letter concerns the relief Demuth clearly felt when recognized by his French peers, what he calls a "Sympathetic Order." Yet in his own way despite his enthusiasm and admiration, Demuth seems to read that moment in Paris as a final flourishing before a potential decline—to which he merely alludes—namely the decline in favor of New York, which the French seem to be the first to recognize.

Although Demuth's swift return to his home town of Lancaster is often attributed to health problems,[17] his second letter reveals other reasons.

It was all very wonderful—but I must work, here. Had I stayed in France when I went to it for the first time—by now I would be into it. It would take years and, after all, there are many able Frenchmen—and New York is something which Europe is not—and I feel of that something—awful as most of it is. Marcel and all the others, those who count, say that all the "modern" [progress] is [now up] to us, and of course, they are right, but it is so hard. . . . What work I do will be done here; terrible as it is to work in this "our land of the free" . . . Together we will add to the American scene. . . .

There is a palpable need here to define through his art the "something" that New York is—and that Europe is not, which is strenghtened by the opinions of his French peers.

Even beyond this mutual contemplation that reinforced the identities of both French and Americans, there was role playing, as incarnated by Gerald Murphy and Man Ray. With great lucidity, Murphy acknowledged thes roles he and his friends acted out in Paris: "Although it took place in France, it was all somehow an American experience. We were none of us professional expatriates, and Paris and the French seemed to relish it."[18] It was not a question of remaining in the womb of Paris, to take up Henry Miller's famous image, of abandoning all national identity, but on the contrary, of accentuating difference. As Jocelyne Rotily shows in her essay in this catalogue (p. 55–62), Murphy turned that difference into an art form.

One might wonder, for that matter, whether a misconception underlay this encounter between French and American artists. Indeed, wasn't Murphy consigned—by Fernand Léger among others—to the role of enlightened patron? Was Albert Gallatin ever viewed as anything other than a collector, or Man Ray anything other than a photographer and portraitist? As Kenneth E. Silver shrewdly shows in his essay (p. 29–42), it was only within the context of certain perceptions and preconceptions that American artists were integrated into the French community: the French were interested not in architects, but in engineers; not in painters, but in photographers and filmmakers; not in intellectuals, but in businessmen. As it transpired, given a France weakened by an unprecedented war effort, the motivation for an exchange—which produced something resembling the intersection between America and Europe—came mostly from Americans. Also worth citing is an article by Maurice Sachs, reviewing an exhibition of three centuries of American art held at the Jeu de Paume in Paris in July 1938. "I would like to find the profound reasons for the profound mediocrity of young American painting. They are extremely complex, but we could say firstly that the Americans make a big mistake by trying to paint European subjects in a European way. They would do better to look around themselves, to become completely American, to let themselves draw inspiration from a world different from ours, which needs to be expressed differently."[19]

From Purism to Precisionism

Several American artists who arrived in Paris before or after World War I quite naturally espoused the post-cubist developments then being elaborated by the French avant-garde. What is paradoxical is that this trend, primarily represented by the magazine *L'Esprit nouveau* (founded by Amédée Ozenfant and Charles-Édouard Jeanneret, or Le Corbusier), sought to establish cubism—or rather Purism—as the product of a purely French context: "The War over, everything is being organized, everything is being clarified and streamlined—factories are rising, already nothing is how it was before the war."[20]

Yet Patrick Henry Bruce, in France since 1904, seemed to adopt the Purist aesthetic as his own, as noted by Kenneth E. Silver in his essay. The shapes of a limited number of objects are summed up in his paintings as pure volumes even as effects of perspective are rejected. Unfortunately, these powerful still lifes received no recognition from the American avant-garde—despite the intervention of Bruce's friend Henri-Pierre Roché with American collectors such as Katherine Dreier and John Quinn[21]—nor from its French counterpart.

A spirit of "construction" dominated the work of Charles Demuth from 1919 and was perhaps related to the publication of the English version of Ozenfant and Jeanneret's *After Cubism,* discussed by Henry McBride in his "News and Comment in the World of Art" for the May 25, 1919 issue of *The New York Sun.* The well-informed Demuth, fully integrated into New York's intimate avant-garde scene, therefore knew what awaited him when he travelled to Paris in August 1921. As already noted above, he was mainly seeking reassurance and confirmation from his European artist-friends. Although *Rue du Singe qui Pêche* (cat. 21) is the only painting in this exhibition that can be incontrovertibly linked to this final trip, other works from that same year, probably painted after his return to Lancaster, reveal a certain solidification of his style, a convergence of cubism and something else, which would later earn him the title of one of the leaders of "Precisionism," characterized by intense colors, sharply delineated, beam-like shapes, and the insertion of letters and slogans onto the painterly surface.

The purpose of Stuart Davis's brief time in Paris, from June 1928 to August 1929, seems to resemble Demuth's. In a letter to his father dated September 17, 1928, Davis wrote, "The attitude toward artists is very different here than in America. They regard it as a reasonable way for a man to spend his time. In America, it is regarded as an eccentricity unless it shows a $10,000 a year income. I'm awfully glad I came

here. Don't know how much longer I will be able to stay."[22] In his case, however, the experience seemed to represent a stylistic pause in his development. In the same letter, he added: "It is a tremendously interesting place over here. I am principally interested in the streets. There is great variety, from the most commonplace to the unique. A street of the regular French working class houses of 100 years ago is always interesting because they are all different in regard to size, surface, number of windows etc. There are a lot of such streets near where I live. An important factor is that they are small so that you can see them."[23] In fact, the many paintings done by Davis in Paris seem to represent a certain regression from the *Eggbeater* series, done just before he left America (several examples of which he took with him). The *Paris– New York* series, executed in 1931 after his return to New York, provides a visual summary of this back-and-forth approach, which drew some criticism from New York's intellectual milieu, notably from McBride:

> You know what a scout is, of course? A good scout gets up in the middle of the night and goes far off in the enemy country and returns with useful information. Stuart Davis has been doing this for years. Sometimes he does it in the daytime, too, but always he returns with what you want to know. . . . The only thing wrong about Stuart Davis is that he picked the language up when out scouting. . . . I should have preferred Stuart Davis to have invented the kind of talk he now hands out. But we can't have everything and, next to the invention of a language, there is speaking it nicely—and that Stuart Davis surely does . . . better than any American I know of."[24]

This quotation provides a clear statement of the ambivalent atmosphere encountered by American artists on their return home—they had to prove once again the Americanness of their art and their rejection of Europe. This Davis soon did, in order "to spike the disheartening rumor that there were hundreds of talented young modern artists in Paris who completely outclassed their American equivalents. . . . It proved to me that one might go on working in New York without laboring under an impossible artistic handicap. It allowed me to observe the enormous vitality of the American atmosphere as compared to Europe and made me regard the necessity of working in New York as a positive advantage."[25]

A pitfall for an entire school

Geometric abstraction probably constitutes the most interesting case within this exhibition because it illustrates, even today, the pitfall that the transatlantic option represented for the career of an entire generation of artists.[26] There were nevertheless many American artists who, often after having discovered Piet Mondrian's paintings in New York, decided to spend a few years in Paris. This exhibition thus presents the European public, often for the first time, with artists such as Ilya Bolotowsky, Charles Biederman, William Einstein, John Ferren, Albert Gallatin, John Graham, Balcolm and Gertrude Greene, Carl Holty, Harry Holtzman, Frederick Kann, Jan Matulka, George L. K. Morris, Charles Shaw, and Jean Xceron, not to mention those for whom we were unable to track down work. Drawn by an art that did not correspond to the demands for social realism prevalent in America in the 1930s, they left in search of information, contacts, and perhaps the respect granted to artists in Europe. On returning to the United States in the latter half of the 1930s, however, they were confronted by indifference and rejection—they were not only too abstract for the general public and its critics, they were also too European for the American avant-garde and its opinion-makers. So in reaction to an exhibition organized by Alfred Barr at the Museum of Modern Art in New York, *Cubism and Abstract Art*, which included no American artist other than Alexander Calder, Harry Holtzman founded the American Abstract Artists Society on the model of the French groups Cercle et Carré and Abstraction–Création (to which several American artists belonged when in France).

The position of Albert Gallatin, one of the rare collectors and museum directors to defend geometric abstraction, was typical. When the Whitney Museum of American Art was founded, he wrote:

> There is no such thing as a local tradition in American painting. Ages ago an artistic impulse existed in Peru and in Mexico, but the art sense of the North American Indian was never developed to any marked degree. . . . [Moreover], the English settlers were bitterly antagonistic to the fine arts. . . . The New York School is as cosmopolitan in its make up as the School of Paris. Foreigners possessing ability as painters include the Russians Alexander Brook and Morris Kantor, the Italian Joseph Stella, the Swiss Joseph Pollet and the Japanese Yasuo Kunyoshi. The influx of foreign blood is good for American art, this intermingling of various cultures.[27]

In 1930, Gallatin thus advocated a New York school as cosmopolitan and international as that of Paris. And yet, in the catalogue for the exhibit devoted to Gallatin, Morris, and Shaw at the Jacques Seligmann Gallery in 1939, in a text about his work probably written by himself, he felt obliged—as had so many of his compatriots— to justify his Americanness. "It is well-known that the new directions of painting, which the twentieth century has built into its most intense plastic language, stemmed from European investigations. For generations the forebears of Gallatin have been a part of American life and his paintings, a few executed in France in 1926 excepted, have been painted in America, the great majority in New York. Their expression is in no sense limited by nationalistic barriers, for the muses it has been said, care little for geography, yet the paintings speak with an American accent."[28] Even today, most works by these artists are still in private hands, and seem to have been overlooked by the critical reassessment of modern American art that began in the 1980s. There is apparently still no room for these abstract artists who considered themselves heirs to Europe during a nationalistic era, and who clung to a formalist art during a socially conscious period. The arrival of the surrealists in New York in the early 1940s delivered the final death blow to a movement that barely had time to blossom.

And yet Mondrian, who had taken refuge in London in 1938 thanks to the intervention of British artist Ben Nicholson, had his mind set on getting to America. In 1940, when London was undergoing the blitz, he replied to an invitation from Winifred Dacre in the following terms: "No, I cannot come to Cumberland. It is too green. I must go to America, my pictures were nearly bombed. I must protect them, but you in England will win in the end—however hard it may be—for we are fundamentally right."[29] Thus America became the final haven for the last of the abstract artists of the interwar period.

A few figures from the birth of surrealism

The case of Man Ray is among the more paradoxical and more ambiguous in this exhibition. How did this man, who was admitted to avant-garde circles solely on the recommendation of Marcel Duchamp, become such a central artist in the surrealist circle? Here again, his nationality provides no more stable a basis for interpretation than does his oeuvre—perhaps he should be taken at his word when he declared, "I never do just one thing, but *two things* that are totally unrelated. I put these together in order to create, by contrast, a sort of plastic poetry."[30]

Furthermore, the biography concocted by Tristan Tzara for Man Ray's first show at the Galerie Six was an absurd combination of common French clichés about Americans. "Monsieur Ray was born one no longer knows where. After having been successively a coal merchant, several times a millionaire and chairman of the chewing gum trust, he decided to respond to the invitation of the dadaists and show his latest canvases in Paris."[31]

It would be mistaken to view Man Ray as a victim of this situation. As he wrote to his backer and patron, Ferdinand Howald, on May 28, 1922,

"They crave America. So we are making a fair exchange, for I love the mellowness and finish of things here."[32] Like others, Man Ray understood that he had to play the foreigner in order to be included in Parisian groups, just as he had to fully assume the role of photographer to the hilt if he wanted to be accepted as an artist. Emmanuelle de L'Écotais examines the ramifications of this strategy in her essay for this catalogue (p. 139–150).

Yet despite Man Ray's key role—and in contrast to the geometric abstractionists—a true school of American surrealism never developed in Paris. Rather, on the one hand there were individuals more or less affiliated with the activities of the Paris group (Lee Miller, Joseph Cornell, Mary Reynolds and, working as a double agent, Marcel Duchamp), and on the other hand there were artists who adopted the biomorphic trend of 1930s abstraction (Isamu Noguchi, Kay Sage, and even Calder in the thirties). The American contribution to surrealism only really occurred in New York at the end of the 1920s.

As so often happens, the current situation has reawakened an historic period, giving it new meaning. These days more than ever, we should beware of taking too lightly Walter Benjamin's "Theses on the Philosophy of History," written in 1940 just a few months before his arrest and suicide. "To articulate the past historically . . . means to seize hold of a memory as it flashes up at a moment of danger."[33] History does not mean methodically bringing to light dead facts that have never ceased to be there, but rather excavating, in the urgent present, a specific moment in the terrain of the past, so that an image can surge forth, shedding light on the ever-threatening present.

The complexity of the interwar period is echoed in our own time, just as the ambivalent fascinations that arose on both sides of the Atlantic are echoed in our own preoccupations. In devising this exhibition, there is no question of oversimplifying that link, casting it as either heroic or hopeless. Instead, based on the artworks, we are offering a dual perspective by contemporary scholars, both French and American, on a past that continues to trouble the present. ■

1— In particular, see several recent exhibition catalogues: *Les Années trente en Europe* (Paris: Musée d'Art Moderne de la Ville de Paris, 1997); *L'École de Paris, 1904–1929, La Part de l'autre* (Paris: Musée d'Art Moderne de la Ville de Paris, 2000); *Paris, Capital of the Arts 1900–1938* (London: Royal Academy of Art, 2002).

2— These figures are taken from Ralph Schor, "Le Paris des libertés," in *Le Paris des étrangers depuis un siècle,* ed. André Kaspi and Antoine Marès (Paris: Imprimerie Nationale, 1989), 14–15.

3— This thesis is partly reflected in Kenneth E. Silver, *Esprit de Corps: The Art of the Parisian Avant-Garde and the First World War, 1914–1925* (Princeton: Princeton University Press, 1989), and more particulary in Romy Golan, *Modernity and Nostalgia: Art and Politics in France Between the Wars* (New Haven: Yale University Press, 1995).

4— "Il y a tout de même des gens à Montparnasse qui ne sont pas encore assimilés [...] Allez aux Indépendants : des salles entières sont d'un slavisme, d'un bulgarisme, d'un américanisme un tantinet agressif." Quoted in Gladys Fabre, "Qu'est-ce que l'École de Paris?" in *L'École de Paris, 1904–1929, La Part de l'autre* (Paris: Musée d'Art Moderne de la Ville de Paris, 2000), 34, note 31.

5— James Charters, *This Must Be the Place: Memoirs of Montparnasse* (London, 1934) quoted in "Montparnasse and the Right Bank: Myth and Reality," *Paris, Capital of the Arts 1900–1938* (London: Royal Academy of Art, 2002), 111.

6— Harold Rosenberg, "The Fall of Paris," *Partisan Review* (1940), reprinted in Rosenberg, *The Tradition of the New* (New York: Da Capo, 1994), 209–210.

7— Alexander Calder, *An Autobiography with Pictures* (New York: Pantheon, 1966), 76.

8— Billy Klüver and Julie Martin, "Carrefour Vavin," in *The Circle of Montparnasse: Jewish Artists in Paris, 1905–1945*, exh. cat. (New York: The Jewish Museum, 1985), 69.

9— Source: Organization of Economic Cooperation and Development.

10— Letter from John Storrs to Mr. Rockwell, July 1913. Archives of American Art, Smithsonian Institution, Washington D.C.

11— John Storrs, "Museums of Artists," *The Little Review* (Winter 1922): 63.

12— Frances O'Brien, "Americans We Like: Georgia O'Keeffe," *The Nation* 12 (October 1927), quoted in Wanda M. Corn, *The Great American Thing: Modern Art and National Identity, 1915–1935* (Berkeley and Los Angeles: University of California Press, 1999), 33.

13— Quoted in Barbara Rose, *American Art Since 1900: A Critical History* (New York: Praeger, 1967), 38.

14— "Le rapport à la terre d'adoption, dans l'exil comme dans l'intégration, est bien souvent vécu comme une relation sexuelle où l'objet de désir, Paris, est assimilé à l'image de la femme que l'on veut posséder, qui tourmente ou apaise. Est-ce 'la terre étrangère qui donne à l'étranger un sens inconscient de libération,' comme l'écrit Canudo, ou 'l'éclatement du refoulement qui conduit à traverser une frontière,' selon Julia Kristeva? Toujours est-il que la relation entretenue avec la ville d'accueil est vécue sur un mode fusionnel avec l'*Autre*, l'étranger, le sexe opposé, le complémentaire manquant de la culture d'origine." Fabre, "Qu'est-ce que l'École de Paris ?", 33.

15— John Storrs, letter dated January 1923, quoted in Noel Stern Frackman, *John Storrs,* exh. cat. (New York: Whitney Museum of American Art, 1987), 48.

16— This letter and the following one are found in Bruce Kellner, ed., *Letters of Charles Demuth, American Artist, 1883–1935* (Philadelphia: Temple University Press, 2000), 28–31 and 37–38.

17— In particular, see Emily Farnham, *Charles Demuth: Behind the Laughing Mask* (Norman: University of Oklahoma Press, 1971); Alvord L. Eiseman, *Charles Demuth* (New York: Watson-Guptill, 1982); and Barbara Haskell, *Charles Demuth,* exh. cat. (New York: Whitney Museum of American Art, 1987).

18— Quoted in William Rubin, *The Paintings of Gerald Murphy,* exh. cat. (New York: The Museum of Modern Art, 1974), 9.

19— Quoted in Francesca Rose, "The French Perspective on American Art, 1919–1938," *L'Amérique et les modernes,* exh. cat. (Giverny: Musée d'Art Américain, 2000), 78.

20— "La Guerre finie, tout s'organise, tout se clarifie et s'épure; les usines s'élèvent, rien n'est déjà plus ce qu'il était avant la guerre." Amédée Ozenfant and Charles-Édouard Jeanneret, *Après le cubisme* (Paris: Éditions des Commentaires, 1918), 11, quoted in Carol S. Eliel, *L'Esprit Nouveau: Purism in Paris, 1918–1925,* exh. cat. (Los Angeles: Los Angeles County Museum of Art in association with Harry N. Abrams, Inc. New York), 17.

21— See William C. Agee and Barbara Rose, *Patrick Henry Bruce: American Modernist. A Catalogue Raisonné,* exh. cat. (New York: Museum of Modern Art, 1979).

22— Lowery Stokes Sims, *Stuart Davis, American Painter,* exh. cat (New York: Metropolitan Museum, 1991), 31.

23— Ibid., 33.

24— Henry McBride, "Stuart Davis Comes to Town," *The New York Sun,* April 4, 1931, quoted in Carolyn Lanchner, *Fernand Léger,* exh. cat. (New York: Museum of Modern Art, 1998), 31.

25— Stuart Davis, "Self-Interview," *Creative Arts* 9 (September 1931): 211. Quoted in Sims, *Stuart Davis,* 55.

26— The bibliography on this subject remains fairly modest and fragmentary, but see the following books and catalogues: *Abstract Painting and Sculpture in America,* exh. cat. (New York: The Museum of Modern Art, 1995); John R. Lane and Susan C. Larsen, *Abstract Painting and Sculpture in America, 1927–1944,* exh. cat. (Pittsburgh: Museum of Art, Carnegie Institute, 1983); Barbara Rose, *American Abstract Artists: The Early Years,* exh. cat. (New York: Sid Deutsch Gallery, 1980); Judith K. Van Wagner, *Geometric Abstraction,* exh. cat. (Lincoln, Neb.: Sheldon Art Gallery, 1979); and John Elderfield, *Geometric Abstraction 1926–1942,* exh. cat., (Dallas: Dallas Museum of Fine Arts, 1972).

27— Albert Gallatin, "Letter from USA," *Formes* 6 (June 1930): 22, quoted in Debra Bricker Balken, "Albert Eugene Gallatin and the Museum of Living Art," in *Albert Eugene Gallatin and His Circle,* exh. cat. (Miami: The Lowe Art Museum, University of Miami, 1986),18.

28— Quoted in Balken, "Albert Eugene Gallatin," 31.

29— Charles Harrison, "Mondrian in London," *Studio International* 172. no. 884 (1996): 285–289.

30— Janus, *Man Ray: The Photographic Image* (Woodbury, N.Y.: Barron's, 1980), 9, quoted in Sandra S. Phillips "Themes and Variations: Man Ray's Photography in the Twenties and Thirties," in Merry Foresta et al., *Perpetual Motif: The Art of Man Ray* (New York: Abbeville Press, 1988), 177.

31— "Monsieur Ray est né on ne sait où. Après avoir été successivement marchand de charbon, plusieurs fois millionnaire et chairman du chewing-gum trust, il a décidé de donner suite à l'invitation des dadaïstes et d'exposer à Paris ses dernières toiles." Billy Klüver and Julie Martin, "Man Ray, Paris," in Foresta, *Perpetual Motif,* 102.

32— Elizabeth Hutton Turner, "Transatlantic," in Foresta, *Perpetual Motif,* 139.

33— Walter Benjamin, *Illuminations,* trans. Harry Zohn (Glasgow: Fontana/Collins, 1977), 257.

the purity of the object

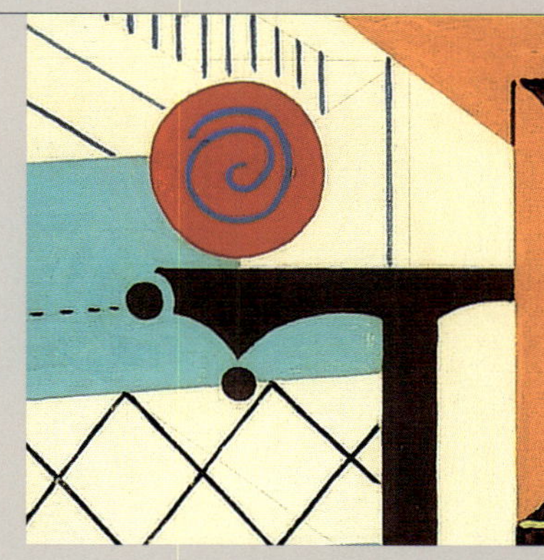

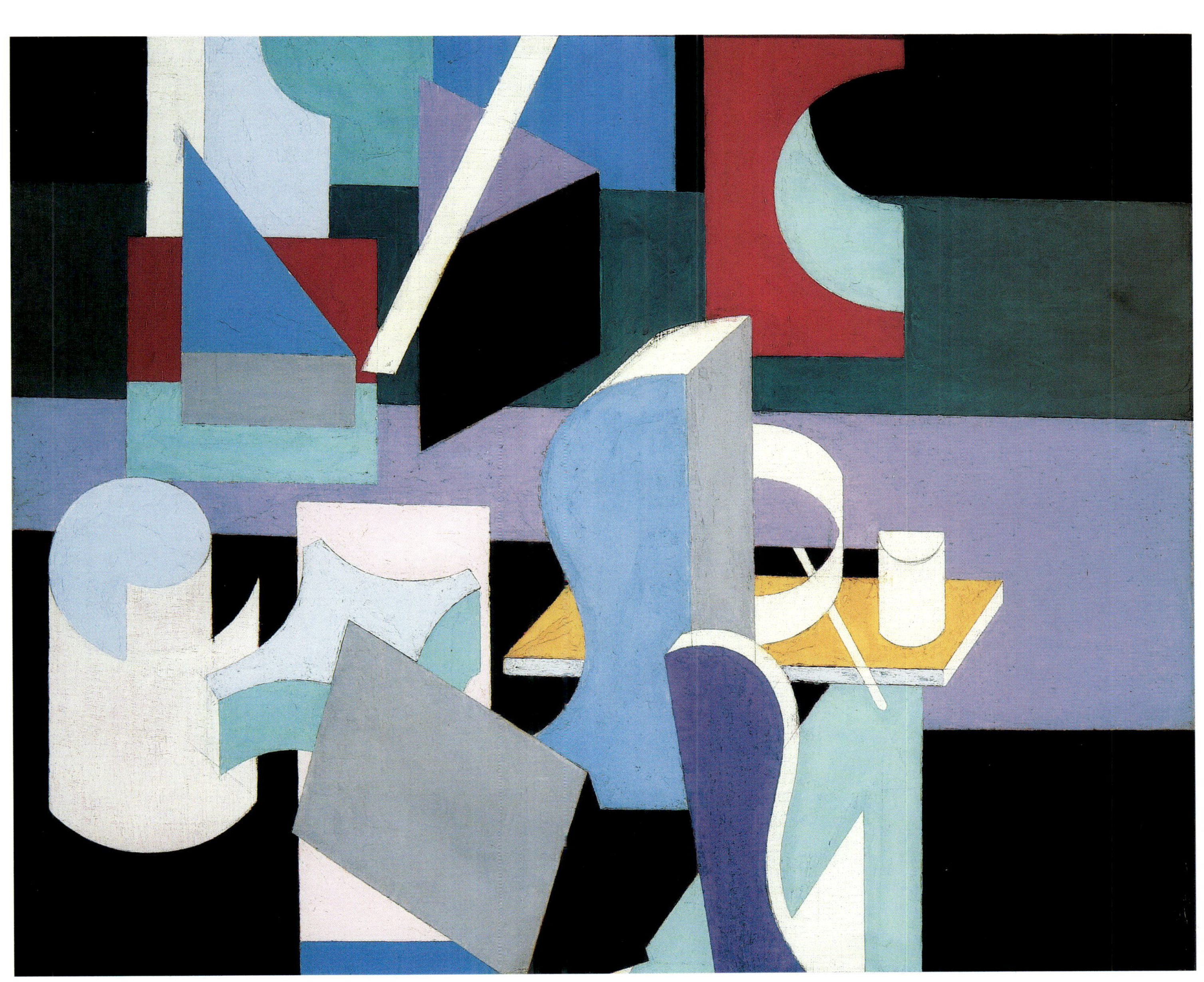

CHAPTER 1

PATRICK HENRY BRUCE
PEINTURE [PAINTING], C. 1917–18
OIL AND GRAPHITE ON CANVAS, 65.1 X 81.6 CM
TERRA FOUNDATION FOR THE ARTS, CHICAGO.
THE DANIEL J. TERRA COLLECTION, 1999.21
MAAG, TAM, TMAA

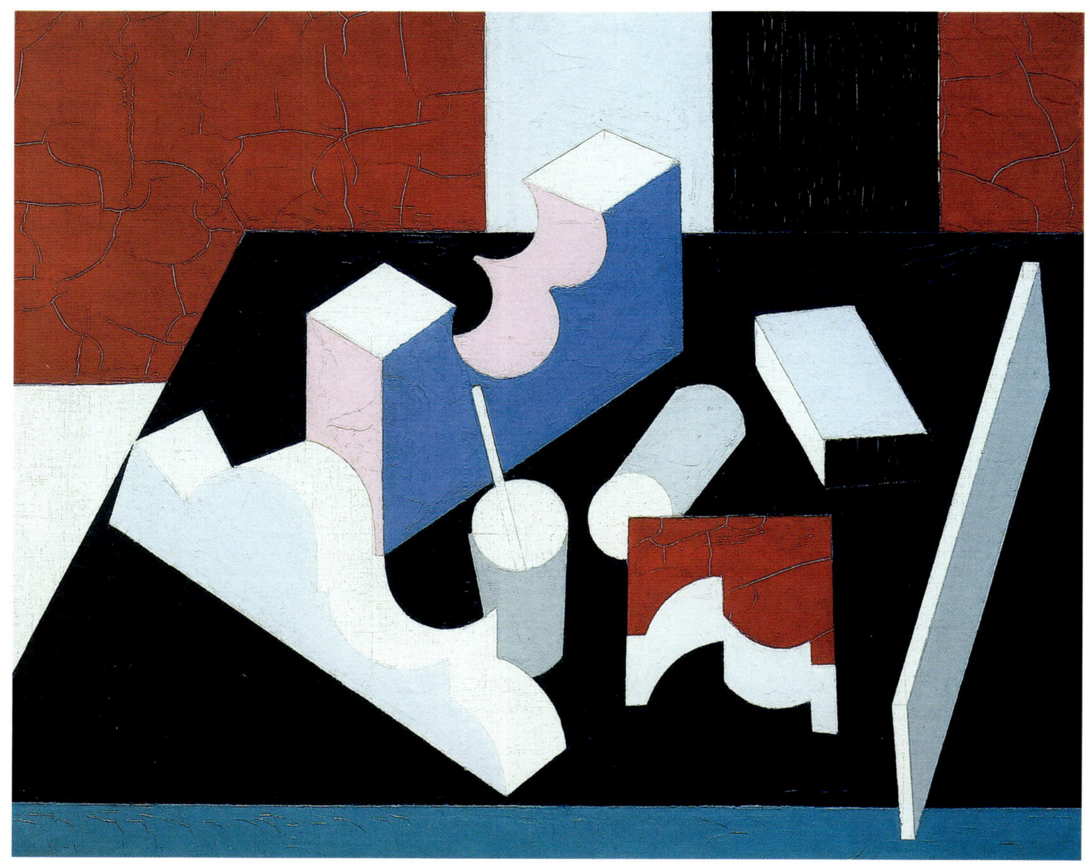

2
PATRICK HENRY BRUCE
COMPOSITION, C. 1923–26
OIL AND PENCIL ON CANVAS,
64.7 X 80.5 CM
MUSÉE NATIONAL D'ART MODERNE –
CENTRE GEORGES POMPIDOU, PARIS.
GIFT OF MR. AND MRS. MICHEL SEUPHOR,
AM 1977.609
MAAG, TAM, TMAA

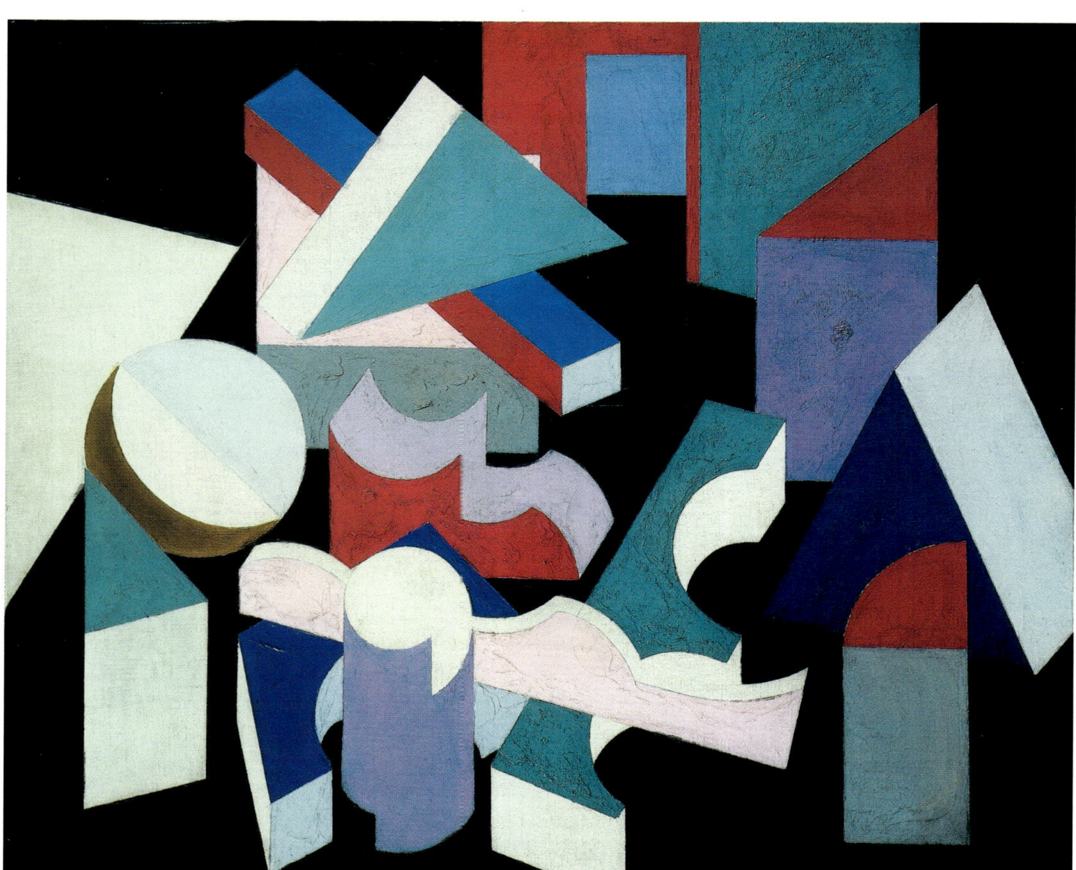

3
PATRICK HENRY BRUCE
STILL LIFE: #4, C. 1922–23
OIL ON CANVAS WITH PENCIL
UNDERDRAWING, 64.4 X 80.7 CM
HIRSHHORN MUSEUM AND SCULPTURE
GARDEN, SMITHSONIAN INSTITUTION,
WASHINGTON D.C.
GIFT OF JOSEPH H. HIRSHHORN, 1972.46
MAAG, TAM, TMAA

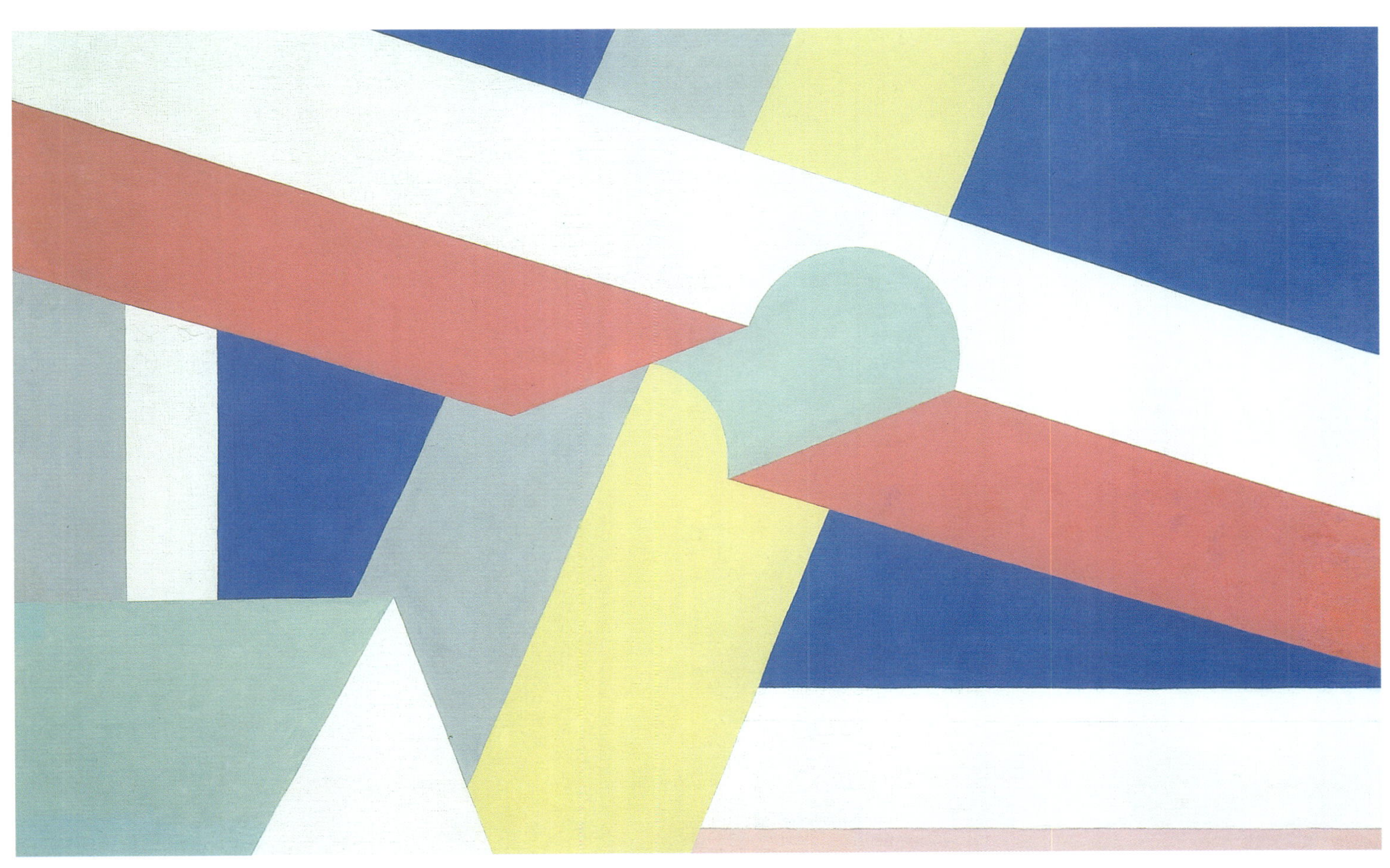

4
PATRICK HENRY BRUCE
STILL LIFE: TRANSVERSE BEAMS, C. 1928–32
OIL AND PENCIL ON CANVAS, 81.2 X 130.2 CM
HIRSHHORN MUSEUM AND SCULPTURE GARDEN,
SMITHSONIAN INSTITUTION, WASHINGTON D.C.
GIFT OF JOSEPH H. HIRSHHORN, 1972.47
MAAG, TAM, TMAA

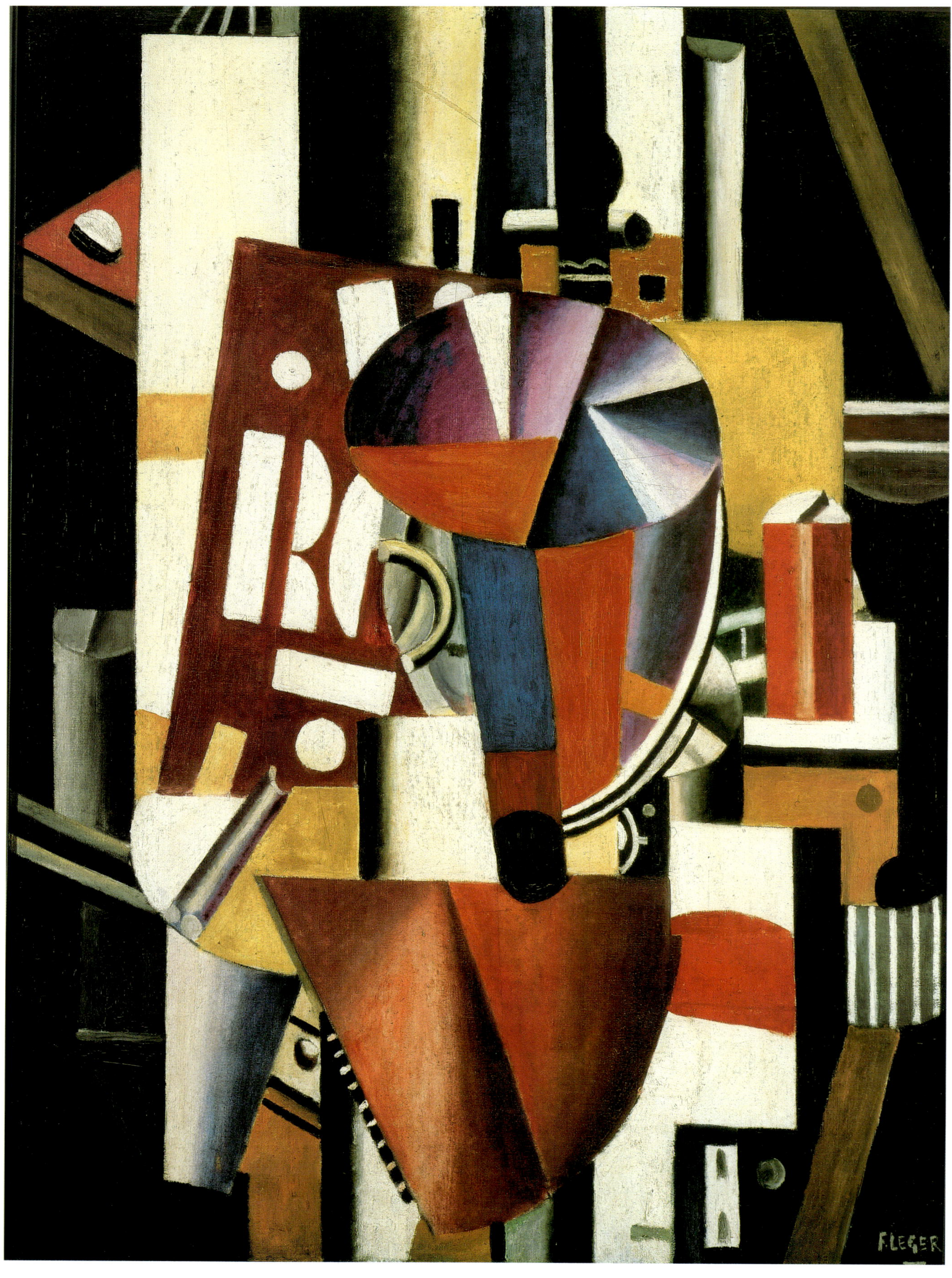

5
FERNAND LÉGER
TYPOGRAPHER (FINAL STATE), 1919
OIL ON CANVAS, 130.3 X 97.5 CM
PHILADELPHIA MUSEUM OF ART.
THE LOUISE AND WALTER ARENSBERG COLLECTION.
1950.134.125
MAAG, TAM, TMAA

FROM *NATURE MORTE* TO CONTEMPORARY PLASTIC LIFE: PURISM, LÉGER, AND THE AMERICANS

KENNETH E. **SILVER**

The United States of the New Spirit

"Let us listen to the advice of American engineers. But let us fear American *architects*."[1] Such was the directive of Le Corbusier, writing in the second issue—November 1920—of *L'Esprit nouveau,* the Parisian design magazine he had founded the previous month with Amédée Ozenfant. The distinction which the Swiss-born architect draws between American technological know-how and American aesthetics—with praise bordering on adulation in the former case and dismissal in the latter—would characterize the magazine's stance for the four years of its existence. Photographs of American grain silos and factories, of American cities (their grid plans, skylines, thoroughfares, and ports), hotels, and office buildings, formed a visual leitmotif of the innovative publication. This was what the modern world should look like, the editors kept reminding their readers, or *almost* what it should look like: when American technology was nakedly asserted, as in the perfect cylinders of the grain silo or the efficient organization of a harbor, Le Corbusier had nothing but praise for transatlantic efforts; when American architects or designers tried to embellish their structures or neglected to control commercial development, he was appalled. Underneath a photo of midtown Manhattan, in issue 20, Le Corbusier wrote: "1923: New York. Discovery of the New World. Poems are published: 'New York!' Enthusiasm, admiration. Beauty? Never. Confusion. Chaos, cataclysm. . . . But the Beautiful is about something else altogether; it begins with order as its basis."[2]

Americans, for the Purists, were the energetic primitives of a new world, imbued with an innate genius for calculation and efficiency—great *constructeurs*—but almost completely lacking in taste and artistic sensitivity. Or rather, for Le Corbusier, it was not that Americans lacked taste, what they lacked was *confidence* in their taste. Rather than aping Europe by decorating New York skyscrapers with neo-Gothic details, Americans should recognize the inherent beauty of their brilliant engineers's unembellished forms, the simple geometric solids on which, he believed, all good design was based. While Le Corbusier's mixture of admiration and disdain for American accomplishments was real,

its rhetorical function in the pages of *L'Esprit nouveau* was to chastise the French (and other Europeans) for their unwillingness to face up to the challenge of modernity as the Americans had.

Although architecture and urban design were unquestionably the major thrust of the magazine's coverage of American culture—in both written form and by way of black-and-white photos of American buildings and cities—they were part of a larger system of American signification, notable as much for its selectivity as its inclusions, which played itself out in *L'Esprit nouveau.* As might be expected in the immediate wake of the Great War, American economic and foreign policy were alluded to regularly, with Woodrow Wilson as the tragic American hero: "A man who understood the danger, and who did not hesitate to wage the good fight in favor of the people against the Magnates of finance, was broken by them. This man was President Wilson," R. Chenevier wrote in issue 7.[3] The same author wrote a more extended treatment of his subject six months later, "Wilson et l'humanisme français," in issue 11/12, which was introduced by a note from the editors at the top of the article: "Some of our readers have expressed their surprise in seeing *L'Esprit nouveau* treat economic and sociological questions. *L'Esprit nouveau* wants to be the great *Review of connection* of thinking men, the link among the elite of specialists; it wants to be complete. Who could fail to perceive that today, more than ever, everything is connected and that questions of the spirit are closely connected to the social."[4] In yet another article on Wilson, in issue 22, in the Spring of 1924, concerned primarily with the League of Nations—accompanied by an exhilarating photo of the former president—the self-styled "review of connection" linked him to another of the magazine's favorite Americans: Walt Whitman: "The peace which Mr. Wilson promised the waiting soldiers was the peace of good will, of which another great American, the poet Whitman, had said that it 'would make grass grow on the borders.'"[5] Whitman had been the subject of a major article in *L'Esprit nouveau* three years earlier, in issue 5, by Léon Bazalgette, the foremost French translator and biographer of the poet. If Wilson was the most timely of American subjects, Whitman was, in a sense, the most timeless, having already been lauded for his straightforward celebration of ordinary

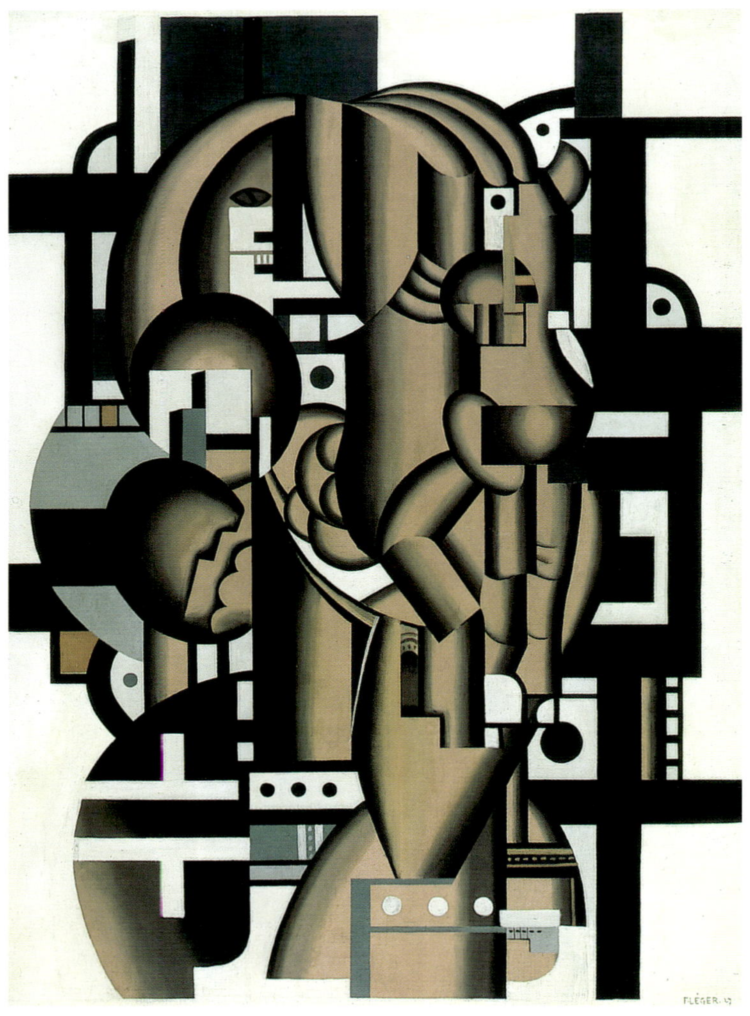

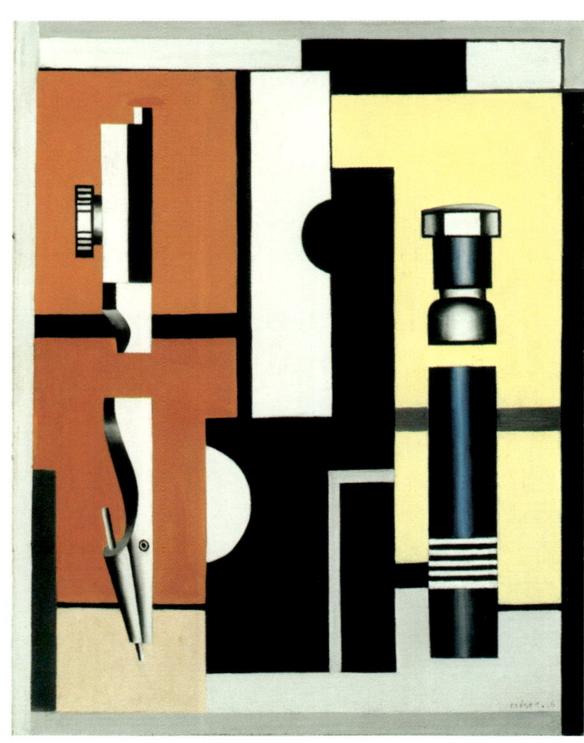

6

FERNAND LÉGER
COMPOSITION, 1923–27
OIL ON CANVAS, 128.3 X 97.2 CM
PHILADELPHIA MUSEUM OF ART,
THE A. E. GALLATIN COLLECTION, 1952.61.63
MAAG, TAM, TMAA

7

FERNAND LÉGER
THE COMPASS, 1926
OIL ON CANVAS, 92 X 73 CM
THE ART INSTITUTE OF CHICAGO,
A MILLENIUM GIFT OF THE SARA LEE CORPORATION,
1999.370
MAAG, TAM, TMAA

American experience by the Parisian avant-garde for decades. Likewise for Edgar Allan Poe, limner of the *extraordinaire*, whose esteem by French modernists dates back to Charles Baudelaire, and who Paul Dermée treated in issue 22.

For the most part, though, American iconography for the Purists was a question of stereotypes (or perhaps, in Purist terminology, it was that these images had stood the typological test of time) American Indians—it was reported in issue 14 that Marshal Foch had smoked a peace pipe with Red Tomahawk, "the man who had killed Sitting Bull," and who gave the French general the name Watakpech Wakiya ("Charging Bull");[6] American athletes—much was made of the fact, with a great deal of ridicule for French arrogance before the fight, that Jack Dempsey had knocked out French champion Georges Carpentier;[7] and American "Negro" jazz and dance—mostly quite positive: "Jazz's folklore melody is pure, essential, rarely banal,"[8] but it was also relegated, in issue 21, to the status of *outworn* exoticism, "*un bon petit brouhaha sentimental et décoratif,*" contrary to the Purist search for a modern folklore based on mechanical standards.[9]

Cinema, on the other hand, was a genuinely new manifestation of culture and American movies were almost unequivocally lauded—to the detriment of the French—in *L'Esprit nouveau*.[10] In "Pro Cinéma," Louis Delluc's opening salvo—"The fact is that there is not yet a French cinema," is contrasted to the "charm, adventure, action, space . . . [of] these large compositions which come to us from Stockholm, New York, Los Angeles, and elsewhere."[11] Familiarity with American stars and directors is evident throughout the run of the magazine. The names Fatty Arbuckle, Norma Talmedge, Mae Murray, William S. Hart, Thomas Ince, and D. W. Griffith are dropped repeatedly; Douglas Fairbanks is called simply "Douglas" and Chaplin is known as both "Charlie" and "Charlot," (the title of the article Élie Faure devoted to him in issue 6).[12] Just as pointing to America's architectural successes and failures was a rhetorical ploy, by which Le Corbusier hoped to spur France to action, so Delluc pulls off a journalistic and didactic tour de force in issue 3. After discussing a number of recent French films—Bernard's *Le Secret de Rosette Lambert,* Violet's *Li-Hang-le-Cruel*, L'Herbier's *Villa Destin*, Poirier's *Penseur,* which he judiciously praises or criticizes—he arrives at *Broken Blossoms,* for which he devotes a line to each of its protagonists (Lillian Gish, Donald Crisp, Richard Bathelmess), and a sentence to its creator: "There's D. W. Griffith, director, who has constructed streets more humane than the small heart of a child and slums whose horizon is vaster than the Pacific," and then ends the article (with capital letters in the original): "ÇA, C'EST UN FILM, Voilà tout. Louis Delluc."[13] The point was clear—Americans made films, the French made . . . things that were not *quite* films.

Purism before the Purists?

But painting and sculpture were another story. There is not a single work by an American artist reproduced in the entire run of *L'Esprit nouveau*, nor an article devoted to one (although contemporary artists from France, Italy, Belgium, Spain, Germany, Austria, Russia, Poland, and a number of other countries are represented in reproductions and articles). Again, this may be partly rhetorical: we know that, for its Purist editors, Americans were people who could accomplish remarkable things, but not art—*the Beautiful is about something else altogether*. Moreover, avant-garde art, especially cubism and its derivatives—for which the magazine propagandized, especially for the Purist art of its founders—was still a recent phenomenon for American practitioners. American art collecting, on the other hand, makes two brief appearances in reference to the Barnes Foundation,[14] and one of the magazine's readers, Armand Salanou, wrote in to suggest that the Louvre should be sold to the Americans to pay off the French war debt.[15] There is also the report of a contretemps between the futurist F. T. Marinetti, who claimed to have invented a new art movement called "tactilism" and Francis Picabia, who says that it was a "Miss Clifford-Williams" who invented tactilism in New York in 1916.[16]

The only American-born artist whose name is even mentioned is Patrick Henry Bruce, and only in passing, although it does appear four times, always in praise: as an able colorist at the Salon d'Automne, in 1920; as one of the cubists, alongside Henri Hayden, Louis Marcoussis, Leopold Survage, and others, "who one will view with pleasure" at the Salon des Indépendants, 1921; as among the efforts, with those of Albert Gleizes, André Lhote, Jacques Lipchitz and others, "most indicative of today's sensibility," in 1921; and along with Fernand Léger and Gleizes, as the cubists whose work produced an "excellent effect" at the Salon d'Automne in 1921.[17] Unfortunately, we have no indication of precisely which works Bruce showed at the Parisian Salons in the 1920s. Although he was a regular exhibitor—at the Indépendants in 1921, 1922, and 1923, and at the Salon d'Automne in 1921, 1922, 1923, 1928, 1929, and 1930—he neutrally titled all his works either *Peinture* or *Nature morte*.

Yet, if we look at the six extant works,[18] which Bruce painted between 1917 and 1921, it is obvious why the Purists took at least a passing interest in him (cat. 1). For these are paintings that fulfill and even exceed the Purist mandate for advanced art after the Great War. In contradistinction to prewar, analytic cubism, Charles-Édouard Jeanneret (Le Corbusier) and Ozenfant called for an art of synthesis, a distilled art which would eschew the haphazard and embrace the enduring, invariable principles of form: "Of all recent schools of painting, only cubism foresaw the advantages of choosing selected objects, and of their inevitable associations. But by a paradoxical error, instead of sifting out the general laws of those objects, cubism showed their accidental aspects, to such an extent that on the basis

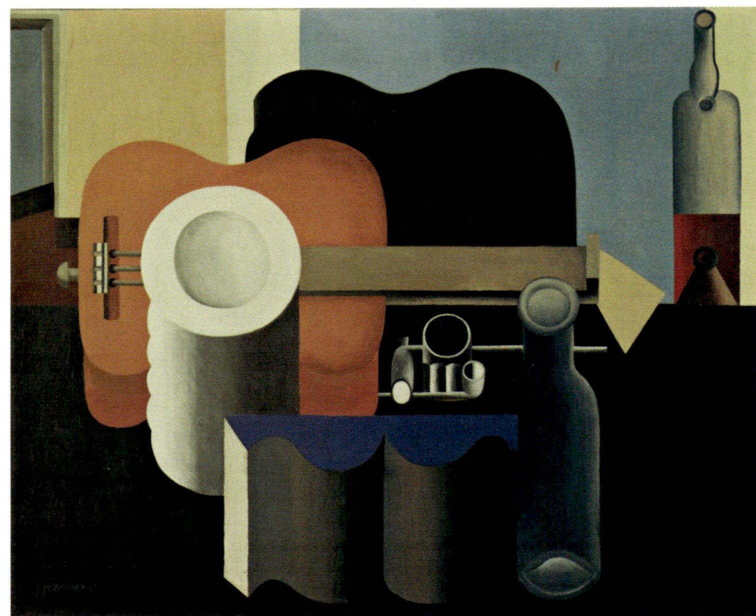

FIG. 1.
**LE CORBUSIER
(CHARLES-EDOUARD JEANNERET),**
STILL LIFE, 1920.
OIL ON CANVAS, 80.9 X 99.7 CM.
THE MUSEUM OF MODERN ART, NEW YORK.
VAN GOGH PURCHASES FUND.

of this erroneous idea it even re-created arbitrary and fantastic forms."[19] The post-cubist art of Purism, on the other hand, would be a kind of Platonic embrace of the constant and the universal: "A painting is an association of purified, related, and architectured elements. A painting should not be a fragment, a painting is a whole. A viable organ is a whole, a viable organ should not be a fragment."[20] The earliest of Bruce's late, synthetic works, in the collection of the Terra Foundation for the Arts (cat. 1) , dated circa 1917–18, might usefully be compared to Jeanneret's *Still Life* of 1920 (fig. 1). Here Bruce had anticipated much that distinguishes the Purist effort: the severe, distilled, geometric forms, the architectural fragments juxtaposed to simple geometric solids, the shallow but legible pictorial space (which is, nonetheless, consistently made ambiguous by means of unmodulated, flat planes of color). The differences are striking as well. Where Bruce reduces all his forms to a lexicon of abstracted, geometric solids, so that individual objects lose their precise identity, in Jeanneret's painting most of the forms retain enough of their anecdotal, real-world characteristics to allow us to speak of the still life objects from which they derive: guitar, shot-glass, pipes, bottle, etc. Bruce's colors are also livelier. Although he works with a restrained palette of grays, greens, mauves, reds, blues, black, and white, there is a contrapuntal relationship between tonality and local colors which the Purist's murkier, earth-toned palette, despite the addition of

the blue edge of the architectural molding, does not possess. Yet, the affiliation is undeniable. Perhaps *avant la lettre*, Bruce has made a painting which is "an association of purified, related, and architectured elements," one that is strikingly close to the Purists's own efforts.

Why then did they fail to reproduce any of Bruce's work in *L'Esprit nouveau*? As I've already suggested, it may have been ideological: America's role in the formation of the New Spirit had already been assigned to its engineers and denied its architects (and by extension all those who would make art as opposed to utilitarian forms). Or, perhaps it was due to a certain anxiety of influence: if the Bruce is accurately dated,[21] then it may be that Ozenfant and Jeanneret found themselves too beholden for comfort to his pictorial solutions. Or maybe it was simply the combination of Bruce's fabled reticence and his lack of a dealer (many of the artists whose works were reproduced in the magazine, unlike Bruce, were represented by either Léonce Rosenberg's Galerie de l'Effort Moderne, or that of his brother Paul Rosenberg, or by Daniel-Henry Kahnweiler's Galerie Simon). Bruce did have an influential ally—really his only art world supporter of any significance—in the person of Frenchman Henri-Pierre Roché, who Ozenfant claimed was the man who supplied *L'Esprit nouveau* with its photographs of American grain elevators and factories, of which Bruce's stripped-down forms are so redolent.[22] But Roché is never mentioned in any of the magazine's regularly published lists of its collaborators. Nor for that matter is any American mentioned in those lists; what's more, not only were no works of art by Americans illustrated in the magazine, but there is not a single American author who wrote for *L'Esprit nouveau*. All by way of saying that, for the Purists, the United States was a more-or-less abstract, mythic, conceptual entity—New York or the prairies of the industrial belt might well be part of its pictorial economy, and Woodrow Wilson, D. W. Griffith, and Jack Dempsey aspects of its larger rhetorical project, but real American artists working in Paris were not.

The Only *American* Painter in Paris

Although American artists were a kind of blind spot in the rhetoric of *L'Esprit nouveau*, this does not mean that the Americans working in Paris were themselves blinded to the Purist aesthetic. As Barbara Rose, Elizabeth Hutton Turner, and Wanda Corn have all demonstrated,[23] a sense of national identity on the part of the Paris-based Americans was encouraged and legitimated in France, even by the avant-garde journal which failed to notice them. The very qualities and characteristics that would have made them feel crass and uncultivated had they remained in the United States, became assets in Paris: directness and simplicity, the power of movies, advertising and commercial culture, and even America's relative lack of art historical precedent, were advantages rather than liabilities in the modernist milieu of the French capital.

Fernand Léger, fellow traveler of the Purists, was as interested in the American artists-in-French-residence as Ozenfant and Jeanneret were not. According to Rose, for instance, when Roché, after the artist's death, "tried to trace Bruce's footsteps . . . he found one of the few artists who remembered the silent, self-effacing American was Léger."[24] Indeed, Léger was a key link between the Parisian art world and the Americans, even before he himself made the transatlantic crossing for the first time, in 1931, and exclaimed: "The most colossal spectacle in the world. Neither film nor photography nor reportage can dim the amazing spectacle that is New York at night seen from the fortieth floor. . . . She retains her freshness, her unexpectedness, her surprise for the traveler who is seeing her for the first time. . . . Astonishing country where the houses are taller than the churches, where the window washers are millionaires, where football games are organized between the prisoners and the police!"[25] As they did for the contributors to *L'Esprit nouveau*, American movies informed Léger's point-of-view about the New World (note that he begins his description of New York by comparing the real thing to images pre-conceived by means of film, photography, and reportage). His own film, *Ballet mécanique* (1923–24), begins with an eleven-second sequence utilizing his cubistic wooden marionette figure of Charlie Chaplin; and the cinematic close-up figures importantly in his thinking about modern art in the 1920s: "Before I saw it in the cinema, I did not know what a hand was! The object in itself is capable of becoming something absolute, moving, and dramatic."[26]

It is relevant, in this context, that we recognize the filmic quality of the paintings of Léger's closest American friend in Paris, Gerald Murphy (see Jocelyne Rotily's essay on Murphy, p. 55–62). In *Cocktail* (fig. 2), for instance, the monumentally scaled objects and their sudden, disjunctive juxtaposition make us think of cinematic close-ups and jump-cuts, just as the grisaille palette of the cocktail shaker and the background, as well as the repetition of closely related forms, suggest the movement of black-and-white frames of film through a movie projector. These cinematic devices, coupled with the use of the commercial vernacular in his art— both industrially produced objects as subject matter and modern advertising techniques as formal templates—meant that, for Léger, Murphy was the very prototype of a new kind of artist, one whom he referred to as the "only *American* painter in Paris."[27]

No French artist knew better than he that this statement was untrue. Not only was Léger, as we know, acquainted with Bruce, but he presumably knew other American painters at the Académie Moderne, an art school in Montparnasse, which he ran with his Purist colleague, Amédée Ozenfant (Léger would become a good friend of the painter George L. K. Morris, who would leave the only extended account of Léger's classes by an American artist).[28] Although his assertion that Murphy was *sui generis*—as both an American *and* an artist—played to the cultural biases of *L'Esprit nouveau*, I don't think that it was intended as a denigration of other American painters in French residence. Rather, I suspect, it was meant to echo the exaggerations of the American pitchman and

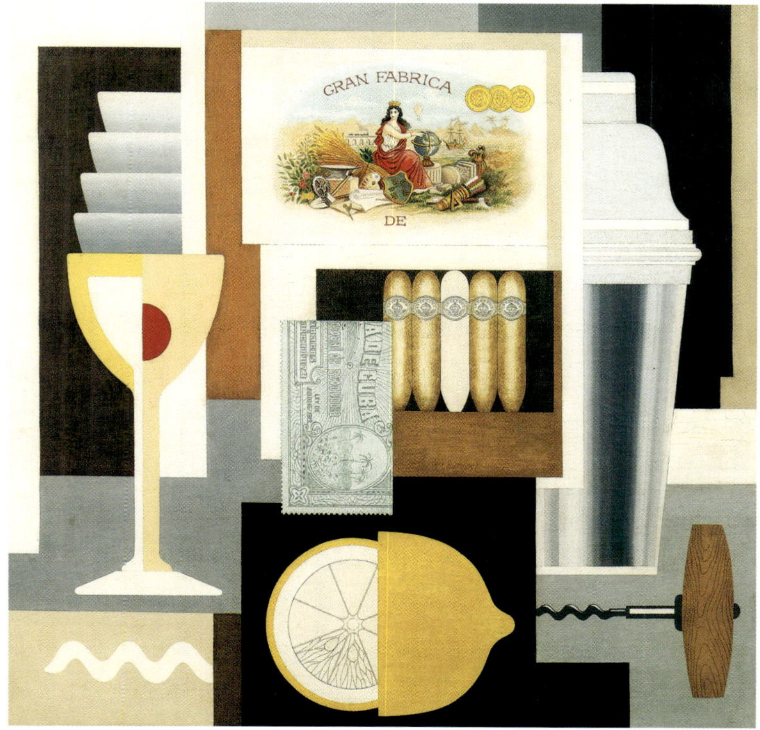

FIG. 2.
GERALD MURPHY,
COCKTAIL, 1927.
OIL ON CANVAS, 73.8 X 75.9 CM.
WHITNEY MUSEUM OF AMERICAN ART, NEW YORK.
PURCHASE WITH FUNDS FROM EVELYN AND LEONARD A.
LAUDER, THOMAS H. LEE, AND THE MODERN PAINTING
AND SCULPTURE COMMITTEE.

the generic advertising billboard which he felt was a beautiful part of the modern environment— ". . . this yellow or red poster, shouting in a timid landscape, is the best of possible reasons for the new painting; it topples the whole sentimental literary concept and announces the advent of plastic contrast."[29]

But it is also the case that no other American artist had learned Léger's lessons about the value of the modern object in painting as well as Murphy, whose work transforms the traditional *nature morte* into bold emblems of "contemporary plastic life," to use Léger's own phrase. Whereas Léger's prewar art had, at moments, skirted the edge of incomprehensibility—veering, as it were, between a cubist renewal of fin-de-siècle obscurantism in works like *La Noce*, of 1910–11 (The Wedding, Centre Pompidou, Paris) and the percussive vitalism of his highly tactile but completely abstract *Contrastes de formes*—by the 1920s he had moved towards the crystalline depiction of modern objects. We see this in the draftsman's tools, embedded in the geometric substrate, in his *Compass* of 1926 (cat. 7). Murphy's art follows this formula quite closely, and it seems not unlikely that he was also perusing the images in *L'Esprit nouveau*: his painting *The Watch*, of 1924–25 (Dallas Museum of Art), may have been, at least in part, inspired by a comparable view of the astronomical clock at Strasbourg Cathedral, reproduced in issue 9 (June 1921).[30]

In "The Machine Aesthetic: The Manufactured Object, the Artisan, and the Artist," published in the *Bulletin de l'Effort Moderne,* Léger, like his friends the Purists, extolled the virtues of the common object of contemporary life in the least likely of environments: "The Beautiful is everywhere; perhaps more in the arrangement of your saucepans on the white walls of your kitchen than in your eighteenth-century living room or in the official museums."[31] For an artist like Gerald Murphy, whose family had made its fortune in the retailing of leather goods and accessories, this kind of talk did more than simply validate a mercantile background. It ratified familiar, ready-made subjects for art, like the box of Three Star safety matches, the Parker fountain pen, and the Gillette safety razor in the Dallas Museum of Art's *Razor*, of 1924. And in pointing not only to the saucepan but also its arrangement—as in his "Notes on Contemporary Plastic Life." of 1923, where he invoked the "highly organized spectacles" of store windows[32]—Léger helped Murphy understand not only the value of modern objects, but also how to put modern display techniques to the service of art: "Like an advertiser, Murphy let the products speak," as Wanda Corn has said.[33]

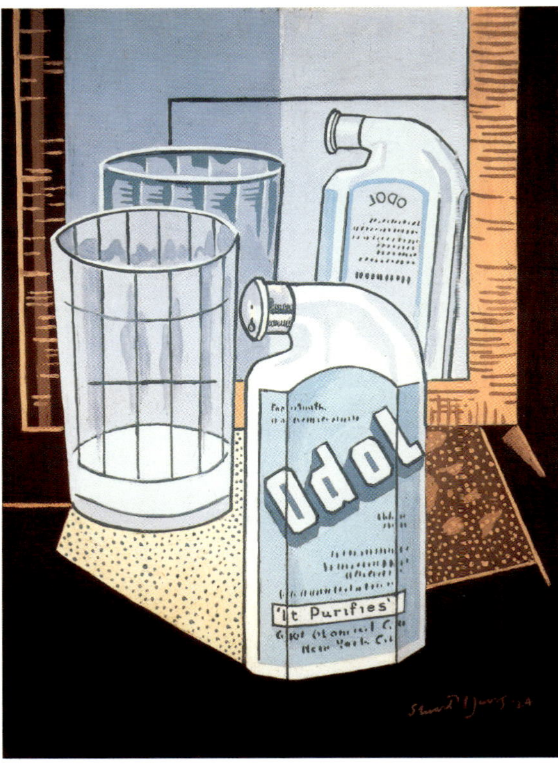

FIG. 3.
STUART DAVIS,
ODOL, 1924.
OIL ON ACADEMY BOARD. 62.1 X 44 CM.
CINCINNATI ART MUSEUM.
EDWIN AND VIRGINIA IRWIN MEMORIAL.

It Purifies

In his journal, in 1921, Stuart Davis had a related epiphany: "I WANT a *direct* expression of my desires. I want to paint a series of pictures the subject matter of which will be popular. By 'popular' pictures, I mean those phases of modern life which I am capable of understanding. One of these things is the beauty of packing. Where a few decades ago everything was packed in barrels and boxes they now are packed singly or in dozen or half dozen lots as the control over distribution increases. This symbolizes a very high civilization in relation to other civilizations."[34] This "theory" of civilization as embodied in its packaging might easily have been written by the Purists, although *L'Esprit nouveau* had only been in existence for nine months when Davis wrote these notes to himself. Like the contemporaneous paintings which were the realization of this desire for "*direct* expression"—*Lucky Strike* (Museum of Modern Art, New York), *Bull Durham* (The Baltimore Museum of Art), and *Cigarette Papers* (Menil Collection, Houston)—we must conclude, therefore, as most Davis scholars have, that the relationship of his art of the early 1920s to Parisian events and tastes was more a matter of affinity than direct influence. We know, on the other hand, that Davis, who did not get to Paris until years later, had been carefully monitoring the art scene there for a long while. He probably saw Léger's work at the 1913 Armory Show in New York, and at the Société Anonyme exhibition of his work in New York in 1925. According to Barbara Rose, Davis was probably also well aware of Léger through his friendship with Charles Demuth.[35]

But if Davis's immediate postwar work remains rooted in prewar cubist collage—we can think of comparable use of fragments of the ephemeral world of packaging in the *papiers collés* of Picasso, Braque, and Gris, although never raised to the monumental scale and isolation of Davis's three paintings—by the mid-1920s the influence of the aesthetic of *L'Esprit nouveau* and of contemporary work by Léger is apparent. In Davis's *Odol*, of 1924 (fig. 3), for example, the artist retains his interest in the slickly packaged product. Now, though, it is submitted to much less cubist fragmentation, its name is even bolder, and the product itself—a mouthwash—is so redolent of the hygienic modern life propagated in the pages of *L'Esprit nouveau,* that one suspects the slogan imprinted on its label, "It Purifies," may be an intentional reference to Ozenfant and Le Corbusier.

When Davis got to Paris, in 1928, his friend Elliot Paul arranged a meeting with Léger. "He liked the Egg Beaters very much," Davis wrote to his father of Léger's reaction, "and said they showed a concept of space similar to his latest development and it was interesting that two people who did not know each other should arrive at similar ideas. He thought the street scenes I am doing here too realistic for his taste but said they were drawn with fine feeling."[36] Of course, since Davis had been well aware of Léger's work for years, the similarity of their spatial conceptions was perhaps not quite as coincidental as the Frenchman thought—did Davis refrain from pointing this out to Léger?

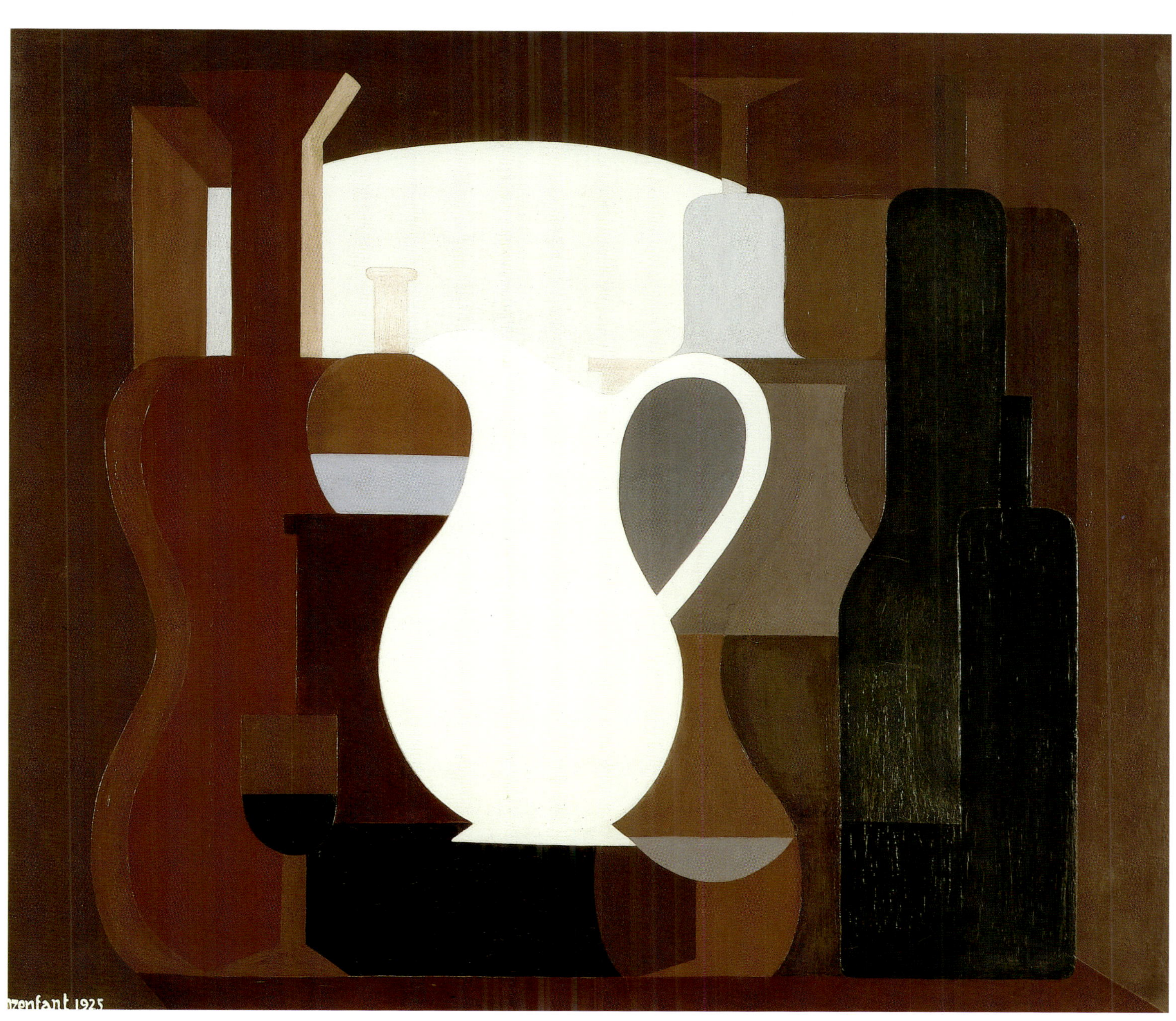

8
AMÉDÉE OZENFANT
LE POT BLANC [THE WHITE JUG], 1925
OIL ON CANVAS, 151.5 X 176.5 CM
MUSÉE NATIONAL D'ART MODERNE –
CENTRE GEORGES POMPIDOU, PARIS.
GIFT OF RAOUL LA ROCHE. AM 4069 P (ON LOAN TO THE MUSÉE
D'ART MODERNE ET CONTEMPORAIN, STRASBOURG)
MAAG

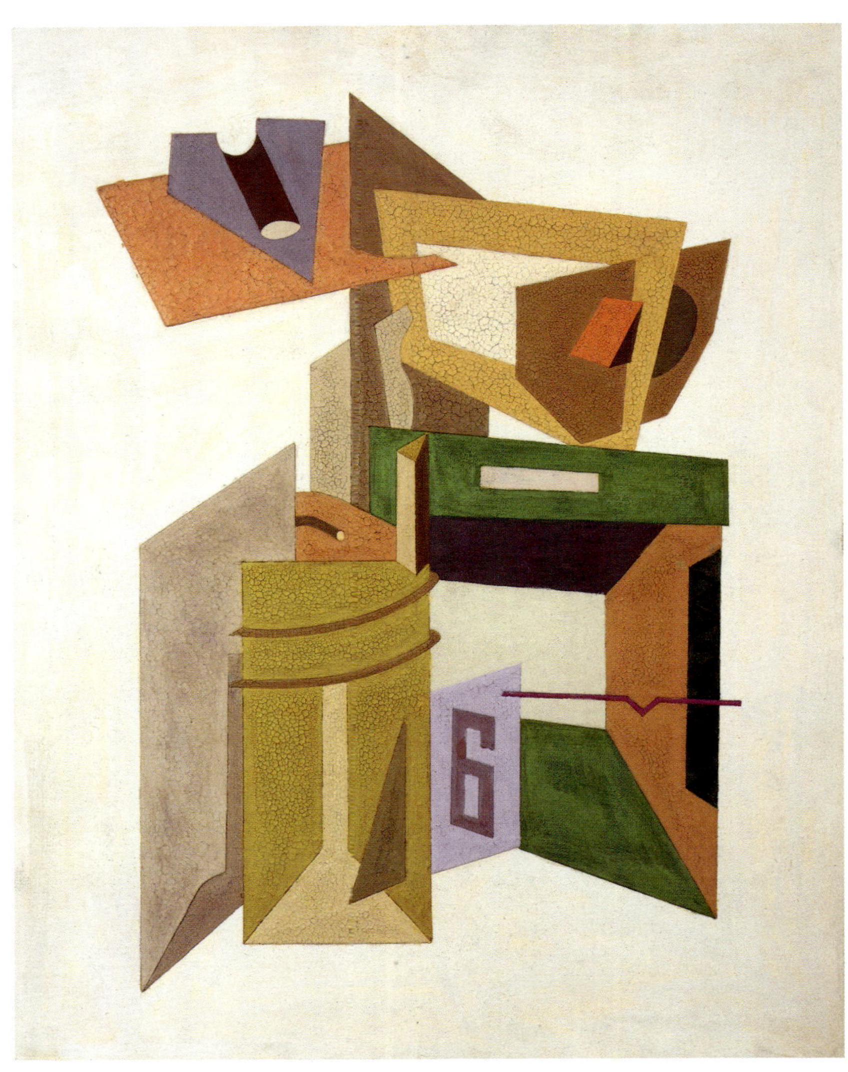

9
STUART DAVIS
PERCOLATOR, 1927
OIL ON CANVAS, 45.1 X 36.4 CM
CURTIS GALLERIES, MINNEAPOLIS,
1998.05.23.1
MAAG, TAM, TMAA

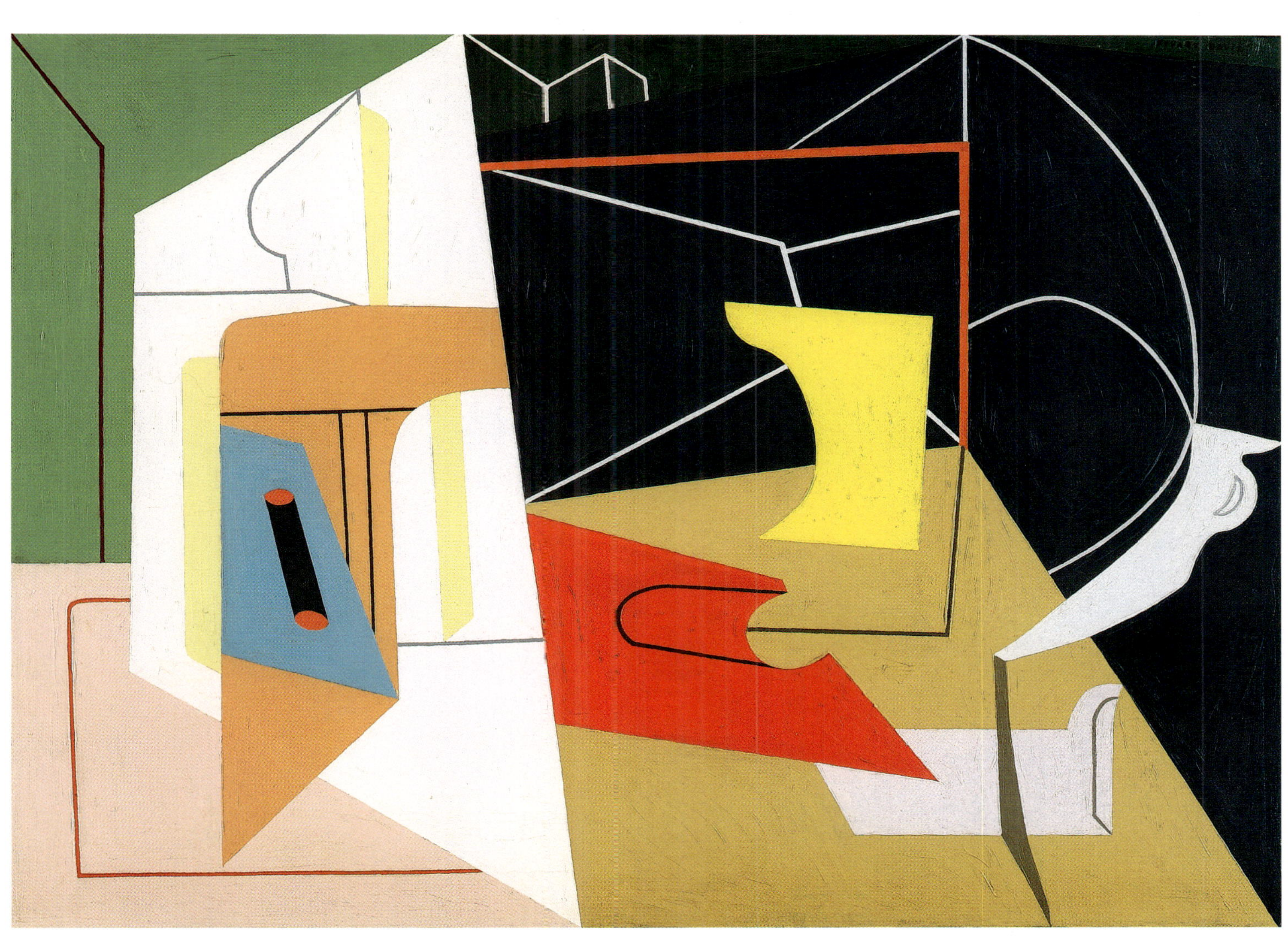

STUART DAVIS
EGGBEATER NO. 4, 1928
OIL ON CANVAS, 68.9 X 97.1 CM
THE PHILLIPS COLLECTION,
WASHINGTON D.C., 0470
MAAG, TAM, TMAA

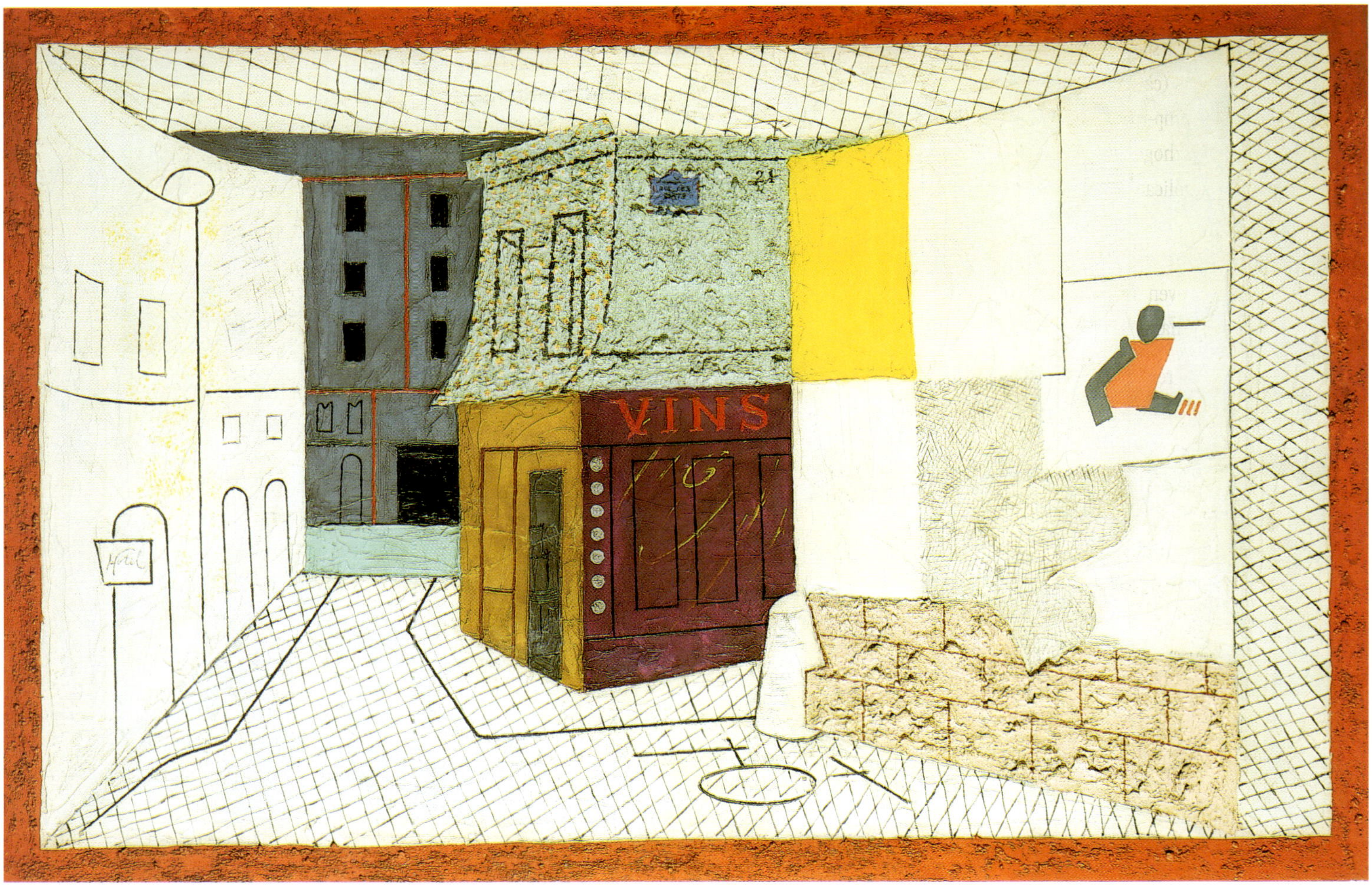

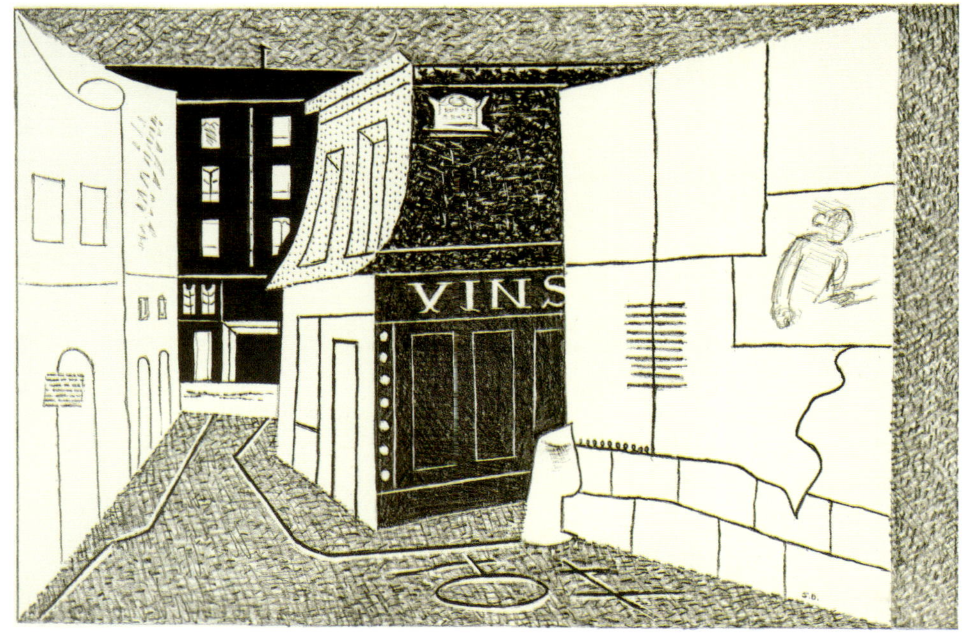

11
STUART DAVIS
RUE DES RATS, 1928
OIL ON CANVAS, 60 X 92.1 CM
CURTIS GALLERIES, MINNEAPOLIS,
1999.01.29.1
MAAG, TAM, TMAA

12
STUART DAVIS
RUE DES RATS, 1929
LITHOGRAPH, 25.4 X 38.6 CM
TERRA FOUNDATION FOR THE ARTS, CHICAGO,
THE DANIEL J. TERRA COLLECTION, 1996.68
MAAG, TAM, TMAA

Be that as it may, the *Eggbeater* series is a remarkable group of pictures, built around a spatial organization that is, if anything, even more complex than Léger's (cat. 10). For not only does Davis make use of Léger's cinema-like jump-cuts to divide up his canvas, but he also transforms the receding orthogonals of linear perspective into the diagonal elements which complicate his post-cubist grid. It's no wonder that, in comparison, Davis's Paris street scenes—like his *Blue Café* painting (cat. 15) and his *Rue des Rats* lithograph (cat. 12)—looked too realistic to Léger, even if, ultimately, they too were distantly related to the Frenchman's Parisian cityscapes.

Léger's art remained a touchstone for Davis after he returned to America. This is evident not only in that he continued to exploit the Frenchman's activated pictorial, but even in such telling details as the nautical tattoo which decorates the large pipe in his mural, *Men without Women,* 1932, a motif borrowed from Léger's *Le Mécanicien* of some ten years earlier (The Mechanic, National Gallery of Canada, Ottawa).[37] Davis wrote in his notebook that "Léger is good because he came to grips with the subject matter of contemporary life in its industrial aspects."[38] This included a lively interest in working-class life, not surprising for an artist of his leftist sympathies. Indeed, politics, as well as painting, was a crucial link between the two: after joining the Artists Union, in 1934, Davis became editor of its publication *Art Front;* one assumes that it was through him, in 1937, that Léger's article, "The New Realism Goes On," appeared in its pages.[39]

Why not meet?

Where the influence of any number of members of the Parisian avant-garde on the art of American sculptor Alexander Calder is readily apparent—of Brancusi, Arp, and Miró in particular—that of the Purists and of Léger is not (although a group of biomorphic drawings Calder made in 1932 are clearly indebted to Léger's contemporaneous cross-hatched renderings).[40] Yet, at his great Galerie Percier exhibition in Paris in 1931, Calder included, along with portraits of Miró, Josephine Baker, and others, wire portraits of both Léger and Ozenfant (fig 4). Perhaps this was because, as artist Louis Lozowick said in 1925 (and as he might have said of the Purists, as well): "Léger is one of the very few whose work pleads with American artists for an American orientation, a closer contact with their industrial civilization so rich in plastic possibilities."[41] Calder met Léger the previous year, when he invited him, as well as Le Corbusier, Mondrian, and others (including Ozenfant, one assumes), to attend a performance of his *Cirque Calder*, the wood-and-wire extravaganza on which he had been working, and performing, since his arrival in Paris, in 1926. Although his circus animals were anticipated by metal animal sculptures of almost two decades earlier, his interest in the circus phenomenon—and the possibilities for exciting the interest of the Parisian artistic milieu in it—may well have been encouraged by articles like Céline Arnaud's, "Le Cirque, art nouveau,"

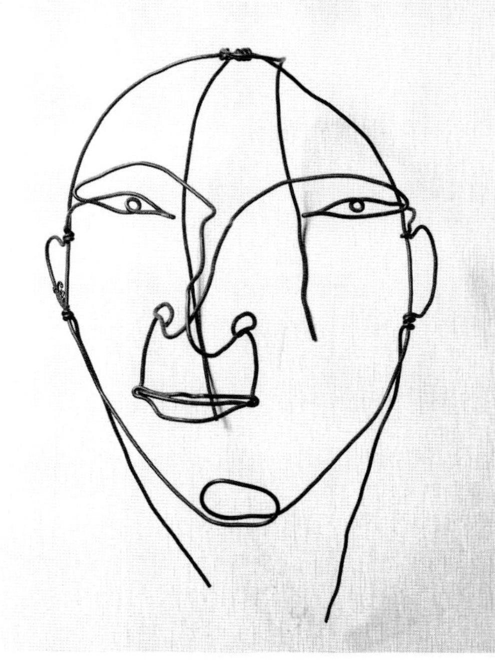

published in the first issue of *L'Esprit nouveau*, and by statements such as Léger's, in 1924, that "The 'Big Top' of the New Circus is an absolutely marvelous world. When I am lost in this astonishing metallic planet with its dazzling spotlights and the tiny acrobat who risks his life every night, I am distracted. . . . I am caught up by the strange architecture of colored tent poles, metallic rods, and ropes that cross each other and sway under the effects of the lights."[42] Calder would later credit Léger, along with Miró, as having been especially influential in his decision to turn to pure abstraction in the 1930s;[43] yet, it is likely that Léger's enthusiasm for contemporary life and, in particular, for America's contribution to modernity, had been formative for Calder for years. At any rate, the two artists were close enough that it was Léger who was asked to write the introductory statement for the Galerie Percier show, where the Frenchman again used the hyperbolic language he had employed in discussing Murphy: "Mondrian, Marcel Duchamp, Brancusi, Arp . . . Calder is in that line, he's American 100/100. Satie and Duchamp are 100/100 French. Why not meet?"[44] If, for the Purists, America produced great engineers, but not artists, and France cultivated great artists, but failed to construct a modern world, for Léger—who loved contrast and exulted contradiction—there was no reason why America and France might not be equal partners in the exhilarating adventure of modernity. ■

1— "Écoutons les conseils des ingénieurs américains. Mais craignons les *architectes* américains." Le Corbusier-Saugnier, "Trois rappels à MM. les architectes," *L'Esprit nouveau* 2 (November 1920): 199 (emphasis in the original).

2— "1923. New York. Découverte du Nouveau-Monde. On publie des albums de vers: 'New York!' Enthousiasme, admiration. Beauté? Jamais. Confusion. Le chaos, la cataclysme . . . . Mais le Beau s'occupe de tout autre chose; pour commencer il possède l'ordre à la base." Le Corbusier, "Pérennité," *L'Esprit nouveau* 20 (Jan/Feb 1924): n.p. [note: with issue 17 (June 1922), the magazine became non paginated].

3— "Un homme qui a compris le danger et qui n'a pas hésité à mener le bon combat en faveur du peuple contre les Magnats de la finance, a été brisé par eux. Cet homme était le Président Wilson." R. Chenevier, "XX," *L'Esprit nouveau* 7 (April 1921): 786.

4— "Quelques-uns de nos lecteurs ont témoigné de la surprise de voir l'*Esprit nouveau* s'intéresser aux questions économiques et sociologiques. L'*Esprit nouveau* veut être la grande *Revue de connexion* des gens qui pensent, le lien entre l'élite des spécialistes; elle veut être complète. Qui peut aujourd'hui ne pas s'apercevoir que tout se tient plus que jamais et que les questions de l'esprit dépendent étroitement de la chose sociale." R. Chenevier, "Wilson et l'humanisme français," *L'Esprit nouveau* 11/12 (November 1921): 1223 (emphasis in the original).

5— "La paix que M. Wilson promit à la patience de soldats était la paix de bonne volonté, dont un autre grand Américain, le poête Whitman, avait dit qu'elle 'ferait pousser l'herbe sur les frontières'." Henri Hertz, "Wilson," *L'Esprit nouveau* 22 (April 1924): n.p.

6— "Le maréchal Foch a fumé le calumet de paix avec le chef indien Tomahawk Rouge, qui tua le chef Taureau Assis . . . . Tomahawk a nommé le maréchal Foch 'Watakpech Wakiya' (le Taureau chargeant)." Anon., "Foch, le 'Taureau chargeant,'" *L'Esprit nouveau* 14 (January 1922): 1676.

7— "Souvenirs du match Carpentier-Dempsey," *L'Esprit nouveau* 10 (July 1921): 1194–95.

8— "La mélodie de folk-lore du jazz est pure, essentielle, rarement banale." Albert Jeanneret is discussing the Billy Arnhold Orchestra in "Les Concerts Wiéner," *L'Esprit nouveau* 14 (January 1922): 1664.

9— Anon., "Usurpation, le Folk-lore," *L'Esprit nouveau* 21 (March 1924): n.p.

10— An exception is Henry de Courtry's contention that American movies were beginning to repeat themselves and that Chaplin was becoming cloying in his sentimentality, in "Cinéma," *L'Esprit nouveau* 18 (November 1923): n.p.

11— "Le fait est qu'il n'y a pas encore un cinéma français. . . . Le charme, aventure, action, espace – qui se dégage n'est pas diminué, loin de là, du fait que ces larges compositions usuelles viennent de Stockholm, de New-York, de Los Angeles ou d'ailleurs." Louis Delluc, "Pro Cinéma," *L'Esprit nouveau* 14 (January 1922): 1666.

12— Élie Faure, "Charlot," *L'Esprit nouveau* 6 (March 1921): 657–66. See also B. Tokine, "L'Esthétique du cinéma," *L'Esprit nouveau* 1: 84–89, and Louis Delluc, "Cinéma," *L'Esprit nouveau* 4 (January 1921), 480–82.

13— "Il y a D. W. Griffith, metteur en scène, qui a construit des rues plus humaines qu'un petit cœur d'enfant et des taudis dont l'horizon est plus vaste que le Pacifique. ÇA, C'EST UN FILM, voilà tout. Louis Delluc" Louis Delluc, "Cinéma," *L'Esprit nouveau* 3 (December 1920), 349–51.

14— For the Barnes Foundation see the preliminary study for the building reproduced in *L'Esprit nouveau* 18 (November 1923): n.p., and a review of Mary Mullen's *An Approach to Art*, published by the Barnes Foundation, in *L'Esprit nouveau* 22 (April 1924), n.p.

15— Armand Salanou, response to questionnaire, "Faut-il brûler le Louvre?," *L'Esprit nouveau* 6 (March 1921): 8.

16— Anon., "La Presse: Le Tactilisme," *L'Esprit nouveau* 5 (February 1921): 594.

17— "Dans les salles cubistes on regardera avec plaisir les travaux de Bruce, de Ferat, de Hayden, de Marcoussis, avec intérêt ceux de Survage, de Tour-Donas."; ". . . Gleizes, Bruce, Ferat, Hayden, Lhote, Marcoussis, Lipchitz, Helessen, Survage et Zadkine marquaient par leurs envois, l'effort le plus significatif de la sensibilité d'aujourd'hui."; "Parmi les cubistes, F. Léger, qui voisine avec Gleizes et Bruce, ont seuls exposé. Nous dirons tout à l'heure ce que nous pensons de l'effet excellent qu'ils y font." The three mentions of Bruce can be found in the following issues of *L'Esprit nouveau* 2 (November 1920): 228; 5 (February 1921): 603; 11/12 (November 1921): 1301; 13 (December 1921): 1504. William Agee states that Bruce's name appeared only twice in *L'Esprit nouveau*, in issues 5 and 11/12, in William C. Agee and Barbara Rose, *Patrick Henry Bruce: American Modernist (A Catalogue Raisonné)* (New York: The Museum of Modern Art, 1979), 28. This excellent catalogue, with essays by Agee and Rose, is the key reference work on Bruce.

18— Bruce destroyed most of his work in the depths of a depression, in 1933.

19— Ozenfant and Jeanneret, "Purism," in Robert L. Herbert, ed., *Modern Artists on Art* (Englewood Cliffs, N.J.: Prentice-Hall, 1964), 65; originally in *L'Esprit nouveau* 4 (January 1921). The literature on Le Corbusier, his ideas, and his architecture, is vast, and I will not rehearse it here. But for Purism as a painting movement Christopher Green's work on Purism in the context of French art of 1920s was the first to take the movement seriously. See John Golding and Christopher Green, *Léger and Purist Paris,* exh. cat. (London: Tate Gallery, 1970) and Green, *Léger and the Avant-Garde* (New Haven and London: Yale University Press, 1976). For the relationship between Purism and World War I see my "Purism: Straightening Up After the Great War," *Artforum* 15, no. 7 (March 1977), 56–63, and *Esprit de Corps: The Art of the Parisian Avant-Garde and the First World War, 1914–1925* (Princeton: Princeton University Press, 1989), in French: *Vers le retour à l'ordre* (Paris: Flammarion, 1991). See as well my exhibition catalogue, *Purism and the Spirit of Synthesis* (New York: Barbara Mathes Gallery, 1986). For Ozenfant, see Susan L. Ball, *Ozenfant and Purism: The Evolution of a Style, 1915–1930* (Ann Arbor, Michigan: UMI Research Press, 1981). The most recent work on Purist painting is Carol S. Eliel, *L'Esprit Nouveau: Purism in Paris, 1918–1925*, exh. cat. (Los Angeles: Los Angeles County Museum of Art, 2001) and Françoise Ducros, *Amédée Ozenfant* (Paris: Éditions du Cercle d'Art, 2002).

20— "Purism," Herbert, 67.

21— Since, in addition to the fact that Bruce destroyed much of his work, and that "with two early exceptions Bruce never dated his work, and because there exists very little significant documentation pertaining to specific extant works done after 1905," Agee and Rose's chronology "is based primarily on intensive examination and stylistic analysis of the paintings themselves," and is thus conjectural. See Agee and Rose, *Patrick Henry Bruce: American Modernist*, 151.

22— Wanda M. Corn, *The Great American Thing: Modern Art and National Identity, 1915–1935* (Berkeley, Los Angeles, and London: University of California Press, 1999), 368, note 14.

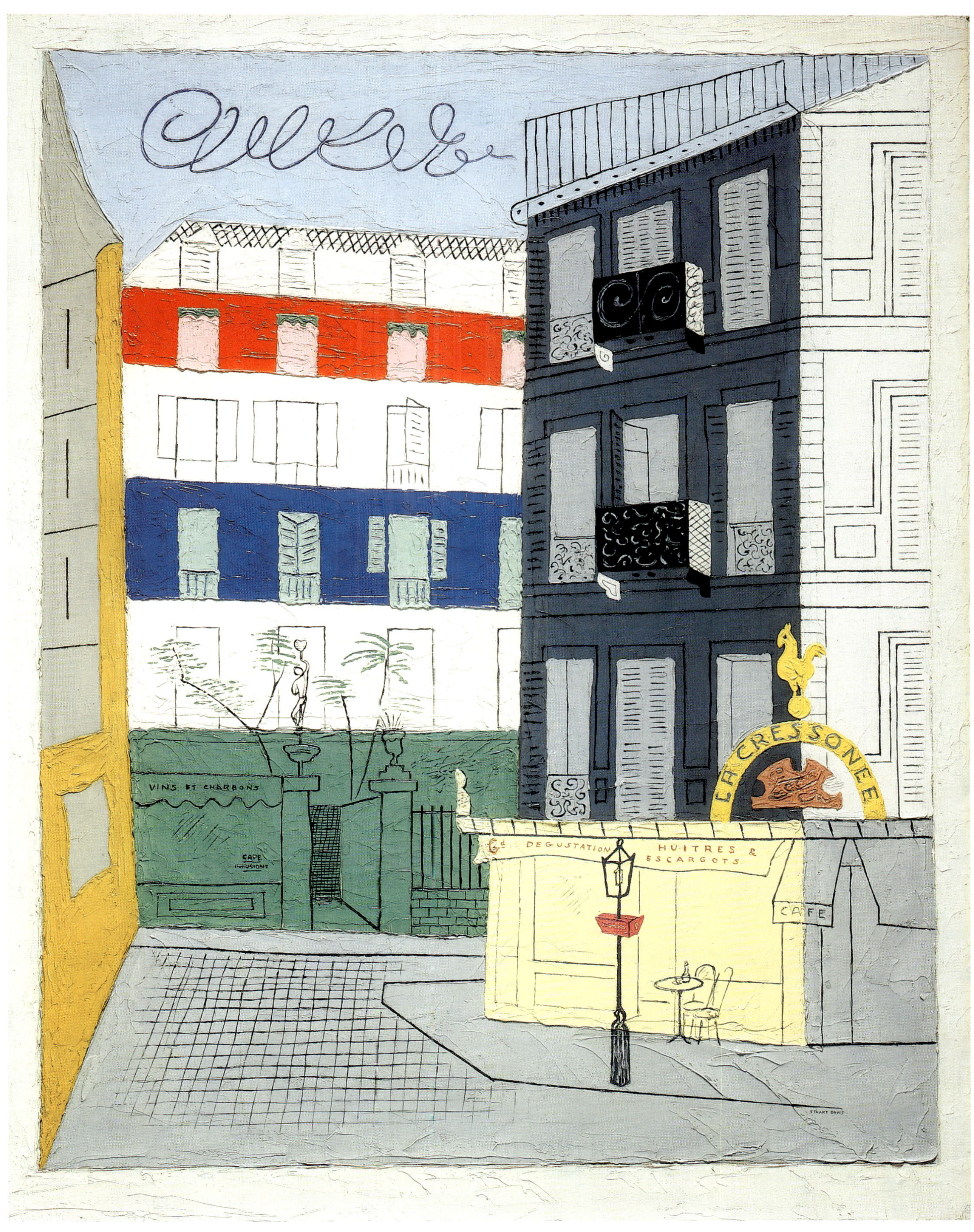

13
STUART DAVIS
PLACE PASDELOUP, 1928
OIL ON CANVAS, 92.1 X 73 CM
WHITNEY MUSEUM OF AMERICAN ART, NEW YORK.
GIFT OF GERTRUDE VANDERBILDT WHITNEY, 31.170
TMAA

23— That French views of America were a key component of how American artists might value their native, modern culture was first suggested by Barbara Rose in her excellent essay, "American Art and the Modern Theme," in Gladys Fabre, ed., *Léger et l'esprit moderne*, exh. cat. (Paris: Musée d'Art Moderne de la Ville de Paris, 1982), 171–208 (in English and French); Elizabeth Hutton Turner elaborated on this idea in her superb and brilliantly researched book, drawn from her doctoral dissertation, *American Artists in Paris, 1919–1929* (Ann Arbor and London: UMI Research Press, 1988); and Wanda Corn has recently put a number of related ideas about the significance of transatlantic "identity" to fine use in her book, *The Great American Thing* (see above, note 20). I am also grateful to Corn for having asked me to be the respondent to her panelists at her College Art Association session, "*Américanisme:* The Old World Discovers the New," in San Francisco, in 1989, where I first began to think about these transatlantic questions.

24— Agee and Rose, *Patrick Henry Bruce: American Modernist*, 54.

25— Fernand Léger, "New York," (orig. published in *Cahiers d'Art*, 1931), translated by Alexandra Anderson in Edward F. Fry, ed., *Functions of Painting by Fernand Léger* (New York: The Viking Press, 1973), 84–85. For Léger and American artists the key study is Carolyn Lanchner, "Fernand Léger: American Connections,' in her *Fernand Léger*, exh. cat. (New York: The Museum of Modern Art, 1998), 15–70.

26— Fernand Léger, "The Machine Age Aesthetic II," (*Propos d'artistes*, Paris, 1925), in Fry, *Functions of Painting*, 65.

27— Cited in William Rubin, *The Paintings of Gerald Murphy*, 30, note 82, 460, emphasis in the original.

28— George L. K. Morris's 1971 memoir is the preface to Fry, *Functions of Painting*, IX–XIII. For the most recent work on Morris and a number of the other American artists in Paris, see Debra Bricker Balken and Robert S. Lubar, exh. cat. *The Park Avenue Cubists: Gallatin, Morris, Frelinghuysen and Shaw* (New York: Grey Art Gallery, New York University, 2002). Unfortunately there is not yet an extended treatment of the Académie Moderne, although a good start was made by Gladys Fabre in her "Petite histoire illustrée de l'Académie Moderne. Liste des élèves de Léger entre 1924 et 1931," in, *Léger et l'esprit moderne,* 479–97. Presumably the list is only a sampling of the student body, since Morris is listed as one of only four Americans to have attended the school in the seven years it covers; there must have been other Americans there, and we know, for instance, that printmaker Blanche Lazzell was among them, although she does not appear on Fabre's list. See Barbara Stern Shapiro, *From Paris to Provincetown: Blanche Lazzell and the Color Woodcut*, exh. cat. (Boston: Museum of Fine Arts, 2002), 13.

29— Fernand Léger, "Contemporary Achievements in Painting," (*Soirées de Paris*, 1914), in Fry, *Functions of Painting,* 12.

30— Rubin and Lanchner point out a number of other likely inspirations from the art of the Parisian avant-garde. as well as a pocket watch that was personally important to him: See William Rubin (with Carolyn Lanchner), *The Paintings of Gerald Murphy*, exh. cat. (New York: The Museum of Modern Art, 1974), 30–35.

31— Fernand Léger, "The Machine Aesthetic: The Manufactured Object, the Artisan, and the Artist," (*Bulletin de l'Effort Moderne*, 1924), in Fry, *Functions of Painting*, 52–53. See as well Matthew Affron's excellent, "Léger's Modernism: Subjects and Objects," in Carolyn Lanchner, *Fernand Léger*, exh. cat. (New York: The Museum of Modern Art, 1998), 121–48.

32— Fernand Léger, "Notes on Contemporary Plastic Life," (*Kunstblatt*, Berlin, 1923), in Fry, *Functions of Painting*, 25; this is one of several times that Léger expressed his admiration for window display, which he also made use of in his film, *Ballet Mécanique*, 1923–24.

33— Corn, *The Great American Thing*, 130.

34— Stuart Davis, from his *Journal* (May 29, 1921), in Diane Kelder, *Stuart Davis: Art and Theory, 1920–31*, exh. cat. (New York: The Pierpont Morgan Library, 2002), 36.

35— Rose, "American Art and the Modern Theme," 181; Rose also mentions that Léger's work was exhibited at the Société Anonyme exhibition in New York, in 1920.

36— Stuart Davis in a letter to his father, September 17, 1928, quoted in Karen Wilken, "Becoming a Modern Artist: the 1920s," in Lowery Stokes Sims, ed. *Stuart Davis: American Painter*, exh cat. (New York: The Metropolitan Museum of Art, 1991), 54.

37— Davis's mural, whose title derives from a collection of stories published by Ernest Hemingway in 1927, now belongs to the Museum of Modern Art, New York; it was originally painted for the men's smoking room of Radio City Music Hall.

38— Stuart Davis Papers (Houghton Rare Books Library, Harvard), September, 1941, quoted in Wilken, "Becoming a Modern Artist," 52.

39— See Fry, *Functions of Painting*, 114–18.

40— See Calder's drawings, in Marla Prather, ed. *Alexander Calder 1898–1976*, exh. cat. (Washington D.C. National Gallery of Art, 1998), figs. 59–69.

41— Louis Lozowick, "Fernand Léger," *The Nation* 121, no. 3154 (New York: December 16, 1925), 712, cited in Lanchner, *Léger*, 23.

42— Fernand Léger, "The Spectacle," *Bulletin de l'Effort Moderne* (Paris, 1924), in Fry, *Functions of Painting*, 40.

43— See Calder in *17 Mobiles by Alexander Calder*, 1943, n.p., cited in Prather, *Calder*, 58.

44— Cited in Lanchner, *Léger,* 50, note 193.

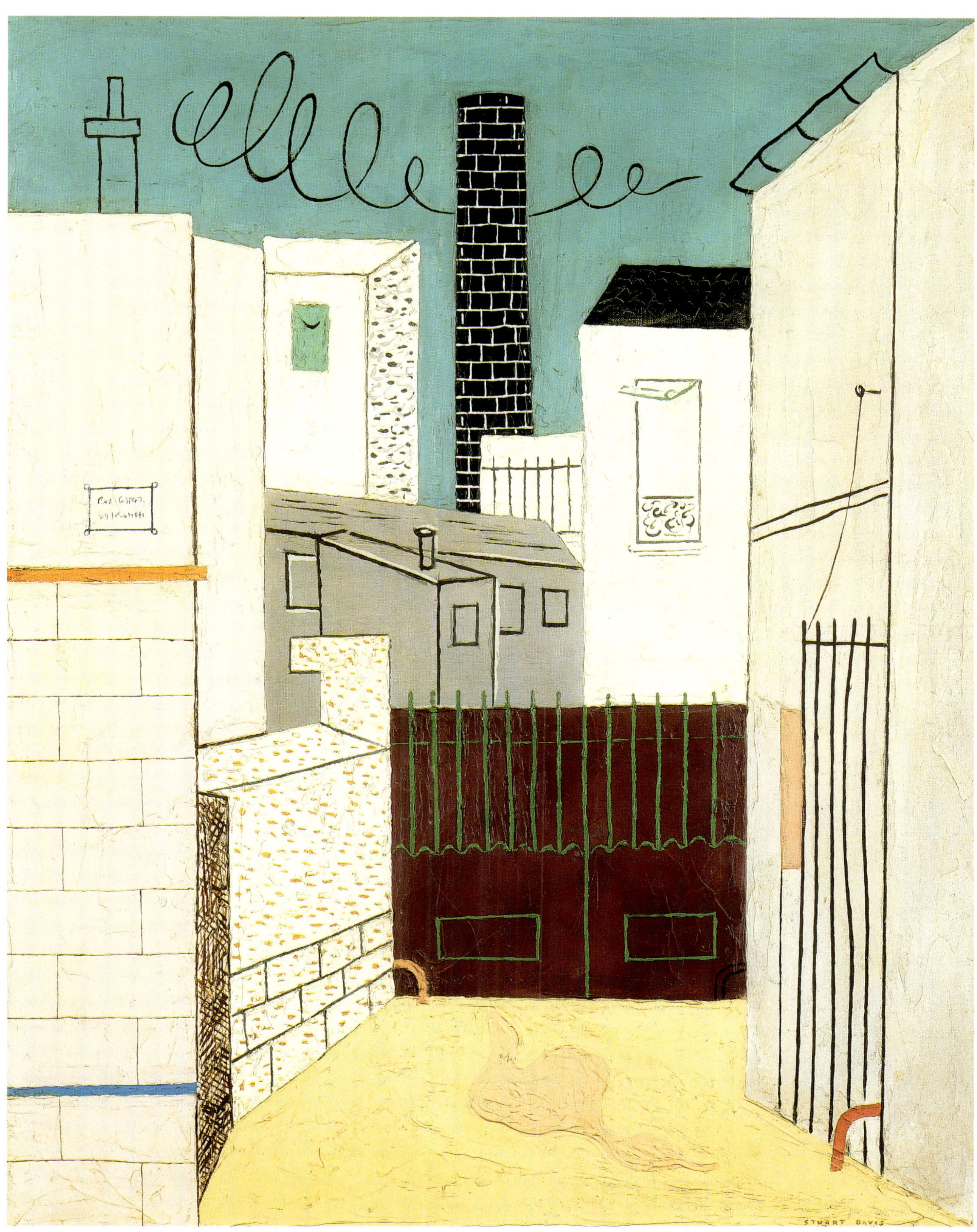

14
STUART DAVIS
ADIT, NO. 2, 1928
OIL ON CANVAS, 73.4 X 60.3 CM
THE MUSEUM OF FINE ARTS, BOSTON.
GIFT OF THE WILLIAM H. LANE FOUNDATION, 1990.394
MAAG, TAM, TMAA

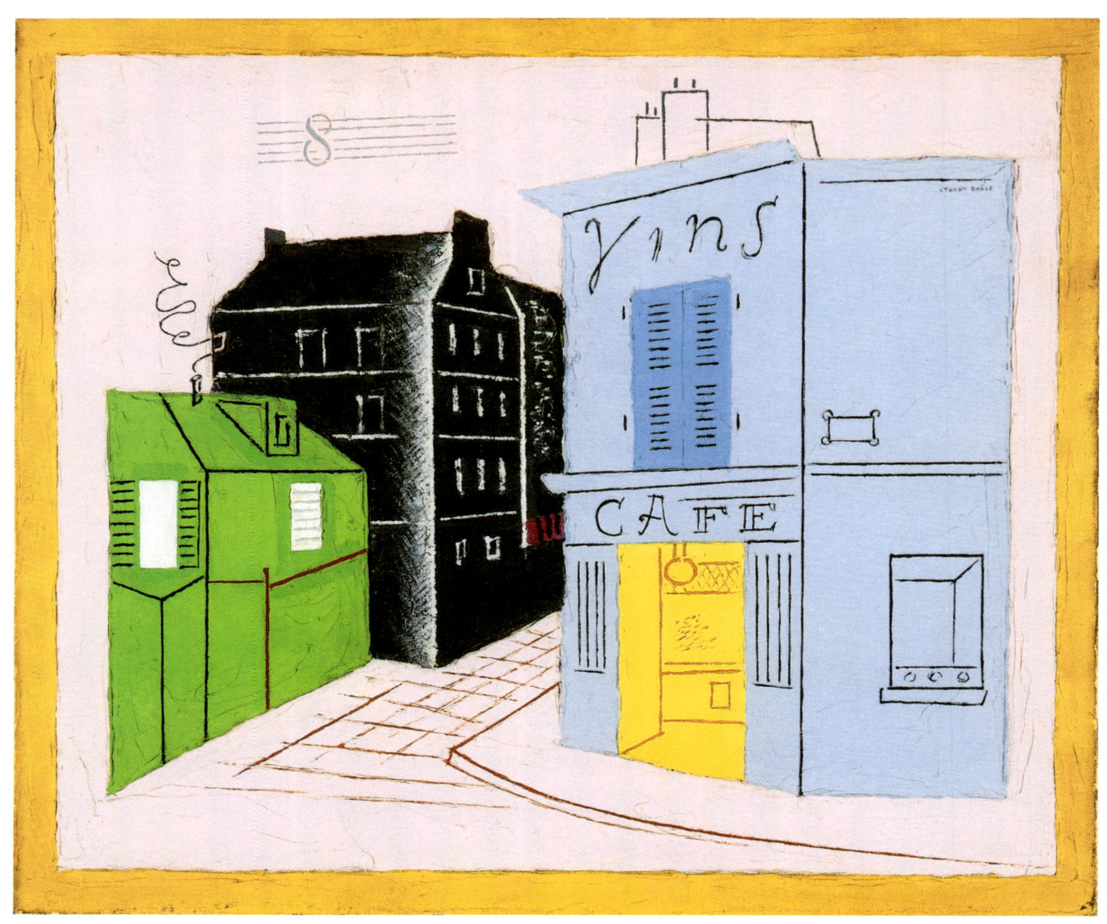

15
STUART DAVIS
BLUE CAFÉ, 1928
OIL ON CANVAS, 46 X 54.9 CM
THE PHILLIPS COLLECTION,
WASHINGTON D.C., 0467
MAAG, TAM, TMAA

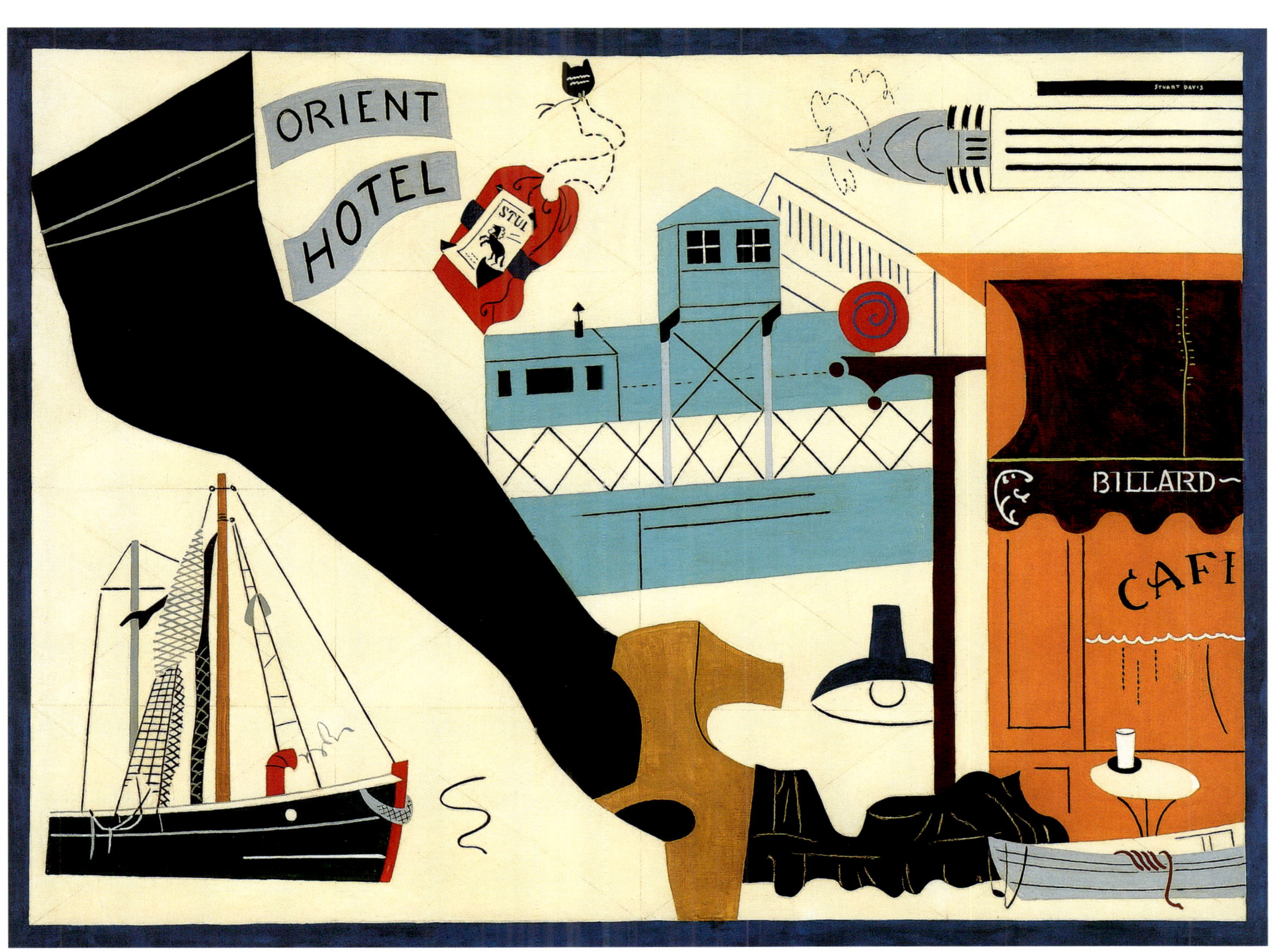

16
STUART DAVIS
NEW YORK–PARIS, NO. 1, 1931
OIL ON CANVAS, 99 X 131.4 CM
THE UNIVERSITY OF IOWA MUSEUM OF ART,
IOWA CITY. MUSEUM PURCHASE, 1955.5
MAAG, TAM, TMAA

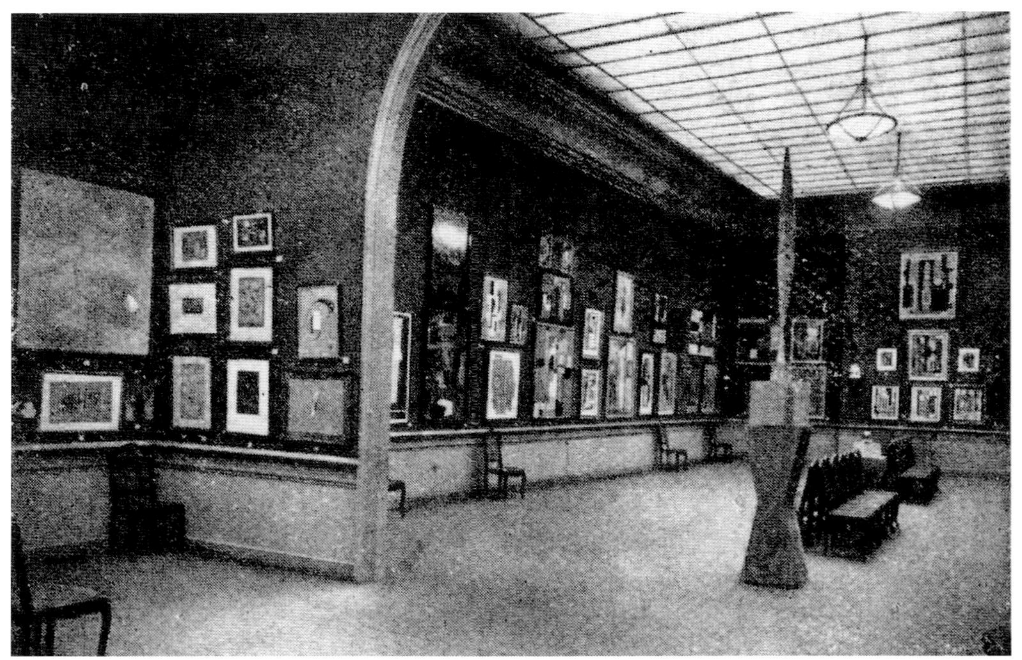

VIEW OF THE *EXPOSITION INTERNATIONALE
L'ART D'AUJOURD'HUI.*
FROM *LE BULLETIN DE LA VIE ARTISTIQUE*
(JANUARY 1, 1926): 5.

Little is known about the context of the *Exposition internationale L'Art d'Aujourd'hui,* organized by Polish artist Victor Poznanski, and held at the Syndicat des Négociants en Objets d'Art at 18 rue de la Ville l'Evêque from December 1 to 21, 1925.[1] The only surviving documents are the catalogue and a few contemporary reviews. However, the deliberately modern and international nature of the selection—which included works by over sixty artists of all nationalities—made it one of the most important avant-garde events of the interwar period.

The introduction to the catalogue attempts to justify the abstract nature of the show: "Why organize this exhibition? Not to show examples of every trend in painting today, but to inventory, as complete as circumstances and distances allow, of the representatives of *non-imitative plastic art,* as first envisaged by the cubist movement. The term 'cubism,' which served to designate the initial harbingers of this vast movement in painting, never had a meaning other than that of the 'firm' idea of a cube contained in the word, and therefore in no way explains the state of mind of said 'cubism' nor of its extensions and parallels, the current state of which is presented in this show."[2]

Six American artists participated in the exhibition, making the United States the third most heavily represented country after France and Germany. Patrick Henry Bruce exhibited four works titled *Natures mortes* (Still lifes, now destroyed), Florence Henri two *Compositions*, Blanche Lazzell a *Peinture* (Painting), Lucy L'Engle a *Panneau pour salle de musique* (Panel for a music room), Gerald Murphy *Montre* (*Watch*) and *Nature morte* (now titled *Razor;* both works are in the Dallas Museum of Art), and Ambrose E. Webster a *Peinture*. Three resided in Paris, Bruce, Murphy, and Henri (then a young painter studying at the Académie Moderne), while the three other painters were members of the artists' colony in Provincetown, Massachusetts and were probably invited to exhibit thanks to the presence of Lazzell, a member of the Provincetown community who had also studied at the Académie Moderne in 1923–24.

Only one of the few reviews of the show —published in *Montparnasse* in January 1924—will be quoted here, but it reflects the generally critical tone: "In this international exhibition, in which the most notorious cubists from many countries are showing, we see nothing more than an academic version of an art launched some fifteen years ago. Coming after the innovators who, in the glorious days of feverish, intuitive inspiration, despite the lack of comprehension and limited outlook of the masses, created a new art, here we have the dumb imitators, the profiteers, and the money-changers in the temple who, meeting no resistance, have appropriated the trophies won by the former after a bloody struggle. . . . Nearly one hundred artists, French, German, Belgian, Dutch, English, Russian, Spanish, American, Hungarian, Italian, Polish, Romanian, Serbian, and Armenian, are showing three times that number of paintings and sculptures. Is this truly an international presentation of the cubism that was so misconstrued and mocked? Indeed, this opening was the glory and feast of snobbery! Gentlemen in evening dress, ladies in gowns, automobiles blocking rue de la Ville-l'Evêque. Social chitchat and fashionable dresses distracted attention from the objects on show. And then there were the Americans with their dollars, their flat-heeled shoes, and the brash laughter from their made-up lips. . . .

It's no longer a revolution. For the early innovators, it has become an academy. Yet new revolutionaries arrived at this celebration of academic cubism—the surrealists. They represented a 'tomorrow' overshadowed by 'yesterday.' They probably went there to plant the flag of their own revolution in place of the dead one. They set themselves on the floor, in a corner of the main hall. There they drew tarot cards, probably trying to discover the future that has already buried them. Time passes quickly and everything that bears the future within itself can be fertilized only by new ideas."[3]

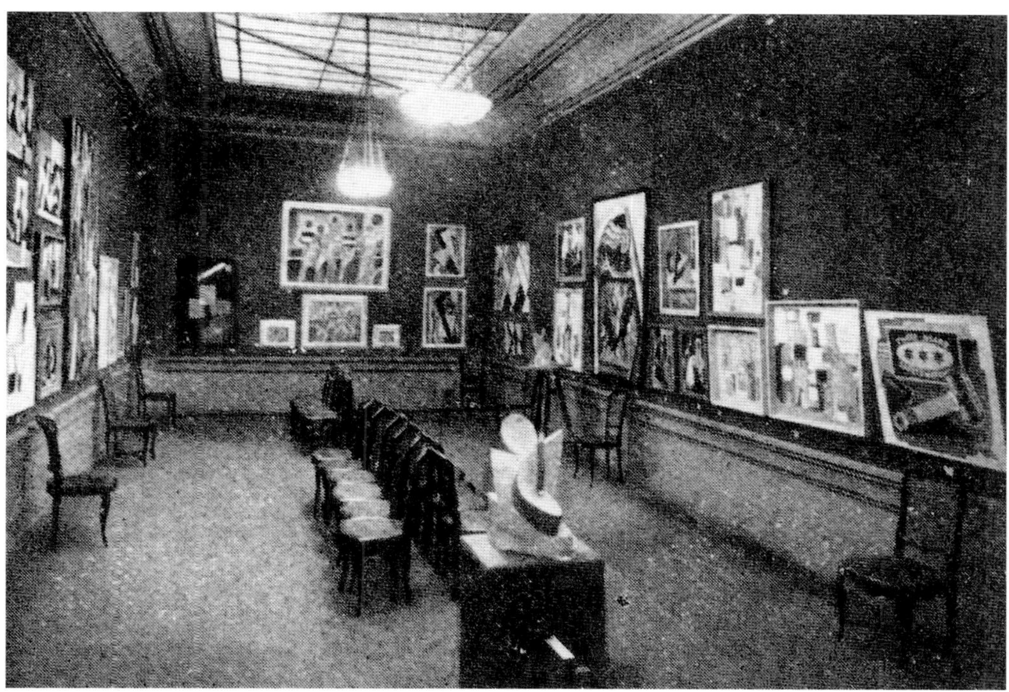

This article notes only the leading figures of French cubism, dismissing the rest of the artists as "followers" or examples of a "new academicism." Foreign artists are generally ignored, Americans being no exception to the rule. Nevertheless, Americans appear here in the role of buyers, dressed in some of the insulting clichés then common in France. Perhaps the conclusion to draw is that this exhibition represented one of the failed encounters between Paris and the international avant-garde. And yet there is a striking reference to the recently formed group of surrealist artists—a "tomorrow" overshadowed by "yesterday"—which allows the informed critic to contrast the two avant-gardes. By the late 1920s, the subversive and literary nature of surrealism would increasingly win out over the formalist optimism embodied by this exhibition, which combined pure abstraction with figurative, "Purist" works.

Sophie Lévy

1— I would like to thank Christian Derouet for sharing his notes on this exhibition.

2— *Exposition internationale L'Art d'Aujourd'hui,* exh. cat. (Paris: Syndicat des Antiquaires, 1925), 3.

3— L. Gyomai, "L'Art d'Aujourd'hui," *Montparnasse* 43 (January 1926).

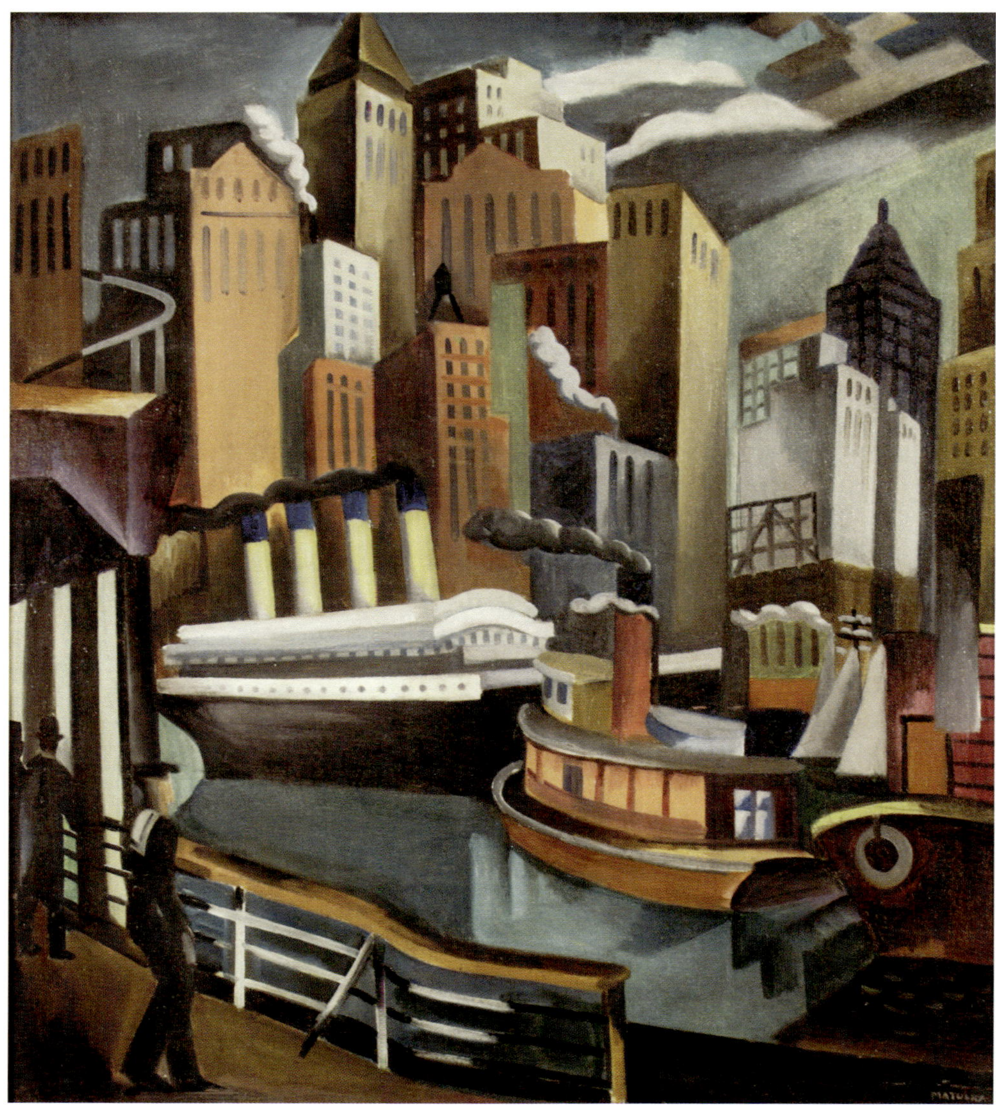

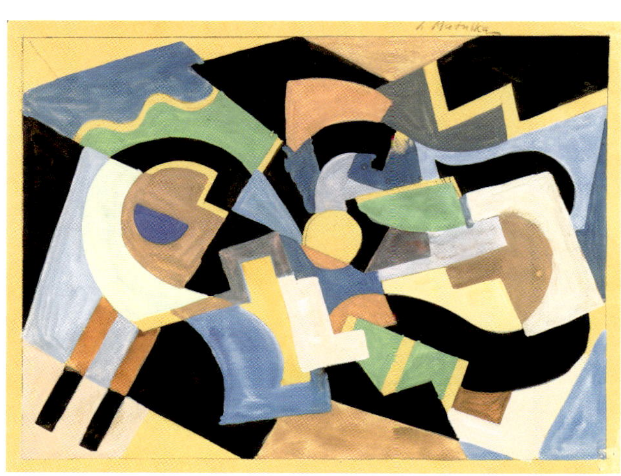

17
JAN MATULKA
NEW YORK HARBOR/PARIS, 1925
OIL ON CANVAS, 105.4 × 91.8 CM
COURTESY NORFOLK
SOUTHERN CORPORATION, VA.
MAAG, TAM, TMAA

18
JAN MATULKA
ABSTRACT, C. 1923
GOUACHE ON PAPER, 25.4 × 38.1 CM
PRIVATE COLLECTION,
COURTESY FRANKLIN RIEHLMAN FINE ART,
NEW YORK
MAAG, TAM, TMAA

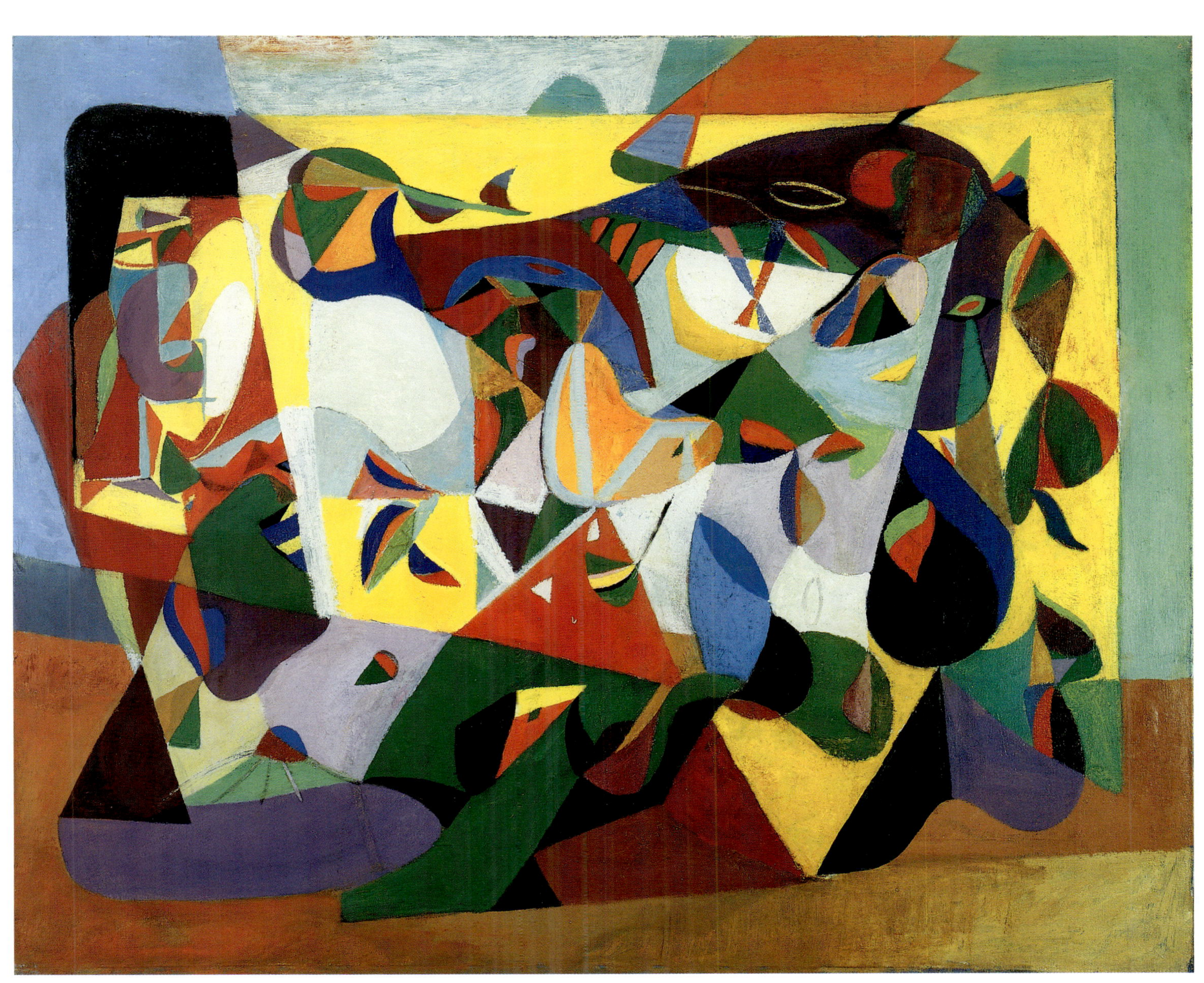

19

JAN MATULKA
UNTITLED (ABSTRACTION), C. 1920
OIL ON CANVAS, 90 X 112.4 CM
THOMAS MCCORMICK GALLERY, CHICAGO
MAAG, TAM, TMAA

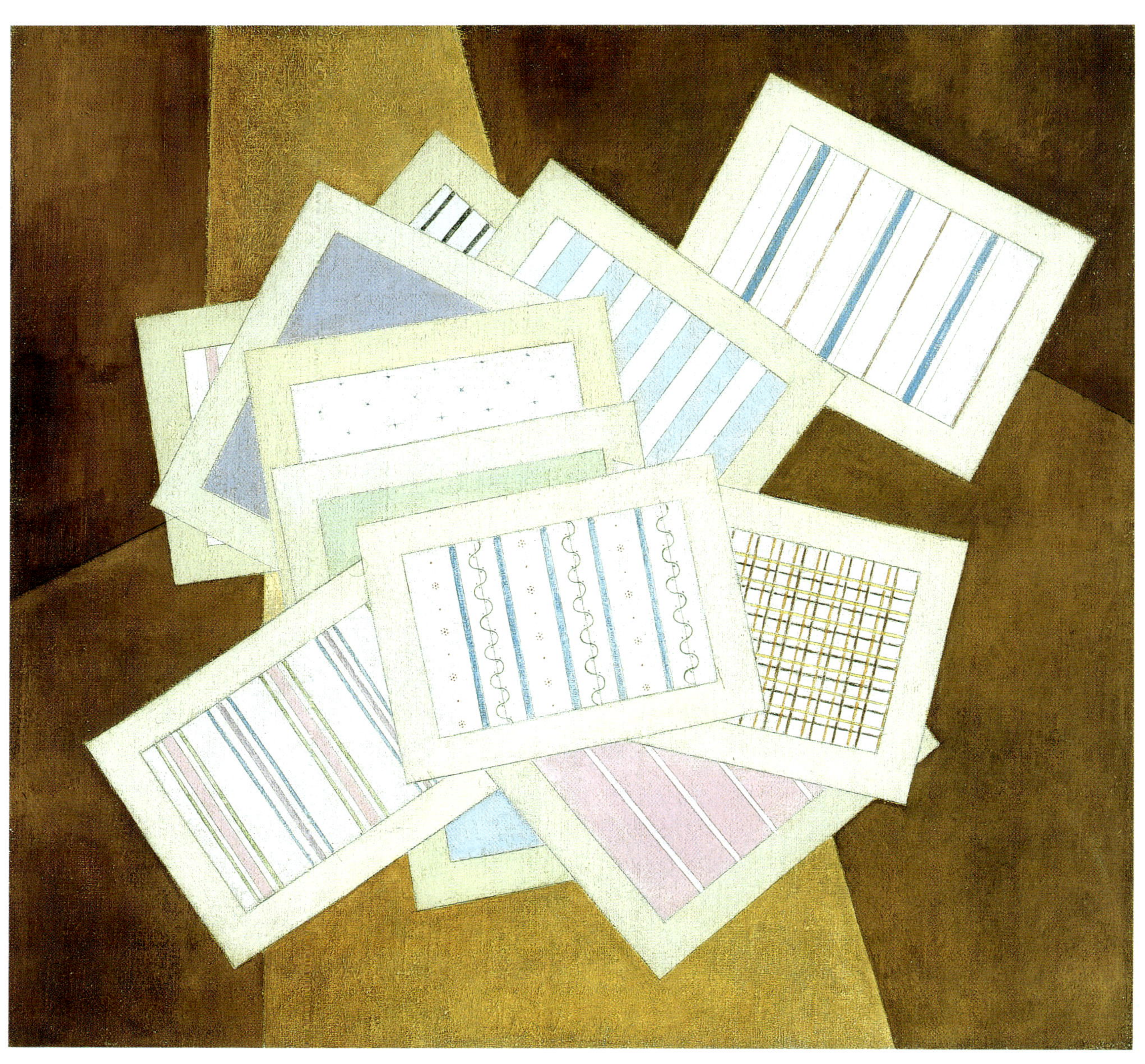

20
CHARLES DEMUTH
SPRING, C. 1921
OIL ON CANVAS, 56.2 X 61.3 CM
THE ART INSTITUTE OF CHICAGO,
THROUGH PRIOR GIFT OF THE ALBERT KUNSTADTER
FAMILY FOUNDATION, 1989.231
MAAG, TAM, TMAA

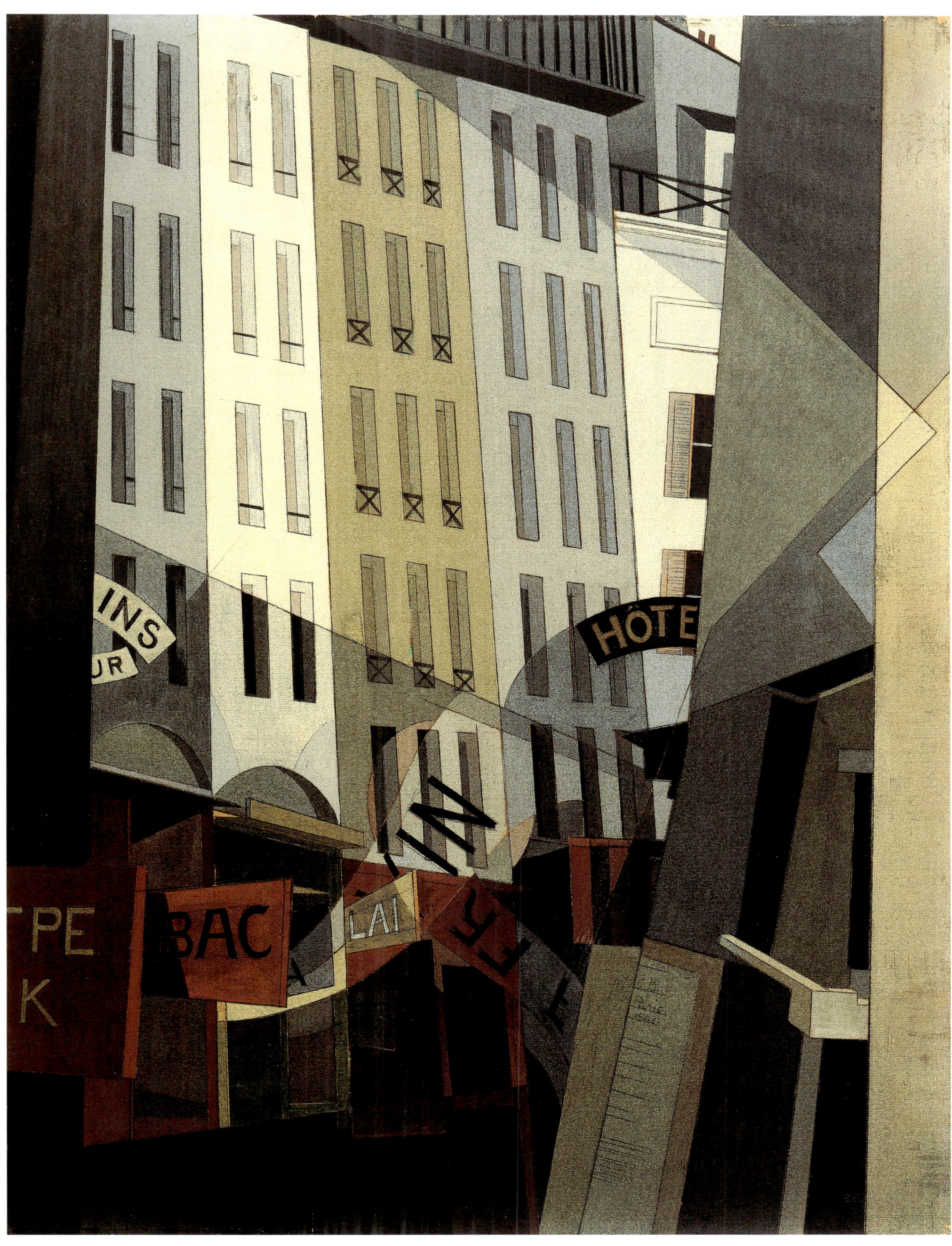

21
CHARLES DEMUTH
RUE DU SINGE QUI PÊCHE, 1921
TEMPERA ON BOARD, 52.2 X 41 CM
TERRA FOUNDATION FOR THE ARTS, CHICAGO.
THE DANIEL J. TERRA COLLECTION, 1999.44
MAAG, TAM, TMAA

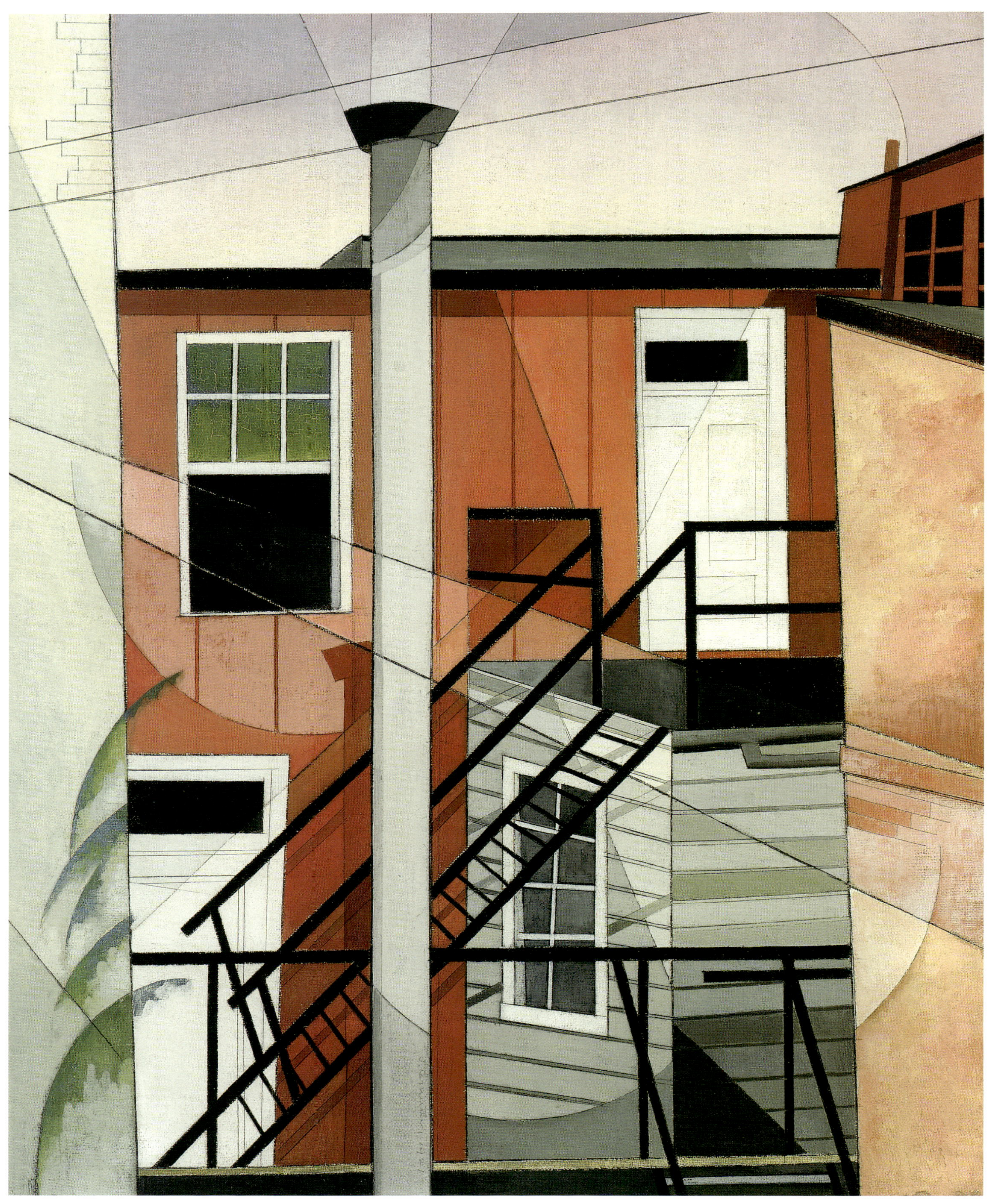

22
CHARLES DEMUTH
MODERN CONVENIENCES, 1921
OIL ON CANVAS, 65.6 × 54.2 CM
COLUMBUS MUSEUM OF ART, OHIO.
GIFT OF FERDINAND HOWALD, 1931.137
TAM, TMAA

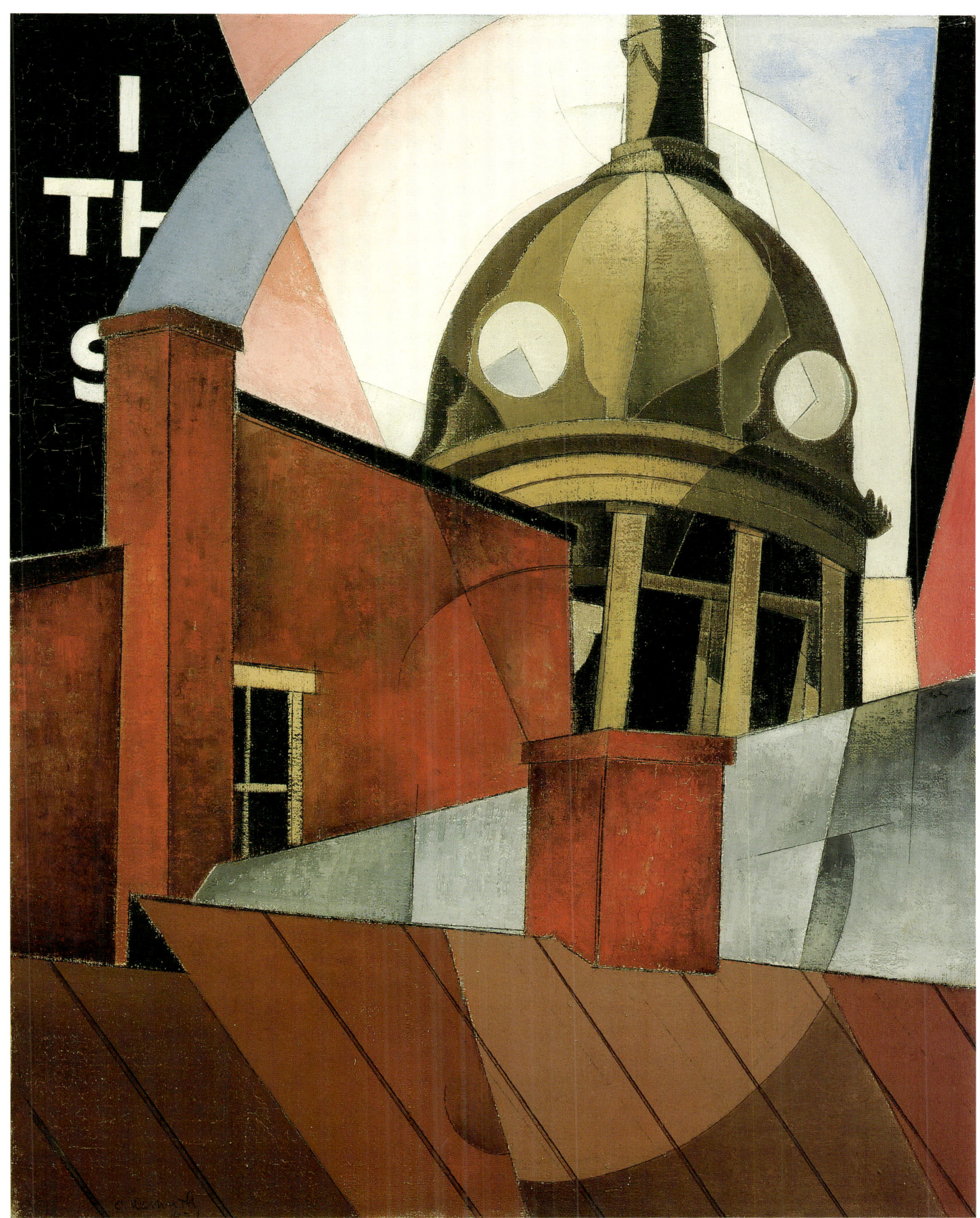

23
CHARLES DEMUTH
WELCOME TO OUR CITY, 1921
OIL ON CANVAS, 63.8 X 51.1 CM
TERRA FOUNDATION FOR THE ARTS, CHICAGO,
THE DANIEL J. TERRA COLLECTION, 1993.3
MAAG, TAM, TMAA

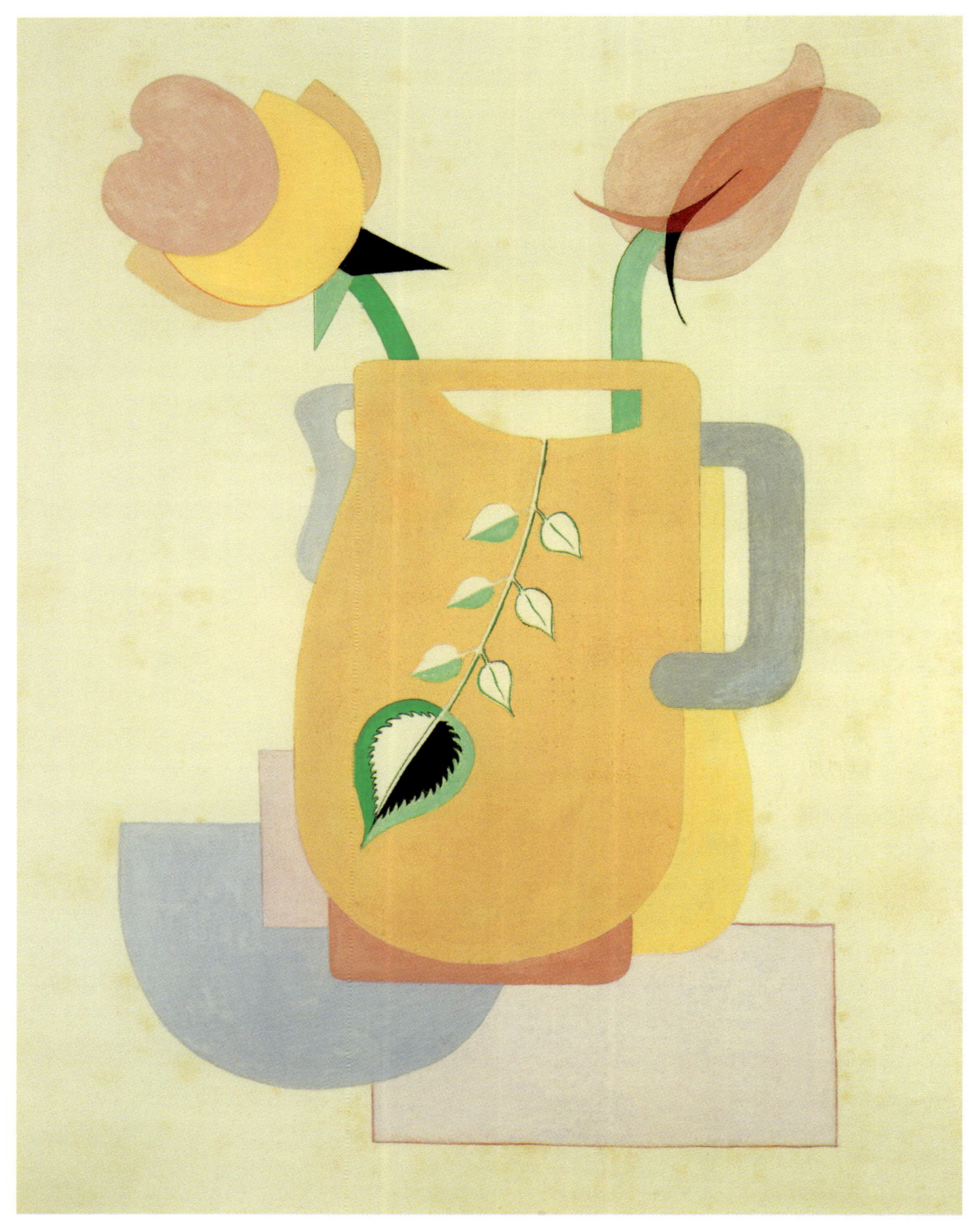

24
GERALD MURPHY
STILL LIFE, C. 1925
WATERCOLOR ON PAPER, 29.2 X 22.9 CM
COURTESY SALANDER O'REILLY GALLERIES,
NEW YORK
MAAG, TAM, TMAA

A PICTURE OF AMERICA BY GERALD MURPHY

JOCELYNE **ROTILY**

An American in Paris: The legend surrounding Gerald Murphy

The myth created around American artist Gerald Murphy has become such a crucial component of his oeuvre that it cannot be ignored. That legend, however, should not be allowed to overshadow the authentic, original talent of an American who arrived in Paris in 1921 and quickly became the darling of the Paris avant-garde.

The legend describes an expatriate American in Paris during the Roaring Twenties,[1] one who led a privileged life based on the economic wealth of a bold, youthful, flaming new country. Seen from the outside, Murphy's life resembles a magnificent "feast"[2] of cocktail parties and jazz soirées. His French friends described him as a "gentleman artist" whose creativity and elegant yet "sporty" lifestyle incarnated affluent, modernist America.

Murphy's special relationship with Fernand Léger (whom some people would call his mentor) has become equally legendary. The two men apparently liked to stroll along the banks of the Seine together, on the lookout for the "spectacle" of urban life, seeking inspiration from new motifs. John Dos Passos witnessed one of these excursions, which he described as follows: "Instead of the hackneyed and pasteltinted [*sic*] Tuileries and bridges and barges and *bateaux mouches* on the Seine, we were walking through a freshly invented world. They [Murphy and Léger] picked out winches, the flukes of an anchor, coils of rope, the red funnel of a towboat. . . . The banks of the Seine never looked banal again after that walk."[3] Together, Murphy and Léger developed the idea of a modern beauty that would no longer be centered on the subject, but rather on manufactured, functional objects freed of sentimental, imitative values.

Murphy's "exceptional" personality was noticed by writers of the Lost Generation who were part of his close circle of acquaintances. F. Scott Fitzgerald, who practically worshipped Murphy, turned him into one of the legendary figures of the Lost Generation portrayed in *Tender is the Night*. The novel's protagonist, Dick Diver, is a carbon copy of Murphy—rich, elegant, idealistic, romantic, and in search of harmony if sometimes gloomy, melancholic, and mysterious.

Just like a novel by the Lost Generation of writers, tragedy entered Murphy's life: his two sons died young and the stock-market crash of 1929 led to financial setbacks that obliged him to return to the United States and put a sudden end to his artistic career. The Second World War, plus Murphy's decision to draw a veil over his painting (life's tragedies having gotten the upper hand), have complicated the task of art historians. Today only eight canvases remain as proof of his talent, and problems of dating these works have not yet been resolved.

Paris: A fertile environment for creativity

"Paris," wrote Henry Miller, "is simply an obstetrical instrument that tears the living embryo from the womb and puts it in the incubator. Paris is the cradle of artificial births. Rocking here in the cradle each one slips back into his soil: one dreams back to Berlin, New York, Chicago . . . "[4] Paris had the same effect on Murphy. This foreign, "different" setting enabled him, I feel, to "dream back" to his native Boston, to reinvent his own America and his own Americanness, so to speak.

True enough, everything in Paris encouraged Murphy to retain his links with his native land, to "play the role" of an American. The Paris avant-garde scene was fascinated with the new civilization's urban landscapes and vast technological accomplishments, perceiving a new, revolutionary beauty in them. New York was the cubist city par excellence. Machinery and progress, so victorious in America, offered a glimpse of a future of collective happiness.

What most appealed to America's fans were its gadgets, its advertising slogans, its "heroic" skyscrapers, and its dynamic movies, which seemed like a wonderful antidote to the lethargy of local cinema. For poet Philippe Soupault, French movies suffered from a syndrome of theatricality.[5] Art historian Élie Faure described Charlie Chaplin, who became a darling of cubist painters, as the Shakespeare of the modern world. Fernand Léger gave the Chaplin character a featured place in his film, *Ballet Mécanique*.

Drawing inspiration from the American model ultimately meant injecting a little life into an aging Europe crippled by tradition. Referring to America, Léger would write: "There is youth in every nook and cranny. Not a hint of old age—they remain active right to the end."[6]

It was therefore almost natural that the Paris press and artists such as Picasso and Léger were enthusiastic about Murphy and his spectacular still lifes of the American world. In their eyes, he was the most American of all expatriates in Paris. According to Jacques Mauny, Murphy had invented a new unique American aesthetic.[7]

Murphy's Americanness, obviously, was not alien to the ultra-nationalist climate typical of the United States in the 1920s. The country was proud of its economic supremacy and its new technological power. "Searching for an American voice was a common and conscious drive" that affected even the creative arts.[8] Liberating themselves from European influence and finding a specifically American artistic idiom was the task adopted by many artists and intellectuals in the 1920s.

The affirmation of an American artistic identity

Murphy's "Americanness" now still needs to be defined, in an effort to grasp the innovative, avant-garde aspect of his art. On arriving in Paris, Murphy knew almost nothing about the visual arts.[9] One day he entered Paul Rosenberg's gallery and chanced upon works by Picasso, Braque, and Gris, and decided, in a totally unexpected move, to become a painter. "I was astounded. My reaction to the color and form was immediate. To me there was something in these paintings that was instantly sympathetic and comprehensible. I remember saying to Sara: 'If that's painting, it's what I want to do.'"[10] He studied with the Russian artist Natalia Goncharova, who taught him set design for ballet and encouraged him toward abstraction. Then he began to explore an idiom that was partly based on cubism and Purism but that nevertheless remained very personal and very American.

Murphy himself described what he saw as the extent of his debt to cubism. Of the set he produced in 1923 for the ballet *Within the Quota*,[11] he said: "It is not cubism but its composition is inspired by cubism."[12] To underscore the dynamism of the set, Murphy indeed used a technique largely exploited by the cubists, namely inserting collages and newspaper clippings into the painterly surface.[13] But, as Murphy himself pointed out, his start in painting occurred in the final years of cubism, at a time when the Purist movement was taking hold, as championed by Amédée Ozenfant, Le Corbusier, and Fernand Léger. "The first impact of cubism was finished," wrote Murphy, "but it was still in the very air one breathed. It had been digested and gone into the bloodstream of each painter who was working independently."[14]

In fact, when studying Murphy's oeuvre, certain affinities with the Purists become clear. Like Léger and Ozenfant, he was fascinated by machines, industrial objects, and the modern world. He favored simplified, pared-down forms, he sought a certain harmony and order, and he displayed the "spirit of construction" so valued by Purists.[15] At the same time, it would be mistaken to view Murphy as a total disciple of Purism. His approach to objects is strongly individual and his imagery is linked to a personal family story in which the quest for an American cultural identity played a great role. In contrast, Purist artists began principally with anonymous objects and drew from them an ideal and "unanimist" vision of society.

Neither completely cubist nor totally Purist, Murphy was an independent and singular artist in the Paris of the 1920s. Although he combined experiments in cubism and Purism—synonymous with modernity—he did so in order to forge a style and an art able to "picture" his Americanness, an Americanness all the more striking for being elaborated outside his native country, in a setting ready for exoticism and rejuvenation.

Only the invented parts of our life have any real meaning [16]

These words were uttered by Murphy in the presence of novelist F. Scott Fitzgerald. The idea that only the "imaginary" part of life is of interest—that life has to be above all invented and created in the way a work of art is composed and organized—was crucial. It helps explain the meaning that Murphy gave to both his life and his art. Testimony from his acquaintances and from the few entries in his notebooks describe, moreover, a man who was wary of the outside world and who strove to construct and invent a life governed by notions of elegance, harmony, light, balance, and clarity. That perhaps explains why Murphy's paintings give the impression of an autonomous, peaceful world apparently protected from fate's harsh blows.[17]

Close-up on *Villa America*

Villa America demonstrates the extent to which Murphy excelled in the realm of invention and the expression of harmony. Prior to being the title of a painting, "Villa America" was the name of the house acquired by the Murphys in 1924. It was located in Cap d'Antibes on the French Riviera. If Murphy's writer and artist friends are to be believed, the villa's architecture and Mediterranean setting were the very picture of harmony and elegance. Meanwhile, its modern conveniences embodied the view of America that so fascinated the Paris avant-garde scene. The villa offered an Edenic setting, to judge by Dos Passos's description of it:

> [The Riviera] seemed too hot to [the French], but to Americans the temperature seemed perfect, the swimming delicious, and Antibes just the quiet untrammeled provincial seaport they had dreamed of discovering. The cult of the sun had barely begun.

> By the following summer Gerald and Sara were making their home at Villa America. Sara engaged an Italian gardener

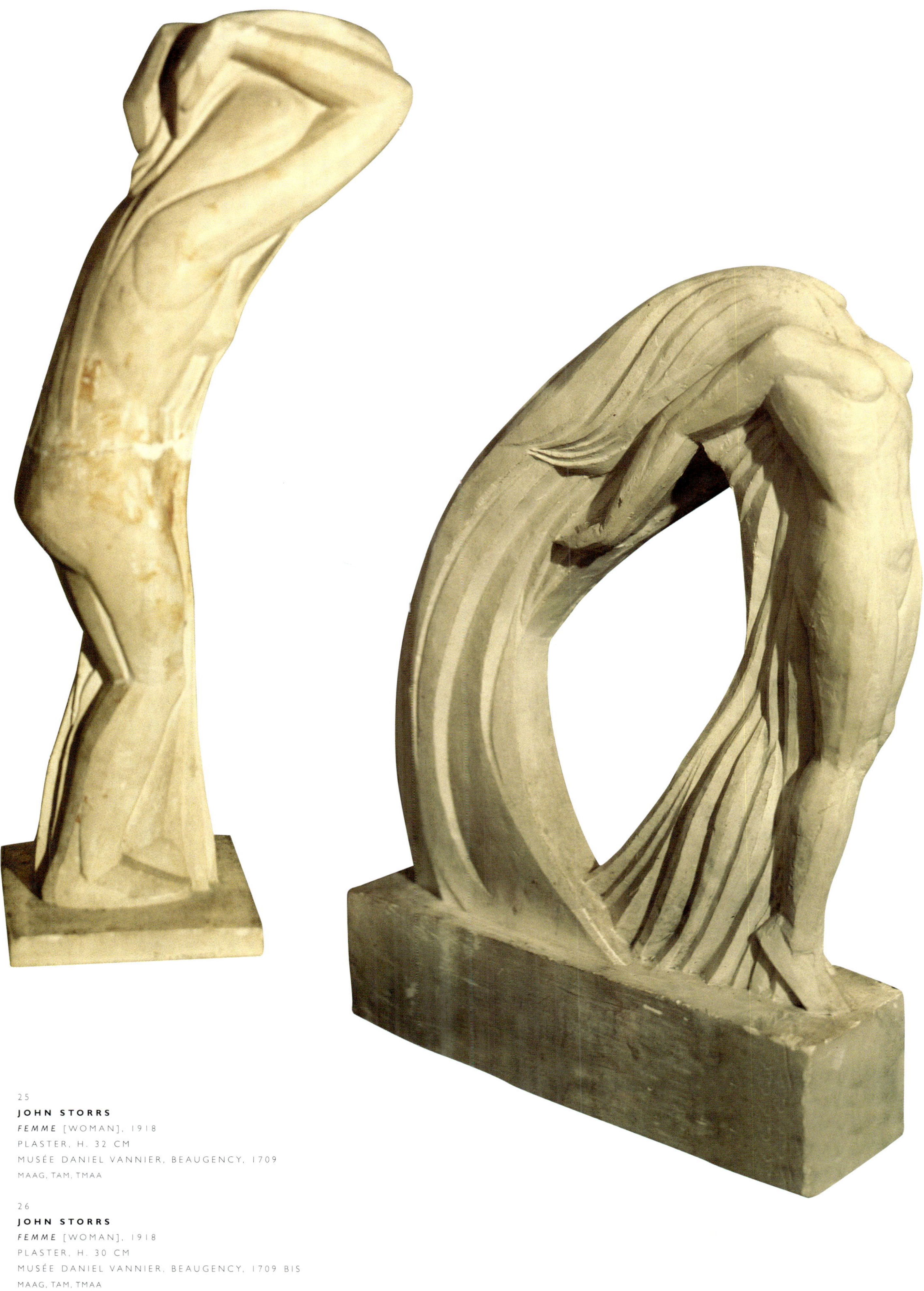

25
JOHN STORRS
FEMME [WOMAN], 1918
PLASTER, H. 32 CM
MUSÉE DANIEL VANNIER, BEAUGENCY, 1709
MAAG, TAM, TMAA

26
JOHN STORRS
FEMME [WOMAN], 1918
PLASTER, H. 30 CM
MUSÉE DANIEL VANNIER, BEAUGENCY, 1709 BIS
MAAG, TAM, TMAA

and started growing sweet corn. Gerald painted in an out-building. They invited their French friends down and before long Picasso was sunbathing at Juan-les-Pins, the Fitzgeralds were renting a villa at Saint Raphael and the artistic-fashionable Franco-American rage for beach life had begun. . . .

We would swim out through the calm crystalblue [*sic*] water, saltier than salt, to the mouth of the cove and back. Then Gerald would produce cold sherry and Sara would marshal recondite hors d'oeuvres for blotters. Saturated with salt and sun, some in cars and some walking, the company would troop back to the terrace, overlooking the flowers and vegetables back of the villa, for lunch. . . . It was a marvelous life.[18]

As remodeled by American architects Harold Heller and Hale Walker, the villa incorporated modern features such as a sunroom, a projection room for movies, and an American-style bar. The interior decoration was an artful and elegant mix of American and Mediterranean styles of the nineteenth and twentieth centuries.

Some of the canvases painted by Murphy seem to have functioned as parts of a set. *Villa America,* painted in 1924, seems to belong to this group (fig. 1). It is a free, whimsical "re-presentation" of the American flag, and was placed in the entrance of the house to "advertise" owner's nationality to visitors. Like his fellow American painter Charles Demuth,[19] Murphy was playing here on the symbolism of numbers.

The five stars of the flag are an allusion to the five residents of Villa America, the people who brought meaning and harmony to this particular "America": Gerald, his wife Sara, his sons Patrick and Baoth, and his daughter Honoria.[20] Murphy's frequent use of coded language was a way of personalizing, in a modest, whimsical way, still lifes that have been mistakenly described as works produced in an impassive manner. In fact, Murphy's total oeuvre is marked by a whiff of nostalgia and poetry that would tend to prove the opposite. His use of gold leaf to cover part of the flag is similarly symbolic, reinforcing the sacred and iconic aspects of the work, the very aspects also found in Demuth's paintings. Calvin Tomkins rightly sees *Villa America* as an allusion to the Edenic life at Villa America.[21] The blue in the painting refers simultaneously to the blue field of the American flag and the "crystal-blue" expanse of the Mediterranean Sea. The America described here is a reinvented America, one pictured in the idyllic setting of southern France. The painting titled *Villa America* could even be defined as a "show-object"—to adopt Léger's idea of *objet-spectacle*—whose function was to underscore Murphy's cultural origins.

The emphasis of the notion of "show" or "spectacle," occupies a special place in the social and cultural history of the United States. Although Léger noted the rise of "showiness" in French cultural life in the 1920s,[22] nowhere else was the concept and policy pushed as far as it was in the United States. Writing of Theodore Dreiser, an American author of the 1920s, Michael Walzer observed that, "the show is a depiction of the American soul."[23] Murphy's oeuvre asserts its American cultural identity through this same tendency to put things on show.

The taste for showmanship is freely expressed in the ballet mentioned above, *Within the Quota.* The story concerns a Swedish immigrant who has just landed in the New World and who, after many adventures, achieves the American dream of becoming a Hollywood actor. For the stage curtain, Murphy devised imagery stitched together from clichés of American society—millionaires, a cowboy, and a sheriff bustling around an urban landscape dotted with skyscrapers and dominated by all-powerful banks and scandal-mongering media.

Murphy, attracted as he was to the "invented" world of show business, could hardly remain indifferent to the movies. Films were projected at Villa America on a frequent basis. Furthermore, we know that Murphy worked with American film director King Vidor.[24] In a way, Murphy's enthusiasm for and use of cinema in his work reinforced his Americanness, because in those days the movies were viewed as a prime example of the American "genius," as was architecture.

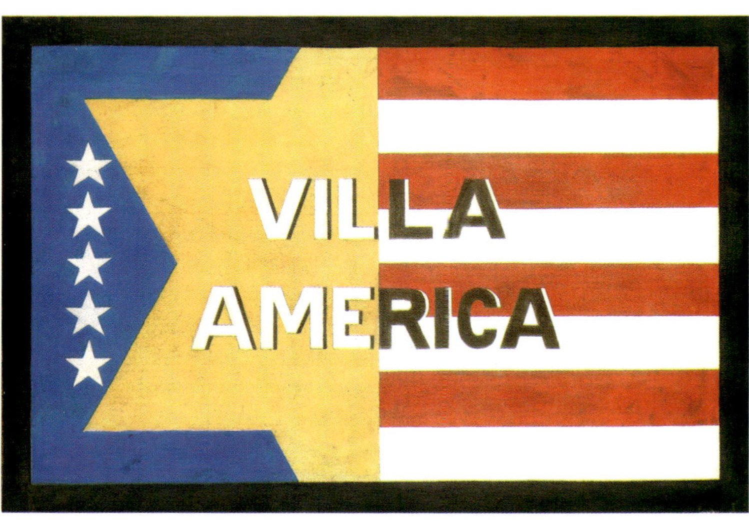

FIG. 1.
GERALD MURPHY,
VILLA AMERICA. C. 1924.
OIL AND GOLD LEAF ON CANVAS.
37 X 54.6 CM.
CURTIS GALLERIES, MINNEAPOLIS.

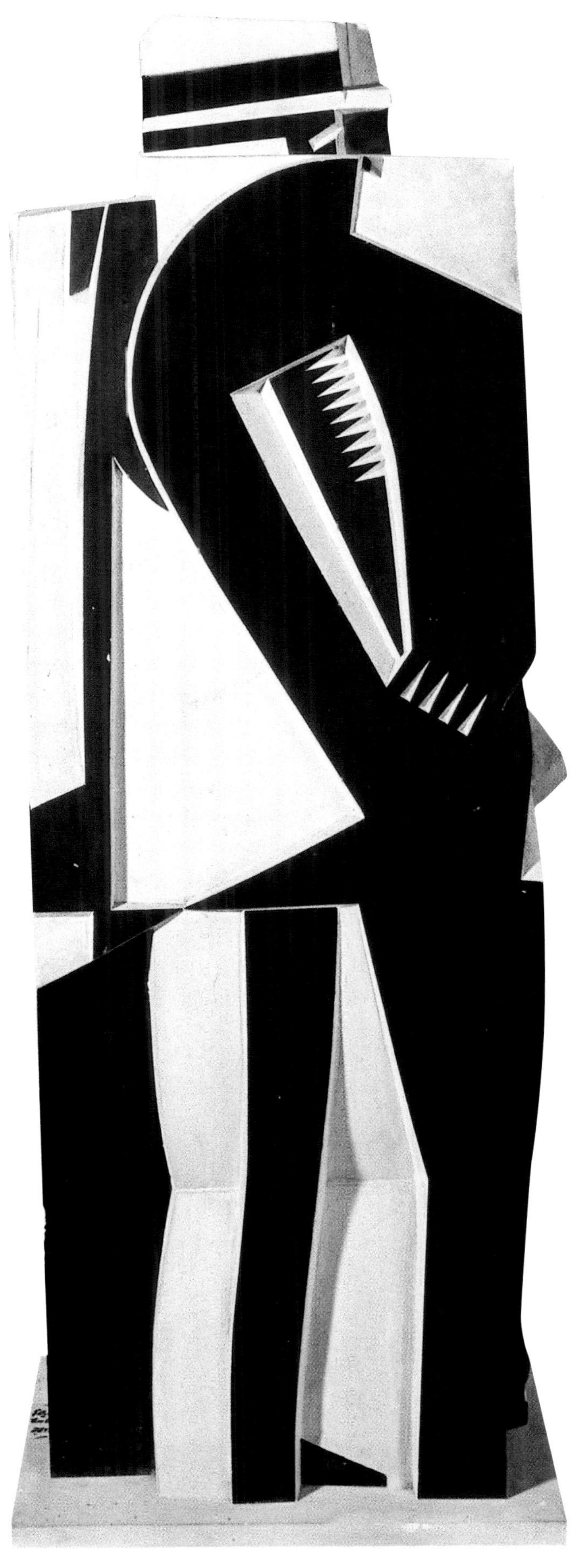

27
JOHN STORRS
GENDARME [POLICEMAN], 1919
LIMESTONE AND BLACK PAINT, H. 108 CM
MUSÉE DANIEL VANNIER, BEAUGENCY, 1703
MAAG, TAM, TMAA

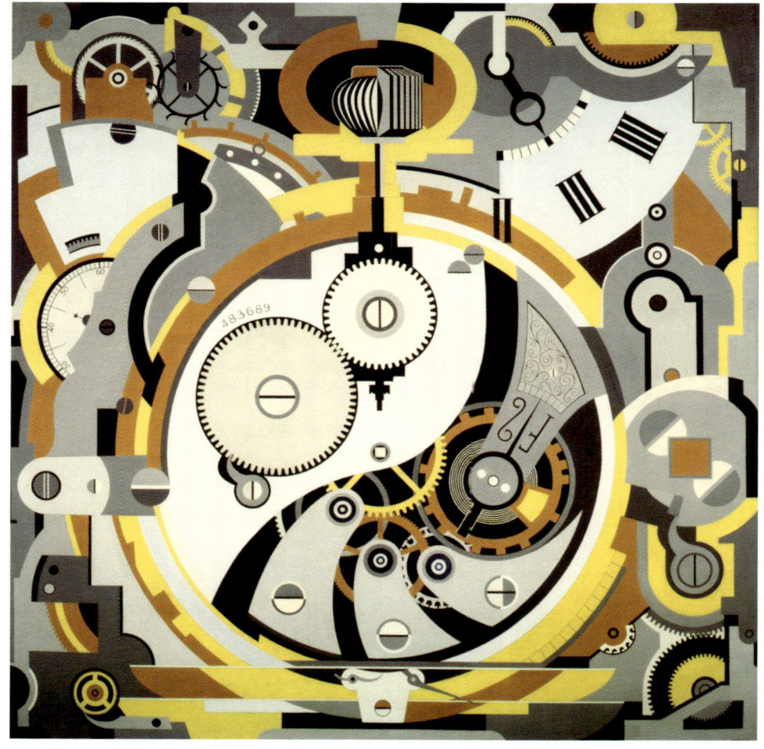

FIG. 2.
GERALD MURPHY,
WATCH, 1925.
OIL ON CANVAS, 199.4 X 200.3 CM.
DALLAS MUSEUM OF ART.
FOUNDATION FOR THE ARTS
COLLECTION, GIFT OF THE ARTIST.

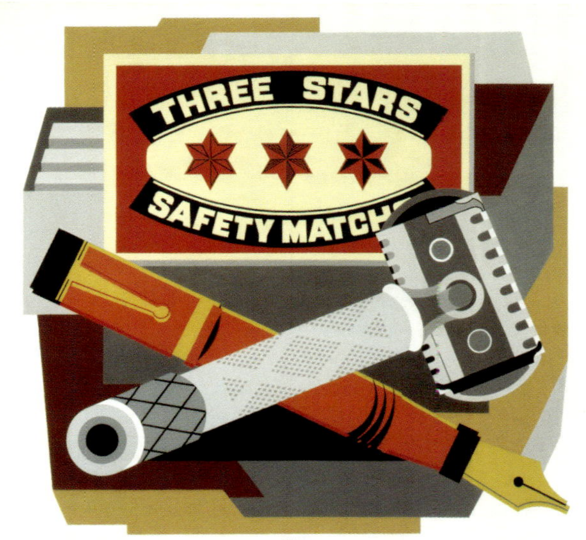

FIG. 3.
GERALD MURPHY,
RAZOR, 1924.
OIL ON CANVAS, 83 X 92.7 CM.
DALLAS MUSEUM OF ART.
FOUNDATION FOR THE ARTS
COLLECTION, GIFT OF THE ARTIST.

Inspired by the cinema's prowess in the art of framing,[25] Murphy thoroughly exploited the technique of the close-up shot on a given object, as seen in paintings such as *Watch* and *Razor* (figs. 2 and 3). This compositional technique, which also flourished in the films of Abel Gance[26] and in Léger's paintings, made it possible to "personalize the fragments" of an object.[27] It also conveyed the new desire to promote objects to the same visual rank as the human figure; objects—primarily manufactured ones—thus became the main "players" on the modern stage. But for Murphy, an object was more than just a player—thanks to its grandiose and heroic dimensions in his work, it became a "star."[28]

Using this close-up technique, which reinforced the notion of subjectivity, Murphy produced a series of still lifes—or perhaps I should say "x-rays"—of the modern American world to which he loudly proclaimed his allegiance. All the objects he meticulously reproduced were basically American consumer products associated with typically American values: health, rapidity, functionality, efficiency. This can be seen in *Razor,* which features a Gillette safety-razor, and *Watch*, which reflects the importance of time and speed on the American lifestyle.

Yet it should not be forgotten that Murphy's objects are never anonymous, that they convey personal, family-oriented connections. The watch in question was designed for the Mark Cross Company, owned by Murphy's father. The Gillette razor was also linked to the paternal world. At the same time, *Watch* is more than just an object associated with his father's America. It was a metaphysical experience, according to Murphy. "I've always been struck," he wrote, "by the mystery and depth of the interior of a watch. Its multiplicity, variety and feeling of movement, and man's grasp at perpetuity."[29]

Doves: In search of an American art both modern and "classical"

Murphy's art, however, was not limited to a simple glorification of modern America. His imagery, although obviously American for the most part, sometimes included motifs drawn from antique art, in the wake of certain cubist and Purist artists, Picasso and Ozenfant, for example. This return to classicism, elsewhere described as a "return to order," often took as its setting the landscape of southern France, marked as it was by Greco-Roman culture.

Doves (fig. 4), painted in Villa America about 1924, shows the extent to which Murphy was in step with his generation of artists. An Ionic column and other fragments of ancient architecture provide the structural framework for a composition that once again underscores the value of harmony and the balance of forms. Three doves are seen in profile, in three different formats, reflecting an approach later favored by Pop artists. The style is "naïve" and recalls American folk art of the nineteenth century. The image of the dove refers to the natural world in which Murphy liked to steep himself,[30] and simultaneously alludes to ancient Greek civilization, the one that viewed doves as the symbol of harmony and spirituality. The subtle, delicate hues differ from the contrasting colors of *Villa America* and *Razor,* being closer to works such as *Cocktail* and *Library.* Like these latter two canvases, *Doves* expresses what seems to have been one of the central concerns of Murphy's work: the creation of an American art that combines the modernity of his times—the concern for functionality, mechanical precision, efficiency— and the values of moderation and harmony so dear to classical art.

A unique position on the Paris art scene

Murphy was not the only American artist to find Paris a fertile place to develop a specifically American artistic identity. Sculptor John Storrs and painter Stuart Davis had a similar experience. They were close to Murphy in the sense that their quest for Americanness involved a reinterpretation of the cubist idiom.

Storrs, like Murphy, was from Chicago. He arrived in France prior to the 1920s and worked with Auguste Rodin before turning toward a cubism that flirted with abstraction.[31] He returned to the United States regularly, and he took his American cultural identity as the raw material of his oeuvre. This can be seen in the series of sculptures titled *Studies in Form (Forms in Space)* (cats. 28 and 29), which he began in 1920. These pared-down, cubist, and architectural forms were inspired by the skyscrapers in his home town of Chicago. Storrs imitated their staggered, vertical patterns and their linear zigzags, thus reinforcing the verticality and dynamism of his forms. Their beauty—sober, functional, and organic—furthermore evokes the architecture of Frank Lloyd Wright, whose work Storrs knew well.[32] Also highly attached to primal America— that of Native Americans—Storrs turned these thrusting edifices into "totems" of modern American civilization, and borrowed from Amerindian art—and primitive arts in general—a taste for polychrome sculpture. With *Winged Horse* (fig. 5), inspired by a poem by Walt Whitman yet handled in an Art Deco manner, Storrs similarly proclaimed his American roots and his links to a poet who incarnated a democratic, progressive America fully cognizant of its cultural wealth.

Stuart Davis, meanwhile, was soon bored with Parisian life and returned to America, the only country he believed could stimulate his energy and creativity. It should nevertheless be pointed out that his time in Paris, in an artistic milieu that fantasized about America, certainly encouraged Davis to seek, in his own country, the foundations of a new art. As soon as he returned home, he developed an oeuvre that was radically American in tone. Like Murphy, though in a style that wavered between cubism and abstraction, Davis centered his attention on American consumer products, such as an *Eggbeater No. 4* (cat. 10) and a pack of *Lucky Strike* cigarettes. He was one of the first artists to draw inspiration from jazz, that 100 percent American invention.

Murphy nevertheless left a much stronger mark on the history of the Paris avant-garde of the 1920s. His made-in-America "showobjects," elevated to the status of icons of the machine age, and his delight in cultivating his own American identity, could not fail to appeal to the imaginations of artists such as Picasso and Léger. They thought that Murphy's painting "was the epitome of transatlantic chic."[33] But the depression, followed by World War II, brought a sudden end to transatlantic chic and Murphy's work was forgotten. It was not until the 1960s that America, Murphy's source of inspiration, discovered this profoundly original artist, whose style and subject-matter heralded, in a way, Pop Art. ■

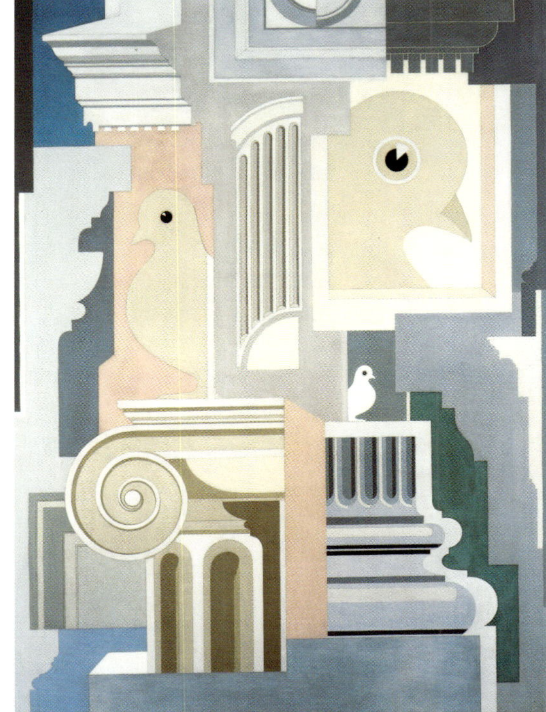

FIG. 4.
GERALD MURPHY,
DOVES, 1925.
OIL ON CANVAS, 123.5 X 91.5 CM.
CURTIS GALLERIES, MINNEAPOLIS.

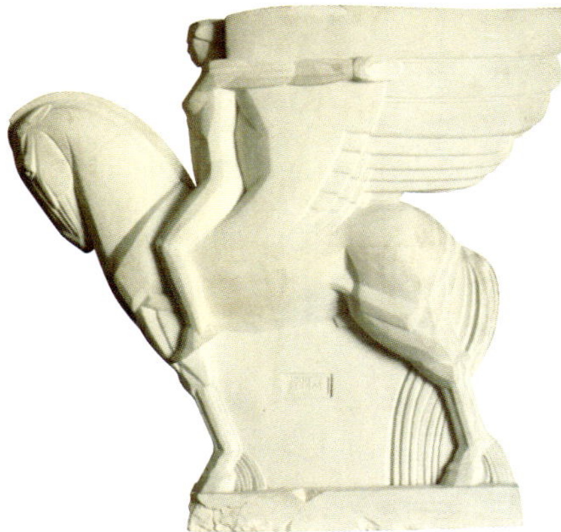

FIG. 5.
JOHN STORRS,
CHEVAL AILÉ [WINGED HORSE]. C. 1918.
PLASTER, 33.7 X 38.5 X 8 CM.
MUSÉE DE MER.
COLLECTION JOHN STORRS.

1— Gerald Murphy arrived in Paris in 1921. First he lived in the former residence of composer Charles Gounod. Later, in 1924, he moved to Antibes in the south of France, thus helping to make the Riveria a fashionable summer spot.

2— The term "feast" alludes to Ernest Hemingway's wonderful account of the festive, non-conformist atmosphere of Paris in the Roaring Twenties, *A Moveable Feast* (New York: Charles Scribner's Sons, 1964).

3— John Dos Passos, *The Best Times* (New York: New American Library, 1966), 146.

4— Henry Miller, *Tropic of Cancer* (New York: Modern Library, 1983), 29–30.

5— In "The American Influence in France," an article published in the United States, Soupault stressed the terrific contribution of American movies. "The American cinema brought to light all the beauty of our epoch, and all the mystery of modern mechanics." *University of Washington Chapbooks* 28 (Washington, D.C., 1930), 17.

6— "Il y a de la jeunesse dans tous les coins. Pas d'odeur de veillard. Ils agissent jusqu'à la fin." Letter from Fernand Léger to Simone, February 1936. *Lettres à Simone* (Zurich: Skira, 1987), 165 (my translation).

7— See the article by Jacques Mauny in *L'Art vivant* 4 (April 1942): n.p.

8— The quotation is drawn from Wanda Corn, "Identity, Modernism, and the American Artist after World War I: Gerald Murphy and *Américanisme*," in *Nationalism in the Visual Arts* (Washington, D.C.: Studies in the History of Art, Symposium Papers XIII, 1991), 150. Corn, an American art historian, studied the nationalist trend among American art circles in the 1920s.

9— Prior to becoming an artist, Murphy had studied landscape architecture at Harvard.

10— Calvin Tomkins, *Living Well Is the Best Revenge* (New York: Modern Library, 1998), 23.

11— The ballet was the work of Swedish choreographer Rolf de Maré; the music was composed by Cole Porter.

12— Quoted in William Rubin, *The Paintings of Gerald Murphy,* exh. cat. (New York: Museum of Modern Art, 1974), 16.

13— It is perhaps appropriate to add that Murphy's writer friend John Dos Passos also had a significant influence on *Within the Quota*. Dos Passos was in Paris when Murphy was doing the sets for the ballet, and he was writing *Manhattan Transfer*, which, as is well known, was the first American novel to experiment with a "cubist" narrative: Dos Passos collaged passages from news clippings into the personal events of his characters. Reliable sources have indicated that Dos Passos spoke of his impressions and experiences with Murphy.

14— Rubin, *The Paintings of Gerald Murphy,* 9.

15— "*Esprit de construction*" is the term used in the manifesto published by the Esprit Nouveau group of Purist artists in October 1920. "There is a new spirit: it is a spirit of construction and synthesis governed by a clear conception. Whatever people may think, it now inspired most human activities. A GREAT PERIOD IS JUST BEGINNING." See *Fernand Léger et l'esprit moderne* (Paris: Musée d'Art Moderne de la Ville de Paris, 1982), 83 (Translator's note: my translation).

16— Quoted in Amanda Vaill, *Everybody Was So Young: Gerald and Sara Murphy* (Boston: Houghton Mifflin Co., 1998), 226.

17— Murphy's psychoanalyst (a disciple of Jung) rightly stressed the closed, almost timeless aspect of Murphy's work. He noted, for example, a sacred, spiritual side to *Watch*. On seeing the painting at the Salon des Indépendants, the analyst allegedly said, "It belongs in some kind of shrine or chapel." Quoted in a letter from Murphy to art historian Douglas MacAgy, dated November 14, 1962. Douglas MacAgy Papers, Archives of American Art, Smithsonian Institution, Washington, D.C.

18— Dos Passos, *The Best Times,* 149–150.

19— There are real stylistic similarities between Murphy and his contemporary, Demuth. They shared a symbolic, almost sacred approach to modern American objects and landscapes. And they shared a use of typography that turned a painting into a coded, ciphered game. Murphy was familiar with Demuth's work, and notably his "liner," which recalls Murphy's *Boatdeck* painted at about the same time. Both artists also cultivated the image of a dandy. In 1928, Demuth painted *I Saw the Figure 5 in Gold* where, once again, the artist played on the symbolism of the number five as well as exploiting, like Murphy, the "sacred" dimension of the color gold.

20— The number five was sacred to Murphy. It figured almost ritually in most of his works. I might add that the figure five is more generally considered to be the number of union, centrality, harmony, and equilibrium. This symbolism, shared by several civilizations, must have been familiar to Murphy, who was interested in ancient civilization, as noted above.

21— Tomkins, *Living Well Is the Best Revenge.*

22— In an article dated 1924, Léger wrote, "Having to speak of spectacle means envisaging the world in all its everyday visual manifestations, which has become one of the fundamental needs of life. It completely dominates daily life." Fernand Léger, "Le Spectacle, lumière, couleur, image mobile, object-spectacle," in *Fonctions de la peinture* (Paris: Gallimard, 1997), 111 (Translator's note: my translation).

23— "Dreiser est toujours en spectacle dans ses romans et le spectacle est une représentation de l'âme américaine [Dreiser is always on show in his novels, and the show is a depiction of the American soul]." Michael Walzer, *La Critique sociale au xxᵉ siècle* (Paris: Éditions Métaillier, 1995), 64 (my translation).

24— King Vidor called on Murphy's musical expertise during the shooting of *Hallelulah!*

25— American director D. W. Griffith, with whom artists and intellectuals of Murphy's generation were fascinated, excelled above all in the art of framing and editing, as can be seen in his *Birth of a Nation*.

26— Abel Gance made prodigious use of the aesthetic and psychological impact of close-ups in his cult film, *La Roue*.

27— See Fernand Léger, "A propos du cinéma," in *Fonctions de la peinture* (Paris: Gallimard, 1997), 168.

28— Murphy was literally drawn to large-scale paintings, as magnificently witnessed by his painting titled *Boatdeck*. The organizers of the Salon des Indépendants had great difficulty in finding exhibition space for it. To those who complained about its large size, Murphy retorted, "If they think my picture is too big, I think the other paintings are too small." Quoted in Rubin, *The Paintings of Gerald Murphy,* 20.

29— Abraham Davidson, *Early American Modernist Painting* (New York: Harper & Row), 286.

30— Villa America was surrounded by gardens and resembled Noah's Ark in its collection of birds, cats, and various domestic animals.

31— Storrs first traveled to Paris in 1905, returning to the capital in 1910–1911. He worked with Rodin around 1912–1913.

32— Storrs was attracted to the architectural theories of Wright, who liked to compare a building to a growing tree. This natural, organic approach to architecture is constantly present in Storrs's sculpture, which favors dynamic vertical thrusts, as mentioned above.

33— Dos Passos, *The Best Times,* 153.

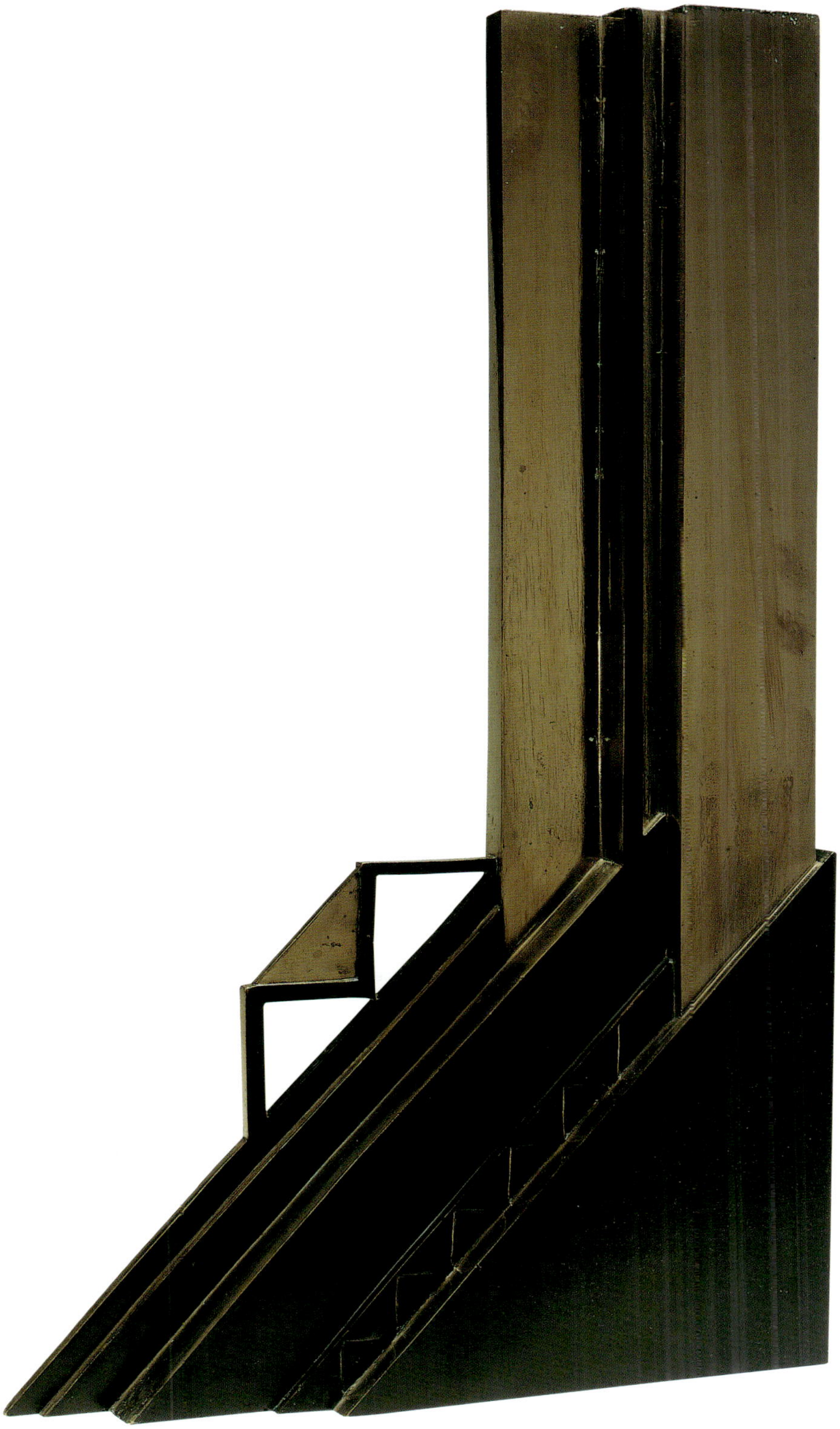

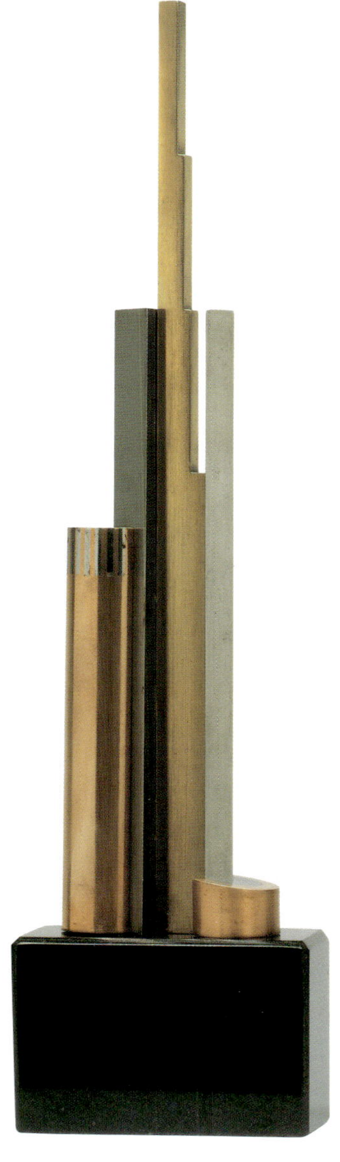

28
JOHN STORRS
STUDY IN FORM (FORMS IN SPACE), 1924
BRONZE, 50.8 X 30.8 X 5.9 CM
HIRSHHORN MUSEUM AND SCULPTURE GARDEN,
SMITHSONIAN INSTITUTION, WASHINGTON D.C.
GIFT OF JOSEPH H. HIRSHHORN, 1966.4824
MAAG, TAM, TMAA

29
JOHN STORRS
STUDY IN PURE FORM (FORMS IN SPACE NO. 4), C. 1924
STEEL, COPPER AND BRASS, H. 31.1 CM
PRIVATE COLLECTION
THIS WORK IS NOT EXHIBITED.

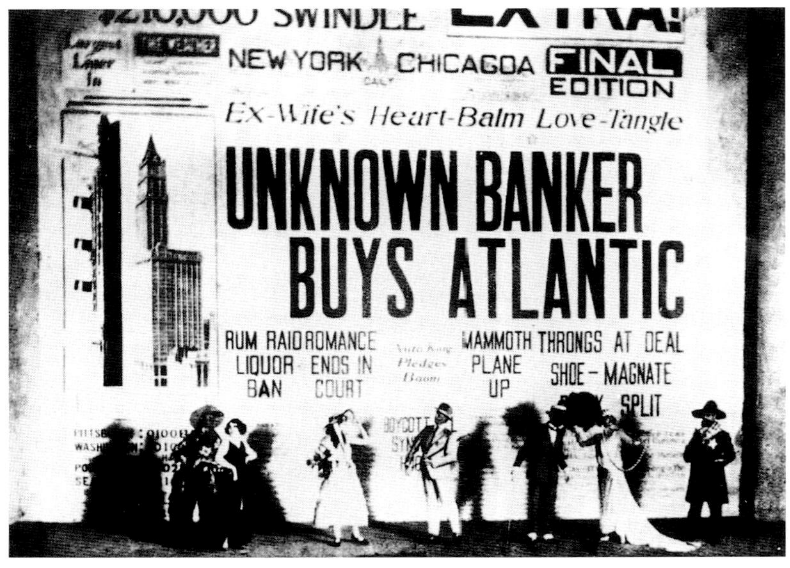

GERALD MURPHY, PAINTED BACKDROP AND COSTUMES FOR *WITHIN THE QUOTA* (SHOWN IN PERFORMANCE). 1923. ESTATE HONORIA MURPHY DONNELLY.

The Parisian avant-garde's fascination with America—seen as the ultimate symbol of modernity—was revealed in two productions by American artists in Paris during the interwar period.

The premiere of the ballet *Within the Quota* was presented on October 25, 1923, at the Théâtre des Champs-Élysées. Gerald Murphy wrote the scenario, and designed the set and costumes, his friend Cole Porter composed the music, Charles Koechlin conducted the orchestra, and dancer Jean Börlin designed the choreography. Rolf de Maré, director of the Ballets Suédois, was the coordinator of the event. According to Darius Milhaud, Fernand Léger had suggested that Murphy design the sets and costumes for an "American" ballet, to be performed as a curtain-raiser to his own ballet, *La Création du Monde*.[1] As an opening piece, designed and executed by Americans, de Maré wanted not only to extend the running time of the overall program but also to promote the company's American tour, scheduled for the winter of 1923–24.

Apparently Léger had already devised a theme for a ballet-sketch that Murphy reformulated into a celebration of the aesthetics of the modern city.[2] *Within the Quota* recounts the picaresque adventures of a Swedish immigrant in New York, set to a "Milhaud-like" jazz score combined with rhythmic music recalling the piano accompaniment for silent films. The title *Within the Quota* alludes to a series of anti-immigration laws then being passed in the United States and Europe.
Upon arrival, the young immigrant meets a series of caricatures: the Cowboy, the Millionairess, the African American Gentleman, the Sheriff, America's Sweetheart, and the Jazz Baby.
The surprise ending transforms the naive protagonist into a movie star. The ballet's appeal resided in its visual elements, namely its costumes of these stereotypes and a magnificent set which was a monumental parody of the front pages of the newspapers owned by press magnate William Randolph Hearst. Headlines of various sizes were emblazoned across the stage, notably the sensational, "Unknown Banker Buys Atlantic."

In a nod to transatlantic connections, the largest French ocean liner, the *Paris*, was illustrated vertically, juxtaposed with New York's Woolworth Building. The critics, French and American alike, responded enthusiastically. For the Paris premiere, Murphy gave an interview to the *Paris Herald* in which he described the ballet as, "nothing but a translation on to the stage of the way America looks to me from over here. I put into the play all the things that come out of America to me, you see, as I get things into perspective and distance."[3]

Léger was also involved in the saga of *Ballet Mécanique,* a musical score composed by George Antheil. Antheil, a "new, ultramodern pianist-composer" who had been a dada figure in New York, headed for Europe in 1922 in search of international fame, taking along his scores with their radical, mechanical sounds of the New World. On October 4, 1923, Antheil staged a concert at the Théâtre des Champs-Élysées, notably including compositions for percussion instruments and machines, with titles such as *Sonata Sauvage, Airplane Sonata,* and *Mechanisms*.[4] It was perhaps subsequent to this concert that Antheil met Léger and Dudley Murphy, who were creating a key avant-garde film, *Ballet Mécanique,* shot in 1923–1924.[5] Antheil then composed his "synchronized musical adaptation" for the film between 1923 and 1925, which meant that it was not ready for the premiere of the film in Vienna in the fall of 1924. Léger and Dudley Murphy nevertheless advertised the film in later years as accompanied by Antheil's music.[6]

Antheil sought to compose the first piece of music "*out of* and *for* machines, *on earth.*" The original version of *Ballet Mécanique* called for sixteen mechanical player-pianos (divided into groups of four), two standard pianos, in addition to percussion instruments (xylophones, bass drums, tom-toms), electric buzzers, a siren, and the sound of three airplane propellers of wood and metal.[7]

The technology of the day, however, did not allow for synchronization of all these instruments, so Antheil composed a second version in 1926, scored for a single player-piano accompanied by standard pianos (in multiples of two).
This version was first performed in Paris on June 19, 1926, sparking a scandal, then at Carnegie Hall in New York on April 10, 1927. This latter performance was a flop, representing a setback from which Antheil's potentially promising career never recovered.

Sometime around 1925, Antheil played his composition for Léger, and he described the artist's enthusiasm in a letter to his friend Ezra Pound: ". . . I hear that Léger has been simply crazy since he heard the *Ballet Mécanique* several days ago. . . . after it was over he simply embraced me. Léger expected a great deal, but he said it was beyond his expectations and that it was as right as right can be."[8] In this radical composition celebrating the machine, Antheil was innovative in his use of silence and noise, and of literal repetition, but he also adopted an approach similar to cubist-derived avant-garde painting as practiced by Léger, which involved the juxtaposition and simultaneity of fundamentally different elements. In the early 1930s, Léger was still waiting for Antheil's score.[9] On October 18, 1935, the 1926 version of the score was presented with the film at the Museum of Modern Art in New York during a lecture given by Léger and attended by Antheil[10]—a privilege that Paris was never accorded.

Francesca Rose

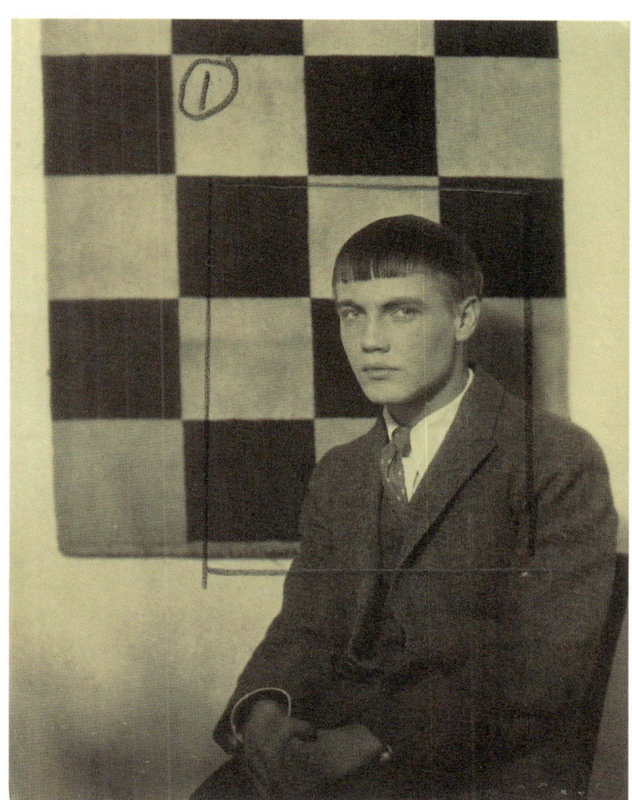

1— Cited in Giovanna Lista, "Léger cinéaste et scénographe," *Fernand Léger et le spectacle* (Paris: Réunion des Musées Nationaux, 1995), 39.

2— Ibid. *Within the Quota* was apparently a reformulation of a ballet project originally by Léger, set in the streets of Paris, designed for Jean Börlin and titled *Sketches de revue.*

3— Quoted in Amanda Vaill, *Everybody Was So Young: Gerald and Sara Murphy, A Lost Generation Love Story* (Boston: Houghton Mifflin Co., 1998), 130.

4— According to Jean-Michel Bouhours, the scandal created by the concert was mainly the work of Marcel L'Herbier, who was then shooting his film *L'Inhumaine* and who wanted to film a scene of a rowdy audience reaction to a recital by a singer played by Georgette Leblanc. See Jean-Michel Bouhours, "D'images mobiles en ballets mécaniques," *Fernand Léger*, exh. cat. (Paris: Musée National d'Art Moderne – Centre Georges Pompidou, 1997), 159.

5— The story of the creation of *Ballet Mécanique* and the roles played by the various protagonists—Léger, Dudley Murphy, and Antheil—is complex, and has sparked several studies that attempt to unravel it. The ample bibliography on the subject includes three texts that focus on this issue: Standish Lawder, *Cubist Cinema* (New York: New York University Press, 1975); Judi Freeman, "Bridging Purism and Surrealism: The Origins and Production of Fernand Léger's *Ballet Mécanique*," in Rudolf E. Kuenzli, ed., *Dada and Surrealist Film* (New York: Willis Locker & Owens, 1987); William Moritz, "Americans in Paris," in Jan Christopher Horak, ed., *Lovers of Cinema: The First American Film Avant-Garde, 1919–1945* (Madison, Wis.: The University of Wisconsin Press, 1995).

6— Bouhours, "D'images mobiles," 160.

7— The first version of *Ballet Mécanique* was finally performed in November 1999 at the University of Massachusetts at Lowell. A recording was subsequently made of this version (EMF CD 020). I thank Marcella Lista for providing this reference.

8— Quoted in Freeman, "Bridging Purism," 33. Letter to Ezra Pound from George Antheil, n.d. [1925]. Ezra Pound Archives, Beinecke Rare Book and Manuscript Library, Yale University, New Haven, Connecticut.

9— Bouhours, "D'images mobiles," 162. Letter to Ezra Pound from Fernand Léger, November 23 [1932], Ezra Pound Archives, Beinecke Rare Book and Manuscript Library, Yale University, New Haven, Connecticut.

10— Ibid. Antheil and Henry Brant performed Erik Satie's musical accompaniment to another silent film that was screened during this same event, namely Francis Picabia and René Clair's *Entr'acte.*

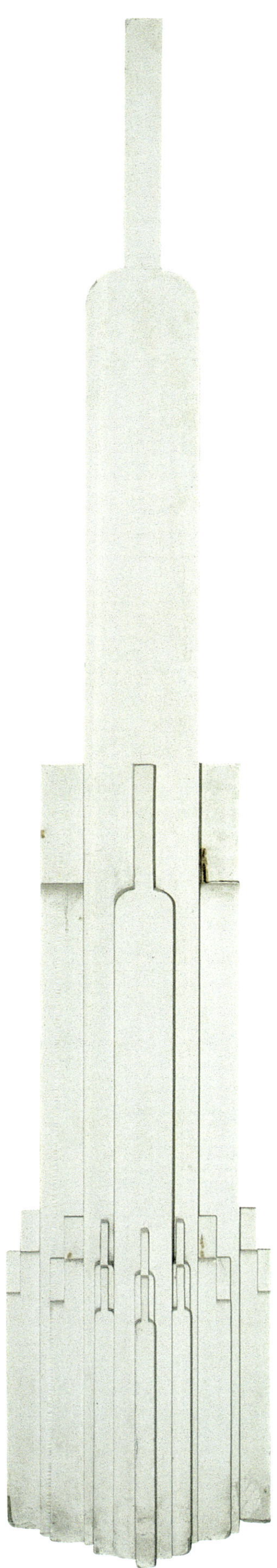

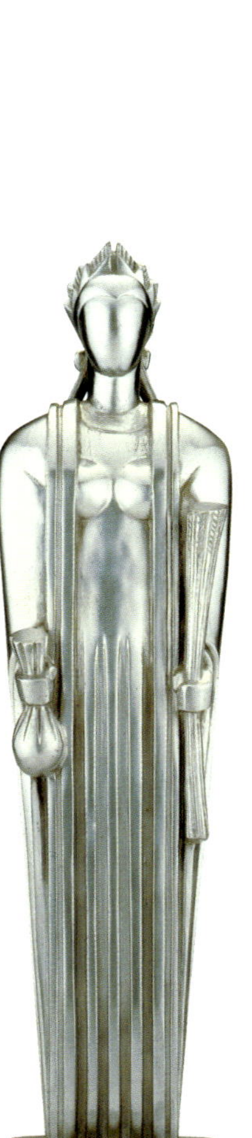

30
JOHN STORRS
ARCHITECTURAL STUDY, C. 1927
PLASTER, H. 162 CM
MUSÉE DE MER.
COLLECTION JOHN STORRS
MAAG, TAM, TMAA

31
JOHN STORRS
CERES, 1928
COPPER-ALLOY PLATED WITH
NICKEL, THEN CHROME,
67.3 X 15.2 X 12.7 CM
THE ART INSTITUTE OF CHICAGO.
GIFT OF JOHN N. STERN, 1981.538
TMAA

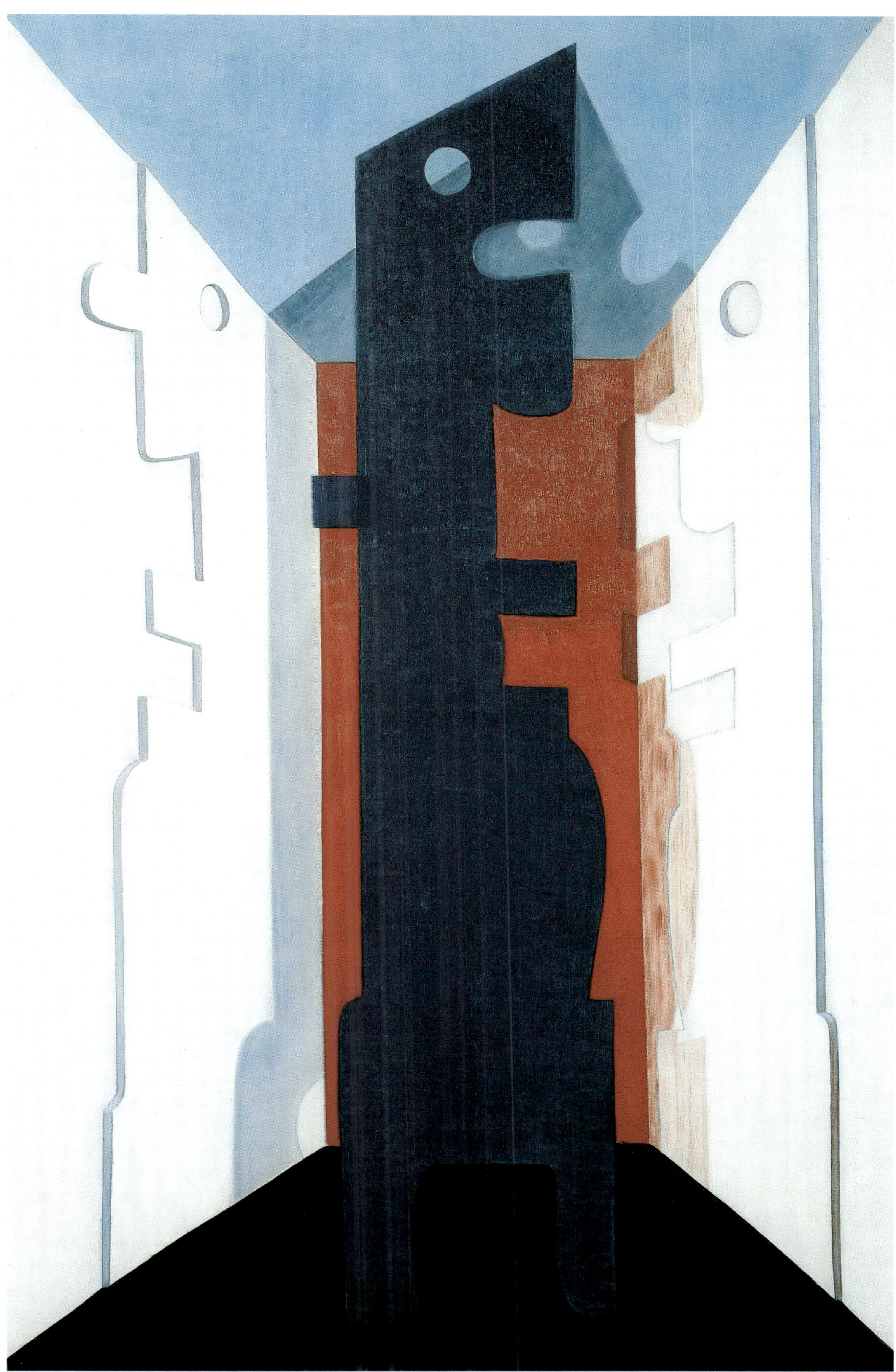

32

JOHN STORRS
MONOLOGUE, 1932
OIL ON CANVAS, 146.1 X 97 CM
WHITNEY MUSEUM OF AMERICAN ART, NEW YORK.
GIFT OF GABRIELLA DE FERRARI AND RAYMOND J. LEARSY
IN HONOR OF FLORA BIDDLE, 91.59.5
TMAA

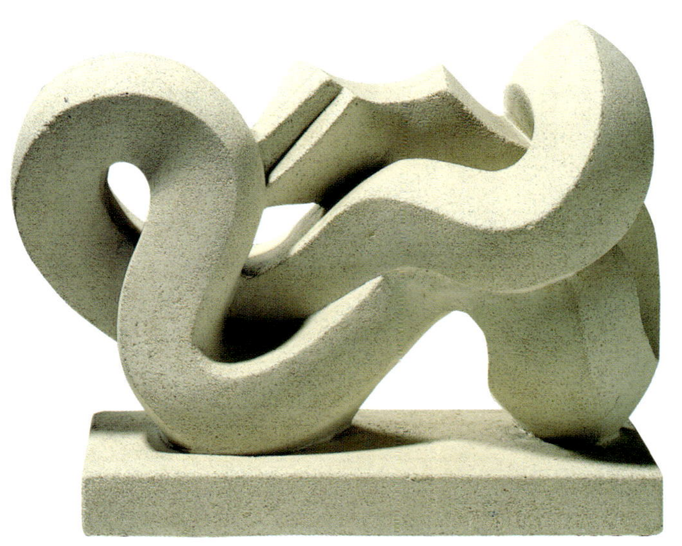

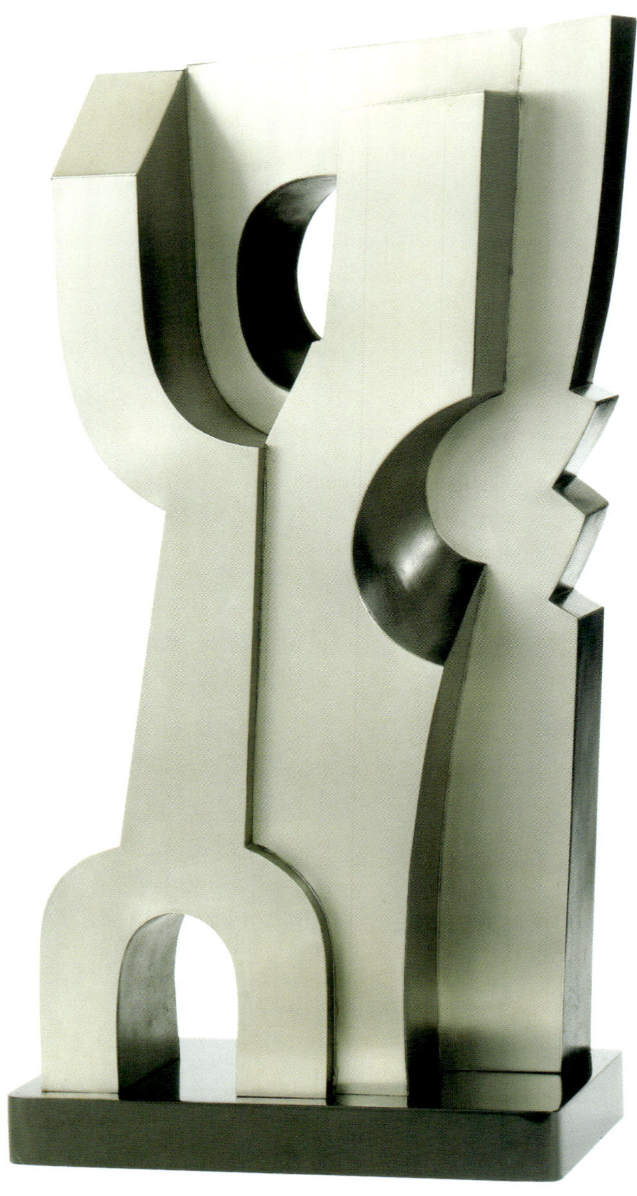

33

JOHN STORRS
[UNTITLED], C. 1937
COMPOSITE STONE, 23 X 31 X 16.5 CM
MUSÉE NATIONAL D'ART MODERNE –
CENTRE GEORGES POMPIDOU, PARIS, AM 1987-615
(ON LOAN TO THE MUSÉE NATIONAL DE LA
COOPÉRATION FRANCO-AMÉRICAINE, BLÉRANCOURT)
MAAG, TAM, TMAA

34

JOHN STORRS
COMPOSITION AROUND TWO VOIDS, C. 1934
STAINLESS STEEL, 50.8 X 25.4 X 15.2 CM
WHITNEY MUSEUM OF AMERICAN ART, NEW YORK,
GIFT OF MONIQUE STORRS BOOZ, 65.34
TMAA

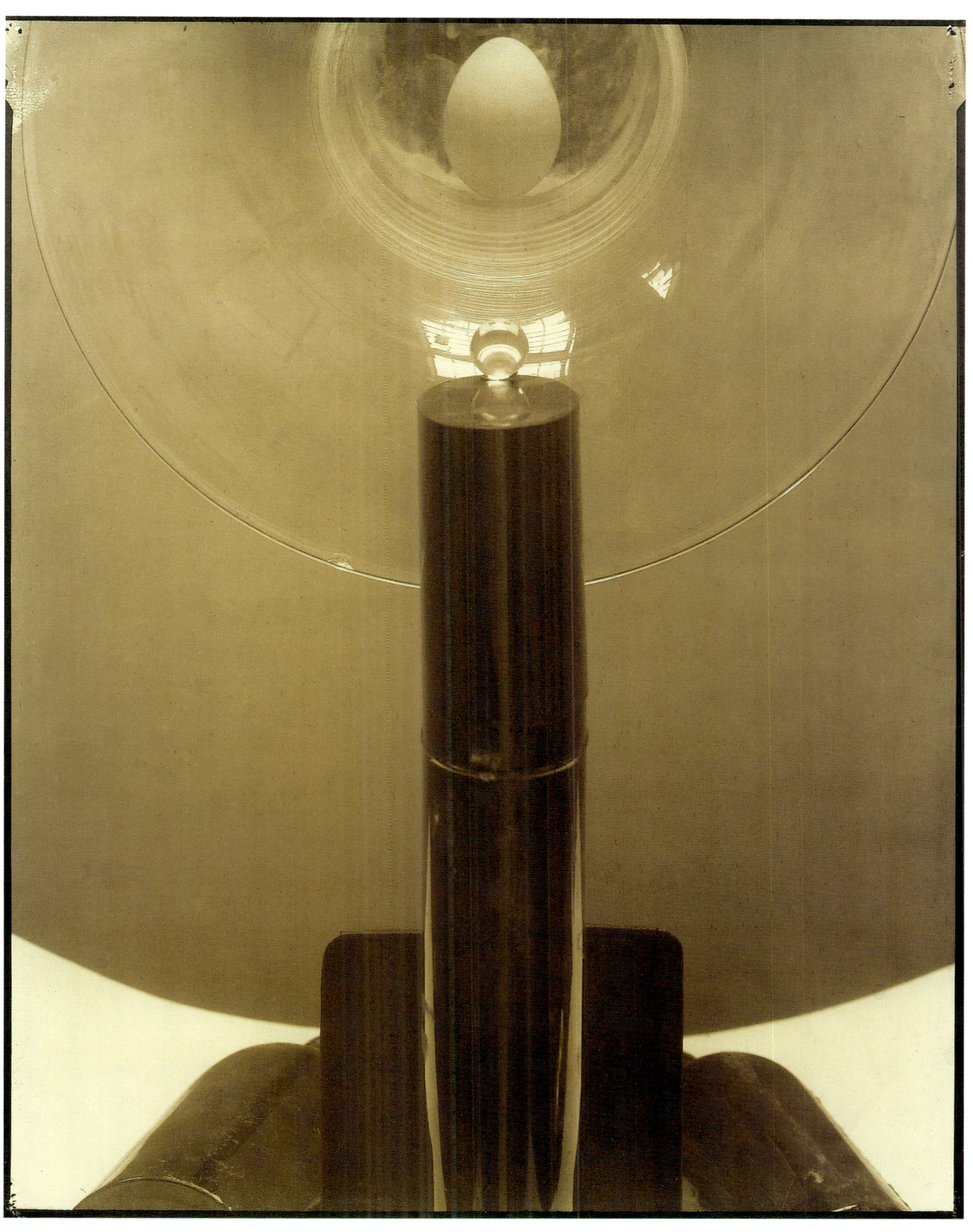

35
EDWARD STEICHEN
TRIUMPH OF THE EGG, 1921
WARM-TONED GELATIN SILVER PRINT, 24.4 X 19 CM
HALLMARK CARDS, KANSAS CITY, MISS.
HALLMARK PHOTOGRAPHIC COLLECTION
MAAG, TAM, TMAA

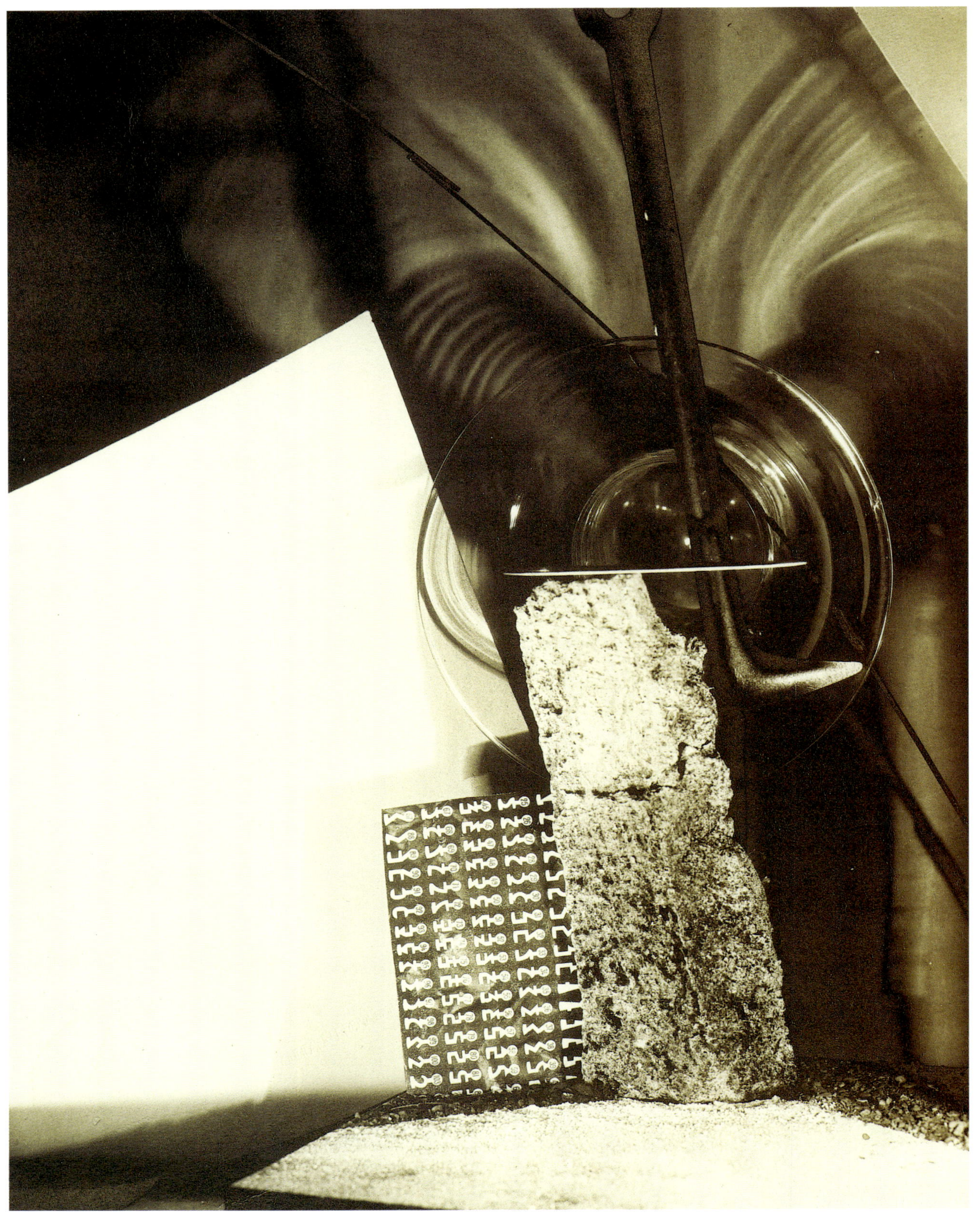

36
EDWARD STEICHEN
TIME-SPACE CONTINUUM, 1920
PALLADIUM PRINT, 24.4 X 19.3 CM
GEORGE EASTMAN HOUSE, ROCHESTER, N.Y.
BEQUEST OF EDWARD STEICHEN BY DIRECTION
OF JOANNA T. STEICHEN, 79.2021.0002
MAAG, TAM, TMAA

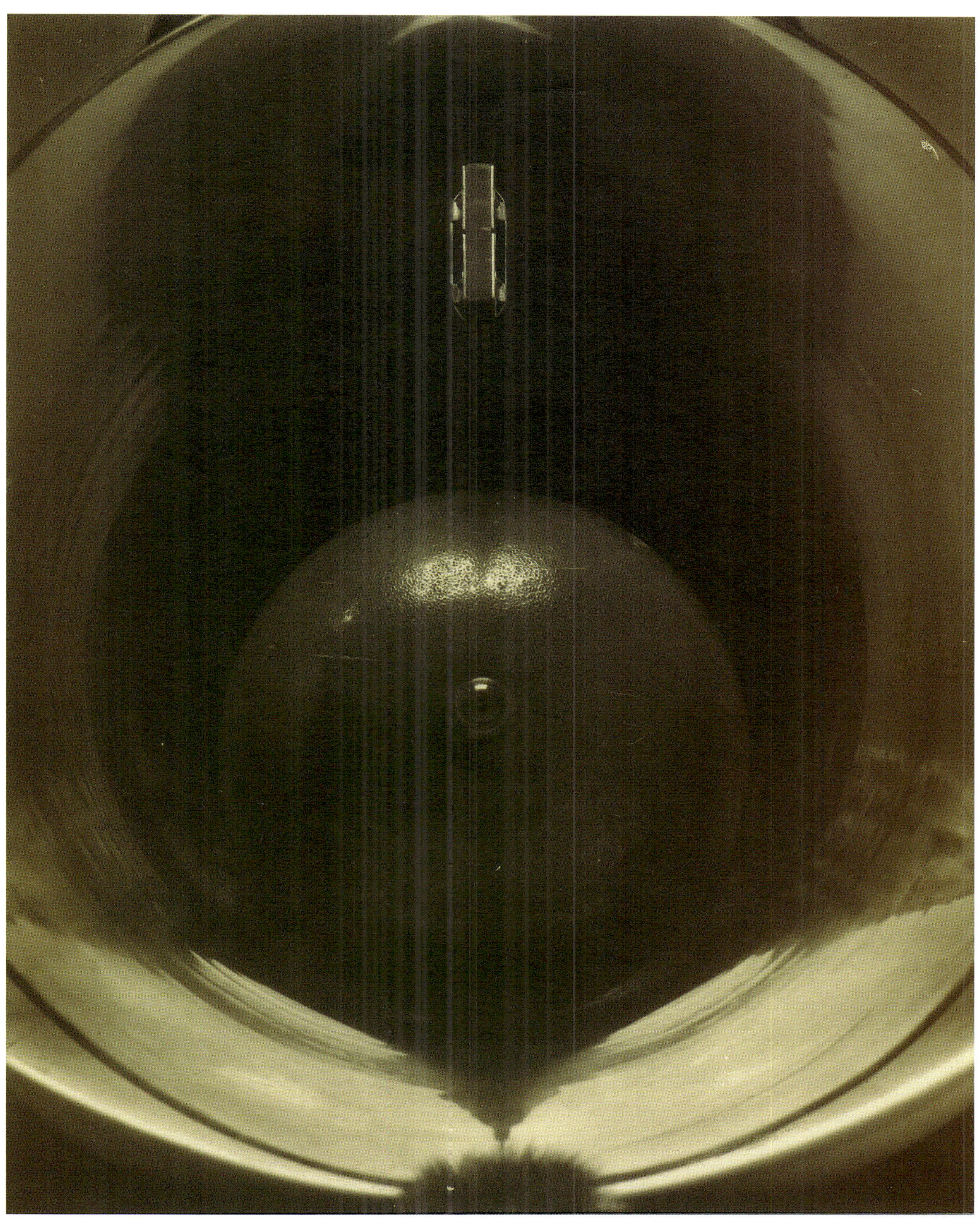

37
EDWARD STEICHEN
HARMONICA RIDDLE, C. 1921
PLATINUM PRINT, 25 X 20.3 CM
THE NEW YORK PUBLIC LIBRARY, ASTOR,
LENOX AND TILDEN FOUNDATIONS.
SHIRLEY CARTER BURDEN COLLECTION,
PHOTOGRAPHY COLLECTION,
MIRIAM AND IRA D. WALLACH DIVISION OF ART,
PRINTS AND PHOTOGRAPHS, SCB91 PH 111
TAM, TMAA

the birth of geometric abstraction

CHAPTER **2**

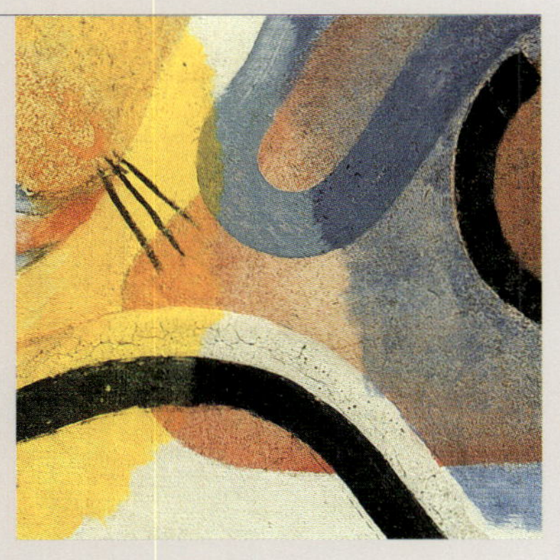

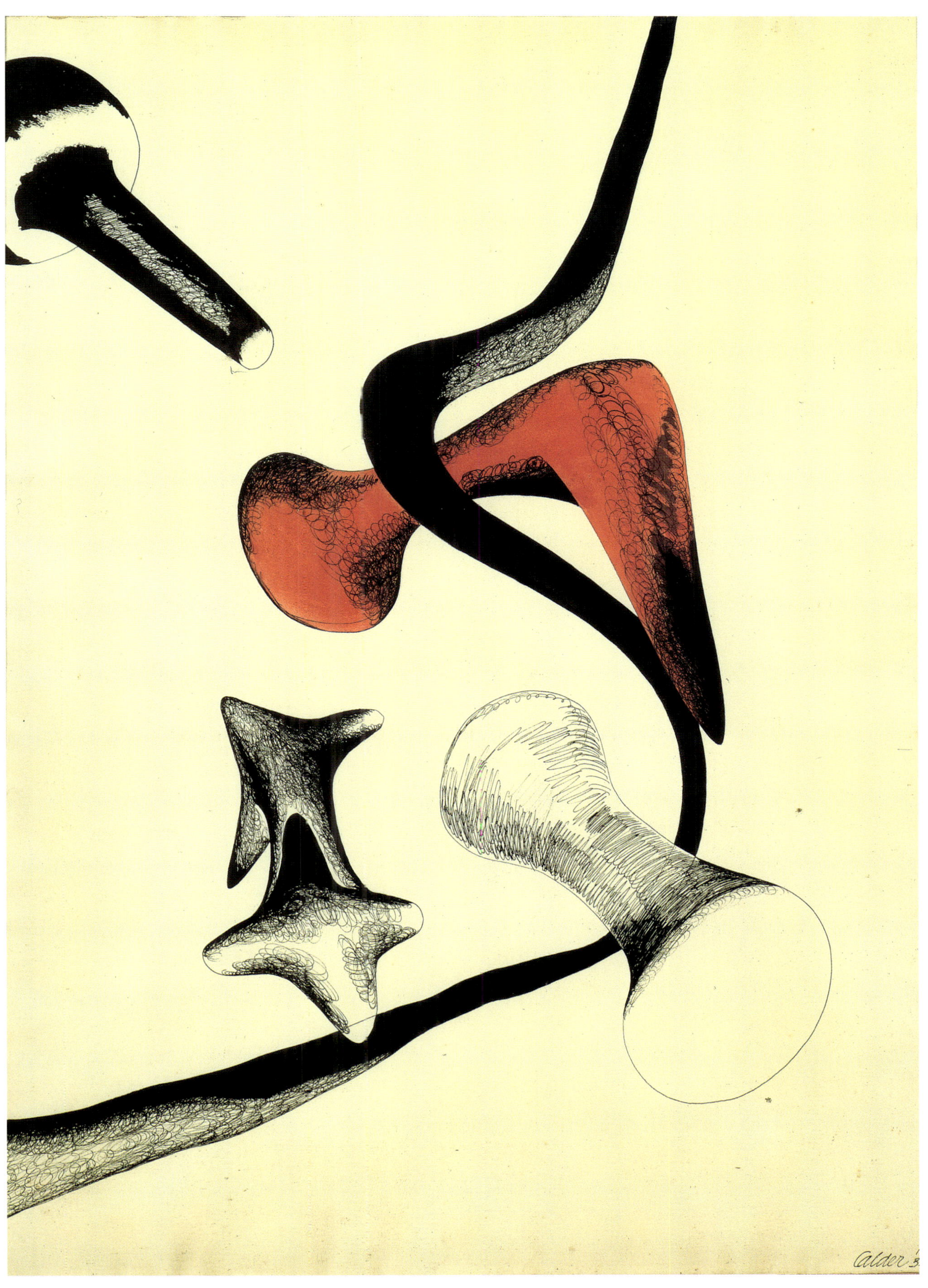

38
ALEXANDER CALDER
MONDE ÉTRANGE [STRANGE WORLD], 1932
INDIA INK AND GOUACHE ON PAPER, 78.1 X 58.2 CM
MUSÉE NATIONAL D'ART MODERNE –
CENTRE GEORGES POMPIDOU, PARIS.
GIFT OF MARY ROWER AND SANDRA DAVIDSON,
AM 1985.499
MAAG

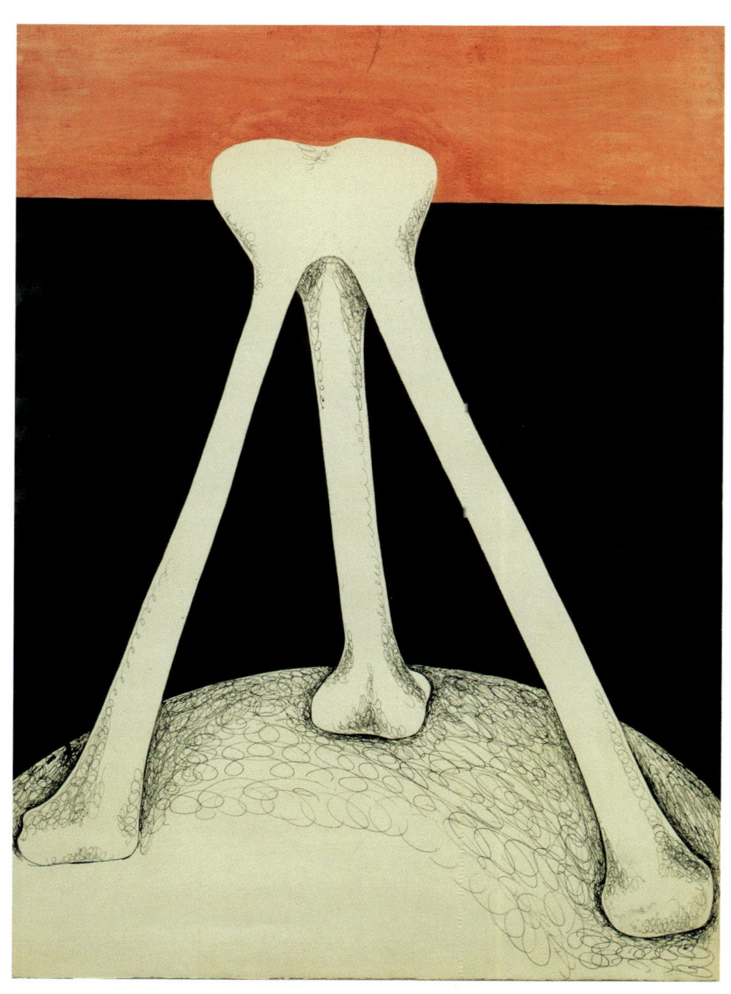

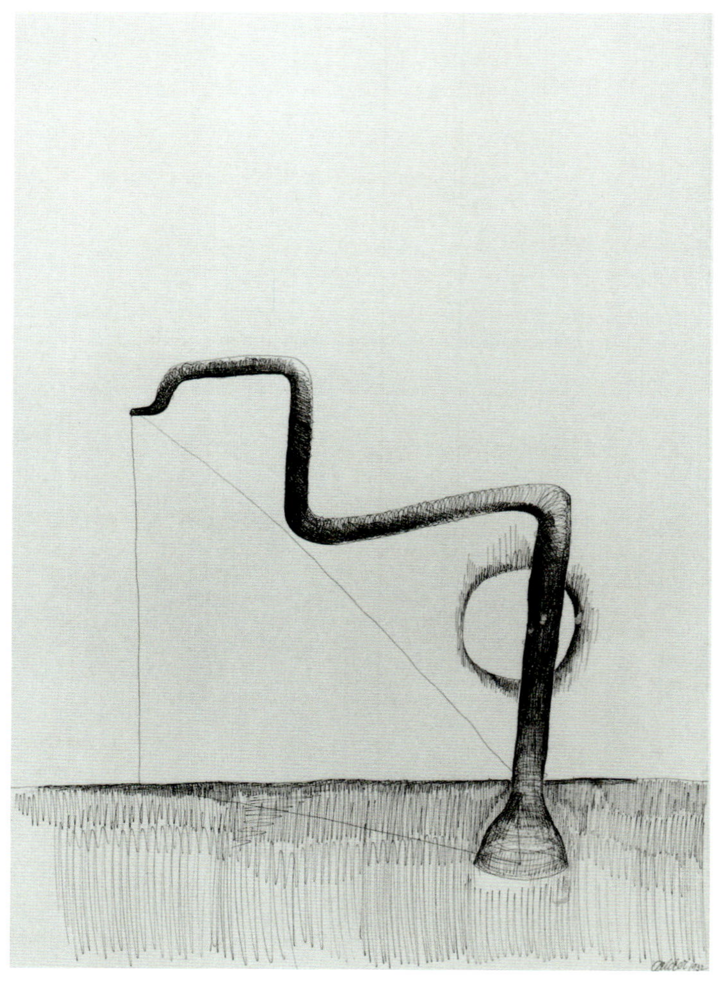

39
ALEXANDER CALDER
[UNTITLED], 1933
GOUACHE, COLORED INKS AND GRAPHITE ON PAPER,
77.5 X 57.1 CM
COURTESY O'HARA GALLERY, NEW YORK
MAAG, TAM, TMAA

40
ALEXANDER CALDER
[UNTITLED], 1932
INDIA INK ON PAPER, 76.2 X 55.8 CM
MUSÉE NATIONAL D'ART MODERNE –
CENTRE GEORGES POMPIDOU, PARIS, AM 1980.18
MAAG

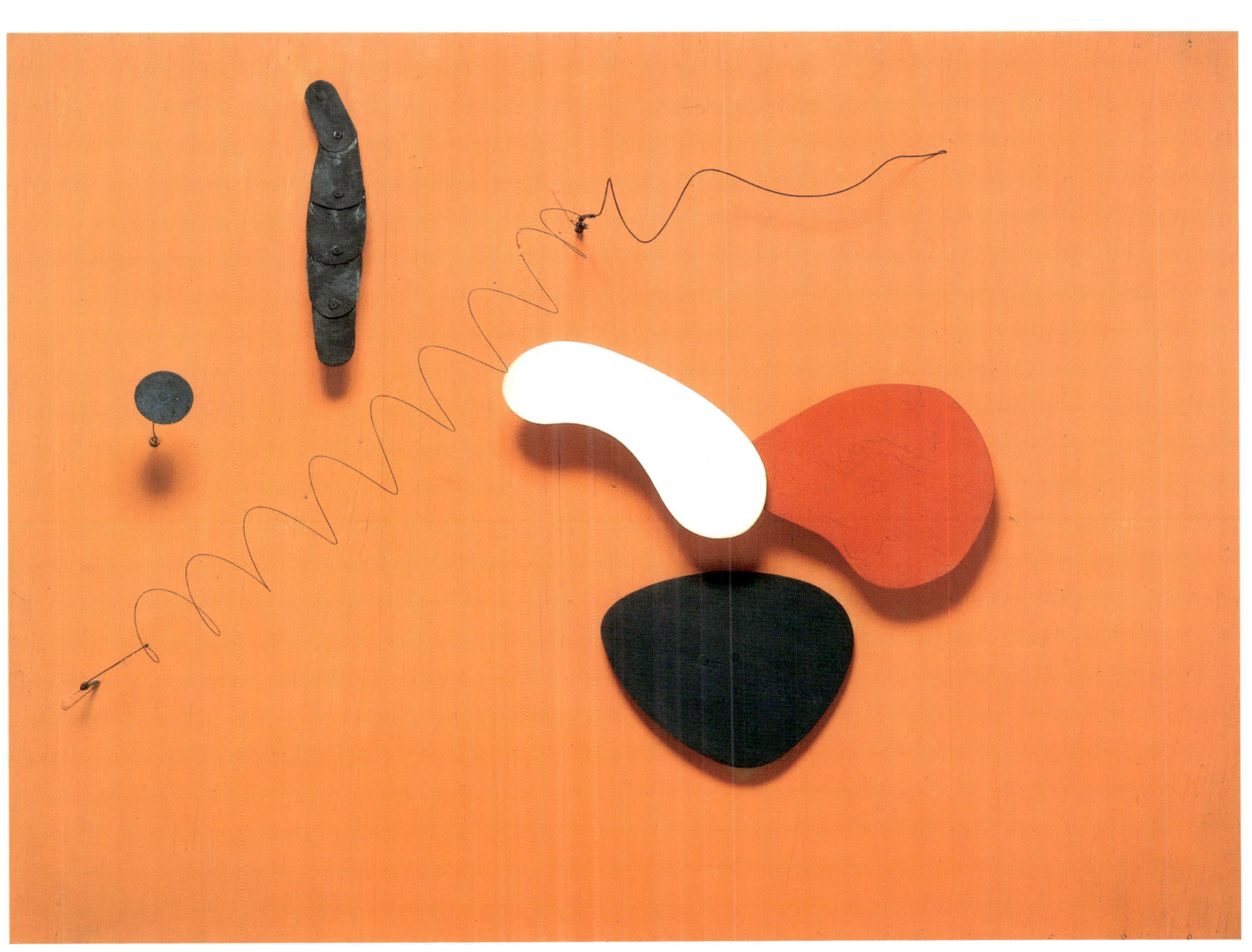

41

ALEXANDER CALDER
ORANGE PANEL, 1936
PAINTED WOOD, SHEET METAL, WIRE AND MOTOR,
91.4 X 121.9 X 22.9 CM
PRIVATE COLLECTION
MAAG

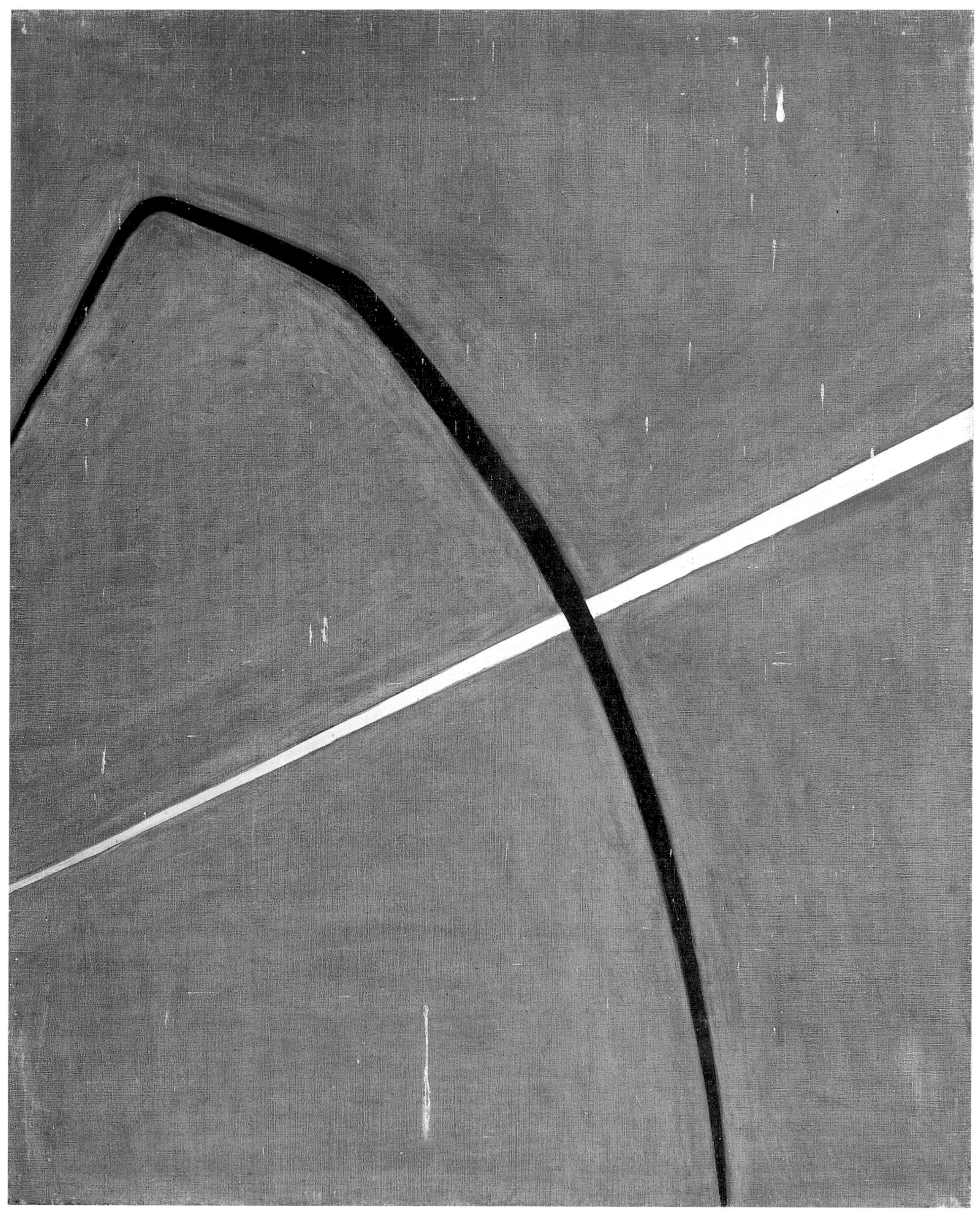

42
ALEXANDER CALDER
FOND BLEU, LIGNES BLANCHE ET MARRON
[BLUE BACKGROUND, WHITE AND BROWN LINES], 1935
OIL ON CANVAS, 81.5 × 66 CM
MUSÉE NATIONAL DE LA COOPÉRATION
FRANCO-AMÉRICAINE, BLÉRANCOURT, MNBCFAC 87.3
MAAG, TMAA

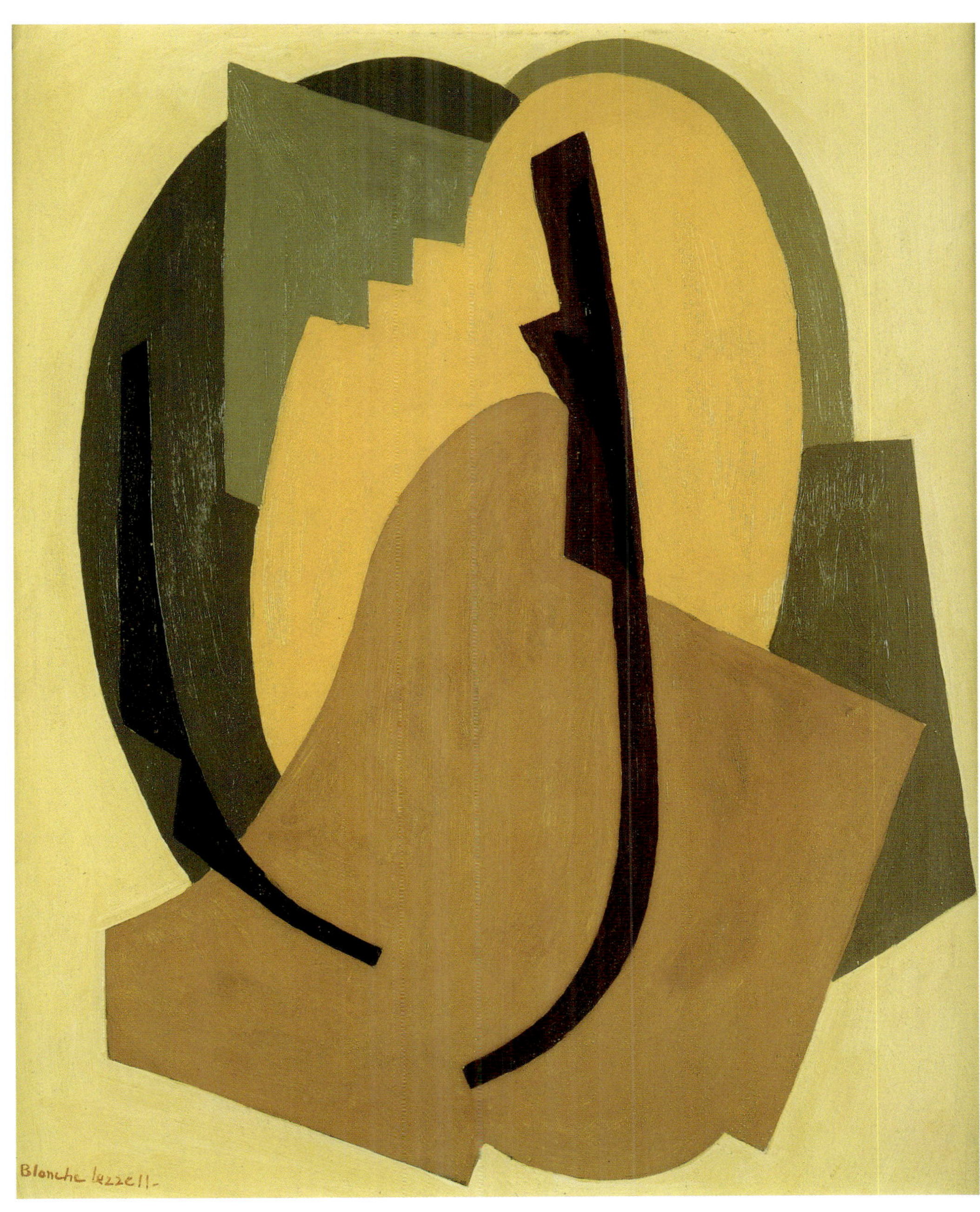

43
BLANCHE LAZZELL
UNTITLED (CUBIST COMPOSITION), C. 1929
OIL ON WOOD PANEL, 47.6 X 39.4 CM
COURTESY MICHAEL ROSENFELD GALLERY,
NEW YORK
MAAG, TAM, TMAA

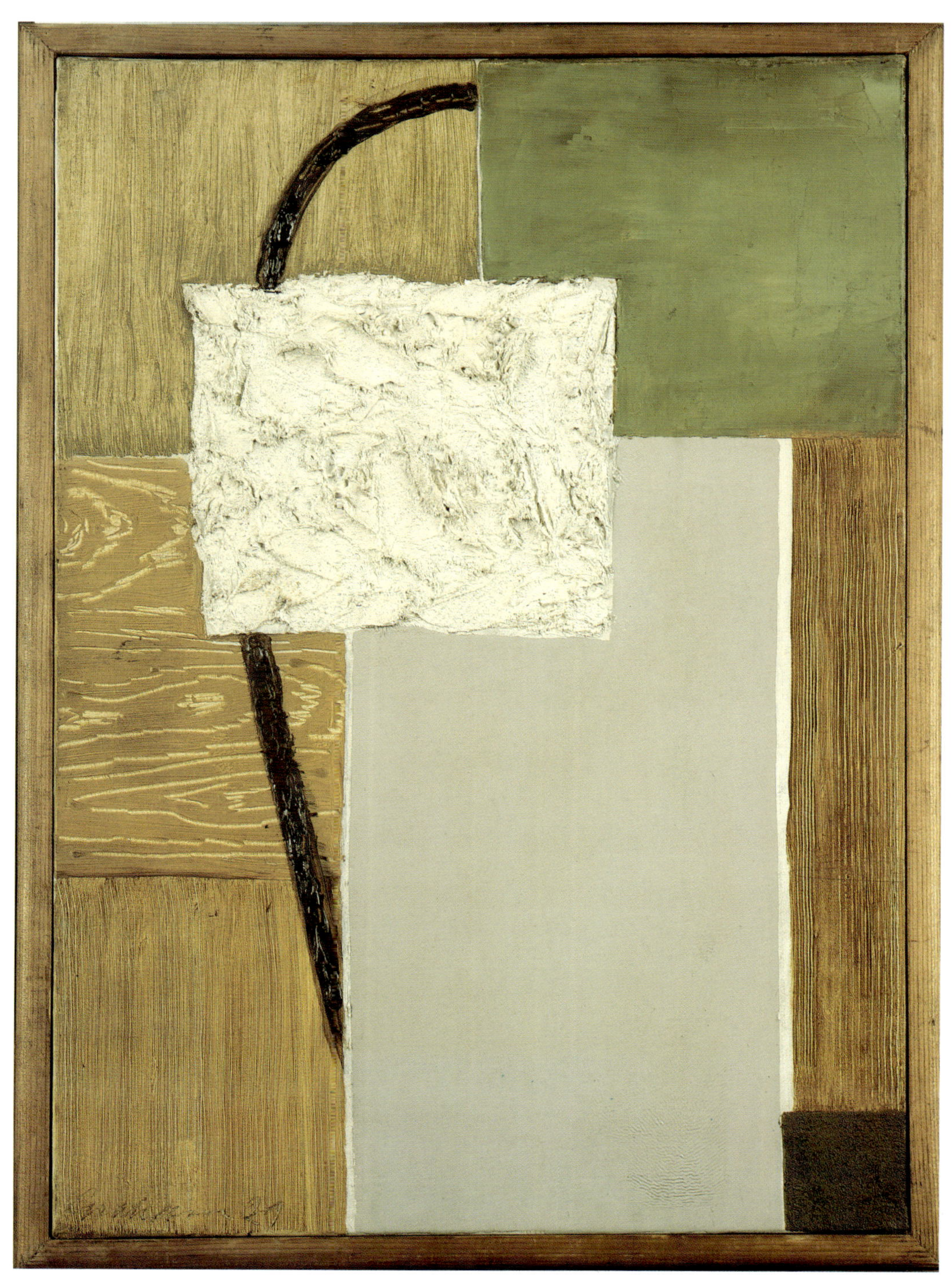

44

JOHN GRAHAM
COMPOSITION, 1929
OIL ON CANVAS, 46 X 33 CM
MUSÉE ZERVOS, VÉZELAY, MZ NO. 436
MAAG, TAM, TMAA

AMERICANS AS SEEN
IN THE *CAHIERS D'ART*
BEFORE 1940

CHRISTIAN **DEROUET**

The protectionism practiced by the Paris art scene in the early twentieth century is an established historical fact. The government led the way when it converted the Jeu de Paume gallery in Paris into a museum of non-French art, placing foreign schools in a kind of quarantine, in order to free some space at the Musée du Luxembourg across town. American works in the government collection were thus exiled to the Jeu de Paume following an exhibition of thanksgiving after the signing of the Treaty of Versailles.[1] Furthermore, French acquisition and exhibition policies favored neighboring countries—neither Russia nor America were thought worthy of interest. Galleries and critics shared this parochial approach. The domestic art market was lifeless and hermetically closed; led by gallery owners Durand-Ruel and Wildenstein, commercial hegemony was organized around exportation in one direction, from Paris to New York. It was up to artists from America (or elsewhere) to move to Paris, and adopt French habits (or even a French name) if they wanted to be accepted. These attitudes and economics need to be posited prior to examining, via *Cahiers d'Art,* signs of a shift that portended what no one had anticipated—the transfer of artistic primacy from one continent to another.

Why examine *Cahiers d'Art?* Because it was one of the finest magazines of the day. Founded in 1926, it ultimately established its headquarters at 14 rue du Dragon near Saint-Germain-des-Prés. Until 1960 it covered news of all the latest and best developments in the visual arts, making claims to universality. After an original attempt to open itself to the German scene, the magazine turned back to Paris. It had no clear policy toward the United States prior to 1940, but after 1945 became openly hostile to America.

It was, furthermore, a highly partial review subject to the prejudices and whims of Christian Zervos, its editor-in-chief (fig. 1). Zervos was a Greek immigrant who neither spoke nor read English. A staunch European of Mediterranean origin, he had no desire to cross the Atlantic. He published the world's finest art magazine, or so he thought. His prime assets were Picasso and Matisse, whose recent works he regularly presented in full-page, black-and-white illustrations.

When Zervos began writing art criticism for *L'Art d'aujourd'hui,* and later for his own *Cahiers d'Art,* America was still just a postwar infatuation. Zervos thought of Americans as the troops that came to hasten the final victory, as engraved by the expert gouge of J. E. Laboureur. The New York skyline at night, sketched with a touch of modernism in the manner of Boutet de Monvel, was an acceptable pattern for interior decorators of postwar bars. Le Dôme on boulevard de Montparnasse, for that matter, redubbed an "American" café-bar, no longer drew its old clientele; the Germans had abandoned its terrace, the Russian grand dukes were now driving cabs, and English aristocrats were counting their pennies. Until the crash of 1929, the only moneyed people left in

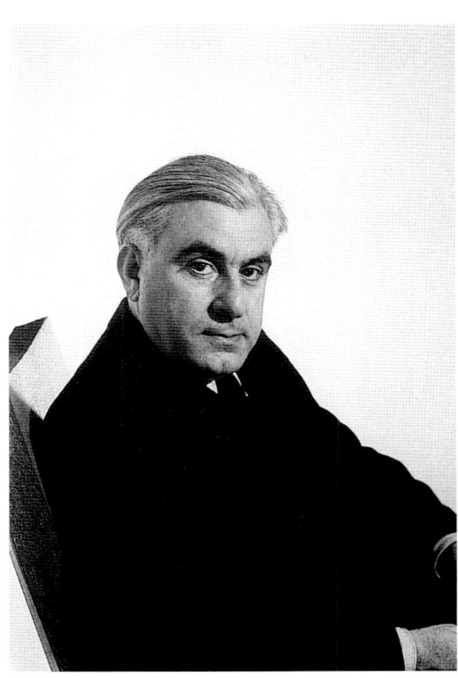

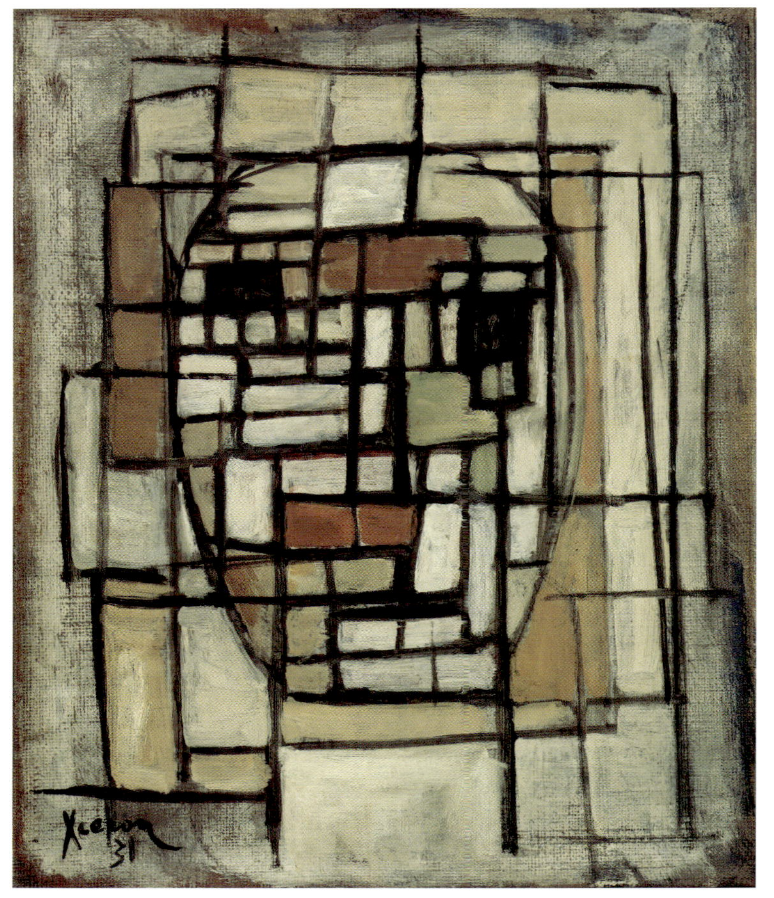

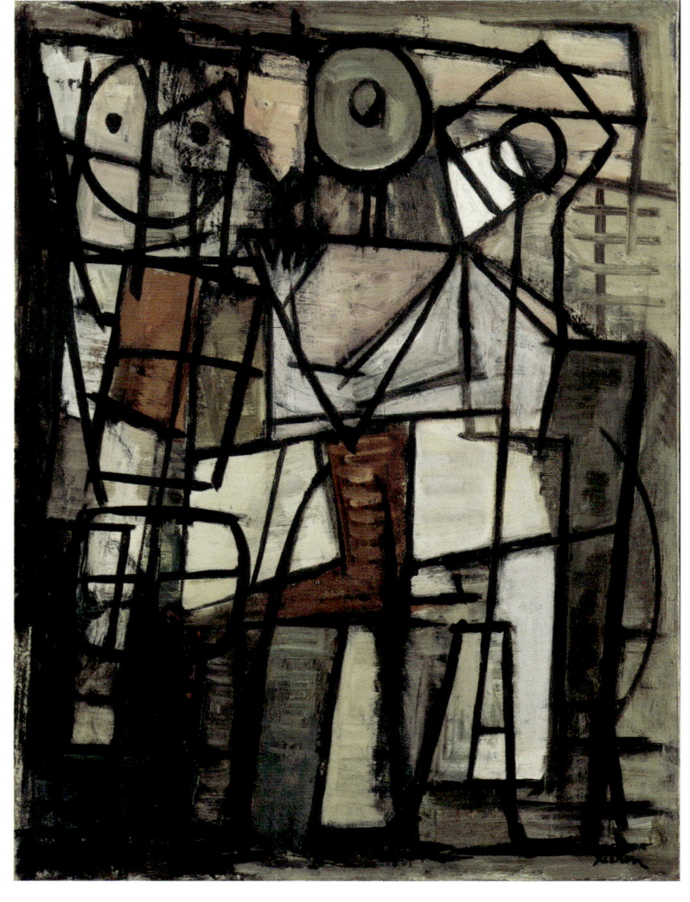

45

JEAN XCERON
PORTRAIT, 1931
OIL ON CANVAS, 46 X 38.5 CM
MUSÉE ZERVOS, VÉZELAY, MZ NO. 685
MAAG, TAM, TMAA

46

JEAN XCERON
TROIS FIGURES [THREE FIGURES], 1932
OIL ON CANVAS, 51 X 38 CM
MUSÉE ZERVOS, VÉZELAY, MZ NO. 688
MAAG, TAM, TMAA

Paris were Americans, caught in the swirl of the Lost Generation. Zervos, who did not share Paul Morand's enthusiasm for New York and was not familiar with Carlo Rim's *Jazz* magazine, wrote:

> There is a crisis of harmony in modern life, claim the voices of sibyls who see—only in order to see in themselves—that modern life is developing a new rhythm. Yet we are still inhabited by the same harmony. Our requirements may be governed by rhythms, indeed original rhythms. But on the old continent, with its slow evolution, we arrive at new forms of living with much adaptation. To the extent that we barely perceive the transformations ourselves. Thus we easily turn to memories of old. And each memory is recovered at the cost of a regret. The realm of memory—that rare bird.
>
> Whatever our resistance, we are subject to the order that has arrived from beyond the western seas. Our lives will necessarily unfold on a shrill tone, caught in a harmony of opposing rhythms that endlessly transform themselves from one into another. Diverse, constantly shifting rhythms that disperse and reunite, converge and diverge, slow and accelerate. This rapid, incessant change brings delirium, passion, agitation, and a sense of scale. Tall buildings that rise over us; lights that entrap us and splatter us; and dances: this is the new rhythm.[2]

Zervos, who was not an art historian, was a little too quick to deny America any sensibility for the avant-garde. Walter Pach took exception to the following comment by Zervos in *Cahiers d'Art:* "We are very pleased to note that North America is beginning, at last, to welcome the efforts of young painters from Paris." Pach thus wrote to remind Zervos, in a letter dated September 10, 1928, that prior to the war New York had hosted the extensive Armory Show.[3] Zervos's prejudices were nevertheless reinforced by the incredible lawsuit that Constantin Brancusi was obliged to bring against American customs authorities in order to recover import duties imposed on *Bird in Space.* Zervos disregarded Gertrude Stein and her collection, even though rehoused not far away on rue Christine. He begrudgingly complimented on the painting of one of his subscribers—Gerald Murphy—who, thanks to the efforts of Fernand Léger, got as far as the antechamber of the Galerie Georges Bernheim. "As to Gerald Murphy's painting, it displays certain qualities, whatever people say. There is firmness and such a sharp feeling of realism that the object, although reproduced in all its truthfulness, does not appear to the mind as a flat copy but rather as an intensification of reality. Murphy's oeuvre does lack sensuality, a fault shared by most American painters. He also lacks European lyricism, because he rarely hits the tone that, though diffused throughout a work and undefinable, gives major works their profound resonance."[4]

Zervos displayed the same lack of tact with Alexander Calder's mobiles, whether motorized or not. Of this towering artist who seduced Paris with his miniature circus, Zervos wrote: "In France, Calder is the promoter of art in movement. His show at the Galerie Colle a few weeks ago

convinced even the most skeptical of the potential of kinetic sculpture."[5] The skeptic, of course, was Zervos, whose idea of boldness in sculpture was long limited to Maillol and Laurens, and who in 1937 still had doubts about Calder, sculptor of the remarkable *Mercury Fountain.*

Complacently, Zervos rejected an exchange of advertising with Forbes Watson's *The Arts,* as suggested by Jacques Mauny, a young bilingual artist and correspondent who penned "Letters from Paris" for American art magazines and "Lettres de New York" for Paris reviews. Zervos brushed off Mauny, a member of the Salon d'Automne who displayed "shrill precisionism" and who had the gall to ask for the return of Charles Sheeler's photographs of skyscrapers, which he had recklessly confided to Zervos.[6]

Since 1926, however, Mauny had been an adviser to American art collector Albert Eugene Gallatin, who soon enjoyed significant prestige among Parisian artists. In December 1927, Gallatin opened his private collection to the public as a museum called the Gallery of Living Art at New York University on Washington Square, . His collection combined work from Paris and New York, and the constantly evolving installation was documented by an elegant publication. Gallatin attempted a similar experiment in Paris during the 1929 reorganization of the Musée du Luxembourg, having become the vice-president of the members' association. Gallatin also submitted "Notes from New York" to Zervos, who published two of them as news briefs in 1931.[7] Around 1933, Gallatin came under the influence of Jean Hélion, Hans Arp, and a few other members of the Abstraction-Création group. After having bought his first works by Mondrian, Gallatin took up painting himself and exhibited in New York in 1936 in the context of *Five Contemporary American Concretionists: Biederman, Calder, Ferren, Morris, Shaw.* The show traveled to the Galerie Pierre in Paris (see p 249). Zervos did not appreciate Gallatin's dilettantism:

> The Gallatin case is particularly interesting. I would be lacking in honesty and friendship toward him if I suggested for a moment that he had any talent as a painter. That would be lying to a man who deserves all our esteem. For it should not be forgotten that Gallatin has been working for years in New York to make Americans familiar, tolerant, accepting, and loving of the best artists of our generation. He has been subject to endless jibes, sarcasm, and hostility. Nothing could shake his faith in the destiny of contemporary art. And he has ultimately succeeded, or almost. Patiently, with no ulterior motive of riches or honors but with stubbornness and faith, he brought together, in a place in New York University, remarkable paintings including Léger's *The City*, one of that artist's key works, plus an admirable painting by Picasso known as *Three Musicians,* along with fine paintings by Miró, Hélion, Ferren, and other talented young artists. A man who has devoted his life to producing a creative project can be allowed to try his hand at painting. It will have no deleterious effect on art.

In contrast, the work by Morris merits no indulgence. Gallatin is merely presenting himself as an amateur, while Morris claims to be an artist. So what we might grant Gallatin must be categorically refused to Morris. It is crucial to the health of art that amateurs not be allowed to invade the sphere of true artists who struggle and suffer all kinds of heartbreak to achieve the dream that dominates their lives and work. If Morris is a conscientious man, as his friends assert, he should abandon a trade that is not his own, and for which he has no disposition or talent. Like Gallatin, he should devote all his efforts to promoting today's art, not from the standpoint of an artist who hopes to create for himself, thanks to his protégés, a place in abstract painting, but in a disinterested way. The United States needs a young, enthusiastic, sincere man able to appreciate, without bias, the finest trends in current art, helping all artists, free of marked prejudices, acting as an apostle of these trends among students, the young middle classes, and officials. The need for such a man is all the more acute in that every day the dealers, speculative collectors, and art snobs are plunging public minds into ever greater confusion. For Shaw, I could merely repeat the same comments concerning Morris. But readers needn't worry, I'll spare them the repetition.[8]

These nasty comments were a little too quick in dismissing the recent movement labeled American Abstract Artists, and they incautiously attacked George L. K. Morris, a critic for the Trotskyist *Partisan Review.* The "Park Avenue gentry" launched another operation in Paris at the Salon des Surindépendants in October 1938, after having clarified its position in a series of manifestos published in the third issue of *Plastique,* a magazine published in Paris by César Domela and Sophie Taeuber-Arp at Gallatin's expense. None of this inhibited Gallatin from visiting Zervos at his home on boulevard de Montparnasse.

Zervos's mind was not totally closed to the idea of American art. He granted that it had made a contribution in architecture: he launched an imprint called "Grands Architectes Modernes" with a monograph on *Frank Lloyd Wright* by Henry Russell Hitchcock; he published an article by Roger Ginsburger on Richard Neutra's rest homes in Los Angeles; and he published another by Siegfried Giedion on the Philadelphia Savings Fund Society Bank by architects George Howe and William Lescaze. In 1933, Zervos defended American architect Paul Nelson, who trained at the École des Beaux-Arts in Paris, by publishing Nelson's plans for a hospital complex in Lille. Nelson would progressively replace Le Corbusier in the pages of *Cahiers d'Art.*[9]

It is hard to discern Zervos's opinion of American painting from the remnants of his collection bequeathed to the museum in Vézelay. He was insensitive to the Precisionism of American painting; paradoxically, he tended to tolerate abstraction among Americans passing through Paris, something he normally rejected in Parisian artists.

On paying a visit to the Salon des Surindépendants, he discovered unfamiliar artists from the second wave of American abstractionism, 1930–1940. In exchange for a canvas, they obtained from him a few lines that temporarily rescued them from anonymity. John Graham, for instance, was first noted in 1929 at the Galerie Zborowski, then again in 1930 at the Galerie Van Leer:

> Graham is an American artist of Russian stock, who is working conscientiously to develop his talent as a painter. Starting with an art a long way from contemporary concerns, he is patiently striving to get closer to them. His recent exhibition at the Galerie Zborowski shows us that his stay in Paris was profitable. If he perseveres in his natural direction yet rids himself of excessive impasto, which he overdoes, he will certainly arrive at true painting. . . . (cat. 44)

Among the American artists who have exhibited in Paris since the war, Graham is indisputably one of the best, if not the best. With each show presented here he displays rapid and remarkable progress. Starting from a strict representation of the object, from the calligraphy of its form, Graham is steadily moving toward a painterly representation of objects and toward true style. But he wants to attain them not by premeditated impoverishment just to "make it new," but on the contrary to enrich his canvases with painterly explorations. It was this exploration that had led him, a year or two ago, to an excessive use of impasto, which he has since eliminated even as he retained the essence of his earlier technique. Today he works by making discreet use of impasto, attenuating its importance to create a painting through the intelligent combination of values. There results an impression of balance that he didn't manage to achieve in his early paintings, and his work conveys a poetic impression that the exclusive exploration of impasto prevented him from attaining in the past. Despite the pressure to make it new at any cost, Graham has become wary of the headlong race toward modernity that typifies post-cubist art. He is patiently seeking to produce true paintings. I have sufficiently often complained of the excessive use made by young people of the freedom that cubism brought to art, of the fact that their efforts are null and void, to enjoy the satisfaction of encouraging an artist who has not forgotten that painting is visual and poetic and not just crude demagogy.[10]

From 1931 to 1933, from the Surindépendants show to the Galerie Pierre, Zervos defended the career of another "American" artist, Jean Xceron (cats. 45 and 46). Having arrived in Paris from New York in 1927, Xceron found panhellenic solidarity from Zervos; furthermore, he exhibited with other Greeks such as Gounaro, Ghika, Tombros, and Orestis Kanellis:

> It is also worth noting another new arrival—new to us, but not to painting. In 1917, in the rather unconducive atmosphere of New York, Xceron produced canvases in a vein similar to

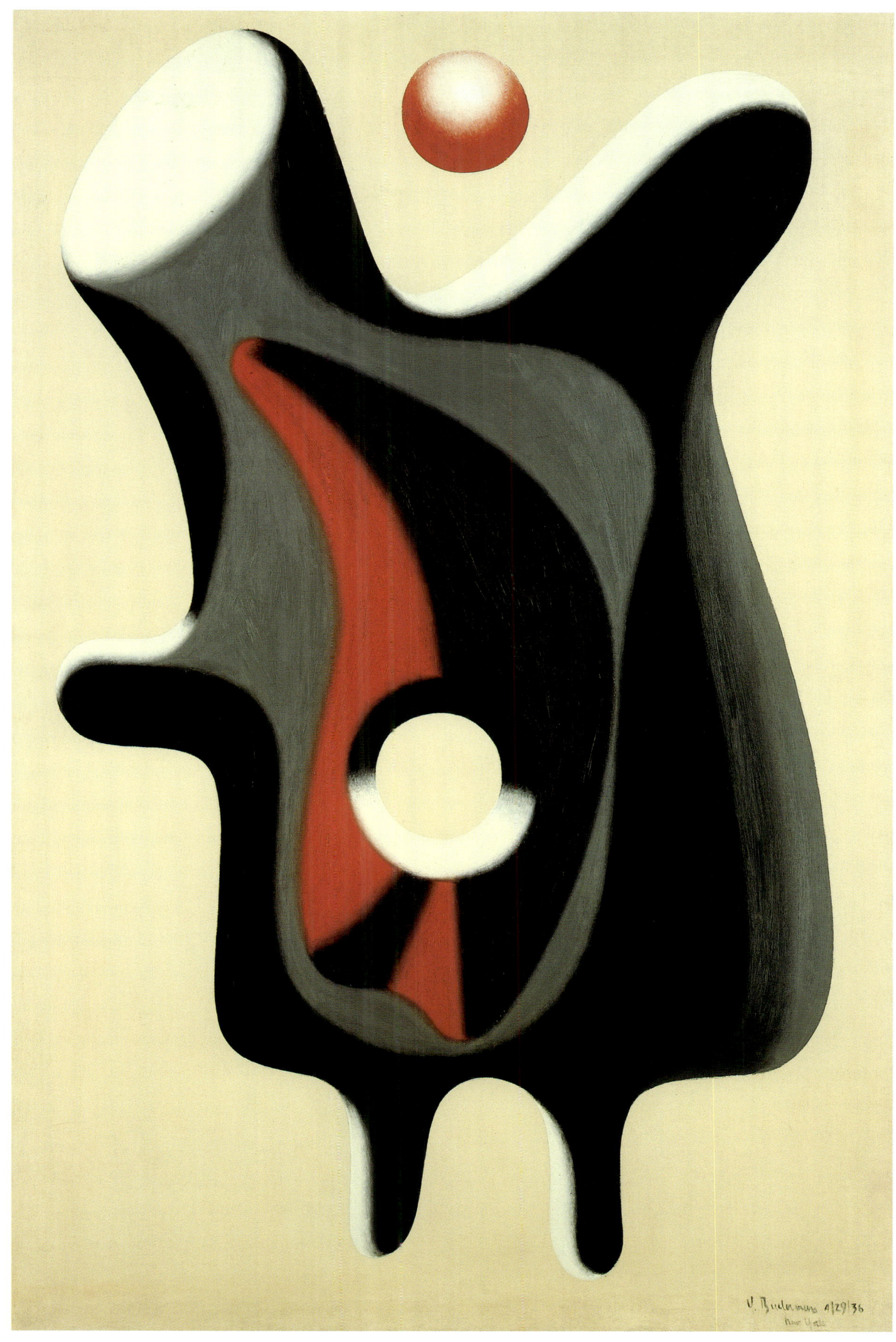

47
CHARLES BIEDERMAN
COMPOSITION, 1935
OIL ON CANVAS, 137 X 91.5 CM
MUSÉE ZERVOS, VÉZELAY, MZ NO. 258
MAAG, TAM, TMAA

the explorations of the school of Paris even though he knew nothing about it at that time. Then, despite the academic instruction he received at art schools in Washington and, later, New York, he painted canvases that are visually very rich, almost like enamels conditioned by strict composition. Next, in 1920, came canvases in which all objects were ringed in outlines handled with light touch—a procedure that, ten years later, would be fashionable among young artists here. Since then, Xceron has experienced moments of acute crisis, when he stubbornly struggled against the drive of his own nature. Contact with the school of Paris disconcerted him at first, briefly leaving him at a loss. But the crisis did not last long, and Xceron, with slow but steady effort, has forged himself a path through the inextricable chaos of doubts and uncertainties among artists of the school of Paris. For a while, overlooking his own potential, he produced paintings that were more cerebral than visual. But his deeper instincts swiftly triumphed over surrounding influences. Today Xceron is managing to reconcile his former visual strengths with all the freedom of a mind liberated from the constraints of a school. When this fusion is complete, Xceron's oeuvre will have increased in freedom and density.[11]

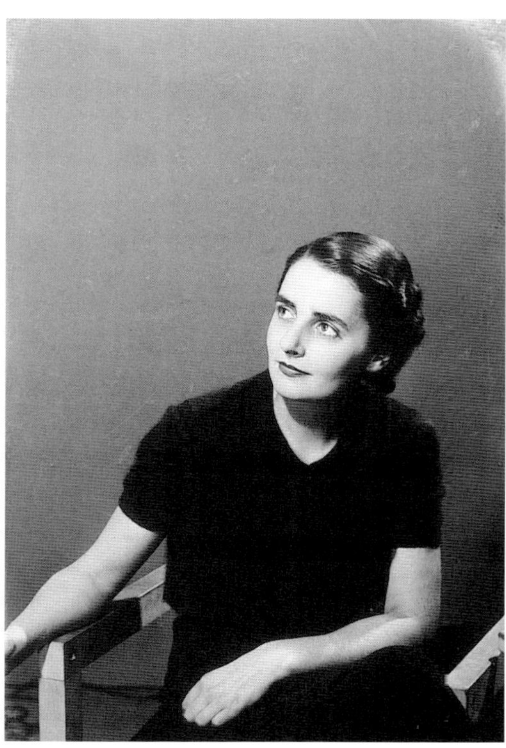

MAN RAY,
YVONNE ZERVOS. 1936.
GELATIN SILVER PRINT.
MUSÉE NATIONAL D'ART MODERNE –
CENTRE GEORGES POMPIDOU.
PARIS. AM 1994-394 (60.5)

Xceron returned to New York in 1937, where he participated in the founding of Hilla Rebay's Museum of Non-Objective Painting, the forerunner of the Solomon R. Guggenheim Museum. Zervos, meanwhile, was willing to offer Benjamin Benno, a future member of the American Abstract Artists group, a letter of recommendation to Guggenheim himself.[12] The critic was even willing to commit himself a little further when it came to the work of Charles Biederman. "Biederman's work is full of possibilities," wrote Zervos. "One has the impression of encountering a gifted, conscientious man, though lacking the confidence that lends a creative thrust to his lyricism. His natural talent has not yet found its true expression, nor the language that best suits his nature. This renders palpable the countless difficulties he has encountered in elaborating his oeuvre, which he has not always overcome. One senses his determination to set out for a fine destination. Will he soon find the courage to depart?"[13]

The least neglected artist was John Ferren: "Ferren, who also exhibited alone at the Galerie Pierre, is the youngest of the five. He has earned our trust because he provides a glimpse of a sincere soul afflicted by serious anxieties and torn by countless tragedies, constantly borne by the desire to deepen his art and perfect his craft. He wants to move forward by taking painting to the extreme frontiers where cubism led it, and then take it further, to who-knows-where for the moment, since Ferren's current stage is just a transitional one and in no way final stage. The same goes for Hélion. But whatever expression finally crystallizes from the substantial core of Ferren's soul, it will always be clear, straightforward, and concerned with quality and balance. Painting will always profit from it."[14] Zervos recommended Ferren to Alfred H. Barr, director of the Museum of Modern Art in New York, in the following terms on September 16, 1936: "My friend Ferren is coming to New York for his show at the Pierre Matisse Gallery. I would be most obliged if you could concern yourself with his exhibition, lend him your moral support, and if possible promote him among collectors. He needs to obtain a certain financial success over there so that he can work in peace, free from constant financial worries."

In some haste, Zervos helped to organize a 1937 exhibition for the museum of foreign art in the Jeu de Paume, titled *Origine et développement de l'art international indépendant*.[15] He compensated for the lack of a real American section with paintings he had on hand by Benno, Biederman, and Ferren, to which he added the sculptor Storrs, largely discounting it as merely secondary abstract work. But Zervos lacked conviction, and he mentioned none of these artists the following year in his voluminous book on *Histoire de l'art contemporain*.[16] All the artists, discouraged by their cool reception in Paris, had already returned to New York.

Since 1935, Zervos had sided with the surrealists. He was associated with their penetration of the New York market through the advertising pages in *Cahiers d'Art* bought by two young dealers, Pierre Loeb in Paris and Pierre Matisse (son of the artist) in New York. The only major American artist living in Paris, Man Ray—with whom Zervos enjoyed a lasting relationship—was part of that movement.[17] Famous as a photographer, Man Ray seemed to have permanently turned his back on his home country. After *Cahiers d'Art* published an anthology of 125 photographs by him in 1934, Man Ray supplied the solarized photographs that Zervos included in the front of each of his artist's monographs. Man Ray moved in the circles of poet Paul Eluard, and he was friendly with Picasso, who had Man Ray teach him the magic of *cliché-verre* prints. In November 1935, Yvonne Zervos (fig. 2) organized a small retrospective of Man Ray's dada paintings in the *Cahiers d'Art* premises for which Max Ernst, another of Man Ray's friends, designed the invitation (figs. 3–4). The show was not to the taste of the gallery's abstract artists. As Kandinsky wrote to Albers on December 19, 1935,

> Zervos has always rejected the Surrealists. He felt the artistic level was too weak. To my great surprise, he is suddenly showing three—Max Ernst, Tanguy, Man Ray. . . . For example, at the Man Ray exhibition that has just ended, there was a lady's saddle placed on the ground. I asked, 'Why is that there?' and received the reply, 'Because he likes it there.' Only later did I learn that it was symbolic, and I left it at that. It was 'officially' declared that the canvases in this show should not be seen as paintings (to which I said, 'Heaven forbid!') because they embodied *esprit*.' As you know, Man Ray is an excellent, worthy photographer, to whom we owe much new inspiration, but by all appearances he's no painter.[18]

The exhibition had no financial ambitions, and was probably designed to reward Man Ray for his photographs of *Objets mathématiques* published in a special issue of *Cahiers d'Art* on "the object." Man Ray also figured in the Jeu de Paume exhibition thanks to a loan from Eluard, *La Volière*, 1919, and one work from his studio, *Le Logis de l'artiste*, 1929. In 1937 he photographed the hands of Yvonne Zervos, gloved in a layer of paint by Picasso. These unused photos were probably taken in connection with the publication of Man Ray's paradoxical anthology, *Les Mains libres*, drawings illustrated with poems by Eluard.[19]

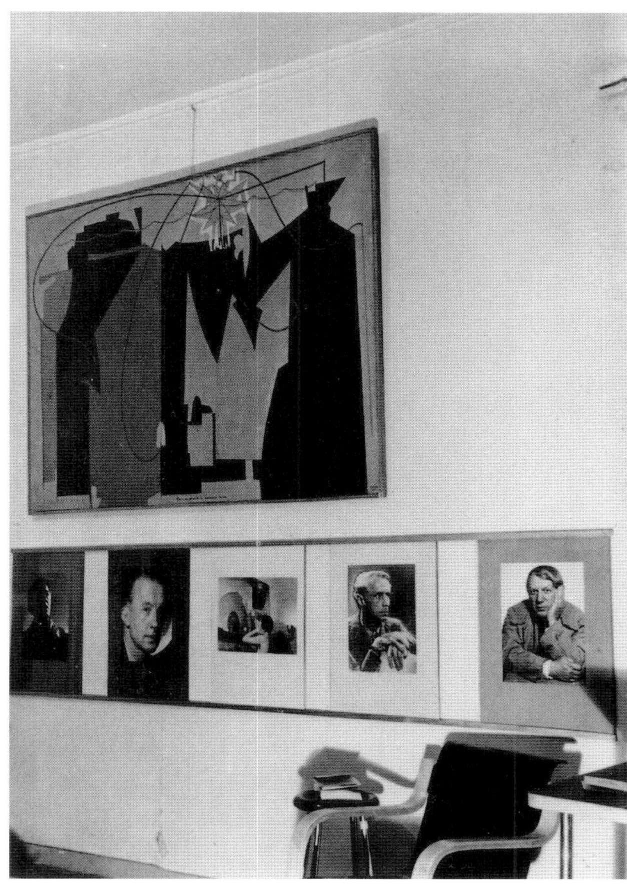

FIG. 3.
VIEW OF THE MAN RAY EXHIBITION TITLED
MAN RAY. EXPOSITION DE PEINTURES ET D'OBJETS HELD
AT THE CAHIERS D'ART GALLERY, 15 NOVEMBER – 30 NOVEMBER 1935.

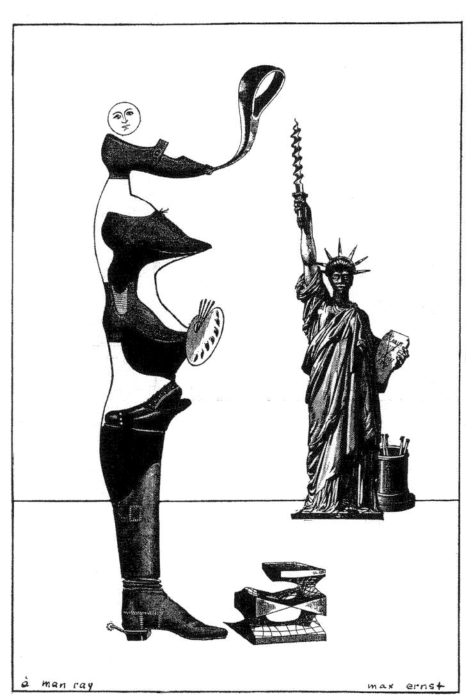

FIG. 4
MAX ERNST,
PORTRAIT OF MAN RAY, 1935.
COLLAGE. ILLUSTRATION FOR THE INVITATION OF THE MAN RAY
EXHIBITION AT THE CAHIERS D'ART GALLERY IN 1935.
COLLECTION LUCIEN TREILLARD, PARIS.

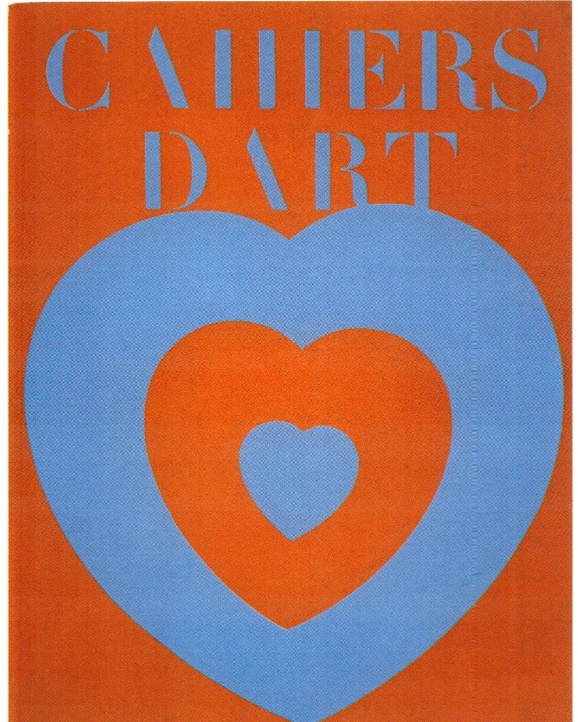

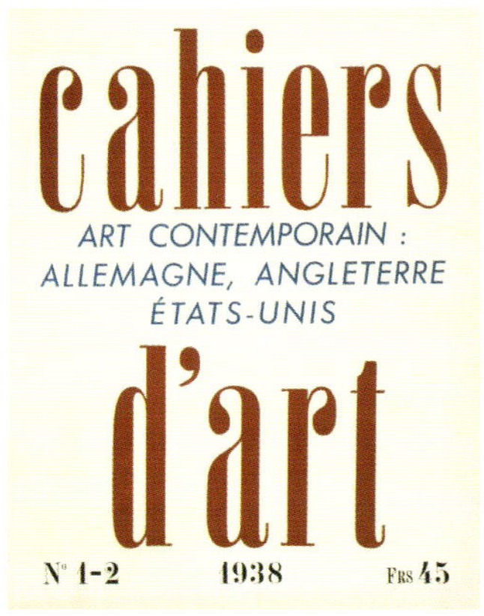

FIG. 5.
MARCEL DUCHAMP,
COVER OF THE *CAHIERS D'ART*, 1936.

FIG. 6.
COVER OF THE *CAHIERS D'ART*, 1938.

Cahiers d'Art considered three French artists to be "Americans," given their lengthy sojourns on the other side of the Atlantic. Zervos considered Marcel Duchamp, a co-founder of New York's Société Anonyme, to be more of a courtier than an artist. Duchamp nevertheless did the color cover for the "Object" issue of the magazine in 1936 (fig. 5). Fernand Léger, although he spoke no English, managed to turn himself into *Cahiers d'Art*'s active agent in New York and Chicago. In 1935, he had his first real retrospective, at the Museum of Modern Art in New York and the Art Club in Chicago. Upon his return from the New World, Léger gave the impression of being buddies with Wallace Harrison (Nelson Rockefeller's architect) and of occupying a strategic position between Paris and America.[20] Jean Hélion, meanwhile, was younger and married to an American. He wrote well in English, and in 1933 became the theorist that Gallatin needed when revamping the Gallery of Living Art. Although Zervos defended Hélion, who had connections, he never really pardoned Hélion's espousal of Abstraction-Création:

Among the young French artists attached to the art called, I know not why, abstract, Hélion is the most recent arrival. But he also holds the greatest hope. This youth indisputably possesses a painter's talent. His paintings are not the meticulous contrivances of a skillful mechanic; the colored planes and lines that share the surface of the canvas, and the intersections and juxtapositions of lines are dictated to Hélion, just as they are to Mondrian, by imperious visual requirements. In order to understand these claims, color illustrations of his work would have to be included here. We hope to be able to fulfill that plan in a future issue of this magazine.[21]

Hélion was thus honored with a show at the *Cahiers d'Art* gallery in 1936, and his painting *Isle-de-France* was exhibited at the Jeu de Paume in 1937. Hélion nevertheless expected greater insight from Zervos. "I've often been accused of doing cheerful paintings. 'It's not dramatic enough,' said Zervos to Nelson in referring to my show there. Nelson, though, found it *too* dramatic. But that doesn't matter. Neither one of them understands drama in the way you and I do. . . ."[22] Hélion was then dividing his time between the Virginian town of Rockbridge Baths and a studio that architect Paul Nelson lent him on boulevard Blanqui in Paris. But the two friends fell out in 1938 when Nelson presented his *Model for a "Suspended House"* in New York, accompanied by works of Arp, Miró, Léger, and Calder, but neglected to include a painting by Hélion.

After the show of "degenerate art" in Germany in 1937, and especially after the Munich Pact, America no longer seemed to be so far away; it began to look like a safe haven for threatened masterpieces, then later like a refuge for Parisian artists and dealers. Up to that point, Zervos had done little to win the allegiance of two American critics who were rising swiftly through the ranks, James Johnson Sweeney and Alfred H. Barr. Sweeney began as a stringer for the daily *Chicago Evening Post* and made an impression in Paris as early as 1934 with reproductions of his essay on "Plastic Redirections in 20th-Century Painting." He was asked to participate in *Plastic,* the first version of a transatlantic review envisaged by Hélion and Gallatin. Sweeney became editor of the art pages in the English-language, Paris-based review *transition*. Zervos asked him to supply articles on ancient Irish art and to contribute to a broad overview of contemporary art throughout the world, published in a 1938 issue of *Cahiers d'Art* (fig. 6). Sweeney listed twenty-six artists, none except Calder had been previously mentioned in the magazine.[23]

Barr was the director of the Museum of Modern Art (MoMA) in New York, which seemed to be a providential institution following its *Cubism and Abstract Art* show in 1936.[24] Zervos reproached Barr for having overlooked the painter Amédée Ozenfant, but conceded that the show was a clear historical presentation of the avant-garde. Barr then organized *Fantastic Art, Dada, Surrealism,* calling on the services of Georges Hugnet, a rowdy but regular contributor to *Cahiers d'Art,* for the catalogue. Despite all these American tributes to Paris as the capital of art, the Paris–New York relationship remained a one-way affair. In May–July 1938, Barr's *Three Centuries of Art in the United States* was hosted by the Jeu de Paume in Paris, but the event was too precocious to merit any mention by Zervos or the French press.[25]

After *Art in Our Time*, an exhibition that inaugurated MoMA's new building, Barr prepared a major retrospective on *Picasso, Forty Years of His Art.* For this he needed photographs from *Cahiers d'Art,* and Zervos also provided information that could not be obtained directly from the artist. A fortunate solution emerged to their problems of communication—Barr wrote in English, Zervos answered in French—when Zervos found a colleague in Mary Callery (1903–1977).[26] Callery (fig. 7), an American and a friend of Mrs. Harrison, had married an extremely rich businessman from Milan, Giuseppe Frua de Angeli. Callery and Zervos not only shared a passion for sculpture but also an intense personal relationship. Meanwhile, Zervos was implicated in Picasso's attempt to divorce his wife, Olga, which did not occur. Zervos was also well-placed to negotiate discreetly Picasso's sale of some very fine paintings to the Callery-Frua de Angeli couple (the Picassos that hung on the walls of Callery's home on rue du Belvédère in Boulogne-sur-Seine were sent to MoMA for the Picasso show). In return, the couple became the patrons of various *Cahiers d'Art* publications—Zervos dedicated to Callery his volume on the works of El Greco in Spain (in which, for that matter, he mostly discussed Picasso). Many illustrations in sundry issues of *Cahiers d'Art* bear the credit, "Coll. Mme Méric Callery," such as a *Mermaid* by Laurens and a *Mobile* by Calder. Matisse and Léger profited from the large studio rented by Callery at the Villa d'Alésia in Paris. That is where Léger and Zervos presented the former's *Composition with Two Parrots* practically before the paint had dried. This large canvas then officially became Callery's property, leaving for "the cellars of Modern Art," as Léger put it, in her luggage. The effectiveness of the Callery-Zervos connection is revealed by a postcard sent to Zervos by Calder and Hélion in New York.[27] During the war, the Callery collection traveled across the United States. In January 1945, this unusual combination of masterpieces by Picasso and Léger came to rest in the rooms of the Philadelphia Museum[28] (fig. 8)—but it would not survive the pretty American woman's separation from her Italian husband. The era was coming to a close and the "French spirit of the twenties and thirties" was fading in the face of New York's growing appeal to artists. The histories of Picasso and Matisse were being written in the late 1940s according to American standards. Publication of *Cahiers d'Art*, interrupted during the war, resumed, but copies did not reach New York distributors Weyhe and Wittenborn in good time. They rotted in the warehouses of United States customs officials, on the grounds that they were printed in French and used photogravure plates.[29] ∎

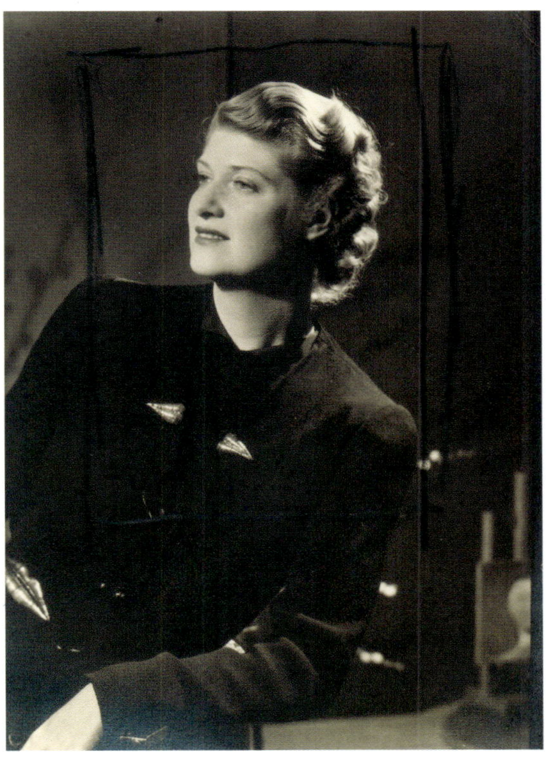

FIG. 7.
MAN RAY,
MARY CALLERY, 1938. GELATIN SILVER PRINT.
MUSÉE NATIONAL D'ART MODERNE –
CENTRE GEORGES POMPIDOU, PARIS.
AM 1994-394 (1516).

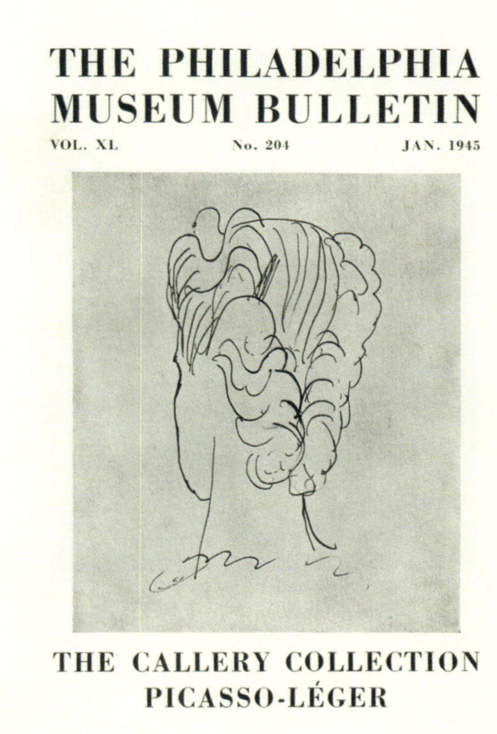

FIG. 8.
COVER OF *THE PHILADELPHIA MUSEUM
BULLETIN* ILLUSTRATED WITH A PORTRAIT OF
MARY CALLERY BY PABLO PICASSO. PUBLISHED
IN CONJUNCTION WITH THE EXHIBITION OF
THE MARY CALLERY COLLECTION AT
THE PHILADELPHIA MUSEUM OF ART,
10 JANUARY – 20 FEBRUARY 1945.

On the occasion of *A Transatlantic Avant-Garde: American Artists in Paris, 1918–1939,* the Terra Foundation for the Arts, at the urging of Sophie Lévy, curator of the Musée d'Art Américain Giverny, sponsored and financed Véronique Roca's cleaning and restoration of four "American" paintings in the Musée Zervos in Vézelay, France. These works, ignored by Zervos after 1937, are the only examples of work by Graham, Xceron, and Biederman in France. They relate more to the history of links between Paris and America than to the characteristic features of the future Musée Zervos, in which Calder would be represented by a splendid gouache of 1947, a superb *Mobile* of 1945 and another one of 1954.

1— *Exposition d'artistes de l'école américaine,* exhibition at the Musée National du Luxembourg, October–November 1919.

2— Christian Zervos, "Amérique," *Cahiers d'Art* 3 (1926): 41–60.

3— Walter Pach was considered an authority on American contemporary art criticism by Paris dealers and a few American connoisseurs. He wrote *Queer Things: Painting* (New York: Harper & Bros., 1938).

4— Christian Zervos, "Gerald Murphy: Quelques toiles (galerie Georges Bernheim)," *Cahiers d'Art* 10 (1928): 452.

5— Christian Zervos, "Exposition Arp, Calder, Hélion, Miró, Pevsner, Seligmann (galerie Pierre), du 9 au 24 juin," *Cahiers d'Art* 3–4 (1933). The supplement to the *Dictionnaire biographique des artistes contemporains* devotes a long entry to Calder, written by Anatole Jakovski. See Édouard Joseph, ed., *Dictionnaire biographique des artistes contemporains* 4 (January 15, 1937): 26–27. The Musée Zervos in Vézelay, France, includes two Calder mobiles, plus a small painting, a fine watercolor, and an engraving. These works, all post-dating World War II, testify to the lasting if ultimately tardy friendship between the American sculptor and Christian and Yvonne Zervos.

6— Letter from Jacques Mauny to Christian Zervos dated February 13, 1928. Cahiers d'Art gallery archives, Paris. "When I lent you the Sheeler photos you asked permission to keep them for three months, probably so that they could not appear in other publications. Since this period lapsed long ago, I would be grateful if you would return the photos you published and above all those you didn't use." (Translator's note: this translation is my own.)

7— A. E. Gallatin, "Notes de New York," *Cahiers d'Art* 1 and 2 (1931). These brief items, contiguous with the exhibition listings discussed later in this article, were not included in Marc de Fontbrune's index of the magazine. See *Index général de la revue "Cahiers d'Art," 1926–1960,* (Paris: *Cahiers d'Art,* 1981).

8— Christian Zervos, "Biederman, Ferren, Gallatin, Morris, Shaw (galerie Pierre, 15–29 juin 1936)," *Cahiers d'Art* 8–10 (1936): 278–279.

9— On Paul Nelson's architectural work and his plans for a new Palais de la Découverte, see J. Hélion, "Termes de vie, termes d'espace (sur une œuvre de l'architecte P. Nelson)," *Cahiers d'Art* 7–10 (1935): 268–273. Nelson himself wrote a few lines on developments in Léger's work in "Peinture spéciale et architecture," *Cahiers d'Art* 1–3 (1937): 84–88, (6 illustrations).

10— Christian Zervos, "Exposition de peintures de Graham (galerie Zborowski)," *Cahiers d'Art* 7 (1929). Christian Zervos, "Graham, peintures récentes (galerie Van Leer)," *Cahiers d'Art* 7 (1930): 389 (2 illustrations). These reviews are contemporary with the entry on Graham in Joseph, *Dictionnaire biographique des artistes contemporains* 2 (Novembre 1931): 142, where Zervos is cited as a collector of the artist's work. The Musée Zervos in Vézelay has just one painting by Graham.

11— Christian Zervos, "Les Expositions à Paris et ailleurs, Salon des Surindépendants," *Cahiers d'Art* 7–8 (1931): 376, and "Xceron (galerie Pierre)," *Cahiers d'Art* 5–8 (1934). The *Dictionnaire biographique des artistes contemporains* 3 (December 15, 1933): 443 lists Zervos as a collector of Xceron's work. The Musée Zervos in Vézelay has seven paintings executed between 1928 and 1932.

12— The Musée Zervos in Vézelay has one watercolor by Benjamin Benno (1901–1980).

13— Christian Zervos, "Biederman, Ferren, Gallatin, Morris, Shaw (galerie Pierre, 15–29 juin 1936). Cinq peintres américains, cinq peintres abstraits, cinq peintres d'âge et de talent très différents," *Cahiers d'Art* 8–10 (1936): 278-279. The Musée Zervos in Vézelay has one painting by Biederman, inscribed May 29, 1935, New York.

14— Ibid.

15— Exhibition held at the Musée National du Jeu de Paume, Paris, July–November 1937. It included a sculpture by Calder on the outdoor grounds, plus a painting in room 14 by Benno (*Two Women,* 1937), and two others in room 15 by Biederman (*Painting,* 1935) and Ferren (*Painting,* 1937).

16— Christian Zervos, *Histoire de l'art contemporain,* with an introduction by Henri Laugier (Paris: Cahiers d'Art, 1938), quarto, 447 p.

17— The entry for Man Ray in Joseph's *Dictionnaire biographique des artistes contemporains* 3 (December 15, 1933): 181 stresses that "[Man Ray] seems to have now abandoned painting and expresses himself exclusively with the camera. He has notably created rayograms (photos made without a camera)."

18— Letter in German from Wassily Kandinsky to Josef Albers, Neuilly, France, December 1935, Yale archives, 42–43. Jessica Boissel, *Kandinsky-Albers, une correspondance des années trente* (Paris: Les Cahiers du Musée National d'Art Moderne, Hors-série/Archives, 1998).

19— Man Ray and Paul Eluard, *Les Mains libres, dessins illustrés par les poèmes de Paul Eluard,* (Paris: Éditions Jeanne Bucher, 1937). Man Ray's drawings were exhibited in the Galerie Jeanne Bucher on November 5–20 of that same year.

20— For an account of Léger's first trip to New York, see "New York vu par Fernand Léger," *Cahiers d'Art* 9–10 (1931): 437–439. On Léger's role as intermediary between Paris and America, see Derouet, *Fernand Léger, une correspondance poste restante, Lettre à Simone, 1931–1941* (Paris: Les Cahiers du Musée National d'Art Moderne, Hors-série/Archives, 1997).

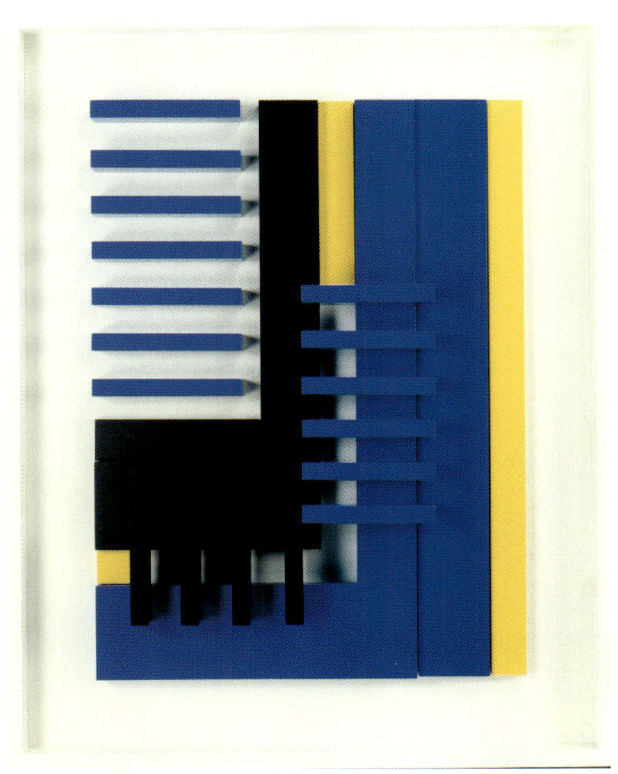

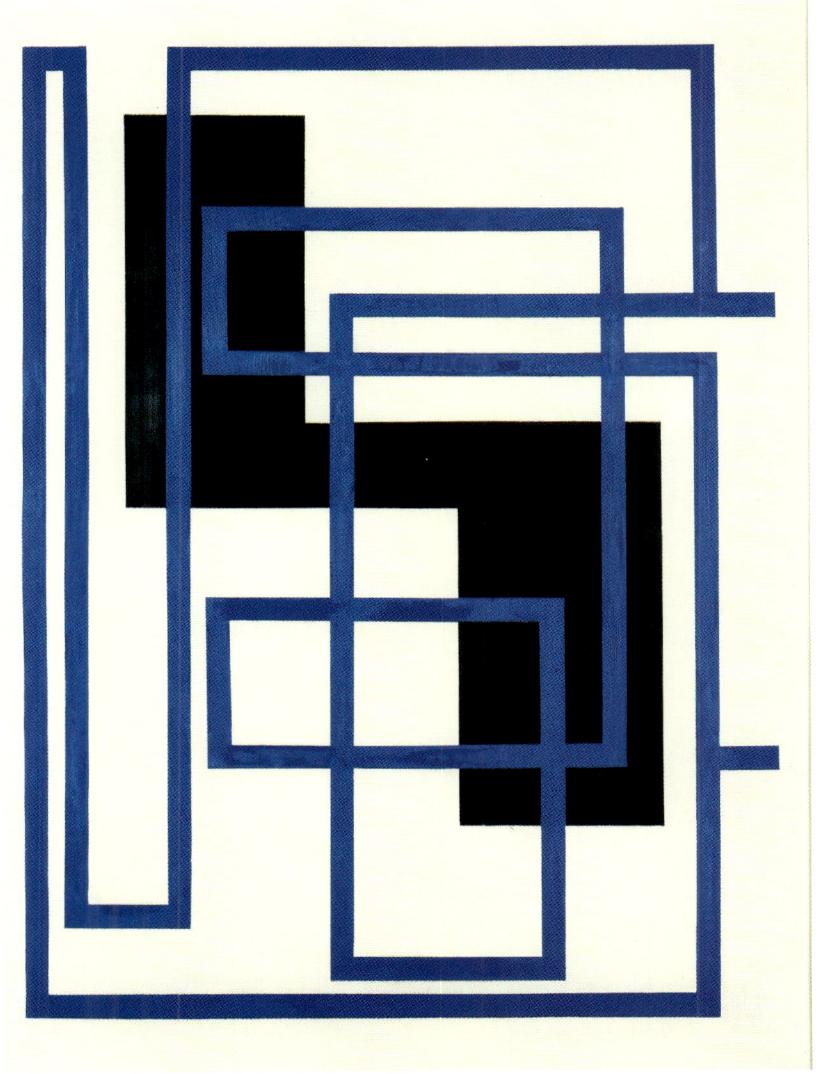

48
CHARLES BIEDERMAN
 # 15, 1937
PAINTED WOOD, 81.3 X 64.8 X 7.6 CM
FREDERICK R. WEISMAN ART MUSEUM,
UNIVERSITY OF MINNESOTA, MINNEAPOLIS.
THE CHARLES BIEDERMAN COLLECTION ARCHIVE,
L1998.39.163
MAAG, TAM, TMAA

49
CHARLES BIEDERMAN
FULL-SCALE STUDY FOR STRUCTURIST WORK, PARIS, MAY 1937
OIL ON CANVAS, 115.6 X 87.9 CM
FREDERICK R. WEISMAN ART MUSEUM,
UNIVERSITY OF MINNESOTA, MINNEAPOLIS.
THE CHARLES BIEDERMAN COLLECTION ARCHIVE,
L1998.39.110
MAAG, TAM, TMAA

21— Christian Zervos, "Hélion, peintures (galerie Pierre),"
Cahiers d'Art 6–7 (1932).

22— Letter from Jean Hélion to Pierre Bruguière, November 13, 1938.
Private archives.

23— J. J. Sweeney, "L'Art contemporain aux États-Unis," *Cahiers d'Art* 1–2
(1938). Works by the following artists were illustrated:
George Caleb Bingham, John H. Twachtman, Mary Cassatt,
Albert P. Ryder, Thomas Eakins, John Sloan, George Luks,
William J. Glackens, Maurice B. Prendergast, John Marin, Max Weber,
Charles Sheeler, Joseph Stella, Charles Demuth, Bernard Karfiol,
Saul Scharry, Peter Blume, Arshile Gorky, Yasuo Kuniyoshi,
Charles Burchfield, Franklin Watkins, Edward Hopper, Stuart Davis,
Niles Spencer, John B. Flannagan, William Zorach, Isamu Noguchi,
Alexander Calder. Many of the photographs were credited to
two new museums in New York, MoMA and the Whitney Museum.

24— See Alice Goldfarb Marquis, *Alfred H. Barr, Jr. Missionary for
the Modern* (Chicago/New York: CB Contemporary Books, 1989).

25— *Trois siècles d'art aux États-Unis. Peinture, sculpture, architecture,
art populaire, photographie, cinéma* (Paris: Éditions des Musées
Nationaux, 1938), catalogue of the exhibition at the Musée National
du Jeu de Paume, May–July 1938.

26— The Musée Zervos owns seven sculptures and two engravings
by Mary Callery, all post-dating World War II.

27— Postcard from Calder to Christian Zervos: Picasso, *Woman in an
Armchair*, Paris, July 1938, ink and crayon, 25 1/2 x 19 3/4 inches.
Lent by Mrs. Meric Callery to the exhibition *Picasso, Forty Years of
His Art*, The Museum of Modern Art. Postmarked New York, Jan. 16.
1940. Addressed to Monsieur Zervos/Cahiers d'Art/
14 rue du Dragon/Paris 6e/France. Handwritten message: *14/1/40
Amitiés – Calder À bientôt Hélion/Bien d'amitiés de nous deux
Iscart/Moutcha/Louise Calder/En tous cas, bien d'amitiés. Sandy.*
(14 Jan. 1940—Regards, Calder. See you soon, Hélion. /Kind regards
from us both, Iscart / Moutcha / Louise Calder / Whatever, best
regards, Sandy.)

28— "The Callery Collection Picasso-Léger," *The Phildelphia Museum
Bulletin* 40, no. 204 (January 1945). Illustrated works by Picasso:
twenty-three paintings, twelve drawings (including two portraits
of Mary Callery, dated June 9, 1938), five engravings, and
one sculpture; by Léger: six paintings and two drawings.

29— Zervos nevertheless took great pains over this important issue
of 1947. It included a review of a show by some American painters
at the Galerie Maeght, and it no longer heaped scorn on George
L. K. Morris, who was showing at the Galerie Colette Allendy.
It even noted the publication, in English, of an anthology of
the main wartime lectures given in New York under the aegis of
the American Abstract Artists, and it featured illustrations—more
than strictly necessary—of works exhibited by Xceron and Callery
in New York galleries.

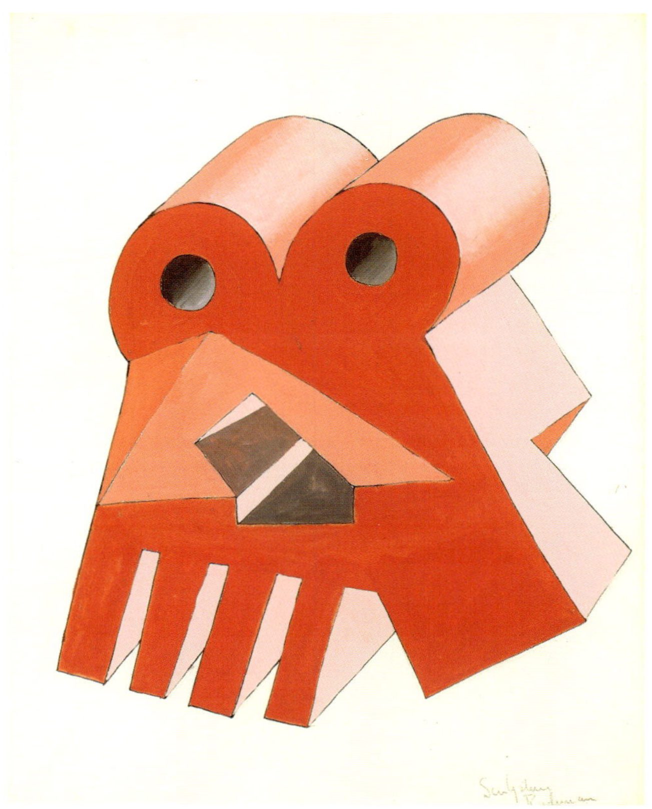

50
CHARLES BIEDERMAN
STUDY FOR SCULPTURE, PARIS, FEBRUARY 1937
GOUACHE AND INK OVER GRAPHITE ON PAPER, 46 X 33.3 CM
FREDERICK R. WEISMAN ART MUSEUM,
UNIVERSITY OF MINNESOTA, MINNEAPOLIS,
THE CHARLES BIEDERMAN COLLECTION ARCHIVE,
L1998.39.709
MAAG, TAM, TMAA

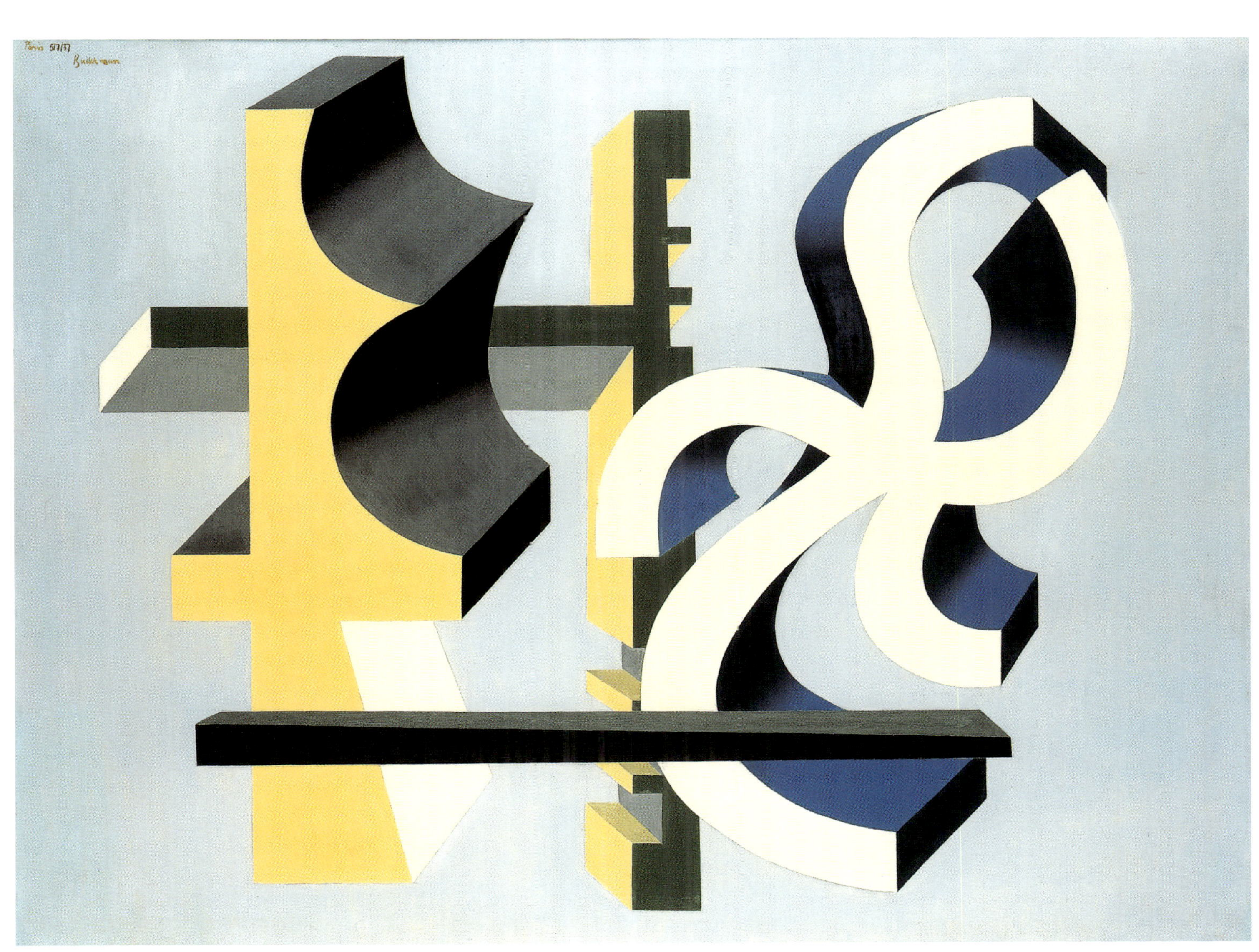

51
CHARLES BIEDERMAN
UNTITLED, PARIS, MAY 7, 1937
OIL ON CANVAS, 97.2 X 130.2 CM
FREDERICK R. WEISMAN ART MUSEUM,
UNIVERSITY OF MINNESOTA, MINNEAPOLIS.
THE CHARLES BIEDERMAN COLLECTION ARCHIVE,
L1998.39.106
MAAG, TAM, TMAA

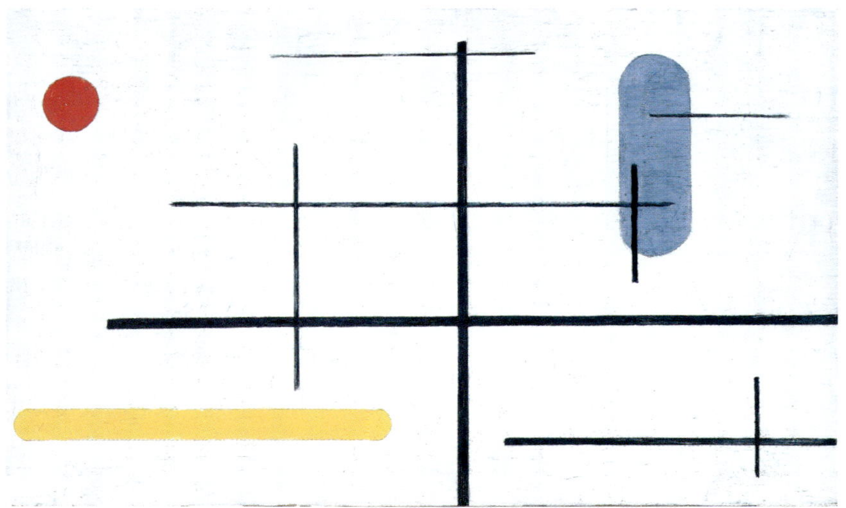

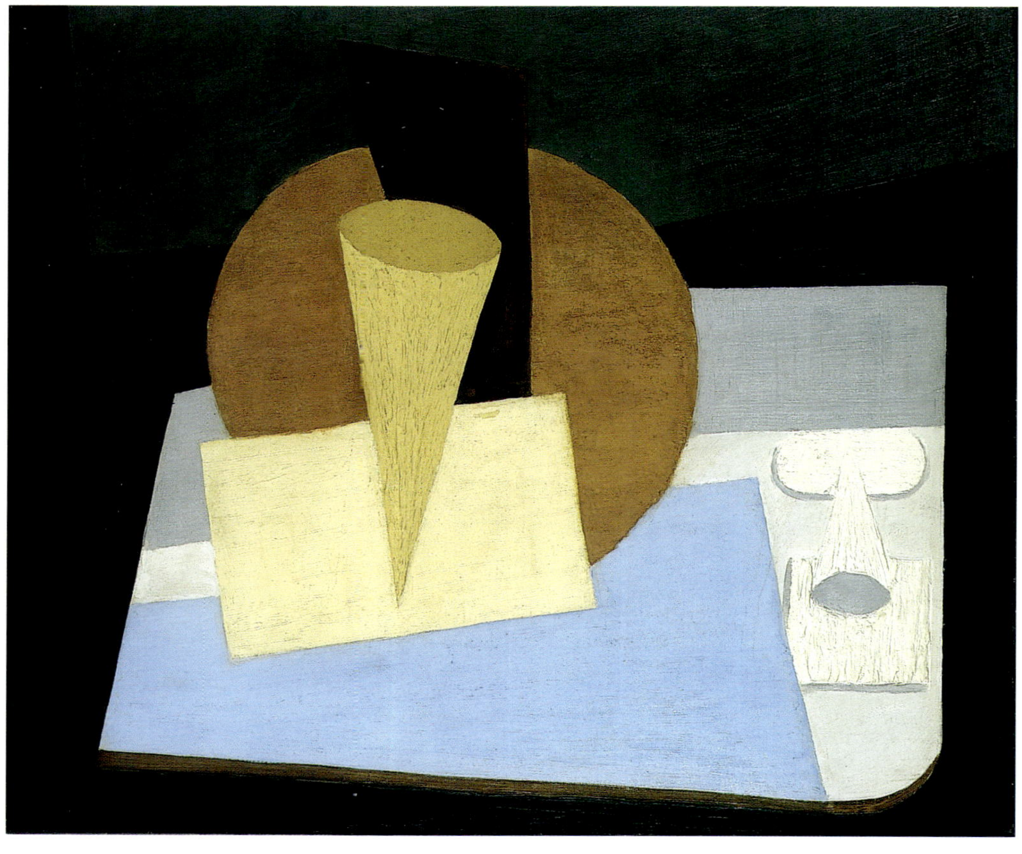

52

WILLIAM EINSTEIN
CONCRETION NO. 1, 1931
OIL ON PANEL, 33 X 55 CM
MUSÉE DE GRENOBLE, 1998.19
MAAG, TAM, TMAA

53

WILLIAM EINSTEIN
ABST 1, 1931
OIL ON CANVAS, 54 X 64.5 CM
GALERIE 1900-2000, PARIS
MAAG, TAM, TMAA

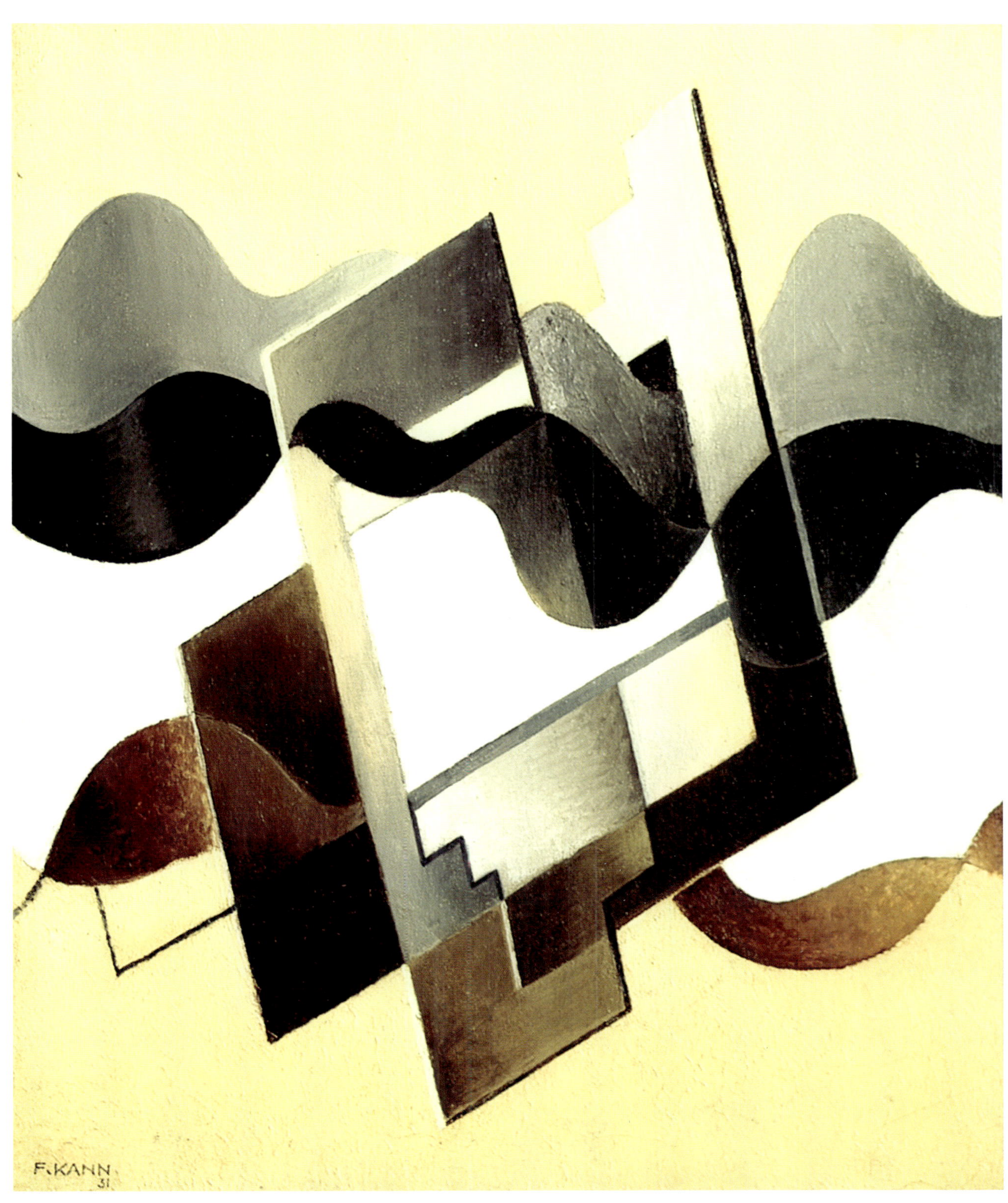

54
FREDERICK KANN
[UNTITLED], 1931
OIL ON CANVAS, 53 X 44.8 CM
COURTESY GARY SNYDER FINE ART, NEW YORK
MAAG, TAM, TMAA

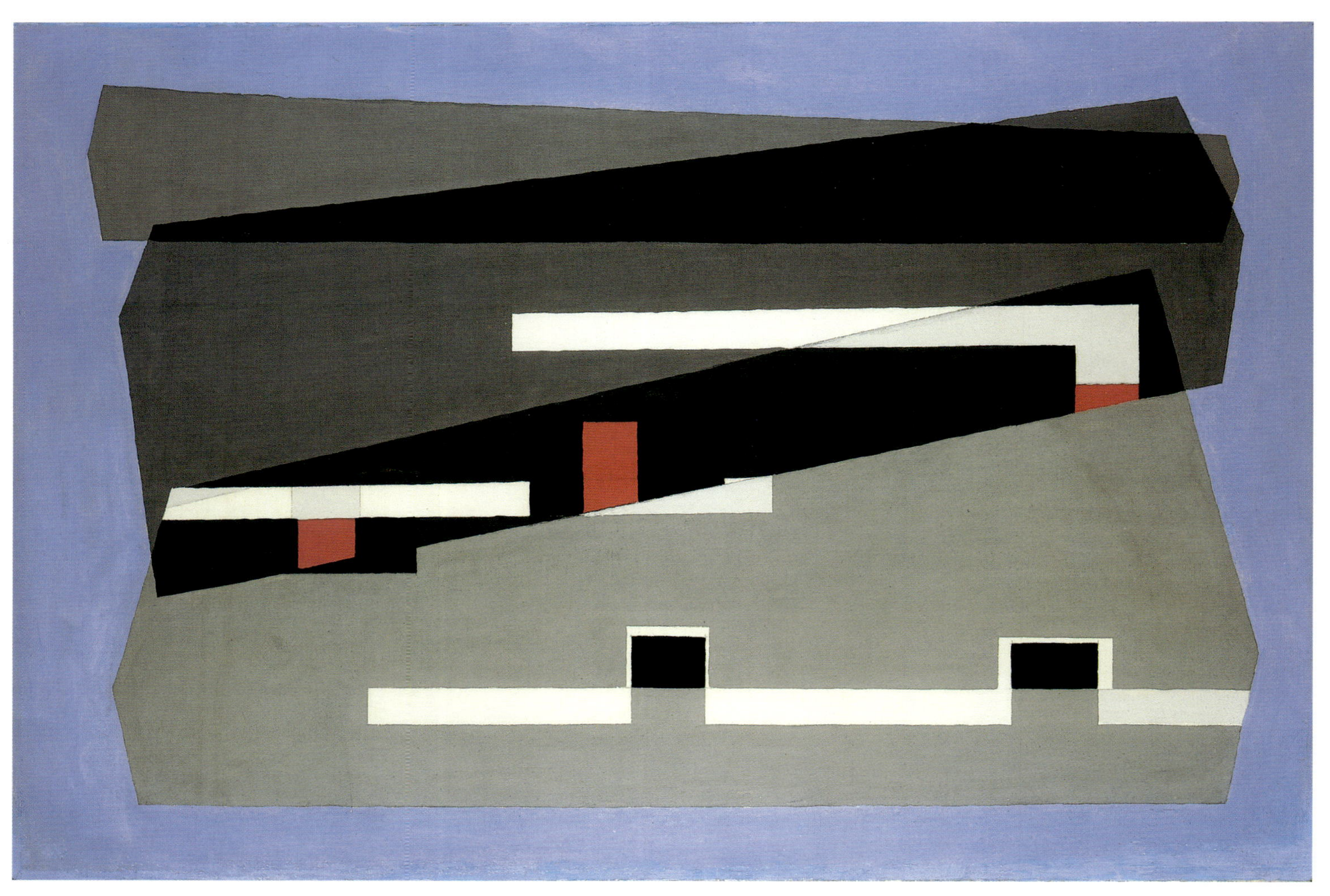

55
BALCOMB GREENE
[UNTITLED], 1937
OIL ON CANVAS, 50.8 X 76.2 CM
ACA GALLERIES, NEW YORK
MAAG, TAM, TMAA

56
BALCOMB GREENE
1936-06, 1936
COLLAGE AND GOUACHE
ON PAPER,
19 X 30.5 CM
ACA GALLERIES, NEW YORK
MAAG, TAM, TMAA

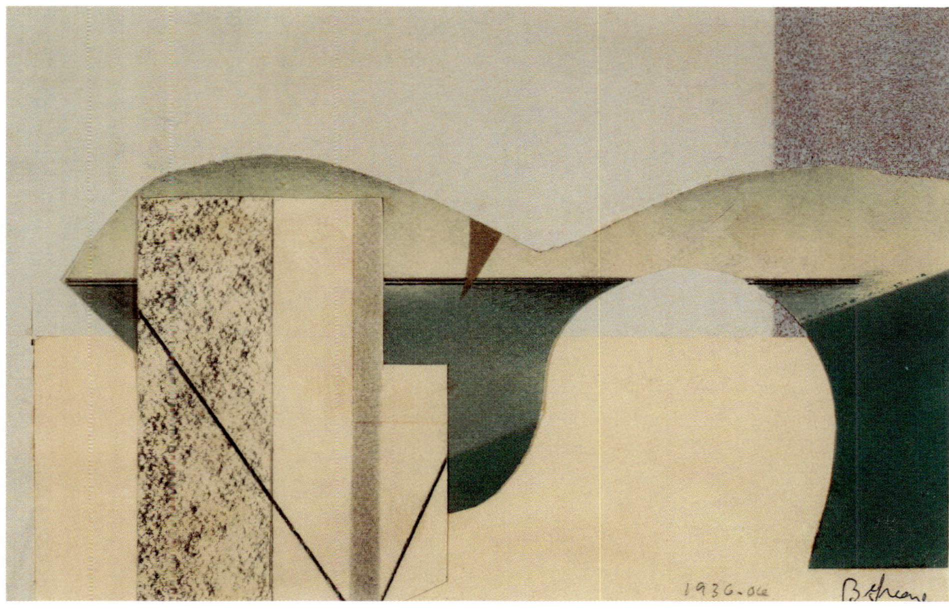

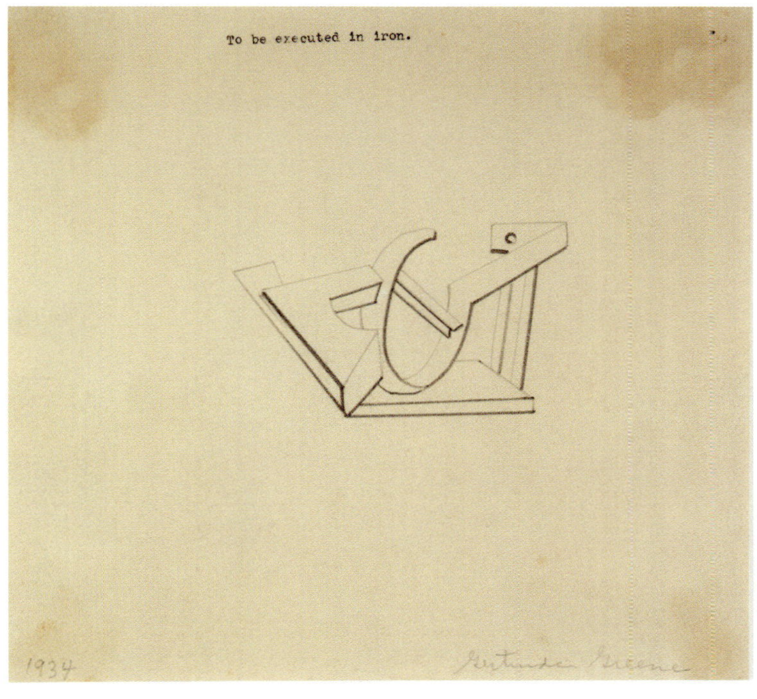

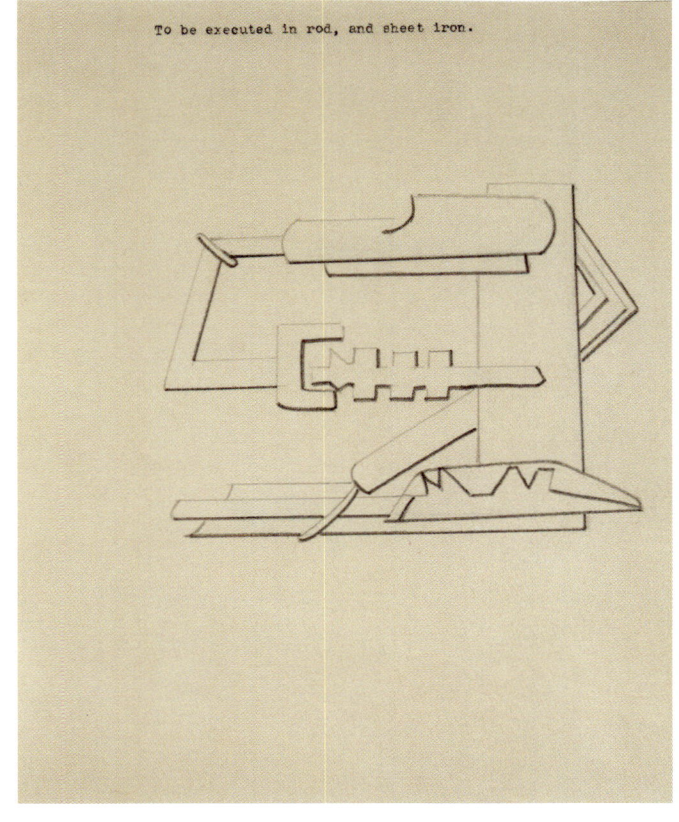

57
GERTRUDE GREENE
PROJECT FOR A SCULPTURE, 1934
PENCIL ON PAPER, 21.6 X 23.5 CM
ACA GALLERIES, NEW YORK
MAAG, TAM, TMAA

58
GERTRUDE GREENE
PROJECT FOR A SCULPTURE, 1934
PENCIL ON PAPER, 26.6 X 21.6 CM
ACA GALLERIES, NEW YORK
MAAG, TAM, TMAA

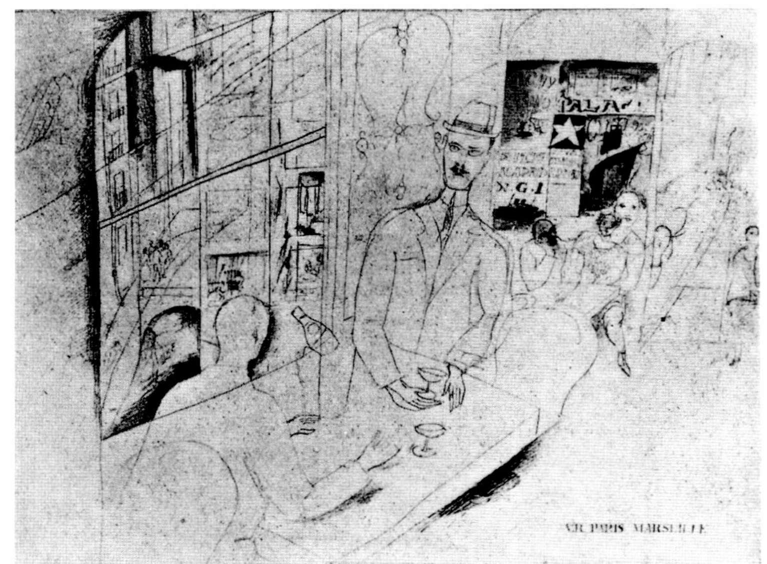

JACQUES MAUNY,
*WAGON-RESTAURANT PARIS-
MARSEILLE,* C. 1927.
INK, WATERCOLOR AND
GRAPHITE ON PAPER,
24 X 34 CM.
FROM *LA RENAISSANCE
DE L'ART FRANÇAIS*
(SEPTEMBER 1927): 415.

Artists were undeniably influential in constituting private and public collections of avant-garde work and in its dissemination. Jacques Mauny, a self-described "minor master," observed in one of his 1927 magazine articles: ". . . it matters little that major collections have been formed on the advice of certain artists— Quinn (Walt Kuhn), Barnes (Glackens), Havemeyer (Mary Cassatt)—'the School of Paris' remains the only one in the eyes of true art lovers."[1] Beginning in the late 1920s, Mauny and Jean Hélion personified the artistic exchange between France and the United States, not only by acting as artistic advisers to the American collector and philanthropist A. E. Gallatin (director of the Gallery of Living Art in New York), but also as art critics and historians. Correspondence with Gallatin, press releases,[2] and catalogues published by the Gallery of Living Art, in addition to articles published in international reviews, document most of the acquisitions and reveal reciprocal influences.

Mauny and Hélion both spoke English fluently at a time when few Frenchmen mastered any foreign language. As a bilingual freelance journalist, Mauny wrote

"Paris Letters" for Forbes Watson's publication *The Arts* (an American review "hostile to the academic arts"[3]) while simultaneously publishing "Lettres de New York" in *L'Art vivant* in Paris. He defended the originality of American artists such as the Precisionist Charles Sheeler, Gerald Murphy,[4] and Man Ray, thus revealing his aesthetic preferences, which he shared with Gallatin. Mauny also contributed articles and exhibition reviews to the periodicals *Creative Arts* (New York), *Magazine of Art* (London), and *Le Centaure* (Brussels). In a French publication, Gallatin praised Mauny in the following terms: ". . . He is a keen and independent critic of the contemporary movement in France. His reflections on current Paris exhibitions, as well as articles on certain individual painters and reviews of new books on art, written in English, which appear each month in an American publication devoted to these fine arts, are set down in an entertaining and intelligent manner."[5] Reciprocally, Mauny did not fail to mention the collector and author in the conclusion of one of his columns: ". . . it is worth noting the valued writer and collector Mr. Gallati [*sic*] . . . ; he is now preparing to exhibit modern

anti-academic art in premises owned by New York University in Washington Square, America's Montparnasse, while awaiting the building of a small museum in another part of town."[6] Between 1921 and 1938, Gallatin made frequent trips to Europe, and sojourned in Paris on numerous occasions.

In 1926, the year he began to teach himself to paint, Gallatin met Mauny at an exhibition of his landscapes at the Galerie Druet in Paris.[7] Mauny introduced Gallatin to artists such as Pablo Picasso, Georges Braque, and Fernand Léger, and to collectors and dealers such as Daniel-Henry Kahnweiler. He also guided Gallatin abroad, during trips illustrated here by a drawing titled *Wagon-Restaurant Paris-Marseille,* enlivened by the figure of Gallatin in the middle. At the inaugural exhibition of the Gallery of Living Art in 1927, works by Paul Cézanne, Giorgio de Chirico, Man Ray, Marie Laurencin, Jean Lurçat, and Pavel Tchelitchev were joined by two canvases by Mauny: *Self-Portrait* and *New York* (1925, Philadelphia Museum of Art), in which the factory smokestacks, baseball players, skyscrapers, and advertising posters were inspired by admiring notes Mauny made during his first stay in the United States in 1925. Between 1928 and 1929, thanks to Mauny, Gallatin acquired works by many artists of the school of Paris, such as Amedeo Modigliani, Marie Laurencin, Maurice Utrillo, Georges Rouault, Chaim Soutine, and Marcel Gromaire, in addition to paintings by Roger Bissière, Cassandre, Roger de La Fresnaye, Lurçat, and André Masson, and a few significant purchases of cubist works. Gallatin's interest in these artists was also reflected in an essay that he co-authored with Mauny in the first catalogue of the Gallery of Living Art in 1930. The efforts Mauny made to bring American painting into French public collections, as revealed by his exchanges with Charles Pacquement, then president of the Association des Amis des Artistes Vivants also warrants mention.[8] Through his intervention, a selection of works from the Gallatin collection were shown at the Musée du Jeu de Paume. Gallatin in turn supported Mauny introducing him to collectors such as the Vicomte de Noailles, Robert Lange, and the Comte de Chambrun. The relationship between Mauny and Gallatin tapered off in 1929, and revived only fleetingly after the war.

Mauny withdrew to Enghien-les-Bains, just outside Paris, and was slowly all but forgotten. He later explained that as early as 1928 the market had begun declining, and once the exchange system collapsed and the depression arrived, publications began to cut their "art" pages; meanwhile, artists—like old cars—soon found themselves on the scrap heap.[9]

While in Paris in 1932, Gallatin became close with Robert Delaunay who encouraged the director of the Gallery of Living Art to create a museum that traced the history of the development of abstract art. Throughout that year, Jean Hélion increasingly influenced Gallatin, steadily replacing Delaunay, and further influenced the collector's taste for abstract art.

Vanessa Lecomte

1— Jacques Mauny, "Paris–New-York 1927," *L'Art vivant* 64 (August 15, 1927), 638.

2— Correspondence and press releases are now held, respectively, at the New York Historical Society, New York, and the Archives of American Art, Smithsonian Institution, Washington, D.C.

3— Mauny, "Paris–New York."

4— In 1924, Mauny painted a portrait of Gerald Murphy (current whereabouts unknown) that he exhibited that same year at the Salon d'Automne, held in the Grand Palais des Champs-Élysées from November 1 to December 14.

5— A. E. Gallatin, "Jacques Mauny," *La Renaissance de l'art français* 9 (September 1927), 416.

6— Mauny, "Paris–New York."

7— Claude Roger-Marx, "Jacques Mauny," *L'Art et les artistes* 69 (July 1926), 336–340.

8— Letter from Mauny to Gallatin, September 29, 1926.

9— Jacques Mauny, "Paris 1919–1940," *Magazine of Art* (March 1940).

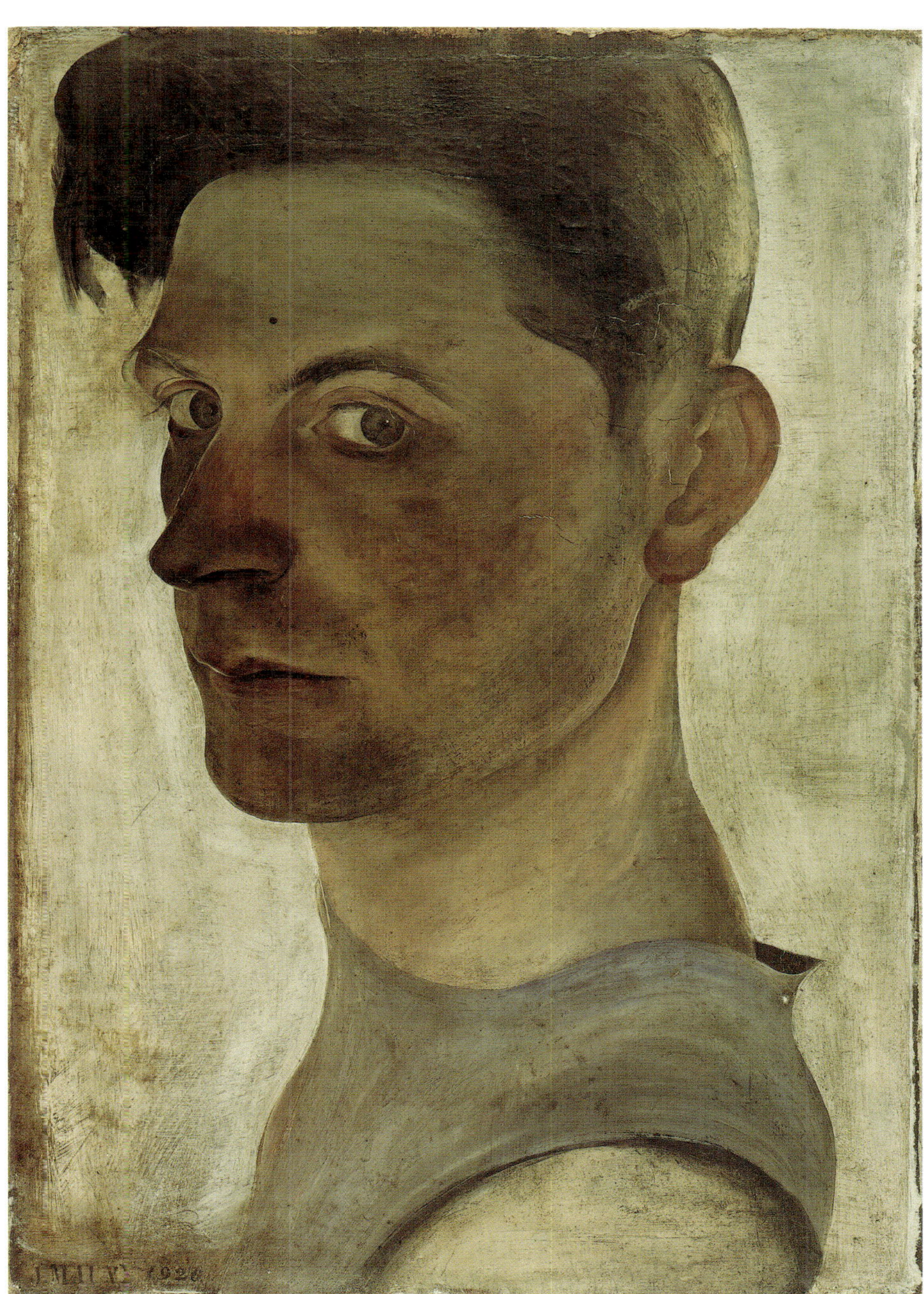

JACQUES MAUNY
SELF-PORTRAIT, 1926
TEMPERA ON BOARD, 31 X 23 CM
PRIVATE COLLECTION, PARIS
MAAG, TAM, TMFA

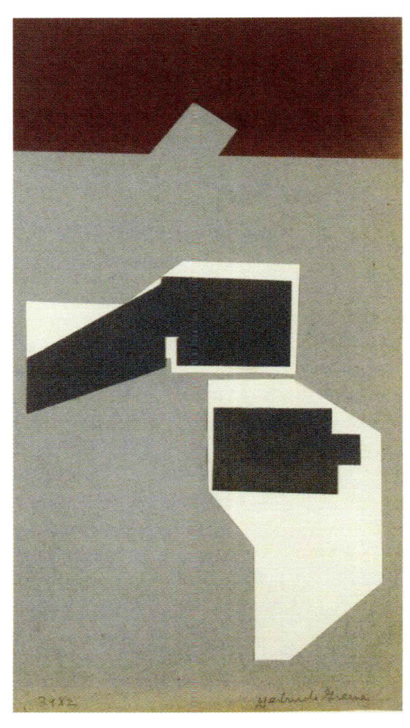

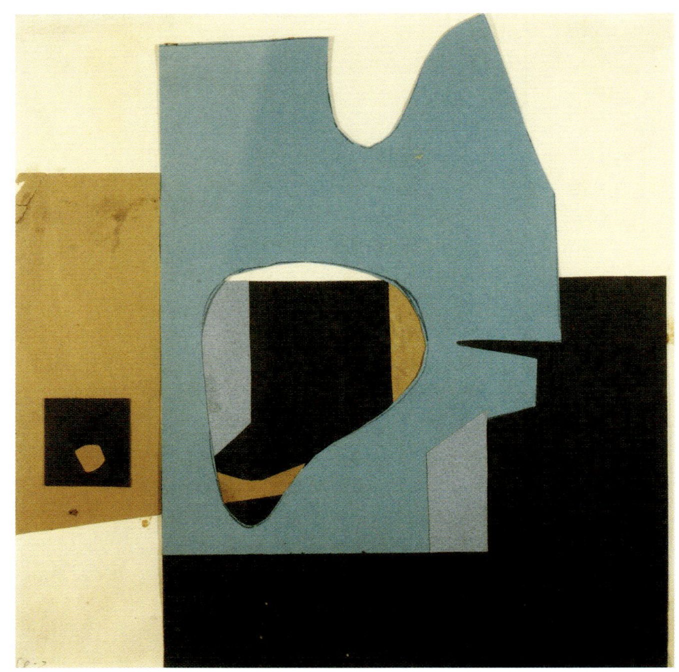

59
GERTRUDE GREENE
1939-X2, 1939
COLLAGE ON PAPER, 30.5 X 16.5 CM
ACA GALLERIES, NEW YORK
MAAG, TAM, TMAA

60
GERTRUDE GREENE
36-2, 1936
COLLAGE, 30.5 X 30.5 CM
ACA GALLERIES, NEW YORK
MAAG, TAM, TMAA

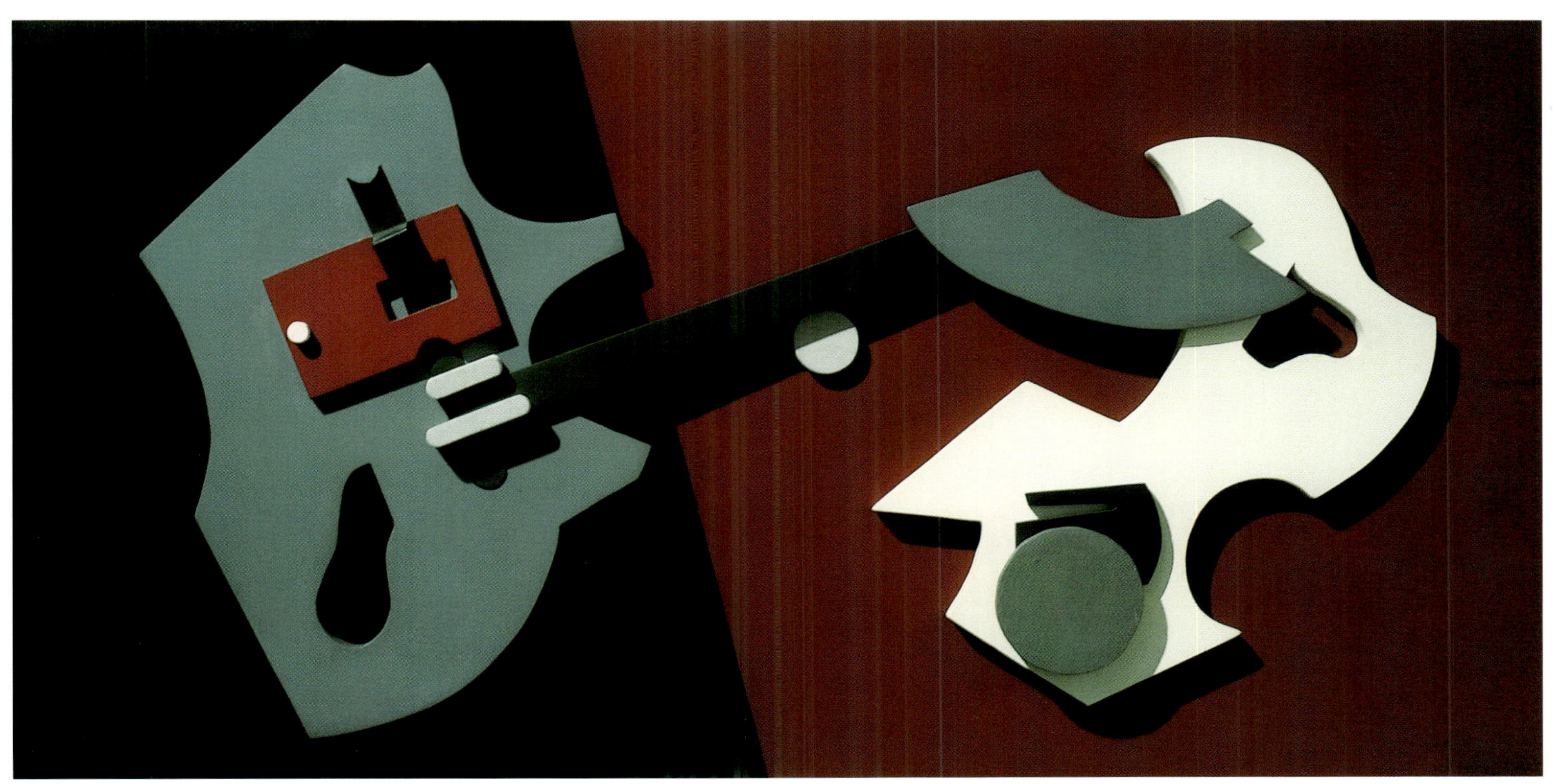

61
GERTRUDE GREENE
CONSTRUCTION, 1937
OIL ON WOOD, MASONITE AND METAL,
50.8 X 101.6 X 6.4 CM
BERKSHIRE MUSEUM, PITTSFIELD, MASS.
GIFT OF A. E. GALLATIN, 1943.26.7
MAAG, TAM, TMAA

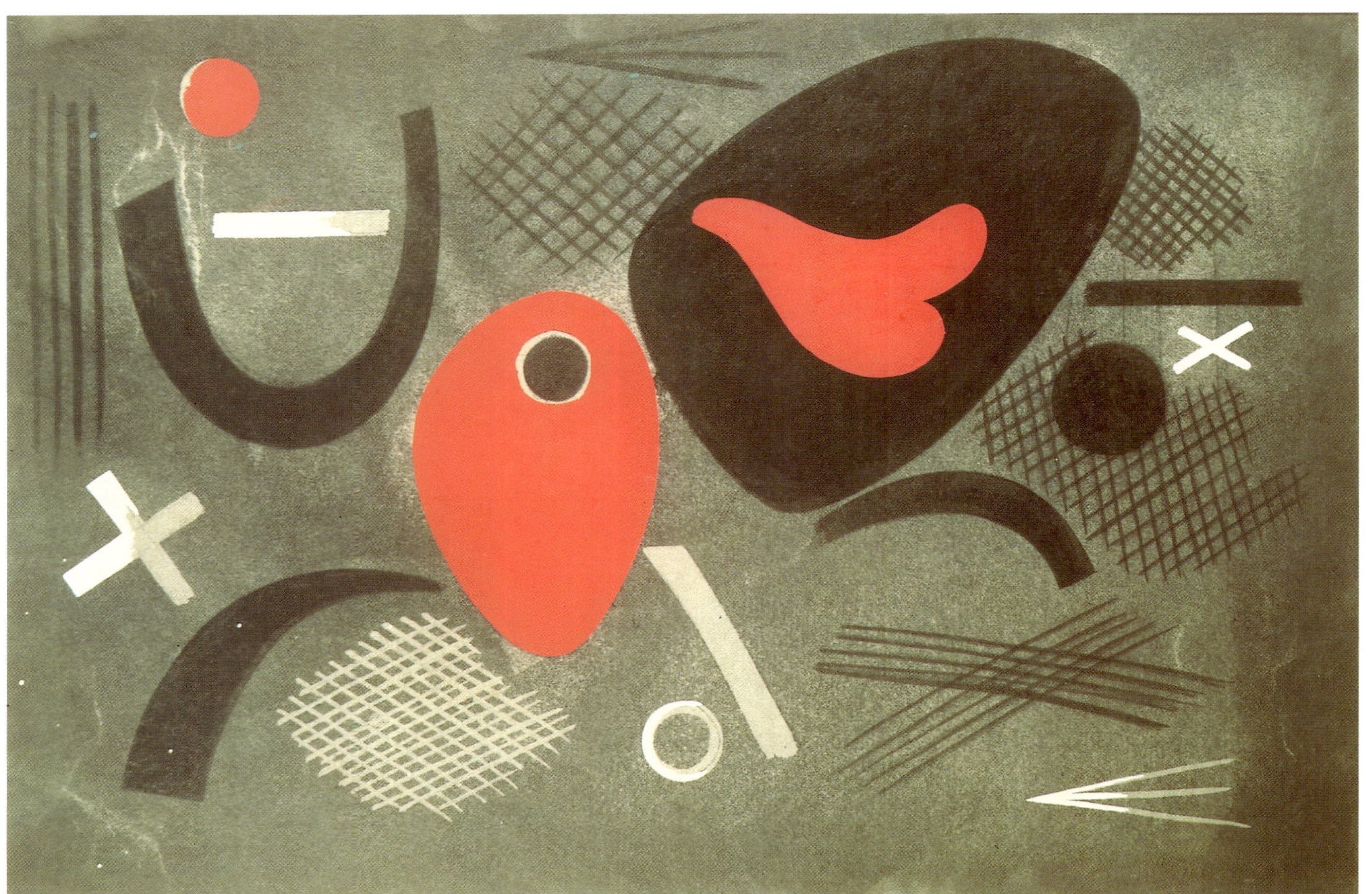

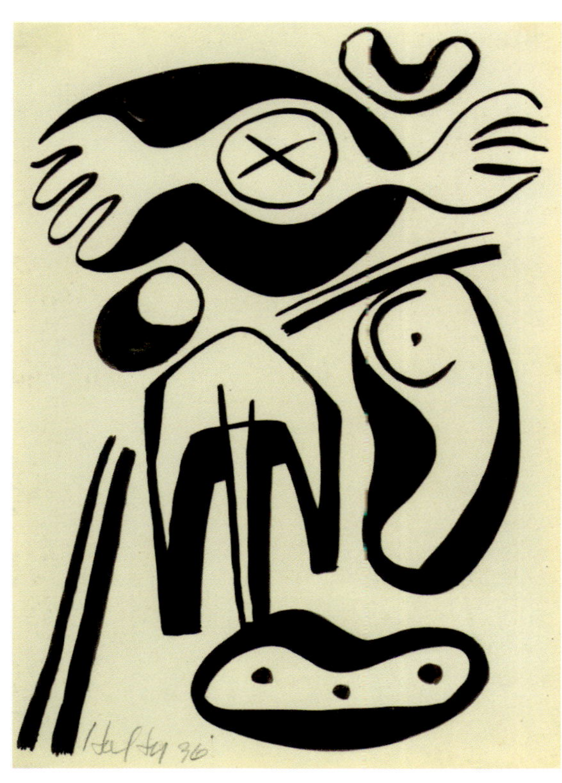

62
CARL HOLTY
UNTITLED ABSTRACTION, 1936
WATERCOLOR ON PAPER, 30.5 X 45.8 CM
COURTESY SPANIERMAN GALLERY,
NEW YORK
MAAG, TAM, TMAA

63
CARL HOLTY
ABSTRACTION, 1936
INK ON PAPER, 24.1 X 17.8 CM
COURTESY SPANIERMAN GALLERY,
NEW YORK
MAAG, TAM, TMAA

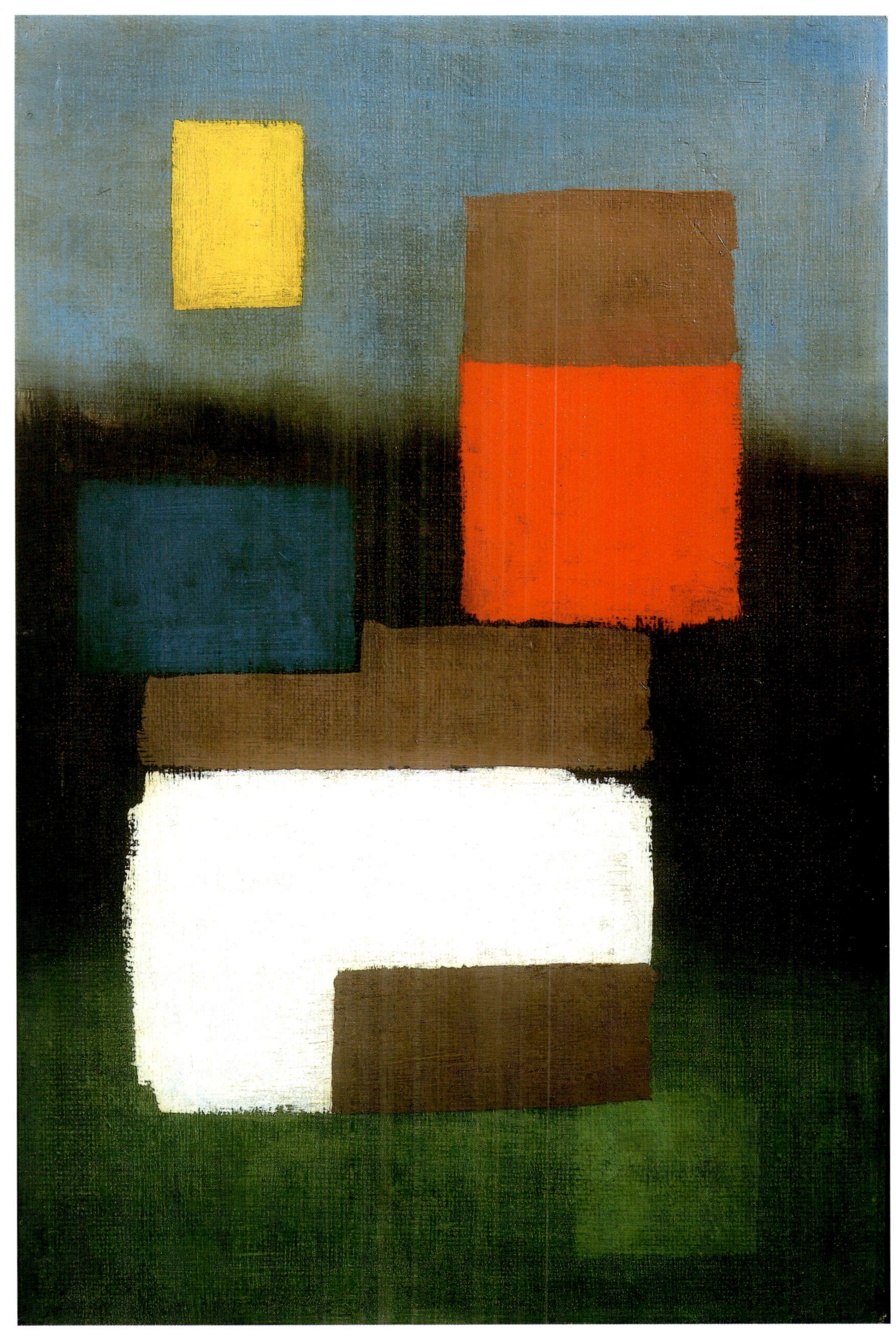

64

CARL HOLTY
[UNTITLED], 1936
OIL ON MASONITE, 45.7 X 30.2 CM
COURTESY SPANIERMAN GALLERY, NEW YORK
MAAG, TAM, TMAA

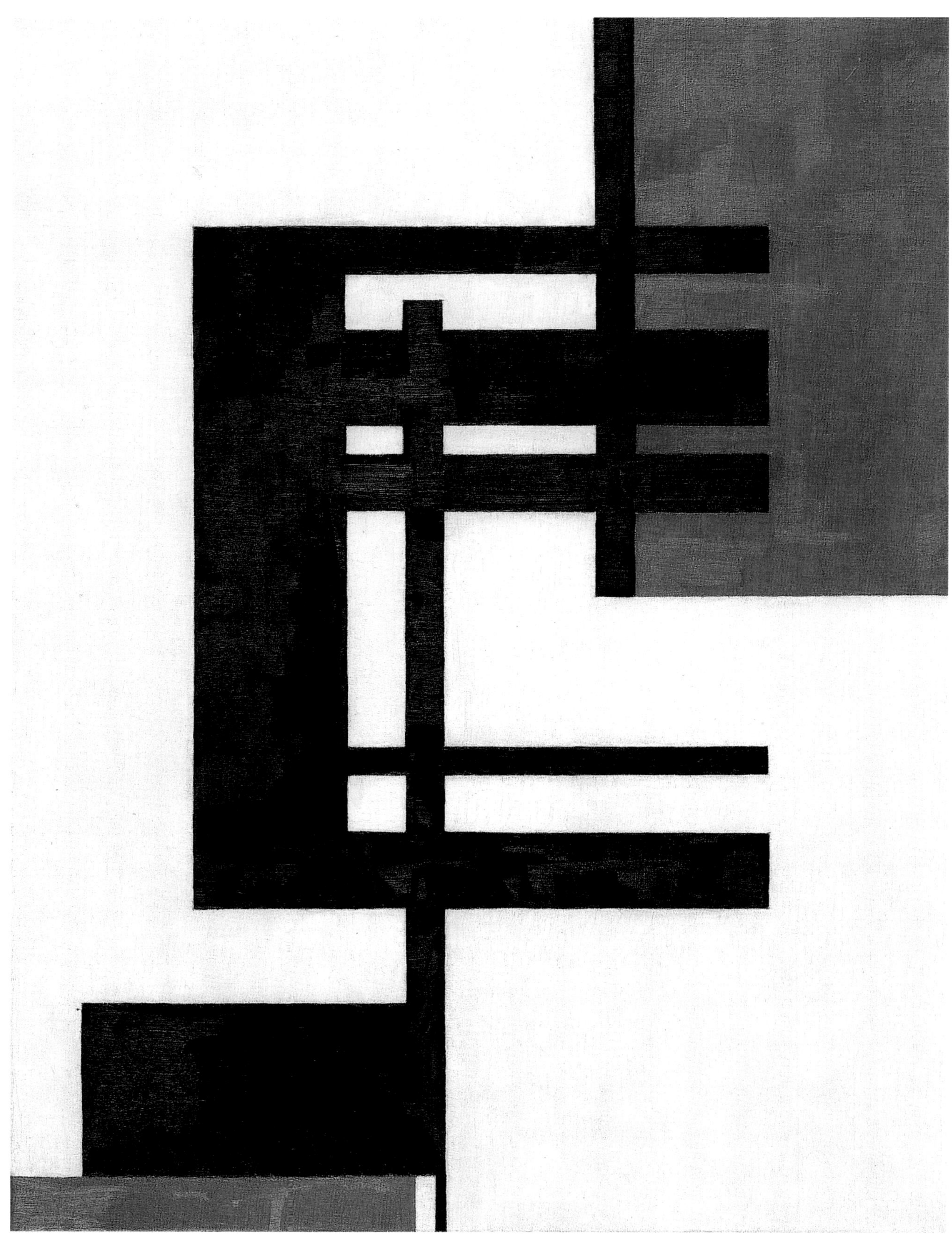

65
JEAN HÉLION
COMPOSITION, 1932
OIL ON CANVAS, 64.6 X 50.3 CM
PHILADELPHIA MUSEUM OF ART.
THE A. E. GALLATIN COLLECTION, 1945.91.1
MAAG, TAM, TMAA

ALBERT EUGENE GALLATIN AND THE PARIS—NEW YORK CONNECTION, 1927—1942

GAIL **STAVITSKY**

As a New York-based collector, museum director, and artist, Albert Eugene Gallatin (1881–1952; fig. 1) played a pivotal role in the dissemination and exchange of information on American and European geometric abstraction in the 1930s. A brief examination of his background and early collecting interests sets the stage for his seminal role as the founder in 1927 of the Gallery of Living Art at New York University, which was the first collection on public view in the United States devoted exclusively to modern art. Gallatin's small, informal museum was the catalyst for his vital Paris–New York connections.

Gallatin's conservative, dandified demeanor and patrician background seemed at odds with his pioneering decisions to found the Gallery of Living Art and to become an artist himself. He was the proud namesake of his great-grandfather, Albert Gallatin—Secretary of the Treasury under Presidents Thomas Jefferson and James Madison—who had posed for portraits by such illustrious artists as Gilbert Stuart and Rembrandt Peale. His distinguished family had played leading political and military roles in France and Switzerland from the fifteenth through the eighteenth centuries. Gallatin's pride in his prominent, self-made ancestors nurtured his life-long love of French art and culture.[1]

As the heir in 1902 to a family fortune made in banking, among other ventures, Gallatin soon established his reputation as an art connoisseur and critic. Collecting and writing extensively from 1897 to 1920 about James McNeill Whistler, Aubrey Beardsley, Max Beerbohm, the French and American impressionists, as well as the Ashcan School, Gallatin during this time virtually ignored more avant-garde art.

During World War I and the 1920s, Gallatin embarked on a program of self-education. In 1916 Gallatin put forth his first published statements concerning modernism in his "Notes on Some Masters of the Water-Color," praising the watercolors of John Marin and Paul Cézanne. By 1918 he found a means for his initial attempts to understand cubism, which would eventually form the cornerstone of his collection. As co-organizer of the Allied War Salon in New York, Gallatin included the semi-cubist war pictures of the British artist C. R. W. Nevinson.

After the watershed experience of the war, when Gallatin was very active as a writer, lender, and curator of benefit exhibitions, he continued to broaden his interest in modern art. Influenced by the formalist theories of Clive Bell, Gallatin responded positively to the work of Charles Demuth, Gaston Lachaise, and Pablo Picasso, acquiring his first work by the Spanish master in 1921.

From 1921 to 1938, Gallatin traveled frequently to Paris, where most of the works in his collection were acquired, often directly from artists. Gallatin's conversion to modernism in the 1920s was stimulated by his readings of the leading American modern art periodical, *The Arts*. There he became familiar with such newly founded institutions of modern art as the Société Anonyme (1920), the Phillips Memorial Art Gallery (1921), and the semi-public Barnes Foundation (1925).

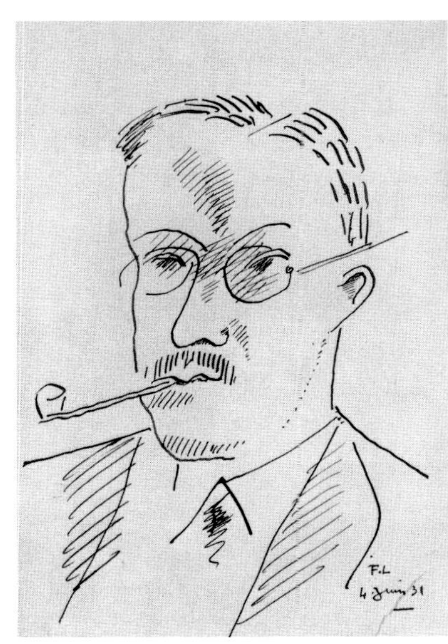

FIG. 1.
FERNAND LÉGER,
ALBERT EUGENE GALLATIN, 1931.
INK ON PAPER, 18.8 X 14.6 CM.
NATIONAL PORTRAIT GALLERY,
SMITHSONIAN INSTITUTION,
WASHINGTON D.C., 91.33.

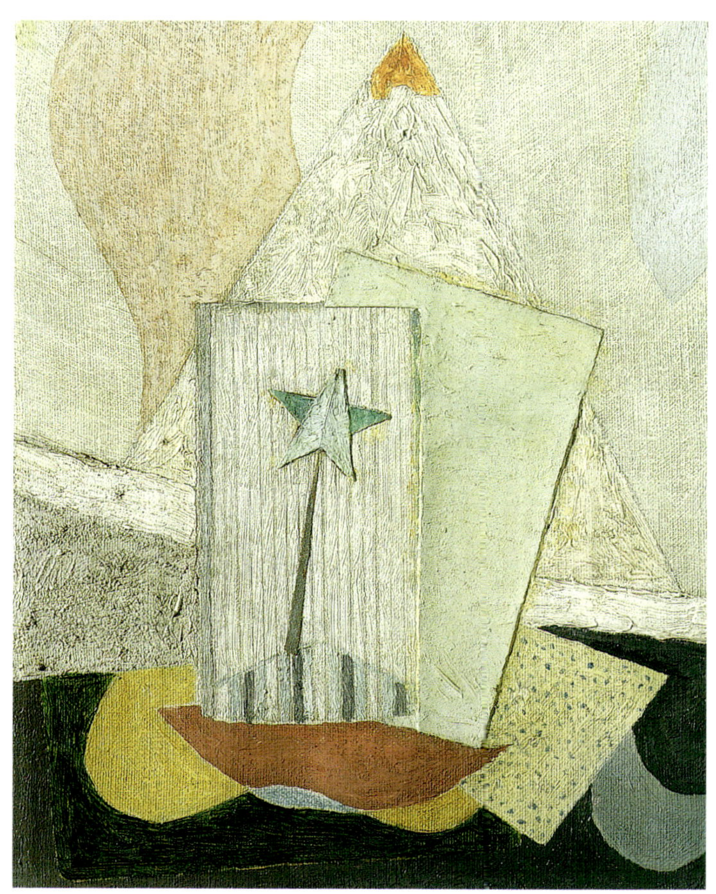

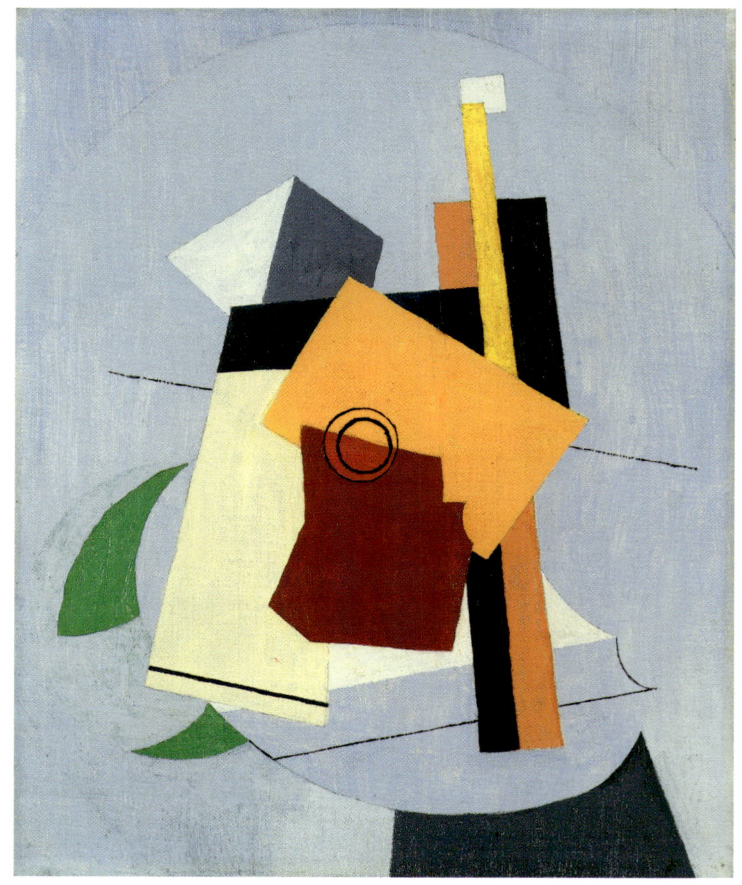

66

ALBERT EUGENE GALLATIN
CUBIST CONSTRUCTION, 1936
OIL ON CANVAS, 25.4 X 20.3 CM
JOHN AND BARB WALLACE COLLECTION
MAAG, TAM, TMAA

67

ALBERT EUGENE GALLATIN
COMPOSITION, 1937
OIL ON CANVAS, 31.3 X 25.9 CM
SMITHSONIAN AMERICAN ART MUSEUM,
WASHINGTON D.C.
GIFT OF PATRICIA AND PHILLIP FROST, 1986.92.25
MAAG, TAM, TMAA

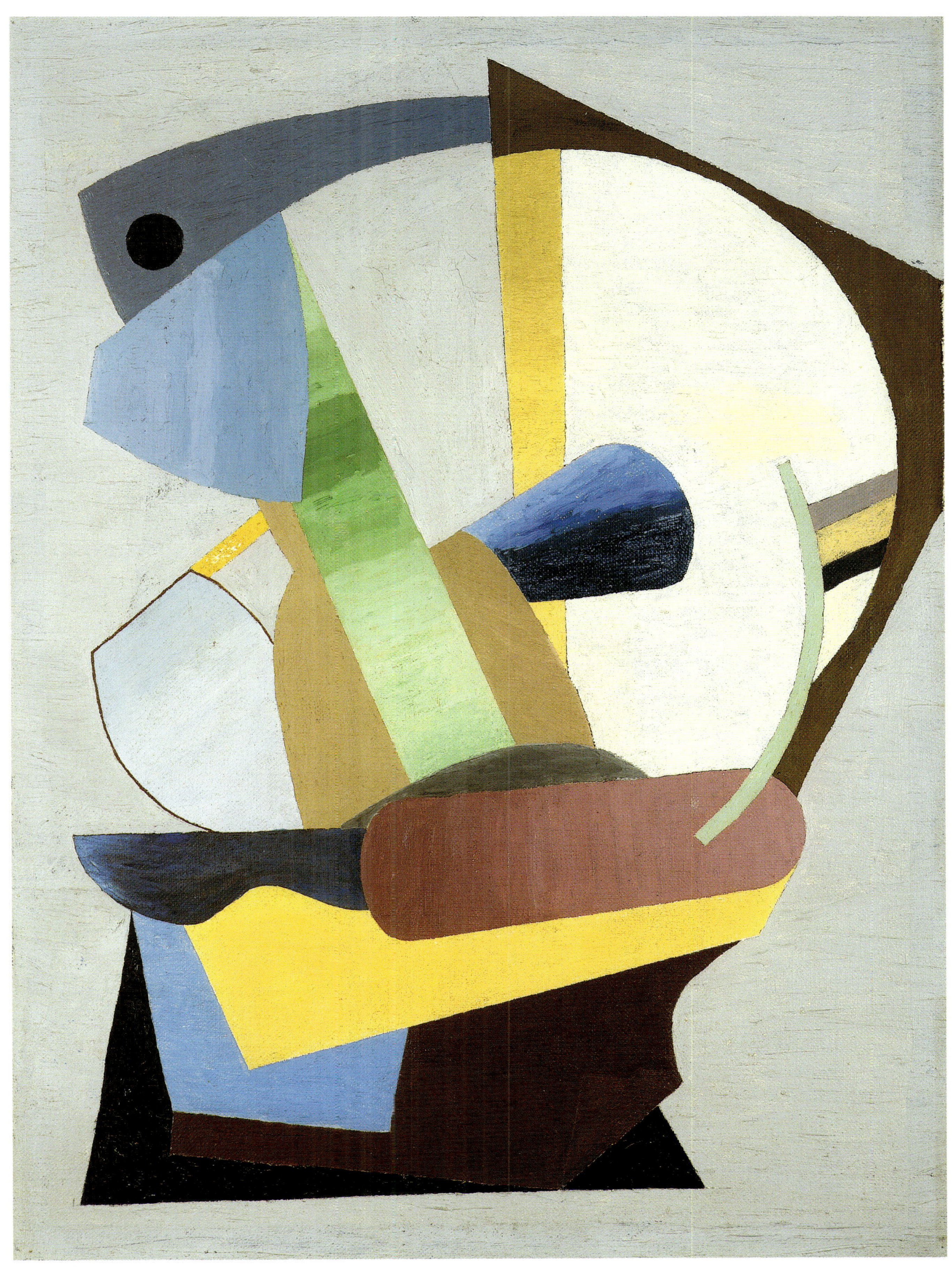

68
ALBERT EUGENE GALLATIN
COMPOSITION, 1936
OIL ON CANVAS, 41.3 X 30.7 CM
PRIVATE COLLECTION, PARIS
MAAG, TAM, TMAA

When editor Forbes Watson deplored the dispersal of the John Quinn collection of modern art and articulated "America's need of a museum of modern art," Gallatin responded to this challenge.[2]

On December 13, 1927 Gallatin opened his collection to the public in the South Study Hall of the main building at New York University, co-founded by his great-grandfather and for which he served as a trustee. The small core of cubist works by Picasso, Georges Braque, Juan Gris, Fernand Léger, and Man Ray in this initial installation established the Gallery of Living Art's future directions and preeminence as a museum of modern art. By 1931 the gallery had won the admiration of the critic James Johnson Sweeney for exhibiting the fullest representation of cubism in America. New York's Museum of Modern Art, founded two years after Gallatin's institution, did not possess a comparable collection until the late 1930s.[3]

Gallatin's trips to Paris were formative experiences that established the foundation for his directions in collecting. In 1926 he met the painter-critic Jacques Mauny, the Paris correspondent for *The Arts*, who became his initial liaison to the Paris art world. Most likely through Mauny, Gallatin met Picasso and the dealer Daniel-Henry Kahnweiler, both of whom stimulated his growing preference for cubism. Gallatin appreciated Kahnweiler's presentation, in his fundamental book *Der Weg zum Kubismus* (1920), of cubism as a carefully structured, classical style based on principles of order, clarity, and purity. This constructive, postwar emphasis upon the renovation of classic pictorial structure and tradition, transmitted through Cézanne and the cubists, was a theme common to the French and American modern art literature that Gallatin was avidly exploring at that time.[4] During the 1930s Gallatin would expand his collection to encompass not only cubism but its offshoots—constructivism, De Stijl, neoplasticism, and abstract surrealism.

Gallatin complemented his experiences of viewing and reading about modern art with an initial attempt at painting in 1926. Little is known about this self-taught activity, which evidently helped to broaden his understanding of modern art and cubism. Only three of his paintings from this time have been documented, including a view of Paris and a semi-cubist still life. Gallatin did not return to painting until 1936, when his collection was firmly established.

The Gallery of Living Art grew considerably during its first few years, as documented in catalogues of 1928, 1929, and 1930. As a one-man operation with an alleged annual budget of fifteen dollars, Gallatin acted on his own, free to establish the enterprising pattern of discovering artists and often acquiring their first works to enter an American collection on public view. During the summer of 1928 in Paris, Gallatin made his most radical purchase to date, Jean Miró's abstract *Painting (Fratellini)*, 1927, marking this Spanish-born surrealist's debut in an American collection open to the public.[5] Possibly encouraged by Mauny and the American critic Henry McBride, this acquisition foretold the increasingly abstract direction of Gallatin's collecting in the 1930s, even

though surrealism never became the collection's primary focus. By 1930 Gallatin's collection had grown to such an extent that he felt the need to publish the Gallery of Living Art's first substantial catalogue and to organize a major exhibition of twenty-eight recent acquisitions, held in the larger space of the Brummer Gallery in New York. Highlights included Picasso's youthful *Self-Portrait*, 1906, acquired from the artist himself, Miró's *Dog Barking at the Moon*, 1926, Man Ray's monumental, cubist *War (A.D. MCMXIV)*, 1914, and André Masson's surreal-cubist *Italian Postcard*, 1925, the first work by this French artist to enter an American public collection.

Receiving mostly positive reviews, Gallatin's institution was, however, castigated by one critic who questioned his dictatorial exclusions:

> Is it right that American students should be forced to accept Mr. Gallatin's verdict that . . . contemporary sculptors are not of real importance? . . . Living art, if Mr. Gallatin is to be believed, scarcely exists outside of America and France. . . . Young America should be given a more accurate idea of England's and Germany's by no means negligible contribution to "Living Art."[6]

Although he would eventually acquire *Painting*, 1936, by the English constructivist Ben Nicholson, Gallatin was a rabidly anti-German collector, inflexibly deploring any emphasis upon literary or symbolic content. Increasingly devoted to cubism and its abstract offshoots as his discriminating standard for collecting, Gallatin rejected expressionism, dada, futurism, and verist surrealism as art that was subjective, illustrative, and vulgar.

Gallatin's growing preference for cubism led to a turning point in his development as a collector during his Parisian sojourn in the spring and summer of 1932. Having written to Robert Delaunay in April requesting a visit, Gallatin initiated a fruitful meeting with this French artist, whom he regarded as "an important member of the original cubist group."[7] Their encounters in April, May, and June resulted in a lively exchange of ideas, as well as several acquisitions. *Three-Part Windows*, 1912, a key example of orphic cubism, was the first work by Delaunay to be acquired for an American collection on public view. Articulate and ambitious, Delaunay decided to educate and cultivate his new friend, urging him in his informative letters during the summer and fall of 1932 to form "an abstract museum with the complete development of this art from its origins."[8]

Delaunay was a founding member of Abstraction-Création, a Paris-based international group of artists active from 1932 to 1936 who were predominantly cubists and geometric abstractionists opposed to doctrinaire surrealism. The group's constructivist promotion of structure, order, precision, and clarity was particularly appealing to Gallatin.[9] Furthermore, Delaunay introduced Gallatin to several fellow members of Abstraction-Création, including Albert Gleizes and Joaquín Torres-García. He acquired several works by the Uruguayan-born Torres-García, including *Construction*, 1931, which was the first significant sculpture to enter the collection.

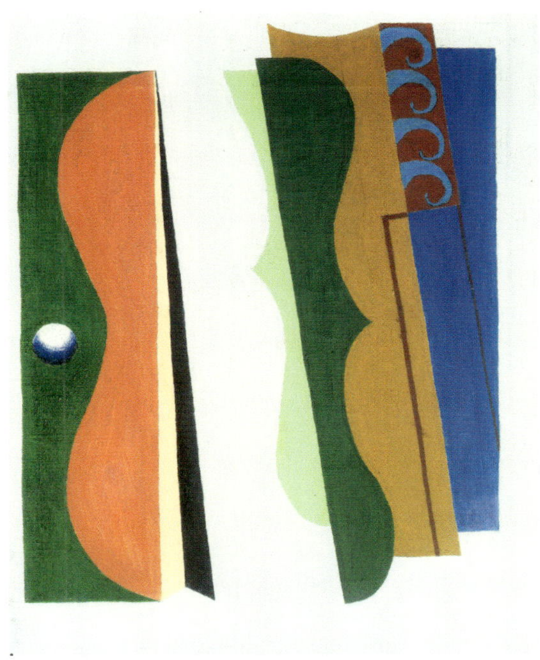

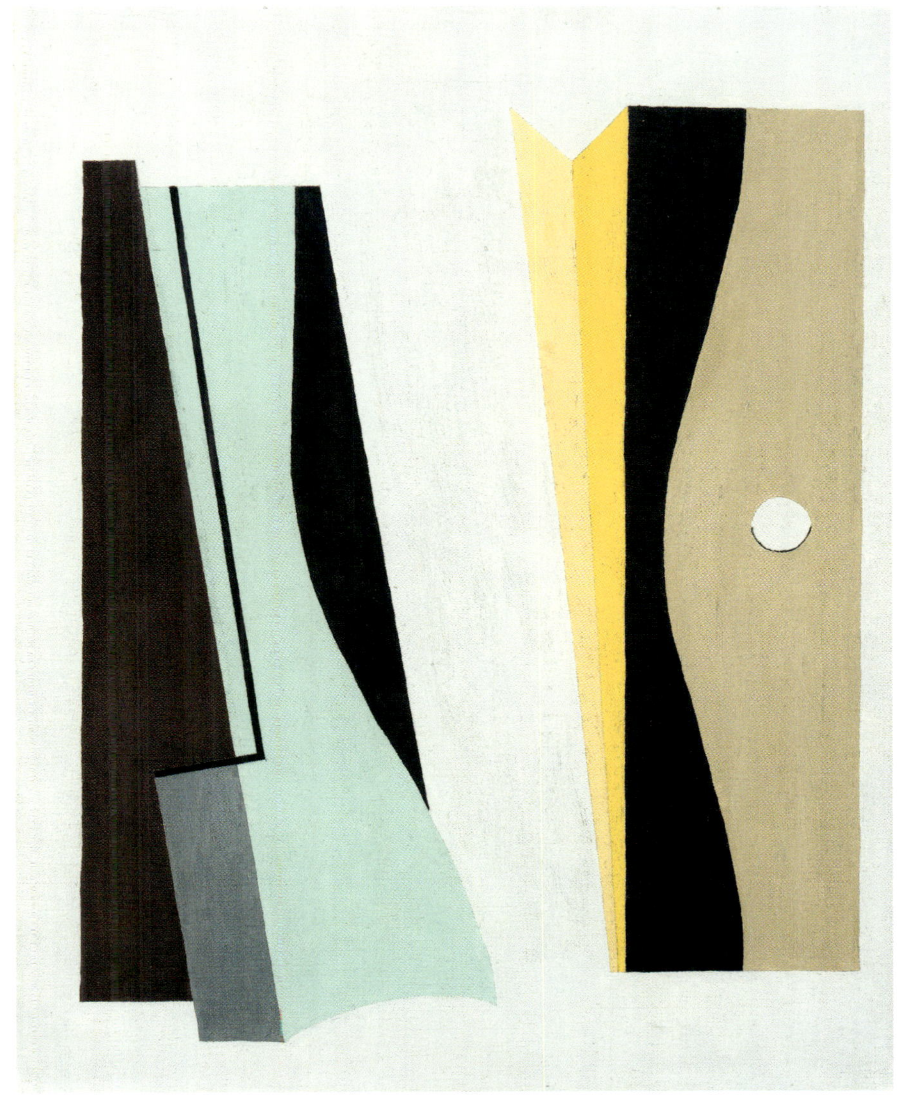

69
ALBERT EUGENE GALLATIN
MUSICAL ABSTRACTION, 1937
OIL ON CANVAS, 30.5 X 25.3 CM
COURTESY SPANIERMAN GALLERY, NEW YORK
MAAG, TAM, TMAA

70
ALBERT EUGENE GALLATIN
[UNTITLED], 1938
OIL ON CANVAS, 51 X 41 CM
MUSÉE NATIONAL DE LA COOPÉRATION FRANCO-
AMÉRICAINE, BLÉRANCOURT, MNBCFAC 85.3
MAAG, TMAA

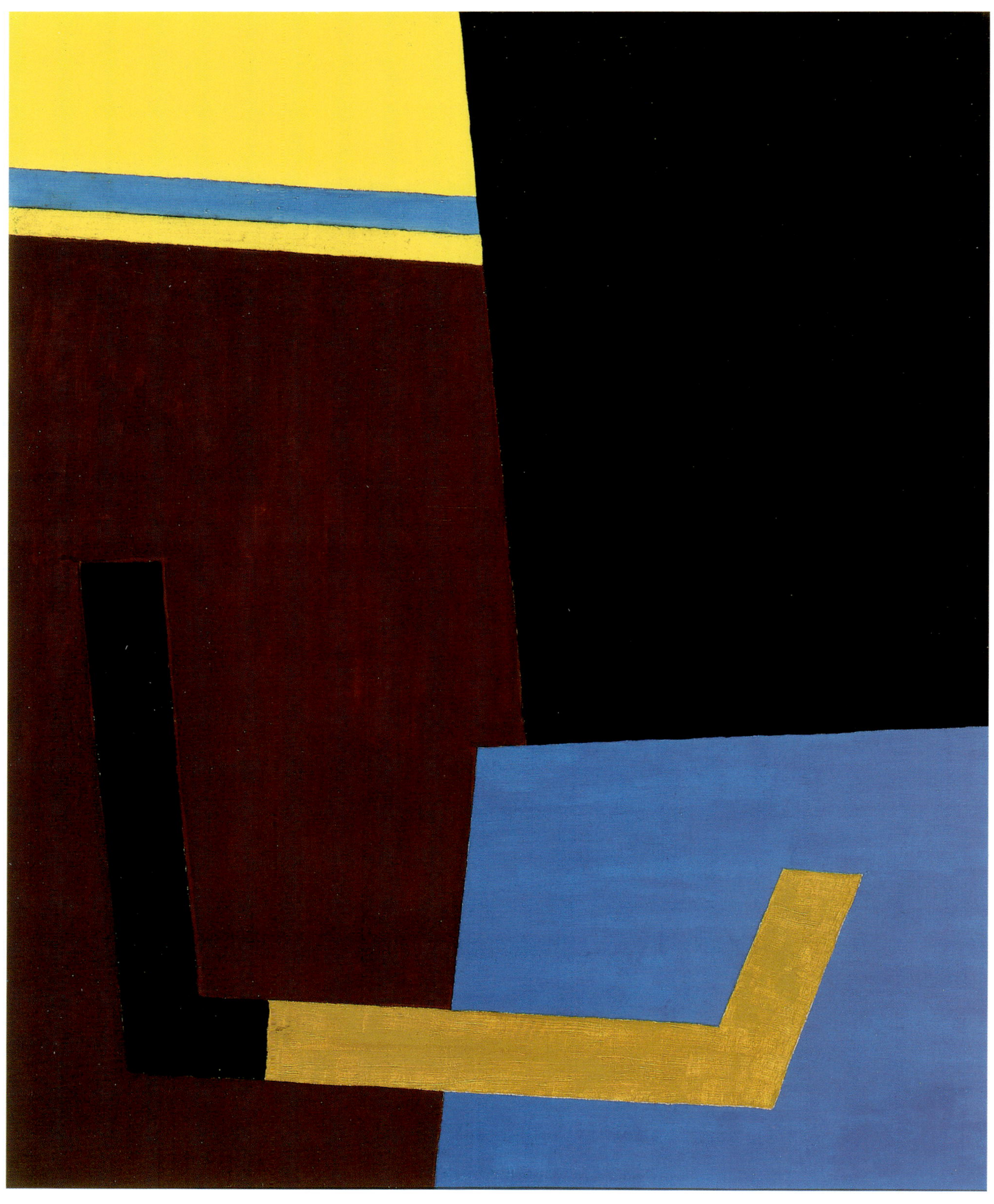

71
ALBERT EUGENE GALLATIN
ROOM SPACE, 1937–38
OIL ON CANVAS, 76.8 X 64.5 CM
TERRA FOUNDATION FOR THE ARTS, CHICAGO.
THE DANIEL J. TERRA COLLECTION, 1999.56
MAAG, TAM, TMAA

Delaunay also introduced Gallatin to Jean Hélion, a leader in the Art Concret and Abstraction-Création movements. This serious, reliable, English-speaking painter-critic would replace Mauny and, later, the mercurial Delaunay, as Gallatin's chief guide to the Parisian art world. Meeting the young artist at his first one-man show at the Galerie Pierre, Gallatin acquired *Composition,* 1932, a geometric abstraction from Hélion's *Orthogonale* series, inspired by Piet Mondrian Along with Torres-García's constructed sculpture, Hélion's painting was yet another debut for an American art institution.[10]

The spring and summer of 1933 in Paris was a pivotal time for Gallatin who renewed his influential contacts with Delaunay and Hélion. Urging Gallatin to concentrate on serious artists and stop featuring so much of "Picasso *aventurier* [and] Braque *petit-bourgeois*," Delaunay tried unsuccessfully to introduce him to Arp, who was not at home at the time of the attempted visit.[11] During other meetings, they discussed abstract art and a projected museum in Paris of nonobjective painting. It was Hélion, however, who succeeded in taking Gallatin to the studios of Mondrian and Arp in May 1933; both were his colleagues in Abstraction-Création. Gallatin's first visit with Mondrian resulted in his progressive acquisition of *Composition with Blue and Yellow,* 1932. Mondrian gave Gallatin a copy of his treatise *Le Néo-Plasticisme* (Paris, 1920) and dedicated it to the collector on the second page which bears the phrase "Aux Hommes Futurs."[12] Gallatin's several visits with Arp resulted in the acquisition of two biomorphic abstractions, the relief *Vase-Bust* and the gouache *Head-Nose,* both dating from 1930, which, like the Mondrian painting, were the first works by this French-German artist to enter an American collection on public view. As Hélion related to this author in 1986:

> This pair of Arp and Mondrian had a very good influence through me on Gallatin because they both represented a complete form of art. Both of them made a complete and very rich opposition. . . . I made [Gallatin] go frankly towards abstract art, where before [his collection] was a mixture of cubist, pre-cubist, and abstract, pre-abstract art. . . . My influence upon him is that he did clarify his collection. With the accent on Mondrian, and Léger and Arp.[13]

That summer, Gallatin also acquired Hélion's *Composition,* 1933 part of the *Équilibre* series in which the rigid rectangles of his earlier *Orthogonale* series were transformed into subtly colored, flexed, and modeled forms reflecting the impact of Léger, Arp, and Miró. Encouraging Gallatin to refine and focus his collection, Hélion persuaded him to eliminate works that did not conform to the structural, non-mimetic character of his recent acquisitions.[14] Hélion emphasized the importance of Mondrian and Arp in a significant essay on the evolution of abstract art he wrote for the 1933 catalogue of the Gallery of Living Art.

Hélion arranged additional introductions to fellow members of Abstraction-Création for Gallatin during the summer of 1934. On June 13, they met with César Domela, Wolfgang Paalen, and Hans Erni,

all of whom were included in the 1934 issue of *Abstraction création art non figuratif*. Gallatin acquired examples of Domela's and Paalen's work two years later. Hélion probably also encouraged Gallatin to attend a one-man exhibition at the Galerie Pierre of his friend and fellow Abstraction-Création member Jean Xceron whose abstract *Composition,* 1934, he purchased three years later.[15] He also urged the collector to buy larger, more significant works, including Léger's abstract *Composition* (1923–27). This abstract purist picture based on carefully ordered, invented mechanical elements was a major addition to Gallatin's collection of smaller and more representational works by Léger. Gallatin also purchased a large *Équilibre* composition of 1934 by Hélion, which was later deaccessioned. In gratitude for this major purchase, Hélion gave Gallatin the small *Composition,* 1934, still in the Gallatin collection of the Philadelphia Museum of Art (cat. 65).

Hélion also encouraged Gallatin to buy recent work by Miró whose *Painting,* 1933, acquired in 1935, was among the most abstract of this Spanish master's paintings, made during the year that he was asked to join Abstraction-Création.[16] Furthermore, he nurtured Gallatin's growing interest in American abstraction by drawing his attention to American members of the Abstraction-Création group, John Ferren and Alexander Calder. In May 1935 Hélion arranged a meeting with Ferren, based in Paris since 1931; during that summer Gallatin acquired his biomorphic abstraction *Composition,* 1934 (cat. 83) which primarily reflected the influence of Miró. Visiting Arp that summer as well, Gallatin was accompanied by his friend and colleague Charles Greene Shaw, who had the honor of having the first one man show at the Gallery of Living Art from May to October 1935. Recognized by Gallatin as "doing the most important work in abstract painting in America today," the largely self-taught Shaw also received accolades from Arp whose work exerted a considerable influence upon him.[17]

Hélion's attempts to encourage Gallatin to buy the work of Calder (based in Paris from 1926 to 1933) date back to 1933 when the two Americans first met. Trying to persuade Gallatin to acquire a mobile, Hélion was not successful in this endeavor, given the collector's preference for a stationary work resembling an Arp relief. In the fall of 1935, after much correspondence and deliberation, he acquired *Red Frame,* 1932, one of Calder's first abstract constructions with suspended circular discs evoking the pure organic forms of Arp and Miró.[18] On view that fall at the Gallery of Living Art were the recent abstractions of another American, Gallatin's close friend George L. K. Morris, who had studied with Léger in 1929 and 1930 at his older colleague's behest.

Gallatin evolved a close working friendship with the younger Shaw and Morris who were both influenced by the cubist and abstract orientation of the Gallery of Living Art. As well-dressed uptown men of independent means, the three were eventually dubbed the "Park Avenue Cubists" by more bohemian contemporaries, including some who were fellow

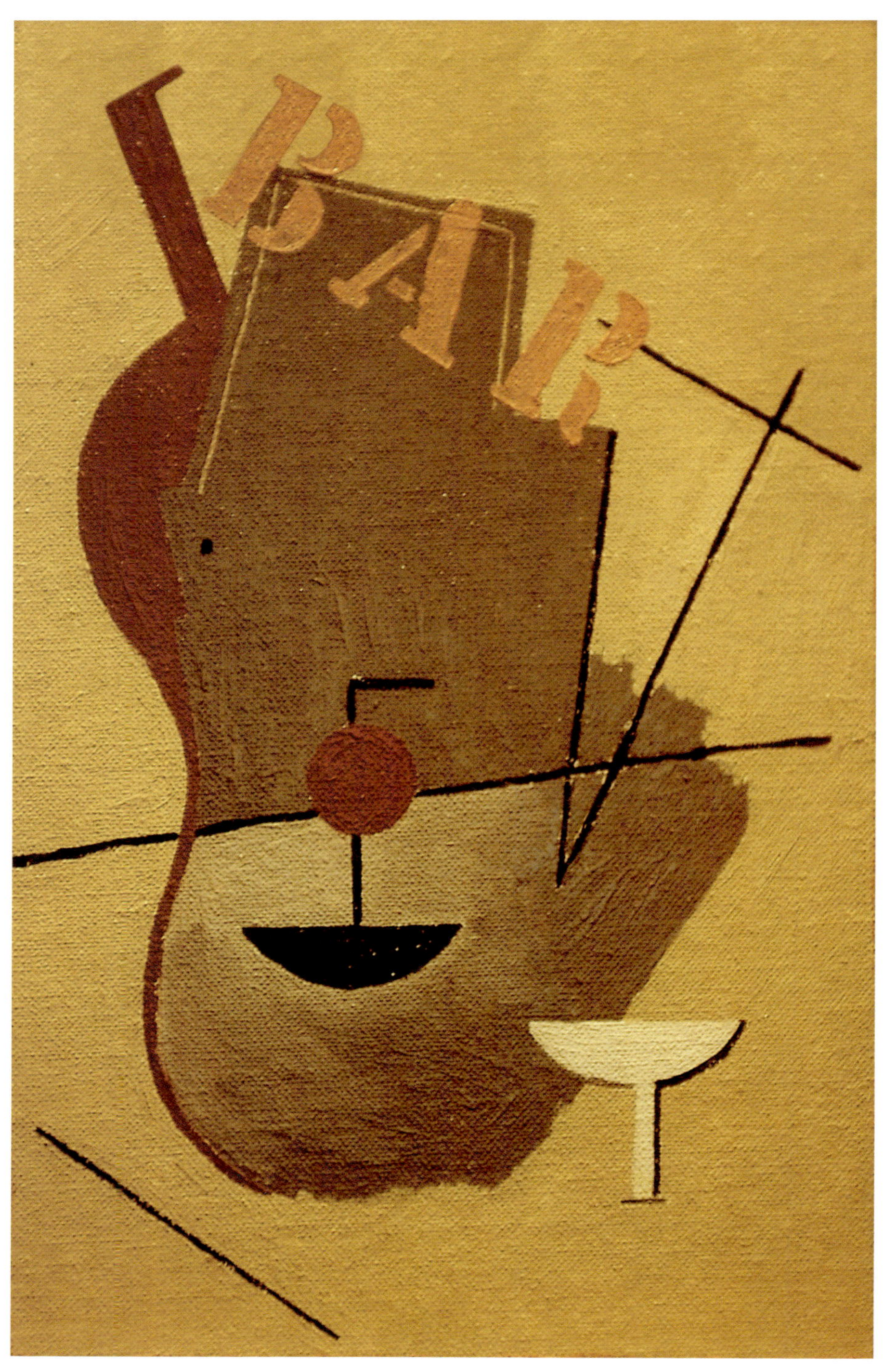

72

ALBERT EJGENE GALLATIN
BAR, 1939
OIL ON CANVAS ON BOARD, 25.4 X 20.3 CM
THE NORMA AND MYRON H. GOLDBERG ART TRUST
MAAG, TAM, TMAA

members of the American Abstract Artists (established in 1937). Having introduced Morris to modern art, Gallatin engaged the budding painter-critic as a curator for the Gallery of Living Art who assisted with the selection of abstract paintings by Shaw for his solo show. Both Morris and Shaw would play a vital role in the organization of Gallatin's landmark exhibition of *Five Contemporary American Concretionists*, held at the Paul Reinhardt Galleries in New York from March 9–31, 1936. This show traveled in an altered version to Paris and London during the summer of 1936.[19]

For the title of his exhibition, Gallatin adapted the formalist term "concrete" that had originated in 1930 with such painters as Theo Van Doesburg and Jean Hélion, members of the Art Concret group. This show was evidently organized as an institutional challenge to the large historical survey at the Museum of Modern Art, *Cubism and Abstract Art* which was almost exclusively devoted to European artists and had opened a week earlier. Indeed, Gallatin had advance notice from Morris and Shaw, both members of the Museum of Modern Art's advisory committee, of the director Alfred H. Barr's plans to exclude Americans. The only Americans chosen were Calder, Man Ray, and Edward McKnight-Kauffer, all of whom had been or were then working abroad.

By the fall of 1935 Gallatin had met all the artists that Morris, Shaw, and he would select for their show of American abstractionists, including Charles Biederman, whose New York studio he visited with Shaw in November. Biederman later acknowledged the formative influence of the Gallery of Living Art collection in his eclectic explorations of visual structure from 1934 to 1936 when he was based in New York and absorbing cubism, as well as the work of Mondrian, Arp, and Miró, as reflected in his experimental abstract paintings, *papiers collés*, and relief constructions. Represented by this range of abstract, geometric, and organic work in the show, Biederman was joined by Morris, Shaw, Calder, and Ferren. This last artist, based in Paris from 1931 to 1938, sent several biomorphic abstractions, including *Composition*, 1934 (The Berkshire Museum, Pittsfield, Mass.), which reflected his appreciation for the work of Hélion, Vassily Kandinsky, Paul Klee, and Miró. Exhibited as a group in America for the first time seven of Ferren's paintings were praised for their subtle color relationships and vigorous designs.[20]

Morris was well represented by seven works; with their interlocking angular and curved geometric forms, all evoked Morris's appreciation of the paintings of Léger and Hélion. Little is known about Shaw's contributions, characterized by one critic as demonstrating "a surrealist interest in germ-like forms."[21] Calder, the best known artist in the group, showed the fewest works, including *Red Frame* and two mobiles, probably no longer extant. Dissatisfied with being categorized as a concretionist and with Gallatin's decision not to acquire another work, independent-minded Calder withdrew from the traveling version of what he called the "Concrete Mixers" show.[22] His replacement was

Gallatin himself, who had been painting steadily since February 1936, after a ten-year hiatus. The Museum of Living Art's collection played a formative role in the evolution of Gallatin's synthetic cubist-derived style, as recognized by critics at the time of his Parisian debut. Although his paintings were dismissed as a purified version of Picasso's work ("Gallatin épure Picasso jusqu'à sa plus simple expression"), Gallatin was credited for his encouragement of contemporary artists.[23] In some of his own works, Gallatin enlivened the geometric context of flattened, interlocking, hard-edged forms by incorporating whimsical biomorphic shapes that reflected the impact of Arp. Ranging from simplified cubist still lifes to pure abstractions, Gallatin's paintings and collages are distinguished by their austere, carefully ordered compositions and subtle, refined palette.[24]

Although the five artists never exhibited together again as concretionists, most of them would soon become involved with the development of the American Abstract Artists (AAA) group of which Gallatin was an early member. Morris, a co-founder, has recalled that the terminological debates concerning the nature of abstraction, inspired in part by the concretionists and their considerable press coverage, continued later on in 1936, and in early 1937, at the meetings of the newly formed AAA. The most articulate spokesman of the AAA was Morris who, along with his fellow geometric abstractionists Gallatin and Shaw, espoused a Purist point of view that stemmed from their previous use of the term concrete.

One of the AAA's prominent founding members, Ilya Bolotowsky, has recognized the concretionist group as a notable precedent for the AAA, which in its debates, encompassed many of the same issues embraced by members of Abstraction-Création.[25] Both movements essentially espouse two different approaches to attaining non-figuration: the progressive abstraction of forms from nature, and the invention, independent of nature, of pure geometric or curvilinear forms. It was the latter direction that was embraced by Gallatin and his circle. Indeed Hélion recognized this in his letter of congratulations on April 24, 1936, applauding "how an interest [in abstract art] is developing in the States when it so stagnates over here"—most likely an allusion to his disillusionment with the Abstraction-Création group from which he had withdrawn in 1934.[26]

In 1936 Gallatin held the first solo show of a European artist at his museum, featuring a group of neo-plastic reliefs by a member of Abstraction-Création, César Domela, whom he had met through Hélion.[27] Later that year, following the major acquisition of Picasso's *Three Musicians*, 1921, Gallatin decided to rename his institution the Museum of Living Art, wishing to avoid the commercial connotations of the term *gallery*. However, from 1937 until the closing of his museum at the end of 1942, Gallatin was increasingly involved with the promotion of his fellow AAA members through acquisitions and exhibitions. He continued to travel regularly to Paris through 1938 and his involvement with the international periodical *Plastique* (1937–39) attests to the ongoing vitality of his Parisian connections.

The first issue of *Plastique*, dated Spring 1937, was the result of a campaign launched in 1936. Domela has claimed that he originated the idea "of editing an [anti-surrealist] propaganda review for geometric abstract art."[28] A letter of July 13 from Domela to Gallatin indicates that plans for the inaugural issue were already under way, including an introduction by Morris and reproductions of works by Kasimir Malevich, Arp, Theo van Doesburg, Anton Pevsner, Gallatin, Kurt Schwitters, and Domela.[29] By August 1936, Gallatin had made a financial contribution, acknowledged by Domela, who along with the Arps (particularly Sophie Taeuber-Arp), were coordinating the forthcoming publication of the magazine in Paris.[30] Originally projected for the fall of 1936, *Plastique* appeared, after many delays, in the spring of 1937.[31]

This multi-lingual magazine featured five articles related to constructivism, including Morris's statement "On the Abstract Tradition." In this article, Morris provided a statement of intention for the new magazine:

> PLASTIC will discuss the abstract tradition as it has constantly rearisen since early times and will reproduce the works of many who are vitalizing it today in its new-found purest forms. The editors are themselves painters and sculptors, who can look out upon the tradition from within, rather than as critics on the watch for subject and anecdote.[32]

Morris's use of the title "Plastic" (translation for "Plastique") raises the issue of Hélion's involvement in this magazine.

Hélion had been asked to contribute to *Plastique* which was a successor to *Plastic*, a never-realized magazine for which he had made plans in 1934. Although Hélion met with Gallatin several times during the winter and spring of 1937 while he was residing in America, he decided against participating in this review because of his shifting interests: "I turned to nature, which they were escaping from."[33] As he evolved "towards a new figuration," Hélion was increasingly replaced by Morris as Gallatin's advisor and spokesman.[34]

Hélion has observed that Gallatin, under the influence of Morris, acquired a group of seven torn paper collages by Arp during the summer of 1937. This acquisition most likely took place around June 24 when Gallatin traveled to Meudon to discuss *Plastique* with the Arps and Domela. As early as 1934, Morris himself had experimented with Arp's torn paper collage technique combining spontaneously produced, irregular forms with consciously created, refined, hard-edge, organic shapes. He regarded the examples purchased by Gallatin as "the final fruition . . . [of] a constant search for an ever greater expressiveness through simplification."[35] In the fall of 1937 Arp had his first one-man show in America at Gallatin's Museum of Living Art.

For the Spring 1938 issue of *Plastique*, dedicated to American abstract art, Gallatin contributed an article entitled "Abstract Painting and the Museum of Living Art." Summarizing the growth and refinement of his collection, Gallatin stated that at "the inauguration of the museum [in 1927] . . . about the only indications of the future evolution . . .

were to be found in the cubist canvas by Braque, a Gris, a Léger, five Picassos and a Man Ray . . . [as a] demonstration of abstract art."[36] He observed that other works in the opening show—"a Friesz, a Marquet, and a Pascin, among others, have been withdrawn, not being considered important elements of the collection, or spiritually related to it."[37] With regard to the development of his abstract directions in collecting, Gallatin referred to the aforementioned cubists and "another significant group," the constructivists Mondrian, Domela, and Hélion.[38] He also noted the selection of pieces "from the now large group of American abstract painters, several of them concerned largely with problems of construction."[39]

Gallatin's illustrated essay in *Plastique* was complemented by the articles of other fellow AAA members, Charles Shaw, Balcomb Greene, and George L. K. Morris. In a statement for a catalogue accompanying a traveling show of the AAA in 1938, he applauded this group as "most likely to produce an authentic American cultural expression" for "the soil here is fertile, not over-cultivated as in many European countries, and from it we may reasonably expect vigorous art forms eventually to emerge."[40] His optimism about the emergence of a native abstract tradition was shared in part by Hélion who was interviewed by Morris for *Partisan Review* in 1938. Hélion, who was himself highly influential for the AAA, praised America's material assistance, including the Works Progress Administration (WPA) and greater possibilities for teaching, exhibiting, and publicity.[41] Although not as close to Gallatin as he used to be, Hélion still exerted some influence, taking the collector to the studio of Alberto Magnelli in June 1938. There Gallatin acquired an abstract collage *Composition*, 1937. That last summer abroad, Gallatin also acquired works by Ferren, Mondrian, and former Abstraction-Création member Georges Vantongerloo.

Although primarily involved with European art acquisitions, Gallatin promoted American abstract art abroad by arranging for a group show at the Galerie Pierre in June 1938.[42] This exhibition consisted of abstract paintings by Gallatin, Shaw's pioneering shaped canvases entitled "Plastic Polygons" which allude to the Manhattan skyline, and Morris's abstract paintings and sculpture.

The outbreak of World War II disrupted Gallatin's annual pilgrimages abroad and eclipsed the artistic avant-garde's activities, including *Plastique*. Although Gallatin continued to make key acquisitions of European work, also giving Mondrian his first one-man show in 1939, his attention shifted to promotion of the AAA. Furthermore, the decreased amount of activity at the Museum of Living Art during its final years coincided with Gallatin's increased devotion to painting. As an AAA member he showed regularly in the group's exhibitions; as an increasingly recognized abstract painter he had annual one-man shows.[43] He made his debut at his own museum in March 1942 when the entire space was filled with works by twenty-five American painters, mostly AAA members. Among them was Suzy Morris Frelinghuysen,

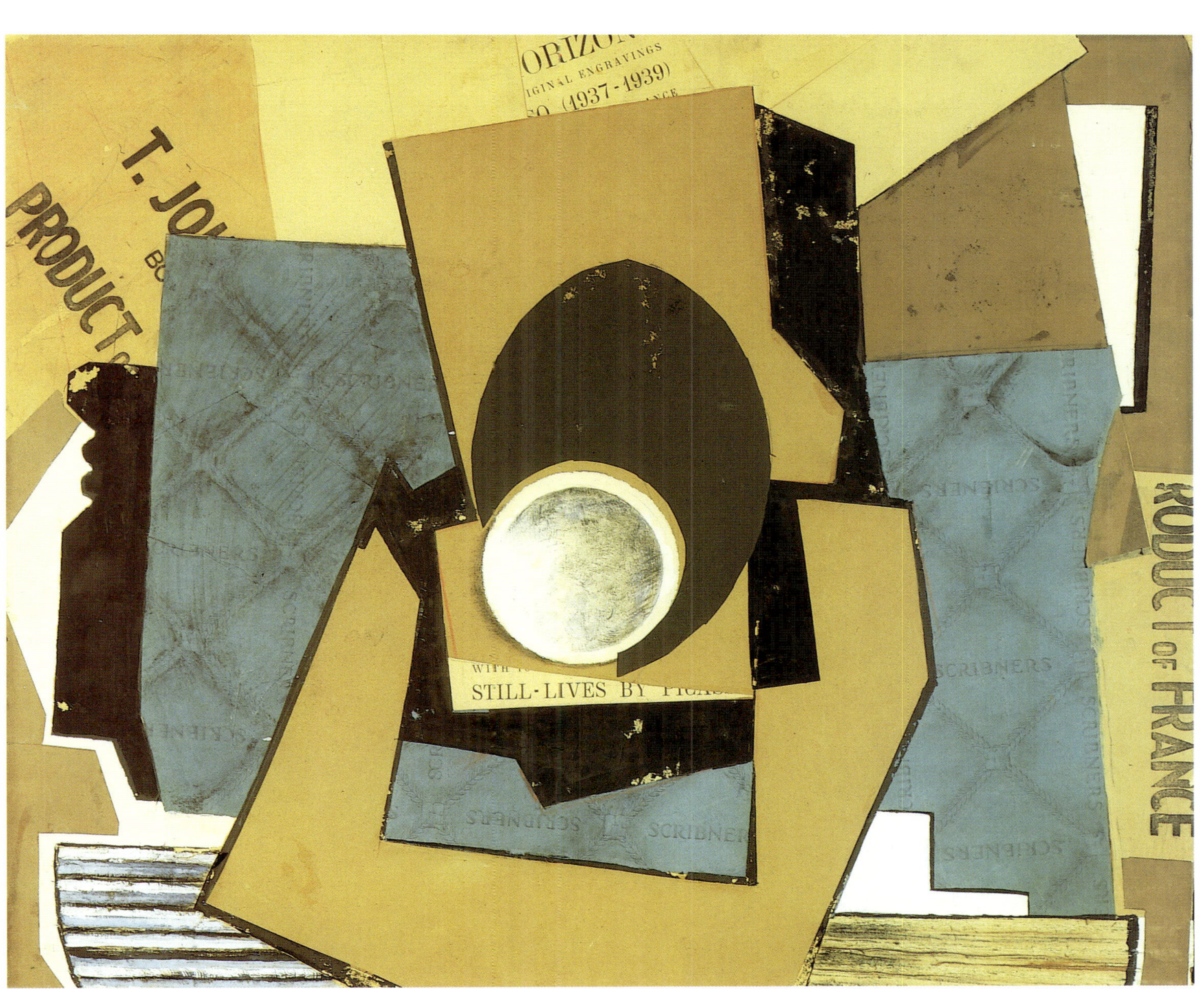

73
SUZY FRELINGHUYSEN
STILL LIVES BY PICASSO, 1939
OIL WITH COLLAGE ON CARDBOARD, 52 X 62.2 CM
GEORGE L. K. MORRIS AND SUZY FRELINGHUYSEN FOUNDATION.
COURTESY SALANDER O'REILLY GALLERIES,
NEW YORK
MAAG, TAM, TMAA

whose large synthetic cubist collage *Composition*, 1940, was acquired by Gallatin and praised in a review as "a real museum piece which could hang alongside any Gris."[44] Aware of the Museum of Living Art as a resource, Gallatin conceived his institution as being "of the utmost value to the working artist."[45] Claiming that his museum had "always especially favored advanced American painters [i.e. the AAA]," Gallatin observed that, "they have studied and built upon the innovations and discoveries of the type of [abstract artist] represented in the Museum of Living Art."[46]

In December 1942 Gallatin was asked by New York University to vacate the premises in order to make way for a library processing facility. The official announcement on December 14 of the Museum's demise coincided with the Museum's fifteenth anniversary. The following year, Gallatin bequeathed the majority of his collection of over one hundred works to the Philadelphia Museum of Art.

Dubbed the "abstract king of America," Gallatin passed away in 1952 at the age of seventy.[47] His multifaceted career and manifold achievements were praised in the press. A significant abstract painter in his own right, Gallatin is best known for the development of his outstanding, highly influential collection which was the vehicle for his fruitful connections in Paris and abroad. The selected works by Picasso, Braque, Gris, Léger, Hélion, Mondrian, and many others distinguish themselves as exemplars of one man's particular vision. Their structural clarity and subtle colors affirm Gallatin's formalist principles as a collector-painter imbued with an unshakable faith in the vitality of the cubist-constructivist tradition. As one critic observed, "Gallatin felt the pulse beat set off by cubism . . . he helped charge the blood of the next generation with that pulse."[48] ∎

1— The information in this essay is based upon the author's dissertation and several articles. See especially Gail Stavitsky, "The Development, Institutionalization, and Impact of the A. E. Gallatin Collection of Modern Art" (Ph.D. diss., Institute of Fine Arts–New York University, 1990), hereafter cited as dissertation; and Gail Stavitsky, "The A. E. Gallatin Collection: An Early Adventure in Modern Art," *Philadelphia Museum of Art Bulletin* 89, nos. 379–80 (winter/spring 1994): 3–47, hereafter cited as *PMA Bulletin*. See also the author's entry on Gallatin in the *American National Biography* (New York: Oxford University Press, 1999), 642–43 and the author's article "A. E. Gallatin's Gallery and Museum of Living Art (1927–1943)," *American Art* 7 (spring 1993): 47–63.

2— See Forbes Watson, Editorial, *The Arts* 9 (January 1926): 4.

3— See *PMA Bulletin:* 12, 18.

4— See dissertation, 76–80; *PMA Bulletin:* 10.

5— *PMA Bulletin:* 14–16. Unless otherwise noted, all cited paintings are in the collection of the Philadelphia Museum of Art.

6— "Gallery of Living Art," *London Observer*, September 28, 1930.

7— A. E. Gallatin, "The Plan of the Gallery of Living Art," in A. E. Gallatin, *Gallery of Living Art: A. E. Gallatin Collection* (New York, 1933), [2]. See also Gail Stavitsky, "A. E. Gallatin and Robert Delaunay," *Source Notes in the History of Art* 11, nos. 3–4 (spring/summer 1992): 53–58.

8— Delaunay exhorted Gallatin to form "un musée abstrait avec tout le développement de cet art avec ses origines." Delaunay to Gallatin, Paris, September 19, 1932, Gallatin Papers, microfilm 1, frame 154, The New York Historical Society Archives.

9— See Patricia Ender Kaplan, "Geometric Abstraction in Paris in the 1930s" (Ph.D. diss., City University of New York, 1978), 159–90; and *Abstraction-Creation, 1931-1936,* (Munster: Westfalisches Landesmuseum für Kunst und Kulturgeschichte, Landschaftsverban Westfalen-Lippe, 1978).

10— Dissertation, 201–2; *PMA Bulletin,* 20; and Merle Solway Schipper, *Jean Hélion: The Abstract Years, 1929–1939* (Ph.D. diss., University of California, Los Angeles, 1974), 74 and passim.

11— See George L. K. Morris, "Dialogues with Delaunay," *The Art News* 53 (Jan. 1955): 17, 18.

12— This booklet is now in the library of the Philadelphia Museum of Art, along with many other publications once owned by Gallatin. For a list, see the author's dissertation, vol. 3, appendix 4.

13— Jean Hélion, interviews by author, Paris, June 18 and 20, 1986; and by Isabelle Dervaux, Paris, November 21, 1986.

14— For more information, see the author's dissertation, 257–8, 274.

15— Ibid., 266–7. Xceron's *Composition*, 1934 was donated by Gallatin to the Berkshire Museum, Pittsfield, Mass.

16— Ibid., 279.

17— Dissertation, 286. For more on Shaw, see the Charles Shaw Papers, Archives of American Art, Smithsonian Institution; Buck Pennington, "The 'Floating World' in the Twenties: The Jazz Age and Charles Greene Shaw," *Archives of American Art Journal* 20 (1980): 17–24; and Susan E. Strickler and Elaine Gustafson, *The Second Wave: American Abstraction of the 1930s and 1940s, Selections from the Penny and Elton Yasuna Collection,* exh. cat. (Worcester Art Museum, 1992), 76.

18— Dissertation, 291–2; and Gail Stavitsky, "A Landmark Exhibition: Five Contemporary American Concretionists," *Archives of American Art Journal* 33, no. 2 (1993): 4–5.

19— Dissertation, 243–5, 283, 296–303 and Stavitsky, "A Landmark Exhibition," 4. For more on Morris, see Debra Bricker Balken and Deborah Menaker Rothschild, *Suzy Frelinghuysen & George L. K. Morris American Abstract Artists Aspects of Their Work and Collection,* exh. cat. (Williams College Museum of Art, 1992).

20— Stavitsky, "A Landmark Exhibition," 5–8. For more on Charles Biederman, see *Charles Biederman: A Retrospective,* exh. cat. (Minneapolis: Minn.: The Minneapolis Institute of Arts, 1976). On Ferren, see the John Ferren Papers, Archives of American Art; and Ann Gibson and Irving Sandler, *The Abstract Spirit John Ferren, 1905–1970* (East Hampton: Pollock Krasner Home and Study Center et al., 1993).

21— Ann H. Sayre, "New Exhibitions of the Week: Shaw, Calder, and other Concretionists," *The Art News* 34 (March 31, 1936): 9.

22— Stavitsky, "A Landmark Exhibition," 8.

23— Gaston Poulain, "Cinq Américains," *Beaux Arts/Comoedia* (June 20, 1936): 3, Shaw clipping file, Archives of American Art. For Gallatin's support of contemporary artists, see the review "Expositions et Livres: Biederman, Ferren, Gallatin, Morris, Shaw," *Cahiers d'Art* 8–10 (1936): 279.

24— For more on Gallatin as a painter, see Susan C. Larsen, "The Patron as Painter" in Debra Bricker Balken, *A. E. Gallatin and His Circle,* exh. cat. (Pittsfield, Mass.: The Berkshire Museum, 1986) 5–10; Douglas Dreishspoon, *New York Cubists: Works by A. E. Gallatin, George L. K. Morris, and Charles G. Shaw from the Thirties and Forties,* exh. cat. (New York: Hirschl & Adler Galleries, 1988); and Gail Stavitsky, "New York Cubists: Works by A. E. Gallatin, George L. K. Morris, and Charles Shaw," *Arts Magazine* 62 (April 1988): 82.

25— Bolotowsky acknowledged the concretionists in his interview with Ruth Gurin, November 5, 1963, 2 conducted by the Archives of American Art and another with Susan Larsen, January 29, 1973, cited in her dissertation "The American Abstract Artists Group: A History and Evaluation of Its Impact upon American Art' (Northwestern University, 1975): 491.

26— Hélion to Gallatin, April 24, 1936, Gallatin Papers, New York Historical Society (microfilm roll 508, frames 909–910, Archives of American Art. See also Dissertation, 267.

27— Dissertation, 273, 304–5 and PMA Bulletin, 28.

28— Pierre Descarques, "Domela ou l'équilibre du bonheur," interview in Musée d'Art Moderne de la Ville de Paris, *Domela 65 ans d'abstraction,* 1987, 248 (my translation). Domela reiterated this claim in an interview with the author, January 27, 1988.

29— Letter of July 13, 1936, Gallatin Papers, microfilm 1, frames 203–4.

30— Letter of August 22, 1936 from Domela, microfilm 1, frames 201–2. For Sophie Taeuber-Arp's involvement with planning *Plastique,* see her letters of October 2, 1937, August 13, 1939, and especially April 20, 1938 in which she included proposals for forthcoming issues. Microfilm 1, frames 20–25.

31— See Domela's letter, January 29, 1937, microfilm 1, frames 197–8.

32— As quoted in Melinda Lorenz, *George L. K. Morris, Artist and Critic* (Ann Arbor: UMI Research Press, 1982), 14.

33— "Arp and the *Abstraction Creation* Group: An Interview with Jean Hélion," in *Arp 1886–1966,* exh. cat. (Minneapolis: Minn.: The Minneapolis Institute of Arts, 1987), 174; See also Schipper, *Jean Hélion*, 221 and Dissertation, 272–4, 363–4.

34— Author's interview of June 18, 1986, 7–8.

35— George L. K. Morris, "Art Chronicle: Hans Arp," *Partisan Review* 6 (January 1938): 32.

36— A. E. Gallatin, "Abstract Painting and the Museum of Living Art," *Plastique* 3 (printemps 1938): 7–8.

37— Ibid., 8.

38— Ibid.

39— Ibid.

40— A. E. Gallatin, Introduction, *American Abstract Artists* (March 1938): n.p.

41— George L. K. Morris, "Art Chronicle: Interview with Jean Hélion," *Partisan Review* 4 (April 1938): 33–40.

42— Press Release, May 9, 1938, microfilm 1293, frame 713, Archives of American Art.

43— See Geoffrey Hellman, "Profiles: Medici on Washington Square," *The New Yorker* 16 (January 18, 1941): 32. For a complete list of Gallatin's one-man shows from 1936 to 1948, see *Paintings by Gallatin* (New York: Wittenborn, 1948), VI–VIII.

44— R[osamund] F[rost], Abstract, *The Art News* 41 (June–July 1942): 39.

45— Letter of January 28, 1943, Geoffrey T. Hellman Papers, microfilm 2814, frame 109, Archives of American Art.

46— A. E. Gallatin, "Encouraging Advanced Painting. Museum of Living Art Now Ten Years Old," *Pictures on Exhibit* 1 (January 1938): 16.

47— Geoffrey T. Hellman, "Abstract King," *The New Yorker*, 8 (May 9, 1942): 11.

48— Deborah Rosenthal, "What Gallatin Collected," *Arts Magazine* 53 (December 1978): 121.

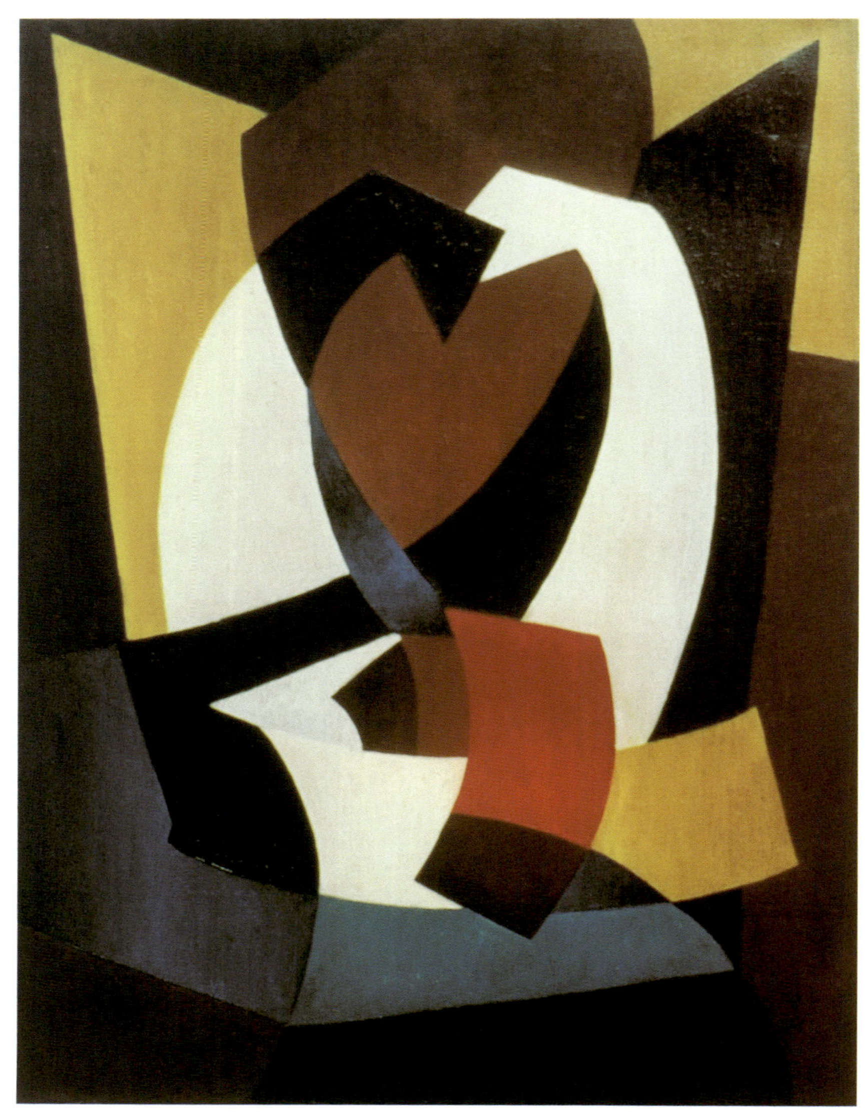

74
GEORGE L. K. MORRIS
COMPOSITION, 1936
OIL ON CANVAS, 66.7 X 51.1 CM
BERKSHIRE MUSEUM, PITTSFIELD, MASS., 1943.26.3
MAAG, TAM, TMAA

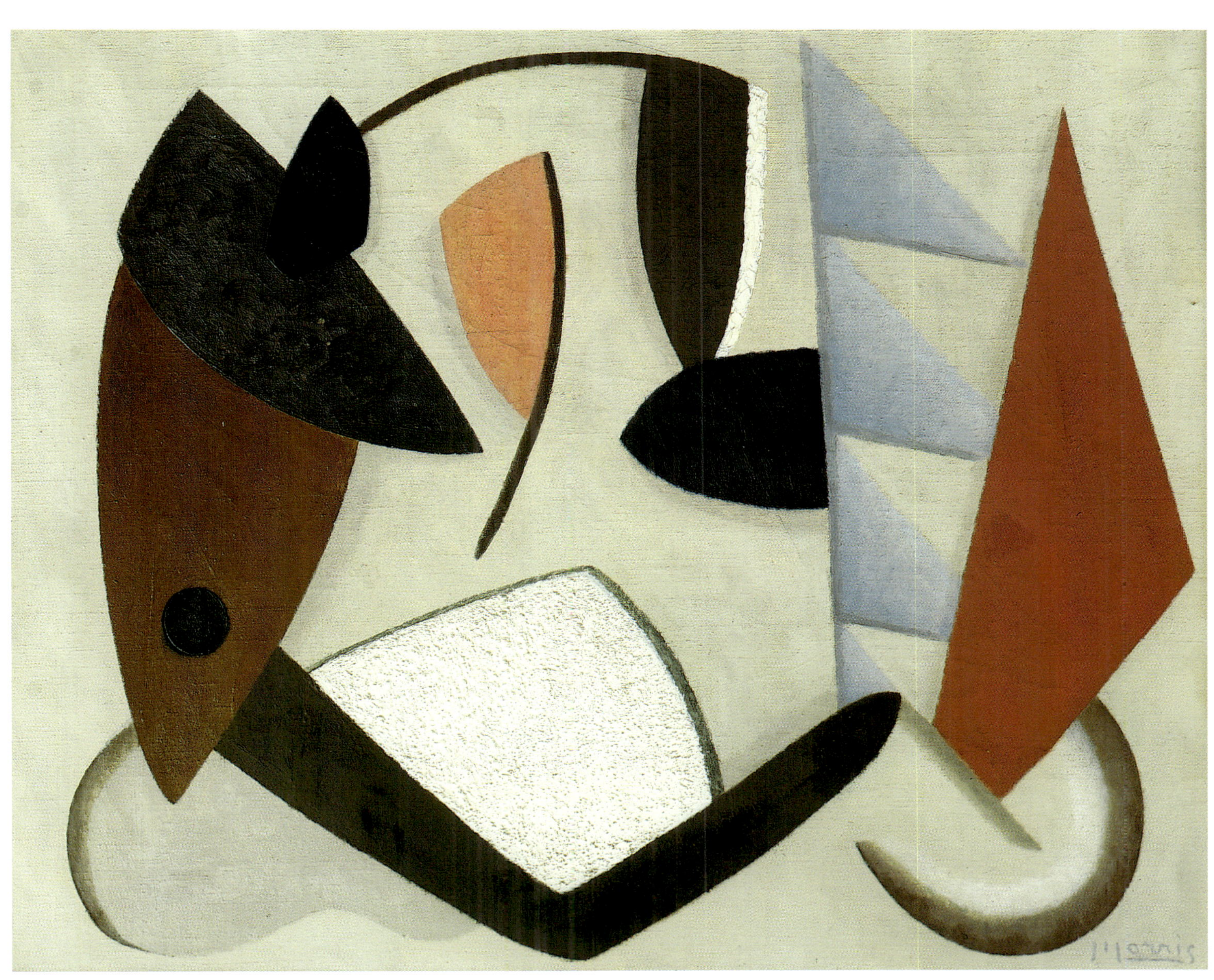

75
GEORGE L. K. MORRIS
NO. 5 (FORMS AND SPACE), 1938
OIL ON CANVAS, 48.3 X 61 CM
GEORGE L. K. MORRIS AND SUZY FRELINGHUYSEN
FOUNDATION.
COURTESY SALANDER O'REILLY GALLERIES,
NEW YORK
MAAG, TAM, TMAA

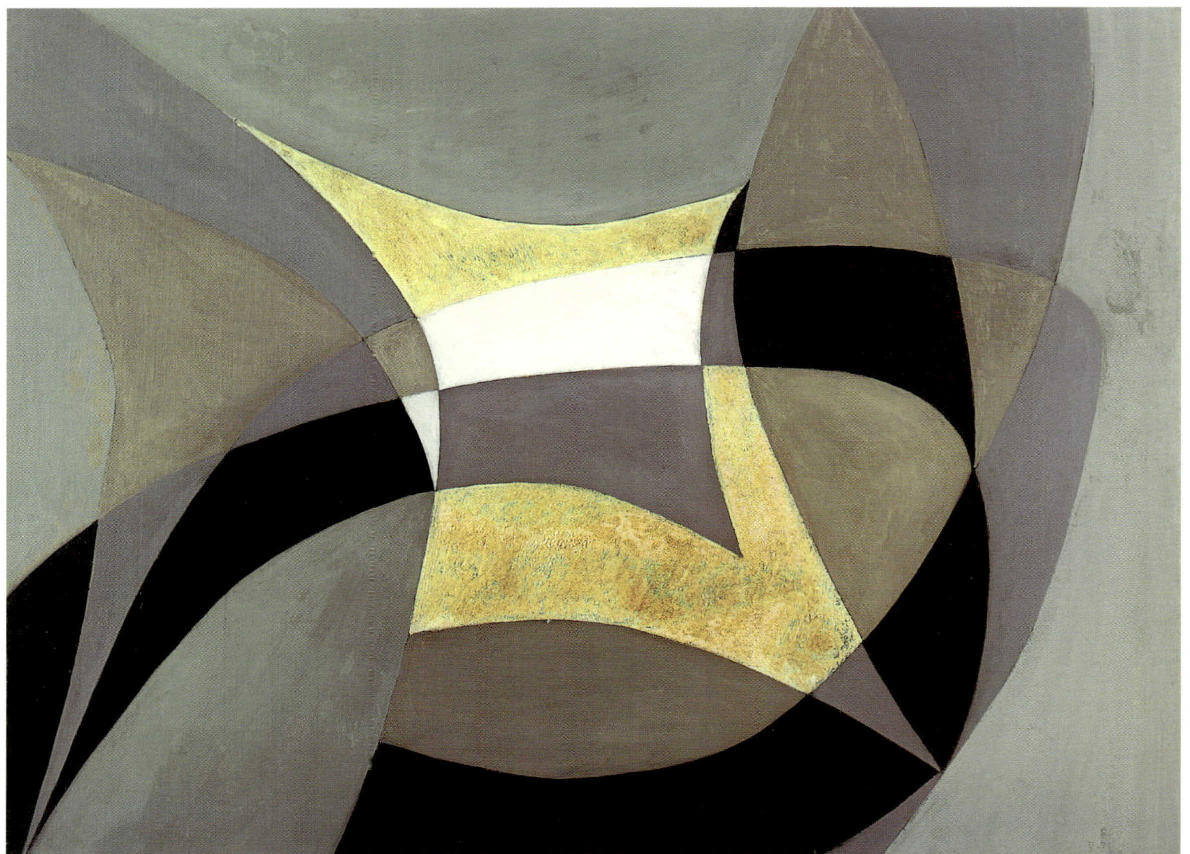

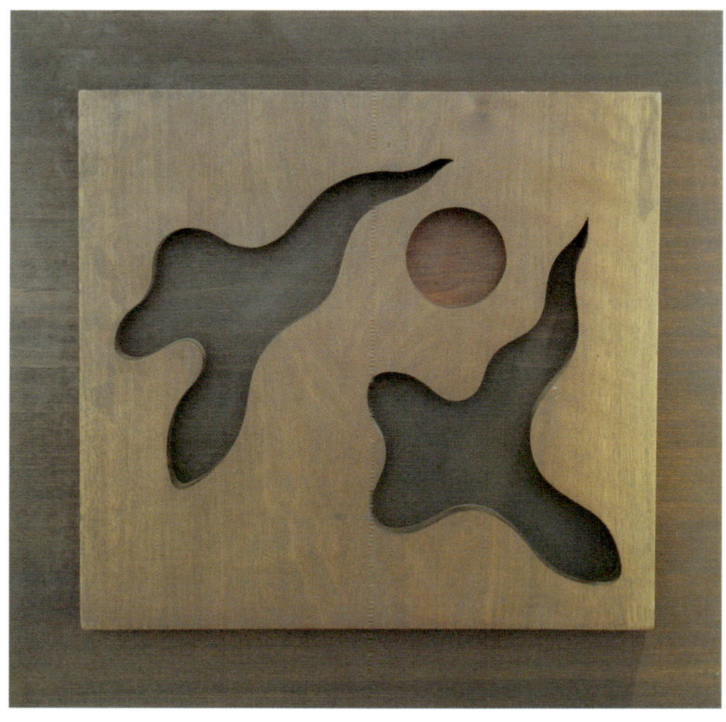

76
CHARLES SHAW
ABSTRACTION, 1935
OIL WITH SAND ON CANVAS, 55.8 X 76.2 CM
COURTESY SPANIERMAN GALLERY, NEW YORK
MAAG, TAM, TMAA

77
CHARLES SHAW
[UNTITLED], 1938
PICTURAL RELIEF, WOOD CARVING, WALNUT,
POLYCHROMY, 45 X 45.5 X 6 CM
MUSÉE NATIONAL DE LA COOPÉRATION FRANCO-
AMÉRICAINE, BLÉRANCOURT, MNBCFA 85.4
MAAG, TMAA

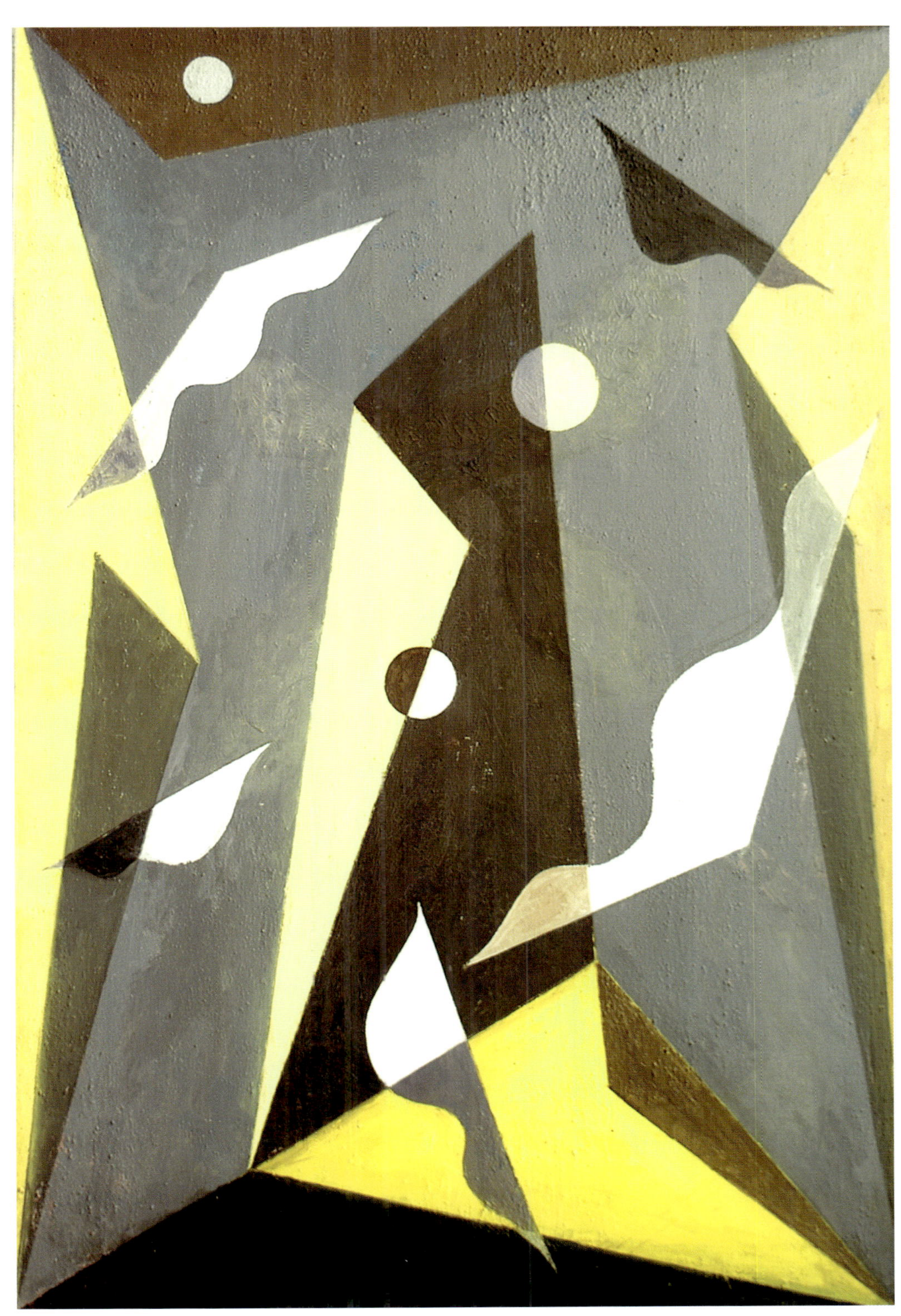

78
CHARLES SHAW
TEXTURED COMPOSITION, 1939
OIL WITH SAND ON CANVAS, 96.8 X 56.3 CM
COURTESY GARY SNYDER FINE ART, NEW YORK
MAAG, TAM, TMAA

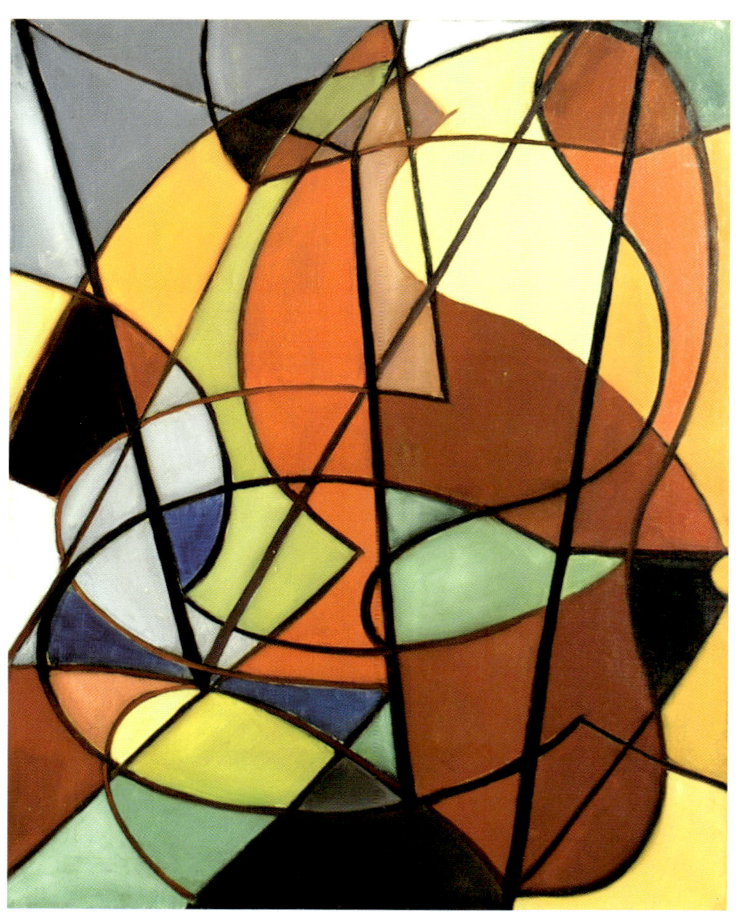

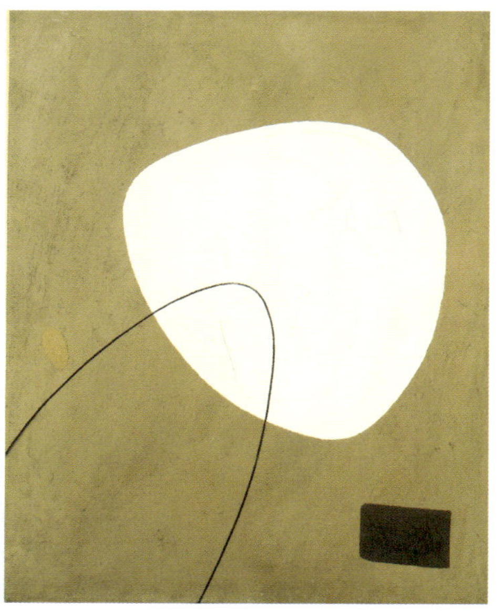

79
JOHN FERREN
UNTITLED (NO. 30), 1932
OIL ON CANVAS, 80.6 X 64.8 CM
COURTESY GARY SNYDER FINE ART, NEW YORK
MAAG, TAM, TMAA

80
JOHN FERREN
COMPOSITION AU GALET BLANC
[COMPOSITION WITH WHITE STONE], C. 1933–35
OIL ON CANVAS, 61 X 50 CM
MUSÉE NATIONAL DE LA COOPÉRATION
FRANCO-AMÉRICAINE, BLÉRANCOURT, MNBCFAC 86.6
MAAG, TMAA

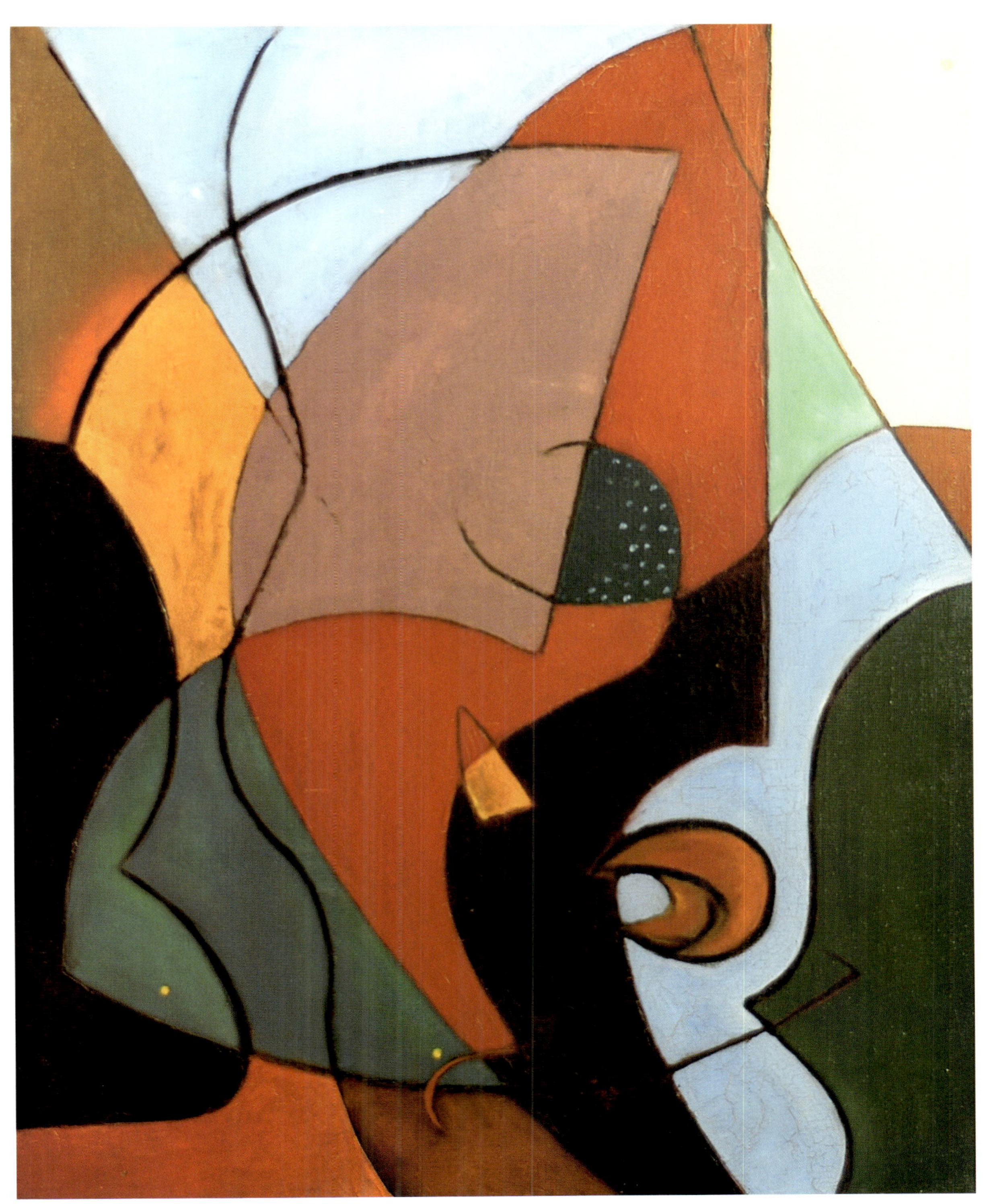

81
JOHN FERREN
UNTITLED (NO. 18), 1932
OIL ON CANVAS, 72.1 X 58.4 CM
COURTESY GARY SNYDER FINE ART, NEW YORK
MAAG, TAM, TMAA

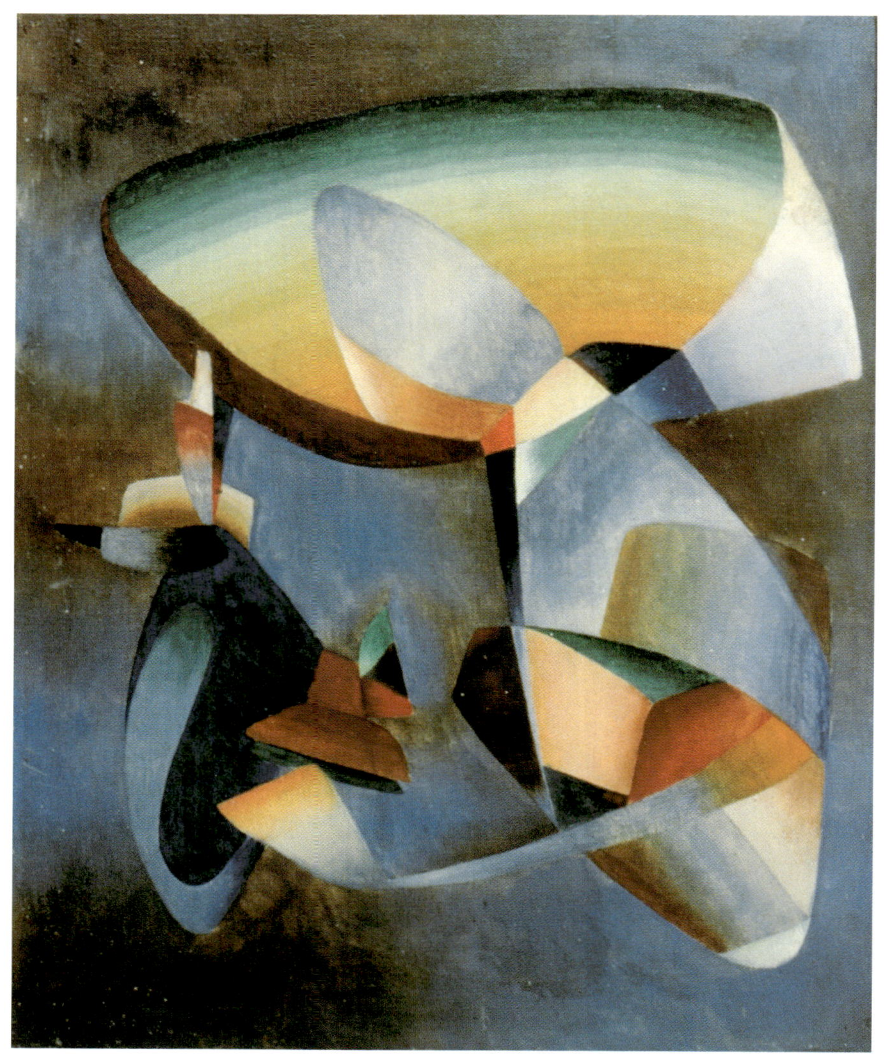

82

JOHN FERREN
COMPOSITION, 1936
OIL ON WALL BOARD, 33 X 27.3 CM
BERKSHIRE MUSEUM, PITTSFIELD, MASS., 1943.26.5
MAAG, TAM, TMAA

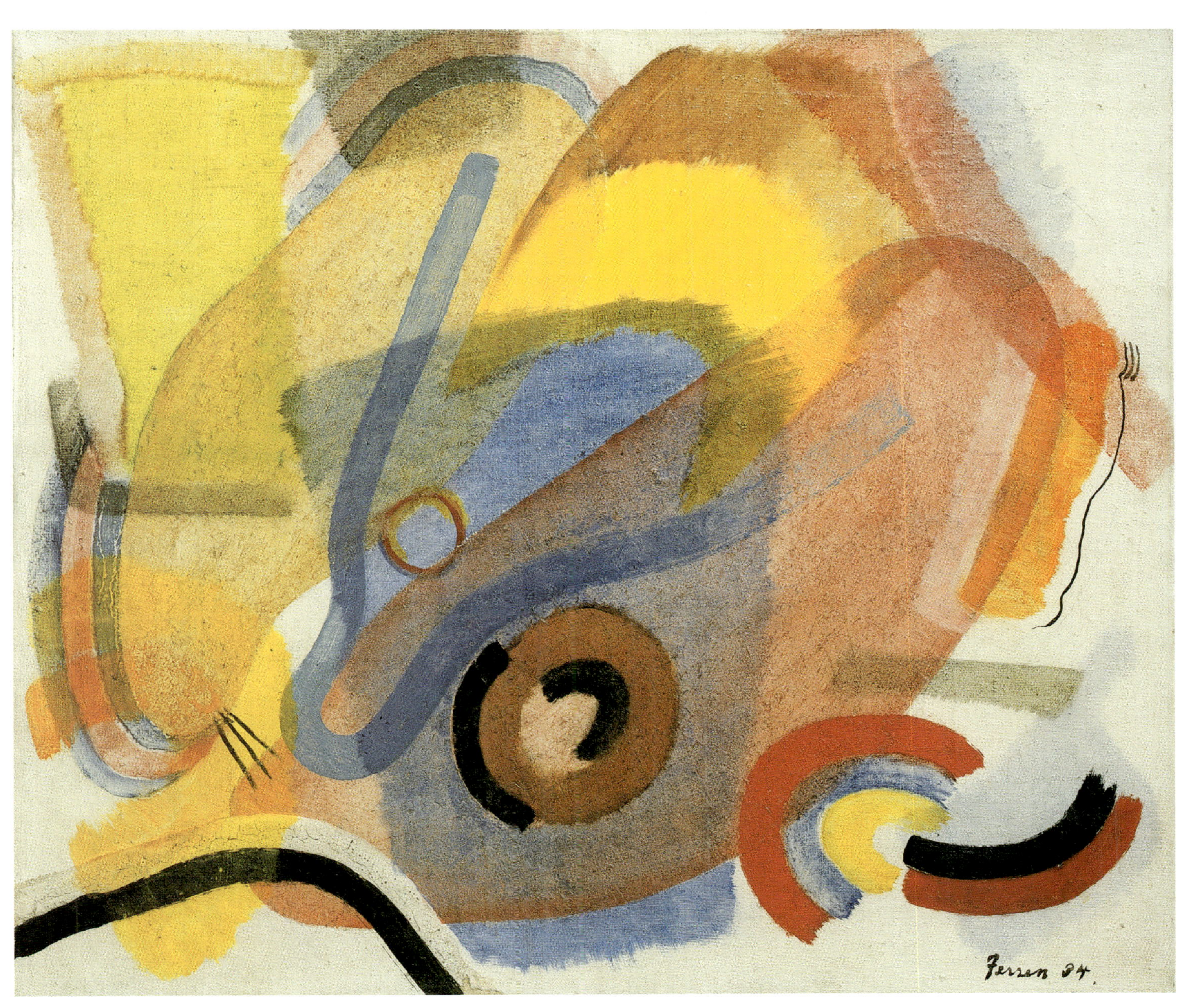

83

JOHN FERREN
COMPOSITION, 1934
OIL ON CANVAS, 46.4 X 54.9 CM
BERKSHIRE MUSEUM, PITTSFIELD, MASS., 1943.26.4
MAAG, TAM, TMAA

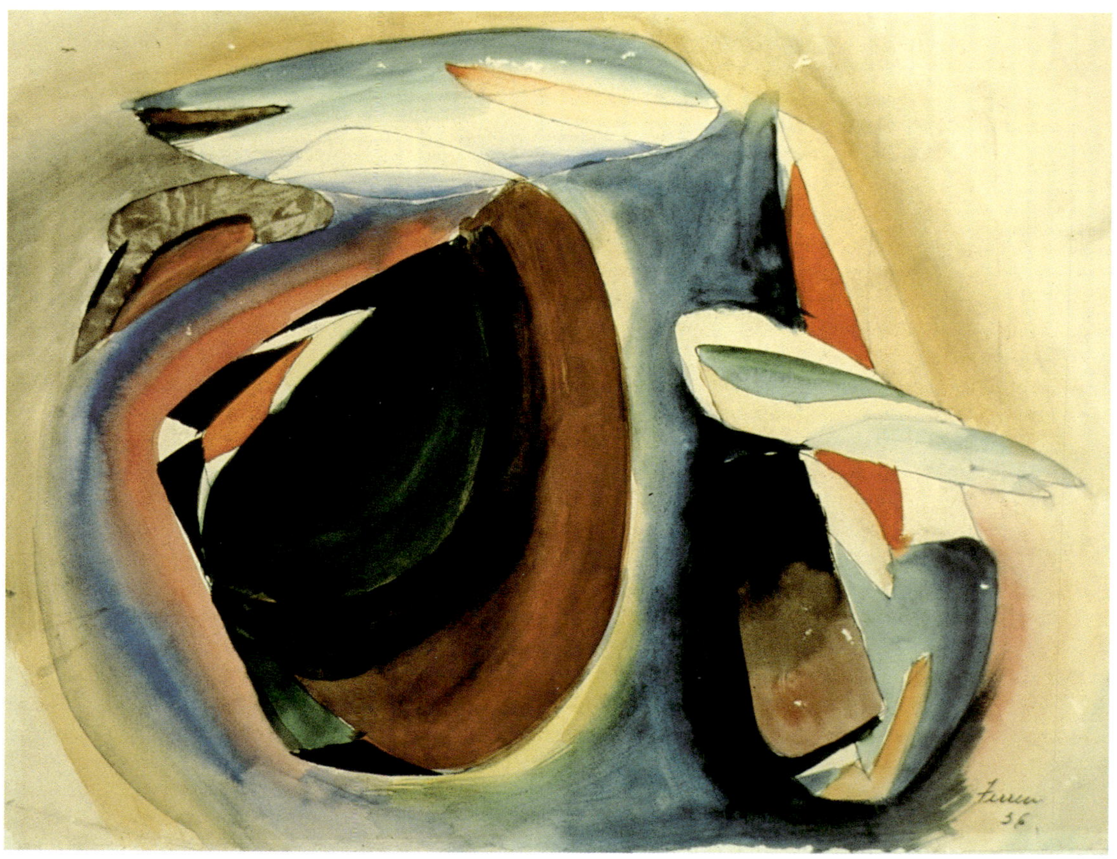

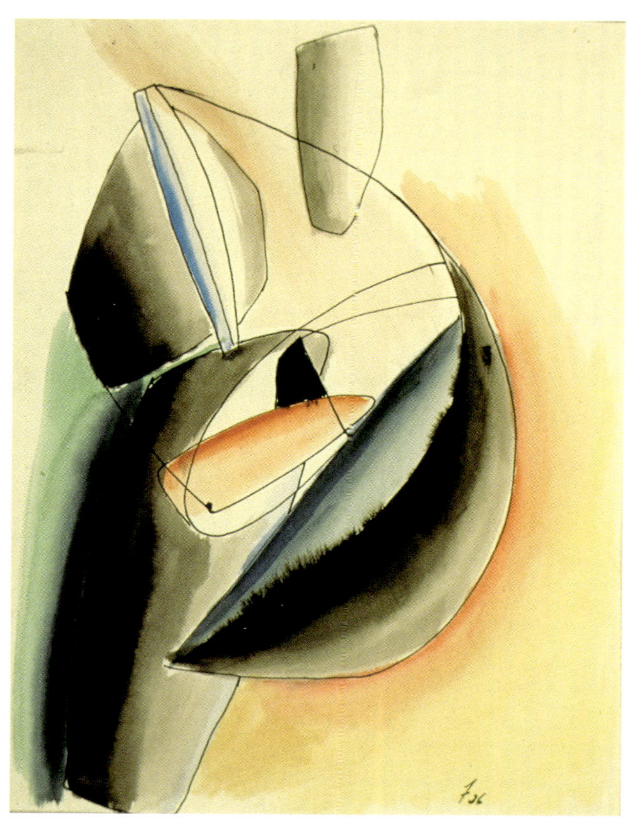

84
JOHN FERREN
JF 175 PARIS, 1936
WATERCOLOR ON BOARD, 33 X 42.6 CM
COURTESY KATHARINA RICH PERLOW GALLERY,
NEW YORK
MAAG, TAM, TMAA

85
JOHN FERREN
JF 199 PARIS, 1936
WATERCOLOR AND INK ON PAPER ON BOARD,
31.7 X 24.1 CM
COURTESY KATHARINA RICH PERLOW GALLERY,
NEW YORK
MAAG, TAM, TMAA

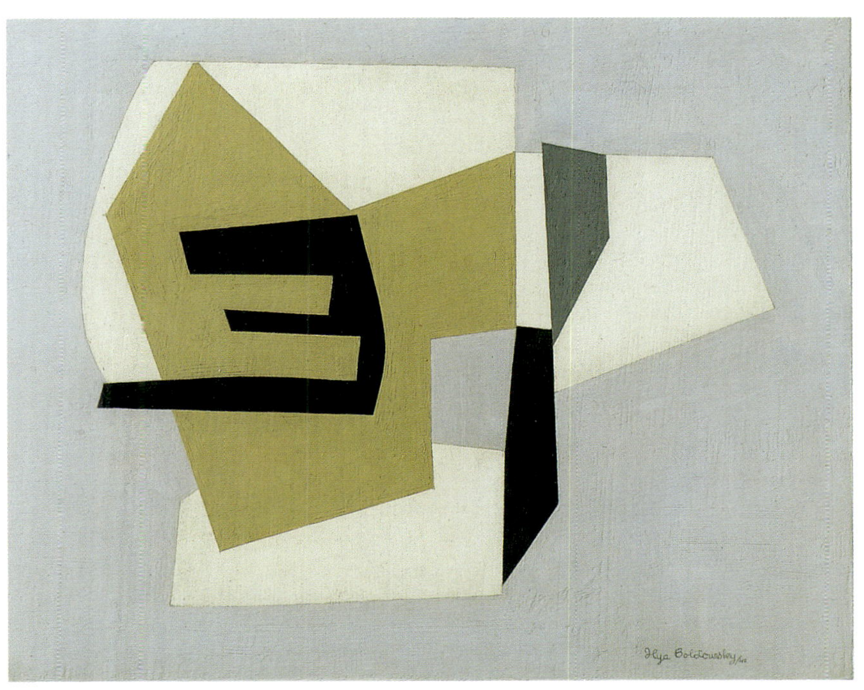

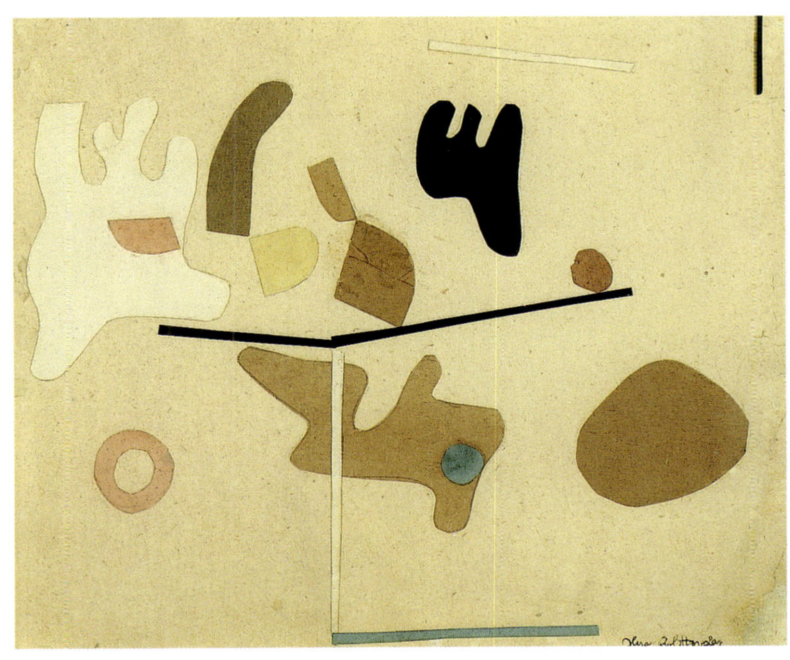

86
ILYA BOLOTOWSKY
ABSTRACTION IN LIGHT BLUE, 1940
OIL ON WOOD, 20.3 X 25.4 CM
PHILADELPHIA MUSEUM OF ART,
THE A. E. GALLATIN COLLECTION, 1946.70.7
MAAG, TAM, TMAA

87
ILYA BOLOTOWSKY
[UNTITLED], C. 1936
COLLAGE ON PAPER, 19.7 X 22.9 CM
GEORGIA DEHAVENON COLLECTION
MAAG, TAM, TMAA

"the chemists of mystery"

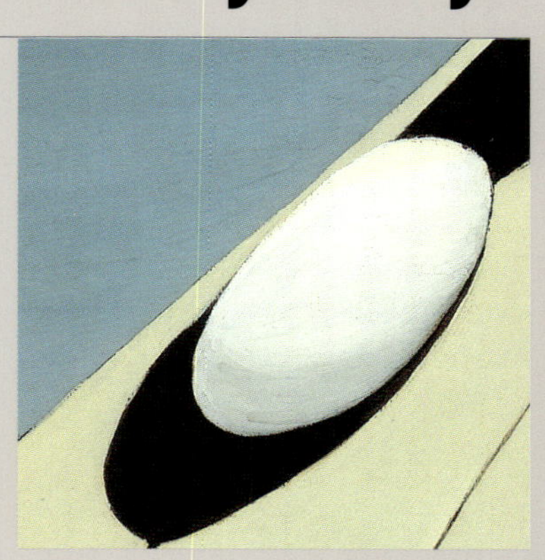

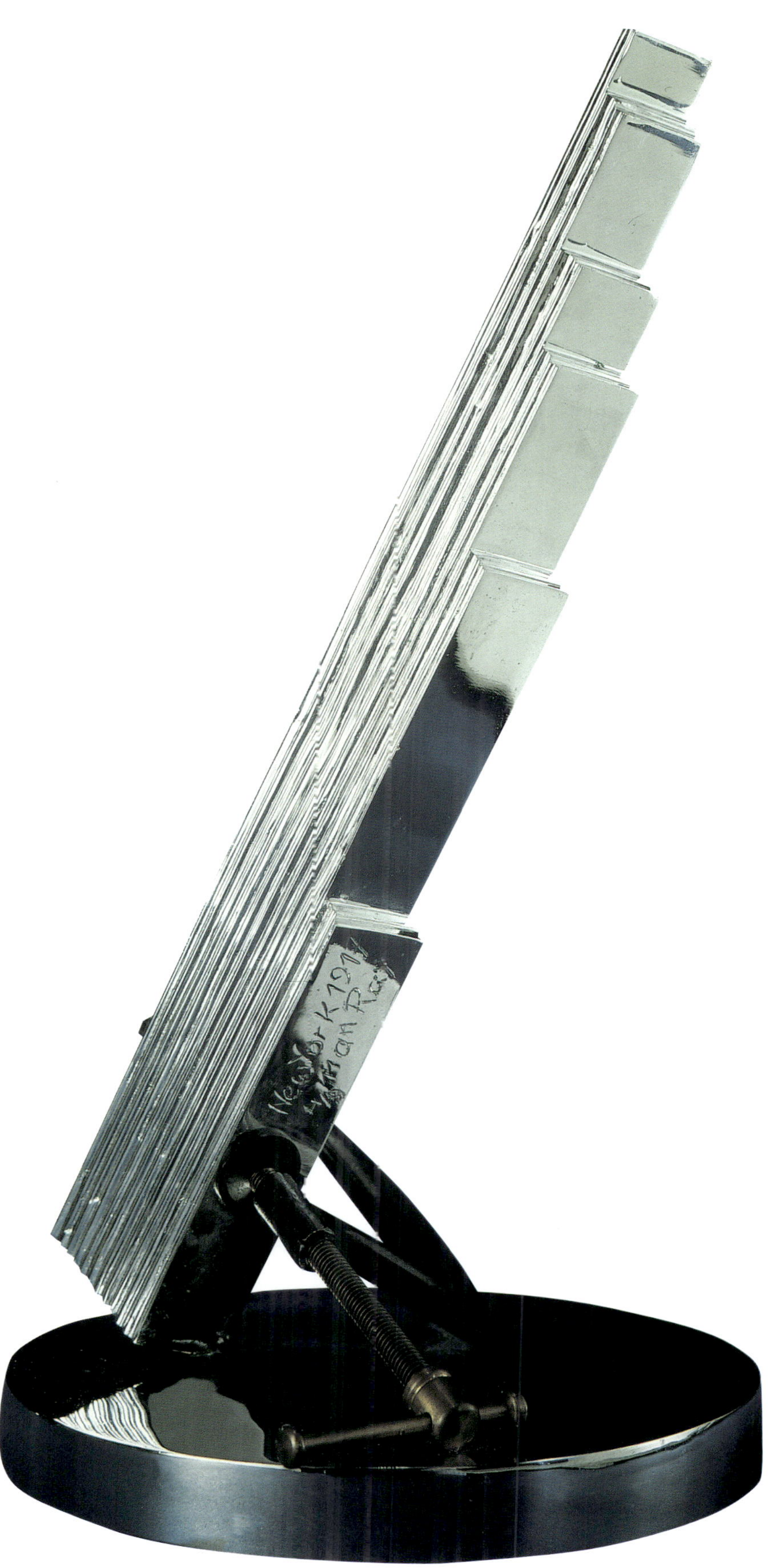

CHAPTER 3

88
MAN RAY
NEW YORK 17, 1917
CONSTRUCTION OF CHROME-PLATED BRONZE AND BRASS
AND PAINTED BRASS VISE, 44.1 X 23.5 X 23.4 CM
HIRSHHORN MUSEUM AND SCULPTURE GARDEN,
SMITHSONIAN INSTITUTION, WASHINGTON D.C.
GIFT OF JOSEPH H. HIRSHHORN, 1972.190
MAAG, TAM, TMAA

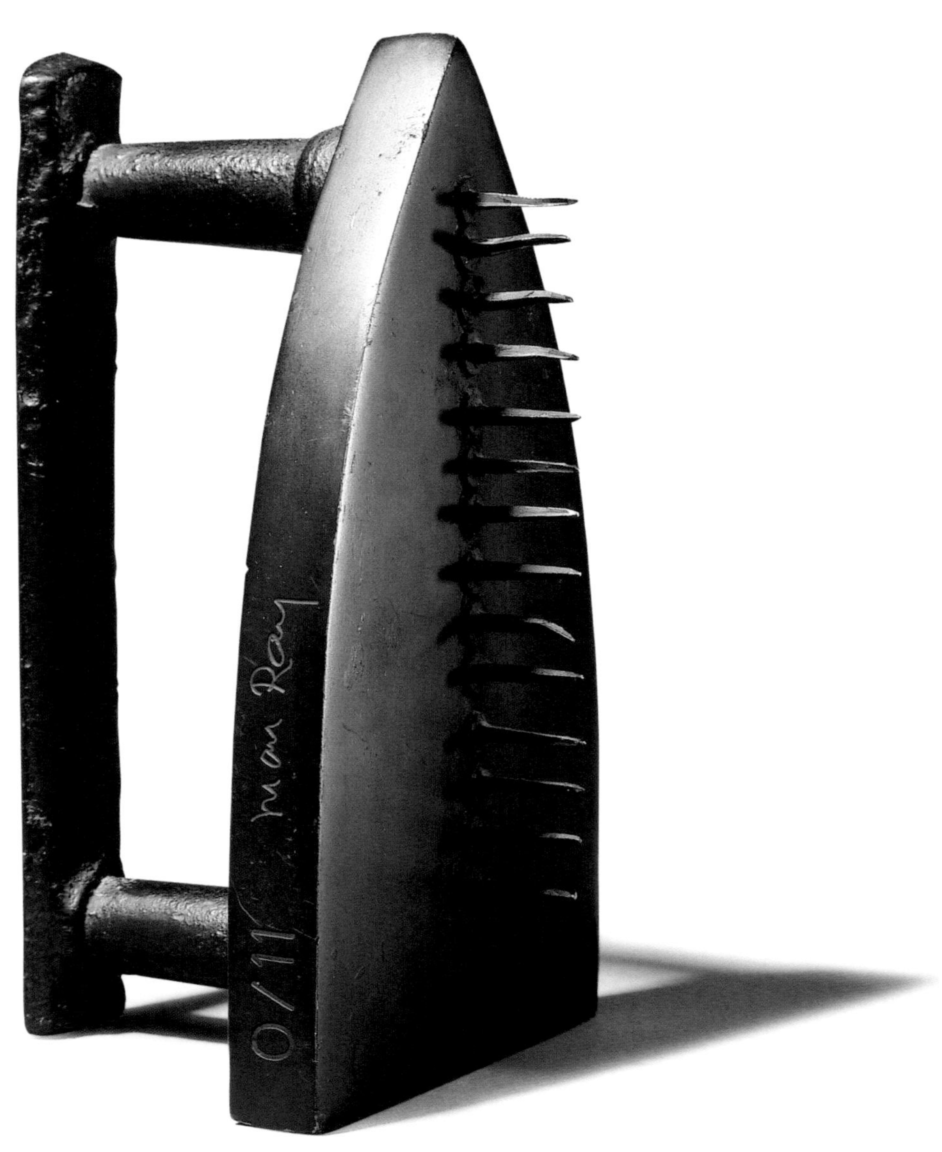

89
MAN RAY
CADEAU [GIFT], 1970 [1921]
IRON AND TACKS. H. 17.7 CM
GALERIE MARION MEYER, PARIS
MAAG, TAM, TMAA

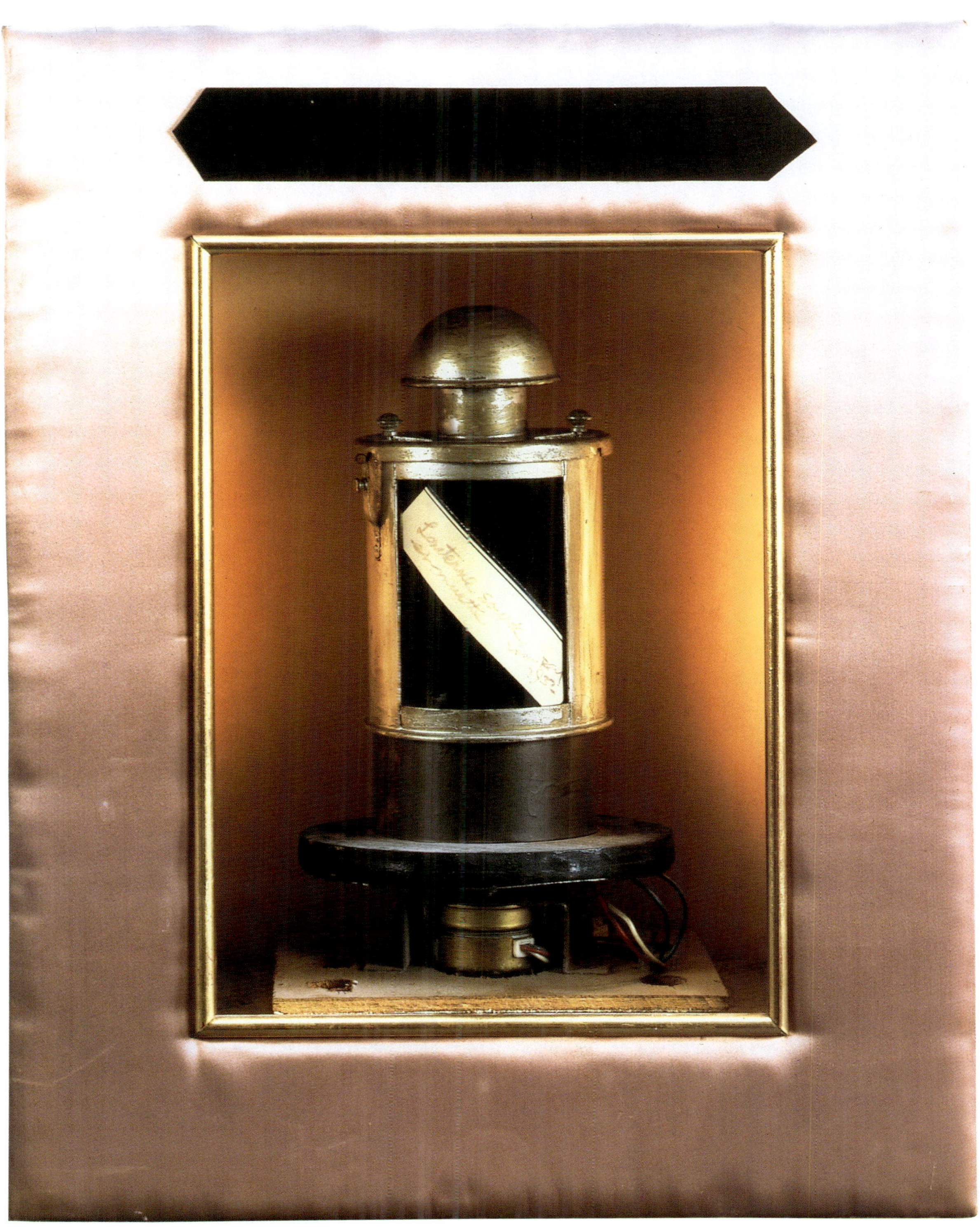

90

MAN RAY
LANTERNE SOURDE ET MUETTE
[DARK AND MUTE LANTERN], 1932
METAL AND GLASS LANTERN IN A SATIN-COVERED BOX.
49 X 39 X 15.5 CM
PRIVATE COLLECTION
MAAG

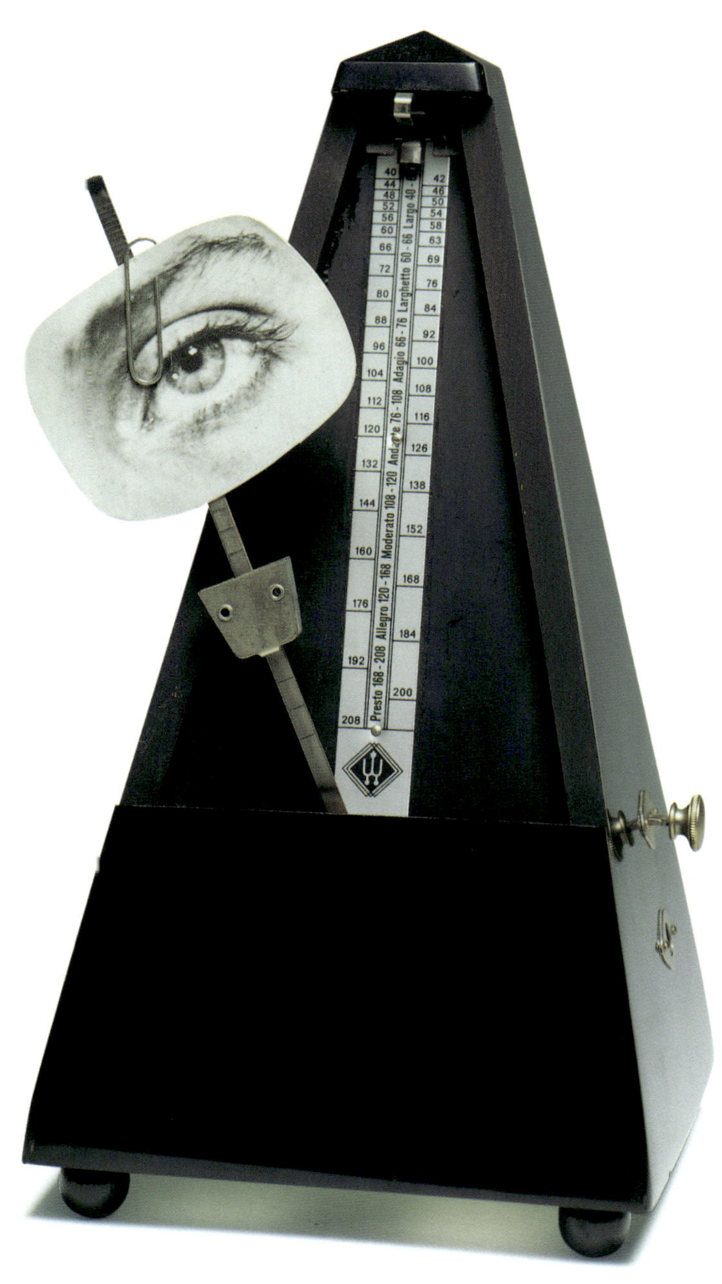

91
MAN RAY
INDESTRUCTIBLE OBJECT, 1970 [1958]
METRONOME AND PHOTOGRAPH, 23.5 X 11 CM
GALERIE MARION MEYER, PARIS
MAAG, TAM, TMAA

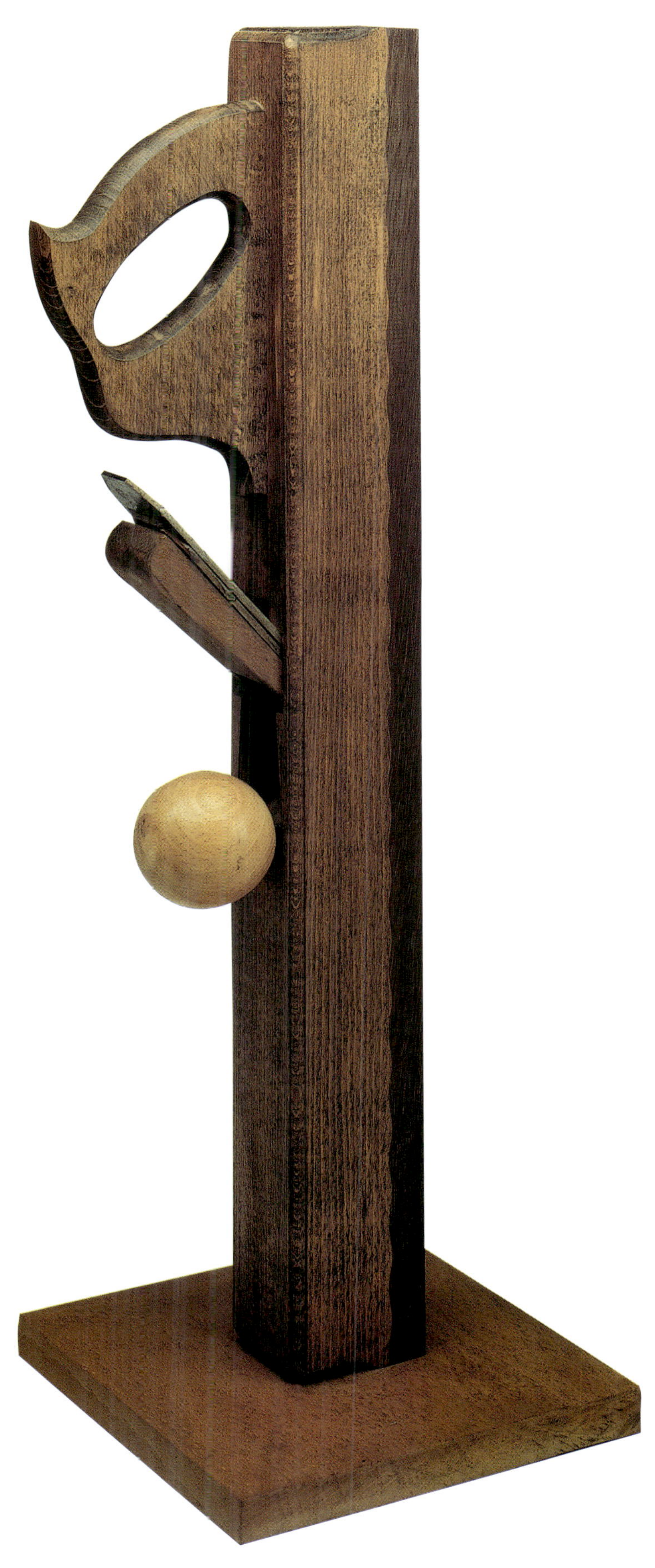

92
MAN RAY
VARLOP, 1935
WOOD, BRASS AND STEEL ON ARTIST'S BASE, 59 X 20 X 24.2 CM
HIRSHHORN MUSEUM AND SCULPTURE GARDEN,
SMITHSONIAN INSTITUTION,
WASHINGTON D.C. THE JOSEPH H. HIRSHHORN BEQUEST, 1986.3140
MAAG, TAM, TMAA

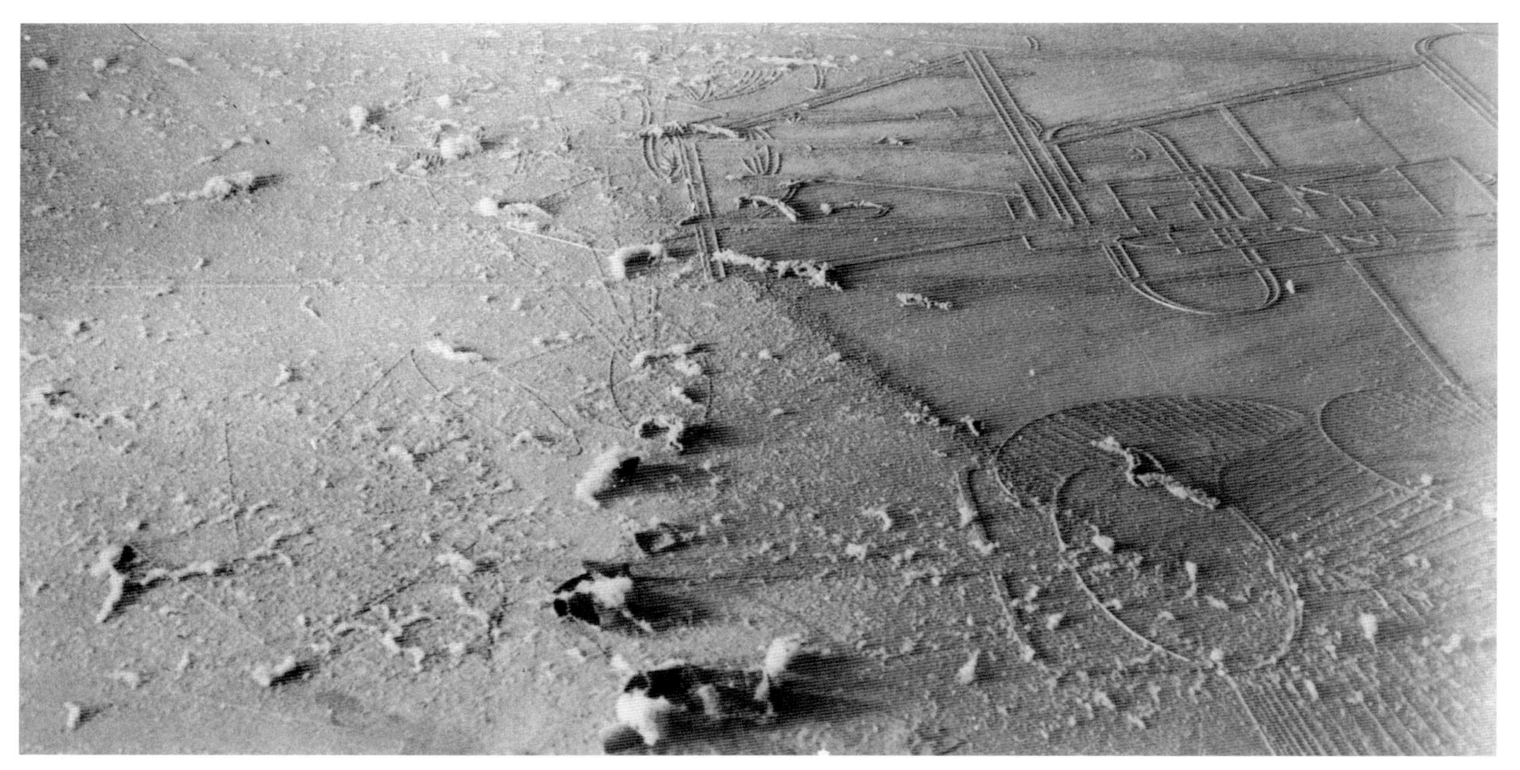

93
MAN RAY
ÉLEVAGE DE POUSSIÈRE [DUST BREEDING], 1920
MODERN PRINT, 21 X 37.5 CM
FONDS RÉGIONAL D'ART CONTEMPORAIN DE
BOURGOGNE, DIJON
MAAG, TAM, TMAA

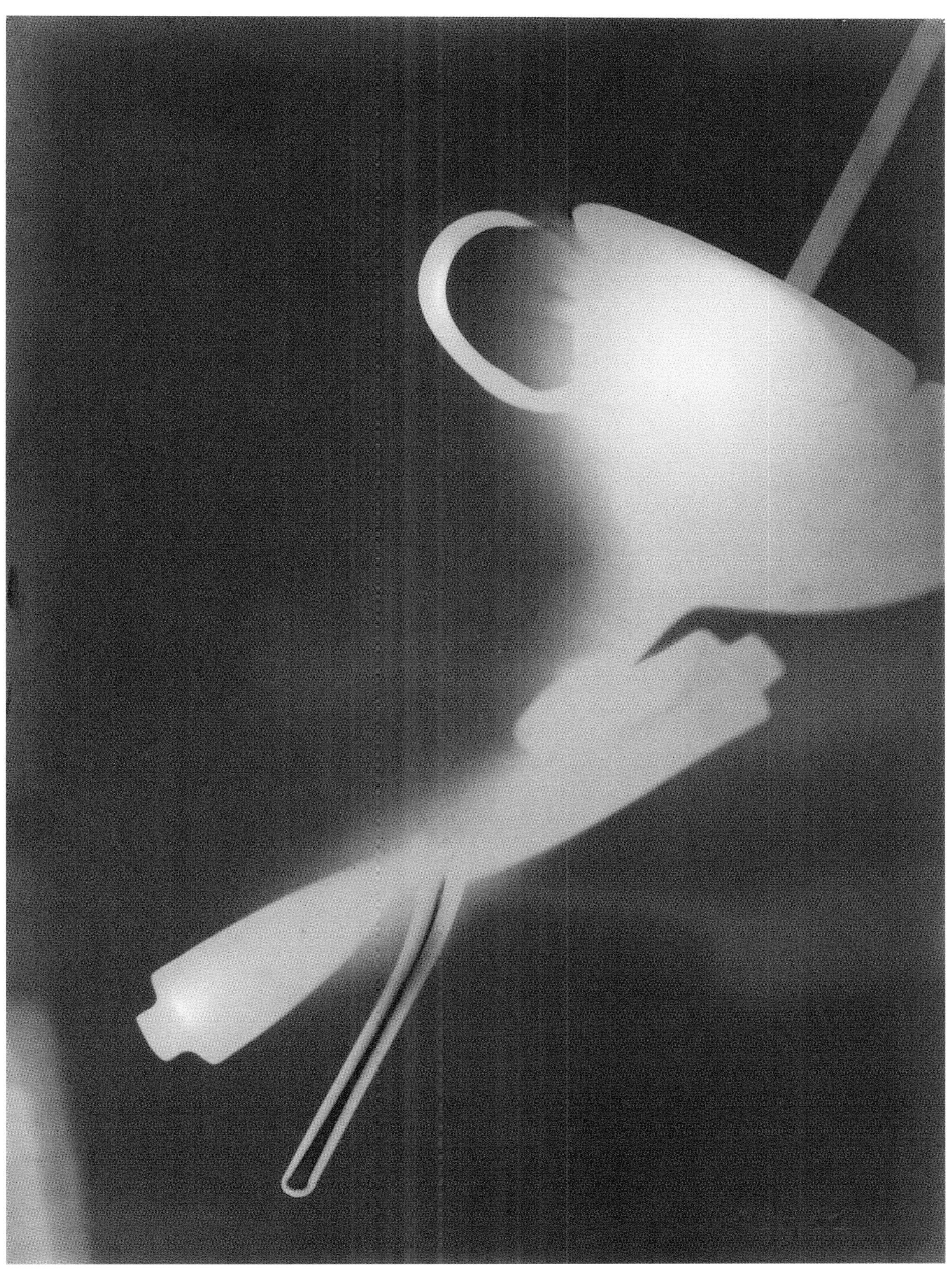

94
MAN RAY
RAYOGRAMME AVEC ENTONNOIR
[RAYOGRAPH WITH FUNNEL], 1922
RAYOGRAPH, 23.5 X 17.5 CM
MUSÉE DE L'ANCIEN ÉVÊCHÉ, ÉVREUX, 94.5.38
MAAG, TMAA

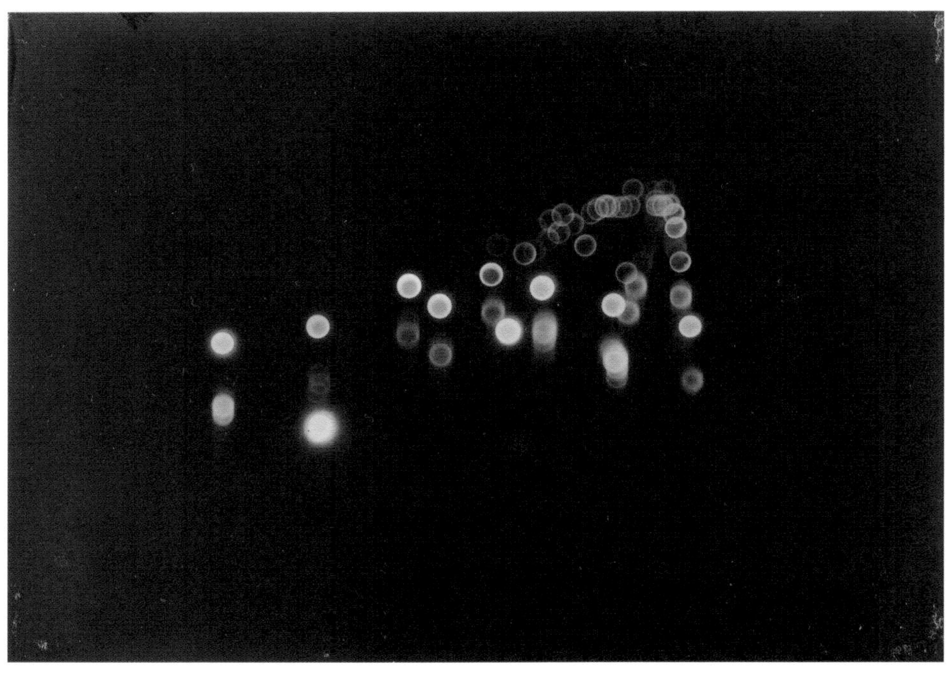

95
MAN RAY
BOULEVARD EDGAR-QUINET, 1924
GELATIN SILVER-BROMIDE PRINT, 7.7 X 11.1 CM
MUSÉE CARNAVALET, PARIS, PH 3502
MAAG

MAN RAY:
AN AMERICAN IN PARIS

EMMANUELLE DE **L'ÉCOTAIS**

> *New York has just given us an amorous finger that should soon tickle the susceptibilities of French artists. Let's hope the tickle will further score the already notorious wound that epitomizes art's tight slumber.*[1]
>
> Tristan Tzara

During his years in Paris (1921–1940), Man Ray produced the most interesting part of his oeuvre. It was there that he developed his highly original art, and there that his work made the greatest impact. At that time Paris was a very important center for art—the dada movement launched in Zurich in 1916, had shifted to the French capital once Tristan Tzara moved there. So New-York-based Man Ray, following the total flop of *New York Dada,* the publication he founded with Marcel Duchamp, viewed Paris as the promised land. Duchamp invited him accross the Atlantic, and introduced him to all the people who would have a crucial influence on the development of his work and career.

On the evening of July 22, 1921, Man Ray met the whole dada group: André Breton, Jacques Rigaut, Louis Aragon, Paul Eluard and his wife Gala, Théodore Fraenkel, and Philippe Soupault. To his surprise, none were painters, rather all were poets or writers. Breton, who edited the review *Littérature,* immediately realized that Man Ray might be useful as a photographer. Man Ray soon became indispensable to Breton, who regularly dispatched him to artists' studios to photograph the works he wished to reproduce. Man Ray profited from this task in two ways: he would take advantage of every photo session by making a portrait of the artist in question, and also asked Breton, who offered him no payment, to publish his own work in the magazine. Man Ray's reputation as a portraitist—his study of Berenice Abbott had been awarded a prize at Philadelphia's Fifteenth Annual Exhibition of Photographs in March 1921— when combined with "word-of-mouth" publicity, functioned so effectively that in no time at all Man Ray had met all the Parisian celebrities of the day, each of whom brought him other clients. Gertrude Stein introduced him to Pablo Picasso and Georges Braque; Jean Cocteau brought along an affluent aristocracy in search of an original portrait

photographer. As one thing led to another, Man Ray's studio became a place of pilgrimage for foreigners in Paris. Since portraits of high society ladies often served as fashion illustrations in the 1920s, Man Ray was brought into contact with Paul Poiret, the fashion designer, and in 1924, he began working regularly for *Vogue*. At the same time, Man Ray managed to publish his art photography in *Littérature, Les Feuilles libres, The Little Review,* and even *Vanity Fair*, furthering his success.

One of the factors in his success was certainly his discovery of the rayograph method early in 1922. Later Man Ray would champion photographic techniques such as superimposition and solarization, both of which valorized creative photography at the expense of the pure photography then practiced in Paris. Unlike other photographers of his day, who wanted to vaunt "Modern Man" through the use of modern techniques stripped of any special effects, Man Ray used photography just like any other artistic medium—he would crop, retouch, print in negative, flip and invert images. He even made photographs without a camera. In short, Man Ray invented surrealist photography.

The technique commonly called "photogram" or "rayograph" involves the technique of placing objects directly onto photosensitive paper and exposing them to light for a few seconds. If the paper is then developed normally, the black-and-white values of the resulting image are reversed. Man Ray claimed to have discovered this technique by accident while developing some fashion photographs for Paul Poiret. But his account, however entertaining, is not convincing—Man Ray always displayed an obvious desire to disguise his creative process. For him, the important thing was not the technique employed but the final work produced. He even claimed that "a certain contempt for the physical means of expressing an idea is essential for producing it best."[2] His anecdote concerning the discovery of this method is therefore of little import. Meanwhile, we know that Tristan Tzara, a close friend of Man Ray's at the time, owned a collection of works by Christian Schad, who had been part of the dada group in Zurich and who had been inspired by the early photography of Fox Talbot.[3] "Schadographs" were

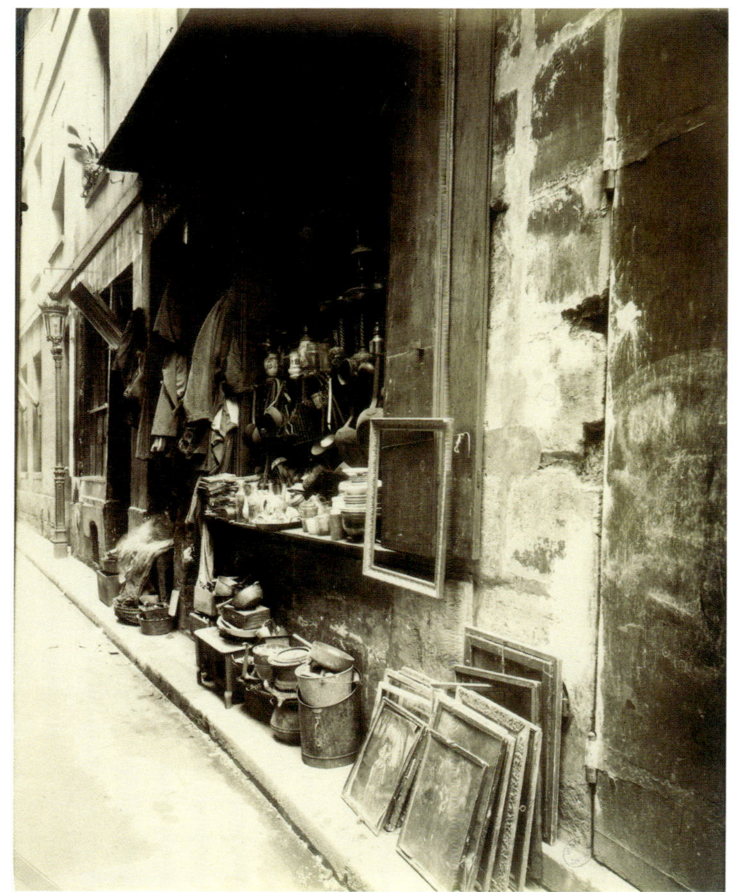

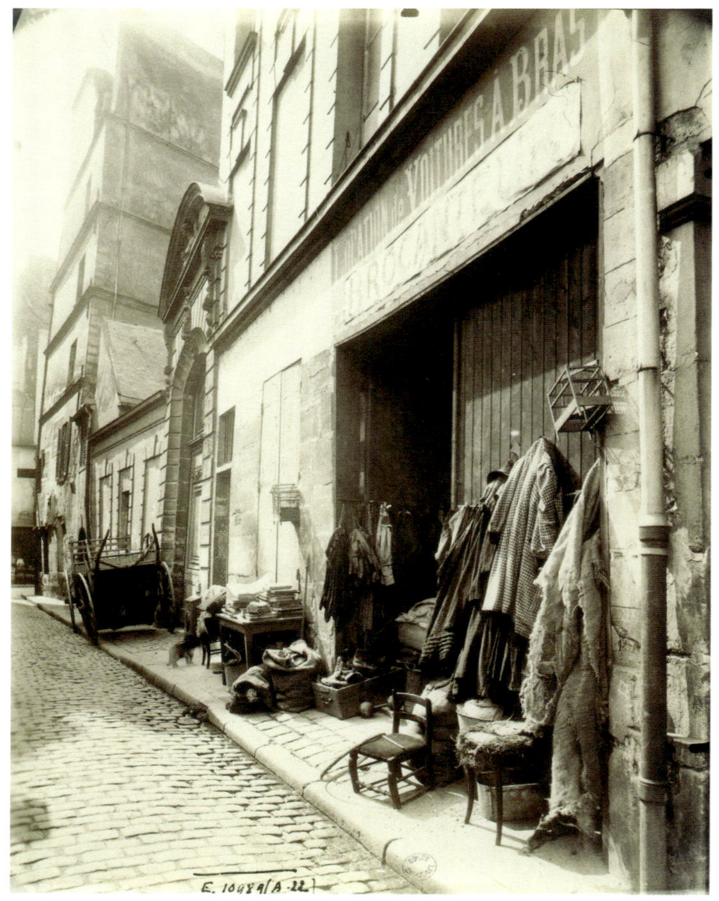

96

EUGÈNE ATGET
BROCANTEUR, RUE DE LA REYNIE [ANTIQUE STORE], 1908
ALBUMEN PRINT, 22.3 X 17.5 CM
MUSÉE CARNAVALET, PARIS, PH 3762
MAAG, TAM

97

EUGÈNE ATGET
UN COIN, RUE SAINT-JULIEN-LE-PAUVRE, 1910–11
ALBUMEN PRINT, 22.1 X 17.7 CM
MUSÉE CARNAVALET, PARIS, PH 3714
MAAG, TAM

made on paper that darkened in direct sunlight and was not highly sensitive, whereas Man Ray worked in the dark room, so that his rayographs could be observed only after the paper was developed and fixed. The main reason behind Man Ray's approach probably had to do with its possibilities for modifying the intensity and direction of the light source. Furthermore, Schad placed only cut-out paper shapes or flat forms on the photosensitive paper, yielding images similar to cubist collages, whereas Man Ray used all kinds of three-dimensional objects, sometimes made of glass, whose translucency and shadows created a varying range of gray values. The presence of Schadographs in his friend's collection may suggest that Man Ray did not "discover" the technique by chance, as he claimed, but instead was inspired by Schad's experiments to forge a new mode of expression.

Man Ray's own experiments in the dark room stemmed from his earlier explorations—in pictures made back in New York, he had already demonstrated a concern to express the life of objects in a "tangible" way, via photography, revealing their independence and their ability to mean something other than their original purpose. *La Femme* (fig. 1), for example, shows a simple eggbeater above the title (Woman). Rayographs proceeded from the same principle, namely putting a new appearance on things. The objects that Man Ray placed on the photosensitive paper often remain recognizable even though transformed and transported into a strange world. It is precisely this relationship—this dialectic between the known and the unknown—that opens the mind to another reality.

Rayographs were the first photographic prints to be accorded the status of art. As Man Ray explained in his *Self-Portrait,* he "was trying to do with photography what painters were doing, but with light and chemicals instead of pigment, and without the optical help of the camera."[4] Rayographs proved that photography, contrary to popular belief, was not simply a record or reproduction, but could also be creative and inventive, giving birth to images that sprang from the imagination, from an artist's inspiration and considerations.

In early 1922, rayographs were viewed as works of pure dada. The title of his album of twelve rayographs, *Les Champs délicieux* (Charming fields, fig. 2) was heavily inspired by the title of a 1920 text by Breton and Soupault, *Les Champs magnétiques* (Magnetic fields). Since that text was later considered by Breton himself to be the first surrealist text, rayographs have often been considered, analogously, as the first surrealist artworks. The technical method behind rayographs offered a parallel to Breton and Soupault's automatic writing in *Les Champs magnétiques*—in 1921, Breton argued that "automatic writing, which appeared in the late nineteenth century, is a true photograph of the mind."[5]

Other photographic techniques, namely superimposition and solarization, would bring fame to Man Ray and would further link him to the surrealist movement. The superimposition involves stacking two

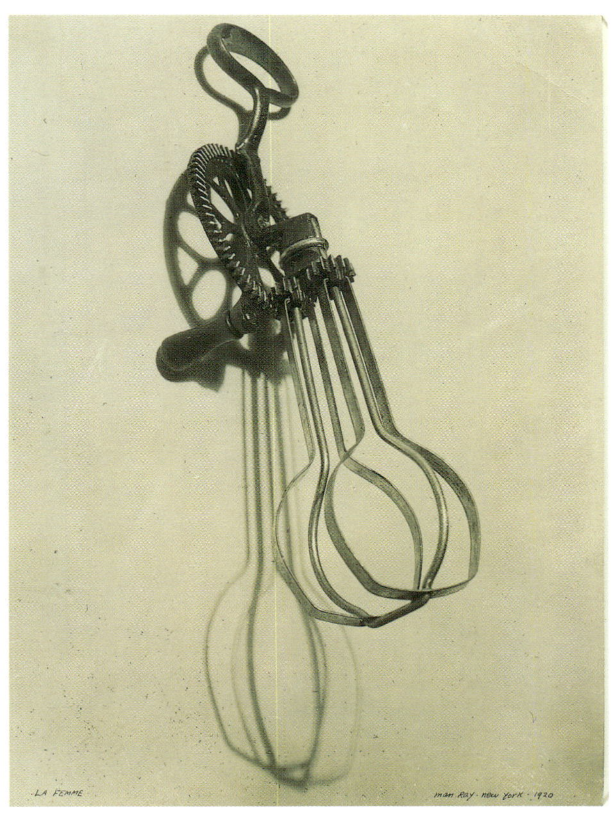

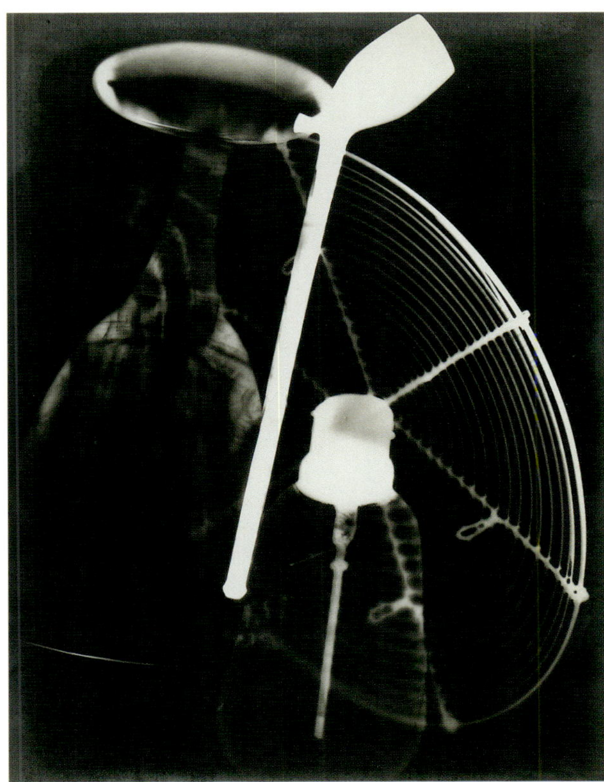

FIG. 1.
MAN RAY,
LA FEMME [THE WOMAN], 1920.
GELATIN SILVER PRINT, 38.3 × 29.1 CM.
MUSÉE NATIONAL D'ART MODERNE –
CENTRE GEORGES POMPIDOU, PARIS.

FIG. 2.
MAN RAY,
LES CHAMPS DÉLICIEUX [CHARMING FIELDS], 1922.
RAYOGRAPH, 22.1 × 17.3 CM.
MUSÉE NATIONAL D'ART MODERNE –
CENTRE GEORGES POMPIDOU, PARIS.

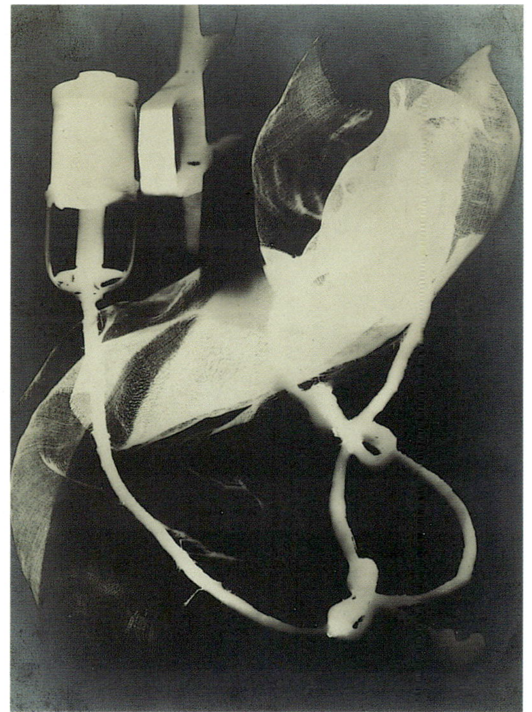

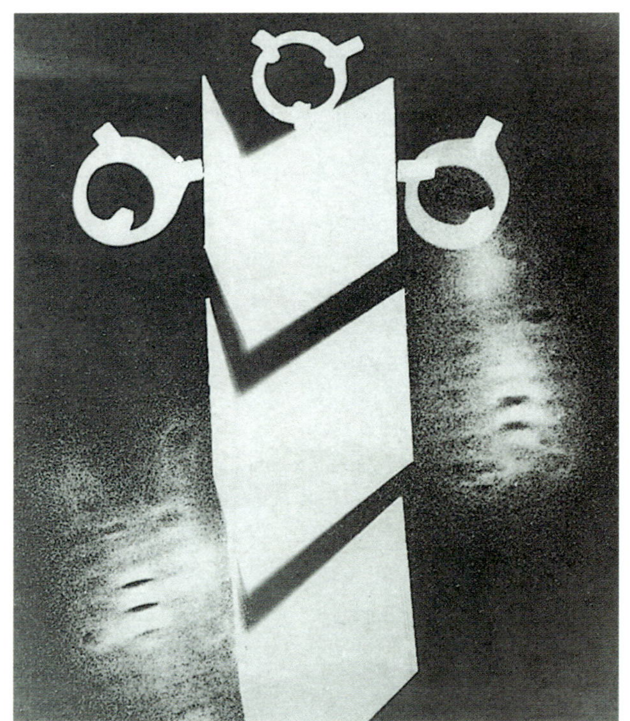

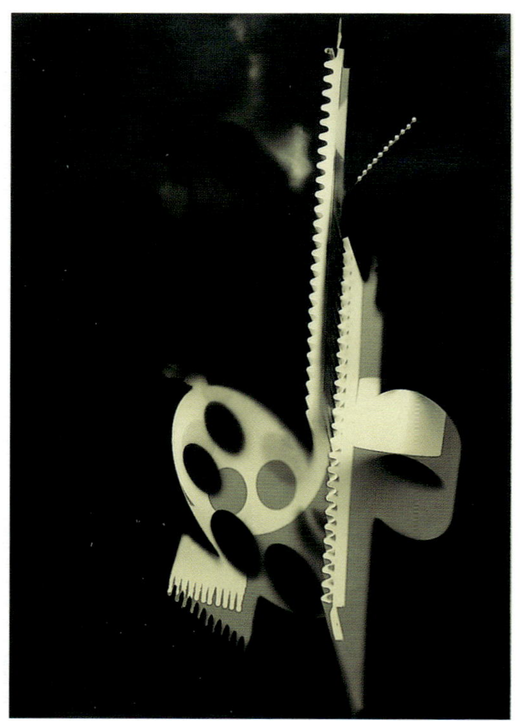

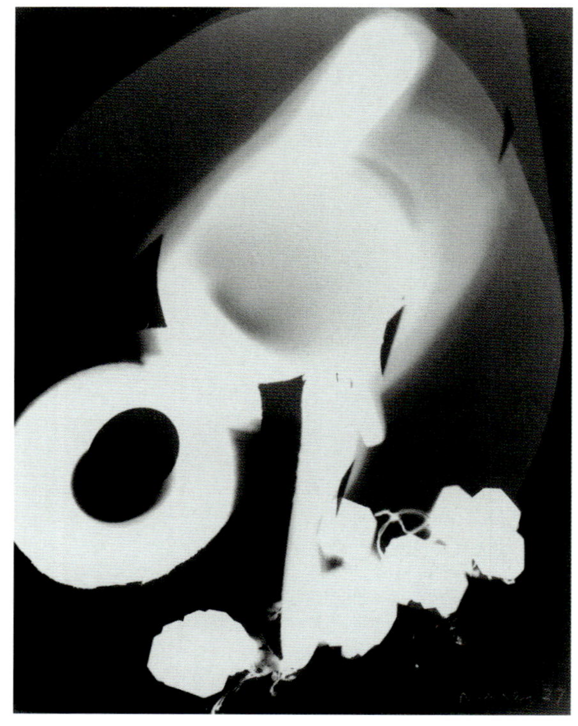

98
MAN RAY
LES CHAMPS DÉLICIEUX
(LE DÉCLENCHEUR RETARDATEUR)
[CHARMING FIELDS], 1922
RAYOGRAPH, 22.1 X 16.8 CM
KICKEN GALLERY, BERLIN
MAAG, TAM, TMAA

100
MAN RAY
RAYOGRAPH, 1925
RAYOGRAPH, 38.7 X 26 CM
HALLMARK CARDS, KANSAS CITY,
MISS. HALLMARK PHOTOGRAPHIC
COLLECTION
MAAG, TAM, TMAA

99
MAN RAY
[UNTITLED], 1924
RAYOGRAPH, 29.5 X 23.6 CM
PRIVATE COLLECTION. COURTESY
GALERIE FRANÇOISE PAVIOT, PARIS
MAAG, TAM, TMAA

101
MAN RAY
RAYOGRAPH, 1927
RAYOGRAPH, 50.8 X 61 CM
LIBRARY OF CONGRESS,
WASHINGTON D.C. PRINTS AND
PHOTOGRAPHS DIVISION,
PH– RAY, M. NO. 8
TMAA

negatives in the enlarger to make a single print. This technique makes it possible to retranscribe a movement or scene, or to juxtapose two elements in order to give them special meaning, as for instance in the case of a portrait of *Tristan Tzara* (fig. 3).

Although Man Ray used superimposition a great deal, it was thanks more to solarization that he earned a reputation as one of the greatest photographers in Paris. Technically, solarization is defined as the partial reversal of values in a photograph, accompanied by characteristic edge-lines. Obtained by briefly turning on the lights during development, it had been previously known as a darkroom occurrence called the Sabattier Effect. Man Ray mastered the technique by 1929, and used it for a great number of portraits, nudes (fig. 4), and fashion photos. These pictures met with instant success, because the effect he obtained seemed striking and astonishing at the time, apparently rendering "auras" visible. The occult sciences held that an aura was visible only to initiates. Unlike the surrealists, Man Ray was not an adept of the occult, yet this technique was part of the reason he was labeled a surrealist photographer.

It is nevertheless important to stress that the development of Man Ray's photographic art was not due to surrealism, as is often stated, but rather that surrealism's photographic development was due to Man Ray. Indeed, even while still part of the dada movement, Man Ray was providing a poetic vision of objects, demonstrating one of surrealism's favorite concepts. Still a dada artist, he approached the photographic medium as a creative art detached from reality, a tool granted complete freedom, whose documentary function could even become a source of jokes (*Rrose Sélavy,* fig. 5). Using an instrument that supposedly provided a faithful reproduction of nature, Man Ray was already photographing phantasmagorical landscapes as early as 1920—*Voici le domaine de Rrose Sélavy,* also known as *Élevage de poussière* [Dust Breeding], seems to have been conceived as a straightforward record of part of Duchamp's *Bride Stripped Bare by Her Bachelors Even* (or *Large Glass*). In his autobiography, Man Ray explained that he had asked Duchamp for permission to take the photo: "It would be good practice for me, in preparation for the work I was to do for Miss Dreier."[6] The work in question entailed illustrations of artworks for the publications of the Société Anonyme. The fact that Man Ray and Duchamp both signed this image, and that the photograph was included as part of Duchamp's *Green Box,* confirms the fact that *Élevage de poussière* was above all a photographic record of the development of the *Large Glass.* This picture was first published in 1922, in issue 5 of *Littérature,* but did not yet bear the title by which it is known today (according to Man Ray, *Élevage de poussière* was applied much later by Duchamp). Instead, it was labeled "Voici le domaine de Rrose Sélavy . . . ," which could be interpreted as "This is the estate of Rrose Sélavy / How arid it is — how fertile it is / How joyous it is — how sad it is!" And it was signed, "Taken from an airplane by Man Ran."[7] The image, its title, and the signature that lent an acrobatic feel to the technical execution

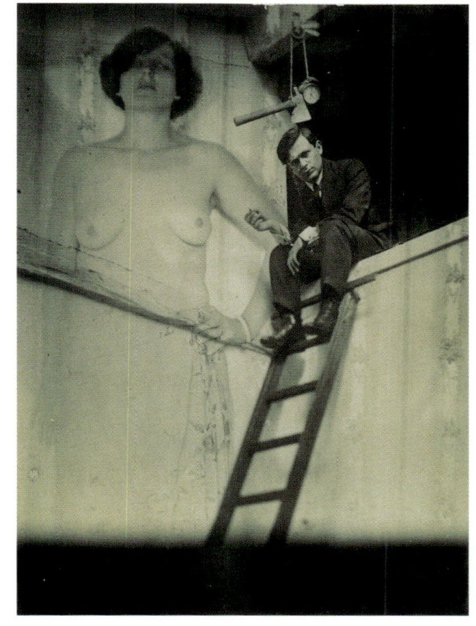

FIG. 3.
MAN RAY,
TRISTAN TZARA, 1921.
GELATIN SILVER PRINT.
MUSÉE NATIONAL D'ART
MODERNE – CENTRE
GEORGES POMPIDOU, PARIS.

FIG. 4.
MAN RAY,
[UNTITLED]. ILLUSTRATION
FOR *FACILE* OF PAUL ELUARD,
1935.
GELATIN SILVER PRINT,
24 X 18.1 CM.
MUSÉE NATIONAL D'ART
MODERNE – CENTRE
GEORGES POMPIDOU, PARIS.

FIG. 5.
MAN RAY,
*MARCEL DUCHAMP AS RROSE
SÉLAVY*, C. 1920–21.
GELATIN SILVER PRINT,
20.9 X 17.3 CM.
PHILADELPHIA MUSEUM OF
ART. THE SAMUEL S. WHITE 3RD
AND VERA WHITE
COLLECTION, 57.49.1.

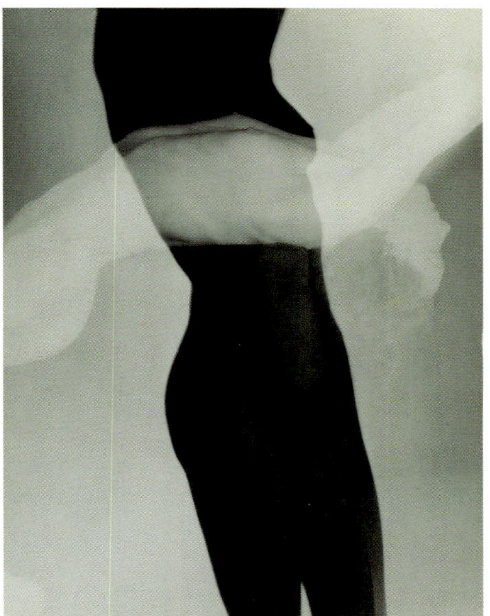

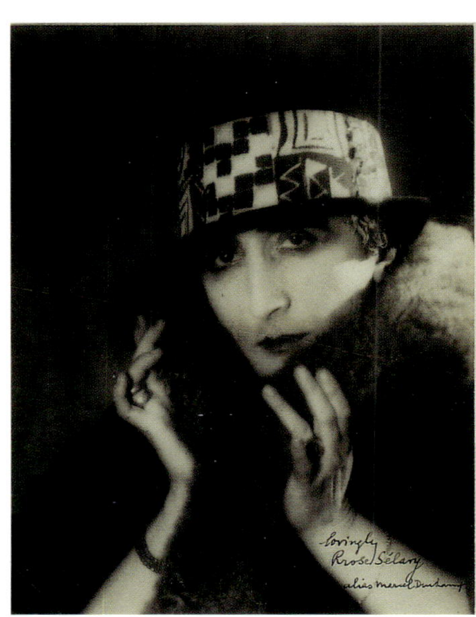

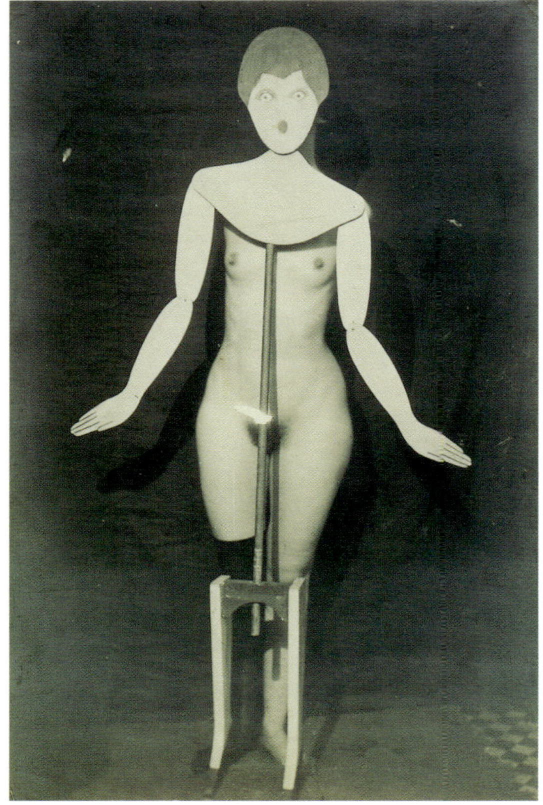

FIG. 6.
MAN RAY,
COAT STAND, 1920.
GELATIN SILVER PRINT,
40.4 X 26.9 CM.
MUSÉE NATIONAL D'ART
MODERNE – CENTRE
GEORGES POMPIDOU,
PARIS.

FIG. 7.
MAN RAY,
MOVING SCULPTURE,
1920.
GELATIN SILVER PRINT.

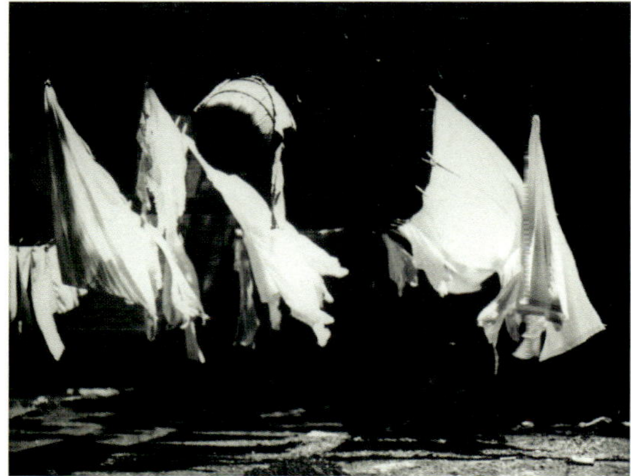

all deceived viewers, to whom the geometric pattern beneath the dust appeared to be the borders of the fields of an "estate" owned by Rrose Sélavy. Breton wrote a letter to Man Ray with a request: "Rather than taking the Duchamp photo ('Voici le domaine de R. S.') out of its frame, I would be grateful if you would provide a new print, for which I will naturally pay you."[8] What started out as good practice for Man Ray and the record of a work-in-progress thereby became an autonomous work of art: Man Ray framed it and Breton was ready to pay for a print of it.

Finally, as early as 1920 Man Ray was producing images in which eroticism and transformation were already patent. While Rosalind Krauss has noted the importance of *Head, New York* for what Georges Bataille, followed by the surrealist photographers, would later call *informe* (formlessness), it should be stressed here that the picture dates from 1920. Surrealism was not born—officially—until four years later.

In fact, Man Ray was not only the sole photographer to make the shift from dada to surrealism, he was also the first photographer identified with the surrealist movement, to the extent of being the only one in that position for nearly five years. Indeed, which photographers are usually considered surrealist? Hans Bellmer, of course, but between 1920 and 1923 he was working in a steel plant and a coal mine. Jacques-André Boiffard, meanwhile, was still a medical student in 1920 and, although he was already reading the poets who would later be hailed as the forerunners of surrealism, he did not meet Breton until 1924. Boiffard was certainly close to the surrealism right from the start, but he only began studying photography—*under Man Ray*—in the years 1924 to 1929. As to Brassaï, he only arrived in Paris in 1924 and only became interested in photography from 1930 onward. Max Ernst, on the other hand, was producing dada photo-collages by 1920, and would exhibit his works at Breton's request in 1921. Ernst's contribution to surrealism nevertheless rests primarily on his paintings. André Kertész was linked to surrealism for a while, notably thanks to his *Distortions,* 1929; his links to the movement are nevertheless debatable, and the surrealists "falsified" his photographs when using them for their publications, for example by giving the title *Garage* to a picture of a hearse standing alone in a courtyard.[9] Dora Maar only participated in the movement very briefly, in 1934. E. L. T. Mesens was primarily a musician, and only showed interest in the visual arts in 1921, his first photomontages dating from 1924. Paul Nougé was above all a theorist. The few pictures he took date primarily from the years 1929–30. Roger Parry studied photography under Maurice Tabard only after 1927. Tabard had begun taking photographs in 1916, but only became associated with surrealism in 1928, following his return to Paris after spending fourteen years in the United States. As to Raoul Ubac, he did not discover surrealism until 1929, and not until 1933 did he abandon painting for photography.

Therefore, the only surrealist photographer who was clearly present from the start was Man Ray. Far from being an "amateur," he had already produced striking pictures in New York, such as *Coat Stand* (fig. 6), *Man, Integration of Shadows,* and *Moving Sculpture* (fig. 7). A work such as *Head, New York* sometimes passes for a surrealist photo even though surrealism did not yet exist in the year it was taken, 1920. The pictures published in the movement's first periodical, *La Révolution surréaliste,* were almost exclusively by Man Ray. The few other photographs used were mostly images found in flea markets or taken from popular or scholarly reviews, and were therefore anonymous. On the cover of every issue appeared the credit: "Illustrations: Photos Man Ray." What is more, when Max Morise attempted to define surrealist visual art

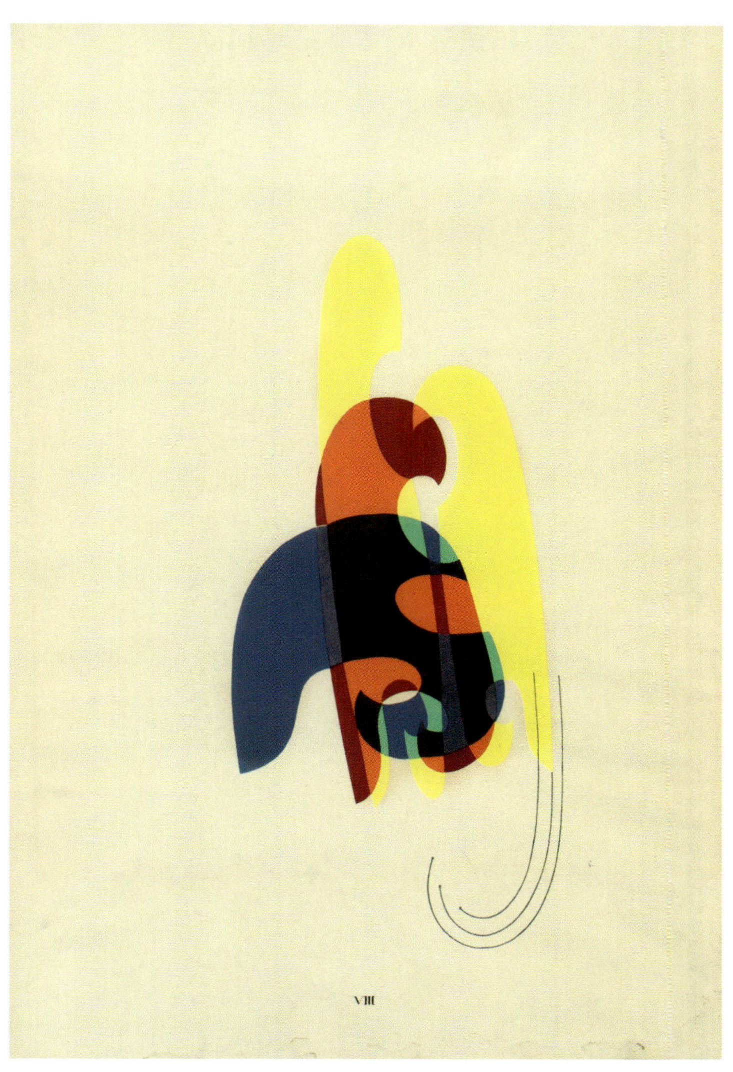

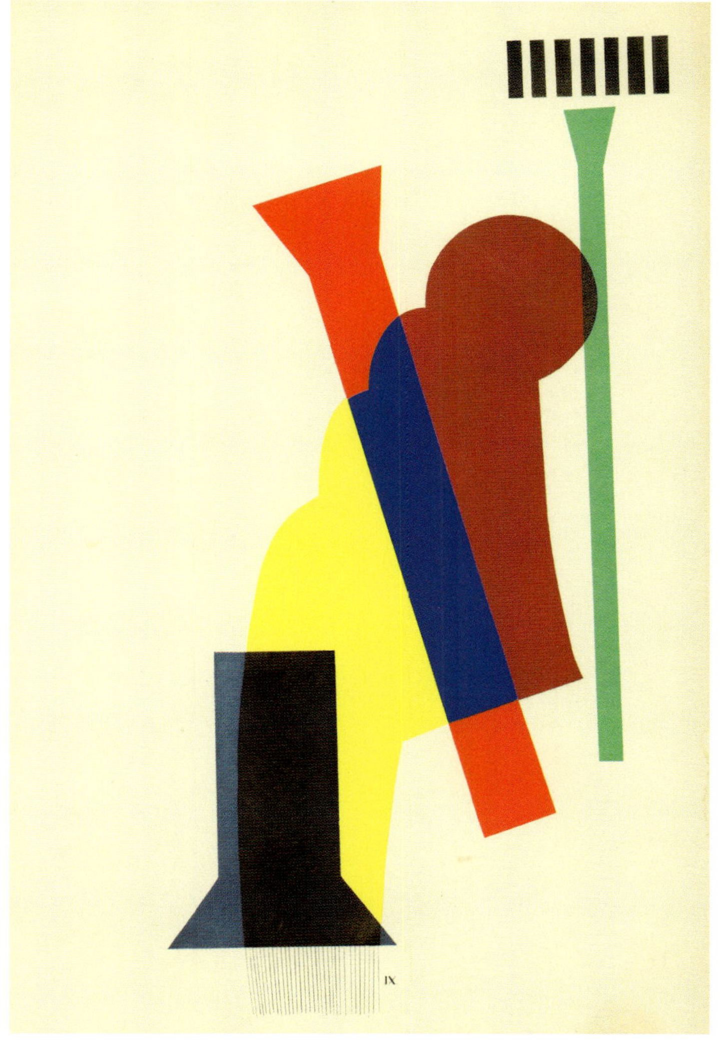

102

MAN RAY

SHADOWS FROM THE SERIES *REVOLVING DOORS*,
NEW YORK, 1916–17, AND PARIS, 1923–24
POCHOIR ON PAPER, 55.9 × 38.1 CM
THE FRANCES LEHMAN LOEB ART CENTER,
VASSAR COLLEGE, POUGHKEEPSIE, N.Y., 1988.37
MAAG, TMAA

103

MAN RAY

CONCRETE MIXER FROM THE SERIES *REVOLVING DOORS*,
NEW YORK, 1916–17, AND PARIS, 1923–24
POCHOIR ON PAPER, 55.9 × 38.1 CM
THE FRANCES LEHMAN LOEB ART CENTER,
VASSAR COLLEGE, POUGHKEEPSIE, N.Y., 1988.38
MAAG, TMAA

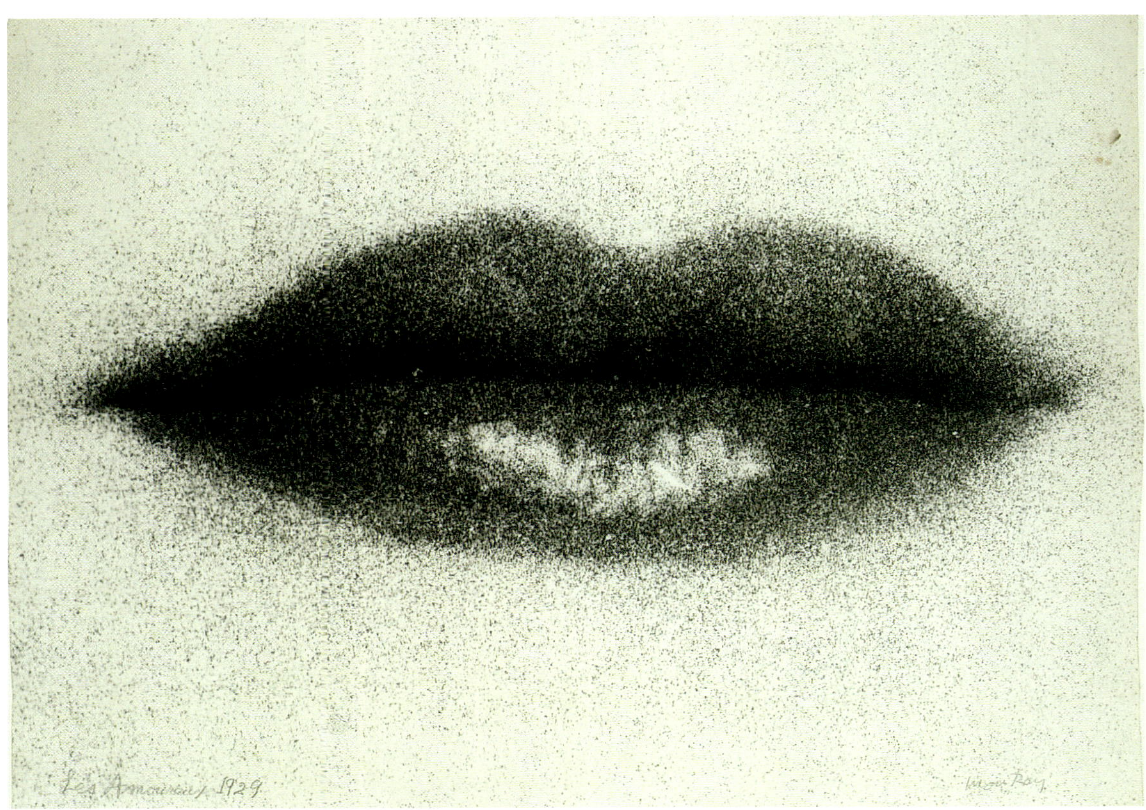

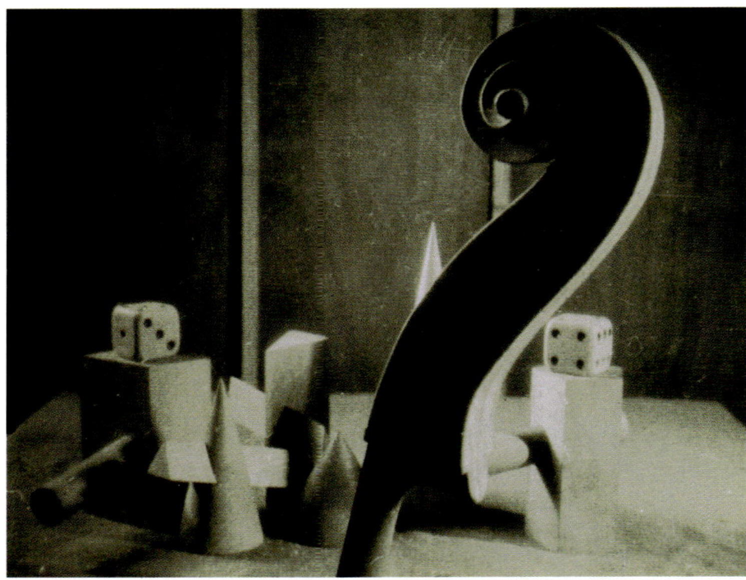

104
MAN RAY
LES AMOUREUX [THE LOVERS], 1929
GELATIN SILVER PRINT, 41.9 X 59.7 CM
HALLMARK CARDS, KANSAS CITY, MISS.
HALLMARK PHOTOGRAPHIC COLLECTION
MAAG, TAM, TMAA

105
MAN RAY
EMAK BAKIA, 1926
FILM STILL (RAYOGRAPH), 15 X 19.5 CM
PRIVATE COLLECTION
MAAG

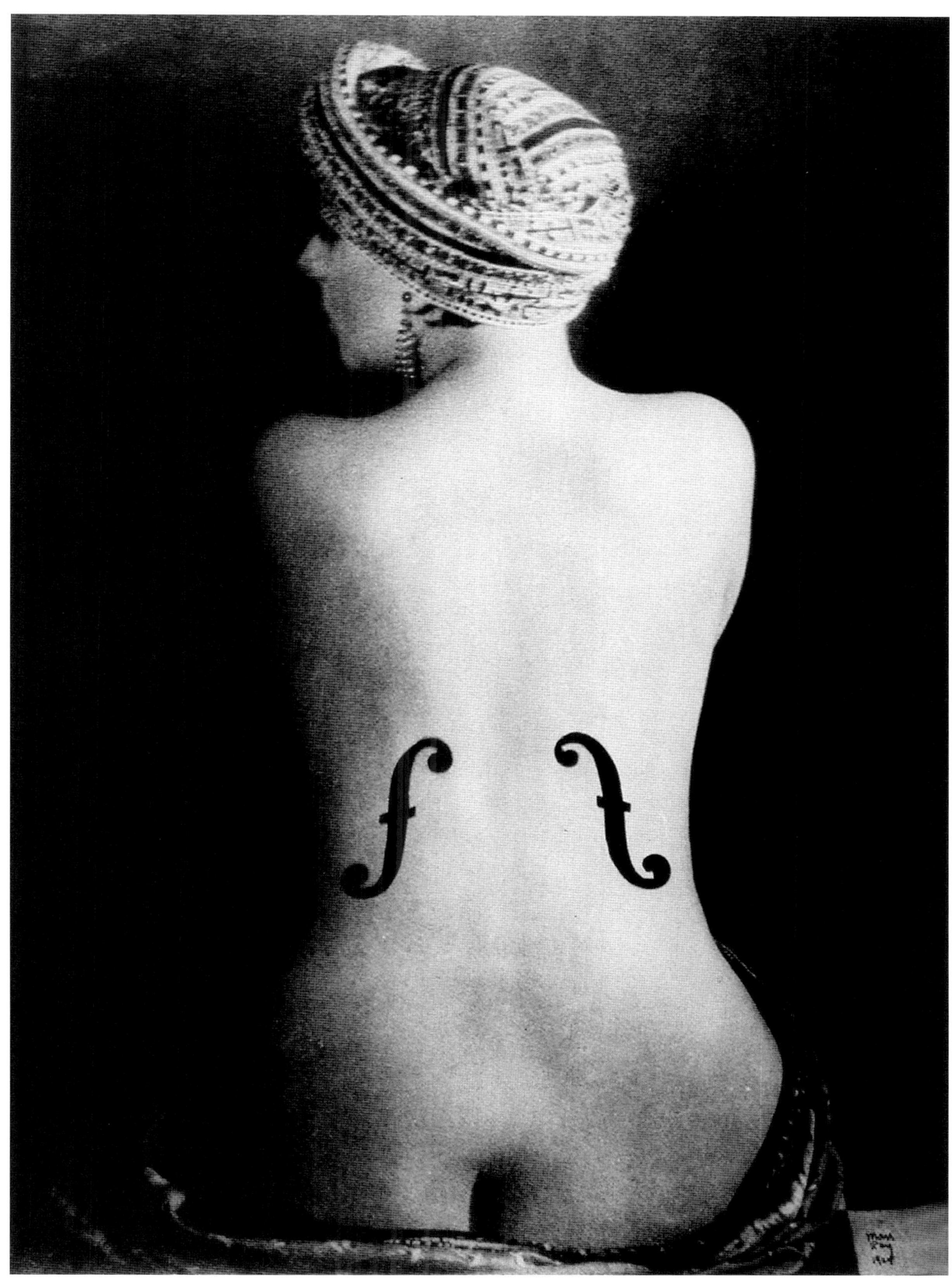

106
MAN RAY
VIOLON D'INGRES, 1924
MODERN PRINT, 27 X 20 CM
FONDS RÉGIONAL D'ART CONTEMPORAIN
DE BOURGOGNE, DIJON
MAAG, TAM, TMAA

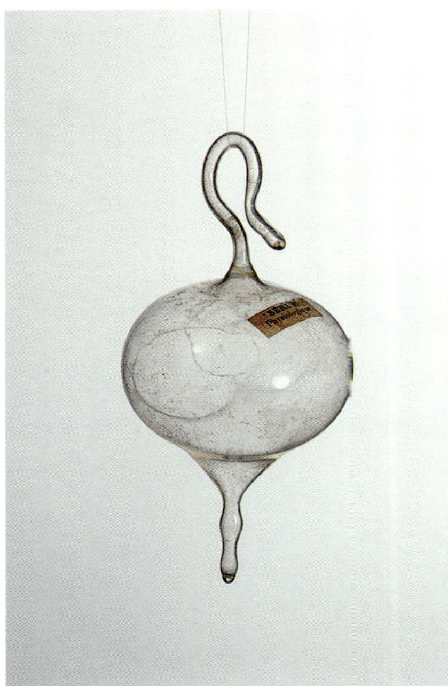

FIG. 8.
MARCEL DUCHAMP,
READY-MADE 50CC AIR DE PARIS. 1919.
GLASS AMPOULE. D. 6.4 CM.
PHILADELPHIA MUSEUM OF ART. LOUISE AND WALTER
ARENSBERG COLLECTION. 50.134.78.

in the first issue of *La Révolution surréaliste* he ran into difficulties because he felt that painting had one major drawback: "To paint a canvas you have to begin at one end, carry on somewhere else, then somewhere else again, a process that leaves great scope for arbitrariness and for taste, and that tends to distract from the mind's dictates. . . . A painting can not be typical of surrealism—images are surrealist, their expression is not."[10] Morise here raised an issue that he seemed to address in a series of questions at the end of the article (to which Man Ray himself seemed to be the only answer): "But what of Man Ray, our friend who turns the most ordinary items into fashionable luxury goods, thanks to light-sensitive paper? What of that pale woman in a motor coach, passing among men with top hats?"[11] The threat brandished by Naville in the third issue of the magazine, where he claimed that "everyone knows there is no such thing as surrealist painting" did not seem to trouble anyone; by the next issue (July 1925), Breton was launching his series of articles on "Surrealism and Painting." It is worth noting, moreover, that Max Ernst and Man Ray were the first two artists that Breton cited in the name of authentic surrealism.

As noted in an astute article by Rosalind Krauss, it was above all publications such as, among others *La Révolution surréaliste, Le Surréalisme au service de la Révolution, Documents, Minotaure, Marie,* and *The International Surrealist Bulletin,* that represented "the true objects produced by surrealism."[12] If this observation is punctuated by Breton's henceforth famous exclamation—"When will all worthy books cease being illustrated with drawings, henceforth appearing only with photographs?"[13]—then Man Ray's importance becomes all the more apparent. Breton allocated a special role to photography, notably the work of Man Ray, both in surrealist publications and in his own books (*Nadja* in 1928 and *L'Amour fou* [Mad love] in 1937 were illustrated with photos). Breton's philosophy was dominated by a determination to create art through "automatic" processes. Photography, as an instantaneous form of creativity, was an ideal medium compared to painting, which required a period of gestation that allowed reason to hamper direct access to the unconscious. And Man Ray, well in advance of the surrealists had understood the creative power of photography. Its inherent recording function—its apparent attachment to reality—had immediately triggered an acute awareness of the unrealness contained within reality itself. It was Man Ray who noticed the unreal beauty of the accumulation of dust on the paintings stacked in Duchamp's bathroom, thereby giving birth to one aspect of the *Large Glass.* Also worth noting is the importance of shadows in Man Ray's compositions right from his earliest photos (*Man* and *Woman,* 1918)—shadows, of course, being the materialization of "unreality." Shadows represent the world of dreams and the marvelous, the land of spirits.

Also paramount to surrealists was the concept of "convulsive" beauty: "convulsive beauty will be 'veiled-erotic,' 'frozen-explodent,' and 'circumstantial-magical,' or it will not be," wrote Breton in *L'Amour fou.* As Krauss explains it, "*érotique-voilée* invokes the occurrence in nature of representation, as one animal imitates another or as inorganic matter shapes itself to look like statuary . . . *explosante-fixe* is related to the 'expiration of movement,' [while] *magique-circonstantielle* consists of the found object or found verbal fragment, both instances of objective chance, where (specifically in the case of the found object) an emissary from the eternal world carries a message informing the recipient of his own desire."[14] In *Man* (1918), the eggbeater is compared by Man Ray to a man (*érotique-voilée*), yet is also a mechanical object at rest (*explosante-fixe*) and a found object that "carries a message informing the recipient of his own desire," namely to "beat eggs all alone," like the bachelors in the *Large Glass* who "grind their chocolate all alone" (*magique-circonstancielle*). Similarly, the 1920 photograph titled *Moving Sculpture,* which shows laundry drying on a clothesline, has a "veiled-erotic" aspect (underwear presented as sculpture or, when later placed on the cover of *La Révolution surréaliste,* as an image of France), as well as being "frozen-explodent" and "magical-circumstantial" insofar as it entails a found object that informs the recipient of his desire, in this case that of freedom, Man Ray desiring here to free sculpture from its plinth. Above all, however, this "moving sculpture" is a representation, a depiction, a materialization, of *air.* Air sculpts the clothes even as it is given shape by them. Back in the sixteenth century already, Leonardo da Vinci wondered "how to paint the wind." In 1919, Duchamp returned to New York with a vial containing *Air de Paris* (fig. 8), thereby managing to "cast" the local air. Man Ray, inspired by

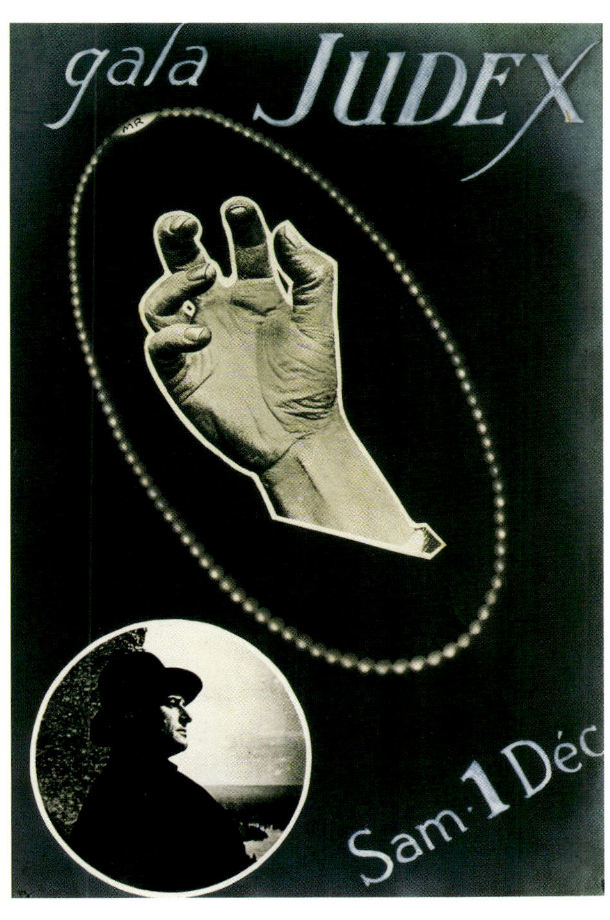

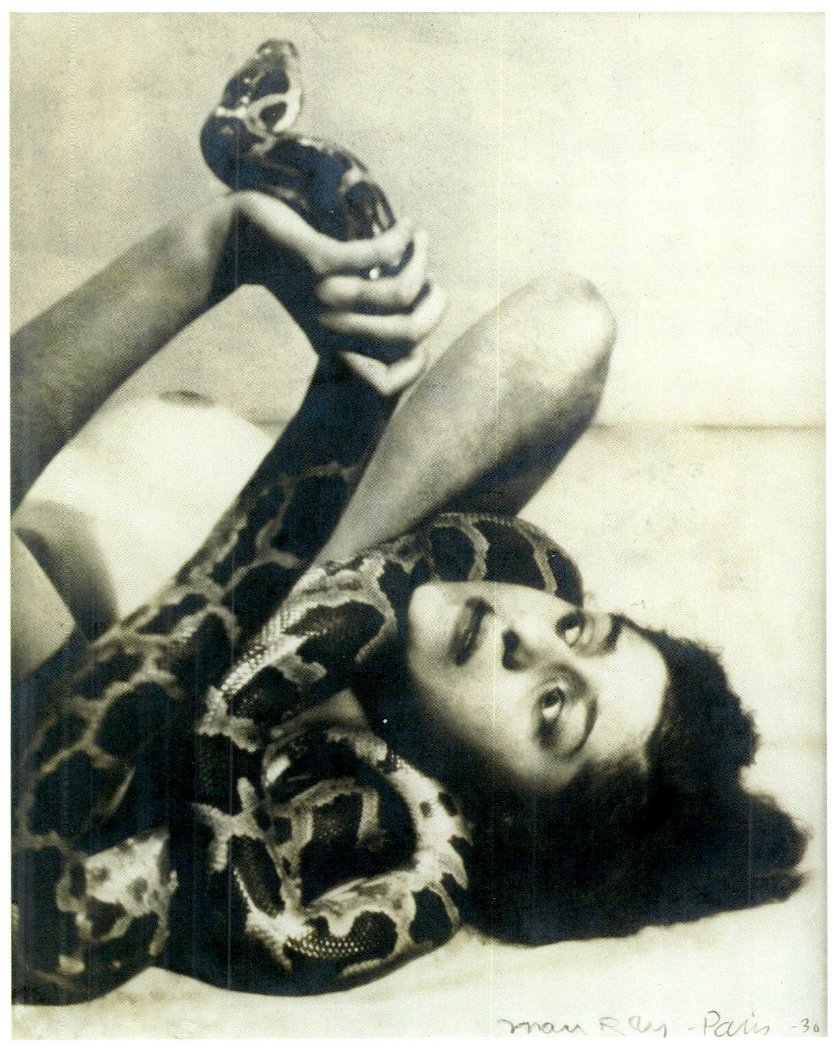

107
MAN RAY
GALA JUDEX, 1922–28
GELATIN SILVER PRINT WITH WHITE INK,
RAYOGRAPH AND PHOTOMONTAGE, 24 X 16.3 CM
COURTESY GALERIE NATALIE SEROUSSI, PARIS
MAAG

108
MAN RAY
LE COLLIER TRAGIQUE [THE TRAGIC NECKLACE], 1930
VINTAGE PHOTOGRAPH, GELATIN SILVER PRINT,
28.3 X 22.8 CM
GALERIE 1900-2000, PARIS
MAAG, TAM, TMAA

both of these ideas, photographed the wind sculpting an object, or cast by it. The title given to this photo when published in *La Révolution surréaliste,* namely *La France,* is moreover a nod to *Air de Paris.* Whereas in France people are advised to "wash [their] dirty linen in the family," people in America are told "not to air [their] dirty laundry in public," Man Ray's photo therefore acquired an additional meaning in the United States, namely the determination to say farewell to good breeding. Man Ray saw France as the land of revolution, where dada could take root, unlike New York where *New York Dada* did not outlive its first issue—the effort was "as futile as trying to grow lilies in a desert," he said.[15]

The techniques Man Ray employed in Paris met with immediate success with rayographs and solarized photos catching on like wild fire. The role of French artists in his success was similar to the one played by a gallery owner or a publisher—which many of them were. Thanks to such people, Man Ray was able to publish his work in numerous reviews associated with dada and surrealism (*Littérature, Mécano, Merz, La Révolution surréaliste, Le Surréalisme au service de la Révolution, Minotaure,* and so on), thereby becoming the most visible American artist in Paris during the interwar period. ■

1— *Exposition dada Man Ray* (December 3–31, 1921) exh. cat.
(Paris: Librarie Six, 1921).

2— "Un certain mépris pour le moyen physique d'exprimer une idée
est indispensable pour la réaliser au mieux."
Man Ray, "L'Age de la lumière," *Minotaure* 3–4 (1933): 1.

3— As early as 1834–35, William Henry Fox Talbot recorded the imprint
of objects on paper impregnated with silver chloride. He called them
"photogenic drawings."

4— Man Ray, *Self-Portrait* (Boston: Little, Brown & Company, 1988), 109.

5— André Breton, *Exposition dada Max Ernst,* exh. cat.
(Paris: Au Sans Pareil, 1921).

6— Man Ray, *Self-Portrait,* 79.

7— "Voici le domaine de Rrose Sélavy / Comme il est aride – comme
il est fertile – / Comme il est joyeux – Comme il est triste!
Vue prise en aéroplane par Man Ray – 1921."

8— "Plutôt que de désencadrer la photo de Duchamp ('Voici le domaine
de R. S.') je serais très heureux si vous veuillez bien me procurer
une nouvelle épreuve, que je vous paierais naturellement."
Letter dated December 29, 1922, Lucien Treillard Collection.
Unfortunately, no print of *Élevage de poussière* turned up at
the recent public auction of the items in Breton's studio.

9— *Bifur* 1 (May 25, 1929): 25.

10— "Pour peindre une toile il faut commencer par un bout, continuer
ailleurs, puis encore ailleurs, procédé qui laisse de grandes chances
à l'arbitraire, au goût et tend à égarer la dictée de la pensée . . .
un tableau ne peut pas passer pour typique du surréalisme:
les images sont surréalistes, leur expression ne l'est pas."
Max Morise, "Les yeux enchantés," *La Révolution surréaliste* 1
(December 1, 1924): 26–27.

11— "Mais quel est ce Man Ray, notre ami, qui d'objets de première
nécessité fait, à l'aide de papier sensible, des objets de dernier luxe?
Quelle est cette femme blanche qui passe en auto-car parmi
des hommes à haut chapeau?" Ibid.

12— Rosalind Krauss, "The Photographic Conditions of Surrealism,"
in *The Originality of the Avant-Garde and Other Modernist Myths*
(Cambridge, Mass.: MIT Press, 1985), 101.

13— André Breton, "Le Surréalisme et la Peinture," *La Révolution
surréaliste* 4 (July 1925).

14— Rosalind Krauss, "Photography in the Service of Surrealism,"
in Rosalind Krauss and Jane Livingston, *L'Amour Fou: Photography
and Surrealism* (London: Arts Council of Great Britain, 1986), 31–35.

15— Man Ray, *Self-Portrait,* 88.

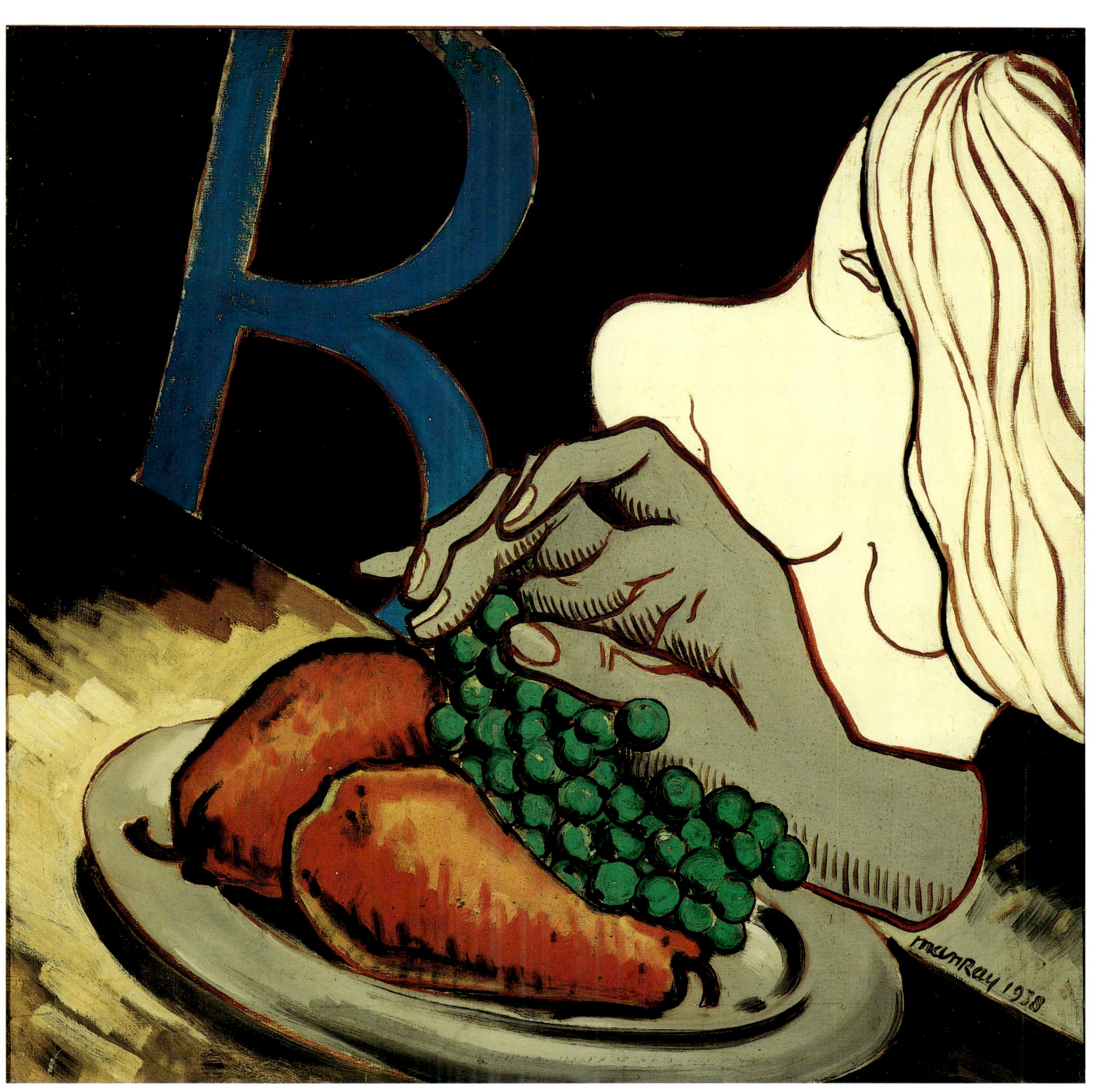

109
MAN RAY
STILL LIFE WITH LETTER B, 1939
OIL ON CANVAS, 61 X 50.8 CM
PRIVATE COLLECTION
MAAG, TAM, TMAA

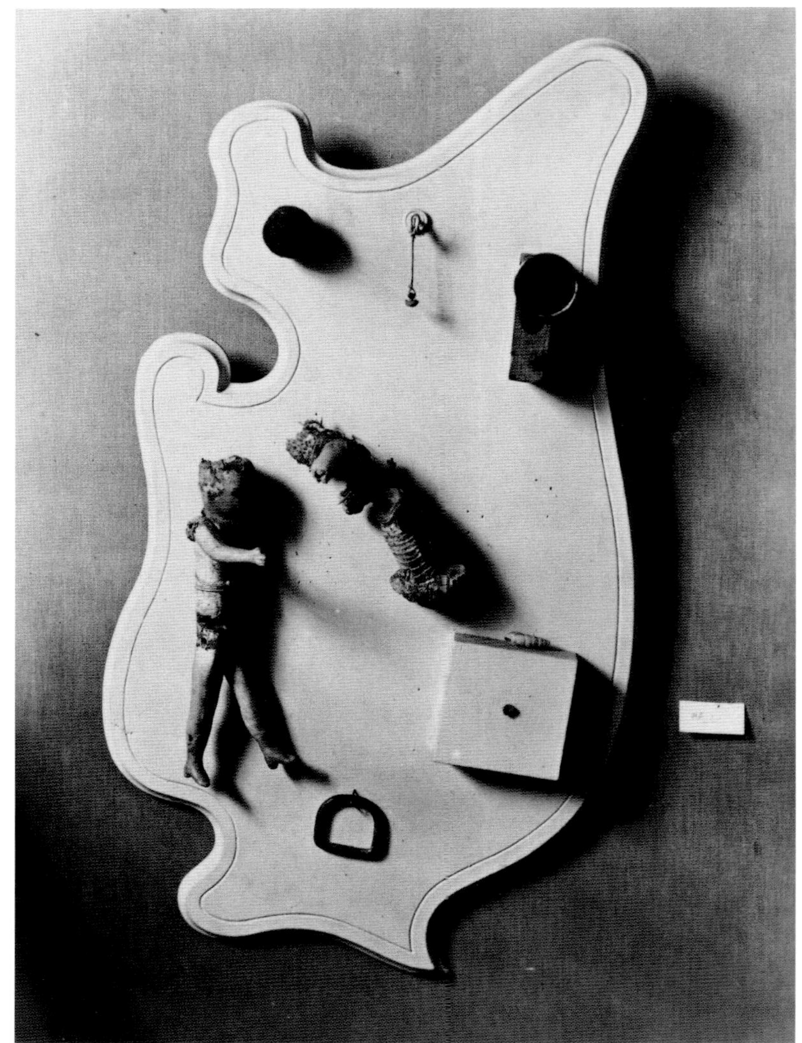

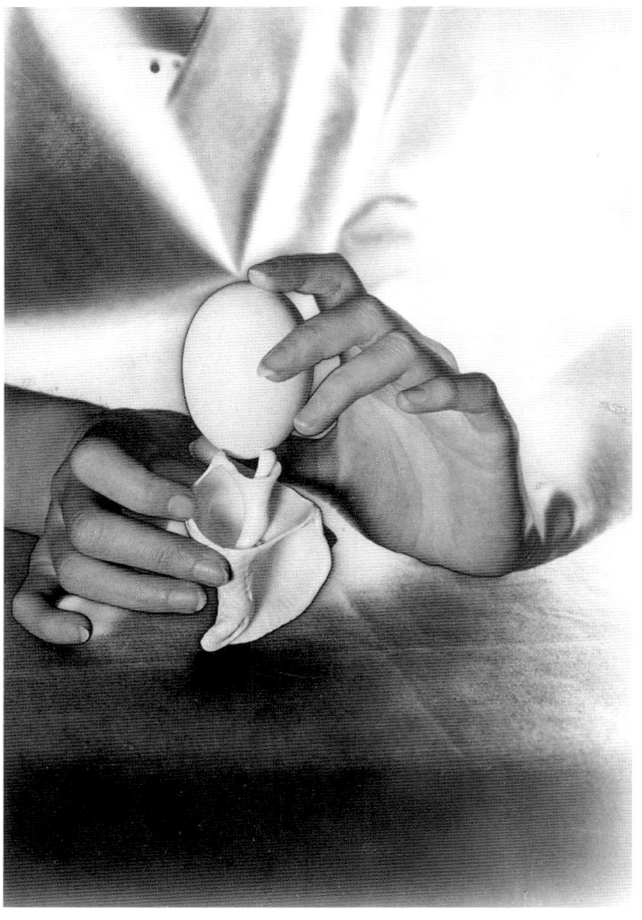

110
MAN RAY
[SURREALIST COMPOSITION], C. 1930
GELATIN SILVER PRINT, 45.8 X 35.6 CM
LIBRARY OF CONGRESS, WASHINGTON D.C.
PRINTS AND PHOTOGRAPHS DIVISION,
PH– RAY, M. NO. 9
MAAG, TAM, TMAA

111
MAN RAY
L'ŒUF ET LE COQUILLAGE
[THE EGG AND THE SHELL], 1931
MODERN PRINT, 30 X 21.5 CM
FONDS RÉGIONAL D'ART CONTEMPORAIN
DE BOURGOGNE, DIJON, 9990010
MAAG, TAM, TMAA

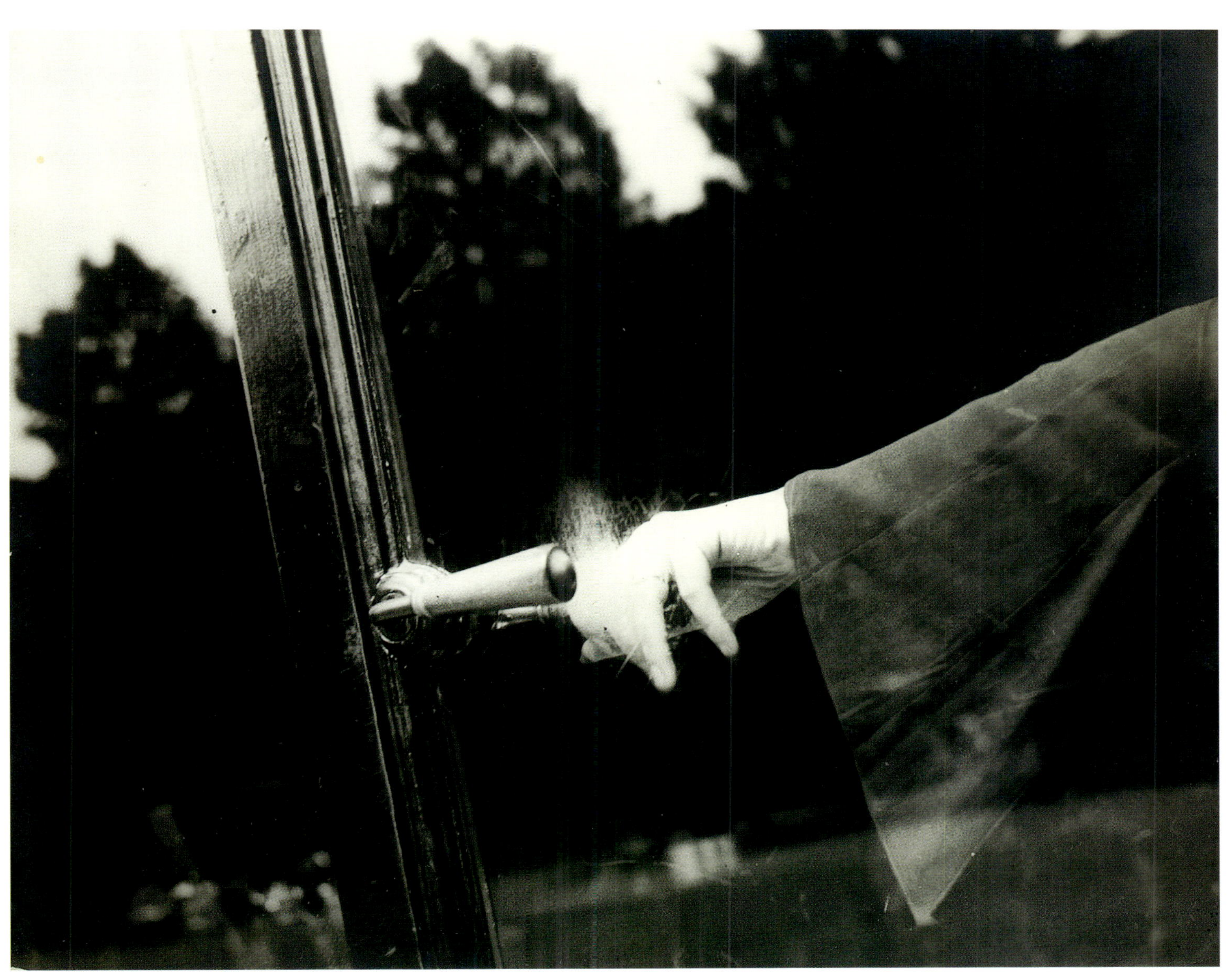

112
LEE MILLER
EXPLODING HAND, 1930
GELATIN SILVER PRINT, 42.3 X 57.5 CM (FRAME)
THE VICTORIA AND ALBERT MUSEUM, LONDON,
PH 101-1984
MAAG, TAM, TMAA

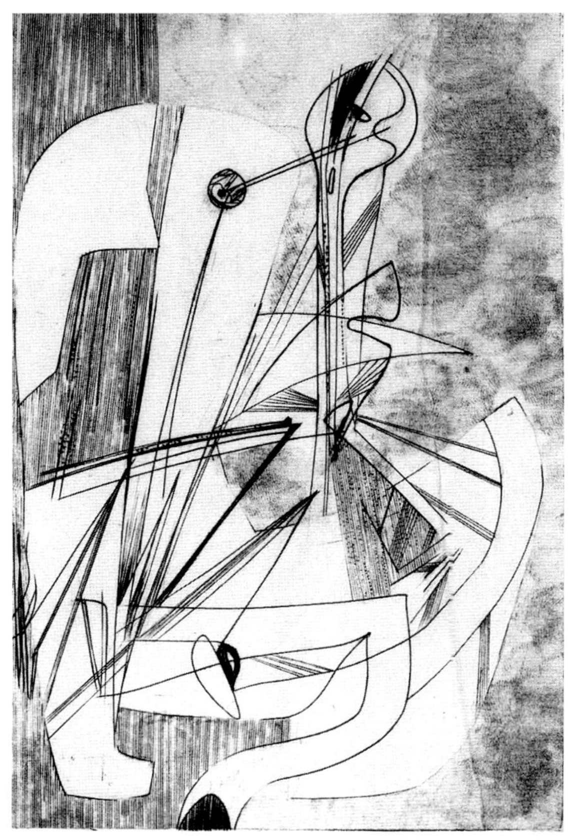

STANLEY WILLIAM HAYTER,
THE INCORRUPTIBLE EYE, 1935.
ENGRAVING AND SOFTGROUND ETCHING.
18.9 X 12.2 CM.

When British artist Stanley William Hayter opened his experimental printmaking workshop in his Paris apartment in 1927, he began to attract members of the international avant-garde. The studio, later known as Atelier 17, became a meeting place for artists, writers, and collectors of all nationalities.[1] Young American artists could brush elbows with famous Europeans like Max Ernst, Alberto Giacometti, Jean Hélion, Joan Miró, Yves Tanguy, Pablo Picasso, and Vassily Kandinsky. The creative atmosphere of Atelier 17 was unique in the art world. Neither a school nor a business, it has been likened to an informal laboratory for experimentation.[2] Artists received equal treatment, assistance in the various techniques of printmaking, and freedom to experiment.

An educational background in chemistry enabled Hayter to master the technical processes of printmaking, and he enthusiastically shared his knowledge.[3] As a teacher, Hayter refrained from value judgments, instead promoting a variety of styles and a spirit of trial and error. He expected artists to complete each phase of printmaking on their own and encouraged them to work without preliminary sketches, drawing directly onto the metal plate. He believed that prints, like paintings, were original works of art and not reproductions of already existing images. The direct contact with the plate also called forth the subconscious, similar to the automatic processes embraced by the surrealists.[4] As an artist, Hayter admired surrealist methods and adapted an abstract biomorphic visual vocabulary in countless mature prints and paintings.

The artists of Atelier 17 pursued diverse artistic styles and never formed a coherent group although many of them exhibited together as early as 1934 in Paris and London. Other collaborative efforts at the workshop included two portfolios of collected prints in response to the horrors of the Spanish Civil War: *Solidarité,* 1938 and *Fraternity,* 1939.[5] Occasionally two or more artists worked together on a series of prints, and frequently artists found inspiration in each other's methods and styles. As American Anita de Caro said of her work at Atelier 17 in the 1930s, "I always sat between Tanguy and Ernst who often offered solutions to my technical problems."[6]

De Caro was one of many American artists who found their way to Atelier 17 in the 1930s including George Ball, Alexander Calder, John Ferren, Man Ray, John Graham, Helen Phillips, and David Smith. Many of these artists had met the charismatic Hayter and came to the workshop to learn printmaking. Others wanted a chance to mingle with the avant-garde—the print workshop had become an exciting international meeting place. In 1940, Hayter moved Atelier 17 to New York City, maintaining the spirit of experimentation. The presence of European expatriates in the New York workshop appealed to young American avant-gardists like Franz Kline, Robert Motherwell, Louise Nevelson, and Jackson Pollock. In 1950, Hayter returned to Paris and re-opened Atelier 17, proof of a life-long commitment to experimental printmaking.

Katherine Bourguignon

1— Atelier 17 began with four then up to ten artists working informally a few times a week. The Atelier took its name in 1933 from its new address at 17 rue Campagne-Première. For more information see Joann Moser, *Atelier 17* (Madison: University of Wisconsin, 1977) and Dominique Tonneau-Ryckelynck et al., *Hayter et l'Atelier 17*, Musée du Dessin et de l'Estampe Originale, Arsenal de Gravelines, (Paris: Imprimerie Union, 1993).

2— In 1973, Hayter said, "This workshop is an experimental shop. . . . This is not a school or art. There is no common agreement; each pursues his own necessity." Quoted in Moser, *Atelier 17*, 13.

3— Hayter studied chemistry and geology at Kings College, London, 1917–21. After a successful exhibition of his paintings in London in 1926, he abandoned his career as a chemist and moved to Paris to study art. He learned engraving from Polish artist Joseph Hecht in Paris. See Moser, *Atelier 17*, 1–2 and 20.

4— Hayter exhibited with the surrealists in the 1930s and became friends with several surrealist artists including Ernst, Miró, and Tanguy.

5— Guy Levis-Mano (GLM) and Atelier 17 printed 150 copies of *Solidarité* in April 1938 with a poem by Paul Eluard and prints by: Picasso, Miró, Tanguy, Masson, Buckland-Wright, Husband, and Hayter. Atelier 17 printed 101 copies of *Fraternity* in March 1939. Artists included Buckland-Wright, Hayter, Husband, Hecht, Kandinsky, Mead, Miró, Rieser, and Vargas.

6— "J'étais toujours assise entre Tanguy et Ernst qui proposaient souvent des solutions à mes problèmes techniques." Quoted in Tonneau-Ryckelynck, *Hayter et l'Atelier 17*, 62. De Caro met her husband Roger Vieillard at Atelier 17.

On October 15, 1936, *Minotaure* magazine published a three-page collage entitled "Le Surréalisme Autour du Monde" reproducing invitations and publications about surrealism from seventeen different countries. The page devoted to England and the United States depicted translations into English of writings by André Breton, Paul Eluard, and Benjamin Péret; invitations to exhibitions, as well as recent books on the subject. By publishing these photographs, the editors of *Minotaure* emphasized the growing internationalism of the surrealist movement. At the same time, they highlighted writers and artists based in Paris.

The desire to promote surrealist activity around the globe and maintain Paris as its center motivated the organizers of the *Exposition Internationale du Surréalisme* held in Paris at the Galerie Beaux-Arts in 1938. Organized by Eluard, Breton, and Marcel Duchamp, this exhibition of over 250 objects listed fourteen participating countries in an accompanying brochure.[1] Comprehensive representation of all fourteen countries seems never to have been a serious goal of the show, and most of the artists included belonged to the dominant surrealist circle based in Paris. James Herbert has suggested that the organizers may have meant to parody the 1937 World's Fair by refusing to assign artists or artworks to specific countries. The list of countries, he said, "ironized the metaphoric nature of nationalism and internationalism" so prevalent at recent exhibitions.[2] Lewis Kachur called the *Exposition* "a gesture toward internationalism," and wrote, "This so-called 'internationalism' was in fact essentially Europeanism."[3] He cited the inclusion of only a few objects from Denmark, Czechoslovakia, Belgium, and Great Britain, and the lack of attention paid to the United States.

Indeed, despite the claims at internationalism, this Paris-based exhibition included only three American artists: Ann Clark, Joseph Cornell, and Man Ray. While Clark gained access to the closed circle through her marriage to surrealist artist Roberto Matta, Cornell may have been included because of his friendship with Duchamp. Having never traveled to France, Cornell had begun to produce collages and constructions inspired by dada and surrealism. Of the three Americans, Man Ray alone played a prominent role in the 1938 exhibition. The only American fully integrated into the Parisian surrealist world, Man Ray had long been admired for his surrealist-inspired photographs, paintings, and found-object sculptures. Not only did Man Ray contribute seven works of art to the *Exposition Internationale du Surréalisme*, including one of the famous mannequins, but he also directed the dramatic lighting for the gallery spaces, distributing flashlights to visitors on opening night.

American artists may have been overlooked by Eluard, Breton, and Duchamp for the show. There were, after all, a few Americans working in a surrealist style at this time, and the American public had already been exposed to surrealism through two major exhibitions: Chick Austin presented *Newer Super-Realism* at the Wadsworth Atheneum in late 1931 and Julien Levy organized *Surréalisme* in January 1932 for his new New York City gallery.[4] Incidentally, these important exhibitions included few American artists.

More important than whether artists of specific nationalities had been overlooked, however, are the questions of nationalism and internationalism that permeated the *Exposition*. French critics commented on the "foreignness" of surrealism, noting that numerous artists associated with Parisian surrealism were not French (Max Ernst, Salvador Dalí, and Joan Miró to name but a few). Additionally, critics remarked upon the international mixture of opening night visitors. As Kachur noted,

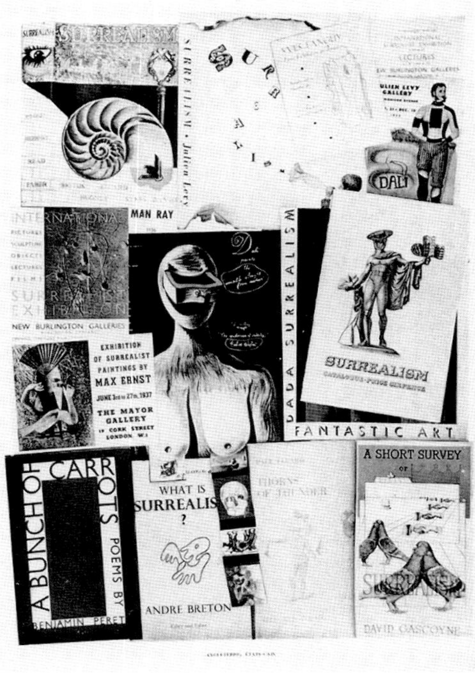

"LE SURRÉALISME AUTOUR DU MONDE," *LE MINOTAURE* 1C (OCTOBER 15, 1936): 64.

"One snidely described the opening as packed with Czechs, Germans, Japanese, and 'even a few Parisians,' while another stereotyped the crowds as 'pretty American women, German Jewish men, and crazy old English.'"[5] These references to national identity reflect the growing international tensions felt by so many artists in Paris during these years preceding World War II when it became more and more difficult to transcend one's national origins.

Katherine Bourguignon

1— The tiny brochure listed participating countries and artists separately. Eluard and Breton also prepared the lengthy, fully illustrated *Dictionnaire abrégé* as a sort of catalogue for the exhibition.

2— James Herbert, *Paris, 1937: Worlds on Exhibition* (Ithaca: Cornell University Press, 1998), 134.

3— Lewis Kachur, *Displaying the Marvelous: Marcel Duchamp, Salvador Dali, and Surrealist Exhibition Installations*, (Cambridge, Mass.: MIT Press, 2001), 30 and 100.

4— See Deborah Zlotsky, "Pleasant Madness in Hartford: The First Surrealist Exhibition in America," *Arts Magazine* (Feb. 1986): 55–61.

5— Kachur, *Displaying the Marvelous*, 100.

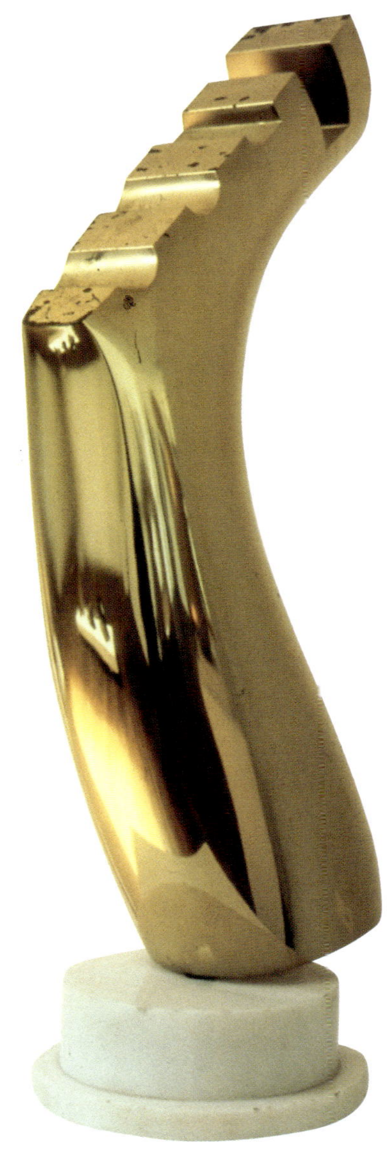

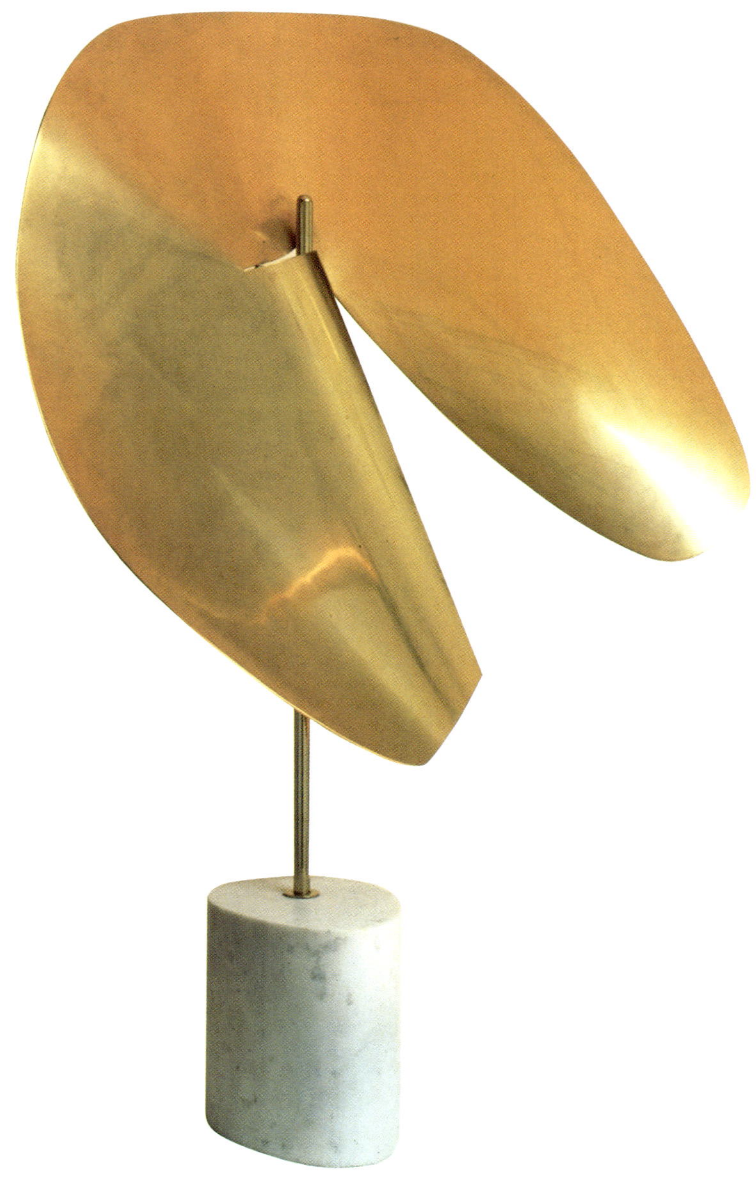

113

ISAMU NOGUCHI
FOOT TREE, C. 1928
BRASS ON STONE AND WOOD BASE,
73.6 X 27.3 X 22.2 CM
COURTESY ISAMU NOGUCHI FOUNDATION,
LONG ISLAND CITY, N.Y., 34
MAAG, TAM, TMAA

114

ISAMU NOGUCHI
POSITIONAL SHAPE, C. 1928
BRASS, 76.6 X 51.4 X 19 CM
COURTESY ISAMU NOGUCHI FOUNDATION,
LONG ISLAND CITY, N.Y., 40
MAAG, TAM, TMAA

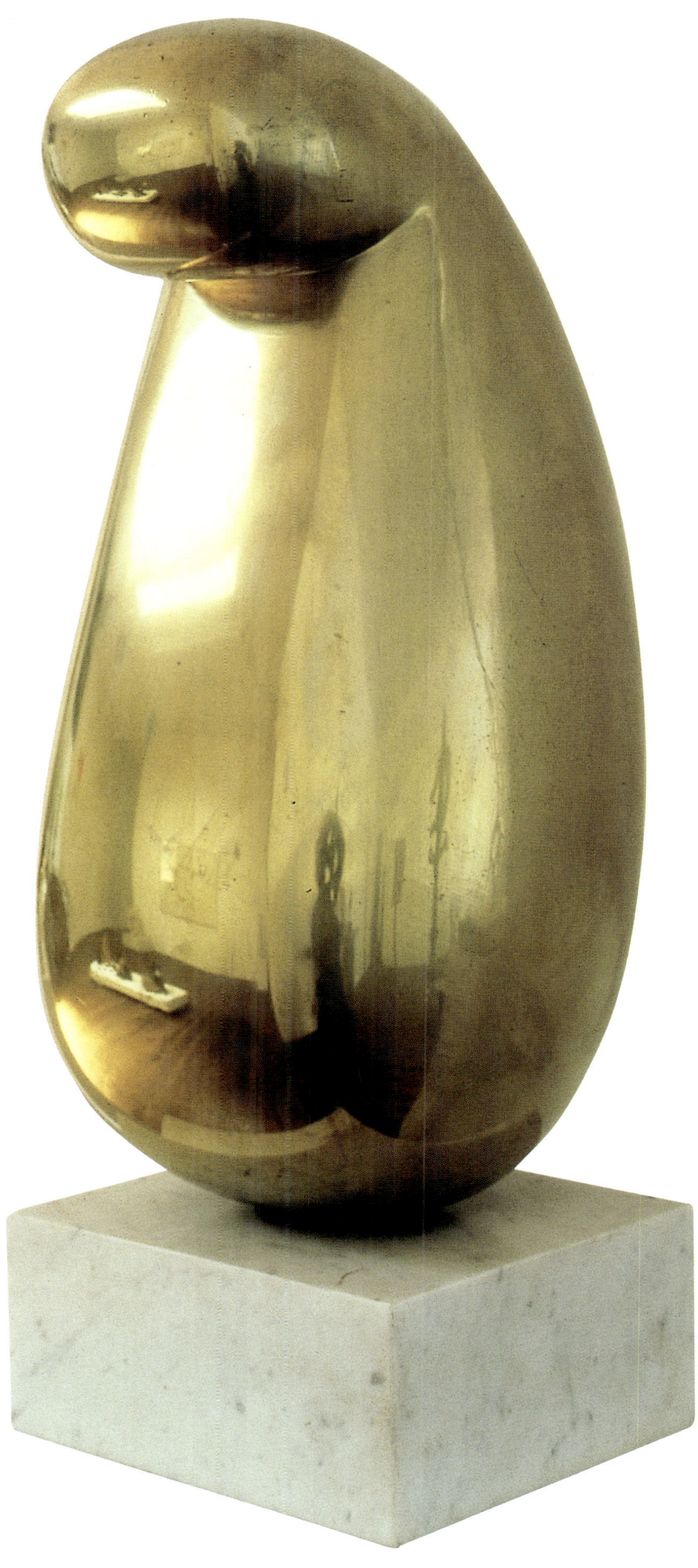

115
ISAMU NOGUCHI
GLOBULAR, 1928
POLISHED BRASS, 61 X 31.5 X 9.2 CM
COURTESY ISAMU NOGUCHI FOUNDATION,
LONG ISLAND CITY, N.Y., 35
MAAG, TAM, TMAA

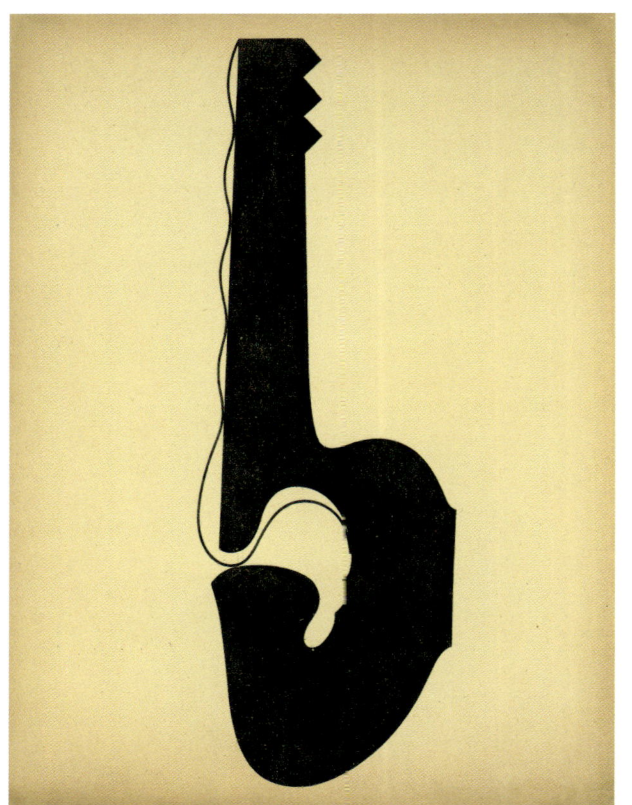

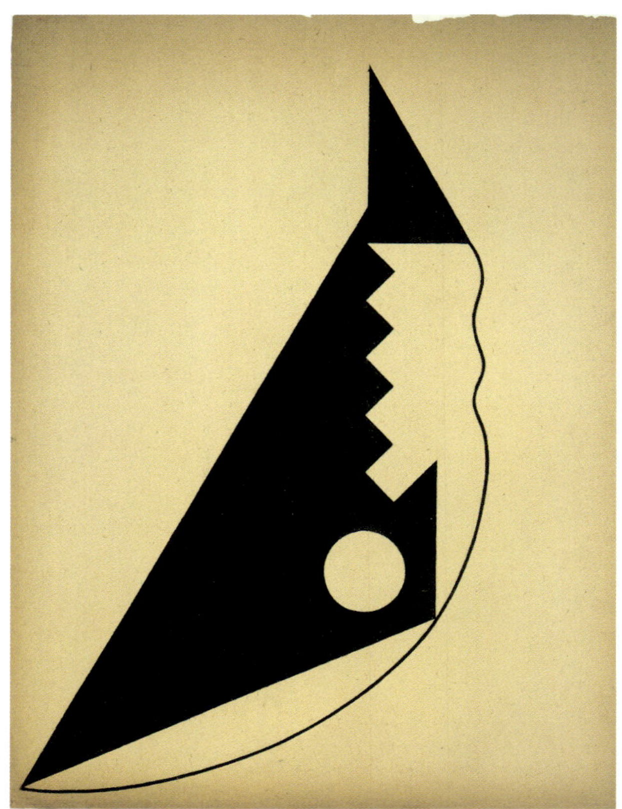

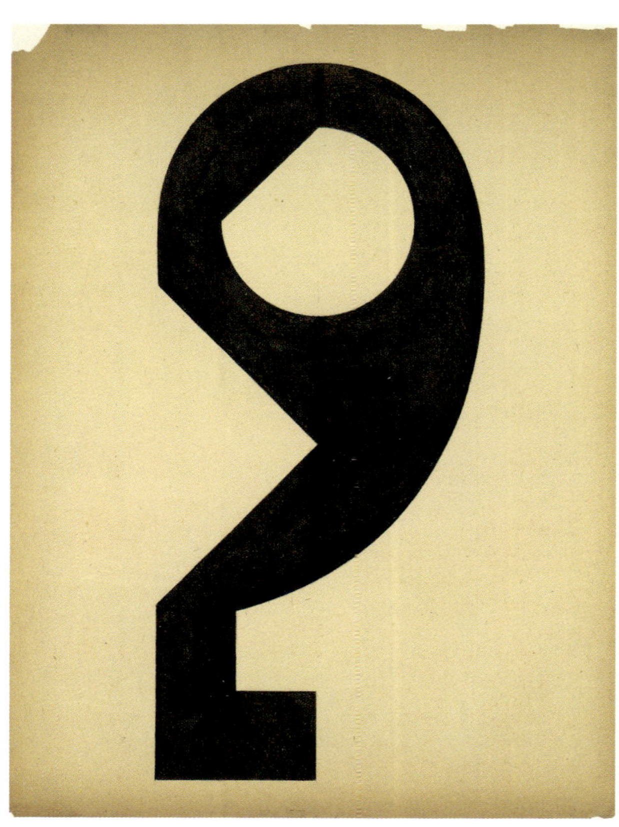

116
ISAMU NOGUCHI
PARIS ABSTRACTION, C. 1927–28
GOUACHE, 65.4 X 50.2 CM
COURTESY ISAMU NOGUCHI FOUNDATION,
LONG ISLAND CITY, N.Y., 22/35
MAAG, TAM, TMAA

117
ISAMU NOGUCHI
PARIS ABSTRACTION, C. 1927–28
GOUACHE, 65.4 X 50.2 CM
COURTESY ISAMU NOGUCHI FOUNDATION,
LONG ISLAND CITY, N.Y., 17/35
MAAG, TAM, TMAA

118
ISAMU NOGUCHI
PARIS ABSTRACTION, C. 1927–28
GOUACHE, 65.4 X 50.2 CM
COURTESY ISAMU NOGUCHI FOUNDATION,
LONG ISLAND CITY, N.Y., 18/35
MAAG, TAM, TMAA

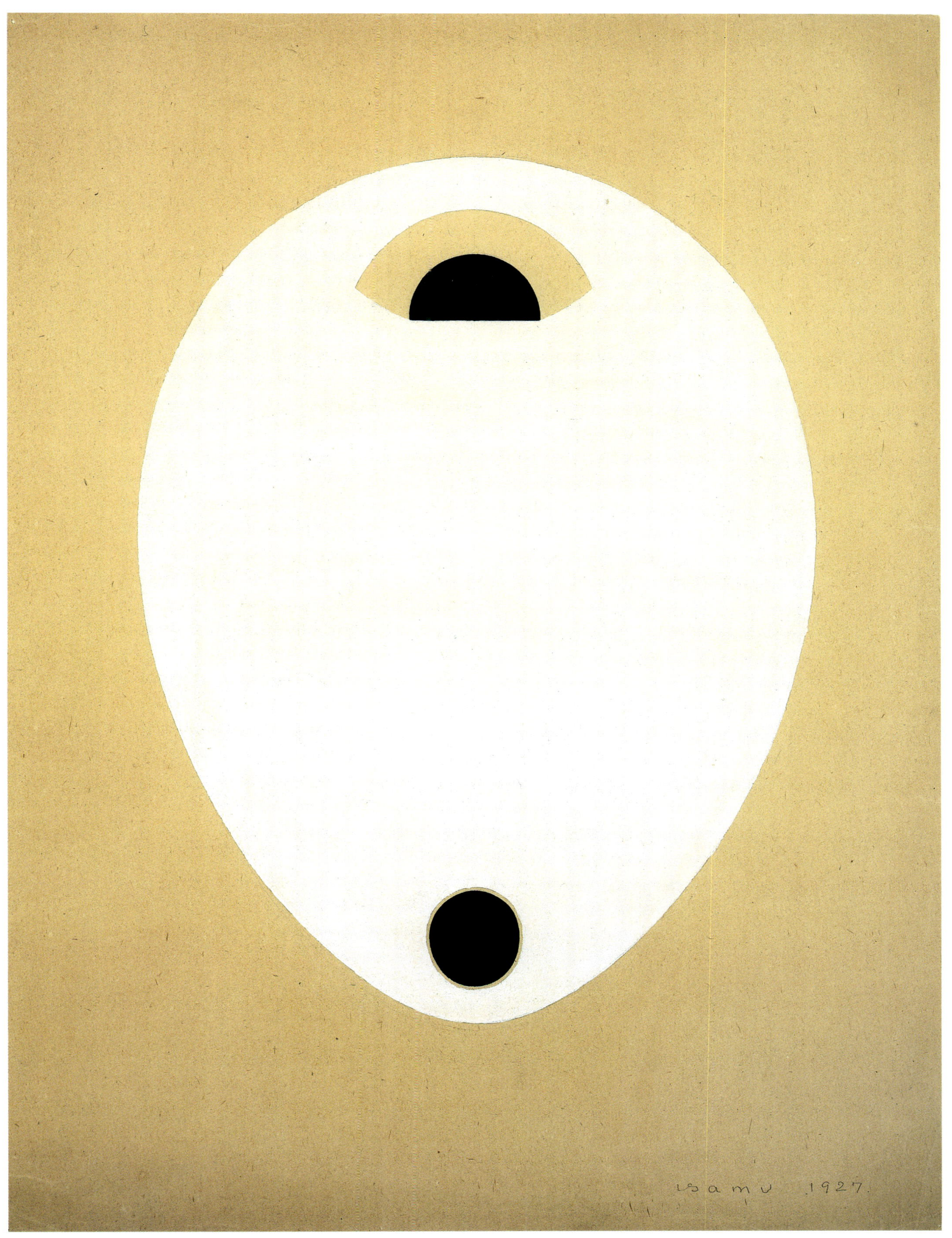

119
ISAMU NOGUCHI
PARIS ABSTRACTION, C. 1927–28
GOUACHE, 64.8 X 49.9 CM
COURTESY ISAMU NOGUCHI FOUNDATION,
LONG ISLAND CITY, N.Y., 7000
MAAG, TAM, TMAA

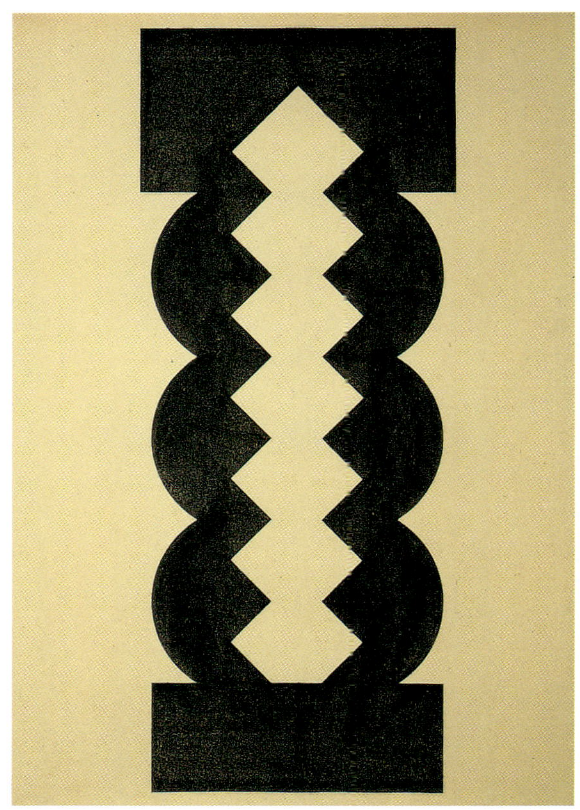

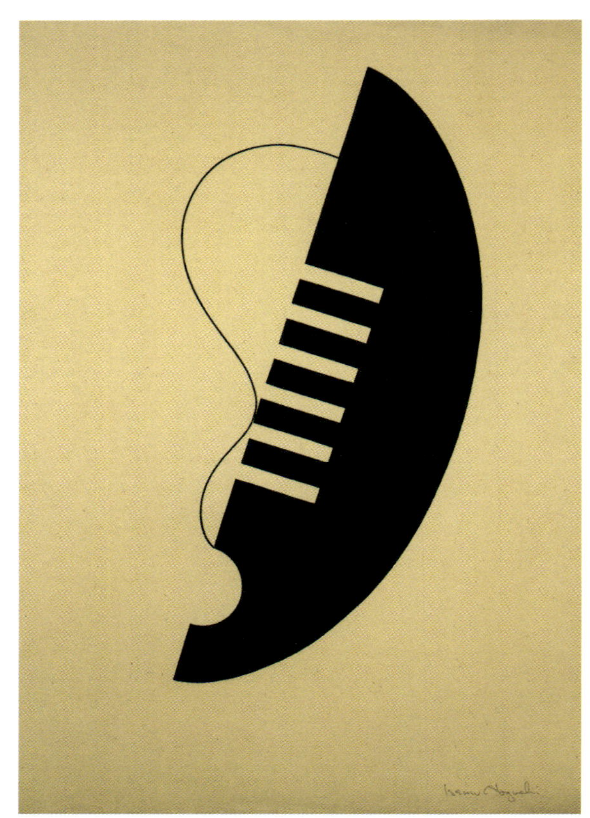

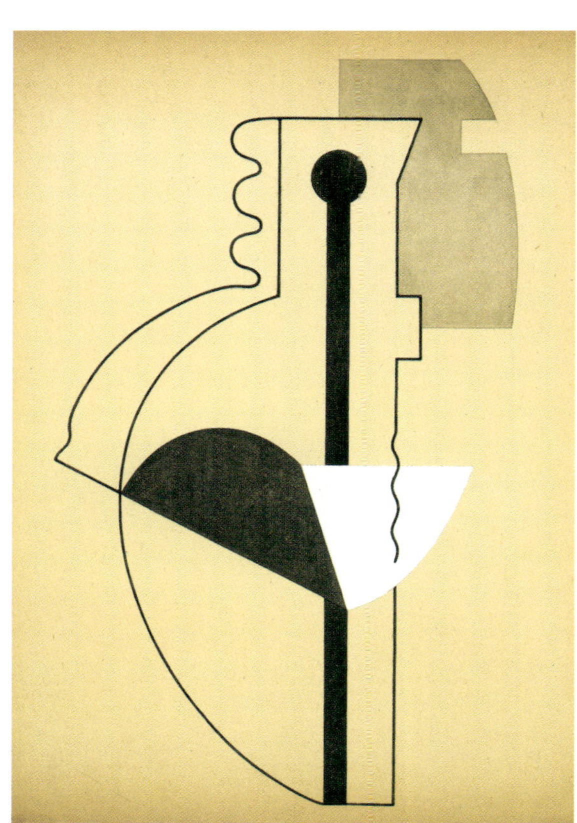

120
ISAMU NOGUCHI
PARIS ABSTRACTION, C. 1927–28
GOUACHE, 65.4 X 50.2 CM
COURTESY ISAMU NOGUCHI FOUNDATION,
LONG ISLAND CITY, N.Y., 7007
MAAG, TAM, TMAA

121
ISAMU NOGUCHI
PARIS ABSTRACTION, C. 1927–28
GOUACHE, 65.4 X 50.2 CM
COURTESY ISAMU NOGUCHI FOUNDATION,
LONG ISLAND CITY, N.Y., 7033
MAAG, TAM, TMAA

122
ISAMU NOGUCHI
PARIS ABSTRACTION, C. 1927–28
GOUACHE, 65.4 X 50.2 CM
COURTESY ISAMU NOGUCHI FOUNDATION,
LONG ISLAND CITY, N.Y., 11/35
MAAG, TAM, TMAA

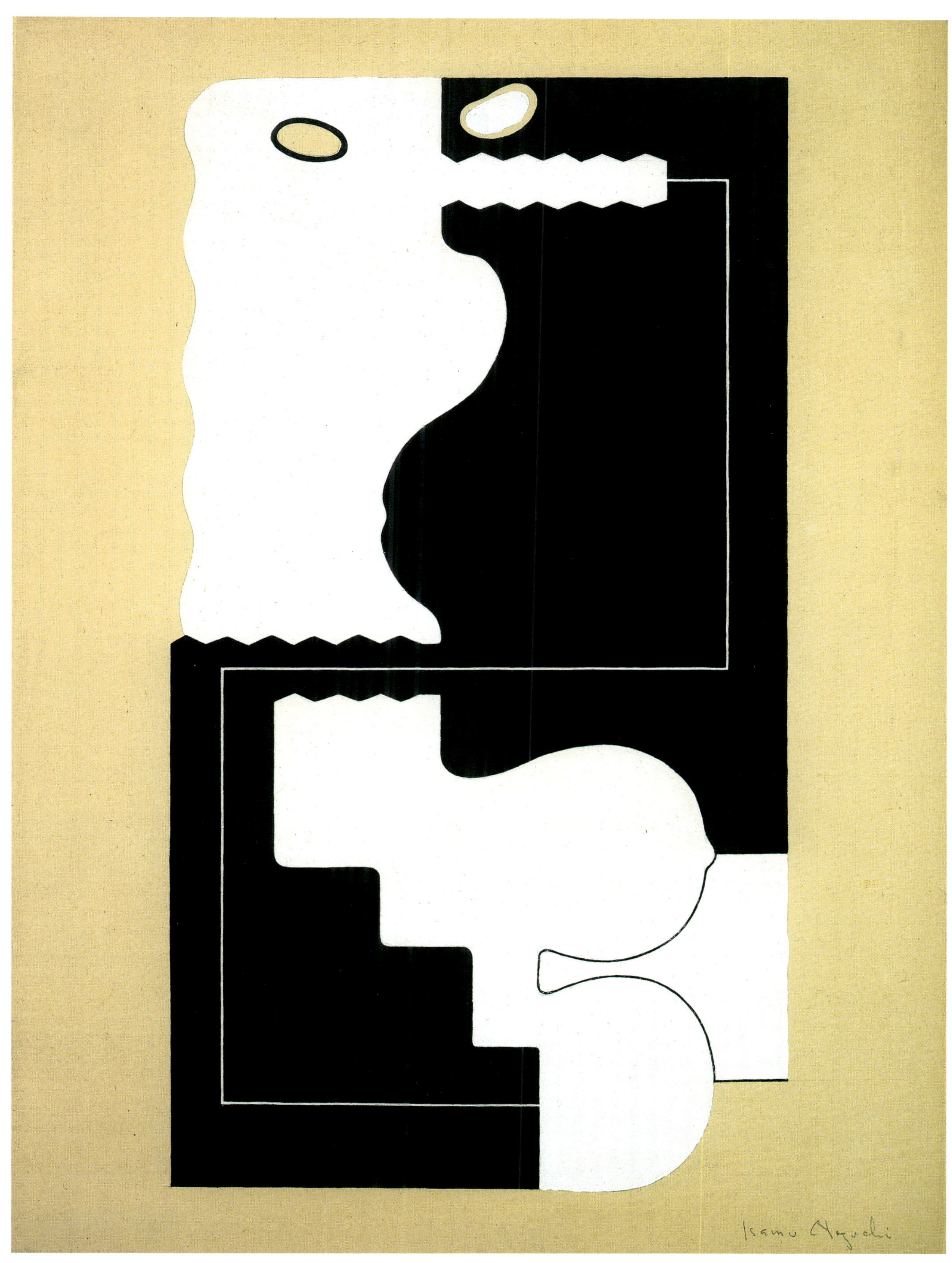

123
ISAMU NOGUCHI
PARIS ABSTRACTION, C. 1927–28
GOUACHE, 65.4 X 50.2 CM
COURTESY ISAMU NOGUCHI FOUNDATION,
LONG ISLAND CITY, N.Y., 7028
MAAG, TAM, TMAA

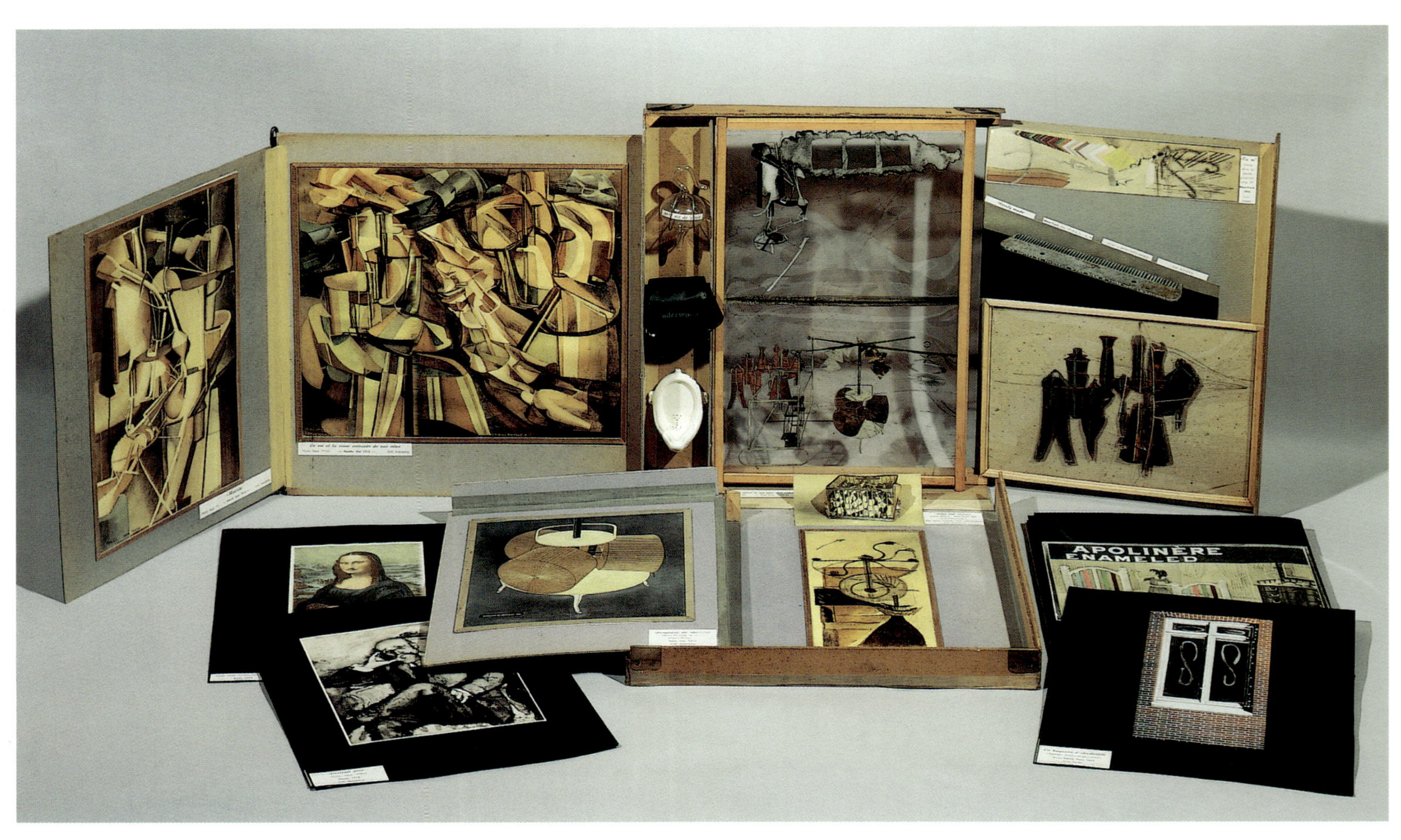

124
MARCEL DUCHAMP
BOÎTE EN VALISE – SERIES "B", 1941
MIXED MEDIAS
PRIVATE COLLECTION.
COURTESY FRANCIS M. NAUMANN FINE ART,
NEW YORK
MAAG, TAM, TMAA

BOXES, BOOKS,

AND THE BOÎTE-EN-VALISE

JANINE **MILEAF**

We see to it that our fingers do not touch, even by chance, in handling books and objects.[1]
Henri-Pierre Roché, 1924

American artists came late to surrealism. André Breton's original manifesto was signed in 1924, but the first American exhibitions did not take place until the winter of 1931–32, when A. Everett "Chick" Austin, Jr. organized *Newer Super-Realism* for the Wadsworth Atheneum in Hartford, Connecticut; two months later Julien Levy opened *Surréalisme* at his recently established gallery on Madison Avenue in New York.[2] Alfred Barr's 1936 *Fantastic Art, Dada, Surrealism* at the Museum of Modern Art (MoMA) would eventually introduce surrealism to a broader audience.[3] While these exhibitions did not emerge out of a surrealist abyss, it is safe to say that the movement did not find full expression in the United States until the late 1930s, precisely when it began to lose ground in France. The surrealists' embrace of America, meanwhile, was equally delayed, if not permanently deferred. An indication of surrealist indifference and/or hostility towards the United States appears in *Le Monde au temps des surréalistes*, a map published in the Belgian journal *Variétés* in 1929. This imaginary geography omits the contiguous United States, although its then territories Alaska and Hawaii figure prominently. In the surrealist mind, "the Americas" conjured notions of indigenous peoples—Apache, Iroquois, Eskimo, and Aztec. Surrealist recognition of the contemporary American nation would not come until World War II when many European members of the movement found themselves living in New York.

It is no wonder then that a number of North Americans who ended up closely associated with surrealism got there through the back door. That is, they began as associates, not of André Breton, but of Marcel Duchamp, the French transatlantic traveler who eventually made the United States his permanent home. Although Duchamp never accepted the surrealist moniker for himself, he facilitated the proliferation of surrealist ideas through collaborations and introductions. Not only did Man Ray find his way to Paris thanks to Duchamp, but also the young Julien Levy

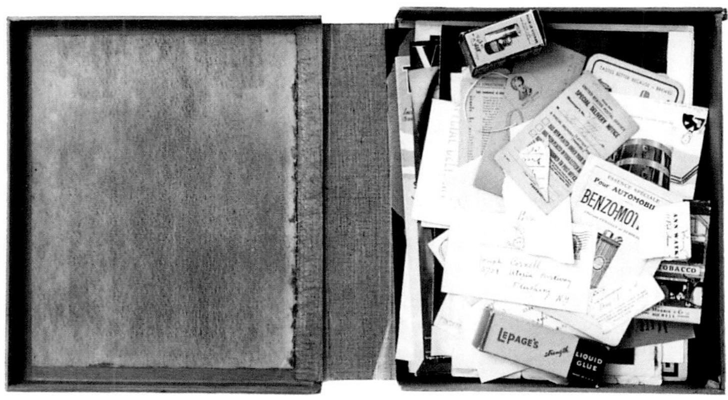

FIG. 1.
JOSEPH CORNELL,
DUCHAMP DOSSIER, 1942–53.
CARDBOARD BOX CONTAINING PAPERS,
NOTES, OBJECTS.
PHILADELPHIA MUSEUM OF ART.
GIFT OF THE JOSEPH AND ROBERT CORNELL
MEMORIAL FOUNDATION, 1990-033-001.

crossed the Atlantic in 1927 at Duchamp's behest. They had met the year before at a Constantin Brancusi exhibition that Duchamp organized for the Brummer Gallery in New York. Levy was on his way to Europe to make a film with Man Ray and Duchamp, but this project never materialized. Instead, he returned to America to found the gallery that would become one of the most significant sponsors of surrealism in the United States.[4]

A few years later, at a second Brancusi exhibition in 1933, the Brummer Gallery again became the host for a significant encounter. It was there that Joseph Cornell first met Duchamp,[5] for whom he would fabricate late versions of the miniature museum, the *Boîte-en-valise*, 1935–41 (cat. 124), more than a decade later.[6] Around that time, Cornell also initiated a collection of ephemera, related to his encounters with Duchamp, now known as the *Duchamp Dossier*, c. 1942–53 (fig. 1). In a cardboard box, likely one cast off from the *Boîte* edition, Cornell amassed torn pieces of paper, empty boxes for ink, glue, and tobacco,

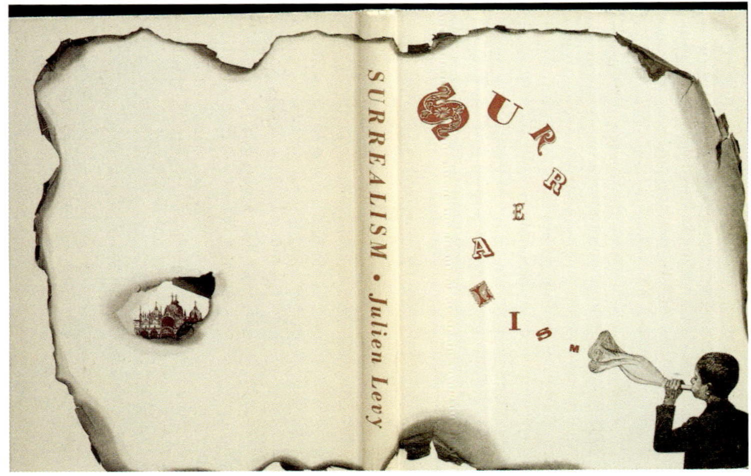

FIG. 2.
JOSEPH CORNELL,
COVER DESIGN FOR *SURREALISM* OF JULIEN LEVY. 1936.
THE MENIL COLLECTION, HOUSTON.

bits of correspondence, receipts for purchases, notes from Duchamp, reproductions, sketches, scraps of fabric and other things. The nature of these two artists' interaction has been explored in the exhibition *Joseph Cornell/Marcel Duchamp . . . in Resonance*, which carefully mapped each of their meetings and the sources for the scraps and documents collected by Cornell.[7] Yet, there remains more to be said about the specific aspect of *portability* in these oeuvres and about how the box as a format for art fulfills the concerns of each artist. There also remains an aspect of this story that can only be surmised at best—the role played by Duchamp's long-term partner, the American expatriate Mary Reynolds, whose little-known bookbindings stand among the few instances of genuine surrealist production by an American in Paris.

Since very little of Reynolds's activities can be concretely traced, and often the ideas for her most celebrated works have been attributed to Duchamp, it requires a degree of speculation, indeed imagination, to find a role for Reynolds in this exchange. I dare to do so here because a significant trail of objects seems to bind all three of these artists' oeuvres. A few noteworthy works, which I will discuss in detail below, trace the tension between the work of art as an object of vision and the work of art as something hand-held.

Like Duchamp, Cornell was uncomfortable with the surrealist label, but he nonetheless won his early reputation through inclusion in the Levy and MoMA exhibitions of surrealism. At the time of the latter, Cornell explained his position to Alfred Barr: "I have never been an official surrealist, and I believe that surrealism has healthier possibilities than have been developed. The constructions of Marcel Duchamp who the surrealists themselves acknowledge bear out this thought, I believe."[8] Despite his preference for Duchamp, Cornell was credited by Levy as being the rare American to fully grasp the concepts of surrealism— Man Ray, who lived in Paris at the time, was the only other exception. In his 1936 anthology of surrealism, Levy extolled: "Finally Joseph Cornell must be mentioned as one of the very few Americans at the present time who fully and creatively understands the surrealist viewpoint."[9] Cornell himself never made it to Paris, but in 1933 he sent a Lee Miller photograph of one of his assemblages to André Breton (cat. 172).[10] Another of his works went to Paris for the 1938 *Exposition internationale du surréalisme* at the Galerie Beaux-Arts.

For the Levy exhibition, the artist's first, Cornell designed the announcement (fig. 2) and contributed collages and an assemblage—*Glass Bell*, c. 1932, which exploited the prevalent surrealist motif of the fragmented body part.[11] Here, a plaster mannequin's hand with a silver wrist strap dangles a black-and-white collage of a rose pierced by an eye at its center. As it survives today, the hand perches upright upon a red, two-tiered, stepped platform, while a miniature slipper and cutlery scatter around its base. The entire collection is housed underneath a bell jar. This early Cornell object seems to relate directly to another work exhibited along with it under the rubric "Potpourri" in the Levy exhibition. Man Ray's *Boule de Neige*, c. 1927, (original no longer extant, editioned in 1970) similarly features the figure of an eye, this time hanging from a row of vertically planted crayons. Man Ray's "snowball," of the type manufactured as a souvenir, was originally destined to be reproduced by the Galerie surréaliste as part of a series of artists' objects, but no such edition was ever released. Such glass orbs require the viewer to shake them gently in order to unleash a flurry of tiny flakes and generate the illusion of a snowstorm. While Man Ray's object was thus designed to be touched, Cornell's assemblage sat safely ensconced behind the bell jar, barring touch even as it featured the image of a hand. This sort of encasement became characteristic of Cornell's oeuvre as he developed the box assemblages for which he is now best known. Jodi Hauptman has proposed an aspect of morbidity to Cornell's penchant for preserving subjects in contained and closed-off spaces.[12] Indeed, the fetishistic partitioning of the figured body demonstrates a version of eroticism that was quite common to surrealism. Levy's anthology grouped together images of ethnographic objects, an Ernst collage, Duchamp's readymade *Why Not Sneeze?*, 1921, and surrealist objects under the heading "fetishism" [*sic*]. More importantly, Cornell's unassuming, almost accidental object, with its conflation of detached hand and eye announces how the tactile is limited by the visible in this aspect of his art.

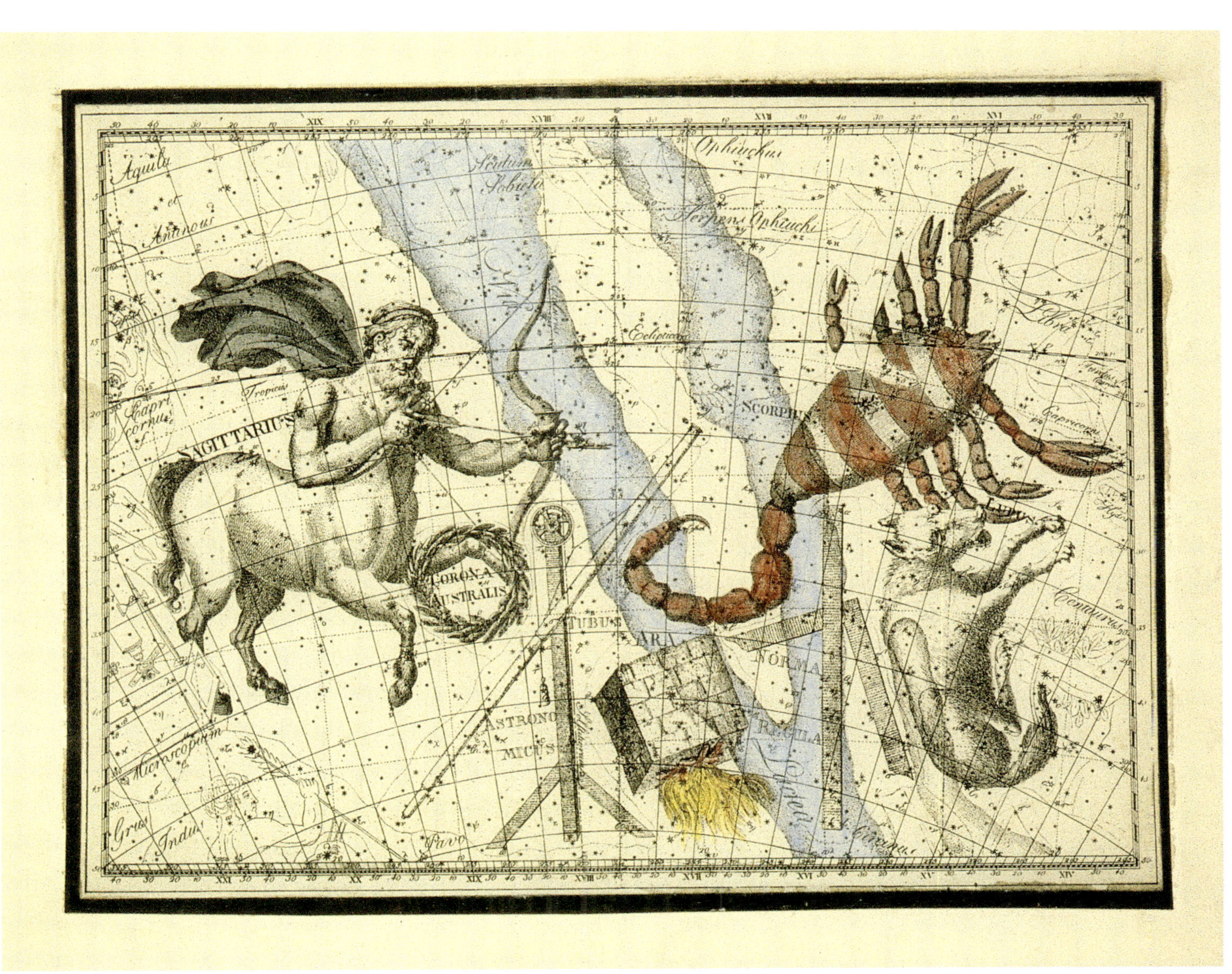

125
JOSEPH CORNELL
[UNTITLED], C. 1930s
COLLAGE, 16.2 X 21.6 CM (SHEET)
THE JOSEPH AND ROBERT CORNELL MEMORIAL FOUNDATION.
COURTESY C & M ARTS, NEW YORK, 1M-4A
MAAG, TAM, TMAA

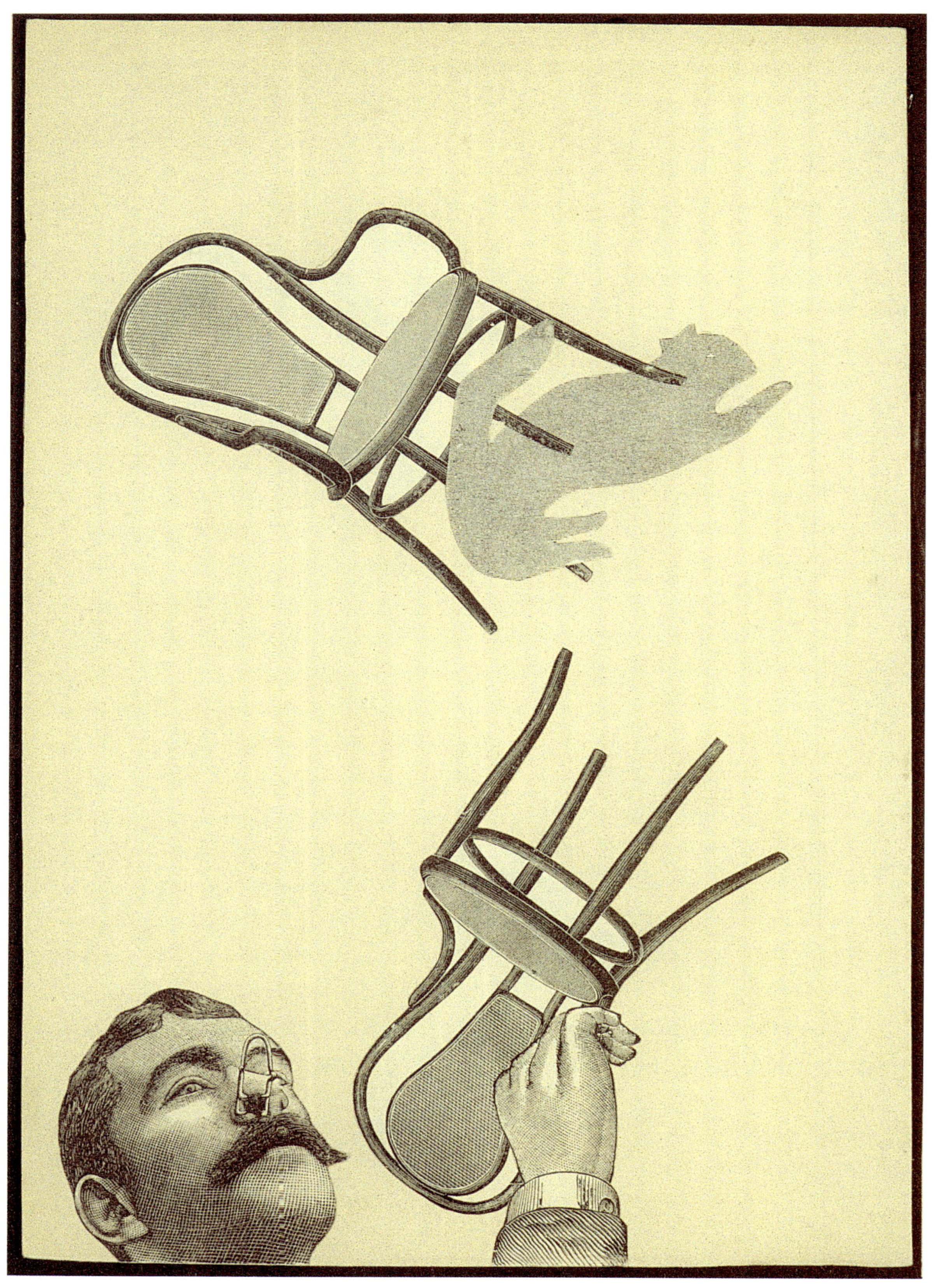

126
JOSEPH CORNELL
[UNTITLED], C. 1930s
COLLAGE, 25.1 X 18.7 CM (SHEET)
THE JOSEPH AND ROBERT CORNELL
MEMORIAL FOUNDATION.
COURTESY C & M ARTS, NEW YORK, IM-15F
MAAG, TAM, TMAA

The motif of the eye pervades surrealism.[13] Man Ray's *Object to be Destroyed*, 1923–32, the metronome with an excerpted eye attached to its pendulum, or Georges Bataille's pornographic novel *Histoire de l'Oeil* (Story of the eye), 1928, suggest its ubiquity. From his comments quoted above on surrealism's "healthier possibilities," we might imagine that Cornell would disdain the more transgressive uses of the eye, but he apparently admired Luis Buñuel and Salvador Dalí's *Un chien andalou*, 1928, a film in which a razor blade notoriously splices open the eye of what appears to be a young woman in the opening scene.[14] Cornell's turn to the motif in *Glass Bell* reads more as nostalgic than disturbing. And yet, the inclusion of the tiny slipper and cutlery adds an aspect of frustrated eroticism to the assemblage. While the rose-eye acts as a talisman, fused to the palm of the hand, the objects around it seem to invite ingestion, or at least imagined incorporation.

It is possible that Cornell had already seen Salvador Dalí's essay on "objects functioning symbolically," published in the December 1931 issue of *Le Surréalisme au service de la révolution*,[15] which illustrated Dalí's combination of footwear, spoon, and moving parts. It is also possible that Cornell, who is known to have reworked his objects, added some of these elements later. A photograph of *Glass Bell*, published in *Minotaure* in 1937, shows a fan held in the hand and indecipherable objects around the base.[16] Dalí's assemblage was meant to putrefy over time—it included a glass of warm milk in a woman's red pump, lumps of sugar to be stirred and dissolved in the milk, and other assorted debris arranged on a vertical apparatus. This type of construction achieved what Dalí described as the third phase of the surrealist object: "The object is movable and such that it can be acted upon." The fourth and final phase required that one commune with the article by ingesting it. Cornell's miniature forks, knives, and spoons come to mind. Levy's anthology reprinted an excerpt from the English version of Dalí's text, captioned by the phrase "Oral Description of Articles (perceived only by touch)": "The subject is blindfolded and describes, by touching it, some ordinary or specially manufactured article, and the record of each description is compared with the article in question. On the strength of descriptions obtained in this manner an article can be made, and compared with the original article described."[17] Thus, Dalí imagines the experience of an object to be intensified through touch, at the expense of vision. Significantly, Levy grouped this text under the heading "play," focusing on the surrealist conception of the art object as a vehicle for interactive amusement. Dalí's instructions can be read as a formula for producing and/or experiencing the surrealist object. It is no coincidence, then, that Levy later marketed Cornell's objects as "toys for adults," often scheduling his exhibitions during the Christmas season for maximum sales.[18] Nor is it surprising that Cornell, as we will see below, developed a series of sandboxes that were surely meant for play.

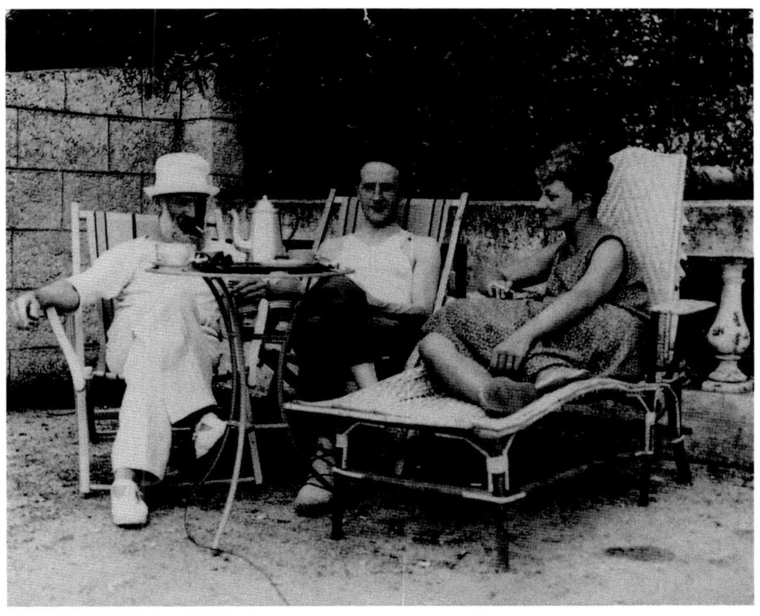

FIG. 3.
CONSTANTIN BRANCUSI, MARCEL DUCHAMP, AND MARY REYNOLDS AT VILLEFRANCHE, 1929.
GELATIN SILVER PRINT.
THE ART INSTITUTE OF CHICAGO. GIFT OF FRANK B. HUBACHEK.
1970.798.

Mary Louise Reynolds came to Paris in April 1921 and settled in Montparnasse, where she quickly fell into the company of an international circle of artists and writers.[19] She had been widowed during World War I by the death from influenza of her husband Matthew Reynolds, a member of the American Infantry. Sometime in 1923, she came into contact with Marcel Duchamp, whom she had met earlier in New York. They began a rocky relationship, interrupted by the brief marriage of Duchamp in 1927 to Lydie Sarazin-Levassor. By the 1930s, however, they had settled into a harmonious partnership that lasted two decades. While they always maintained separate residences—Duchamp at 11, rue Larrey and Reynolds at 14, rue Hallé—they spent a majority of their leisure time together, hosting dinners at her house, and vacationing in the summers (fig. 3).

Much testimony from the earlier difficult years of this liaison is found in the memoirs of Duchamp's cohorts—friends like Man Ray and Henri-Pierre Roché. These men remember that Duchamp kept Reynolds at a distance while he continued to sleep with other women, that she resorted to drinking binges, and generally put up with all of his bad behavior.[20] Such recollections might be slanted by predictable rivalries among men; Roché for example was fond of making lovers of Duchamp's girlfriends, but was unable to do so in this instance. Indeed, after his first visit to Reynolds's apartment without Duchamp, Roché described Reynolds and her careful deflection of any lingering sexual tension: "a handsome spectacle. Slender heroic body with dark circles under her eyes. Great calm. She seems to have something like a desire to die.

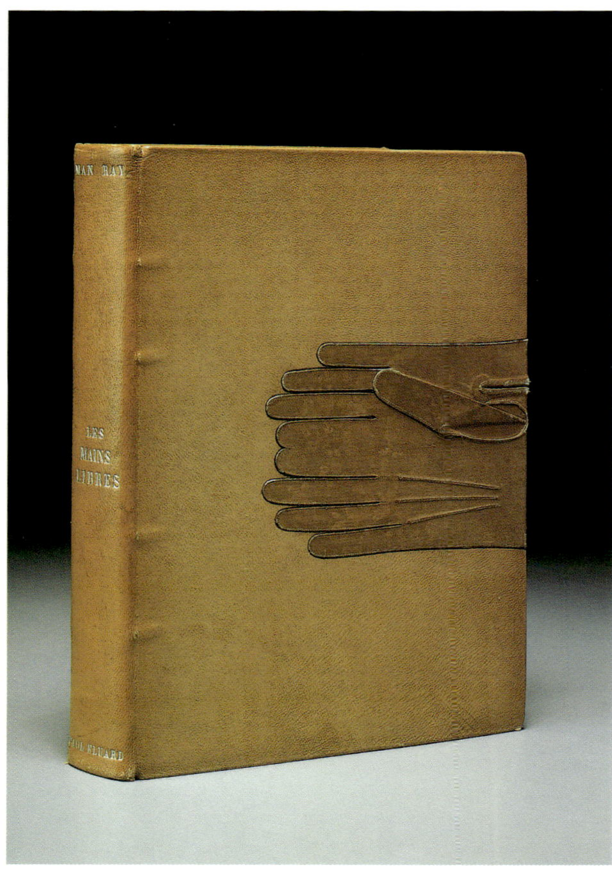

FIG. 4.
MAN RAY AND PAUL ELUARD,
LES MAINS LIBRES, 1937.
BINDING BY MARY REYNOLDS.
THE ART INSTITUTE OF CHICAGO.
RYERSON & BURNHAM LIBRARIES.
MARY REYNOLDS COLLECTION, RX20234/1.

She drinks each night until she gets drunk. In that state loses neither her charm nor her nobility . . . We see to it that our fingers do not touch, even by chance, in handling books and objects."[21] Here Roché unwittingly remarks upon the surrealist use of things as vehicles for human touch. In his off-handed comment, he echoes Dalí's somewhat more deliberate conception of people interacting around things—when they "play," they invite deeper associations.

In 1929, Mary Reynolds took up bookbinding as an avocation, training under the well-known book designer Pierre Legrain.[22] For the most part, she made luxury bindings for the books in her own collection, often by writers associated loosely with surrealism such as Alfred Jarry, Raymond Queneau, and Jean Cocteau.[23] She specialized in exotic materials and the occasional three-dimensional folly—a broken piece of pottery, a thermometer, or a corset stay. A few of her bindings—those for Alfred Jarry's *Ubu Roi* (King Ubu), 1921, Giorgio de Chirico's *Hebdomeros*, 1929, and Duchamp's own collection of puns *Rrose Sélavy*, 1939—are documented as collaborations with Duchamp. For the Duchamp text, Reynolds set rectangles of gray cardboard framed by thin rope on the

front and back covers. A blind stamp that reads "de ou par Marcel Duchamp ou Rrose Sélavy" embosses each card. On the back, a second, more faint impression from the same stamp doubles the first, so that the letters overlap and become difficult to decipher. Speckled endpapers feature insects drawn in black ink. The stamp used for the lettering was likely a cast-off from Duchamp's ongoing *Boîte-en-valise*, the official title of which—*De ou par Marcel Duchamp ou Rrose Sélavy*—was stamped on the back of the support for the reproduction of the *Large Glass*.[24] While it is easy to imagine, as many have, that Duchamp influenced Reynolds's book designs, fewer have speculated on Reynolds's role as a trained bookbinder in the fabrication of Duchamp's boxed art. One notable exception is the leading expert on the *Boîte*, Ecke Bonk, who surmised that Mary Reynolds might have assisted Duchamp in the meticulous reproduction of his notes for the *Green Box*.[25] Although no one has said so, Reynolds probably participated in figuring out the complicated armature for the *Boîte-en-valise* as well.

One of Reynolds's most remarkable bindings encases *Les Mains libres*, 1937, a surrealist collection of drawings by Man Ray and poems by Paul Eluard. Bound in a rich honey-colored leather, and stamped cleanly on the spine with the title and authors' names, this book explores themes of eroticism and desire. Reynolds's design for it is quite elegant (fig. 4). A dismantled kid glove, which echoes the many hands figured in the drawings and poems, has been spread open and pressed into the flat surface of the book's front and back covers. As has been argued by Susan Glover Godlewski, the visual pun, which was probably inspired by Duchamp, plays on the title "free hands" to "symbolically" free the authors' hands by slitting open the gloves.[26] And yet, the adherence of the glove to the surface of the book frustrates the image of a freed hand. There is no inside to these gloves, only the impossibility of ever lifting them from the text.

My interest is in the reader's experience of holding this book. Pick up the book and begin to read. The gloves fall exactly where you find your own hands. Imagine the strange sensation of the flattened fingers that double, or even triple your own—split open, each glove reads as two. These hands are sensual yet alarmingly cold, inhuman. The leather is soft and lush; the stitching on the thumb and back of the hand rub against your fingers as you rest the volume on your lap. Turn the pages and you notice that the book gives under the pressure of their weight; the interior covers, or doublures, consist of thin sheets of pink sponge rubber, further enhancing tactile pleasure. Years later, in 1947, Duchamp would literalize this invitation to feel a book when he jokingly attached rubber "falsies" to the cover of a surrealist exhibition catalogue with the help of Enrico Donati (fig. 5). The breasts might be disturbing to grab, but Duchamp urges the viewer's transgression with the inscription: "prière de toucher," please touch.[27]

The unsettling presence of a detached hand, even one meant to invite interaction, recalls Breton's haunting vision of a woman's glove recounted in *Nadja*, 1928. Fascinated by the sky-blue covered hands of a visitor to the surrealist centrale, Breton first asks the woman to donate her gloves to its collection of curiosities. When she agrees and begins to take off her gloves, Breton finds himself in a panic, begging her not to expose her hands: "I don't know what there can have been, at that moment, so terribly, so marvelously decisive for me in the thought of the glove leaving that hand forever."[28] An obvious interpretation here derives from the classic understanding of fetishism in Freudian theory—the fear of castration evoked by the fragmented body. Hal Foster has gone further to relate this episode to the anxiety of the death drive, a repetition of repressed trauma that will never be recognized nor put to rest.[29] The hand in Reynolds's composition may be taken as a consummate example of this surrealist obsession, and indeed engages on this level with the surrealist texts it envelops. At the same time, Reynolds's lighter touch reminds us of Cornell's hand emerging whimsically from a field of miniature eating artillery as it staves off the contact enabled by Reynolds's binding.

It was probably not until 1943, when both Reynolds and Duchamp were back in New York, and Cornell had been engaged to fabricate later versions of the *Boîte*, that Cornell and Reynolds became acquainted. Duchamp had begun to think about the project, which would faithfully reproduce sixty-nine of his works in miniature, as a portable museum retrospective, in the mid-1930s. As the war situation worsened in France, Duchamp secured a cheese merchant's license to cross between the occupied and unoccupied zones and gradually smuggle out pieces of his yet unassembled boxes, leaving the remainder stored in Reynolds's cellar.[30] In July 1941, Peggy Guggenheim carried one completed box in her carry-on luggage to the United States and shipped the components for about fifty more with her art collection, all disguised as "household goods." During these months, Reynolds remained ensconced in Paris where it would later be found out she was working with the French Resistance. Duchamp exited to New York, arriving in June 1942, but Reynolds did not agree to depart until it was almost too late.[31] In January 1943, she made it to the United States after a harrowing passage through the Pyrénées, and a few near misses with the Gestapo. Although Duchamp conceived of the *Boîte* before Hitler became a tangible threat to Parisians, the uncanny reality of his boxed oeuvre being smuggled in pieces across international borders brings the project into the realm of what T. J. Demos has labeled "geopolitical displacement."[32]

In contrast to Duchamp, who also spent World War I in the United States, Reynolds resisted relocation.[33] While Duchamp labored on a portable oeuvre, Reynolds rooted herself to her adopted home. She wrote letters to her brother about how "crazy and pig-headed" she knew she was being and yet how she desired to stay and take care of her house and cats. In these letters, she admitted to spending much of her time "tracking down food and unorganized aid," but said that she was enjoying solitude and gardening for her dinner: "I am leading just the

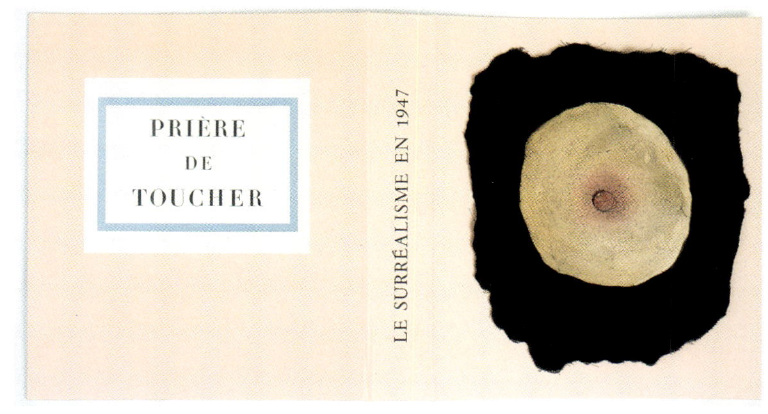

FIG. 5.
MARCEL DUCHAMP WITH ENRICO DONATI,
COVER FOR *LE SURRÉALISME EN 1947*, 1947.
GALERIE MAEGHT, PARIS.

kind of life I would love to lead and never do except when forced to. The only drawback is that the force that would otherwise make me a good life is such a black and ugly one that it can't be ignored even in retreat—and the fact that so much misery exists is sometimes overpowering."[34] Duchamp's letters from Sanary-sur-Mer, where he stayed while awaiting his American visa, were a bit more clipped: "Little to eat here but lots of sun . . ." he wrote to Georges Hugnet, "I am trying to finish a box in leather."[35] His single-mindedness with regard to the *Boîte* seems a strategy for enduring the war.

When Duchamp arrived in New York, however, his will to edition the *Boîte-en-valise* did not subside. He soon hired Cornell in this capacity, giving the younger artist ample opportunity to collect ephemera for his *Duchamp Dossier*. The dossier preserves nine letters from Mary Reynolds to Cornell, all from the period after she returned to New York. The first, dated December 14, 1944 is a brief note, addressed in a manner that became common among the three artists—"Cher Amiral" in this case, "Amiral Grillon" in others.[36] The origin of this appellation remains a mystery, but Cornell incorporated a cutout text in Duchamp's hand stating "appartenant à l'amiral Grillon" [belonging to admiral cricket] for his circular boxed assemblage *Amiral Grillon (Watch)* or *A Watch-Case for Marcel Duchamp*. The present whereabouts of this object is unknown, but its image survives in a montage that Cornell published in a special issue of the magazine *View* devoted to Duchamp in 1945.[37] This is likely one of the objects referred to in another of Reynolds's letters from the *Duchamp Dossier*. This one was written after her return to Paris:

> I'm also looking forward to having again two of your boxes I
> thought I had not to take with me when I came—the war
> still being on & they had a spyish look to them. The Amiral &
> the box with ring & black powder are here before me.

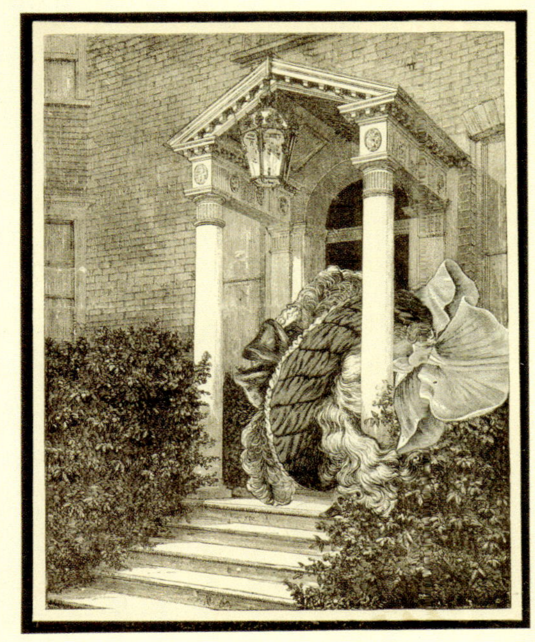

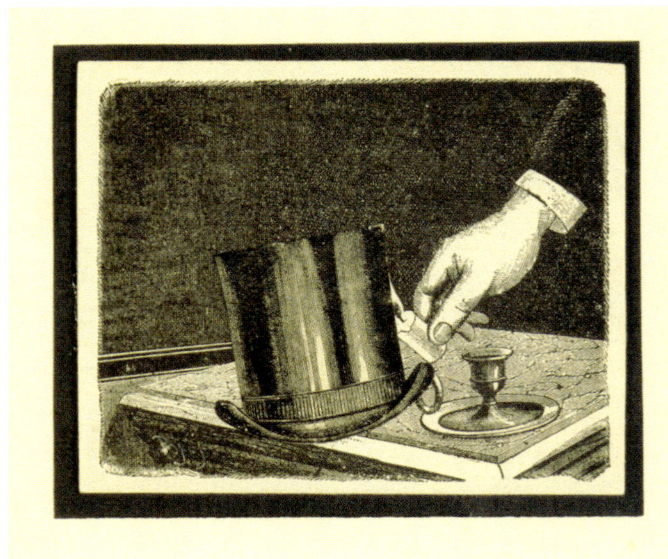

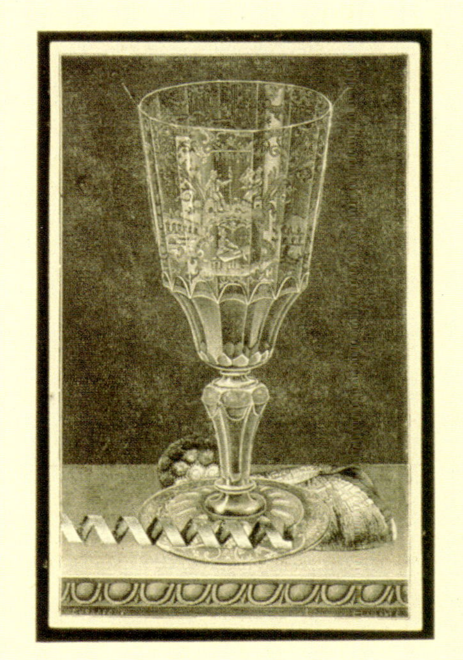

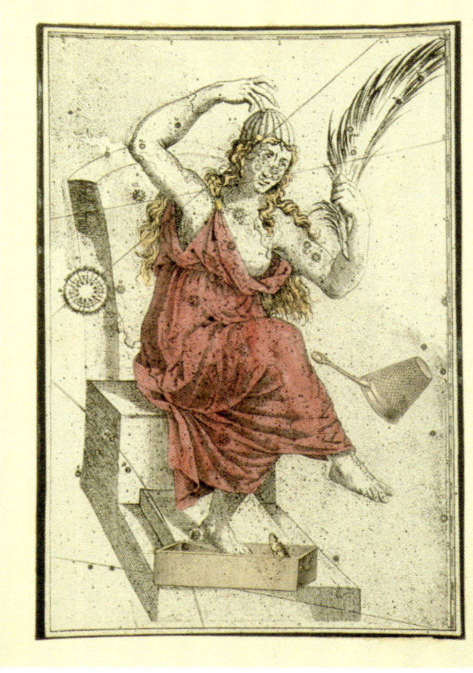

127
JOSEPH CORNELL
[UNTITLED], C. 1930s
COLLAGE, 24.8 X 18.7 CM (SHEET)
THE JOSEPH AND ROBERT CORNELL
MEMORIAL FOUNDATION.
COURTESY C & M ARTS, NEW YORK,
1M-11E
MAAG, TAM, TMAA

128
JOSEPH CORNELL
[UNTITLED], C. 1930s
COLLAGE, 19.1 X 24.8 CM (SHEET)
THE JOSEPH AND ROBERT CORNELL
MEMORIAL FOUNDATION.
COURTESY C & M ARTS, NEW YORK,
1M-10B
MAAG, TAM, TMAA

129
JOSEPH CORNELL
[UNTITLED], C. 1930s
COLLAGE, 25.1 X 18.7 CM (SHEET)
THE JOSEPH AND ROBERT CORNELL
MEMORIAL FOUNDATION.
COURTESY C & M ARTS, NEW YORK,
1M-10G
MAAG, TAM, TMAA

130
JOSEPH CORNELL
UNTITLED (LA CASSIOPÉE), C. 1930s
COLLAGE, 23.2 X 17.2 CM (SHEET)
THE JOSEPH AND ROBERT CORNELL
MEMORIAL FOUNDATION.
COURTESY C & M ARTS, NEW YORK,
1M-4E
MAAG, TAM, TMAA

> Tho I've made myself an almost perfect life—hardly allowing anyone in the house I don't approve—there have yet been inquiries about the box—What is it? How do you play it?[38]

In the same letter Reynolds thanks Cornell for a care package he sent, which she refers to as "that delicious box." Cornell used the functional box as a conduit for precious commodities in post-war Paris, sending Reynolds gingerbread mix, currants, magazines, soap, chocolate cake, and even marshmallows.[39] Although Reynolds mocks her guests for wondering what to do with Cornell's art, the "box with ring and black powder" that she mentions must surely have been designed for "play." *Surrealist Box (Sand Painting)*, 1951 (fig. 6) is a wood-framed, rather shallow, box, filled with a dark granular substance, a silver metal ring, and inscribed with a pattern of radiating diagonals.[40] Unlike the more familiar upright boxes by Cornell, this one sits horizontally on a table surface, like the famed surrealist game boards made by Alberto Giacometti in the early 1930s.[41] Seemingly begging to be shaken, the delicate grains leave a residue of reddish purple color on the interior surface of the box that deepens with use.[42] This box, unlike the earlier *Glass Bell*, required Reynolds's touch. Indeed it did not acquire its rich coloration unless manipulated by the viewer. Cornell's invention recalls Dalí's somewhat more aggressive directive that art be used for contact.

When Mary Reynolds died in 1950, she had three Cornell constructions in her collection, two of which were sandboxes.[43] She also owned a *Boîte-en-valise* that Duchamp inscribed to her in May 1941, one month before he made his final journey to the unoccupied zone to await departure for the States. The *Boîte* was not intended as a game and yet its carefully designed compartments and sliding framework require the viewer's machinations. If Reynolds played with this work, she probably envisioned travel, dislocation, and war. And yet for Duchamp, to play meant to be rewarded with the satisfying containment and preservation of one's oeuvre. If touch was sensually gratifying in Reynolds's bookbindings or playfully amusing in Cornell's sandboxes, it facilitated memory, permanently delaying gratification, in Duchamp's *Boîte*. ■

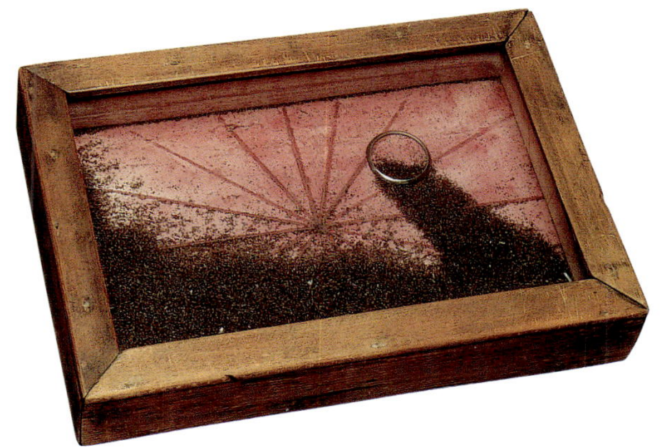

FIG. 6.

JOSEPH CORNELL,
SURREALIST BOX (SAND PAINTING), 1951.
DRY COLOR AND NOTEBOOK RING IN BOX
WITH GLASS TOP, 26 X 18 X 4.76 CM.
THE ART INSTITUTE OF CHICAGO.
GIFT OF FRANK B. HUBACHEK, 1951.201.

1— Henri-Pierre Roché, Journals, June 9, 1924. Carlton Lake Collection, Harry Ransom Humanities Research Center, The University of Texas at Austin, quoted in Calvin Tomkins, *Duchamp: A Biography* (New York: Henry Holt and Co., 1996), 257.

2— There is some controversy as to whether Levy organized both shows, as he claims to have done. Julien Levy, *Memoir of an Art Gallery* (New York: Putnam and Sons, 1977), 79–80. For a comparison of the two shows, see Deborah Zlotsky, "Pleasant Madness in Hartford: The First Surrealist Exhibition in America," *Arts Magazine* 60 (February 1986), 55–61.

3— For more on surrealism in the United States, see Dickran Tashjian, *A Boatload of Madmen* (New York: Thames and Hudson, 1995) and Martica Sawin, *Surrealism in Exile* (Cambridge, Mass.: The MIT Press, 1995).

4— For more on Levy, see Ingrid Schaffner and Lisa Jacobs, eds., *Julien Levy: Portrait of an Art Gallery*, exh. cat. (Cambridge, Mass.: The MIT Press, 1998).

5— "Brummer Gallery/I recall so easily an esp. cherished one, first brief meeting (as a stranger), the piquant flavor of contact with/a unique personality . . ." Draft of condolence note from Joseph Cornell to Alexina Duchamp, October 9, 1968, Joseph Cornell Papers, Archives of American Art, Smithsonian Institution, Washington D.C., microfilm 1056:679–681, quoted in *Joseph Cornell/Marcel Duchamp . . . in Resonance*, exh. cat. (Houston: Menil Collection and Philadelphia: Philadelphia Museum of Art, 1998), 80. Hereafter cited as *Cornell/Duchamp*.

6— The full title of this work is *De ou par Marcel Duchamp ou Rrose Sélavy*. There are twenty-four deluxe examples, fitted in leather suitcases—each one containing a single original work of art. Although the entire series is often referred to as the *Boîte-en-valise*, later versions are more properly designated as the *Boîte* editions. It was these later editions that Cornell would have helped to assemble. Ecke Bonk, *Marcel Duchamp: The Box in a Valise* (New York: Rizzoli, 1989), 257.

7— *Cornell/Duchamp*. I would like to thank Michael Taylor, Philadelphia Museum of Art and his staff, as well as Rena Hoisington, for making the *Duchamp Dossier* and related materials available to me.

8— Joseph Cornell to Alfred Barr, November 13, 1936, The Museum of Modern Art, Department of Registration, "Fantastic art, Dada, Surrealism," Exhibition No. 855, exhibition file, quoted in *Cornell/Duchamp*, 87.

9— Julien Levy, *Surrealism* (Black Sun Press, 1936; reprint, New York: Da Capo, 1995), 28.

10— *Cornell/Duchamp*, 279–80.

11— Levy later used Cornell's announcement for the cover of his anthology.

12— Jodi Hauptman, *Joseph Cornell: Stargazing in the Cinema* (New Haven: Yale University Press, 1999), 49–50.

13— For example, see Martin Jay, "Disenchantment of the Eye," *Visual Anthropology Review* 7, no. 1 (1991): 15–38.

14— Levy gave the film its American premiere in November 1932.

15— Salvador Dalí, "Objets surréalistes," *Le Surréalisme au service de la révolution* 3 (December 1931): 16. An English version of this text appeared as "The Object as Revealed in Surrealist Experiment," *This Quarter* 5, no. 1 (September 1932): 179–207.

16— *Minotaure* 3 series: no. 10 (1937): 34.

17— Salvador Dalí quoted in Levy, *Surrealism* (1936), 48.

18— Ann Temkin, "Habitat for a Dossier," in *Cornell/Duchamp*, 81.

19— This brief summary of Mary Reynolds's biography is indebted to Susan Glover Godlewski, "Warm Ashes: The Life and Career of Mary Reynolds," *Mary Reynolds and the Spirit of Surrealism*, The Art Institute of Chicago Museum Studies 22:2 (1996), 102–115; as well as Susan Davidson's "Marcel Duchamp/Joseph Cornell Chronology," in *Cornell/Duchamp*, 276-97; Jennifer Gough-Cooper and Jacques Caumont, *Ephemerides on and about Marcel Duchamp and Rrose Sélavy* (Cambridge, Mass.: The MIT Press); and Tomkins, *Duchamp: A Biography*. After her death in 1950, Mary Reynolds's collection of artworks, books, and journals was donated to the Art Institute of Chicago (AIC) by her brother Frank Hubachek. In 1956, the museum published a catalogue with a brief introduction by Duchamp, revised in 1973. Hugh Edwards, ed., *Surrealism and Its Affinities: The Mary Reynolds Collection,* exh. cat. (Chicago: AIC, 1956). I would like to thank Jack Perry Brown, Director of the Ryerson and Burnham Libraries, AIC, for sharing both the collection and his expertise with me.

20— Roché, June 9, July 3, 1924, quoted in Tomkins, *Duchamp: A Biography*, 257–59; and Man Ray, *Self-Portrait* (Boston: Little, Brown, and Co., 1988 [1963]), 190. Kay Boyle similarly reported Reynolds going "on a sort of wild thing" when Duchamp married. Kay Boyle interview with Calvin Tomkins, quoted in Tomkins, *Duchamp: A Biography*, 258.

21— See note 1.

22— For more on bookbinding, see Jean Toulet, "Binding as Invention," *Surrealism: Two Private Eyes: The Nesuhi Ertegun and Daniel Filipacchi Collections,* exh. cat. (New York: Guggenheim, 1999), 811–15.

23— See Godlewski, "A Selected Catalogue of Bookbindings by Mary Reynolds," in *Mary Reynolds*, 116–29.

24— See Bonk, "Delay Included," in *Cornell/ Duchamp*, 103.

25— "Knowing a little bit of Duchamp's patience and working principles, one can assume that a great deal of this hand/work (manu/facturing) was eventually done by the artist himself, maybe with help from Mary Reynolds." Ibid., 101.

26— Godlewski, *Mary Reynolds,* 126.

27— Perhaps what Duchamp really had in mind was an experience of excess—or an exaggeration of desire that would lead to its extinction: "When they started preparing the covers . . . in Donati's studio, there were 999 foam-rubber breasts on the floor to be glued separately by hand. 'By the end,' recalled Donati, 'we were fed up but we got the job done. I remarked that I had never thought I would get tired of handling so many breasts, and Marcel said, 'Maybe that's the whole idea.'" Gough-Cooper and Caumont, *Ephemerides*, May 17, 1947.

28— André Breton, *Nadja* (Paris: Gallimard, 1960 [1928]), 55–56.

29— Hal Foster, *Compulsive Beauty* (Cambridge, Mass.: The MIT Press, 1993), 33.

30— Gough-Cooper and Caumont, *Ephemerides*, January 7, 1941.

31— For more details, see Godlewski, *Mary Reynolds*, 111–13 and Janet Flanner, "The Escape of Mrs. Jeffries," *New Yorker* (May 22, May 29, and June 5, 1943).

32— Demos develops his notions of exile, decontextualization, and recontextualization in two articles: "Duchamp's Labyrinth: First Papers of Surrealism, 1942," *October* (summer 2001): 91–119 and "Duchamp's *Boîte-en-valise*: Between Institutional Acculturation and Geopolitical Displacement," *Grey Room* 8 (summer 2002): 6–37.

33— On Duchamp's role as a noncombatant, see Amelia Jones, "Equivocal Masculinity: New York Dada in the Context of World War I," *Art History* 25, no. 2 (April 2002): 162–205.

34— MLR to FBH, January 8, 1941, August 7, 1941, November 30, 1941, and February 14, 1942, Folder 1.1, Box 1, 1951.1, Mary Reynolds Collection, Ryerson and Burnham Libraries, AIC. Hereafter cited as Mary Reynolds Collection.

35— Gough-Cooper and Caumont, *Ephemerides,* March 9, 1942.

36— All texts from the *Duchamp Dossier* are transcribed in *Cornell-Duchamp*. I indicate the catalogue numbers from this text in the references that follow. MLR to JC, December 14, 1944 (DD 9), *Cornell/Duchamp*, 307.

37— *Cornell/Duchamp*, 288, 298.

38— MLR to JC, May 1, 1946 (DD 80), *Cornell/Duchamp*, 322.

39— MLR to JC, January 28, 1948 (DD 82), *Cornell/Duchamp*, 322.

40— I would like to thank Daniel Schulmann and Suzie Schnepp, AIC for making this object and its materials analysis available to me.

41— On Georges Bataille's notion of the horizontal with regard to Giacometti's games, see Rosalind Krauss, "No More Play," *Originality of the Avant-Garde and Other Modernist Myths* (Cambridge, Mass.: The MIT Press, 1986), 42–85.

42— According to a conservation report, the grains consist of transparent quartz or pumice mixed with a dye known as methyl violet. It is possible that Cornell mixed clear sand with a colored dye so that the action of the sand would gradually change the color of the interior of the box. Schnepp to author, November 14, 2002.

43— An inventory of Reynolds's household goods includes the following notation: "Cornell, Joseph—1 boîte with yellow sand, 1 boîte with black sand, 1 boîte—round," "List of Works of Art Going to Chicago," 2, Folder 1.6, Box 1, 1951.1, Mary Reynolds Collection. The round work was likely *Amiral Grillon (Watch)* or *Mémoires inédits de Madame de Rochejaquelein*, 1943, which has also been attributed to her collection. *Cornell/Duchamp*, 288.

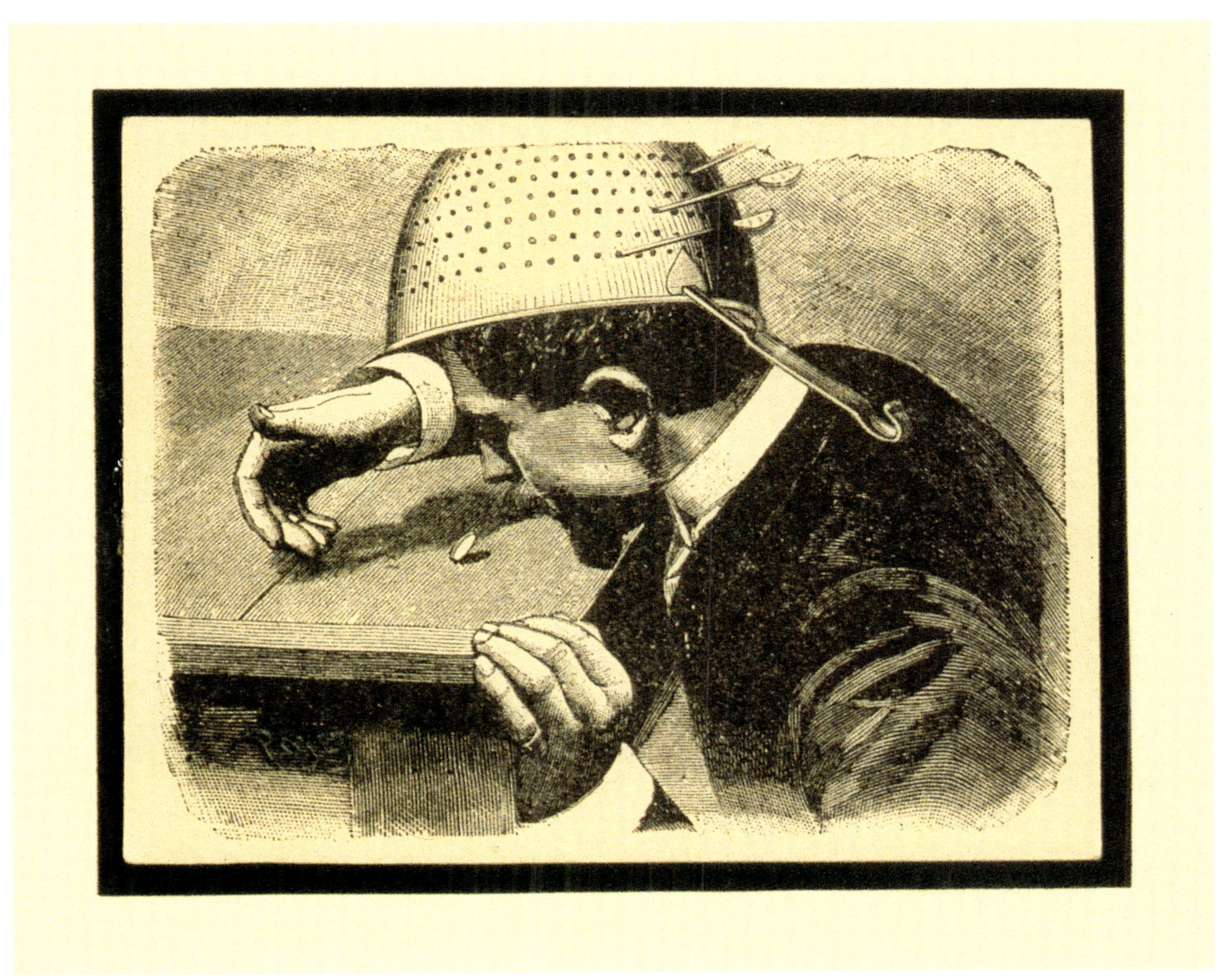

131
JOSEPH CORNELL
[UNTITLED], C. 1930s
COLLAGE, 18.7 X 25.1 CM (SHEET)
THE JOSEPH AND ROBERT CORNELL MEMORIAL FOUNDATION.
COURTESY C & M ARTS, NEW YORK, IM-10H
MAAG, TAM, TMAA

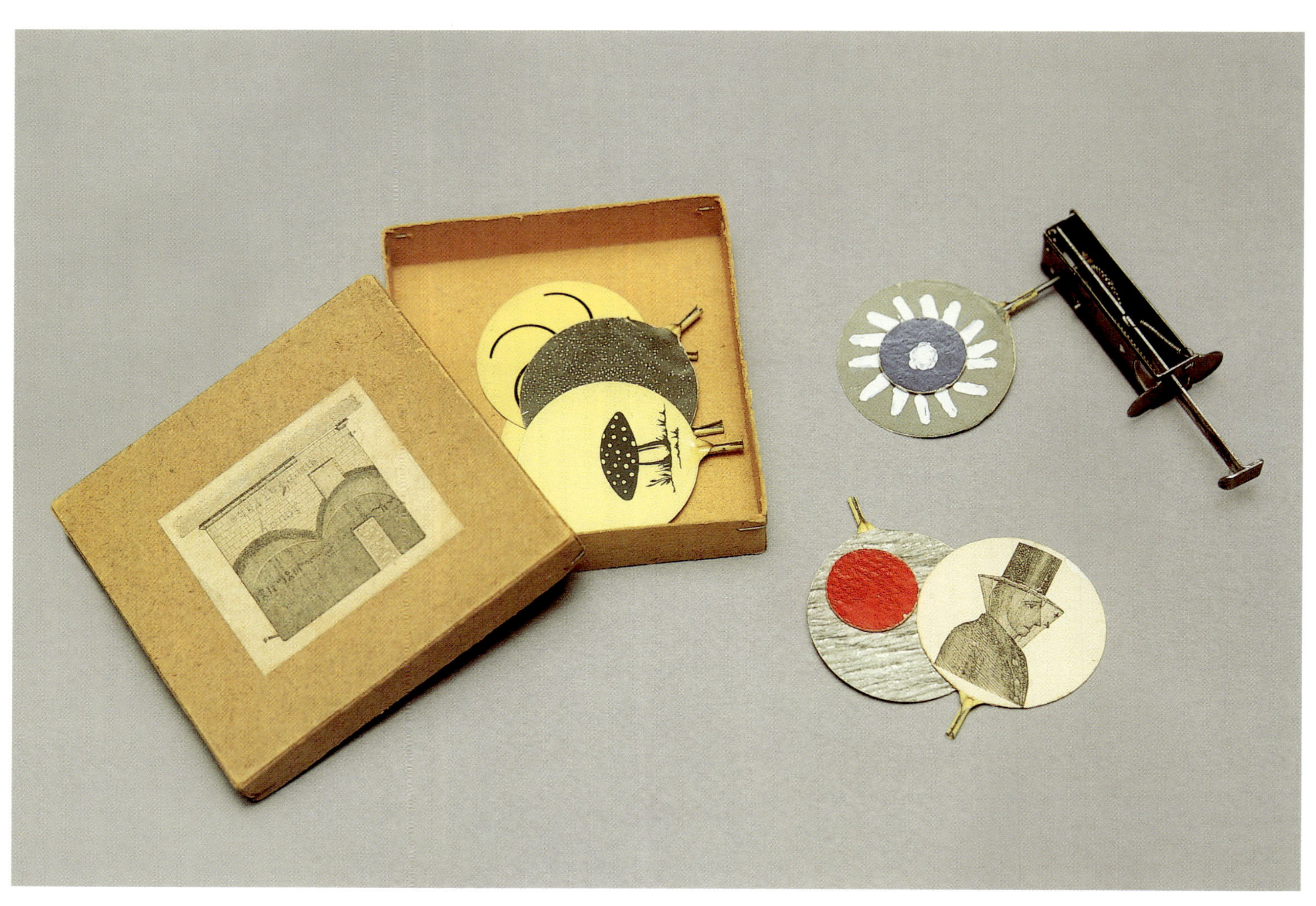

132
JOSEPH CORNELL
JOUET SURRÉALISTE [SURREALIST GAME], C. 1932
STEEL LINE ENGRAVINGS, PAPER, PAINT AND INK ON
PAPERBOARD AND METAL, 10.6 X 9.9 X 2.3 CM
SMITHSONIAN AMERICAN ART MUSEUM, WASHINGTON D.C.
GIFT OF MR. AND MRS. JOHN A. BENTON, 1978.95.1
MAAG, TAM, TMAA

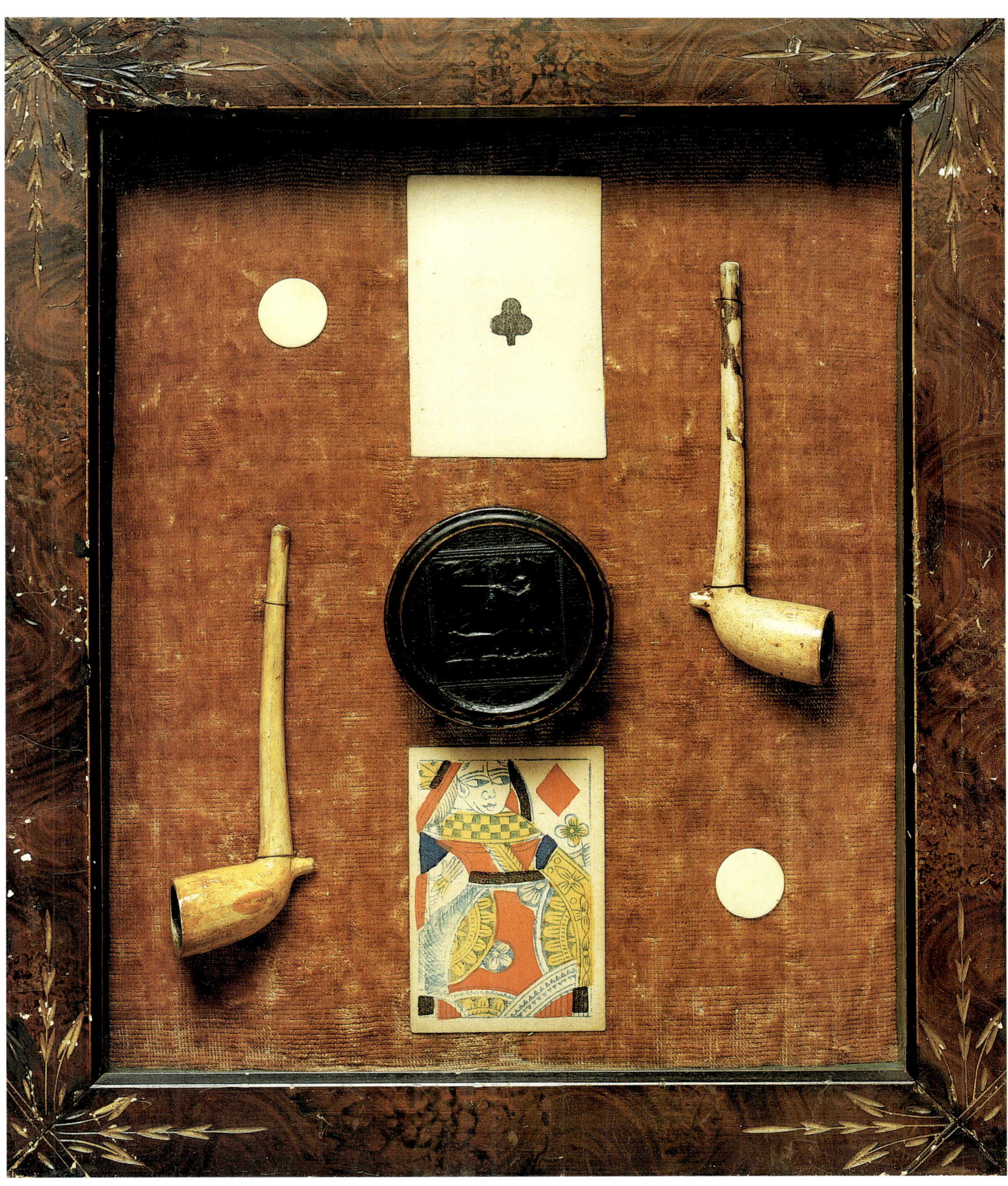

133
CHARLES SHAW
MONTAGE, 1935–50
PAPER PLAYING CARDS, CLAY PIPES, IVORY DISCS, AND
WOOD SNUFF BOX MOUNTED ON VELVET, 38.1 X 33 X 5.4 CM
SMITHSONIAN AMERICAN ART MUSEUM, WASHINGTON D.C.
GIFT OF PATRICIA AND PHILLIP FROST, 1986.92.87
THIS WORK IS NOT EXHIBITED.

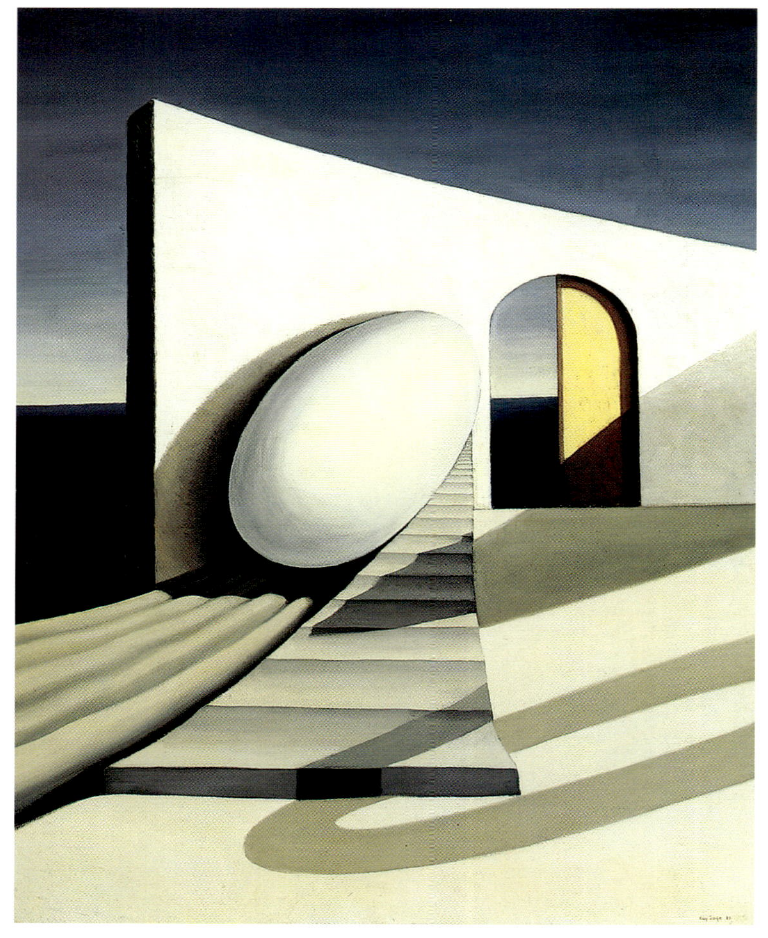

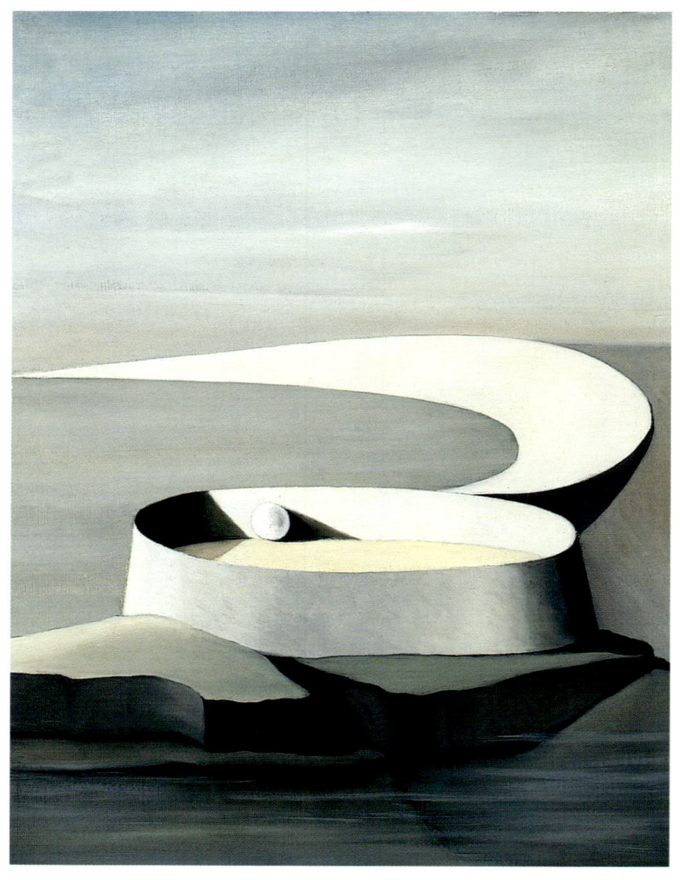

134
KAY SAGE
MY ROOM HAS TWO DOORS, 1939
OIL ON CANVAS, 99 × 83.8 CM
MATTATUCK MUSEUM, WATERBURY, CONN.,
KSCX68.12
MAAG, TAM, TMAA

135
KAY SAGE
NO ONE HEARD THUNDER, 1939
OIL ON CANVAS, 91.4 × 71.1 CM
MATTATUCK MUSEUM, WATERBURY, CONN.,
KSCX68.8
MAAG, TAM, TMAA

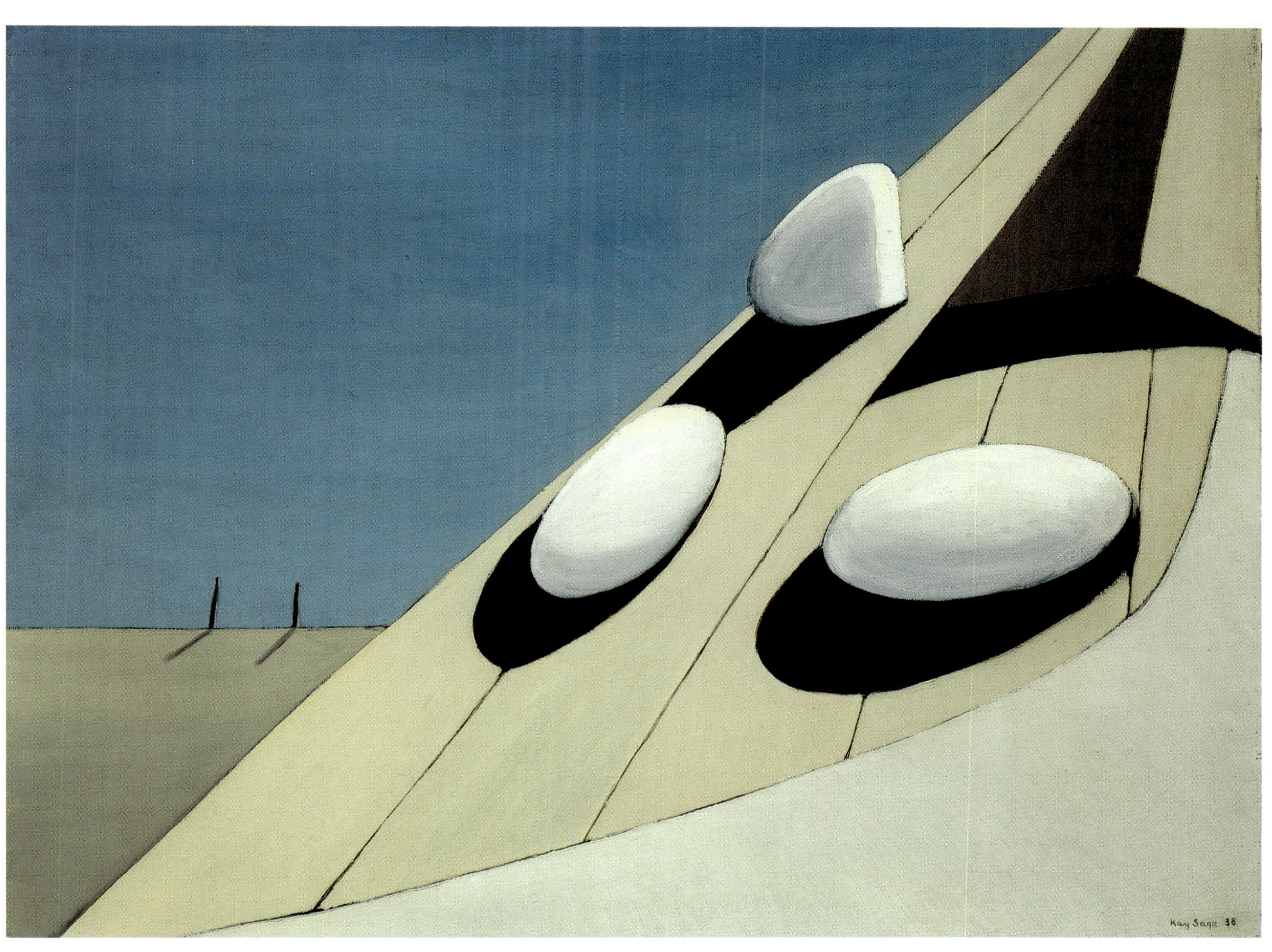

136
KAY SAGE
THE WORLD IS BLUE, 1938
OIL ON CANVAS, 51.1 X 72.4 CM
INDIANA UNIVERSITY ART MUSEUM, BLOOMINGTON.
KAY SAGE BEQUEST, 64.72
MAAG, TAM, TMAA

the portraits of the avant-garde

CHAPTER **4**

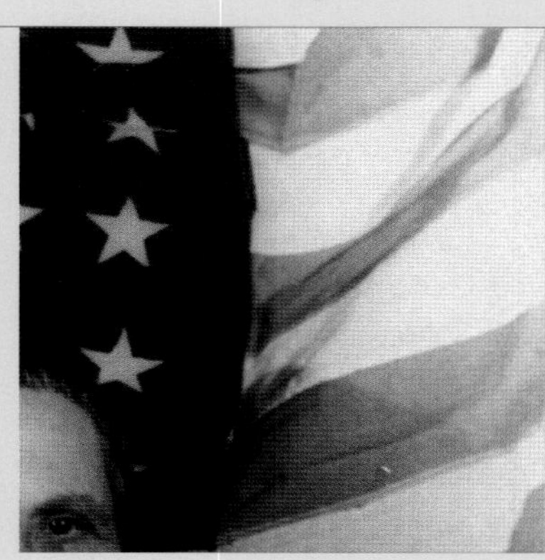

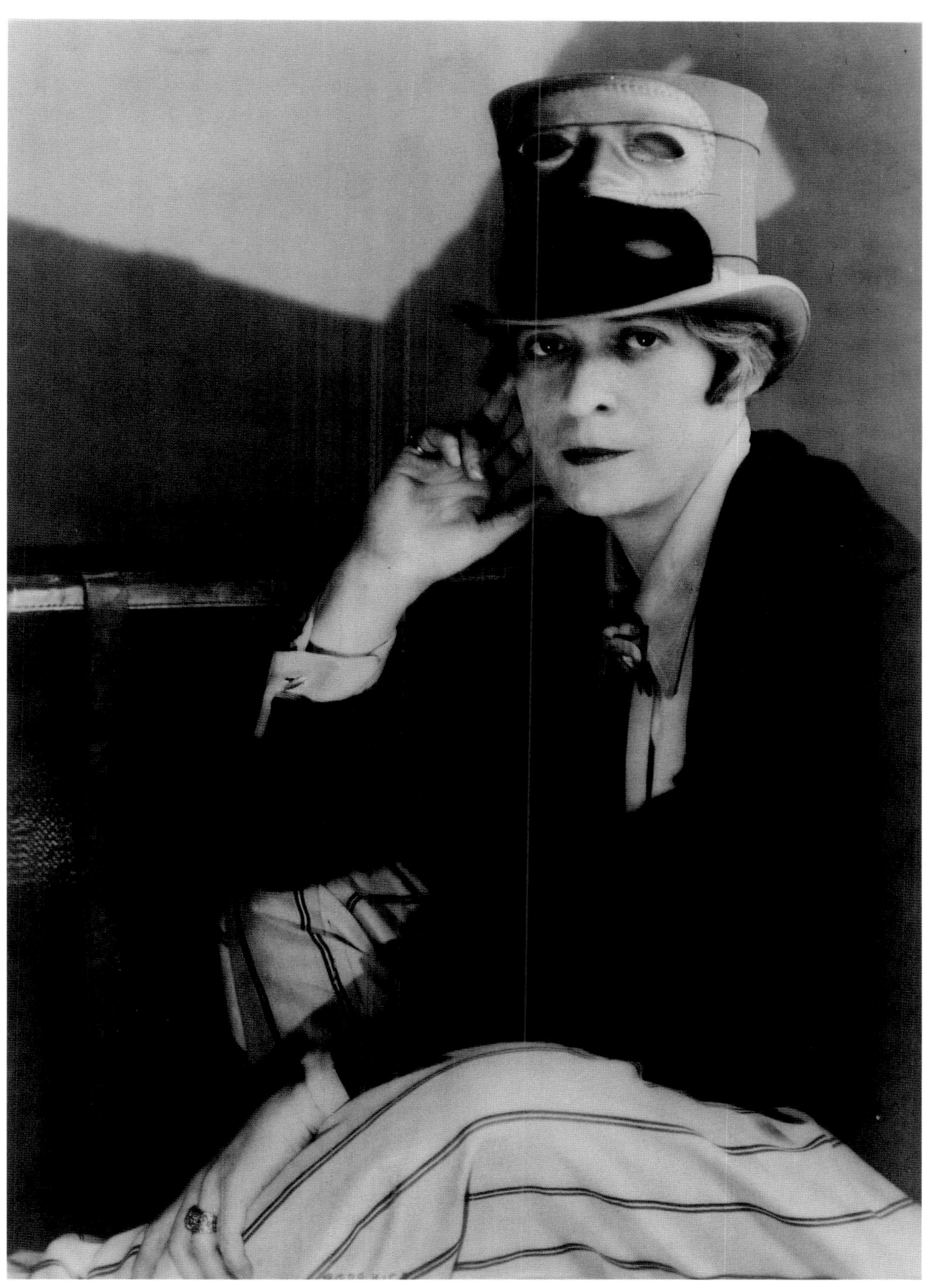

137
BERENICE ABBOTT
JANET FLANNER IN PARIS, 1927
GELATIN SILVER PRINT, 35.5 X 27.9 CM
LIBRARY OF CONGRESS, WASHINGTON D.C.
PRINTS AND PHOTOGRAPHS DIVISION, DLC/FP-1980.55
MAAG, TAM, TMAA

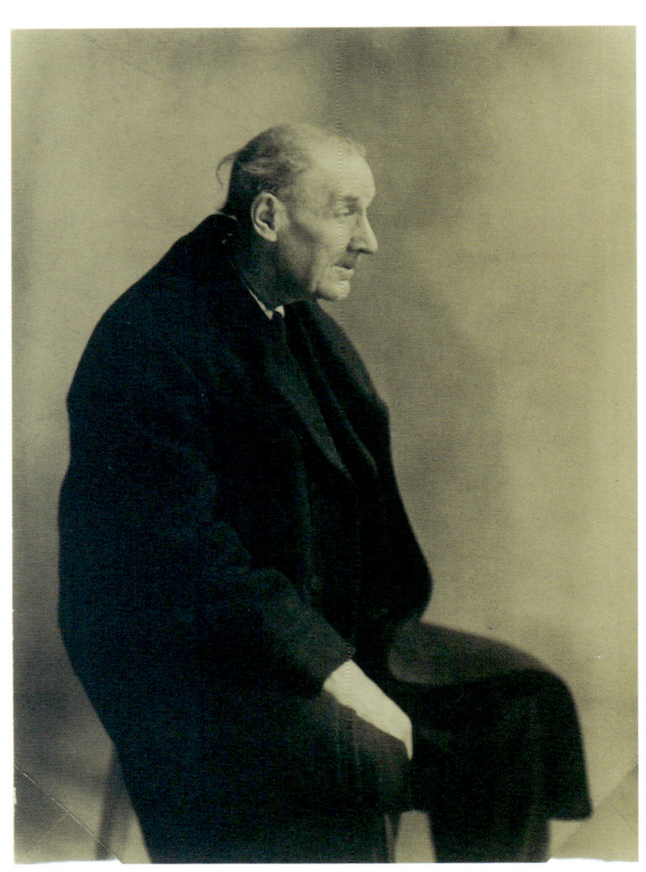

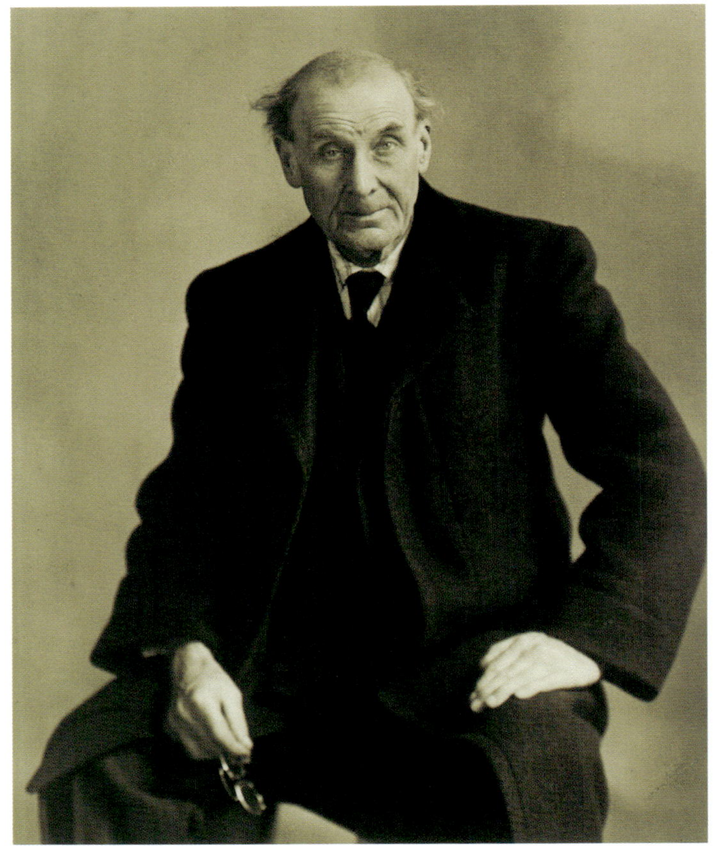

138
BERENICE ABBOTT
EUGÈNE ATGET, 1927
GELATIN SILVER PRINT, 23.2 X 17.5 CM
THE NEW YORK PUBLIC LIBRARY, ASTOR, LENOX
AND TILDEN FOUNDATIONS, PHOTOGRAPHY
COLLECTION, MIRIAM AND IRA D. WALLACH
DIVISION OF ART, PRINTS AND PHOTOGRAPHS,
89 PHO 16.006
TAM, TMAA

139
BERENICE ABBOTT
PORTRAIT OF THE PHOTOGRAPHER EUGÈNE ATGET,
1927
GELATIN SILVER PRINT, 61 X 50.8 CM (FRAME)
THE VICTORIA AND ALBERT MUSEUM, LONDON,
PH 1150-1980
MAAG, TAM, TMAA

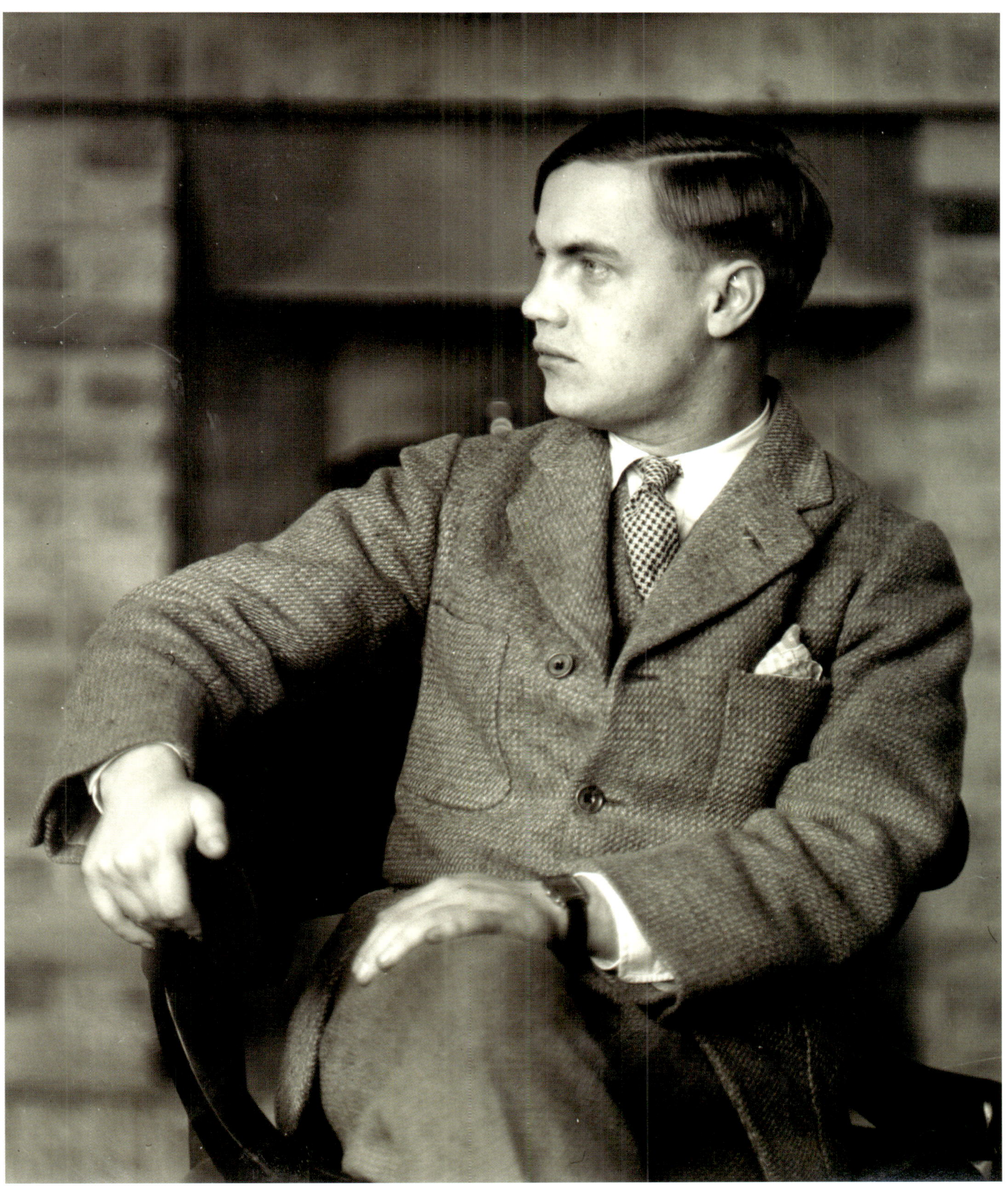

140

BERENICE ABBOTT
GEORGE ANTHEIL, 1929
GELATIN SILVER PRINT, 22.9 X 18.4 CM
COURTESY ROBERT KLEIN GALLERY, BOSTON
MAAG, TAM, TMAA

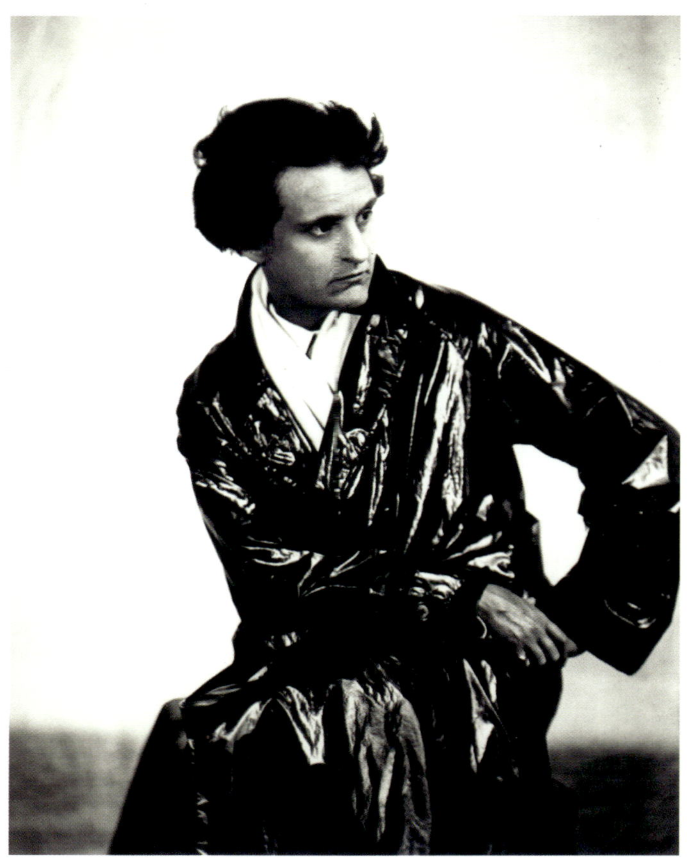

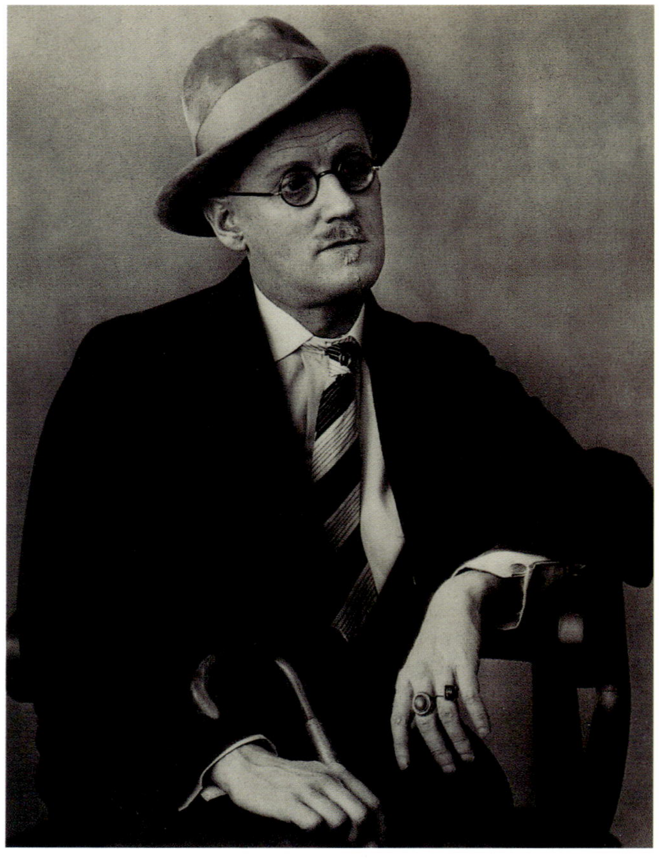

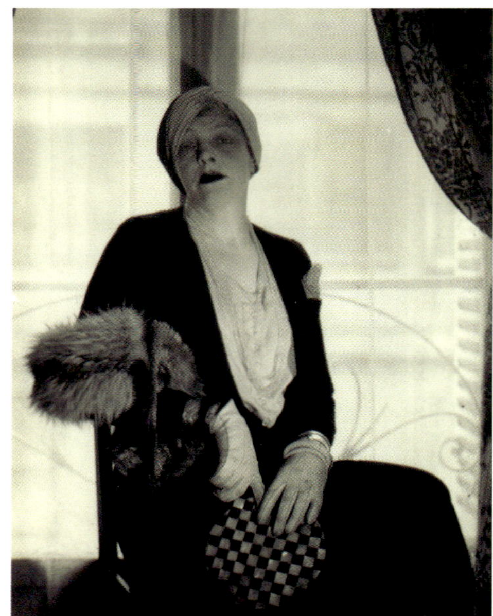

141

BERENICE ABBOTT
SYLVIA BEACH, 1928
GELATIN SILVER PRINT, 24.1 X 19 CM
COURTESY ROBERT KLEIN GALLERY, BOSTON
MAAG, TAM, TMAA

142

BERENICE ABBOTT
JAMES JOYCE, C. 1926–29
GELATIN SILVER PRINT, 34.5 X 26.3 CM
MUSÉE NATIONAL D'ART MODERNE –
CENTRE GEORGES POMPIDOU, PARIS, AM 1982.371
MAAG, TAM, TMAA

143

BERENICE ABBOTT
MARGARET ANDERSON, 1927
GELATIN SILVER PRINT, 12.7 X 10.2 CM
COURTESY ROBERT KLEIN GALLERY, BOSTON
MAAG, TAM, TMAA

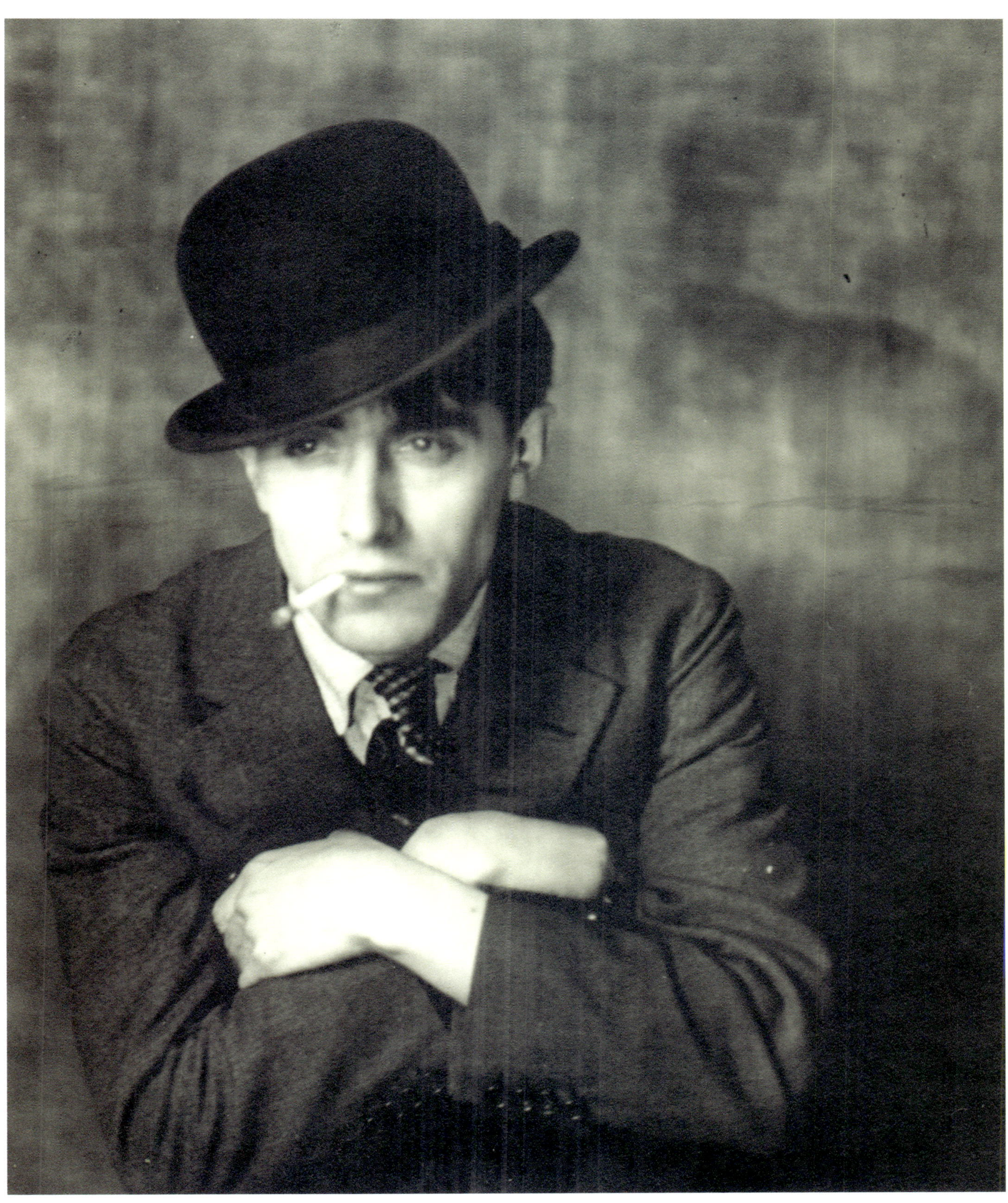

144
BERENICE ABBOTT
PIERRE DE MASSOT, 1927
GELATIN SILVER PRINT, 24.1 X 20.3 CM
COURTESY ROBERT KLEIN GALLERY, BOSTON
MAAG, TAM, TMAA

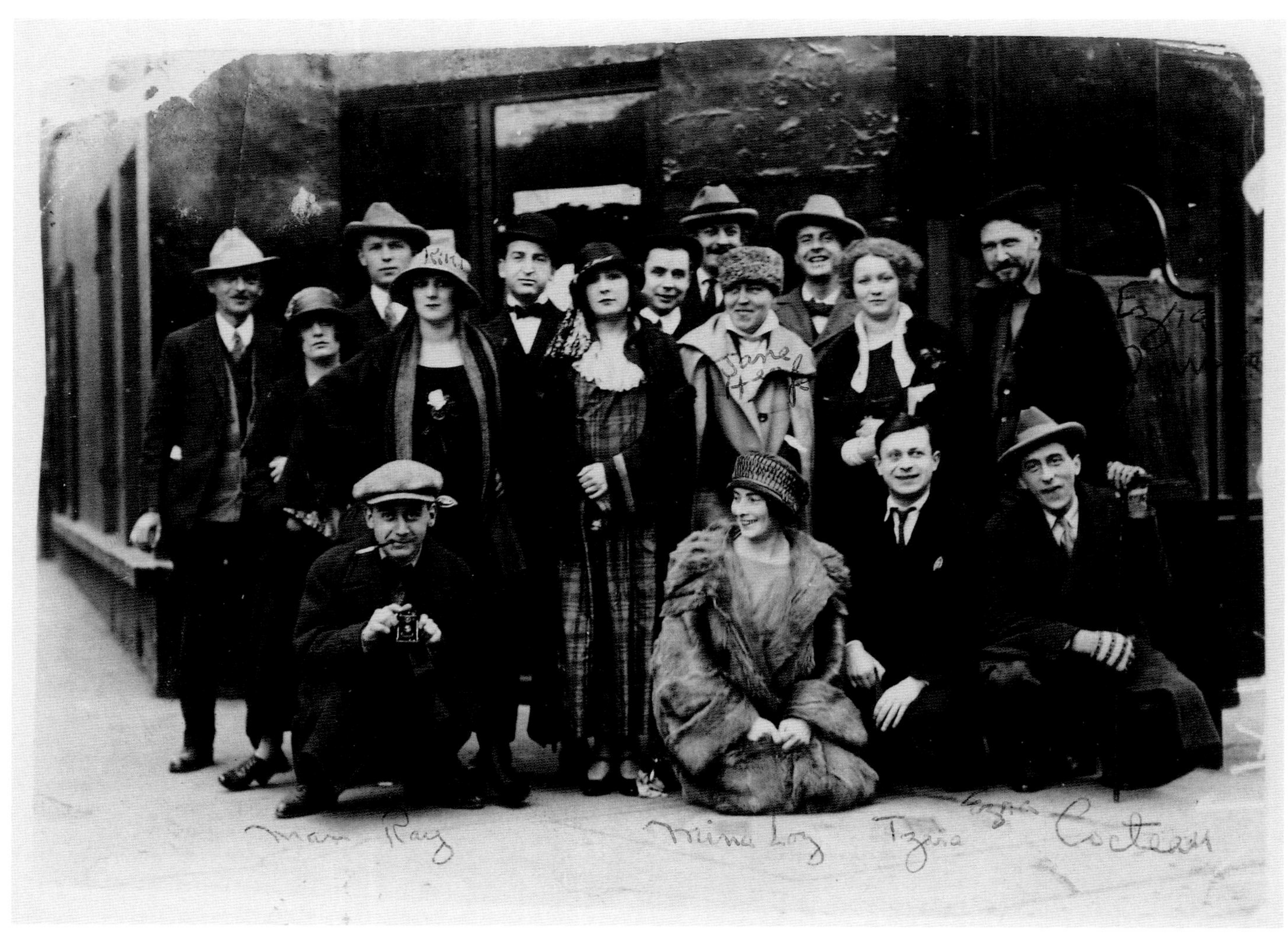

145
[GROUP PORTRAIT OF AMERICAN AND
EUROPEAN ARTISTS AND PERFORMERS IN
PARIS — MAN RAY, MINA LOY, TRISTAN TZARA,
JEAN COCTEAU, EZRA POUND, JANE HEAP, KIKI,
MARTHA DENNISON], C. 1920
GELATIN SILVER PRINT, 27.9 X 35.6 CM
LIBRARY OF CONGRESS, WASHINGTON D.C.
PRINTS AND PHOTOGRAPHS DIVISION,
LC-USZ62-113902
MAAG, TAM, TMAA

TO BE IS TO BE PERCEIVED:[1]

PORTRAITS OF THE AVANT-GARDE IN PARIS

BRONWYN A. E. **GRIFFITH**

Though portraiture remains historically the most widely practiced form of representation, it is also the most illusive, for each portrait embodies a collaboration between the artist and the sitter—some the result of brief encounters, others a testament to enduring friendships. The illusion of the immediacy of the sitter remains problematic with the artistic interpretation of the individual most often hidden from the viewer by the technique, leaving the image to be mistakenly read as "real" or documentary. However, the success of professional portrait photographers depends on their ability to make an image of the sitter that is consistent with whatever self-image that person has or wishes to project.

Any attempt to analyze portraiture and its place within the arts is inseparable from what Kenneth Silver calls its "use-value," defined by "its function as a document and ritual object."[2] The perfect example of this can be found in Paris during the interwar period in Sylvia Beach's bookstore, Shakespeare & Co., where the walls were lined with photographic portraits of great writers.[3] It was a privilege that was not only limited to time-honored authors, but also included up-and-coming contemporaries, such as Ernest Hemingway, Djuna Barnes, H. D. (Hilda Doolittle) and James Joyce, as photographed by Man Ray and Berenice Abbott. As the inscriptions reveal, many of the prints were given to Beach by the authors themselves, who usually knew that she displayed such images in her bookshop.[4] Thus, beyond the reverence Beach gave these talented writers, there was undoubtedly some cachet in having one's portrait taken by the two most cutting-edge portrait photographers of the day. As Beach clearly stated in her autobiography, "[t]he artist Man Ray and his pupil Berenice Abbott, who assisted him for awhile, were the official portraitists of 'the Crowd.' The walls of my bookshop were covered with their photographs. To be 'done' by Man Ray and Berenice Abbott meant that you were rated as somebody."[5] So to in turn distribute a portrait of yourself by either of these photographers could then be considered as a bit of self-promotion, revealing contact with the exclusive circles of the avant-garde—proof that you were part of the club.

In the period between the world wars, the exchange of portraits among the avant-garde was a current practice,[6] but since social conventions have changed, it is difficult to accurately decipher the motivations behind these exchanges. The genre of portraiture expanded in unexpected directions during this uncertain time, demanding not just a resemblance or a likeness, but rather exploring issues of identity and transcending the visual arts by spreading into music and literature of the day. Of particular interest is how portraiture, simultaneously being explored in diverse fields, was being disseminated in very different circles. This essay will first discuss the role of portrait photography in the avant-garde crowd as dominated by the American photographers Man Ray and Berenice Abbott and how their portrait photographs were a form of promotion whether exchanged with other artists, reproduced in the press, or exhibited publicly and were integral in the formation of public personas. Next it will explore the shifting definition of portraiture as it moved away from a likeness, by showing fractions of an individual and at times moving toward complete abstraction. Finally, examples will be given showing how the practice of portraiture—whether in poetry, music, or visual art—overlapped as artists were seeking to define themselves and their contemporaries.

[E]ach of us has a complete Kodak idea of himself . . .
Man has learnt to see himself. So now, he is what he sees.
He makes himself in his own image.[7]
D. H. Lawrence

Proof of the fad for portrait photography can be seen in the six-part contest launched by the magazine *Vu* in March 1928, which challenged readers to guess the profession, first name, and nationality of seven women and men based on simple head shots.[8] At odds with the modern conceptions that were exploring the complexity of the human mind and subconscious, the contest appealed to the common impulse to judge character based on physical appearance. Despite the fact that the study of physiognomy had been repeatedly dispelled as a false science,[9] the desire to see photographs of prominent people stems from a yearning to interpret the face and figure of the individual—to *read* the portrait.

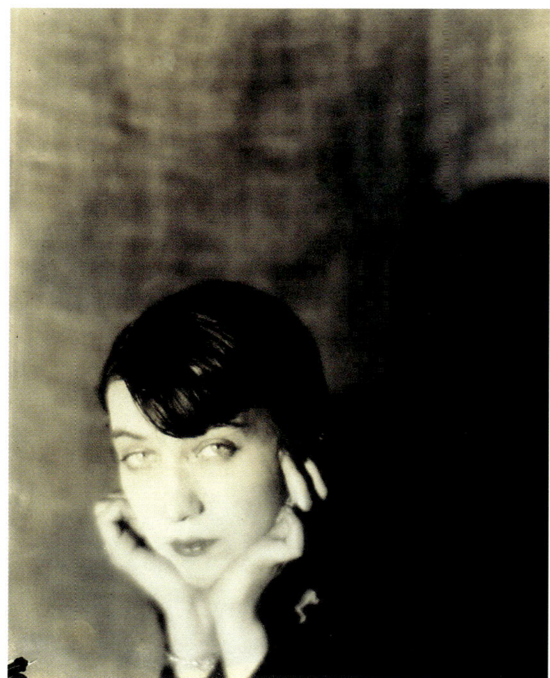

FIG. I.
MAN RAY,
BERENICE ABBOTT, 1921.
GELATIN SILVER PRINT, 19.8 X 15.9 CM.
THE J. PAUL GETTY MUSEUM, LOS ANGELES.
84.XM.230.3.

In an attempt to satisfy a demanding public eager to put faces on the renowned figures of the day, magazines regularly featured photographic portraits, thought to be more revealing than portrait paintings, in which the hand of the artist is more visible. Both the popular press such as *Vanity Fair, Vogue, Variétés,* and *Harper's Bazaar,* and small-edition literary and art journals such as *The Little Review, transition,* and *Minotaure* frequently reproduced portraits of avant-garde figures in Paris, while key figures of the Parisian avant-garde, such as Jean Cocteau and Tristan Tzara, also regularly contributed articles. These are among the most tangible examples of how the role of the artist in society was being fundamentally redefined during the interwar period. The emergence of public artistic personalities, truly beginning with Pablo Picasso, is vitally indebted to the published photographic portraits and accompanying articles, which linked the artistic avant-garde to an ever-expanding mass culture.[10] The prevalent fad for portraits in both the popular press and small journals is evidence, not only of its importance, but also a significant indication of how the same images were simultaneously operating on two different frequencies: one for those eager to know; the other for those in the know.

Answering a demand for innovative styles, trained artists like Man Ray and Berenice Abbott entered the ranks as professional photographers supplying distinctive photographs of personalities in response to the burgeoning desire for portraits.[11] The photographs they produced were nothing like today's day-in-the-life or candid shots intended to reveal the private lives of celebrities; rather, they were rigorously composed images that constructed or reinforced public personas. Because these portraits were going to be seen and *read* by a large audience, careful attention was paid to the image they projected. When the best-known photographic portraits of the avant-garde are compared with lesser-known images, the deliberate choices made by the sitter and photographer to consistently portray these individuals in a certain light are revealed, as is the ability to manipulate the photograph, still perceived as an objective documentary representation, through scrupulous cropping and retouching.[12] Particularly gifted in this delicate task, Man Ray and Berenice Abbott quickly established reputations as portrait photographers. Though each had initially come to Paris pursuing success in other artistic media, the role that they played in both documenting and promoting the work and image of the prominent artistic figures of the period unquestionably advanced their careers.

Upon his arrival in Paris the summer of 1921, Man Ray immediately gained entry to the Parisian art world through his relationship with Marcel Duchamp (cat. 158) and managed to secure a one-man exhibition of his paintings at the Librairie Six shortly after his arrival. Having just arrived from abroad, Man Ray was free to reinvent himself and with the help of his friends immediately began to craft an artistic personality. This is demonstrated in the catalogue essay which casts him as a mythical American character of uncertain origins who had "run through several fortunes as coal merchant, chairman of the bubble gum trust, modern architect and banjo playing."[13] However, not a single work sold, and economic concerns prevailed, as revealed in his autobiography *Self-Portrait*: "I was going to make money—not wait for recognition that might or might not come. In fact, I might become rich enough not to have to sell a painting, which would be ideal . . ."[14] Man Ray's fortune was to be made in professional portrait photography. Once he embarked in this direction, the impatiently awaited recognition came almost immediately. Some of his first commissions were from André Breton (cat. 157) who wanted photographs of works by established artists, such as Braque, Picasso, and Derain for his periodical *Littérature*. In addition to having the privilege of meeting these great figures Man Ray saw opportunity, cleverly saving a plate at the end of each session to make a portrait of the artist. Similarly, commissions from Sylvia Beach, owner of Shakespeare & Co., to photograph writers gave Man Ray an entrée with the literary avant-garde and through these contacts he began to establish an enviable, and increasingly profitable stock of photographs of celebrity artists and writers.[15]

Photographic portraits were not unfamiliar territory for Man Ray, who several years earlier had won Honorable Mention for a photograph of Berenice Abbott submitted to the Fifteenth Annual Exhibition of Photographs in Philadelphia in 1921.[16] (fig. 1) Dramatically composed by positioning her head at the lower left of the image, he would return

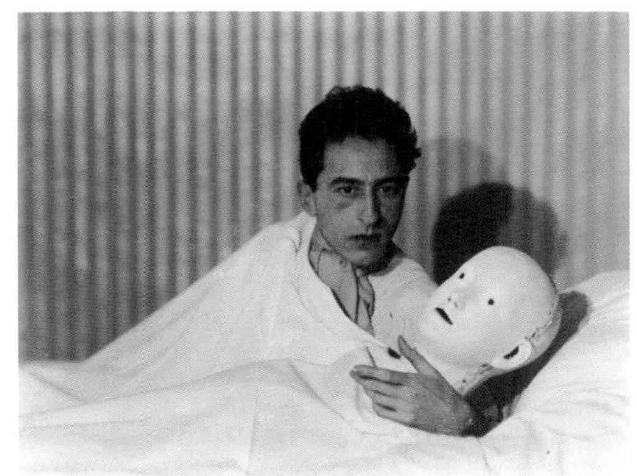

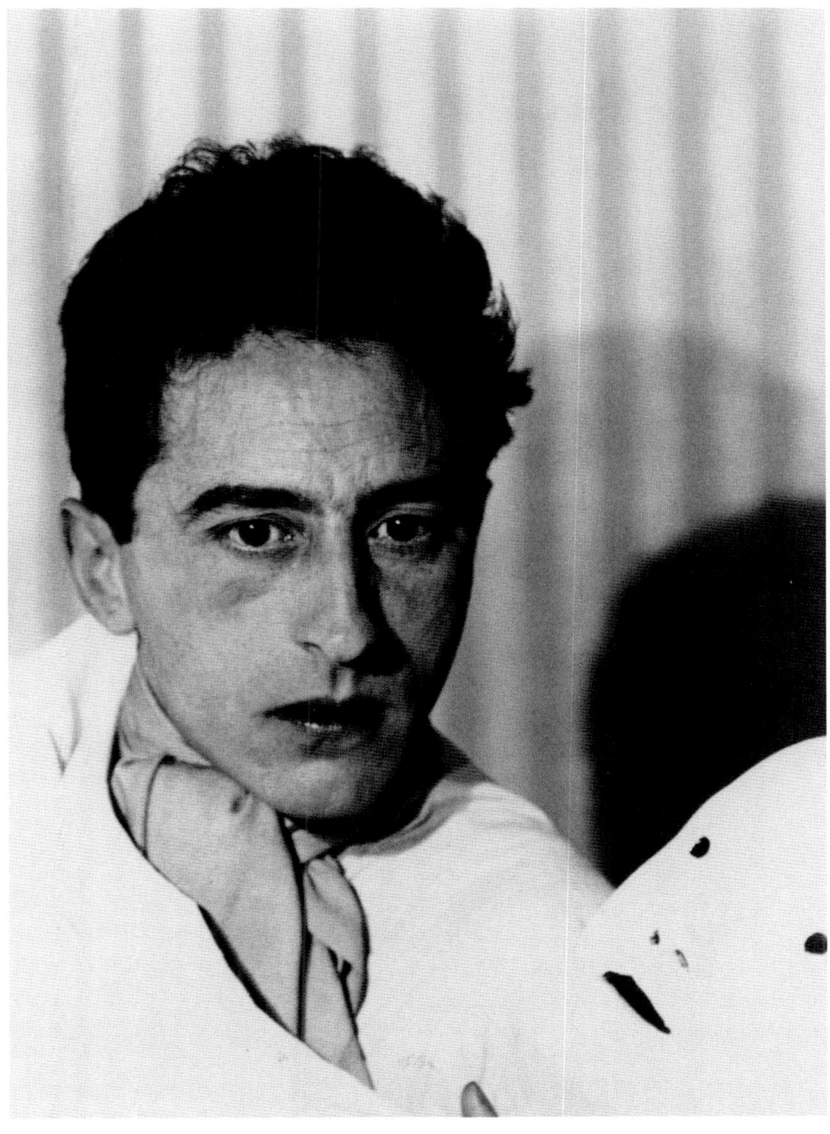

146
BERENICE ABBOTT
JEAN COCTEAU, 1927
GELATIN SILVER PRINT, 8.8 X 11.3 CM
THE NEW YORK PUBLIC LIBRARY, ASTOR,
LENOX AND TILDEN FOUNDATIONS.
PHOTOGRAPHY COLLECTION, MIRIAM AND
IRA D. WALLACH DIVISION OF ART,
PRINTS AND PHOTOGRAPHS, 89 PH 16.003
MAAG, TAM, TMAA

147
BERENICE ABBOTT
[JEAN COCTEAU, HOLDING A MASK], 1928
GELATIN SILVER PRINT, 35.5 X 27.9 CM
LIBRARY OF CONGRESS, WASHINGTON D.C.
PRINTS AND PHOTOGRAPHS DIVISION,
USZ62-109609
MAAG, TAM, TMAA

to this composition with his portrait of Kiki de Montparnasse (Alice Prin) five years later in Paris, adding a strongly cast shadow on the wall that occupies the place traditionally given to the sitter's head (cat. 148). It was this kind of originality that caught the interest of the avant-garde and secured Man Ray a central role: "There were rivalries and dissentions among the avant-garde group but I was somehow never involved and remained on good terms with everyone—saw everyone and was never asked to take sides. My neutral position was invaluable to all; with my photography and drawing, I became an official recorder of events and personalities."[17]

Much of Man Ray's subsequent success with the avant-garde was dependent on word-of-mouth promotion of his work. On September 21, 1922 Max Jacob wrote a letter praising Man Ray for the portrait he had taken of him:

> Not to mention that portraits by painters are never good like-nesses, whereas here I'm alive, myself! Not very handsome! Not too ugly! Not made younger. No longer very young! . . .
>
> I'm delighted with you and with the portrait. I've written to Cocteau that I know you. That I have a portrait by you and that everyone admires it and he would be wise to ask you for it because I cannot bring myself to part with this authentic effigy.[18]

It was not long before Jean Cocteau contacted Man Ray to take his portrait, a contact which proved to be particularly useful in garnering other work, as Man Ray recognized: "The photographs were a great success, and were distributed among his friends. From then on he began bringing or sending people to my hotel room. . . . No one paid for the prints but my files became very imposing and my reputation grew."[19]

Just three years after his arrival in Paris, Man Ray was the first American and one of the first modernists to be featured in the *Peintres Nouveaux* series by Gallimard.[20] The small monograph by George Ribemont-Dessaignes contains a brief biography that speaks of Man Ray's work in photography and film, but curiously omits mention of his portrait photography, despite the fact that by this time he had already established a successful portrait studio and was regularly contributing portraits to *Vanity Fair*. The frontispiece to the small book is a wood-block engraving by Georges Aubert that closely follows a very flattering photographic self-portrait taken the same year in which Man Ray truly looks the part of an artist, with an intense gaze dramatically directed off camera, and clothes disheveled. So not only was Man Ray providing portraits of others, he was also creating and circulating images of himself. This frontispiece, combined with the omission of Man Ray's then primary activity as a portrait photographer in the biography, are evidence of how he was crafting his public persona.

Further proof of Man Ray's self-fashioning can be found in the autobiographical publication *Man Ray Photographies 1920–1934 Paris*[21] which opens with a portrait of Man Ray by none other than Picasso (location unknown). In contrast with the Ribemont-Dessaignes biography

from ten years earlier, his portraits comprise over half of the publication. A section introduced with an essay by André Breton titled "The Visages of the Woman" is devoted to portraits of women. The text describes how their beauty is captured by the "great hunter" Man Ray, "These quivering nostrils, these trembling lips, these swelling throats—it is a whole communion of perfumes, of thoughts and of breathing which attach us to these beings . . . each one of them is a total of desires and dreams which have never before been had and which never will again."[22] Man Ray experiments with the images, taking the liberty of making figures appear to be hanging upside-down or to be armless. Though many of these women are well-known and identifiable, only the last photo in the section formally identifies the female sitter—none other than the rather masculine-looking American poet Gertrude Stein. This image leads into the next series of portraits of men, opening with the essay "Men Before the Mirror" in English and German by Rrose Sélavy, a.k.a. Marcel Duchamp. In stark contrast to Breton's text, which discusses women as perceived by Man Ray and the viewer, this text emphasizes men's perception of themselves. The section serves as a pantheon of avant-garde artists and writers, each sitter rendered in a dignified manner and clearly identifiable—with the exception of the transvestite Barbette whose full-length portrait is focused on his body, as are some of the women's photos. Each of the texts affirms the artistic value of the portraits, which Man Ray describes in the preface as "[s]eized in moments of visual detachment during periods of emotional contact, these images are oxidized residues, fixed by light and chemical elements, of living organisms."[23] The fact that Man Ray features his portraits over other photographs is perhaps a sign that he had realized that the posterity of his work would be largely reliant on his skillful portraiture of famous figures.

Though she had also been acquainted with Duchamp in New York, Berenice Abbott was slower than Man Ray to establish herself in Paris. Arriving in March 1921, she supported herself the first two years by doing odd jobs and modelling for artists while studying briefly in the studios of Émile Bourdelle. Abbott sojourned for a short time in Berlin. In 1923 in a last attempt to establish herself as a sculptor before returning to Paris. By this time Man Ray was running his very successful portrait studio. Frustrated with her experiences and in need of a steady income, Abbott immediately proposed herself as an assistant when Man Ray, a friend from New York, said he was looking for someone who knew nothing about photography. A quick learner, she was soon involved in every stage of the process, at times even taking portraits of Man Ray's less prestigious clients. As her skills and curiosity developed, Man Ray gave Abbott permission to use the studio during lunch hours and evenings to pursue her own portrait work. She recalled her first experiments in photography,

> I had no idea of becoming a photographer, but the pictures kept coming out and most of them were good. . . . Soon I started to build up a little business and I paid Man Ray out of the money I made for the supplies I used, but eventually I was paying him more than he was paying me and that's when it started to become a problem.[24]

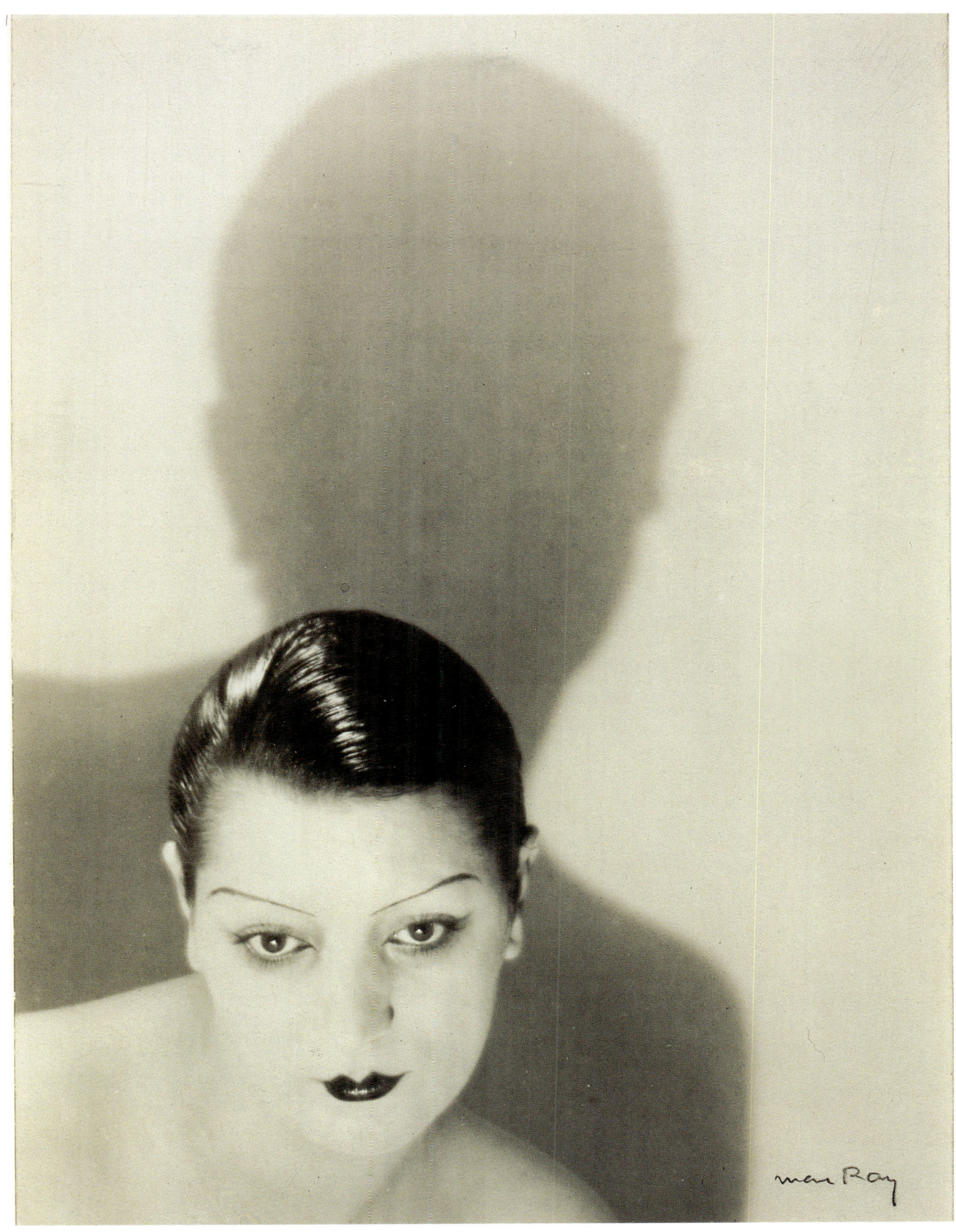

148
MAN RAY
KIKI, 1926
GELATIN SILVER PRINT, 23.2 X 17.9 CM
MUSEUM LUDWIG, KÖLN, 1977/636
MAAG

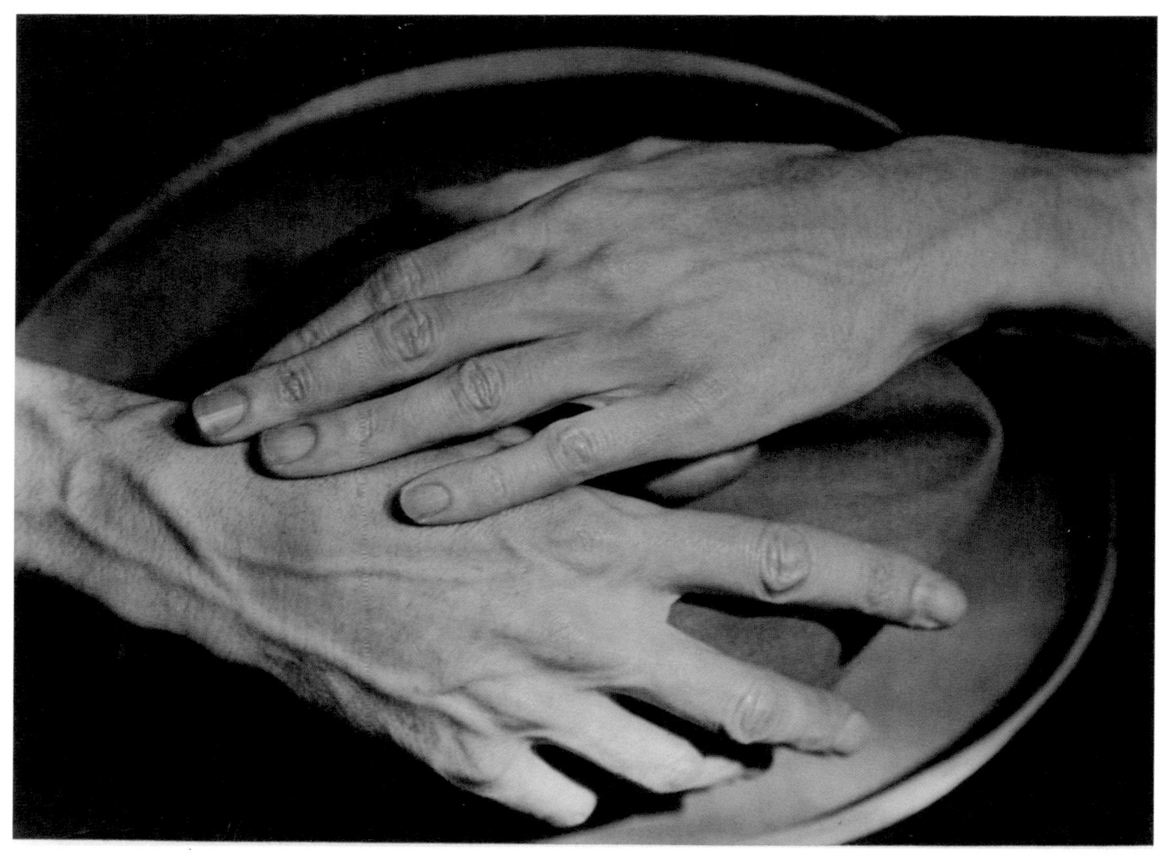

149
BERENICE ABBOTT
HANDS OF JEAN COCTEAU, 1927
GELATIN SILVER PRINT, 10.6 X 15.7 CM
THE NEW YORK PUBLIC LIBRARY, ASTOR,
LENOX AND TILDEN FOUNDATIONS,
PHOTOGRAPHY COLLECTION, MIRIAM
AND IRA D. WALLACH DIVISION OF ART,
PRINTS AND PHOTOGRAPHS, 89 PH 16.004
TAM, TMAA

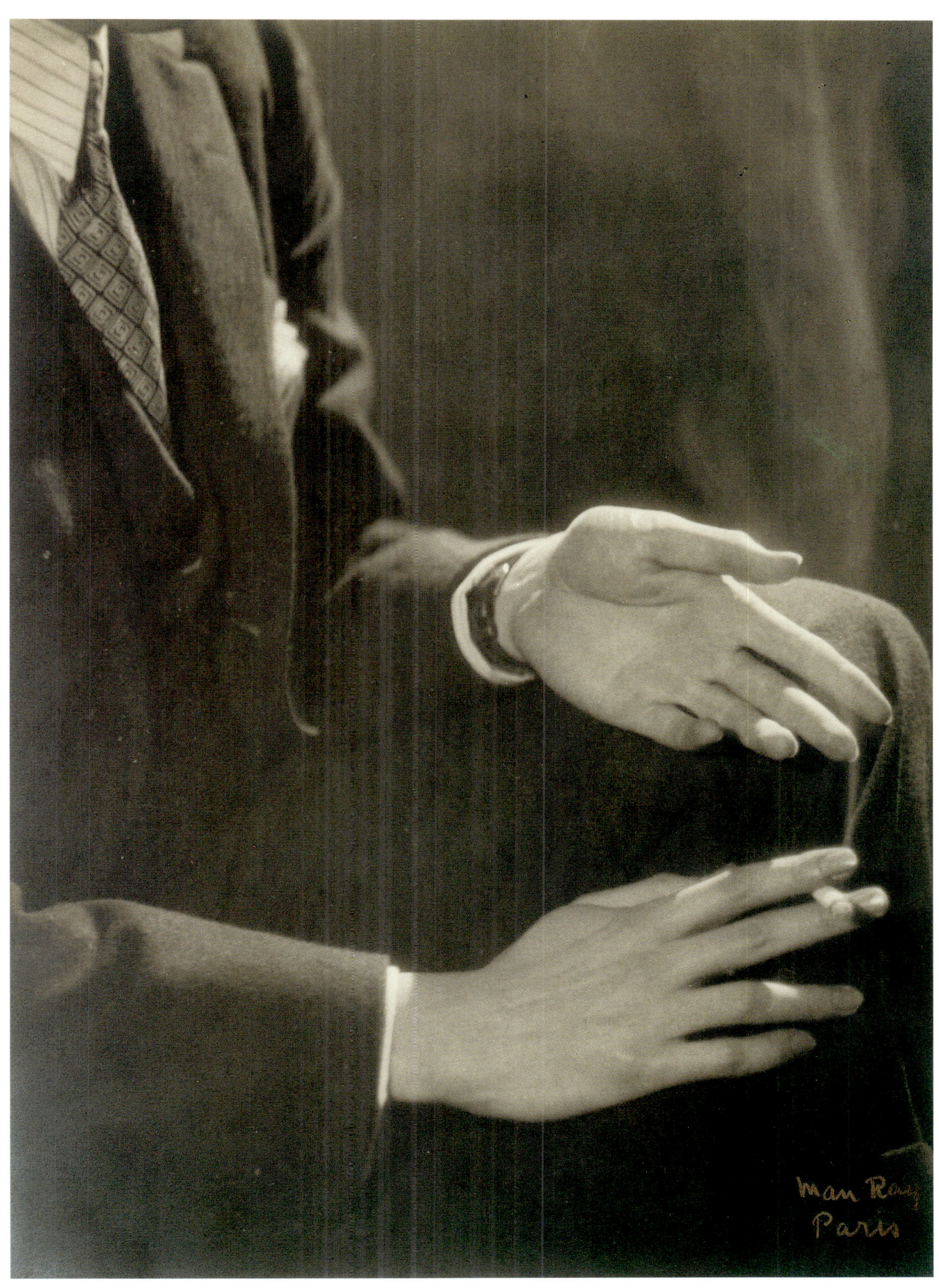

150
MAN RAY
HANDS OF CHARLES DEMUTH, C. 1921
GELATIN SILVER PRINT, 23.2 X 17.1 CM
GEORGE EASTMAN HOUSE, ROCHESTER,
N.Y., 81.3228.0001
MAAG, TAM, TMAA

In 1925, Abbott left Man Ray's studio to found her own at 44 rue du Bac with financial assistance from wealthy compatriots that included expatriates Robert MacAlmon, his wife Winifred Bryher, and arts patron Peggy Guggenheim. Just one year later Abbott was honoured with the solo exhibition *Portraits photographiques* at Jan Slivinsky's gallery Au Sacre du Printemps from June 8–20. The exhibition included portraits of prominent contemporary artists and writers in Paris such as James Joyce (cat. 142), Jean Cocteau (cats. 146 and 147), Sylvia Beach, André Tardieu, Djuna Barnes, Alexander Berkman, Marie Laurencin, and André Gide. The invitation included a short text by Jean Cocteau that read:

> Mademoiselle Abbott bears a name that is half shadow,
> half light: Berenice. [Beret / Nice]
> She displays her charming memory.
> Within her a chess match between light and shadow takes place.
> Lady-bird, bird of men: Berenice, sexless bird catcher,
> tames the shadows of birds.[25]

Though the exhibition was well received it was not until a few years later that recognition of Abbott's work caused a rift between her and Man Ray. It was the press coverage following the Premier Salon Indépendant de la Photographie, commonly referred to as the "Salon de l'Escalier"[26] that truly caused a break between Man Ray and his protégé (see p. 209). Despite the markedly different style of their portraits, they worked in the same circles and were inevitably compared, becoming unwitting competitors with critics praising portraits by Abbott and criticizing those by Man Ray.

One year later the final issue of *The Little Review*, which included a questionnaire that got "More than fifty of the foremost men in the arts to tell the truth about themselves,"[27] featured dozens of portraits by both Abbott and Man Ray—a perfect illustration of their roles as the established portraitists of intellectuals and artists in Paris during the interwar period. That same year, Abbott returned to New York shifting her focus to documenting that city, while Man Ray would remain the reigning portrait photographer in Paris. Time has since validated the portraits of both photographers: Abbott for her straightforward style and Man Ray for his inventiveness. Both took studio portraits that seem to capture the essence of the sitters, suspending them in a neutral space removed from signs that might indicate their profession, which the viewers are expected to know. The controlled space with its modulated light and carefully selected composition is timeless. In fact, the Paris studio portraits by Man Ray and Abbott taken between the world wars have become *the* definitive portraits of the period's artists and render all others awkward and lifeless in comparison.

We Nominate for the Hall of Fame

Hand-in-hand with the desire to see what talented artists looked like was the public's desire to see the environments in which they worked. Thus portraits of artists in their studios were a popular and profitable subject. Taken almost exclusively for promotional purposes, these photographs gave an inside look at their mysterious realm and contributed to the artist's public image. As mentioned earlier, Man Ray first began to earn a living in Paris by photographing the work of established artists, routinely saving at least one plate to take a portrait of the artist in his surroundings. These images were later sold to *Vanity Fair* to illustrate a monthly column titled "We Nominate for the Hall of Fame." These and other photographs by Man Ray appeared in *Vanity Fair* nearly every month in 1922 and continued regularly through the late 1920s. His portraits were also highlighted in feature articles like "Among the Best of American Painters,"[28] which included his double portrait of Joseph Stella and Marcel Duchamp, and "Four Masters of French Painting. The Founders of the New French School of Painting, Who Have Ever Since Remained at its Head,"[29] complete with portraits of André Derain, George Braque, Henri Matisse, and Pablo Picasso. These exclusive portraits furthered his reputation in the United States as an American who was at home among the Parisian avant-garde.

Profiles of individual artists, systematically accompanied by photographs, were also regular features in *Vanity Fair*, for example Jeanne Robert Frost's article "New Sculptures by Constantin Brancusi. A Note on the Man and the Formal Perfection of His Carvings," was illustrated with photographs by Charles Sheeler.[30] The American artist Edward Steichen had a special penchant for sculptors, first taking a series of portraits of Auguste Rodin and later of the Rumanian Constantin Brancusi (cat. 180), who had been inspired by the French master. A. E. Gallatin completed a series of studio portraits of many modern artists previously photographed by Abbott and Man Ray for inclusion in his 1933 catalogue for the Gallery of Living Art (see essay by Christian Derouet, p. 223). Thérèse Bonney, an American photographer who established a stock photo company in Paris that specialized in design images and personality photos, also took portraits of her compatriots in Paris, including Gertrude Stein, the composer Virgil Thomson, and Alexander Calder (fig. 2). There is a portrait by her of Fernand Léger in front of the triptych titled *Comet Tails* that he painted for Gerald Murphy's home, called "Villa America," in Antibes (fig. 3).[31]

Maybe, taken separately, the eye, ear, nose, and mouth of a lover each merit a whole portrait.[32]

Man Ray

Moving beyond the likeness to try to capture the essence of a person, artists began to focus on single features, allowing details to speak as portraits. In *Works of Art in the Age of Mechanical Reproduction*,

German writer and critic, "[Walter] Benjamin likens the camera for example to the surgeon's knife that can operate dispassionately on the human body and by seeing it in fragments can enter more deeply into its reality."[33] Man Ray's description of his approach is not dissimilar, "I have often taken a detail . . . a detail of the face—eye, mouth, or nose—that I enlarged to make a portrait of someone."[34] One of the most striking examples is *Object to be Destroyed*—destroyed at an exhibition in Paris, after which Man Ray had other versions made, alternately titled *Lost Object* (1945), *Indestructible Object* (1958; cat. 91) and *Perpetual Motif* (1971). It consists of a metronome to which Man Ray has attached Lee Miller's eye cut from a photograph. After Miller had left him, Man Ray sent the same image of her eye with the postscript: "With an eye always in reserve / material indestructible . . . / Forever being put away / Taken for a ride . . . / Put on the spot . . . / The racket must go on / I am always in reserve. / MR" (on the back of cat. 152). The isolation of the eye of a lover is reminiscent of "lover's eye" miniature portraits that were popular at the end of the eighteenth century and early nineteenth century. However, these objects, intended to disguise identity, were meant to be cherished, while Man Ray's object served as a symbolic fraction of the person to be destroyed—complete with how-to instructions.

Hands are another feature thought to reveal personality or be symbolic of an individual; they were repeatedly the focus of attention during the interwar period. The magazine *Vu* ran a feature with a double-page article of photographs of hands introduced by the text, "What could be more eloquent than hands? They are the bedazzlement of human thought. The mind orders, the hand creates. The mind understands, the hand translates. In chirognomy, the shape of the hand suffices to reveal the person."[35] Further evidence of interest in this attribute can be found in the "Salon de l'Escalier" which included three photographs that featured hands : Abbott's *Mains de Jean Cocteau*, Kertèsz's *Des mains et des livres*, Krull's *Les Mains de Mariette Lidys* The surrealists in search of ways to reveal the human psyche also turned to hands. In addition to repeatedly using hands in their art, an extensive article in *Minotaure* was devoted to reading the palms of André Gide, Maurice Ravel, André Derain, Aldous Huxley, Antoine de Saint-Exupéry, Breton, Paul Eluard, and Duchamp, complete with photographs of their palms (fig. 4).[36] Less poetic, *Vanity Fair* also ran an article "A Page for Palmists. Carrying the Suggestion that a Line in the Hand is Worth Two in the Face," which interpreted the hands of celebrities complete with gemological identifications.[37]

Man Ray characteristically cropped his portraits to arrive at a final image in his portrait of Charles Demuth the choice is particularly interesting—the result is a vertical composition in which just the torso and hands remain (cat. 150). In 1923 Demuth's hands also drew the attention of Alfred Stieglitz, who made a similar composition. It is more than mere coincidence that both photographers were drawn to this feature, revealing an intense level of collaboration between the sitter and photographer.

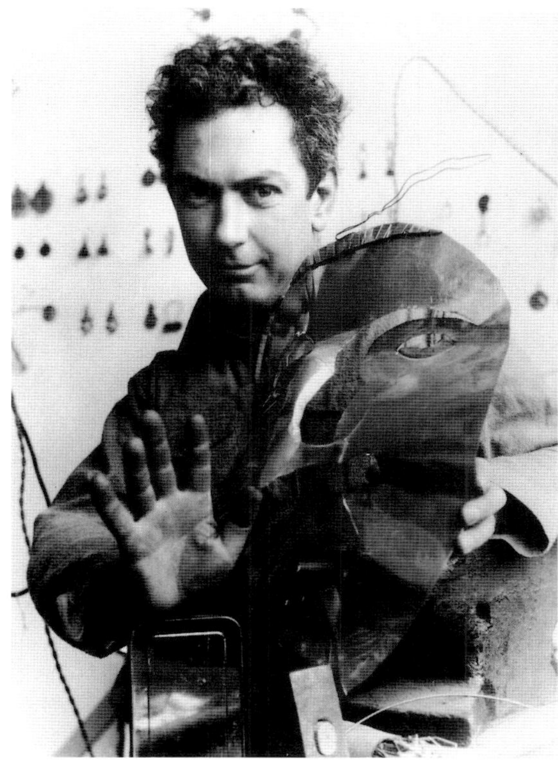

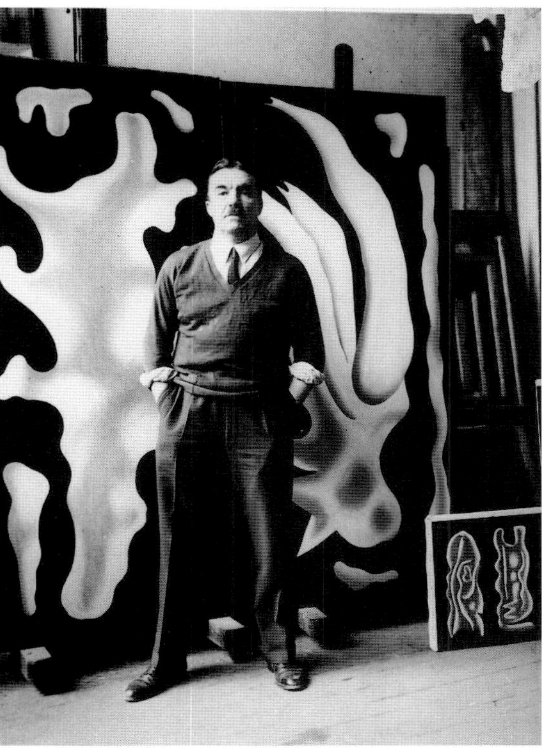

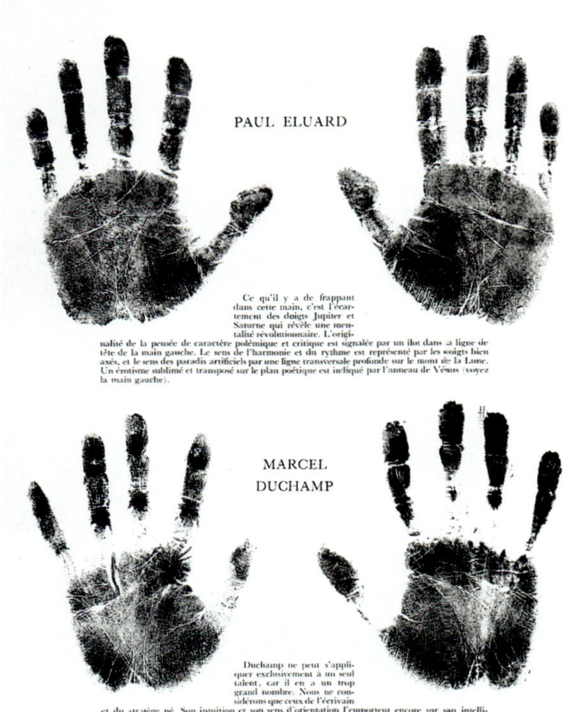

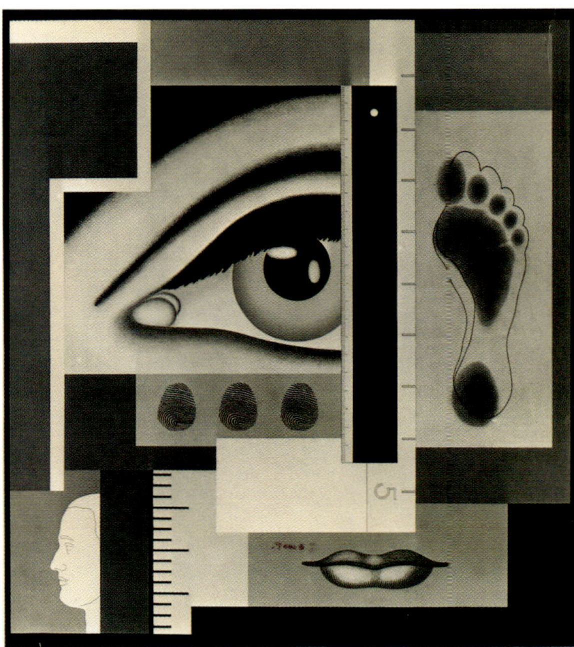

FIG. 4.
LE MINOTAURE 6 (MAY 1935): 44.

FIG. 5.
GERALD MURPHY,
PORTRAIT, C. 1928.
OIL ON CANVAS, 81.3 X 81.3 CM.
ESTATE HONORIA MURPHY DONNELLY.

In response to *The Little Review* questionnaire "What do you like most about yourself?" Demuth simply responded "My hands."[38] Also particularly proud of his hands, Jean Cocteau gracefully displays them in numerous portraits by various photographers. Berenice Abbott boldly captured Cocteau's hands gently overlapping while holding a hat and allowed them to occupy the entire picture plane (cat. 149). Rather than isolating single feature, Gerald Murphy assembled various features often associated with individuality and commonly used for identification. His composition *Portrait,* c. 1928 (which was destroyed) presents an eye, footprint, ruler, lips, and fingerprints (fig. 5). While most elements in the painting are schematic, the fingerprints were carefully traced after his own and the footprint was made by stepping directly on the canvas.[39] Other artists of the interwar period give even fewer clues as to the sitter's identity, for example Constantin Brancusi's biomorphic portraits of the wealthy American art patrons Nancy Cunard and Agnes Meyer.[40] The Cunard portrait is a smooth bronze head with no facial features topped by a twisting chignon, while the Meyer portrait is a seven-and-a-half foot tall totemic figure in black marble, made in response to a commissioned portrait of Mrs. Meyer by Despiau.

***Who knows if, in this way, we are not on the point
of breaking away from the principle of identity.***[41]
André Breton

Photographic portraits were also recurrently used in surrealist collages that visually manipulated self-image and explored identity through the construction of composite portraits made up of symbols and fragments of an individual. A newly found modernist technique, collage was the ideal media for exploring the concerns at the heart of surrealist activities that investigated the "destabilization and splitting of identity, portrayed as a *locus* of contradiction, fragmentation and decentering."[42] Disguises, aliases, name changes, compound or alternate identities— each was used by the avant-garde, particularly the surrealists, in their search to define and redefine themselves. Tristan Tzara, Le Corbusier, Man Ray, Duchamp—sometimes Rrose Sélavy—each worked under an assumed name. The new name was part of a conscious process of establishing artistic identities. Charles-Édouard Jeanneret used his given name for his painting and Le Corbusier for his architecture, keeping the two quite separate. Janet Flanner (cat. 137) wrote her chronicles about cultural life in Paris under the penname Genêt, while Gertrude Stein (cat. 159) went so far as to author the *Autobiography of Alice B. Tolkas* (1933), her lover, before later writing her own under the provocative title *Everybody's Autobiography* (1937). Duchamp went the furthest by establishing an alternate personality: Rrose Sélavy, a name under which he would not only create, at times making reference to Duchamp, but also contribute to joint projects, such as the 1934 book by Man Ray to which André Breton, Tristan Tzara, and Rrose Sélavy contributed essays—Rrose's in German and English.

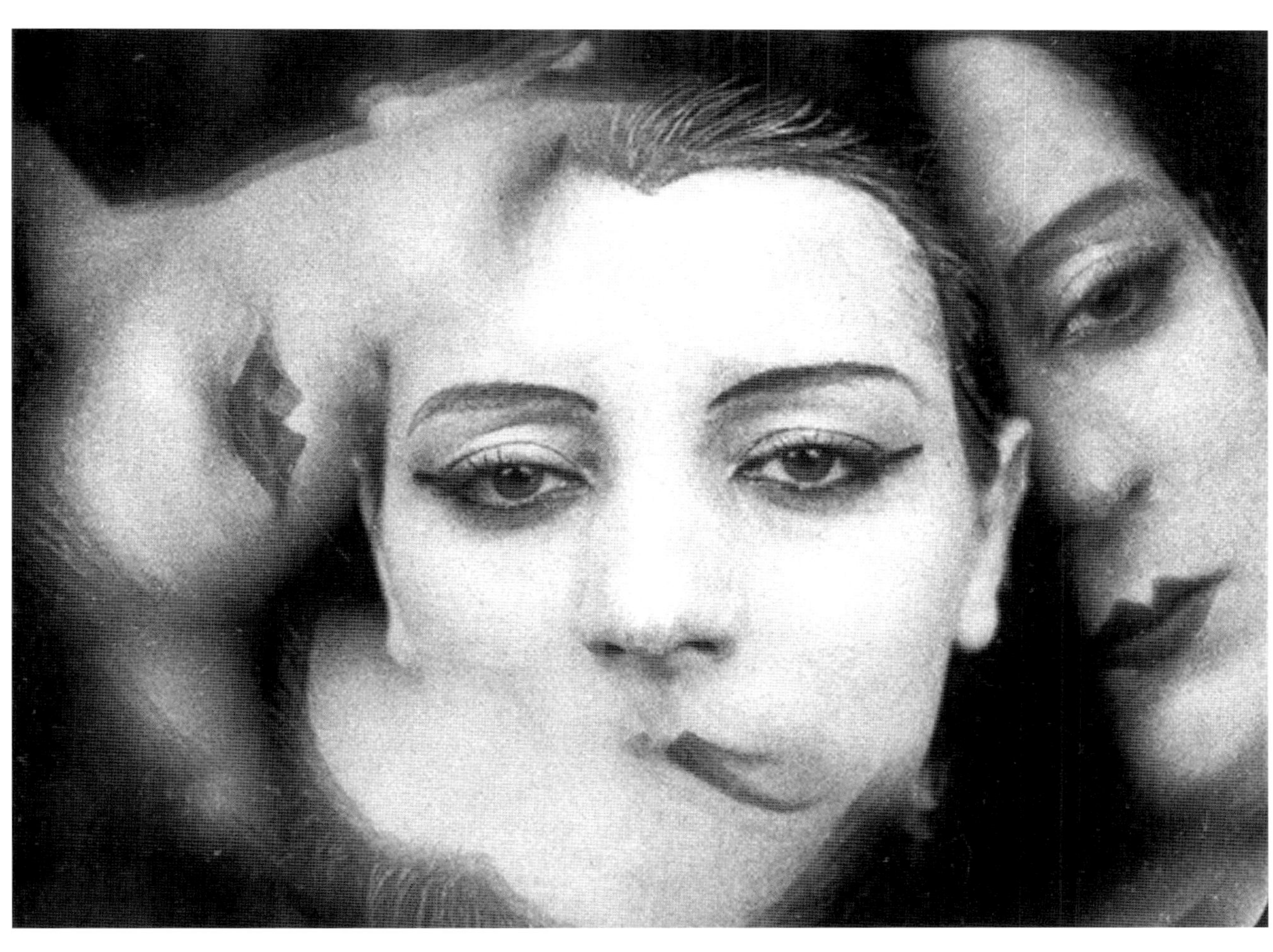

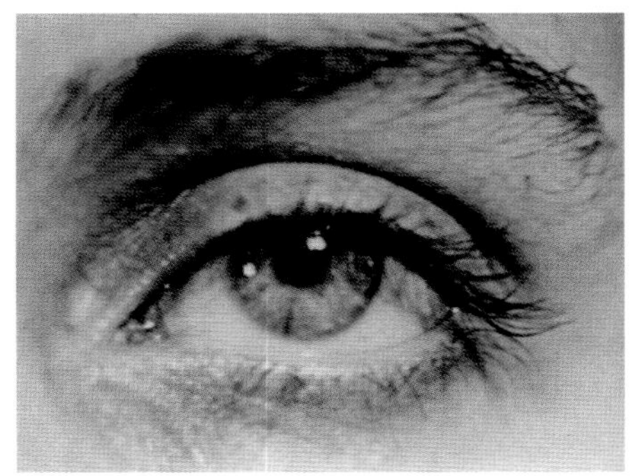

151
MAN RAY
KIKI, 1924
MODERN PRINT, 22.3 X 30 CM
FONDS RÉGIONAL D'ART CONTEMPORAIN
DE BOURGOGNE, DIJON, 9990018
MAAG, TAM, TMAA

152
MAN RAY
EYE OF LEE MILLER, OCTOBER 11, 1932
VINTAGE PHOTOGRAPH, GELATIN SILVER PRINT,
7.8 X 10.5 CM
LEE MILLER ARCHIVES, CHIDDINGLY, GREAT BRITAIN
MAAG, TAM, TMAA

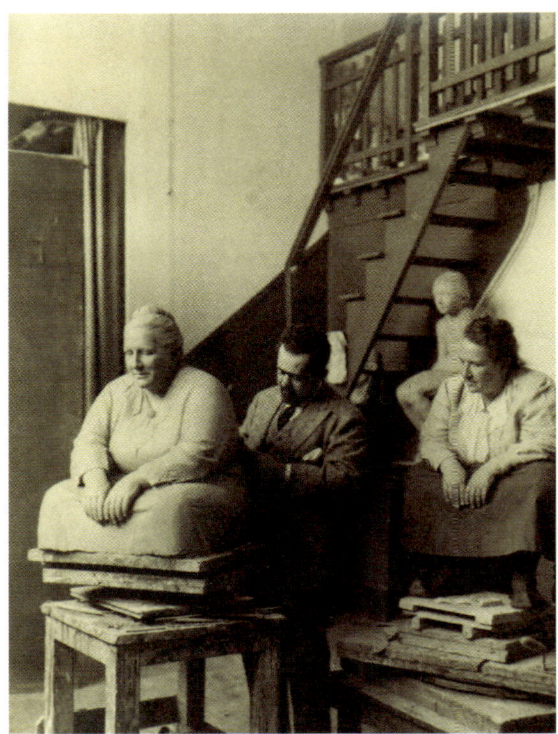

FIG. 6.
MAN RAY,
GERTRUDE STEIN AND JO DAVIDSON
WITH PORTRAIT SCULPTURE. 1926.
GELATIN SILVER PRINT, 30.5 X 23.5 CM.
THE J. PAUL GETTY MUSEUM, LOS ANGELES.
84.XM.1000.88

In his famous self-portrait *Wanted, $2000 Reward* (1923) Duchamp inserts identity photographs of himself into a fictional bounty poster that gives a list of aliases, and adds a final line in the same typeface: "Known also under name Rrose Sélavy." Through the text he removes himself by another step from his true identity, yet the photograph remains unaltered, he is not disguised as Rrose or obscuring his physical appearance as he does in other photographs. In his analysis Richard Brilliant aptly calls this an anti-portrait, for it calls into question the very role of the portrait in defining the boundaries of the self.[43] Other artists used alternative personalities as creative tools, to provide freedom for creation and also freedom to talk about themselves. In the essay "Identité instantanée" (1936) Max Ernst (cat. 162) curiously turns the identity of the author on its head by writing extensively about himself—his physical appearance, affect on women and character in general—in the third person yet signs the article himself.[44] This transparent self-fashioning was yet another means of developing public personas, while creating an air of mystery and confusion.

Among the American personalities in Paris who inspired artists and writers to try to capture them through portraits, some more flattering than others, were Gerald and Sara Murphy. Resolutely "Amurikan"[45] and larger-than-life, the Murphy's made a splash in Paris social circles, so fascinated with all things American at that time. The principal characters of F. Scott Fitzgerald's *Tender is the Night* are but thinly veiled portraits of the Murphy's and their rather decadent lifestyle. Léger, who socialized with the Murphys, made watercolor portraits of both Sara and Gerald (cat. 153 and 154). A portrait of Gerald Murphy, complete with his fedora and block letters spelling out his name, by the French artist an critic Jacques Mauny was submitted to the 1924 Salon d'Automne. It must have garnered attention as it was one of the few works illustrated in the *Bulletin de la Vie Artistique*.[46] Meanwhile, the poet Archibald MacLeish was inspired to write a "Sketch for a Portrait of Mme G_______ M_______."[47] And like most Americans in France that could afford his services, the Murphy's commissioned Man Ray to do a series of family portraits at their home "Villa America" in Antibes.[48]

Perhaps the most exclusive invitation in Paris was 27 rue de Fleurus, the home of Gertrude Stein. In her telltale fractured style, Stein had been writing portraits of her famous guests for years,[49] including Pablo Picasso, Henri Matisse, Sherwood Anderson, Erik Satie, Ernest Hemingway, Man Ray, Jean Cocteau, Jane Heap, Carl Van Vechten,[50] Virgil Thomson, Alfred Stieglitz,[51] Francis Picabia and others, most of whom in turn made portraits of her in their media. Shortly after his arrival in Paris, Man Ray became her "official" photographer until he made the mistake of sending her a bill following a session. One of the most celebrated photographs by Man Ray shows Stein in front of her portrait by Picasso. It creates a double portrait of sorts, an effect that he repeats when documenting Stein sitting for sculptor Jo Davidson with a nearly life-sized portrait of herself (fig. 6). The reciprocal portraiture current in the Stein circle is brilliantly revealed on a single page of the popular magazine *Vanity Fair*. It assembles Stein's poem "A Portrait to Jo Davidson," Picasso's portrait of Stein, a bust of Stein by Lipchitz and the aforementioned photograph by Man Ray of Jo Davidson executing the nearly life-size sculpture of Stein.[52] Jo Davidson had advised Stein that "one should sell one's personality."[53] It would seem that she listened to him.

Since the invention of photography, "the potential for a perpetually induced pantheon of ourselves and our intimates has pervaded modern consciousness."[54] The portraits from this period by and of the avant-garde reveal the personal and creative interactions that shaped modern artistic movements. Many of those considered to be members of the avant-garde were themselves active in more than a single media and most collaborated on multimedia projects with other artists at some time.[55] The interaction of Americans and French, artists and musicians during this time period was succinctly addressed by Fernand Léger in the preface to a Calder exhibition that included wire portraits: "Calder is in that line, he's American 100/100. Satie and Duchamp are 100/100 French. Why not meet?"[56]

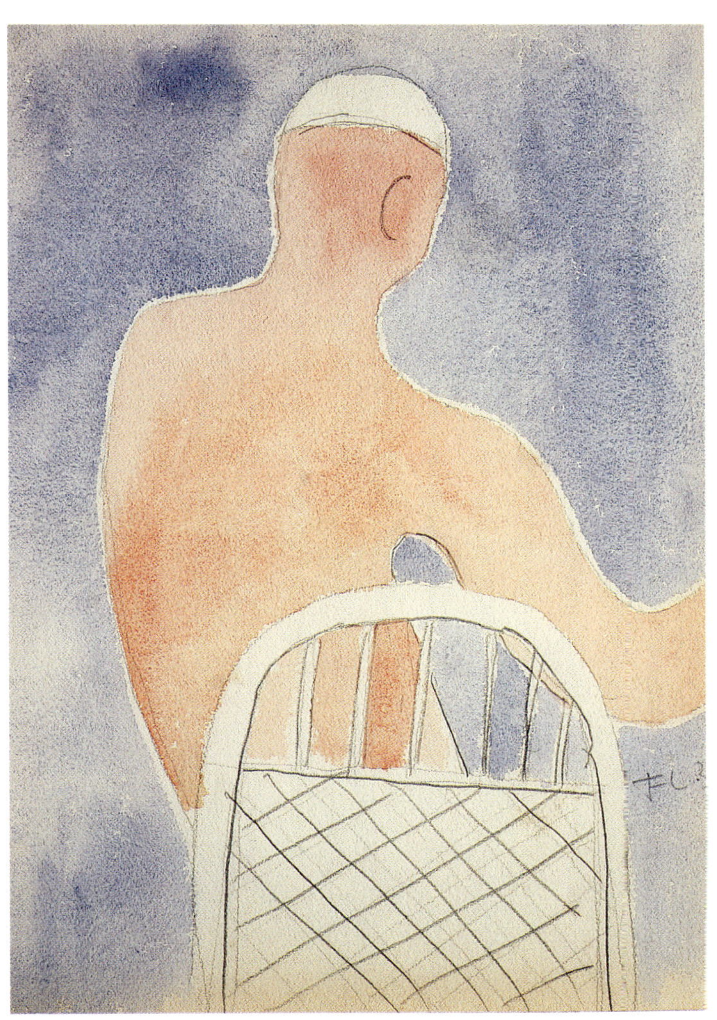

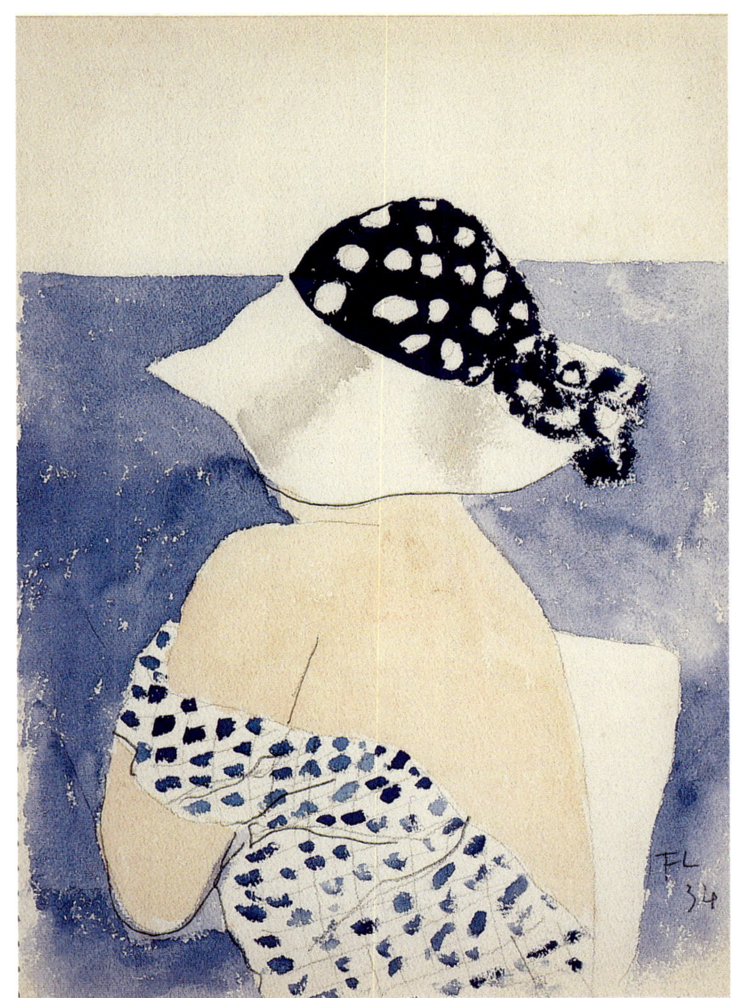

153
FERNAND LÉGER
PORTRAIT OF GERALD MURPHY, 1934
WATERCOLOR ON PAPER, 32.4 X 24.1 CM
ESTATE HONORIA MURPHY DONNELLY
MAAG, TAM, TMAA

154
FERNAND LÉGER
PORTRAIT OF SARA MURPHY, 1934
WATERCOLOR ON PAPER, 32.4 X 24.1 CM
ESTATE HONORIA MURPHY DONNELLY
MAAG, TAM, TMAA

As traditional truths were called into question, artists sought the means to create modern portraits that would reveal the complexity of identity. Palm reading, dream interpretation, publication of Freud's *Beyond the Pleasure Principle* in 1920, each were attempts to decipher the human psyche. Seeking to understand the complexities of themselves, the many forms of portraiture were part of this collective effort. The avant-garde artists played with this construction of self, particularly the public persona, to varying degrees. Assembled together, they bring to light the personal and creative interactions that shaped modern artistic movements revealing how they imagined and ultimately, crafted an image of the sitter. ■

1— *Esse is percipi*. George Berkeley, *Principles of Human Knowledge* (1710) cited in *Ghost in the Shell: Photography and the Human Soul, 1850–2000,* exh. cat. (Cambridge, Mass. and Los Angeles: MIT Press and Los Angeles County Museum of Art, 1999), 1.

2— Kenneth E. Silver, "In Praise of the Particular: American Portraits," in *Face Value: American Portraits*, ed. Donna De Salvo (Paris: Flammarion, 1995), 65.

3— Similarly, photographer George Platt Lynes (1907–1955) opened a bookshop in 1929 and published the writings of Gertrude Stein, Ernest Hemingway, and others. He took up photography at this time and exhibited his portraiture in the bookshop's gallery. Cited in Keith F. Davis, *Passionate Observer. Photographs by Carl Van Vechten* (Kansas City, Missouri: Hallmark Cards, 1993), 110.

4— The Sylvia Beach Papers, including photographs, are housed at Princeton University.

5— Sylvia Beach, *Shakespeare and Company* (1959; reprint London: Plantin Publishers, 1987), 111–112.

6— See Wanda Corn, *The Great American Thing*, (Berkeley: University of California Press, 1999), 193–237.

7— D. H. Lawrence, "Art and Morality," *Calendar of Modern Letters* (November 1925) as cited in Jean-François Chevrier, "Image of the Other," in *Staging the Self: Self-Portrait Photography, 1840s–1980s*, exh. cat., ed. James Lingwood (London: National Portrait Gallery, 1986), 12.

8— " Vous devez être physionomiste. Grand Concours," *Vu* 2 (March 28, 1928): 38.

9— The Swiss theologian Johann Kaspar Lavater developed a system of physiognomy in the mid-eighteenth century that was rather quickly denounced; however, interest in this form of character analysis remained current in society and was evident in the arts, for example, in the novels of Balzac and the art of Edgar Degas and most particularly photography. See *Ghost in the Shell* for a series of essays by Robert A. Sobieszek that subtly explores portrait photography and the role of physiognomy.

10— Christopher Phillips's introduction to *Photography in the Modern Era: European Documents and Critical Writings, 1913–1940*, exh. cat. (New York: The Metropolitan Museum of Art, 1989) and conversations with Sophie Lévy were instrumental in the development of this idea.

11— Only Americans are cited here because of the focus of the essay. Photographers of other nationalities such as Brassaï, Eli Lotar, Germaine Krull, and André Kertész were also actively supplying photographs to periodicals.

12— A particularly interesting source to see careful choice of composition techniques is Emmanuelle de l'Écotais and Alain Sayag, *Man Ray: Photography and Its Double,* trans. Deke Dusinberre (Corte Madera, Ca.: Gingko Press, 1998). Drawing from the extraordinarily rich collection of works by Man Ray, comparisons are made that illustrate his working methods and artistic choices of photographs by publishing different prints of the same image including some complete with crop marks.

13— Man Ray, "An Autobiography" in *An Exhibition Retrospective and Prospective of the Works of Man Ray,* exh. cat. (London: Institute of Contemporary Arts, 1959).

14— Man Ray. *Self-Portrait*, (Boston: Little, Brown and Company, 1988), 119.

15— Man Ray's ambivalence about the role of his portrait photography continued throughout his life. A perfect example is Fritz L. Gruber's book *Man Ray Portraits* (Gütersloh: Sigbert Mohn Verlag, 1963), which opens by stating, "En réalisant le portrait des personnalités de cette collection, le photographe s'est intéressé uniquement au visage de ses modèles, sans tenir compte de leur situation ou de leur célébrité, ni de la sympathie plus ou moins grande qu'ils pouvaient lui inspirer personnellement." Though he supposedly aimed at objectivity, he goes on to be transparently subjective, assigning a rating system to the portraits. Predictably, former lovers, such as Kiki and Lee Miller both rate as 15, while his current wife Juliet rates as a 20, with his oldest friend Duchamp running a close second.

16— Neil Baldwin, *Man Ray, American Artist* (New York: Clarkson N. Potter, 1988), 70–71. According to Baldwin, Stieglitz encouraged him to submit this photograph which is listed as "Portrait of a Sculptor," no. 648 in the catalogue of the exhibition held in March 1921.

17— Man Ray, *Self-Portrait*, 118.

18— "Sans compter que les portraits des peintres ne sont jamais ressemblants tandis qu'ici je vis, moi-même ! Pas très beau! Pas trop laid! pas rajeuni. Plus très jeune! . . . Je suis ravi de vous et du portrait. J'ai écrit à Cocteau que je vous connais. Que j'ai mon portrait par vous et que chacun admire et qu'il fera bien de vous demander le mien car je ne veux pas me séparer de cette véridique effigie." Letter housed in the Man Ray archives at the Musée National d'Art Moderne, Paris. Cited in l'Écotais, *Man Ray. Photography and Its Double,* 117.

19— Man Ray. *Self-Portrait*, 118.

20— Georges Ribemont-Dessaignes, *Man Ray*, Peintres Nouveaux (Paris: Gallimard, 1924).

21— Preface by Man Ray, texts by Paul Eluard, André Breton, Rrose Sélavy (Marcel Duchamp) and Tristan Tzara. Portrait by Picasso, *Man Ray Photographies 1920–1934 Paris* (Hartford: James Thrall Soby, 1934).

22— Ibid., n.p.

23— Ibid.

24— Hank. O'Neal, *Berenice Abbott, photographe américaine* (Paris: Philippe Sers, 1982), 10.

25— "Mlle Abbott porte un nom moitié ombre moitié lumière: Bérénice. Elle expose sa mémoire délicieuse. Elle est le lieu d'une partie d'échecs entre la lumière et l'ombre. Elle d'oiseau, oiseau des ils: Bérénice, oiseleur sans sexe, apprivoise l'ombre des oiseaux." Reproduction of the invitation in O'Neal, *Berenice Abbott,* 11.

26— Held from May 24 to June 7, 1928 in the "Salon de l'Escalier" a space upstairs in the Comédie des Champs-Élysées.

27— *The Little Review* (Paris, Spring 1929).

28— *Vanity Fair* (March 1923): 52.

29— *Vanity Fair* (May 1923): 63; and "Marchesa Casati: A Symbol for Twenty Painters," *Vanity Fair* (October 1922) which illustrates Man Ray's famous double image portrait.

30— *Vanity Fair* (May 1922): 68 and 124.

31— "Peut-être que, pris séparément, l'œil, l'oreille, le nez ou la bouche de l'aimée valent un portrait entier." Gruber, *Man Ray Portraits*, preface, n.p.

32— The comet motif was inspired by an astronomy book belonging to Murphy's ailing son, Patrick. For reasons unknown, the panels were never delivered, and after the death of Léger, they were split in two. The silver side is now part of the Adrien Maeght collection and the brown side is at the Musée National Fernand Léger in Biot (France). I thank Christian Derouet for this information.

33— Walter Benjamin, "L'Œuvre d'art à l'époque de sa reproductibilité technique," in Walter Benjamin, *Œuvres* 3 (Paris: Gallimard, 2000), 300–301.

34— "J'ai souvent pris un détail . . . un détail de visage: œil, bouche ou nez que j'agrandis pour en faire un portrait d'une personne." *Petit Journal de Vogue* (1973, special supplement): n.p.

35— "Qui-a-t-il de plus éloquent que les mains? C'est l'éblouissement de la pensée humaine. L'esprit commande, la main crée. L'esprit comprend, la main traduit. En chirographie, la forme de la main suffit à révéler l'individu." Mathilde Berger-Levrault, "Mains," *Vu* 5 (April 1928), 126–127.

36— Docteur Lotte Wolff, "Les Révélations psychiques de la main," *Minotaure* 6 (May 1935): 38–44.

37— *Vanity Fair* (August 1922): 52.

38— *The Little Review* (Paris, Spring 1929).

39— William Rubin, *The Paintings of Gerald Murphy*, exh. cat. (New York: Museum of Modern Art, 1974), 42, note 99.

40— For details on this commission and other portraits of Agnes Meyer by Maurius de Zayas, Charles Despiau, Francis Picabia, and others see Sidney Geist, "Le Portrait de Mme Eugène Meyer Jr.," in *Le Portrait? La Série et l'œuvre unique* (Paris: Éditions Centre Pompidou, 2002), 39–52.

41— André Breton, *Œuvres complètes* (Paris: Gallimard, 1988), vol. I, 256; as cited in Adamowicz, Elza, "The Surrealist (Self-)Portrait: Convulsive Identities," in *Surrealism: Surrealist Visuality*, ed. Silvio Levy, (Keele, Staffordshire, UK: Keele University Press, 1996), 31-44.

42— Adamowicz adeptly explores the role of the portrait in surrealist artistic practice in her essay "The Surrealist (Self-)Portrait," 32.

43— Richard Brilliant, *Portraiture* (Cambridge: Harvard University Press, 1991), 171–174.

44— Max Ernst, "Identité instantanée," in "Au-delà de la peinture," *Cahiers d'Art* 14 (October 1936): 180–182.

45— Letter from Murphy to Philip Barry, cited in Rubin, *The Paintings of Gerald Murphy*, 30.

46— *Bulletin de la Vie Artistique* (November 15, 1924): 498.

47— Archibald MacLeish, *Collected Poems, 1917–1952* (Boston: Houghton Mifflin Company, 1952).

48— Many prints of this commission are housed in the Fonds Man Ray at the Musée National d'Art Moderne in Paris.

49— Many of these portraits were published in *Camera Work*.

50— She wrote two portraits of Van Vechten and also dedicated *Portraits and Prayers* (New York: Random House, 1935) to him: "To Carl who knows what a portrait is because he makes them and is them."

51— Gertrude Stein, *America and Alfred Stieglitz, A Collective Portrait* (Garden City, N.Y.: Doubleday, Doran, and Co., 1934).

52— Gertrude Stein, "A Portrait to Jo Davidson," *Vanity Fair* (February 1923): 48. The only unrepresented media is music. Inspired by Stein, composer Virgil Thomson sat with friends trying to capture their essence in music using only pencil and paper. "The portraits are attracting considerable attention. Picasso came to hear them (and other things) and is giving me lots of praise and advertising." A letter to Maurice Grosser dated April 13, 1940 just before returning to the United States, in *Selected Letters of Virgil Thomson*, ed. Tim Page and Vanessa Weeks Page (New York: Summit Books, 1988), 133.

53— Gertrude Stein, *Everybody's Autobiography* (New York: Random House, c. 1937), 51; and Jo Davidson, *Between Sittings* (New York: Dial Press, 1951), 174.

54— Silver, "In Praise of the Particular," 65.

55— It was a particularly fertile period for collaboration as can be seen in the artwork, books, theater, dance, and music. Artists were often contributing both images and texts to books and reviews, for example: *Facile* written by Paul Eluard and illustrated by Man Ray, the opera *Four Saints in Three Acts* written by Gertrude Stein, music by Virgil Thomson, sets and costumes by Florine Stettheimer.

56— "Erik Satie illustré par Calder, pourquoi pas? C'est un Américain 100/100. Satie et Duchamp sont 100/100 Français. Comme on se rencontre?" *Volumes—Vecteurs—Densités. Dessins—Portraits*, exh. cat. (Paris: Galerie Percier, April 1931). Translated in Carolyn Larchner, *Fernand Léger*, exh. cat. (New York: The Museum of Modern Art, 1998), 50, note 193.

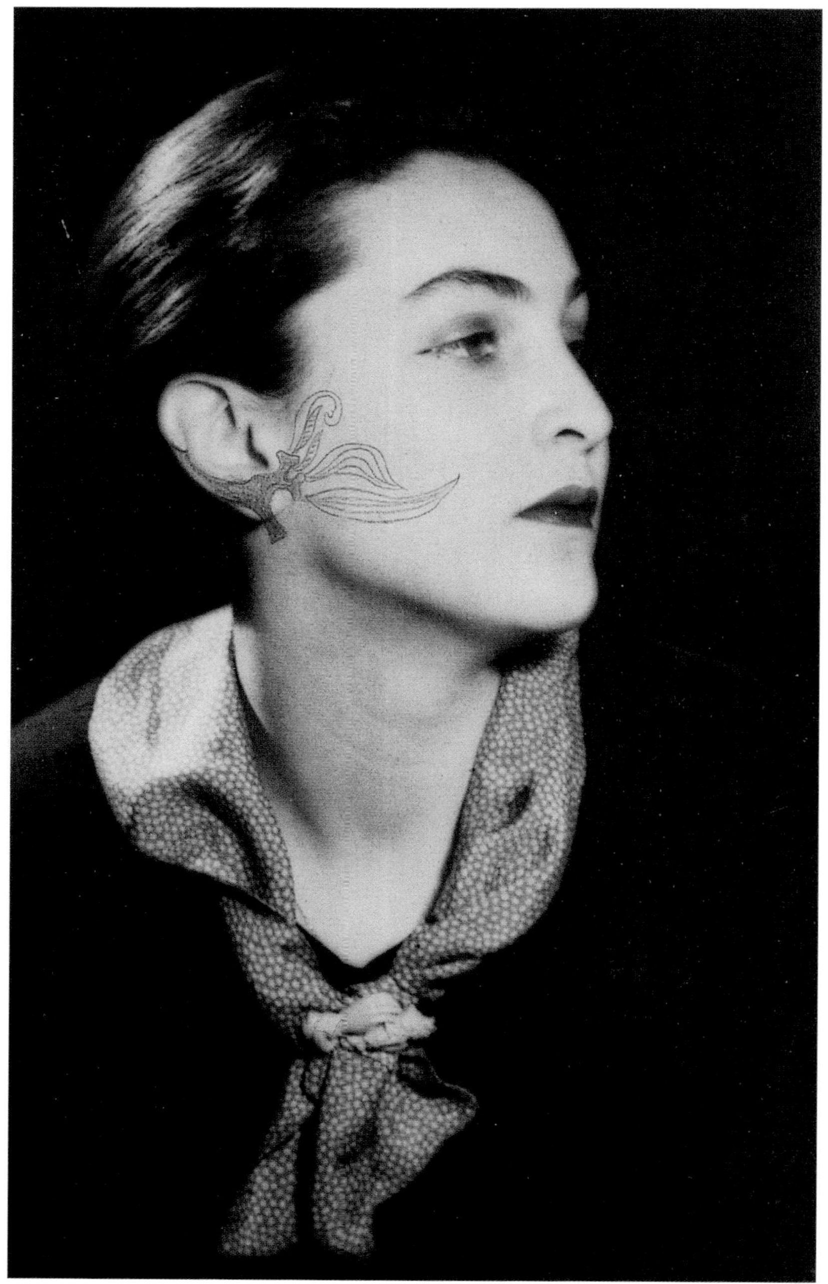

155
MAN RAY
MERET OPPENHEIM, 1931
VINTAGE PHOTOGRAPH, 17 X 10.9 CM
PRIVATE COLLECTION,
COURTESY GALERIE FRANÇOISE PAVIOT, PARIS
MAAG, TAM, TMAA

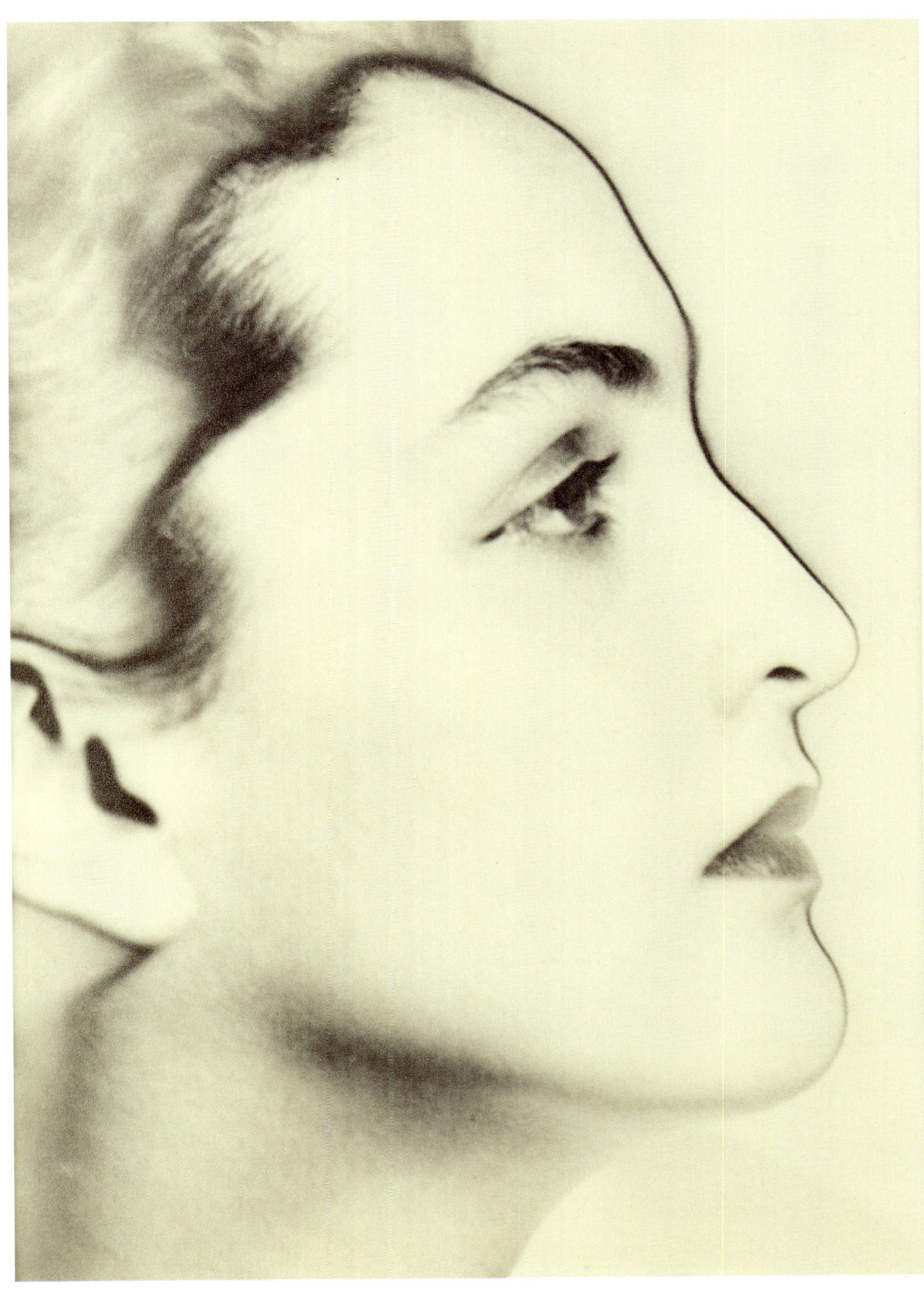

156
MAN RAY
MERET OPPENHEIM, 1933
SOLARIZED GELATIN SILVER PRINT,
61 X 50.8 CM (FRAME)
THE VICTORIA AND ALBERT MUSEUM, LONDON,
PH 68-1984
MAAG, TAM, TMAA

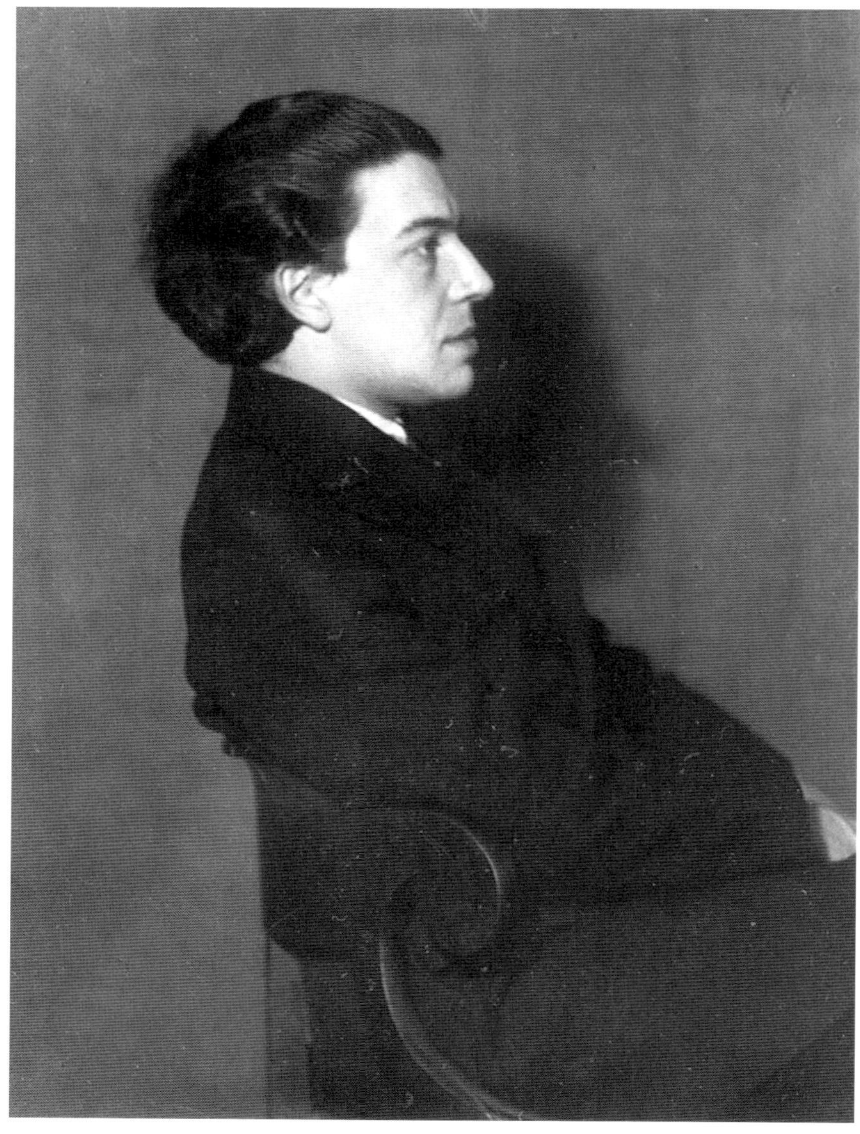

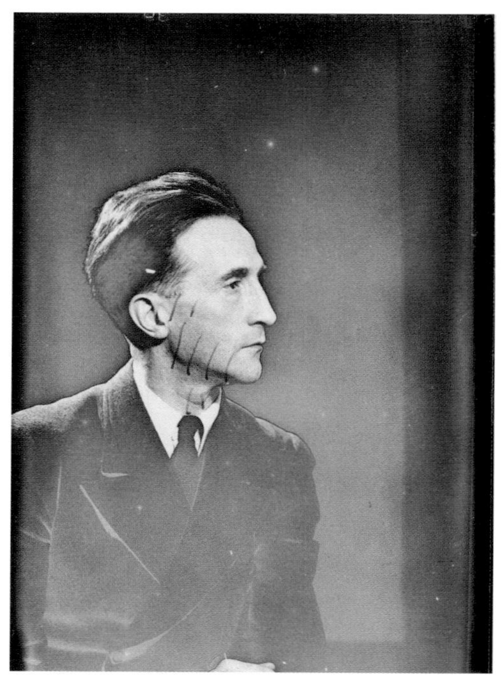

157

MAN RAY
ANDRÉ BRETON, 1921–22
MODERN PRINT, 28.7 × 22.8 CM
FONDS RÉGIONAL D'ART CONTEMPORAIN
DE BOURGOGNE, DIJON
MAAG, TAM, TMAA

158

MAN RAY
PORTRAIT OF MARCEL DUCHAMP, 1924
CONTACT PRINT SOLARIZED AND RETOUCHED,
9 × 6.5 CM
GALERIE 1900-2000, PARIS
MAAG

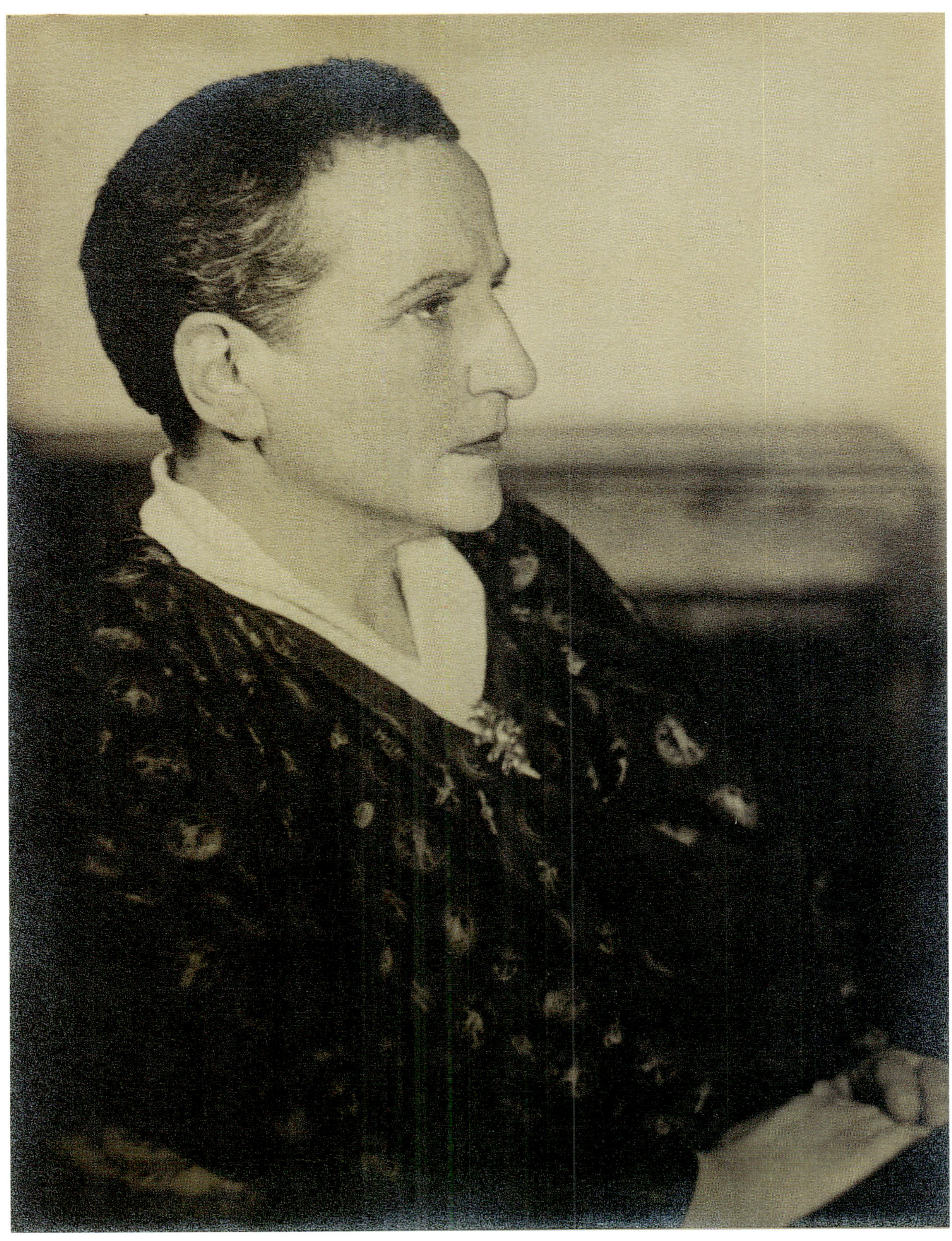

159
MAN RAY
PORTRAIT OF GERTRUDE STEIN. C. 1926
GELATIN SILVER PRINT, 22.9 X 17 CM
HALLMARK CARDS, KANSAS CITY, MISS.
HALLMARK PHOTOGRAPHIC COLLECTION
MAAG, TAM, TMAA

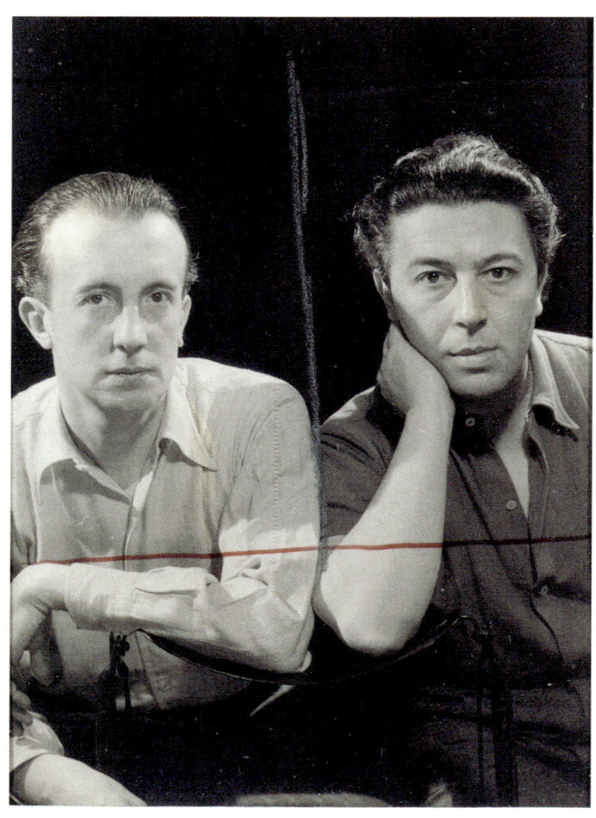

160
MAN RAY
ELUARD AND BRETON, C. 1930
GELATIN SILVER PRINT WITH RED INK,
8.6 X 6.3 CM
GALERIE 1900-2000, PARIS
MAAG

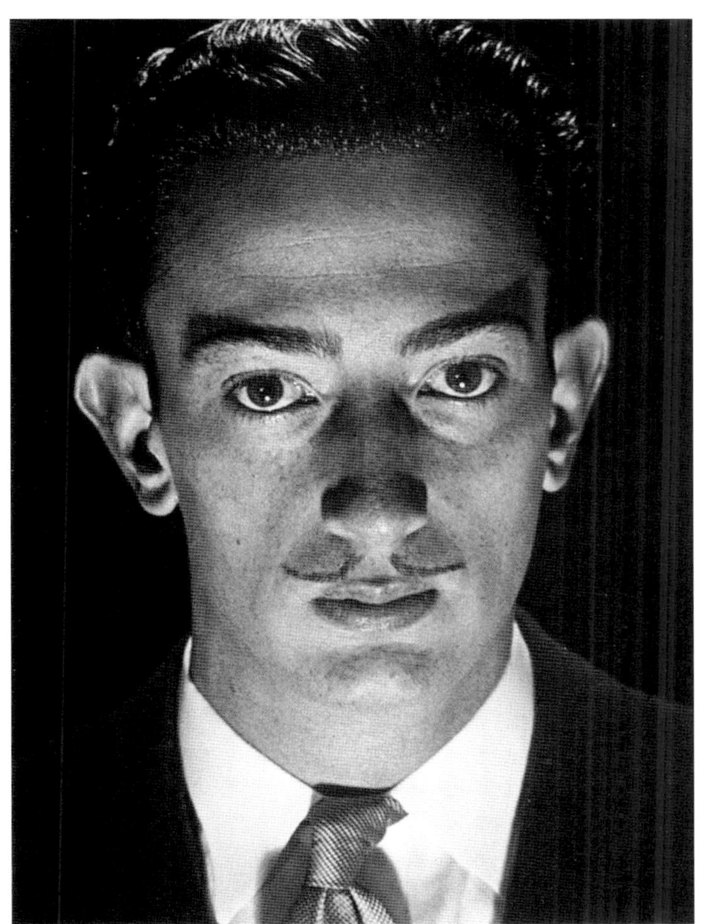

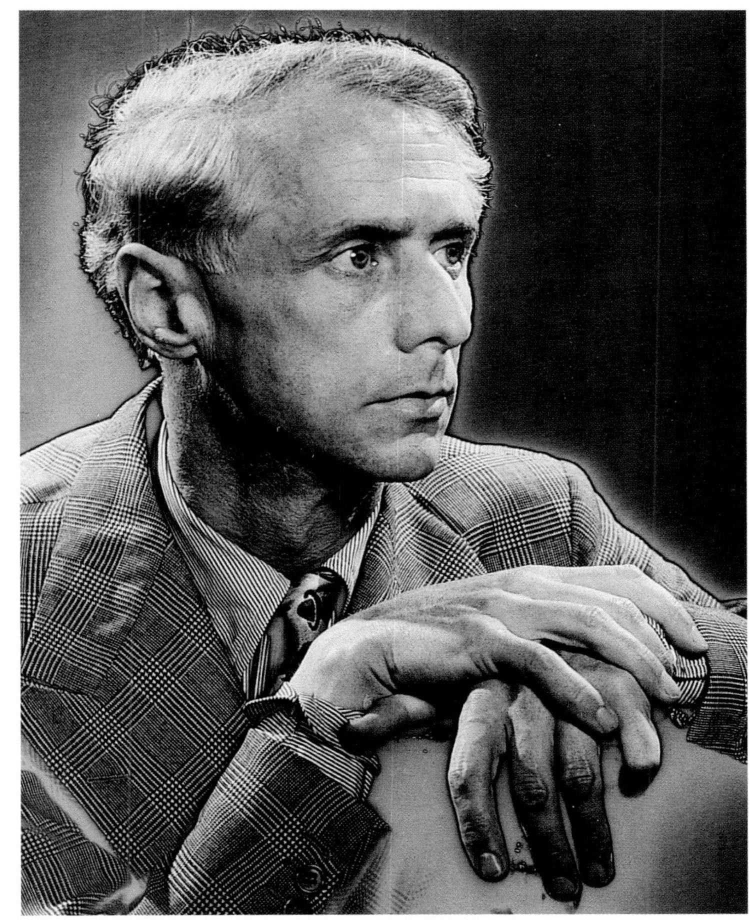

161
MAN RAY
SALVADOR DALI, 1929
MODERN PRINT, 28 × 21.5 CM
FONDS RÉGIONAL D'ART CONTEMPORAIN
DE BOURGOGNE, DIJON
MAAG, TAM, TMAA

162
MAN RAY
MAX ERNST, 1935
GELATIN SILVER PRINT, 24.9 × 19.8 CM
MUSEUM LUDWIG, KÖLN, 1977/634
MAAG

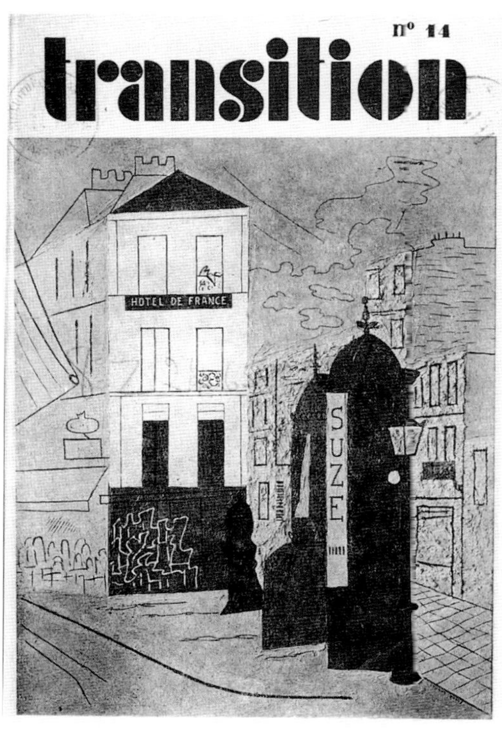

COVER OF *TRANSITION* ILLUSTRATED WITH *HÔTEL DE FRANCE* BY STUART DAVIS (AUTUMN 1928).

American literary journals flourished in Paris in the 1920s and 1930s offering English-language readers a wide selection of essays by international authors and reproductions by contemporary artists. Many avant-garde American writers found a forum to express their experimental styles in these "little magazines" including Djuna Barnes, Kay Boyle, Hart Crane, Ernest Hemingway, Mina Loy, Gertrude Stein, and William Carlos Williams. Written by and about the avant-garde, these magazines contributed to the atmosphere of a growing European-American consciousness and gave a voice to Americans living abroad.[1] Indeed, their editors often wrote self-consciously of their role in the transatlantic exchanges of this period.

Editor of *The Little Review* Margaret Anderson came to Paris in 1923 to compile an important "Exiles Number" that included writings by Hemingway, Stein, and Loy as well as Fernand Léger's "The Esthetics of the Machine." The next issue, known as

the "French Number" (autumn/winter 1923–24), filled its pages with translations of French avant-garde authors such as René Crevel, Paul Eluard, and Louis Aragon, as well as a group of rayographs by expatriate Man Ray. In May 1929, Anderson decided to discontinue her magazine, publishing the final number with both New York and Paris editorial addresses. About the magazine's move to Paris, Janet Flanner wrote, "In a sense then, *The Little Review*, though it had never been in Paris before, came to its home to die."[2] She gave credit to the magazine for its influence on later publications in Paris, such as *The Transatlantic Review* (1924–25). Edited in Paris by British-born Ford Madox Ford, this short-lived journal included occasional illustrations in its pages of essays by mostly American authors. The editors wanted to show "a little of what is being done in Paris—and bought by the United States—at this moment," reproducing works by Léger, Man Ray, Georges Braque, Pablo Picasso, John Storrs, and Constantin Brancusi.[3] Like *The Little Review*, the magazine also carried essays by Americans living in Paris, conscious of their dual and constantly changing identities.

One of the principal European-American reviews in Paris, *transition* magazine (1927–32), furthered the goals of its predecessors. French-born American editor Eugene Jolas provided a forum for the transatlantic exchange of art and literature by promoting experimental authors and artists in his self-proclaimed "international magazine."[4] He reproduced works by avant-garde artists like Alexander Calder, Stuart Davis, Max Ernst, Léger, Man Ray, and Joan Miró. In March 1928, Jolas implied that American writing had advanced beyond its European counterpart when he wrote, "While *transition* will continue to regard itself as a link between Europe and America . . . the emphasis in the future will be placed on American contributions, as we feel that our intensified inquiry into international writing is, for the moment, at a standstill."[5]

Later that fall, photographer Berenice Abbott voiced the dilemma of many Americans abroad—at home in two different countries, "The very complex nature of America is, if possible, better understood from a distance than at close range, the extent of one's Americanism is put to a severe test, and that extent denotes the depth of the artist's capacity."[6] She emphasized a feeling shared by her fellow expatriate artists that to leave one's country, if only for a short while, allowed for an objective evaluation of it. Her thoughts echoed the self-conscious writings found in so many of these transatlantic magazines. Through their tireless efforts, the editors sought to explain the latest American art and literature to their European and American readers. In turn, they created a forum for international dialogue and stressed the constantly changing relationship between the two cultures.

Katherine Bourguignon

1— Examples include: *The New Review* (1931–32) edited by Sam Putnam; *Tambour* (1929–30) by Harold J. Salemson; *Échanges* (1929–31) by Allanah Harper; and *This Quarter* (1925–27 and 1929–32) by Edward W. Titus. See *Paris–New York. Échanges littéraires au xxe siècle* (Paris: Bibliothèque publique d'information, Centre Georges Pompidou, 1977).

2— Janet Flanner, *Paris was Yesterday* (New York: Harcourt Brace Jovanovich Pub., 1972), 56. Co-editor Jane Heap published the "French Number" from New York while Anderson remained in Paris. See also Margaret Anderson, *The Little Review Anthology* (New York: Hermitage House, 1953).

3— "Art Supplement," *The Transatlantic Review* (March 1924) and (June 1924).

4— "An Introduction," *transition* 1 (April 1927): 136. See also Craig Monk, "Photography in Eugene Jolas's *transition* Magazine," *History of Photography* 20, no. 4 (winter 1996): 362–365.

5— Eugene Jolas and Elliot Paul, "A Review," *transition* 12 (March 1928): 182.

6— Berenice Abbott, "Why do Americans live in Europe?" *transition* 14 (fall 1928): 111.

The *Premier Salon Indépendant de la Photographie*, or the "Salon de l'Escalier" as it is most commonly known, was intended to be the first in a series of annual exhibitions of photography that provided an alternative to the established Salon de Photographie. Organizers believed that the work selected for the Salon de Photographie was outmoded and sought to bring modern photography created in France to the attention of a wider public. Florent Fels, who had publicly denounced the Salon de Photographie in his magazine *L'Art Vivant* one year earlier, was joined by Lucien Vogel, René Clair, Jean Prévost, and Georges Charensol[1] on the organizing committee. It was held from May 24 to June 7, 1928, in the Salon de l'Escalier,[2] a gallery space in the stairway of the Théâtre des Champs-Élysées leading to the seventh floor where the Comédie des Champs-Élysées was located. Each landing was hung with photographs, creating an alluring space that also provided the public with an excuse to stop and catch their breath while ascending. The list of ten photographers featured in the exhibition contains a curious number of misspellings, some due to the addition of French accents to American names and hyphens added or omitted from others: Bérénice [sic] Abbott, d'Ora, Albin Guillot [sic], Hoyningen-Huené [sic] (studio du journal "Vogue"), André Kertesz [sic], Germaine Krull-Ivens, Man-Ray [sic], Nadar, Paul Outerbridge, Retrospective Adget [sic].[3]

The "Salon de l'Escalier" was not an attempt to provide a representative exhibition of contemporary photography, but rather intended to focus "attention on a few works by precursors and by others now in full possession of their craft."[4] The precursors considered "essential" to the exhibition were Eugène Atget and Nadar, père et fils, all documentary photographers. Atget, who had died the previous year, spent thirty years recording the mysterious beauties of a rapidly changing Paris. Little-known at that time, his work was appreciated by a select group of writers and artists including photographers Man Ray and Berenice Abbott, who would be instrumental in preserving his life's work. The "Salon de l'Escalier" was the first organized public showing of his work. Nadar by contrast was a high-profile portrait photographer at the center of nineteenth-century literary and artistic circles. He created a panorama of celebrities and personalities titled *Panthéon Nadar*. His portraits are vital documents of the nineteenth century just as the Parisian portraits by Man Ray and Berenice Abbott are essential records of the avant-garde in Paris between the world wars.

Though Fels stated clearly that the committee "wished to avoid 'artistic' photography, photography inspired by painting, engraving, or drawing,"[5] the three most popular subjects were traditional: portrait, still life and landscape. However, the photographers selected succeeded, in the opinion of the committee, in bringing a fresh approach. Rather that bathing subjects in diffuse light, as had been popular among pictorialists, the photographs were more direct and documentary while still paying scrupulous attention to composition. Germaine Krull and André Kertész managed to transform popular subjects like stairways in Montmartre and the Eiffel Tower with untraditional perspectives. Still lifes on display included compositions by Outerbridge, a close-up of a single fork by Kertész, a magnolia by Man Ray, part of his series of flowers little-known today, and also four of his ephemeral rayographs. Falling somewhere between the definition of still life and portrait, there were three photographs of hands: Kertész *Des mains et des livres*, Krull *Les Mains de Mariette Lidys* and Abbott *Les Mains de Jean Cocteau*. The portraits, many of well-known avant-garde figures, garnered the most attention. They were praised for being "exact, clear and precise," and for not playing tricks. A master of this style, Abbott received a special note of mention "Berenice Abbott reduces the human figure to its basic lines: exquisite style and character."[6]

Frequently cited as the first exhibition in Paris to bring modern photography to the public, the "Salon de l'Escalier" was a modest exhibition that succeeded in demonstrating that photography was an art "having its own laws, dependant neither on reality nor on the art of painting."[7]

Bronwyn A. E. Griffith

1— The names cited appear in the brief catalogue of the *Premier Salon Indépendant de la Photographie*. Photocopy obtained from the George Eastman House, Rochester, New York. Lucien Vogel published the magazines *Vu* and *Jardin des modes*; René Clair, filmmaker; Florent Fels, writer and editor of *L'Art Vivant*; Jean Prévost, novelist and journalist; Georges Charensol, critic and editor of *Les Nouvelles littéraires*.

2— Some believe that this is the name of the exhibition; however, it was also the name of the exhibition space as can be seen in the catalogue and contemporary articles.

3— Catalogue *Premier Salon Indépendant de la Photographie*. Berenice Abbott, American, former assistant to Man Ray, 12 portraits; d'Ora, pseudonym of Dora Kallmuss, Austrian portrait photographer, 12 portraits; Laure Albin-Guillot, French portrait photographer and photographic illustrator, 11 photographs, still lifes, nudes, portraits; George Hoyningen-Huene, Russian-born leading fashion photographer in Paris in 1920, 12 photographs, 7 of which were portraits; André Kertész, Hungarian-born, active in Paris in the 1920s and 1930s, 15 photographs, 6 portraits, still lifes, landscapes; Germaine Krull-Ivens, German, 13, landscapes, portrait, nude; Man Ray, American, 10 photographs, 4 portraits, 5 rayographs, still life; Félix Nadar and Paul Nadar, 11 photographs, 10 portraits; Paul Outerbridge, American, 9 still lifes, Eugène Atget, French, number of photographs not specified.

4— Florent Fels, "Le Premier Salon Indépendant de la Photographie," *L'Art Vivant* 4 (June 1, 1928): 445.

5— Ibid.

6— Georges Charensol, "Les Expositions," *L'Art Vivant* 4 (June 15, 1928): 486.

7— Catalogue of the *Premier Salon Indépendant de la Photographie*, 11.

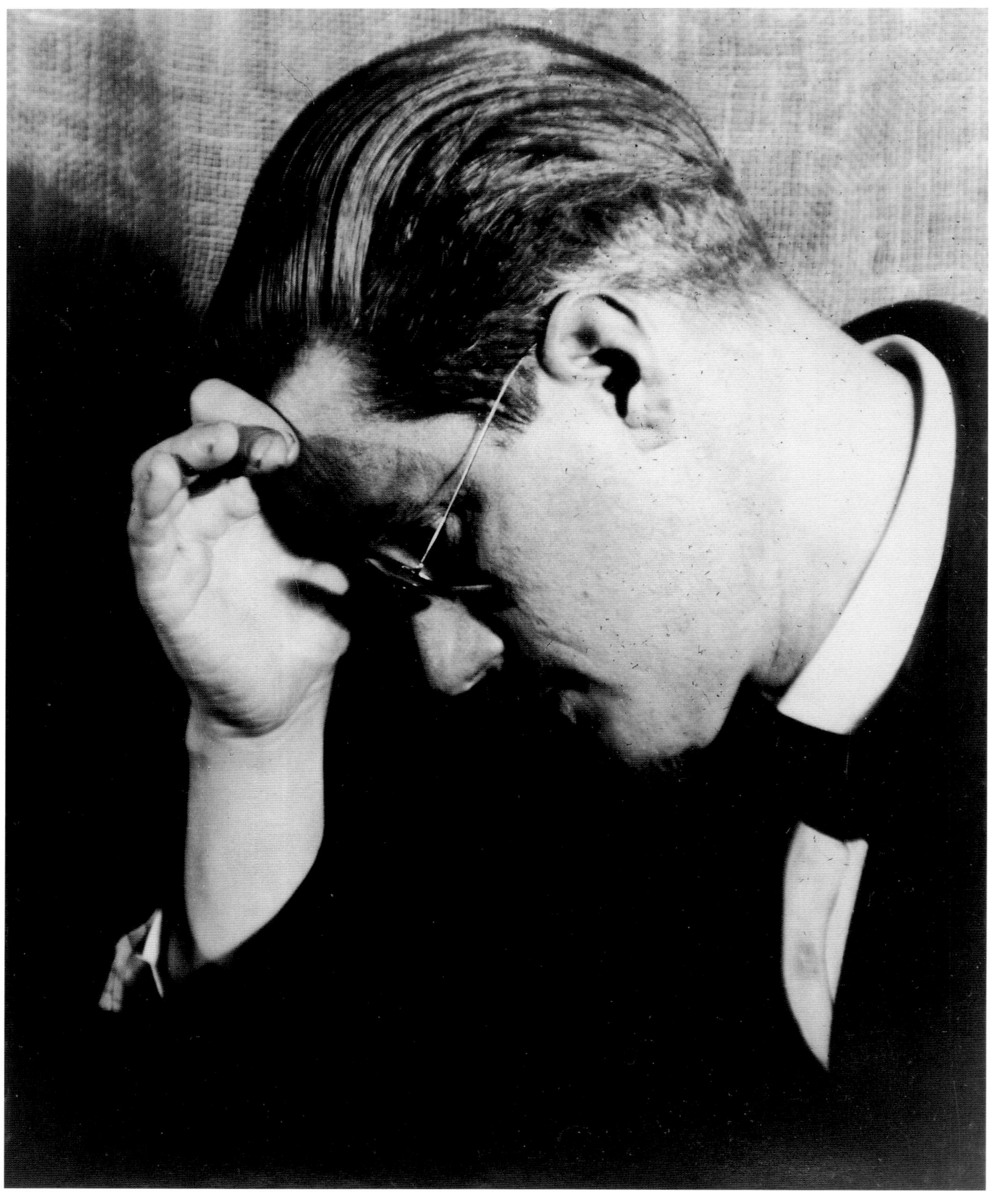

163
MAN RAY
[JAMES JOYCE, HALF-LENGTH PORTRAIT, LEFT
PROFILE, HAND TO FOREHEAD], C. 1930
GELATIN SILVER PRINT, 45.8 X 35.6 CM
LIBRARY OF CONGRESS, WASHINGTON D.C.
PRINTS AND PHOTOGRAPHS DIVISION,
PH – RAY, M NO. 3
MAAG, TAM, TMAA

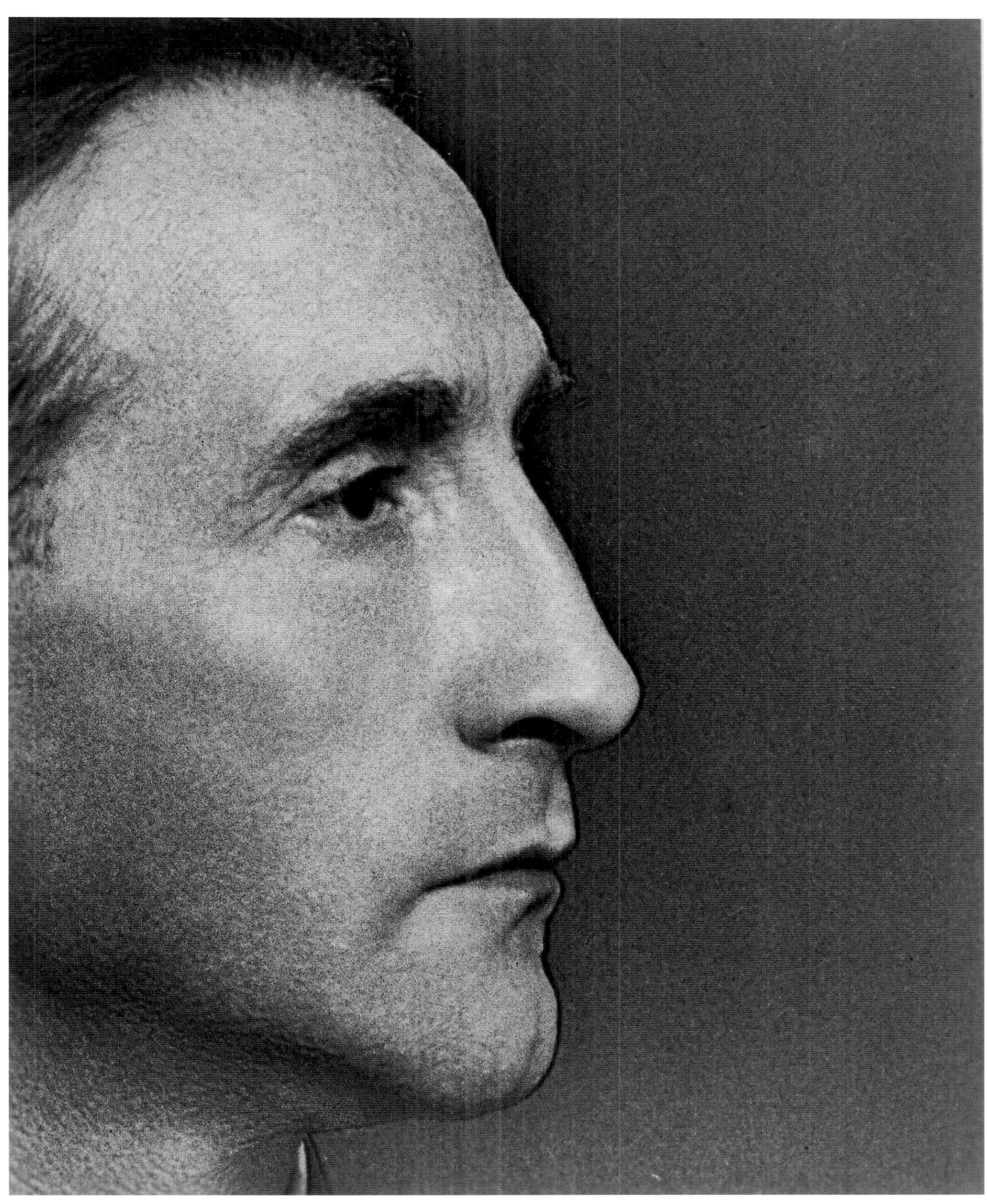

164
MAN RAY
[MARCEL DUCHAMP HEAD FACING RIGHT], C. 1930
GELATIN SILVER PRINT, 45.8 X 35.6 CM
LIBRARY OF CONGRESS, WASHINGTON D.C.
PRINTS AND PHOTOGRAPHS DIVISION, PH – RAY, M. NO. 5
MAAG, TAM, TMAA

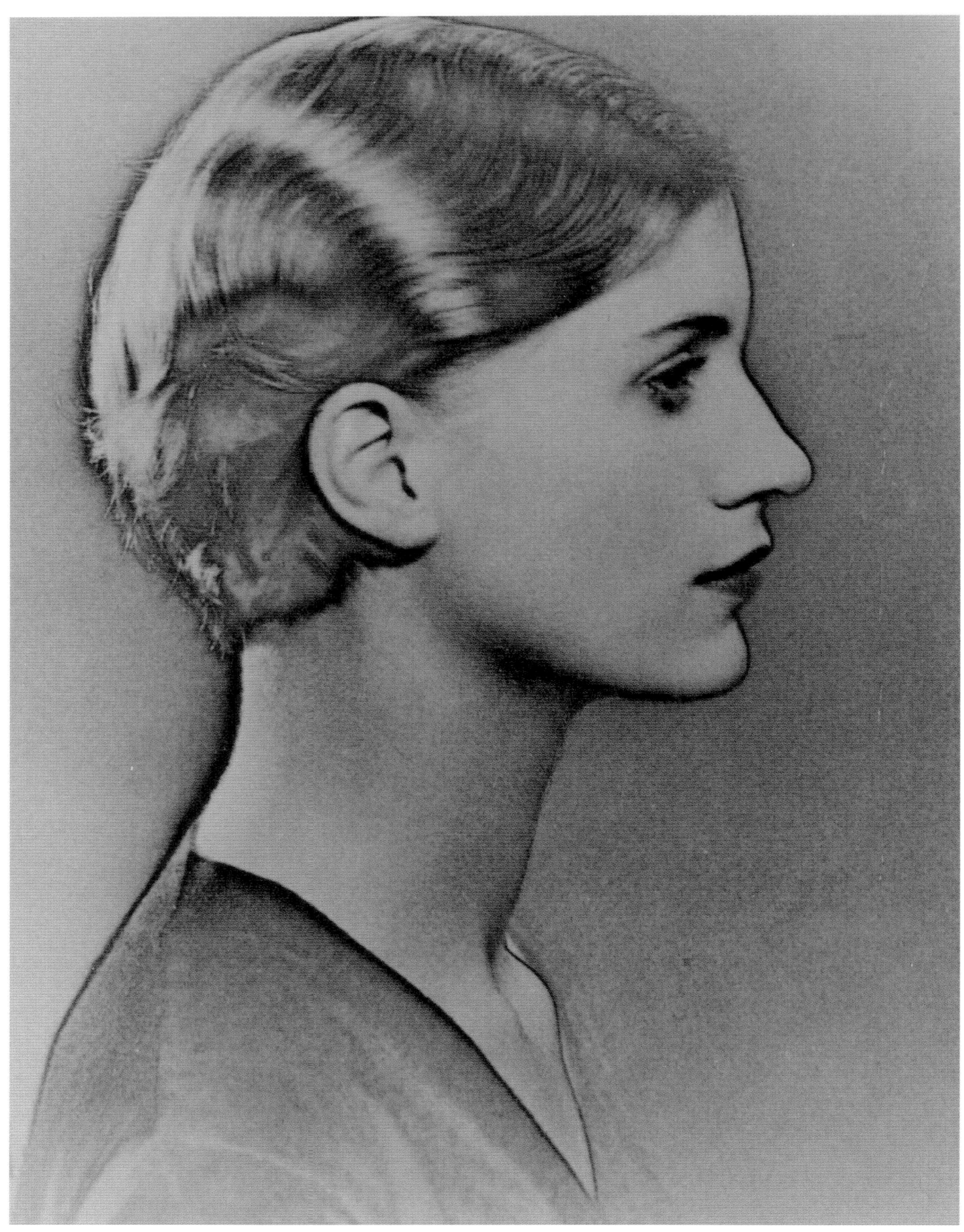

165
MAN RAY
LEE MILLER, SOLARISED PORTRAIT, PARIS, C. 1929
VINTAGE PHOTOGRAPH, GELATIN SILVER PRINT,
24 X 19 CM
LEE MILLER ARCHIVES, CHIDDINGLY, GREAT BRITAIN
MAAG, TAM, TMAA

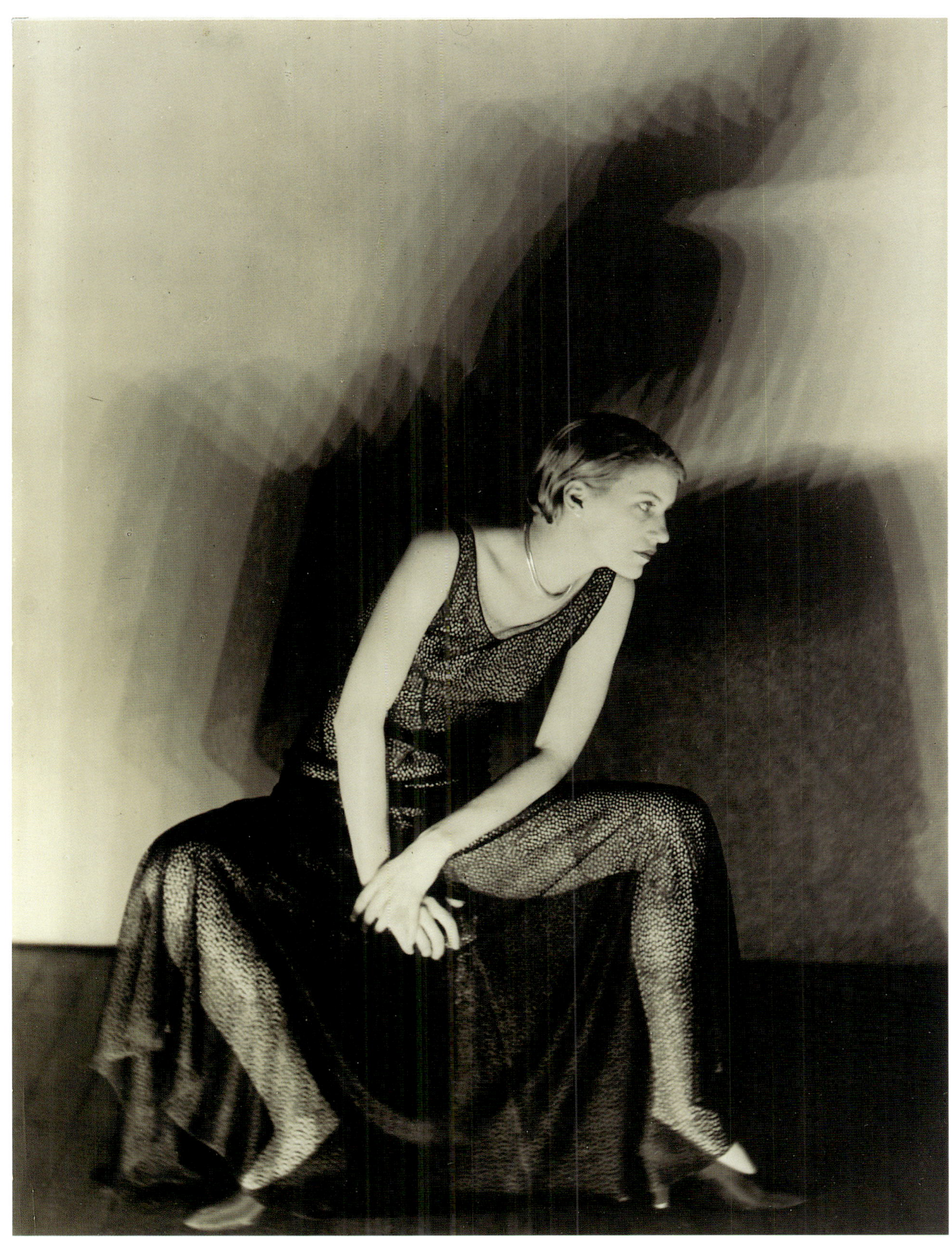

166
MAN RAY
LEE MILLER, 1929
GELATIN SILVER PRINT, 28.9 × 22.2 CM
MUSEUM LUDWIG, KÖLN, 1977/643
MAAG

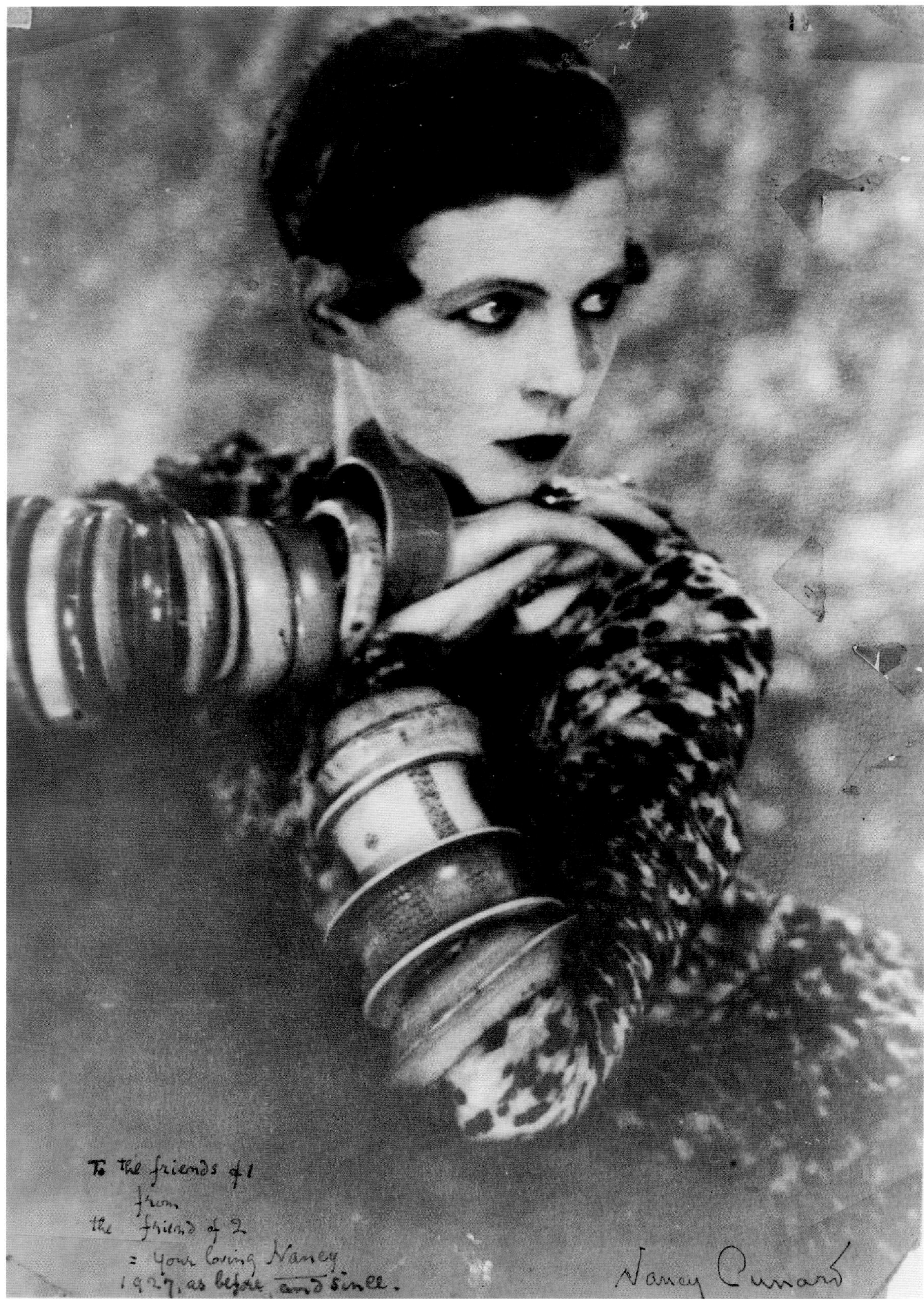

167
MAN RAY
[NANCY CUNARD, HALF-LENGTH PORTRAIT], 1927
GELATIN SILVER PRINT, 27.9 X 35.6 CM
LIBRARY OF CONGRESS, WASHINGTON D.C.
PRINTS AND PHOTOGRAPHS DIVISION,
LOT 13259, V. 21, NO. 65A
MAAG, TAM, TMAA

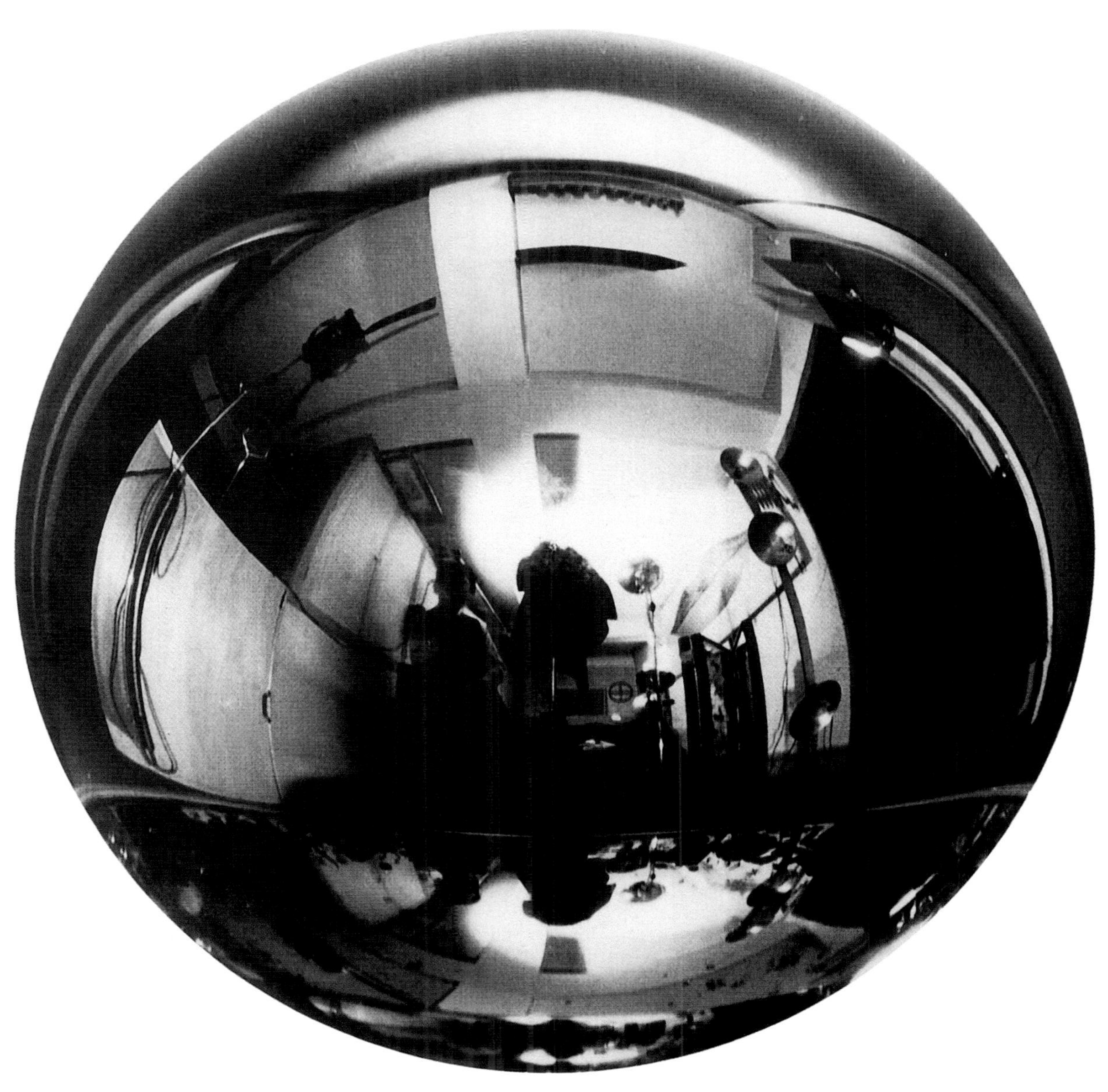

168
MAN RAY
SELF-PORTRAIT, C. 1935
GELATIN SILVER PRINT, D. 15.6 CM
PRIVATE COLLECTION.
COURTESY GALERIE FRANÇOISE PAVIOT, PARIS
MAAG, TAM, TMAA

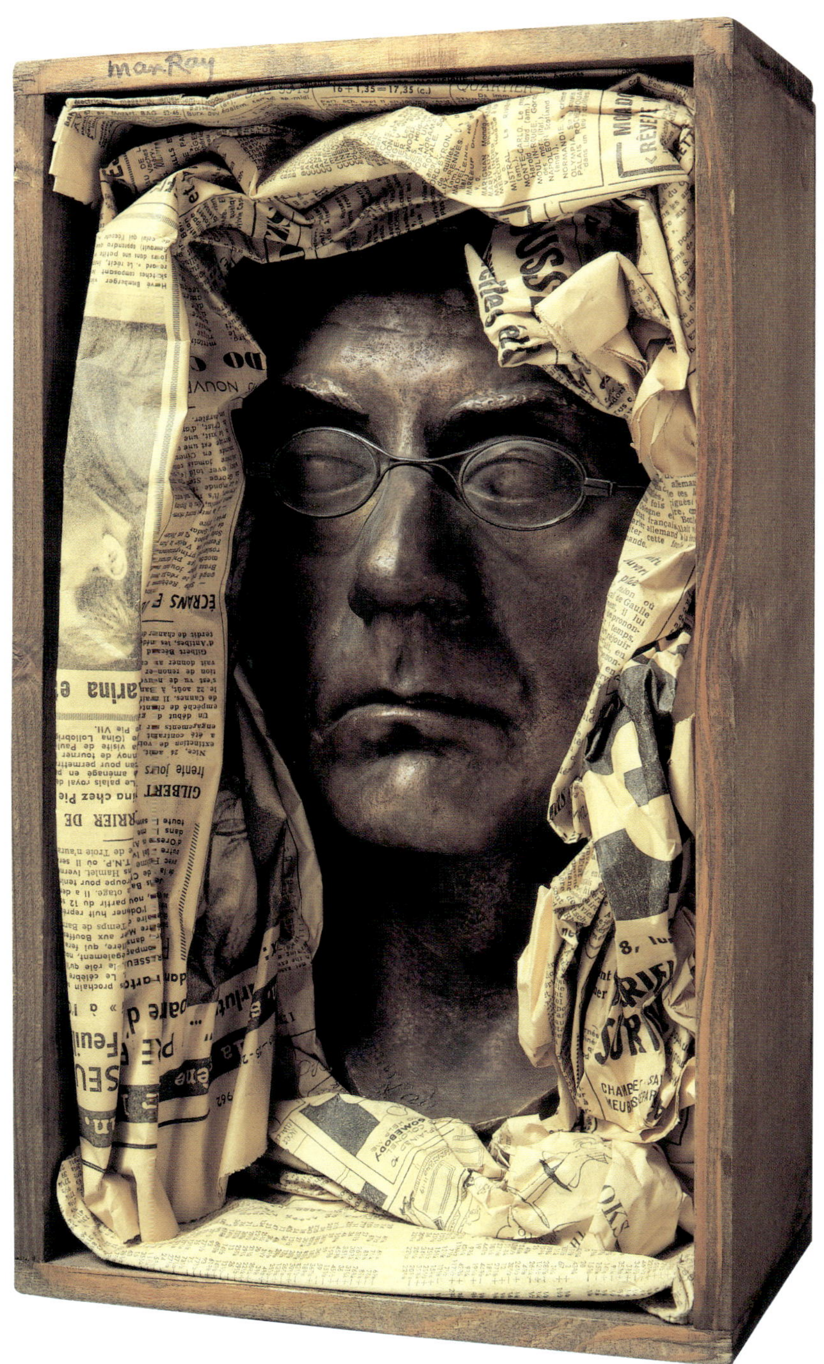

169

MAN RAY
SELF-PORTRAIT, 1933
BRONZE, GLASS, WOOD AND NEWSMINT,
35.6 X 21.1 X 13.7 CM
SMITHSON AN AMERICAN ART MUSEUM,
WASHINGTON D.C. GIFT OF JULIET MAN RAY, 1983.105.2
MAAG, TAM, TMAA

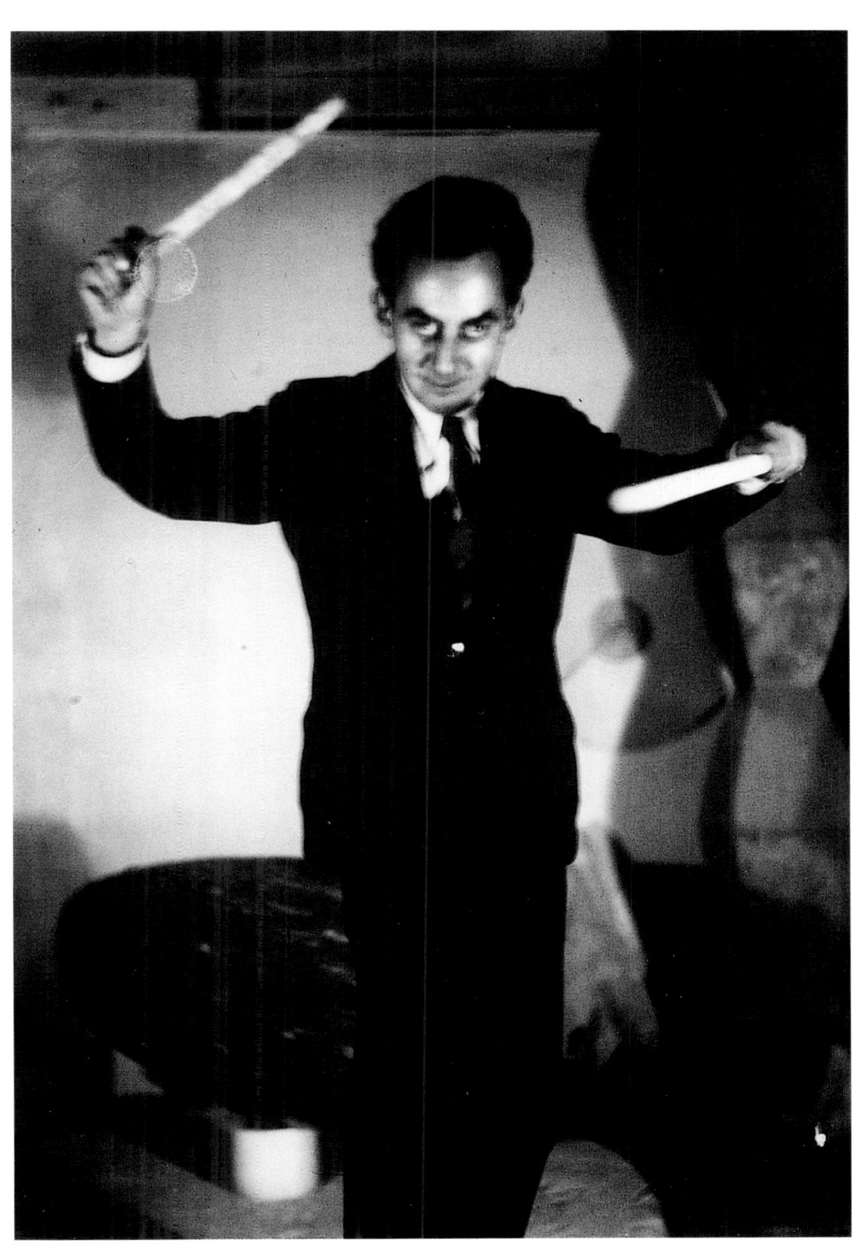

CONSTANTIN BRANCUSI
MAN RAY À L'ATELIER [MAN RAY IN HIS WORKSHOP], 1930
MODERN PRINT FROM THE ORIGINAL NEGATIVE, 16 X 11 CM
MUSÉE NATIONAL D'ART MODERNE –
CENTRE GEORGES POMPIDOU, PARIS
MAAG, TAM, TMAA

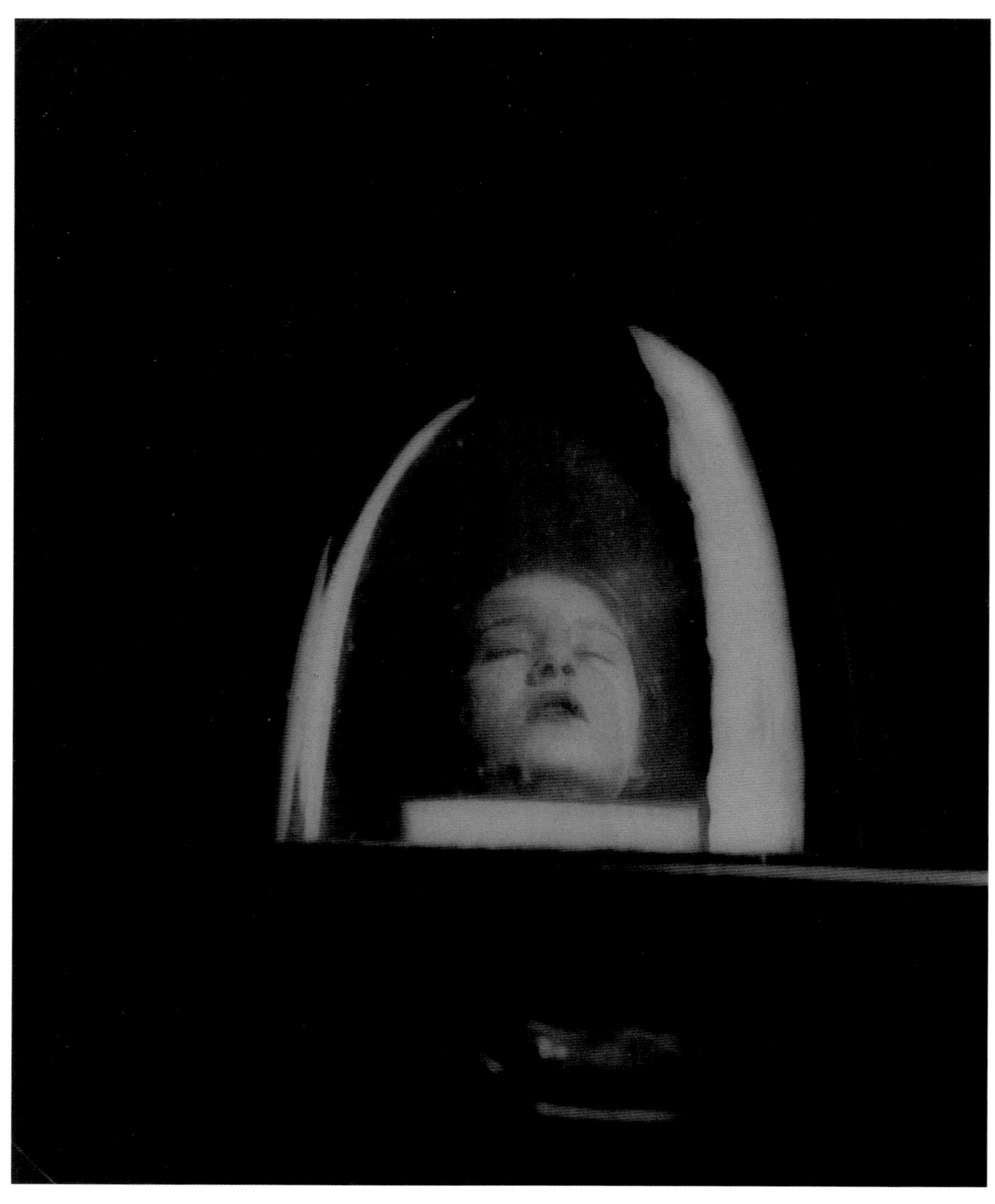

171
LEE MILLER
TANJA RAMM, PARIS, 1931
VINTAGE PHOTOGRAPH, GELATIN SILVER PRINT,
17.6 X 14.7 CM
LEE MILLER ARCHIVES, CHIDDINGLY, GREAT BRITAIN
MAAG, TAM, TMAA

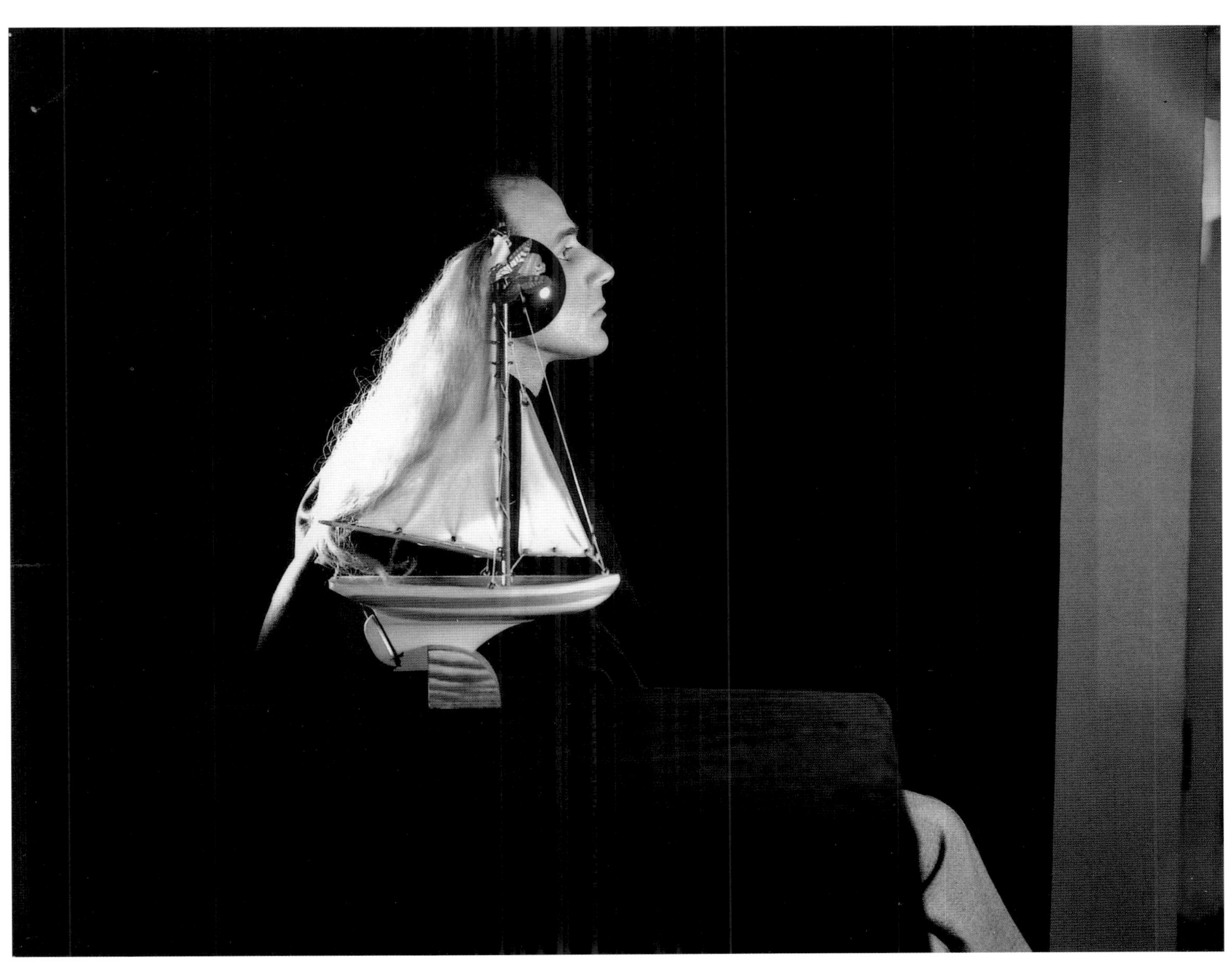

172
LEE MILLER
JOSEPH CORNELL, NEW YORK, 1933
VINTAGE PHOTOGRAPH, GELATIN SILVER PRINT,
16.4 X 21.5 CM
LEE MILLER ARCHIVES, CHIDDINGLY, GREAT BRITAIN
MAAG, TAM, TMAA

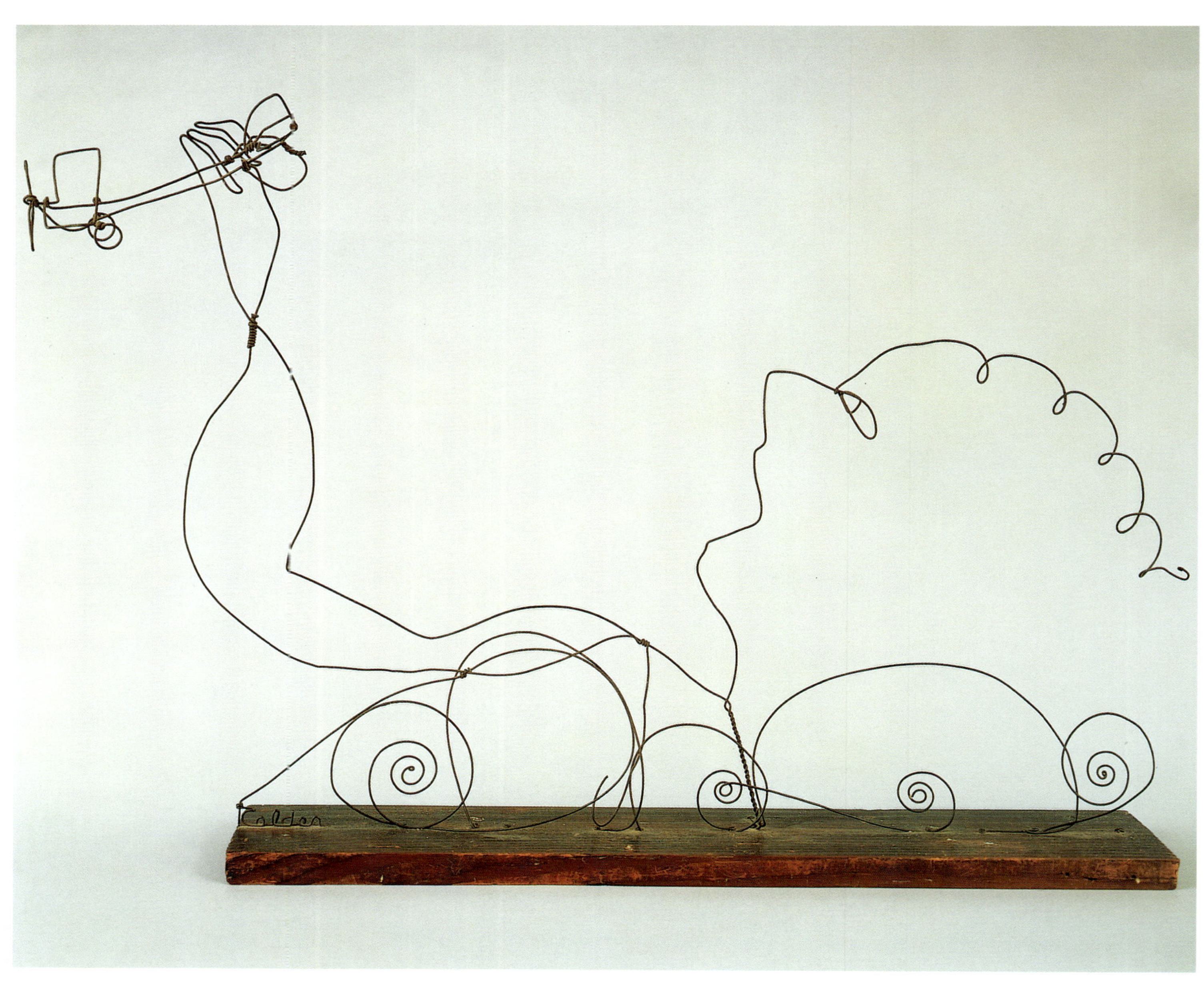

173

ALEXANDER CALDER
THE SPIRIT OF SAINT LOUIS, 1929
WIRE SCULPTURE, 43.2 X 61 X 10.2 CM
PRIVATE COLLECTION.
COURTESY GUGGENHEIM ASHER ASSOCIATES
MAAG, TAM, TMAA

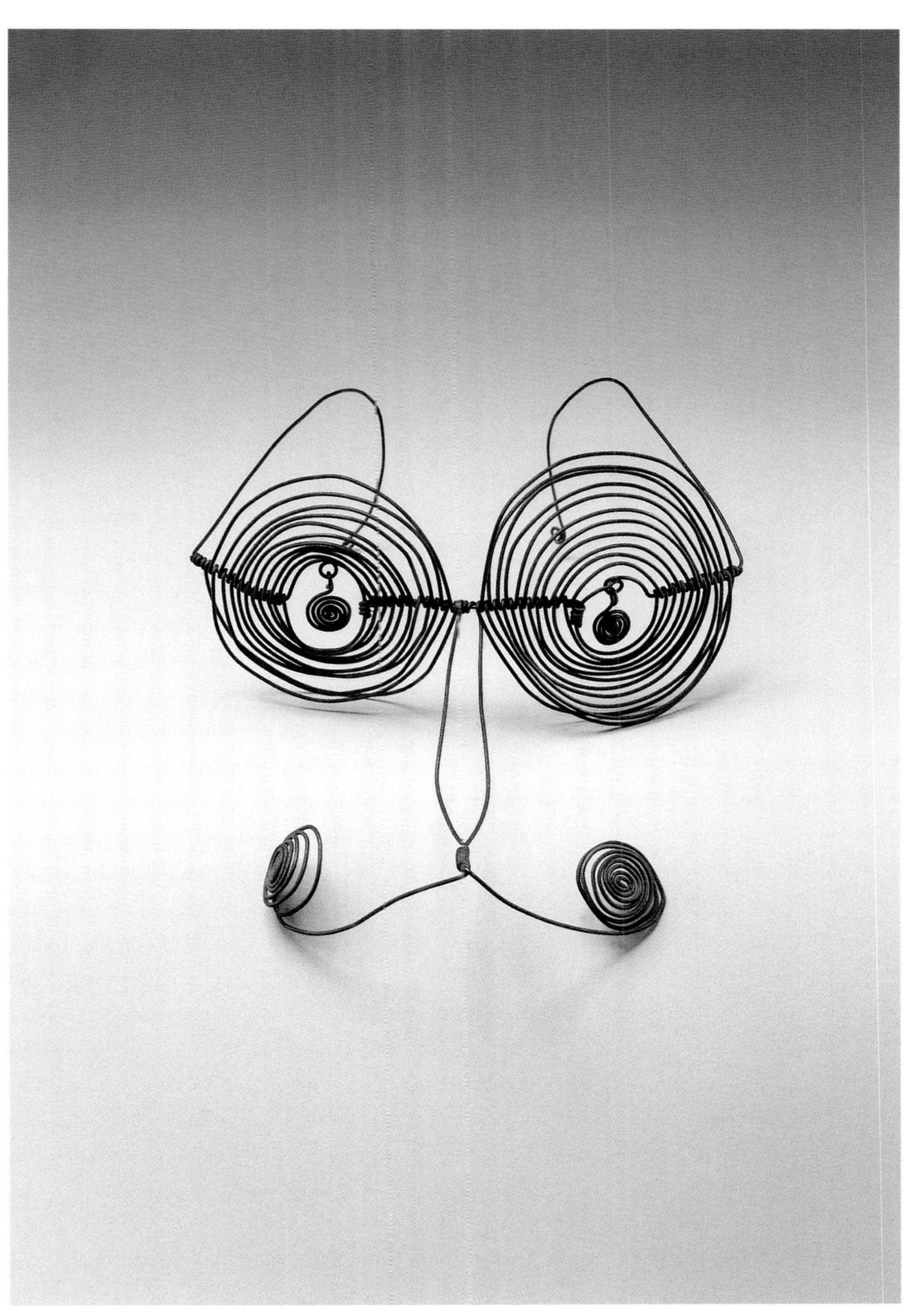

174
ALEXANDER CALDER
UNTITLED, SPECTACLES. 1932
WIRE SCULPTURE, 10.8 X 13 X 15.2 CM
PRIVATE COLLECTION.
COURTESY GUGGENHEIM ASHER ASSOCIATES
MAAG, TAM, TMAA

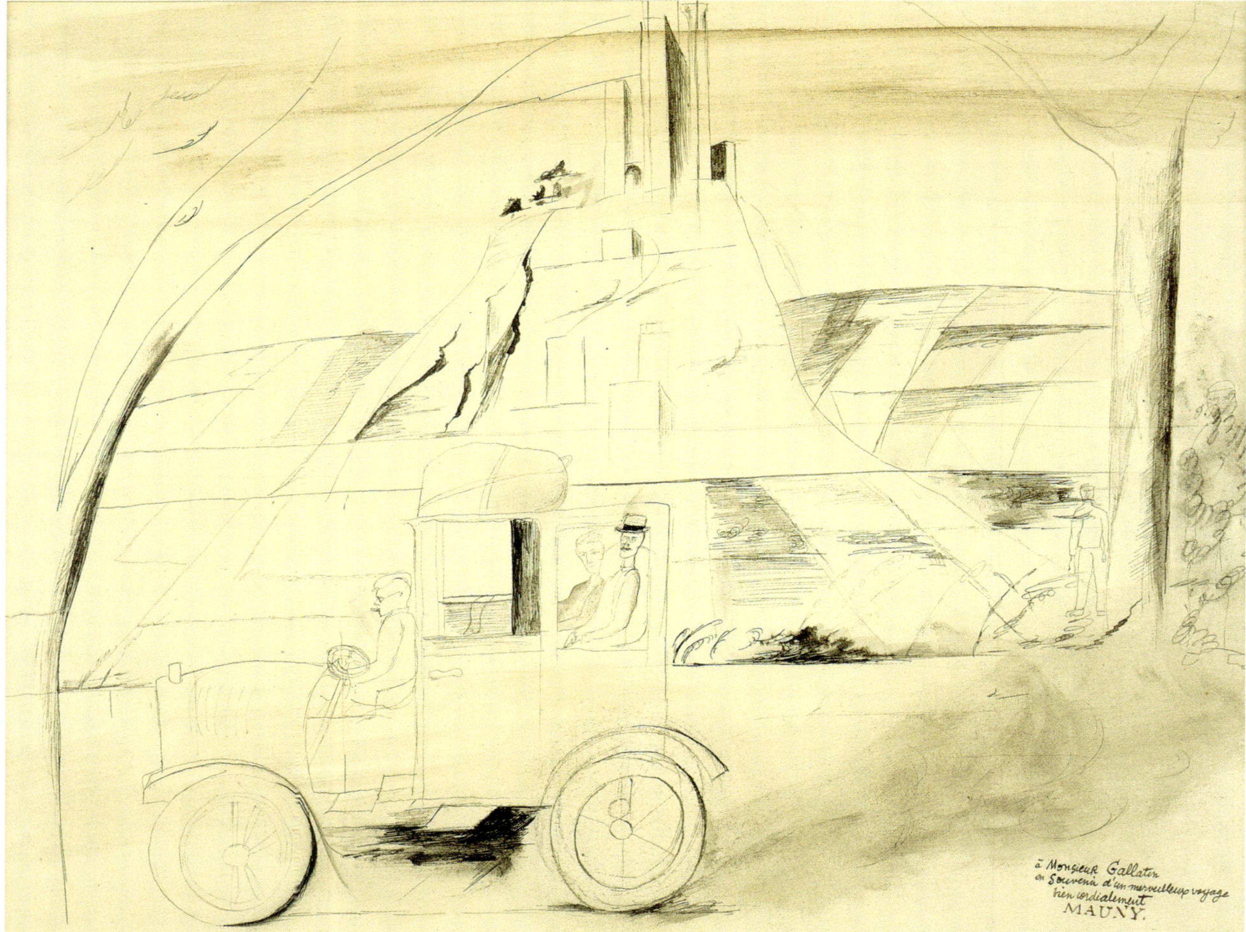

FIG. 1.
JACQUES MAUNY.
[UNTITLED]. 1926 (DATE ADDED IN PENCIL ON MOUNT).
PENCIL AND INDIA INK, 26 X 35 CM.
SIGNED AND DEDICATED LOWER RIGHT: "À MONSIEUR GALLATIN/
EN SOUVENIR D'UN MERVEILLEUX VOYAGE/BIEN CORDIALEMENT:
MAUNY [IN RED INK]".
PRIVATE COLLECTION, PARIS (PROVENANCE: GALLATIN ESTATE,
DISPERSED IN 1995).

This naïve yet refined wash has never been published. It shows Gallatin and Mauny in a chauffeur-driven car on the road to Istanbul. Mauny produced other images of Gallatin, one of them showing him in the restaurant car of the Paris–Marseille train, on which the artist based a dry-point engraving used as the frontispiece for a book that Gallatin wrote on Mauny, published by Éditions des Quatre Chemins in 1928. The critic of *L'Amour de l'art* (no. 1, January 1929) greeted this publication with a damning review. "Jacques Mauny is a talented and expert artist who, unfortunately, has followed a rather tiresome path that obscures his finer qualities. M. Gallatin's text has been translated from English into French so literally that it hovers halfway between the two languages. The author is unsparing in his praise for the artist, thereby often reminding the reader, unintentionally, of [La Fontaine's] fable of the bear and the gardener. The book is well produced and contains very fine illustrations."[6] It is probable that Gallatin also financed, that same year, Jean Giraudoux's *Amica America*, illustrated with twenty original engravings by Mauny, published by Éditions Émile-Paul.

Gallatin met Mauny, even more of a loner than himself, during a Constantin Guys exhibition in 1926. Gallatin enabled his protégé to cross the Atlantic, and promoted him in the most aristocratic collections of Paris and Philadelphia. In return, Mauny facilitated Gallatin's early transactions with Picasso, Braque, and Léger. Mauny was a bilingual free-lancer for reviews such as *The Arts* in New York, *L'Art vivant* in Paris, and *Drawings and Design* in London; as a painter, he was impressed with Charles Sheeler's Precisionism and meticulously executed little works in tempera on cardboard. After the failure of two exhibitions in New York, Mauny withdrew to obscurity in Enghien-les-Bains north of Paris. His *Self-Portrait* of 1926 (see p. 99) was exhibited at the Gallery of Living Art until the gallery's hanging was revamped in 1933.

ALBERT EUGENE GALLATIN'S
TRAVEL KIT

CHRISTIAN **DEROUET**

Everything winds up finding its place in the history of art, even souvenirs of an austere art-lover who enjoyed a comfortable life in New York in the first half of the twentieth century. Albert Eugene Gallatin boasted a handsome fortune and an ancestry that went back to Thomas Jefferson. He lived in an apartment on Park Avenue, decorated with staid furniture and venerable objects. His world never resembled the free-wheeling one associated with Louise and Walter Arensberg. Gallatin participated in Manhattan's art scene alongside Alfred Stieglitz, John Quinn, Katherine Dreier, and Maud Chester Dale without really mixing with them. In Paris, he would not necessarily visit Gertrude Stein or go see Raoul La Roche's collection in its appointed setting, specially built by Le Corbusier. Gallatin expressed his love of contemporary art in solitude, as did Jacques Zoubaloff, Roger Dutilleul, and Pierre Bruguière who, with more modest means, collected the same artists.

Having admired James McNeill Whistler at a young age, Gallatin was impressed by the American artist's dandyism as well as by his international stature. Gallatin adopted Whistler's expressions and mimicked his refinement. From these years of "connoisseurship" Gallatin retained the habits of regularly visiting international museums and of writing short articles, often printed at his own expense. He amassed woodcuts by Aubrey Beardsley and, like all print lovers, he appreciated things for their rarity. During this "contrarian" period, he crossed the Atlantic for the Paris Exposition of 1900, where he is not known to have had any special adviser. In 1949, he divested himself of the fruit of his early collecting to the benefit of the Princeton University library.

From 1921 to 1938, Gallatin acquired the habit of returning to the old continent at the end of every spring. All those who saw him regularly—Jacques Mauny, Jean Hélion, César Domela—have confirmed an apparent unease in Gallatin: his own restraint was smothering him. Albert Gleizes, who only knew him in passing, perhaps profiled him better than anyone else when he wrote to Léonce Rosenberg on December 4, 1935: "I would also like to thank you for having sold the gouaches to E. Gallatin for his Gallery of Living Art. Gallatin came to my place two or three years ago and would have bought some paintings had they

been smaller. He wrote to me last year from New York saying that he was 'happy' to have bought several stencil prints of mine. He's nice but indecisive, not exactly knowing what he wants. Just between us, I don't think he understands very much about modern trends. His museum contains more authentic daubs than interesting works. I have his catalogues, which are far from *fascinant*. Moreover, his adviser over here—the artist [Hélion] you mentioned to me—is a whole religion in himself."[1]

Gallatin sought the company of cultivated young people. Like Pygmalion, he wanted to be the first to buy a work, to present a new name to the public. He wanted to be right, ahead of everyone else. He backed the John Becker Gallery in New York because the dealer was a young man who needed a patron.

Shy and stuffy in public, Gallatin was an autocratic epicurean at home. He hovered around institutions in order to assert his personality as patron. In the 1920s, he bombarded the print department of New York's Metropolitan Museum with loans. Then, in 1926, after having been appointed a trustee of New York University (NYU), he conceived his key project in life by implanting a rather informal foundation of contemporary art into one of the libraries on Washington Square, where he was given three large alcoves in which to hang his collection. Admission to the Gallery of Living Art—later dubbed the "Museum" of the same name—was free of charge, for it was designed to help young people cultivate their taste. Gallatin bought works, paid for hanging costs, and published catalogues and newsletters at his own expense. Things ran smoothly from 1927 until 1942, when NYU chancellor Dr. Harry Woodburn Chase asked Gallatin to vacate the space. Fortunately for his collection, Gallatin found temporary—and later, permanent—shelter at the Philadelphia Museum of Art in 1943. In the meantime, he had discovered a small museum in Pittsfield in the Berkshires where he sent works by the American abstract artists he frequented and supported.

In Paris, Gallatin was associated with the parochial set that gravitated around the Musée du Luxembourg, which was the official showcase for Salon artists. He contacted Robert Rey, one of the curators, and Monsieur Pacquement, the president of the members' association. After expressing

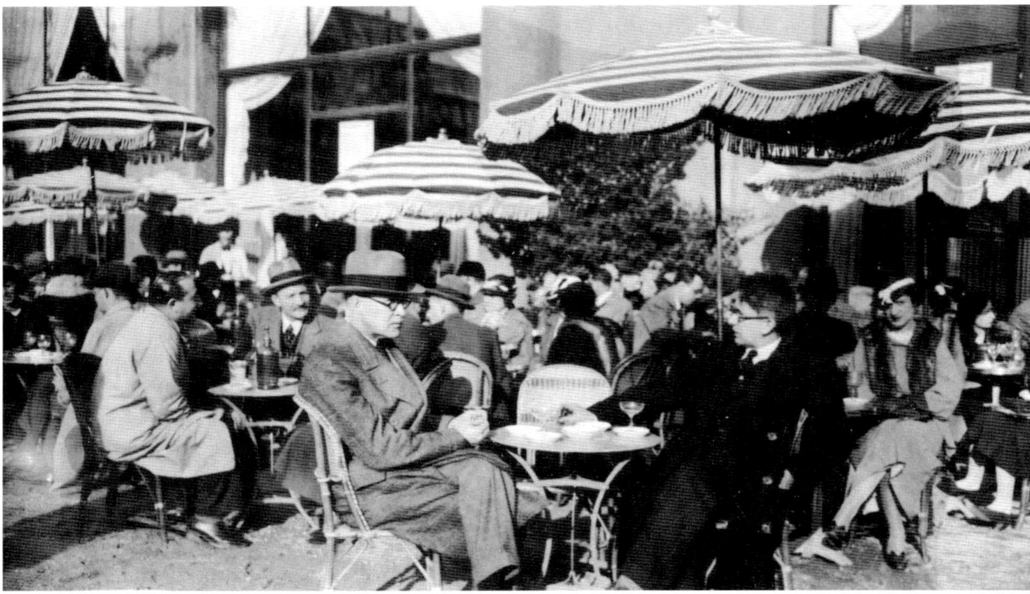

FIG. 2.
[ALBERT EUGENE GALLATIN AND JEAN HÉLION UNDER PARASOLS
ON THE TERRACE OF A GRAND HOTEL IN PARIS (?)], N.D.
PREVIOUSLY UNPUBLISHED POSTCARD. 8 X 13 CM.
ANNOTATED IN PENCIL ON THE BACK: "GALLATIN ET HÉLION, PARIS",
BIBLIOTHÈQUE KANDINSKY, FONDS GALLATIN, PARIS, 3287-1.

Robert Delaunay introduced Jean Hélion to Gallatin, who bought
a *Composition* dated 1932 at the young painter's first exhibition
at the Galerie Pierre [Loeb]. With Hélion, Gallatin discovered
the group of artists working under the banner of "Abstraction–Création."
In May 1933, Hélion took Gallatin to meet Mondrian and then
Hans Arp. By way of polite exchange, Hélion was invited to give
a guided tour through the rooms of the Gallery of Living Art on
December 9, 1933. The two men discussed the inappropriateness
of the terms "abstract," "concrete," "non-objective," "non-figurative,"
and "non-representational," and they envisaged launching a review
of the current art scene that would defend their concept, *Plastic*.
Hélion enjoyed Gallatin's favor until 1938, and benefited from
occasional financial aid, as demonstrated by a letter from the artist
to his friend Pierre Bruguière, dated November 13, 1938:
"Tell Henriette [Pierre Loeb's assistant] to see about the painting
that Gallatin wanted to donate to a Paris museum but which has
remained at Pierre's. Who knows, maybe the Luxembourg?
It's urgent because Gallatin has told me twenty times that if the
government doesn't take the painting then he won't buy it, and
I'll have to repay him the 200 dollars I borrowed to go to France.
Such woe! Once he heard about the setback at the New Bauhaus,
he decided to extend my credit a little longer…."[7] Having taken
refuge in New York, Hélion honored the opening of the Gallatin
rooms in the Philadelphia Museum with a lecture on May 14, 1943.
Shortly afterward, Hélion's return to a figurative idiom was viewed
by Gallatin's entourage as a complete betrayal.

pleasure that Jacques Doucet had bequeathed a large painting by
the Douanier Rousseau to the Louvre, he said he hoped that France
would welcome the American landscape painters he was supporting—
but Gallatin was being over optimistic. The Musée du Luxembourg was
still digesting the Impressionist works bequeathed by Gustave
Caillebotte. The only potential museum of modern art in 1929 would
have been the rather narrow collection of art dealer Paul Guillaume.
It was not until 1937 that Gallatin's gallery was imitated in Paris, when
Jeanne Boucher, a dynamic dealer, rented premises in a cultural center
on rue de Navarin and opened a "Museum of Living Art" on October 15.
It soon closed, however, for lack of funds.

Gallatin's career can be divided into four distinct stages. The transition
from one stage to the next entailed a radical aesthetic revolution.
The first, primarily British, period, on which little research has been
done, concerns his Belle Époque taste. The second, from 1926 to 1932,
focused on New York artists and Parisian post-cubists; with Mauny,
he approached Pablo Picasso, Georges Braque, and Fernand Léger and
obtained major works from them even as he probed less-established
artists such as Bissière, Cassandre, La Fresnaye, Lurçat, Masson, and
others. His acquisitions nevertheless remained a selection of specimens
easy to mask when going through customs. In the third stage,
from 1932 to 1936, Gallatin mustered his assets and bought Picasso's
Three Musicians and Léger's *City* in order to give greater substance to
"his" cubists. But he then permanently dropped these artists on adopting
the hard line advocated by the various people who initiated him into
"pure form"; he discovered the disciplined beauty of Mondrian and
backed the development of Hans Arp. The fourth period, finally, lasted
from 1938 to 1952 when, after having made his last purchases in
Europe (a Hartung, a Mondrian, and an El Lissitsky), he renounced the
quest for collection pieces in order to devote himself to his own painting.

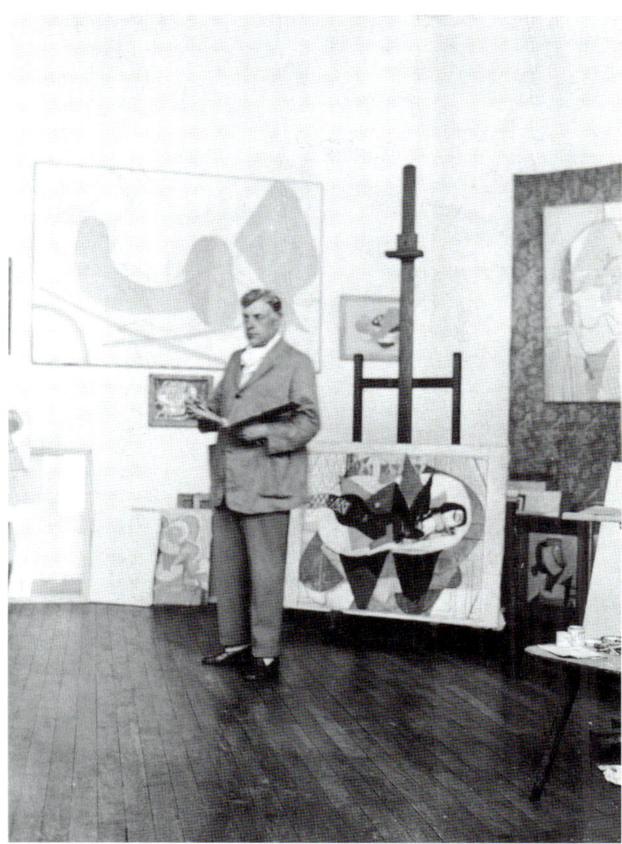

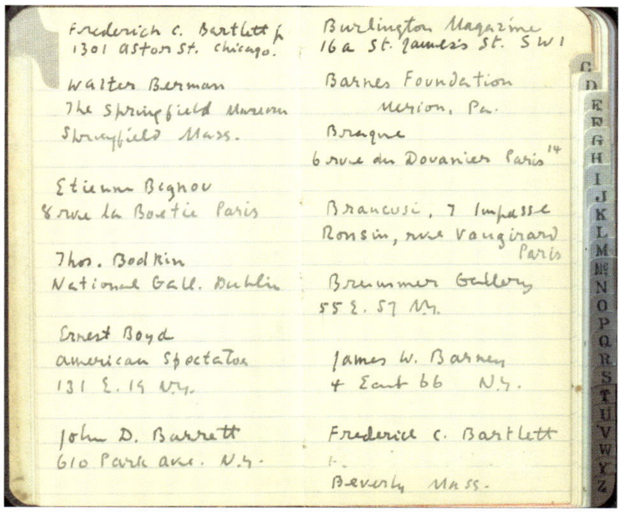

FIG. 3.
ADDRESS BOOK OPEN TO THE LETTER B FOR BRAQUE.
BIBLIOTHÈQUE KANDINSKY, FONDS GALLATIN, PARIS.
GIFT OF MRS. AMY WOLF, 3287-8.

This little key to Gallatin's movements contains 187 American addresses (including some fifteen artists), fifty Paris addresses (including twenty-six artists), twenty-three contacts in the United Kingdom, seventeen in Switzerland, and ten scattered across the globe.

FIG. 4.
ALBERT EUGENE GALLATIN.
[GEORGES BRAQUE], 1932.
GELATIN SILVER PRINT, 20.8 X 15.8 CM.
BIBLIOTHÈQUE KANDINSKY, FONDS GALLATIN, PARIS, 3287-8.

He painted studiously, in a manner full of admiration for Juan Gris's works of 1916. Gallatin henceforth financed the emergence of a native abstract school by associating with the American Abstract Artists group. He bought their paintings and financed exhibitions in Paris and the publication of five issues of *Plastique.* In New York, he supported the Riverside Museum. It might be wondered to what extent he shared the opinions of his younger relative, George L. K. Morris, an art critic for *Partisan Review,* in which luminous Trotskyist glosses by the likes of Meyer Schapiro, Harold Rosenberg, and Clement Greenberg appeared alongside surprising review slips and glossy illustrations of work by Greene, Shaw, and Gallatin.

This anachronistic dandy's open-mindedness might be doubted if we place too much emphasis on the spleen of his "Museum Piece" in the 1946 anthology titled *American Abstract Artists,* where he attacked all rival United States institutions that surpassed in scope and reputation his own Museum of Living Art. He barely slapped the Whitney Museum, the better to lambaste the others: "The Museum of Non-Objective Art is largely a demonstration of Germanic lack of feeling for painting [this against Hilla Rebay, the high priestess of what would become the Guggenheim Museum]. Art of This Century [Peggy Guggenheim's gallery in New York] is divided into two parts, plastic art and surrealism, of which the latter section is the essence of vulgarity. With its garden

The collection includes two photographs of Braque in his studio on 6 rue du Douanier Rousseau in the 14th arrondissement of Paris. In one, he is standing in front of an easel; in the other he is seated. Dress, pose, everything is affected.

The Gallery of Living Art owned four paintings, a magnificent *papier collé,* and a small plaster sculpture by Braque. In addition, Gallatin received from the artist the gift of a superb gouache dedicated "à Gallatin, G. Braque, 1918," in addition to a lithograph of 1933.

Gallatin credited Braque with a crucial role in discovering the *papier collé* technique. But when he reviewed the opening of Maud Chester Dale's French Art Museum in New York for *Cahiers d'Art* (no. 2, 1931), Gallatin implied that of the three painters on show, Picasso, Léger, and Braque, the latter was perhaps the most tied to the past. And he added a judgment too nuanced to be anything other than Gallatin's own: "In my opinion some connoisseurs may feel that certain small gouaches and certain small paintings are where the most delightful features of Braque's oeuvre are to be found."[8]

In 1943, Gallatin wrote a small pamphlet titled *Georges Braque: Essay and Bibliography,* published by Wittenborn in New York.

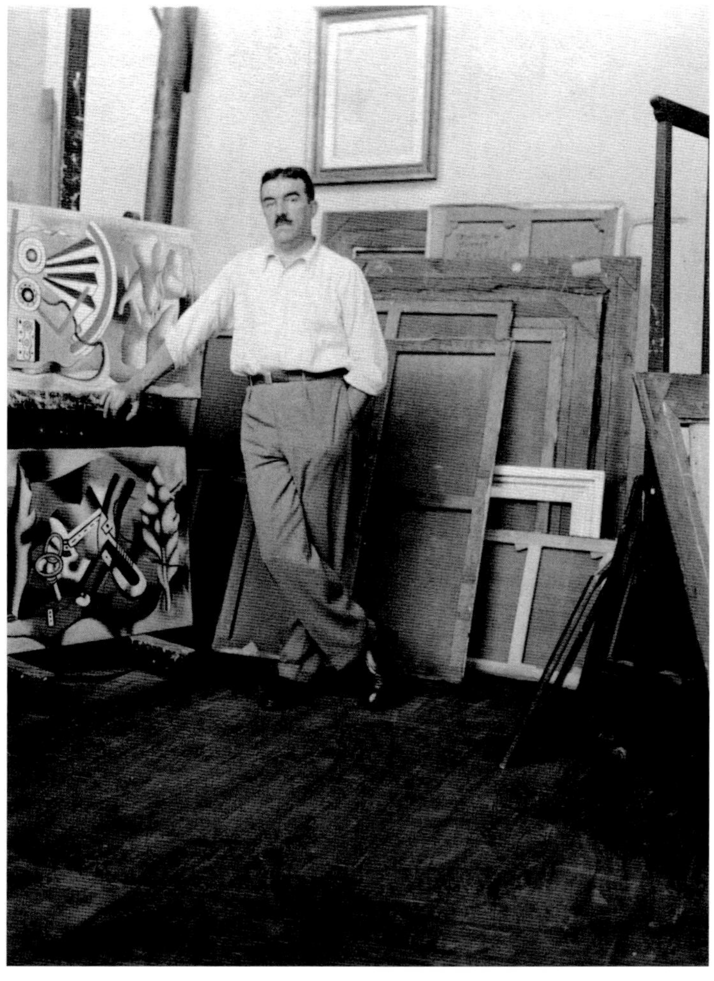

FIG. 5.
ALBERT EUGENE GALLATIN,
[FERNAND LÉGER], 1932.
GELATIN SILVER PRINT, 10.5 × 7.8 CM.
BIBLIOTHÈQUE KANDINSKY, FONDS GALLATIN, PARIS, 3287-3.

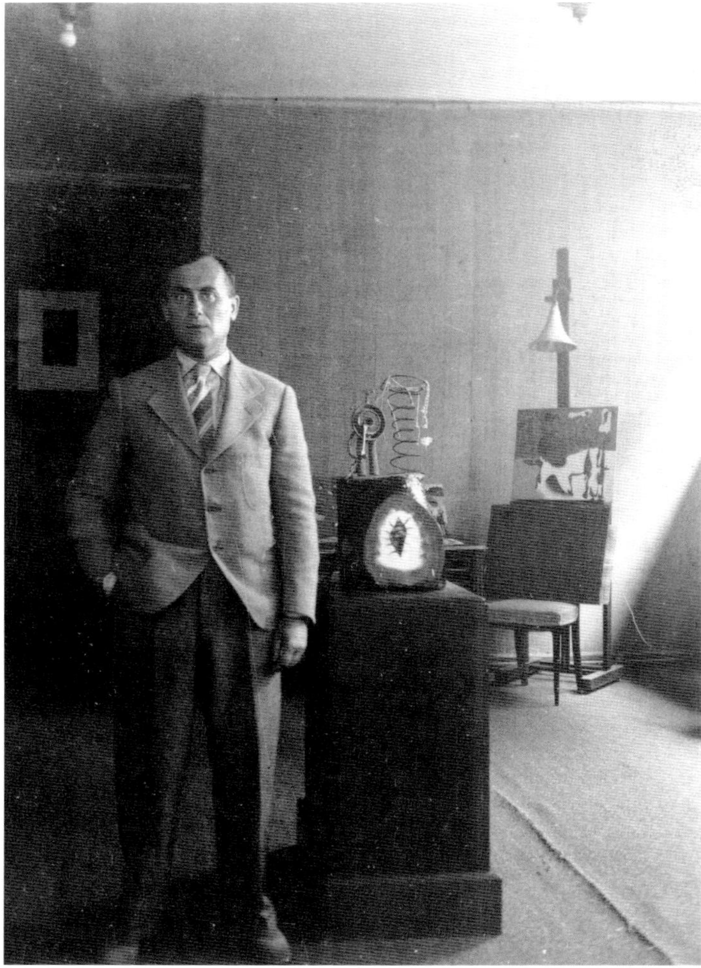

FIG. 6.
ALBERT EUGENE GALLATIN,
[JOAN MIRÓ], 1936.
GELATIN SILVER PRINT, 10.5 × 7.8 CM.
BIBLIOTHÈQUE KANDINSKY, FONDS GALLATIN, PARIS, 3287-11.

The collection has two photos of Léger in his studio at 86 rue Notre-Dame-des-Champs in the 6th arrondissement of Paris; in one, the artist poses in shirt-sleeves, leaning casually on an easel; in the other he is seated astride a stuffed chair.

The Gallery of Living art owned four paintings and ten watercolors or drawings on paper by Léger. He was invited to visit Washington Square on November 4, 1931. Léger shrewdly sold Gallatin one of his masterpieces at a bargain-basement price to insure his presence in New York. On January 27, 1937, he informed Gallatin by postcard that, "*The City* will arrive on the *Paris*. It is a canvas that has traveled much, seen much and which has had an enormous influence on *La Couleur dans le monde*. It is fragile and somewhat weary—it must be handled with care and perhaps someday be re-backed. It is only natural that it end its days in New York, which is the 'very great city' for which it was the 'harbinger.'"[9] Léger's perspicacity paid off. Exiled to New York from 1940 to 1946, he caught up with this masterpiece in 1943 during the opening of the Gallatin Wing in the Philadelphia Museum of Art, when he posed flatteringly in front of it with a glass of red wine in his hand.

The painter Miró lived in Mointroig Tarragona and in Barcelona, but regularly presented his work at the Pierre [Loeb] Gallery on 2 rue des Beaux-Arts in Paris. In the photo, behind Miró can be seen works recently brought to Paris. Gallatin's four photos were taken at the time of the Pierre Gallery's show of five American painters—Biederman, Ferren, Gallatin, Morris, Shaw—from June 15–29, 1936. The interest of this long-unpublished photo is to prove that *L'Objet du couchant*, a sculpture in the background, dates not from 1938 but rather from the spring of 1936.[10]

From 1928 to 1934 Gallatin supported Miró's art. His 1929 purchase of *Dog Barking at the Moon,* a canvas of 1926, created a sensation in the American press. At the Gallery of Living Art, Mirós were hung next to work by Mondrian, Torres-García, Hélion, and Delaunay. But the cleavage between the abstractionists and surrealists intensified in the 1930s. Miró became less respectable. George L. K. Morris, in "Sweeney, Soby and Surrealism," in the *Partisan Review* attributed a scathing comment to him: "Have you ever heard of greater nonsense than the aims of the abstractionist group?" Morris then went on to argue that, "Miró obviously acquired his ability to coordinate shape, color and line from abstract painters (particularly Arp) but his work always depends strongly on representational suggestions. He never got very far inside to [the] picture surface and he adds nothing to the solutions of the abstract problems . . . Had Miró been just a little more a man of letters perhaps his work would not have been declining so sadly since 1933 . . ."[11]

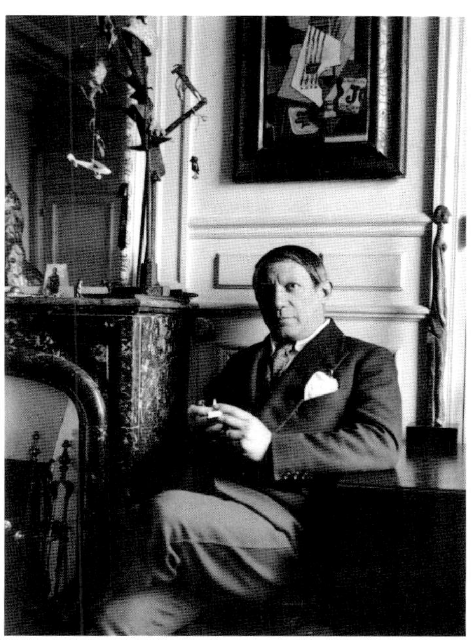

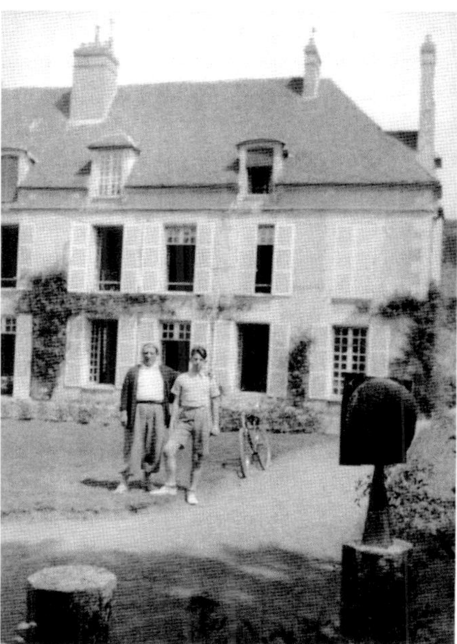

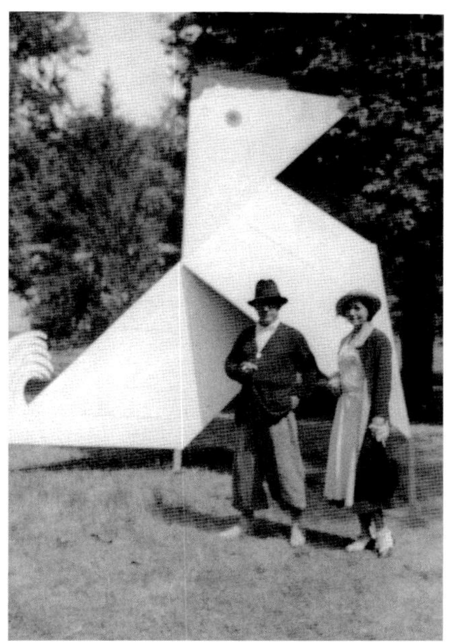

FIG. 7.
ALBERT EUGENE GALLATIN.
[PABLO PICASSO], 1932 (AND NOT 1933).
GELATIN SILVER PRINT, 20.8 × 15.5 CM.
BIBLIOTHÈQUE KANDINSKY, FONDS GALLATIN, PARIS, 3287-1.

FIG. 8.
ALBERT EUGENE GALLATIN.
[PICASSO AND HIS SON PAULO], 1933.
GELATIN SILVER PRINT, 16.9 × 11.8 CM.
INSCRIBED IN INK ON THE BACK BY GALLATIN: "PICASSO AND HIS SON
(SCULPTURE BY PICASSO) IN FRONT OF HIS CHÂTEAU NEAR GISORS,
FRANCE. A. E. GALLATIN PHOTO".
BIBLIOTHÈQUE KANDINSKY, FONDS GALLATIN, PARIS, 3287-13.

FIG. 9.
ALBERT EUGENE GALLATIN.
[PICASSO AND OLGA], 1933.
GELATIN SILVER PRINT, 20.8 × 15.5 CM.
INSCRIBED ON THE BACK BY GALLATIN: "PICASSO AND WIFE".
BIBLIOTHÈQUE KANDINSKY, FONDS GALLATIN, PARIS, 3287-14.

The collection contains nine photographs of Picasso. On April 27, 1932, Gallatin prudently sent a postcard from the Lancaster Hotel in London to advise Picasso of his intentions: "If you are free one day, would you allow me to visit you with my Kodak? Gallatin."[12] Picasso received the collector in his studio at 23 rue La Boétie in the 7th arrondissement of Paris. The artist, in a suit with watch-chain pinned to his collar, posed at a window or near the fireplace where the light fell, agreeing to a series of pictures in which he held a portrait drawing of his son or, more prosaically, a cigarette. The Gallery of Living Art owned eight paintings by Picasso, in addition to ten works on paper, four engravings, and a wonderful print of the painted bronze *Glass of Absinthe*. Gallatin was entranced by the short Spaniard who reigned in Paris. In his review of the New York art scene for the first issue of *Cahiers d'Art* in 1931, Gallatin displayed his pleasure in participating in Picasso's success. "At the top of the list should be placed the exhibition of twenty-three paintings by Picasso, all abstract paintings, most of which are very recent and seven of which were done in 1930. Posterity may well decide that of all of Picasso's oeuvre, it is the large abstract still lifes of 1926–1927 that most thoroughly express the artist's astonishing genius. Because it shares this conviction, the Gallery of Living Art at New York University bought a splendid still life with guitar, executed in 1923, for its collection, which boasts several other canvases by Picasso."[13] Gallatin also published an essay, *Of Art: Plato to Picasso,* in 1944 (New York: Wittenborn, 1944).

In 1933, Gallatin followed Picasso to his sculptor's lair in Boisgeloup. There, in front of the big house, Gallatin took two photos of the artist *en famille*. The archives of the Musée Picasso in Paris contain an empty envelope addressed to Picasso by Gallatin from Gerardmer, a spa in the Vosges mountains, on July 13, 1933. This slim evidence might date his visit to Boisgeloup.

In 1936, Gallatin made one of the most important acquisitions of the Gallery of Living Art by buying, through Paul Rosenberg, a canvas from the Reber collection in Lausanne, namely the second version of *The Three Musicians*. The news was discussed in Paris even before it hit America. On October 20, 1936, Léonce Rosenberg congratulated Gallatin. "I am delighted to hear that you purchased *The Three Musicians* by Picasso from Dr. Reber. It is not a picture, but an event in art. In my modest opinion, it is not only the best work Picasso ever did, but also, if not the finest, one of the finest works of the present century. I often thought of *The Three Musicians* and always deplored that this painting was not in a museum like yours, where it could be always seen by art lovers and for the benefit of artists. The genial experimentator [sic] Picasso has reached there fullness and magnificence together which is not often the case of his work, being, as a rule, more significant than complete. *The Three Musicians,* in few words, is an accomplishment [sic] work and that is why I dare to call it a museum picture."[14] Gallatin's entourage was convinced that the Museum of Living Art had acquired the world's undisputed masterpiece. That, at least, was what Gallatin's colleague George L. K. Morris implied in "On the Mechanics of Abstract Painting," published in *Partisan Review*. "Yet it is interesting to note that he [Picasso] executed two versions of his most complete realization, the *Three Musicians,* and that it is the later version (in the Museum of Living Art, New York University) that is incomparably the more smoothly organized."[15]

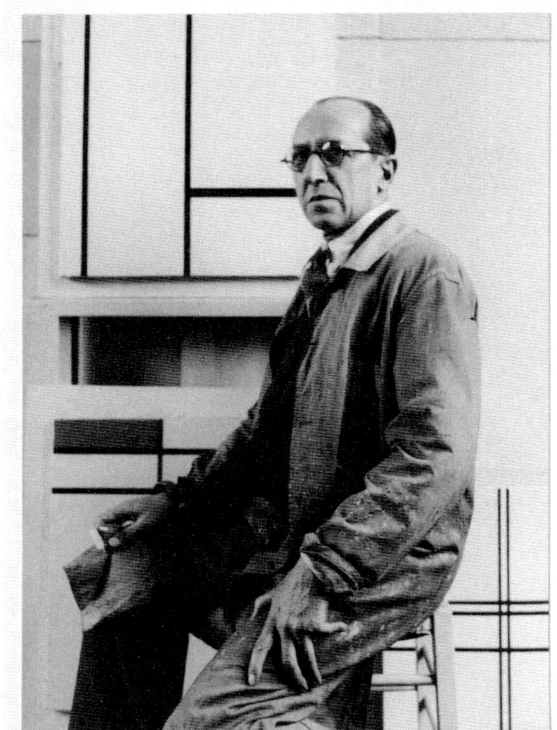

FIG. 10.
ALBERT EUGENE GALLATIN.
[PIET MONDRIAN]. 1934.
GELATIN SILVER PRINT, 17.8 X 11.9 CM.
INSCRIBED ON THE MOUNT, LOWER LEFT: "GALLATIN, JUNE 1934".
BIBLIOTHÈQUE KANDINSKY, FONDS GALLATIN, PARIS, 3287-20.

Piet Mondrian, wearing an artist's smock, is seated in front of an easel in his studio on 26 rue du Départ in the 14th arrondissement of Paris.

On May 26, 1934, shortly before or after Gallatin visited him, Mondrian wrote to Clara Friedrich, an artist from Zurich married to a banker who became a collector of Mondrian's work: "I am very pleased and honored that you and your husband have decided to buy the yellow painting. The American took the white and black one [Lozenge, 1926] to New York along with the large blue one [Composition with Blue, 1932], so I am delighted to be able to send you the one you chose …"[16] The tone of the letter is condescending toward Gallatin but it is worth noting that he enjoyed the privilege of first choice.

The Gallery of Living Art possessed four paintings that demonstrated to young artists the importance of Mondrian, whom Paris so ignored that he moved to London. Clement Greenberg noted this move in "Towards a Newer Laocoon," published in Partisan Review in the summer of 1940: "By 1939 the center of abstract painting had shifted to London, while in Paris the younger generation of French and Spanish painters had reacted against abstract purity and turned back to a confusion of literature with painting as extreme as any of the past…"[17] When Mondrian arrived in New York on October 3, 1940, he was welcomed as a pioneer by the American Abstract Artists group.

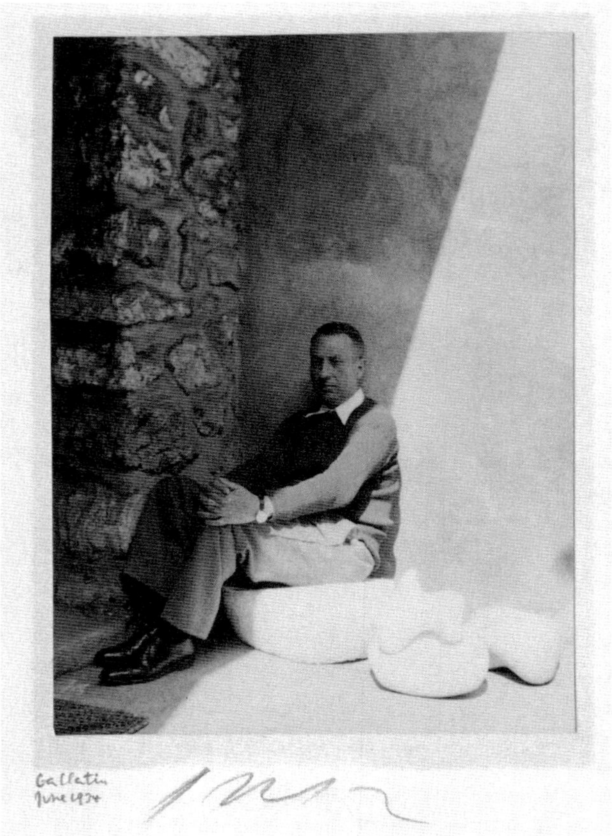

FIG. 11.
ALBERT EUGENE GALLATIN.
[HANS ARP]. 1934.
GELATIN SILVER PRINT, 17.6 X 13 CM.
INSCRIBED ON THE MOUNT, LOWER LEFT: "GALLATIN, JUNE 1934,"
AND COUNTERSIGNED IN PENCIL, "ARP".
BIBLIOTHÈQUE KANDINSKY, FONDS GALLATIN, PARIS, 3287-21.

Hans Arp was photographed outside his newly built studio-house in Meudon-Val-Fleury near Paris. He is shown seated near a recent sculpture.

The Gallery of Living Art owned two reliefs in wood and seven papiers déchirés (torn paper compositions). After the war, Arp offered the Gallatin collection a stone sculpture of his own and a painting by his wife, Sophie Taeuber-Arp.

On June 27, 1937, Gallatin and Domela went to Meudon to discuss with Sophie Taeuber-Arp the production of several issues of Plastique. Gallatin bought a series of Arp's paper collages which served as the core of the Hans Arp show presented at the Museum of Living Art in 1937.

George L. K. Morris provided the recipe for Arp's papier déchiré technique in "On the Mechanics of Abstract Painting," published in Partisan Review: "Arp frequently starts a new work from what he calls composition par hasard; he will tear up three or four scraps of paper and proceed to drop them from a height of a foot or two. When they happen to fall into some combination which suggests an interesting interplay of form, he will paste them just as they landed and from the resulting arrangement develop his composition."[18]

of sculpture, the Museum of Modern Art has revived old memories of the chambers of horrors at the Eden Musée, perhaps we should be grateful for such nostalgic items [Gallatin was wary of MoMA's Alfred Barr and his assistants J. J. Sweeney and James T. Soby].[2]

Let us dwell instead on a different obsession. In 1931, during his annual tour of artists' studios, Gallatin asked each master for a little portrait of himself. Braque and Léger executed little bookplate-sized vignettes in which Gallatin can be recognized from his glasses. The following year, 1932, Gallatin reversed the roles and used a Kodak to turn himself into a portrait photographer. The pictures he obtained felicitously complement the gallery of portraits by Man Ray and Rogi André. They represented a kind of contract between Gallatin and his artists, which he later thought merited explanation:

> To meet the above suggestion, I have taken my camera with me on several of my visits to artists who are represented in this collection. Repeated visits over the years to the studios of these painters and sculptors, about forty of them, have certainly helped enormously in arriving at a just estimate of their worth. The photographs made on these occasions, some of them reproduced on the following pages, I hope may prove to be interesting documents. Those of Braque and Léger were made in 1931, that of Picasso in 1933, of Mondrian in 1934, and of Miró in 1936. All these were taken in Paris. The photograph of Matisse was taken at Nice in 1932, and that of Arp at Meudon-Val-Fleury, near Paris, in 1934. This is a different set of photographs from that published in the 1933 and 1937 catalogues and afterwards in *Life* (May 2, 1938) and in [the] "Britannica Book of the Year" for 1939.[3]

Gallatin's approach reflected a certain cleverness. He was seeking to bypass Mauny's services, but he did not speak French very well. In the time it took him to get the light just right and to arrange the pose, Gallatin had made a tour of the artist's studio. He could then strike up a conversation with his sitter who, eyes staring into the camera, was in good position to listen to purchase proposals. The artists' willingness to submit to this whim is all the more understandable given the terrible depression in the art market at that time. Gallatin reproduced his photos in the publications of the Gallery of Living Art. And he thought enough of them to add ten to the portrait of Joaquín Torres-García that he gave to Fiske Kimbal for the Philadelphia Museum of Art in 1937.

Gallatin's legacy is solidly preserved in Philadelphia, Pittsfield, and the New York Historical Society. The sudden decision to allow the collection of the Museum of Living Art to be transferred to Philadelphia was an inspired one. Gallatin put behind him everything he had collected in a seventeen-year period, and in which he had sunk a significant part of his capital. This disinterested move was transformed into a protest against the obscurantism of NYU academics. Furthermore, as the opening of the "Gallatin Collection" in Philadelphia would clearly show, in 1943 it symbolized a war-time gesture of solidarity with a city Paris,

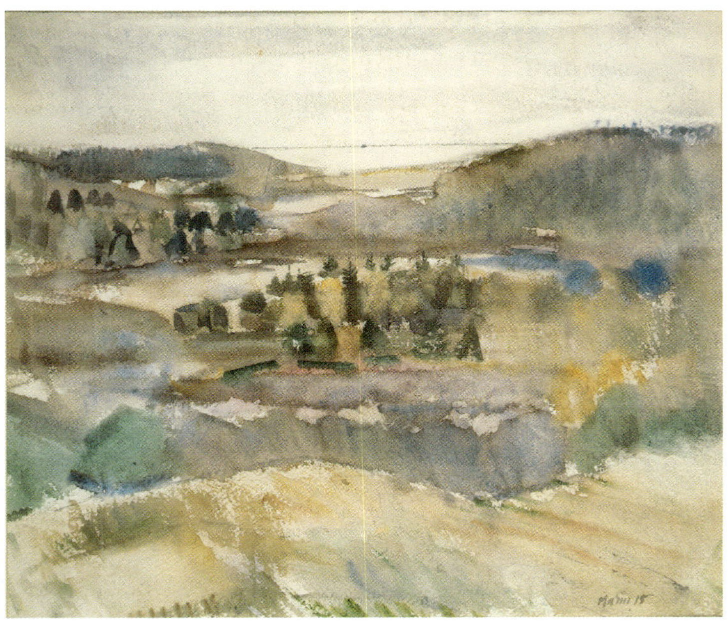

FIG. 12.
JOHN MARIN,
PAYSAGE [LANDSCAPE]. 1915.
WATERCOLOR ON PAPER. 39.9 × 46.3 CM.
MUSÉE NATIONAL D'ART MODERNE –
CENTRE GEORGES POMPIDOU, PARIS.

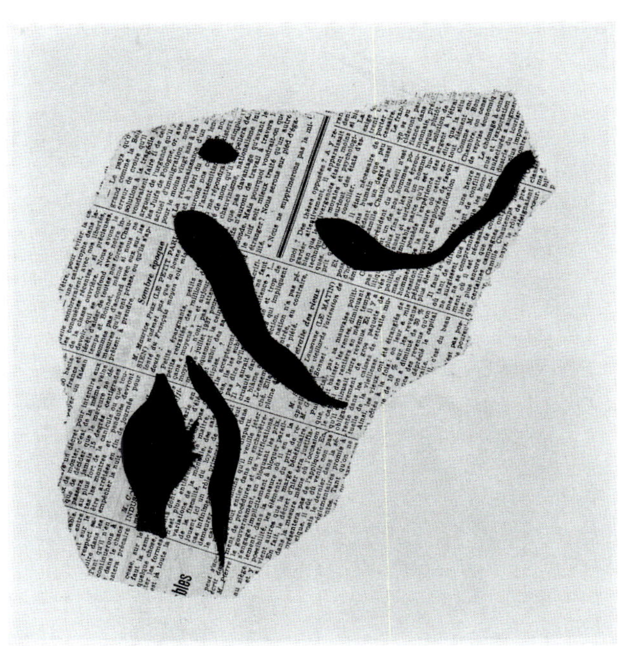

FIG. 13.
HANS ARP,
PAPIER DÉCHIRÉ [TORN PAPER]. 1936.
COLLAGE. 23 × 15 CM.
MUSÉE D'ART MODERNE ET CONTEMPORAIN
DE STRASBOURG.

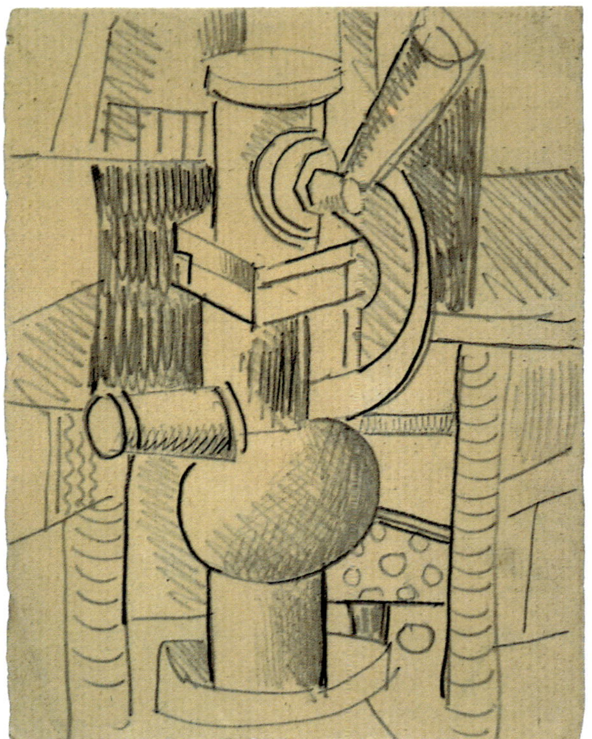

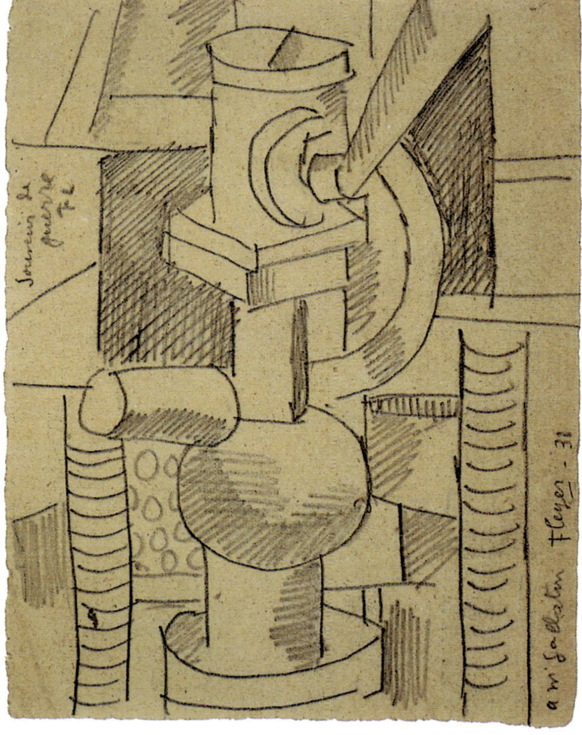

and a nation, France, then experiencing the deepest humiliation. NYU's Grey Art Gallery and Study Center is now left to dream of the unlikely return of a collection that never should have left Washington Square.

In France the mark left by Gallatin is scarcely discernible, even if all the crumbs are gathered together. Vestiges in public and private collections would barely fill his travel kit. One memento was a direct gift by Gallatin to the Musée du Luxembourg, a watercolor landscape (fig. 12) done in 1915 by John Marin (now held by the Musée National d'Art Moderne). César Domela, who in 1938 acquired two paintings by Gallatin and a relief by Shaw, generously donated two of these works to the Musée National de la Coopération franco-américaine in Blérancourt (cats. 70 and 77), the smallest and most original one having been sold to a private collector cat. 68).

Amy Wolf, charged with selling works that Gallatin had retained and then bequeathed to heirs, came across an article of mine on a Jacques Mauny *View of New York* acquired by the museum in Blérancourt[4]; she then was able to help her direct a Hans Arp *papier déchiré* of 1937 (fig. 13) and a Léger war drawing of 1916 (figs. 14 and 15) to museums in Strasbourg and to reserve twenty-four photographic prints for the documentation department of the Musée National d'Art Moderne.[5] She also offered to sell me Mauny's *Self-Portrait* (see p. 99) and four other drawings and watercolors by Mauny that had found no other buyer. Souvenirs of Gallatin are thus scattered throughout France like so many little moorings of the *Boatdeck* period that anchor his name more firmly to the history of cultural exchange between Paris and New York, recalling the importance of the Gallery of Living Art in the 1930s. ■

FIGS. 14 ET 15.
FERNAND LÉGER,
SOUVENIR DE GUERRE [MEMORY OF WAR] (FRONT AND BACK), 1915–16.
DRAWING, 16.1 X 12.5 CM.
ANNOTATED ON BACK: "SOUVENIR DE GUERRE FL"
AND DEDICATED: "À MONSIEUR GALLATIN. F. LÉGER. 31".
MUSÉE D'ART MODERNE ET CONTEMPORAIN DE STRASBOURG –
CABINET D'ART GRAPHIQUE.

For more information on Gallatin, see the article and bibliography published here by Gail Stavitsky (p. 105) and the catalogue by Debra Bricker Balken, *Albert Eugene Gallatin and His Circle* (Coral Gables, Florida: The Lowe Art Museum, University of Miami, 1986).

1— "Je vous remercie aussi d'avoir vendu à E. Gallatin des gouaches pour sa Gallery of Living Art. Gallatin était venu il y a deux ou trois ans chez moi et aurait bien acheté des tableaux s'ils avaient été plus petits. Il m'avait écrit l'an passé de New York me disant qu'il était 'heureux' d'avoir acheté des pochoirs de moi. C'est un flottant sympathique qui ne sait pas très bien ce qu'il veut. Je crois, entre nous, qu'il n'entend pas grand chose des tendances modernes. Son musée comporte plus de croûtes authentiques que d'œuvres intéressantes. J'ai ses catalogues qui ne sont pas *exciting* ! D'ailleurs son conseiller ici—le peintre [Hélion] dont vous me parlez—est toute une confession."
Albert Gleizes folder, Léonce Rosenberg Collection, Kandinsky Library, Musée National d'Art Moderne, Paris. (Translator's note: this and all following translations of correspondence and periodical articles are my own). Léonce Rosenberg was an art dealer who, from 1916 to 1941, ran the Galerie de l'Effort moderne. He corresponded with Gallatin, and his archives have been assembled by the Musée National d'Art Moderne.

2— Albert Eugene Gallatin, "Museum Piece," in *American Abstract Artists*, 1946.

3— *A. E. Gallatin Collection* (Philadelphia: Philadelphia Museum of Art: 1954), 145.

4— Christian Derouet, "*Vue de New York* par Jacques Mauny," *Revue du Louvre* 4 (1987).

5— The Arp collage was bought directly by the Musée de Strasbourg while Léger's *Dessin de guerre* was presented to the same museum by its friends' association, Les Amis des Arts et des Musées.

6— "Jacques Mauny est un peintre doué et fin, qui malheureusement depuis quelques années s'est engagé dans une voie assez fâcheuse, où se perdent ses meilleures qualités. Le texte de M. Gallatin a été traduit de l'américain en français avec une telle littéralité, qu'il reste à mi-chemin entre les deux langues. L'auteur ne ménage pas les éloges à l'artiste; aussi rappelle-t-il souvent à l'esprit du lecteur, sans le vouloir, la fable de l'ours et de l'amateur de Jardin. Le livre, bien présenté, contient de fort bonnes reproductions." *L'Amour de l'art* 1 (January 1929).

7— "Dites à Henriette [collaboratrice de Pierre Loeb] de s'occuper du tableau que Gallatin a voulu donner à un musée de Paris et qui est resté chez Pierre. Qui sait, le Luxembourg? C'est urgent car Gallatin m'a écrit quinze fois que si le gouvernement ne prenait pas ce tableau il ne l'achetait pas, et que je devrais lui rendre les 200 dollars empruntés pour aller en France. Malheur ! Ayant appris l'échec du New Bauhaus, il a décidé de me faire crédit un peu plus de temps..." Private archives. Pierre Bruguière was a judge who dabbled in art criticism. With modest resources, he managed to assemble a select collection of works by Arp, Ernst, Giacometti, Kandinsky, Léger, and Miró as well as countless drawings and paintings by Jean Hélion.
His name figures in Gallatin's address book.

8— "À mon avis certains connaisseurs peuvent penser que c'est dans certaines petites gouaches et dans certaines petites peintures qu'on trouve les traits les plus délicieusement savoureux de l'œuvre de Braque." *Cahiers d'Art* 2 (1931).

9— "Par le 'Paris' vous arrive 'La Ville' c'est une toile qui a beaucoup voyagé, beaucoup vu—et qui a eu sur 'La couleur dans le monde' une influence énorme. Elle est délicate et un peu fatiguée—il faut la ménager et peut-être envisager un jour son 'rentoilement', c'est naturel qu'elle finisse ses vieux jours à New York qui est la 'très grande ville' et dont elle a été la 'précurseur.'" A. E. Gallatin Papers, New York Historical Library. See also Christian Derouet, "Gallatin collectionneur primordial," in *Léger: Le cabinet des dessins* (Paris: Flammarion, 1997), 116–119.

10— *L'Objet du couchant* [*Subject in the Setting*] is an assemblage made for the surrealist exhibition at the Galerie Charles Ratton in May 1936. This event marked the split between the surrealist artists and the abstractionists. *L'Objet du couchant* was purchased from the Breton estate by the Musée National d'Art Moderne, Paris, in 1975.

11— George L. K. Morris, "Sweeney, Soby and Surrealism," *Partisan Review* 2 (March–April 1942).

12— "Si vous êtes libre un jour voulez-vous permettre à moi à visiter vous avec mon Kodac? Gallatin." Gallatin folder, archives, Musée Picasso, Paris.

13— "Au premier rang, il faut placer l'exposition de vingt-trois peintures de Picasso, toutes peintures abstraites dont la majorité sont tout à fait récentes et dont sept ont été peintes en 1930. Peut-être la postérité jugera-t-elle que de toute l'œuvre de Picasso, ce sont les grandes natures mortes abstraites de 1923-1927 qui expriment le plus complètement le stupéfiant génie du peintre. C'est parce qu'elle avait cette conviction, que la galerie d'art vivant, à l'Université de New York a acheté la splendide nature morte à la guitare, qui appartient à l'année 1923, pour sa collection où se trouvaient déjà plusieurs toiles du maître." *Cahiers d'Art* 1 (1931).

14— A. E. Gallatin Papers, New York Historical Library.

15— George L. K. Morris, "On the Mechanics of Abstract Painting," *Partisan Review* 5 (September–October 1941): 410.

16— Brigit Blass and Rudolf Koella, *Das Legat Clara und Emil Friedrich-Jezler im Kunstmuseum Winterthur* (Zurich, 1985), 73.

17— Clement Greenberg, "Towards a Newer Laocoon," *Partisan Review* 4 (July–August 1940): 309.

18— Morris, "On the Mechanics of Abstract Painting," 408.

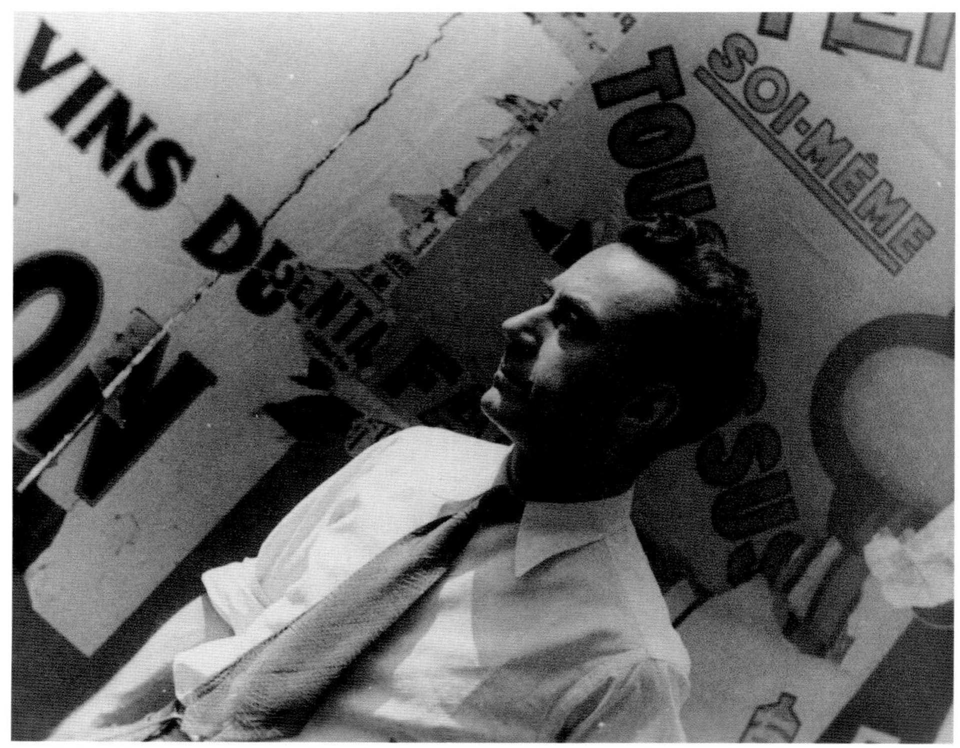

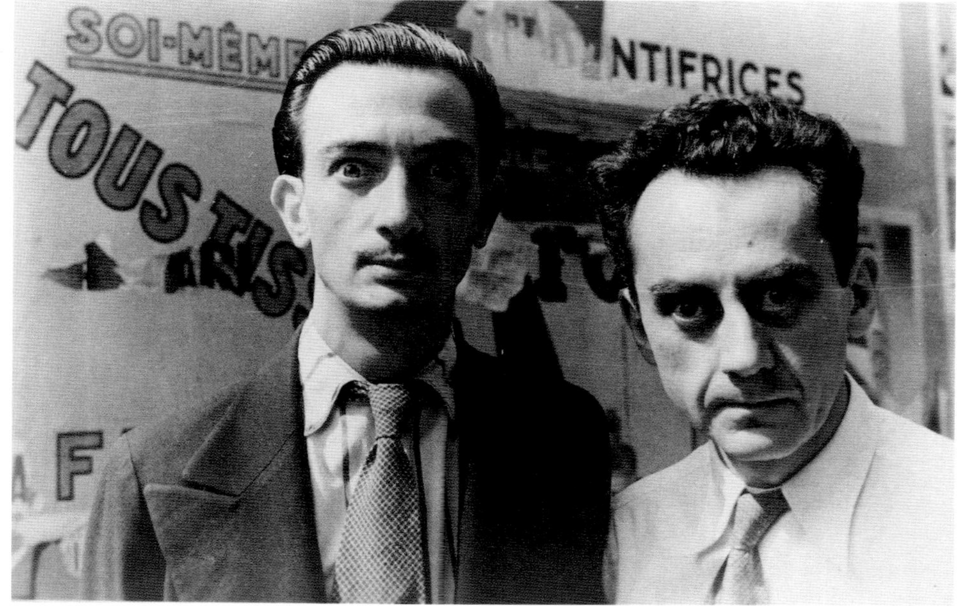

175
CARL VAN VECHTEN
[PORTRAIT OF MAN RAY], JUNE 16, 1934
GELATIN SILVER PRINT, 35.6 X 45.8 CM
LIBRARY OF CONGRESS, WASHINGTON D.C.
PRINTS AND PHOTOGRAPHS DIVISION,
LOT 12735, NO. 969
MAAG, TAM, TMAA

176
CARL VAN VECHTEN
[PORTRAIT OF MAN RAY AND SALVADOR DALI,
PARIS], JUNE 16, 1934
GELATIN SILVER PRINT, 35.6 X 45.8 CM
LIBRARY OF CONGRESS, WASHINGTON D.C.
PRINTS AND PHOTOGRAPHS DIVISION,
LOT 12735, NO. 968
MAAG, TAM, TMAA

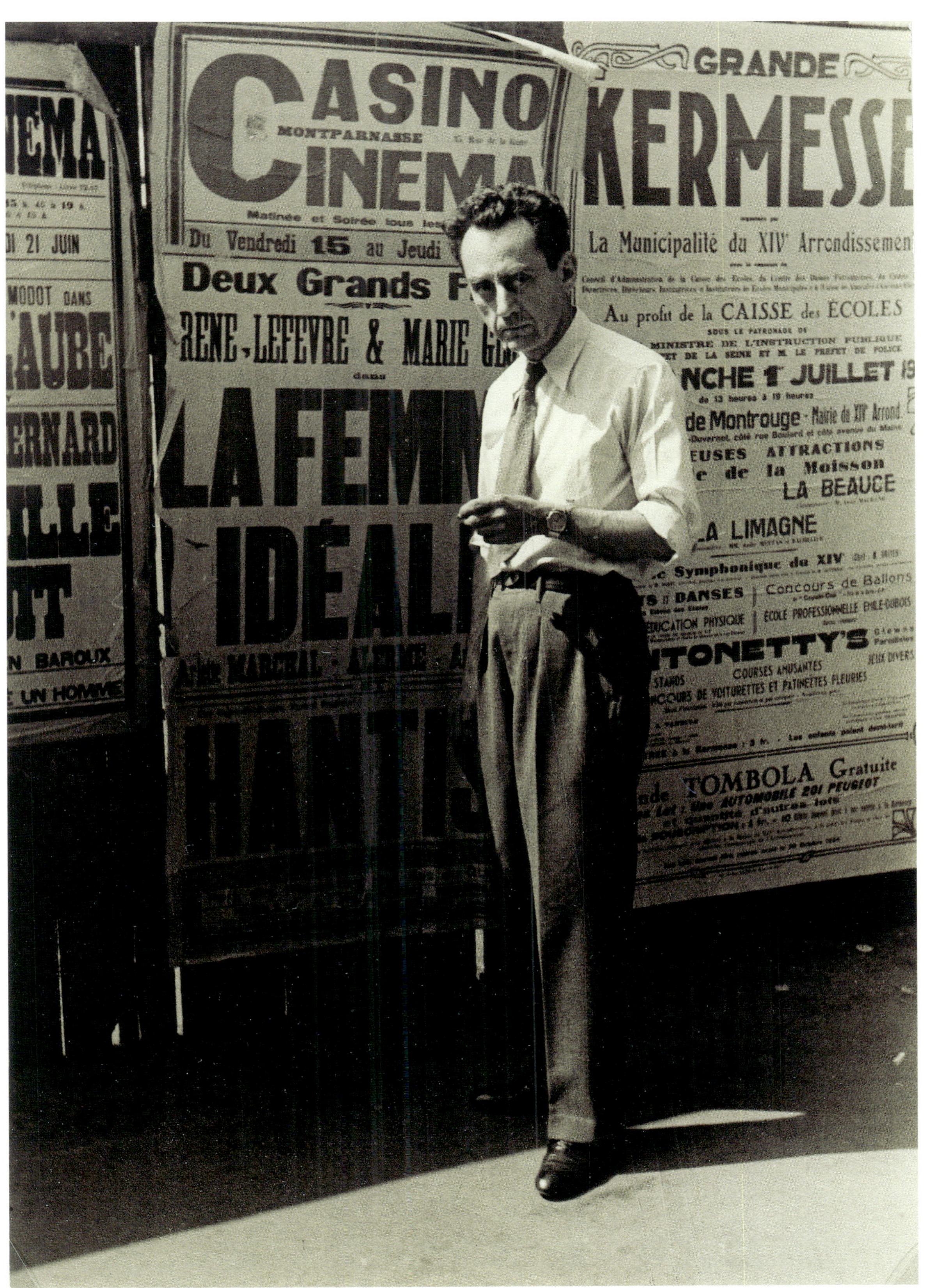

177
CARL VAN VECHTEN
PORTRAIT OF MAN RAY,
MONTPARNASSE, JUNE 6, 1934, 1934
GELATIN SILVER-BROMIDE PRINT, 23.2 × 16.6 CM
MUSÉE CARNAVALET, PARIS, PH 4901
MAAG, TAM

THE STUDIO OF
CONSTANTIN BRANCUSI

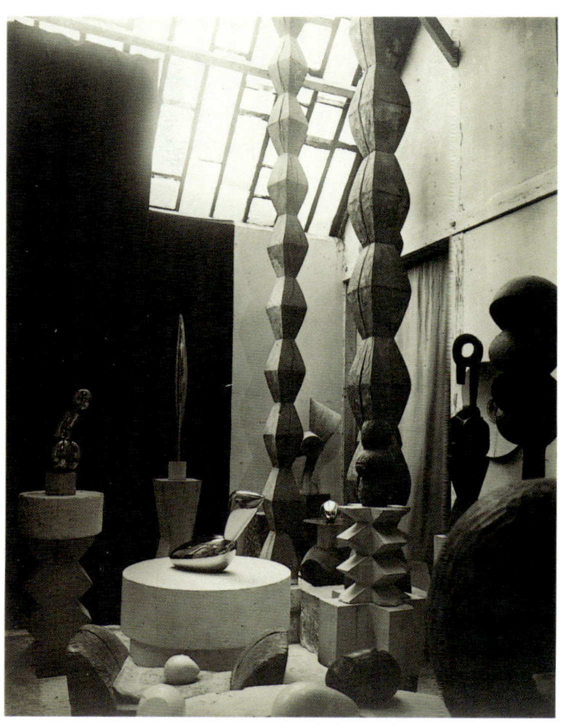

CONSTANTIN BRANCUSI,
VIEW OF THE STUDIO:
ENDLESS COLUMNS, CHIMERA, C. 1930.
GELATIN SILVER PRINT, 29.8 X 23.8 CM.
MUSÉE NATIONAL D'ART MODERNE –
CENTRE GEORGES POMPIDOU, PARIS.

In 1916 Constantin Brancusi moved to 8 impasse Ronsin, later transferring to 11 impasse Ronsin, a space that he would occupy and continually expand until the end of his life in 1957.[1] This *impasse*, a pavilion of many studios, demonstrates the necessity of workspace for artistic creation as well as providing an arena for artists to exchanges. The list of people who occupied studios at the impasse Ronsin is impressive, ranging from Duchamp and Max Ernst, to a younger generation lured by Brancusi's fame including Jean Tinguely, Niki de Saint Phalle, and Larry Rivers. The list of visitors to these studios is even longer, evocative of the dynamism that was characteristic of this *impasse* and the interplay between creation and sociality so important to Brancusi and his career.

The sculptor lived and worked in his studio. It was a space where Brancusi was free to create as he pleased, where working and living spaces were merged into one. The interior was lined with Brancusi's sculptures, some awaiting their finishing touches while others were still in the process of being created. Ezra Pound alluded to this collection of sculptures that occupied all tha available space in the studio where "quiet was established" when he wrote of the calm whiteness of the marble.[2] The way the light danced across the room, decorating the sculptures on the floors and workbenches and dappling the tools that hung on the walls created an atmosphere that was, in a way, a work of art itself. It is as though Brancusi's creative genius was visible on the very walls of his studio, as though the studio exceeded its functionality to become a sculpture itself. The American photographer Edward Steichen took many photos of this studio, revealing its aesthetic value. In fact, Brancusi himself continually photographed the space, quite frequently re-arranging his sculptures and capturing them from different angles and under the varying effects of light. A visitor to the studio recalls that on one occasion among friends he took out flashlights, becoming: "instantly as serious as if he were beginning a piece of sculpture. He spends an hour adjusting his apparatus to suit him and in examining his audience with a good view to lighting. He seats himself with the group and by an arrangement of long cords takes the picture so as to include himself."[3] Ultimately Brancusi interacted with his studio as a photographer whose work revealed his perception of both this space and his artistic creation. The concept of the studio as a work of art was not lost upon others either. Alfred H. Barr, curator of the Museum of Modern Art in New York and James Johnson Sweeney, an influential collector of modern art visited the studio and called it a transcendent sculptural site in itself.

An atmosphere of conviviality resonated in Brancusi's studio. Gatherings permitted lively exchanges between artists, patrons, curators, and friends—exchanges that were an important factor in the making of an international modern art. And yet Brancusi's workspace was not always as glamorous as those who visited it. Peggy Guggenheim, a frequent guest, described a small side room where you could sit on a tree trunk and listen to oriental music. The coldness of the studio itself was only just bearable: "He lived there amid monumental sculptures and working tools, and every surface was covered with a fine white dust," she recounted, adding that he slept in a very simple bedroom upstairs.[4] In *Being Geniuses Together,* Robert McAlmon described Brancusi's studio which he visited with Ezra Pound: "The dining table was a huge round slab, and the stove had been made by Brancusi himself of stones piled one on the other. The meal started with a kirsh, Rumanian hors d'oeuvres, and then steak or roast chicken, salad and fruit, and of course, quantities of wine."[5] Such quotations reveal the many purposes that the studio served, including the fact that it welcomed many influential American artists, critics, and art collectors. It was a meeting place that transcended geography and nationality. From an early date in the sculptor's career, American patronage was a crucial factor in his gaining fame and recognition. Edward Steichen first purchased a Brancusi sculpture, *Maiastra*[6] in Paris in 1911. An associate of Stieglitz, Steichen played a key role in preparing the first one-man exhibition dedicated entirely to Brancusi that was held in New York in 1914 at 291, the Stieglitz Gallery. The art collector John Quinn, Brancusi's most significant patron, paid several visits to Paris where the two played golf in addition to conducting business. It was an almost "mandatory" event for the American intellectual elite to visit Brancusi's studio.[7]

The dynamism of Brancusi's studio on the impasse Ronsin and the transatlantic exchanges evident in the writing, photographs, and visits made by many Americans reveal the way that the architecture of the studio transcends simple walls. Reginald Pollack evokes the power of Brancusi in his studio, comparing him to a magician in his temple.[8] In this space, Brancusi manipulates, creates, and enchants. The studio both becomes a work of art and documents the many elements involved in the creation and diffusion of art, thus being emblematic of the exchanges that occurred there. While the impasse Ronsin was declared unfit for habitation in 1955, it was not destroyed until after Brancusi's death in 1957. In his bequest, Brancusi asked for his studio to be recreated with its contents at a permanent site, and in so doing, the Musée National d'Art Moderne – Centre Georges Pompidou has immortalized both Brancusi and the importance of his studio.

Eliza Johnson

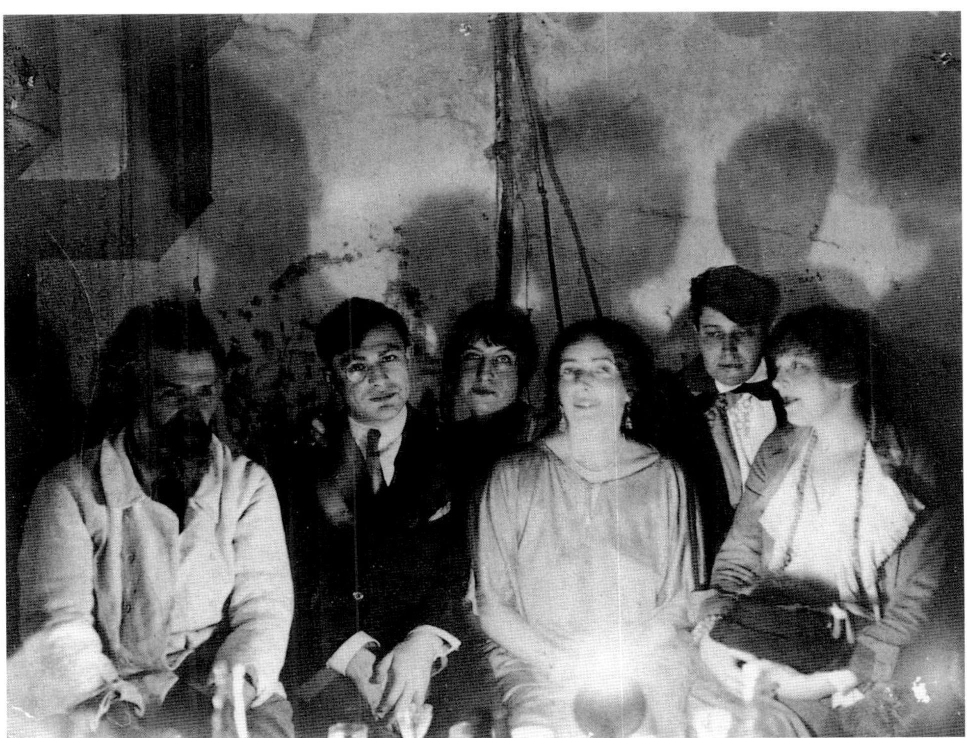

[TRISTAN TZARA, A FRIEND, MINA LOY, JANE HEAP AND MARGARET ANDERSON IN BRANCUSI'S STUDIO]. C. 1920
GELATIN SILVER PRINT, 23 X 35.6 CM
LIBRARY OF CONGRESS, WASHINGTON, D.C.,
PRINTS AND PHOTOGRAPHS DIVISION. LC.USZ.6.2113
MAAG, TAM, TMAA

1— Constantin Brancusi moved to Paris from Rumania in order to study sculpture. After a brief stint under Rodin's tutelage, he set up on his own in 1907, a move that marked his independence as a sculptor and his ability to create works that defy classification, space, and time. That same year he moved into a studio at 23 rue d'Ocessa in Montparnasse, next to Edward Steichen, the American photographer who would become a close friend. This relationship is emblematic of the transatlantic ties that played such a pivotal role in the reception and renown that the sculptor would earn in his lifetime.

2— Ezra Pound, *Guide to Kulchur,* (New York: New Directions, 1970), 84. One of the many visitors to Brancusi's studio, Ezra Pound also wrote of the artist's use of white marble in "Brancusi" in the *Little Review*, Autumn 1921. Cited in *L'Atelier Brancusi: la collection* (Paris: Musée National d'Art Moderne – Centre Georges Pompidou, 1997), 38.

3— Margaret Anderson, *My Thirty Years' War: The Autobiography. Beginnings and Battles to 1930* (New York: Horizon Press, 1969), 254.

4— Peggy Guggenheim, *Out of This Century: Confessions of an Art Addict* (New York: Universe Books, 1979), 218. Cited in Laurence Tacou-Rumney, *Peggy Guggenheim* (Paris: Flammarion, 1996), 96.

5— Cited in J. J. Wilhelm, *Ezra Pound in London and Paris, 1908–1925* (University Park: The Pennsylvania State University Press, 1990), 274.

6— The *Maiastra* is an early version of *Bird*, the recurring image for which Brancusi is renowned.

7— *L'Atelier Brancusi*, 38.

8— Ibid., 53.

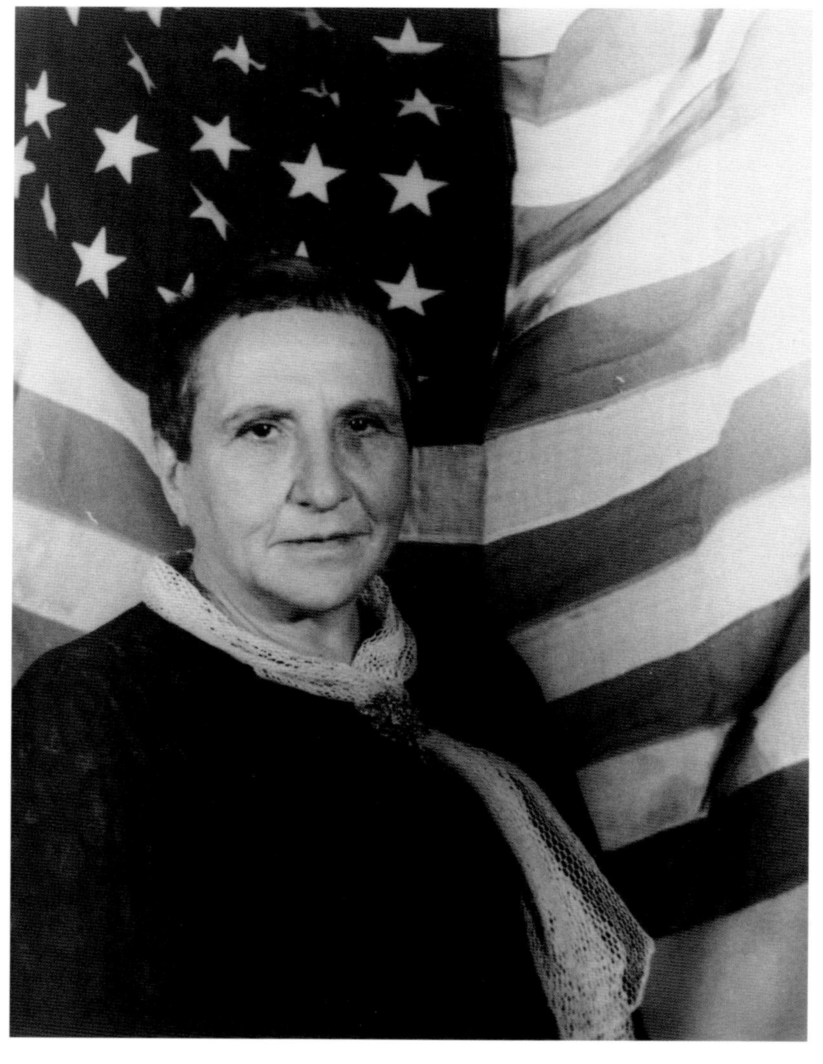

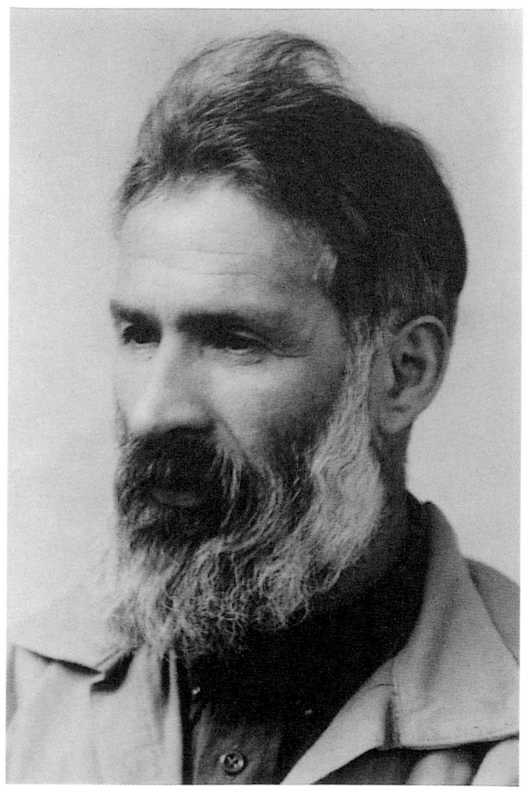

178
CARL VAN VECHTEN
[PORTRAIT OF GERTRUDE STEIN WITH AMERICAN
FLAG AS BACKDROP], JANUARY 4, 1935
GELATIN SILVER PRINT, 45.8 X 35.6 CM
LIBRARY OF CONGRESS, WASHINGTON D.C.
PRINTS AND PHOTOGRAPHS DIVISION,
LOT 12735, NO. 1050
MAAG, TAM, TMAA

179
PAUL OUTERBRIDGE
PORTRAIT OF BRANCUSI, 1925
GELATIN SILVER PRINT, 15.8 X 9.9 CM
MUSÉE NATIONAL D'ART MODERNE –
CENTRE GEORGES POMPIDOU, PARIS,
BEQUEST OF CONSTANTIN BRANCUSI, AM 1988.1706
MAAG, TAM, TMAA

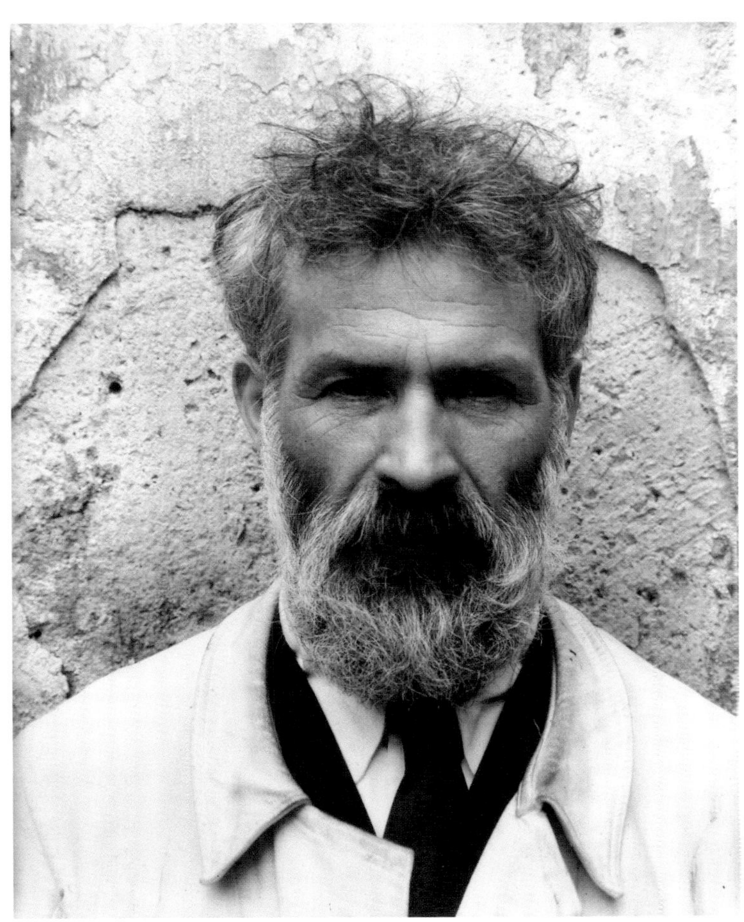

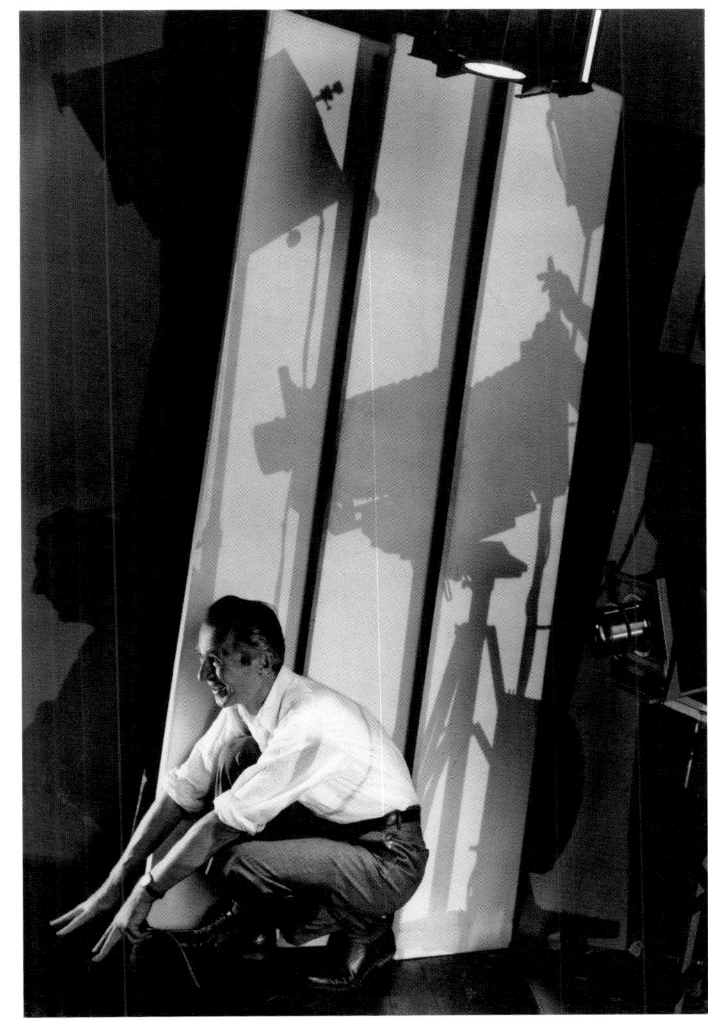

180
EDWARD STEICHEN
CONSTANTIN BRANCUSI, 1922
GELATIN SILVER PRINT, 41.5 X 33.5 CM
BIBLIOTHÈQUE NATIONALE DE FRANCE,
PARIS, 94C209506
MAAG

181
EDWARD STEICHEN
SELF-PORTRAIT, 1929
GELATIN SILVER PRINT, 34.5 X 23.5 CM
BIBLIOTHÈQUE NATIONALE DE FRANCE,
PARIS, 94C209502
MAAG

CHRONOLOGY 1918–1939

Symbols have been used to refer to
the cities where the events take place:

● Paris,

■ New York,

▲ outside of these two cities.

1918

● Patrick Henry Bruce, who had arrived in Paris early in 1904, is photographed with the American students' committee of the École des Beaux-Arts.

■ American collector Katherine S. Dreier acquires *Composition I* and *Composition II* by Bruce [1916, Yale University Art Gallery, New Haven].

Berenice Abbott meets Marcel Duchamp and Man Ray.

● Amédée Ozenfant and Charles-Édouard Jeanneret (Le Corbusier) meet and co-author *Après le cubisme* (published by Éditions des Commentaires).

● **JUNE** Fernand Léger paints *Propellers* [Museum of Modern Art (MoMA), New York] purchased by Katherine Dreier.

● **DECEMBER** John Storrs first sees Émile-Antoine Bourdelle's bas-reliefs at the Théâtre des Champs-Élysées (Storrs had first visited Paris in 1906, and moved there in 1911).

● **DECEMBER 22–JANUARY 11, 1919** A "Purist" exhibition is held at the Galerie Thomas (rue de Penthièvre).

1919

● Henri-Pierre Roché, author and diplomat, plays the role of agent for avant-garde American collectors such as John Quinn whom he met in New York in 1917. Roché promotes Constantin Brancusi, Man Ray, Francis Picabia, the Paris dada group, and notably Duchamp, whom he met in New York in 1916 and who introduced him to Walter Arensberg and Katherine Dreier.

▲ **EARLY 1919** Edward Steichen returns to the United States after travelling in Europe.

● **JANUARY 2** Roché, accompanied by Bruce, visits Harrison Reeves who had introduced the two men in 1916. From 1919 to 1932, Roché and Bruce would see each other twice a year, and Roché became one of Bruce's most ardent supporters.

● **FEBRUARY 5–28** *Œuvres par Fernand Léger*, his first solo exhibit, is held at Léonce Rosenberg's Galerie l'Effort Moderne (19 rue de la Baume).

■ **MARCH** In conjunction with Henri S. Reinolds and Adolf Wolff, Man Ray publishes the sole issue of *TNT*, a review containing contributions from Adon Lacroix (Man Ray's wife, also known as Donna Lecoeur), Philippe Soupault, Arensberg, Duchamp and an article by Man Ray titled "Revolving Doors" (republished in an expanded, French version as "Les Portes tournantes," *Minotaure* 7, 1935).

● Publication of the first issue of *Littérature,* edited by Louis Aragon, André Breton, and Philippe Soupault, soon joined by Paul Eluard. Paul Valéry suggests the title.

● **APRIL 4** Roché, accompanied by Reeves, visits Bruce's studio and describes his canvases as "architectural paintings."

● **JUNE 22** After spending nine months in Buenos Aires, Duchamp returns to Paris, where he stays until the end of the year.

● **LATE AUGUST** Dreier goes to Europe where she remains until December. On September 8 she visits Bruce's studio with Roché.

● **OCTOBER–NOVEMBER** *Exposition d'artistes de l'école américaine,* curated by a Franco-American committee, is held by the Musée National du Luxembourg. Storrs exhibits a sculpture (Storr [*sic*], no. 252, *Étude*, bronze figurine).

● **NOVEMBER 1–DECEMBER 10** At the Salon d'Automne in the Grand Palais des Champs-Élysées, Bruce exhibits two geometric still lifes for the first time (*Peinture*, nos. 241 and 242); Storrs shows *Portrait de Miss Mary A.* (marble, no. 1778), *Portrait de P.-S.-M...* (plaster, no. 1778 b), *Statue d'homme nu* (plaster, no. 1779), *Portrait de Vicomte J.* (plaster, no. 1780).

● **LATE 1919** Steichen returns to France with funds from two commissioned paintings.

1920

▲ The Aero Club de France commissions Storrs to produce a monument commemorating the first flights by Wilbur Wright (now on avenue Léon-Bollée in Le Mans).

● Le Corbusier meets Léger at the Café de la Rotonde in Montparnasse.

● Piet Mondrian publishes the essay titled *Néo-Plasticisme* (Éditions de l'Effort Moderne).

● **EARLY 20s** Bruce meets Duchamp via Roché. He frequents the Café du Dôme in Montparnasse and the Café Flore in Saint-Germain-des-Prés, often in the company of the surrealists, notably Tristan Tzara.

▲ Peggy Guggenheim meets Duchamp through Mary Reynolds and Lawrence Vail (whom she marries in 1922).

▲ **FROM 1920 TO 1924** Jan Matulka divides his time between New York and Paris.

■ **AFTER 1920** Quinn recruits Roché to help him constitute his art collection.

■ **JANUARY 6** Duchamp goes to New York where he lives until July of that year.

● **JANUARY 17** Tristan Tzara arrives in Paris.

● **JANUARY 19–31** *Exposition des peintures de Henry Ottman et des sculptures de John Storrs* is held at the Galerie des Feuillets d'Art (11 rue Saint-Florentin).

● **JANUARY 28–FEBRUARY 29** At the first postwar Salon des Indépendants in the Grand Palais des Champs-Élysées, Léger exhibits *La Ville* (no. 2651) and *Disques dans la ville* (no. 2652). Bruce exhibits six canvases (*Peinture*, nos. 607–612).

■ **APRIL 29** The Société Anonyme, Inc. (Museum of Modern Art) is founded by Dreier, Duchamp, and Man Ray. This first "museum of modern art" organizes exhibitions and lectures devoted to modern European artists, and a few Americans such as Marsden Hartley and Man Ray. Dreier commissions Man Ray to make photographic reproductions of artworks for Société Anonyme publications.

■ **APRIL 30–JUNE 15** The Société Anonyme's inaugural exhibit features among others, Brancusi, Bruce, Duchamp, Picabia, Man Ray, Georges Ribemont-Dessaignes, Joseph Stella, and Jacques Villon. The exhibit is held in the gallery at the organization's headquarters.

■ **JUNE 17–AUGUST 1** The *Second Exhibition of Modern Art* held in the gallery of the Société Anonyme, notably includes work by Matulka and Bruce. His last significant exhibit in the United States until the early 1950s.

● **SEPTEMBER** Daniel-Henry Kahnweiler opens an art gallery with André Simon, called Galerie Simon (27 bis rue d'Astorg).

● **OCTOBER 15** Ozenfant and Jeanneret launch the review *L'Esprit nouveau*, subtitled *Revue internationale d'esthétique*, which ran until 1925.

● **OCTOBER 15–DECEMBER 12** At the Salon d'Automne, Bruce exhibits two paintings (nos. 313 and 314); Jacques Mauny, two paintings titled *Arcade* (no. 1556) and *Les Écossais* (no. 1557); Storrs (109 rue du Cherche-Midi), *Tête de jeune femme* (stone, no. 2040).

● **NOVEMBER 15** Roché tries in vain to convince Quinn to acquire paintings by Bruce.

■ **DECEMBER 9–24** The first solo exhibit devoted to Storrs is held at the Folsom Galleries. His wife, Marguerite de Ville Chabrol, wrote the catalogue under the pseudonym of Marc Debrol.

1921

● Man Ray begins superimposing images in his photography, as seen in his portrait of *Tristan Tzara* (cat. 143).

▲ Storrs acquires the château of Chantecaille in Mer, near Orléans, yet retains his Paris apartment.

● Ezra Pound moves to 70 bis rue Notre-Dame-des-Champs (where he lives until 1924), near Léger's studio (at number 86), and the two men become friends

● **FROM 1921 TO 1938** Albert Eugene Gallatin makes an annual trip to Paris and begins to constitute a collection of European and American avant-garde art, earning him the epithet—conferred by critic Geoffrey Hellman—of "king of the abstract."

■ **JANUARY** Publication of the "Dada Manifesto" in *The Little Review* 7, no. 4 (January–March).

● **JANUARY 15** Ozenfant and Le Corbusier publish their manifesto "Le Purisme" in issue number 4 of *L'Esprit nouveau* (which henceforth bears the subtitle, *Revue internationale illustrée de l'activité contemporaine*).

● **JANUARY 22–FEBRUARY** *Ozenfant et Jeanneret: Peintures puristes* is held at the Galerie Druet (20 rue Royale).

● **JANUARY 23–FEBRUARY 28** Bruce exhibits three *Peintures* (nos. 462–464) at the Salon des Indépendants.

▲ **MARCH** Man Ray is awarded a prize at Philadelphia's Fifteenth Annual Exhibition of Photographs for his portrait of Berenice Abbott.

● **MARCH 21** Abbott sails for France on the *Rochambeau*. Thanks to help from Storrs, she rents a studio on the Left Bank. She studies under Bourdelle as well as at the Académie de la Grande-Chaumière in Montparnasse and with Brancusi at 8 impasse Ronsin (see p. 234).

■ **APRIL** Man Ray and Duchamp publish the sole issue of *New York Dada*.

■ **JUNE 8** In a letter to Tzara, Man Ray dubs himself "directeur du mauvais movies" and comments on the difficulty of publishing his manifestoes: "Dada cannot live in New York. All New York is dada—and will not tolerate a rival—will not notice dada." (Letter from Man Ray to Tristan Tzara, June 8, 1921. Bibliothèque Littéraire Jacques Doucet, Paris. Tzara Collection).

● **JUNE 6–30** Tzara organizes *Salon Dada: Exposition Internationale* at the Galerie Montaigne in the Studio des Champs-Élysées which includes works by Hans Arp, Duchamp, Max Ernst, and Tzara.

● **JUNE 10** The first performance of Tzara's play, *Le Cœur à gaz* provokes a scandal.

● **JULY 14** Funded by the American collector Ferdinand Howald, Man Ray leaves New York, taking with him series of the *Revolving Doors* (cats. 102 and 103) and most of his airbrush paintings. Upon arrival in Paris on July 22, Duchamp takes him to the Hôtel Boulainvilliers in Passy, where Tzara lives. The same evening Man Ray meets Breton, Aragon, Eluard, Gala, Jacques Rigaut, and Soupault at the Café Certa in Passage de l'Opéra.

● **SUMMER** At Jacques Villon's home in Puteaux, Man Ray helps Duchamp film his spinning optical disks.

● **AUGUST 15** Charles Demuth arrives in Paris. During his stay, he paints *Rue du Singe qui Pêche* (cat. 21), the only work known with certainty to have been executed in the capital.

● **SEPTEMBER** Gerald and Sara Murphy arrive in Paris and move into the Hôtel Beau-Site.

● During a dinner at Picabia's, his artist friends sign the canvas *L'Œil cacodylate* [1921, Musée National d'Art Moderne, Paris]. Man Ray signs "Man Ray directeur du mauvais movies," and photographs the work, which is illustrated in *The Little Review* "Picabia Number," 8, no. 2 (spring 1922).

● Man Ray meets fashion designer Paul Poiret.

● **AUTUMN** Murphy discovers the work of Georges Braque, Pablo Picasso, and Juan Gris at Léonce Rosenberg's gallery (rue de la Boétie).

▲ Duncan Phillips publicly opens the Phillips Memorial Art Gallery, now known as The Phillips Collection, in Washington, D.C.

● Man Ray rediscovers the photogram technique and dubs the resulting works "rayographs." One of his early rayographs, ƎOƧ *ROSE-SEL A VIE*, is published in *The Little Review*.

● Man Ray meets Alice Prin, known as Kiki of Montparnasse, who becomes his companion for several years.

● **OCTOBER** Demuth sells two watercolors, titled *Views of the City*, to Léonce Rosenberg for five hundred francs each.

● **NOVEMBER 1–DECEMBER 20** At the Salon d'Automne, Bruce shows two *Peintures* (nos. 298 and 299); Fernand Léger exhibits *Le Déjeuner* (no. 1410); Mauny, four paintings titled *Le Port, Les Bœufs blancs; Le Port, Le Corsage rouge; Rue napolitaine,* and *Bonnes d'enfants* (nos. 1660–1663).

▲ **NOVEMBER 12** Demuth goes back to his hometown of Lancaster, Pennsylvania. On the return voyage, he produces several sketches of the ocean liner that will be used for *Paquebot "Paris"* [1921–22, Columbus Museum of Art, Ohio].

● **LATE AUTUMN** Murphy spends six months studying with Natalia Goncharova. He helps to make the sets for the Diaghilev ballet company, under the guidance of artists such as Goncharova, Braque, Picasso, Mikhail Larionov, and André Derain. The Murphys meet Léger, with whom they become friends. Through them, Léger would meet the writers Archibald MacLeish, Ernest Hemingway, and John Dos Passos.

● **EARLY DECEMBER** Man Ray, joined by Kiki, turns his room at the Hôtel des Écoles (15 rue Delambre) into a photo studio.

● **DECEMBER 3–31** Man Ray's first solo exhibit in France is held at Librairie Six (5 avenue Lowendal) then run by Mick Verneuil, Soupault's wife. The opening was announced as a dada event, to symbolize "Paris welcoming New York." For this occasion, Man Ray creates with Erik Satie an object called *Cadeau* (cat. 89) and displays thirty-five other works including *Percolator* (cat. 9), *Volière* (1919), *Transatlantique* (1921), and *Isadora Duncan nue* (1922). The exhibition receives little attention in the press.

1 9 2 2

- Storrs takes Dreier to Jacques Lipchitz's studio, where she acquires the stone sculpture, *Man With Mandolin* [1916–17, Yale University Art Gallery, New Haven]. Storrs meets Lipchitz regularly from January to April.

- Man Ray produces his first photographic portrait of Gertrude Stein and her companion, Alice B. Toklas. Through Roché, he also photographs Picasso's work for Quinn.

- Le Corbusier builds a studio-residence for Ozenfant at 53 avenue Reille.

- JANUARY 21 The film clips based on Duchamp's optical disks are projected at Madame Cora's home in Puteaux.

- JANUARY 27 In the January 27, 1922, issue of *L'Intransigeant* (p. 2), Maurice Raynal reviews the paintings exhibited by Bruce at the Salon des Indépendants. He describes them as being "mistakes," although not without a certain charm.

- JANUARY 28 Duchamp returns to his studio in the Lincoln Arcade Building in New York, where he spends the next thirteen months working on the *Large Glass,* bought first by the Arensbergs then by Dreier (for 2,000 dollars).

- JANUARY 28–FEBRUARY 28 At the Salon des Indépendants, Bruge [*sic*] exhibits three *Peintures* (nos. 514–516); Matulka (50 rue Vavin) shows *La Femme, Paysage,* and *Composition* (nos. 2464–2466); Man Ray is represented by three works, *Le Fond* (no. 3063), *Boardwalk* (no. 3064), and *Catherine Barometer* (no. 3065). Man Ray's work is not appreciated by the critics, partly due to the presence of Picabia. Man Ray never again submits work to the Salon. Storrs visits the exhibition where he meets Gertrude Stein and Alice B. Toklas.

- FEBRUARY Storrs visits Ossip Zadkine. Gino Severini gives Storrs several paintings to sell.

- SPRING Murphy sets up a studio at 69 rue de Froidevaux.

- APRIL An insert soliciting subscriptions for Man Ray's album of photographs, *Les Champs délicieux,* is placed in the sole issue of the review *Le Cœur à barbe,* edited by Ribemont-Dessaignes and Tzara. Man Ray stresses the fact that this is the first time photography has been placed on the same footing as original artworks.

- AROUND MAY Matulka rents a studio at 50 rue Vercingétorix, which he keeps until 1934.

- SUMMER Sara and Gerald Murphy visit Antibes for the first time, and stay with Cole Porter at the Château de la Garoupe.

- JULY Man Ray and Kiki move into a new studio at 31 bis rue Campagne-Première in Montparnasse, and become neighbors of Eugène Atget (at number 17 bis). Sylvia Beach, the American publisher and owner of Shakespeare & Co, recommends Man Ray to writers such as James Joyce.

- AUTUMN The Murphys return to Paris and then move into the Hôtel des Réservoirs in Versailles.

- OCTOBER Storrs's memorial to Wilbur Wright is inaugurated at Auvours, near Le Mans.

- OCTOBER 1 Man Ray's photograph *L'Élevage de poussière* (cat. 93) is published for the first time in issue number 5 of *Littérature* entirely devoted to Rrose Sélavy (aka Marcel Duchamp).

- NOVEMBER 1–DECEMBER 17 Bruce exhibits two still lifes (nos. 319 and 320) at the Salon d'Automne.

- DECEMBER 15 The Société Générale d'Imprimerie et d'Édition publishes a limited edition of forty numbered copies of *Les Champs délicieux,* comprising twelve rayographs and a foreword by Tzara titled "Man Ray – La photographie à l'envers" (cat. 98).

- WINTER Abbott spends several months in Berlin.

1 9 2 3

- Blanche Lazzell returns to Paris, where in 1912 she had studied at the Académie Julian and at the Académie Moderne. She takes courses with Léger, André Lhote, and Albert Gleizes.

- EARLY 1923 Steichen returns to the United States and becomes chief photographer for Condé Nast publications.

- FEBRUARY Storrs arrives in New York. Accompanied by Louise Bryant, he discovers Joseph Stella's paintings.

- EARLY FEBRUARY Duchamp decides to sign the *Large Glass,* though it is incomplete. He returns to Europe shortly thereafter.

- FEBRUARY 10–MARCH 11 Murphy (23 quai des Grands-Augustins) presents his work for the first time at the Salon des Indépendants, exhibiting two paintings, *Turbines* (no. 3439), *Pression* (no. 3440) and a watercolor *Taxi* (no. 3441*)*, plus a drawing, *Cristaux* (no. 3442). Bruce shows three *Natures mortes* (nos. 668–670); Matulka, four *Peintures* (nos. 3195–3198); while Léger presents a *Projet d'ensemble pour un hall* (no. 2764 b).

- FEBRUARY 23 –MARCH 22 The Société Anonyme presents an *Exhibition of Sculpture by John Storrs* that later travels to the Arts Club of Chicago.

- FEBRUARY 28–MARCH 28 Léonce Rosenberg organizes an exhibit titled *Tableaux par Ozenfant et Jeanneret* at the Galerie l'Effort Moderne.

- MARCH Charles Sheeler photographs Storrs's sculptures in New York.

- SPRING Man Ray hires Abbott as a darkroom assistant. She works alongside him for two years. Murphy and his family rent a house in Saint-Cloud.

- MAY Margaret Anderson and Jane Heap, editors of *The Little Review,* travel to Paris (see p. 208).

- EARLY JUNE Dos Passos arrives in Paris; Murphy introduces him to Léger.

- JUNE The Murphys return to Antibes.

- SUMMER Murphy stays with the Porters in Venice, working on the ballet *Within the Quota* (see p. 64).

- JULY 6 Man Ray's first film, *Le Retour à la raison,* is shown at the dada event *Le Cœur à barbe* at the Théâtre Michel (40 rue des Mathurins). Also projected are *Fumées de New York* [*Manhatta*] by Charles Sheeler and Paul Strand and a "new film" [*Rhythmus 21*] by Hans Richter. The program also includes a musical accompaniment composed and performed by George Antheil, a play by Tzara titled *Le Cœur à gaz,* poems by Apollinaire, Jean Cocteau, Eluard, and Soupault, and musical works by Darius Milhaud, Erik Satie, Georges Auric, and Igor Stravinsky. After a scuffle during which the police are called in, the second performance, scheduled for July 7, is canceled. American filmmaker Dudley Murphy contacts Man Ray following the event. During the summer they begin shooting scenes for a possible film; these shots were later incorporated into *Emak Bakia* (1926) and perhaps *Ballet Mécanique* (1924).

● **MID-JULY** Duchamp returns to Paris where he gets in touch with Mary Reynolds, first met during the 1910s in New York.

● **OCTOBER 25** Rolf de Maré, director of the Ballets Suédois, presents *La Création du monde* by Blaise Cendrars (score by Darius Milhaud, sets and costumes by Léger, choreography by Jean Börlin) at the Théâtre des Champs-Élysées. Murphy's ballet, *Within the Quota*, is presented as a curtain-raiser.

● **AUTUMN** The Murphys return to the Hôtel des Réservoirs in Versailles.

● **NOVEMBER** Le Jockey Club is founded on boulevard du Montparnasse by Miller and the American artist Hilaire Hiler. Kiki, the muse of avant-garde artists, returns from New York.

● **NOVEMBER 1–DECEMBER 14** Bruce exhibits two *Still Lifes* (nos. 243 and 244) at the Salon d'Automne.

● **DECEMBER** Man Ray and Duchamp live at the Hôtel Istria (29 rue Campagne-Première).

1 9 2 4

■ Matulka meets Calder and Graham at the Art Students League.

▲ Lazzell returns definitely to the United States, never to return to Europe.

● Man Ray begins to work for *Vogue*. He photographs Peggy Guggenheim wearing a gown designed by Paul Poiret. Ribemont-Dessaignes publishes the first monograph devoted to Man Ray as part of Gallimard's Peintres Nouveaux series.

● Léger and Dudley Murphy complete *Ballet Mécanique*, an early "film without screenplay," based solely on contrasting imagery and rhythms.

● Publication of the last issue of *Littérature* and the first issue of *La Révolution surréaliste*. Publication of *The Transatlantic Review*, edited by Ford Madox Ford until 1925 (see p. 208).

● **JANUARY** Othon Friesz allocates several hours of teaching work to Marie Laurencin and Léger. Léger's courses at the Académie Moderne (86 rue Notre-Dame-des-Champs) are known to date from this time, though it is possible they began in the final quarter of 1923.

● Gertrude Stein composes a prose portrait of Man Ray. The most famous lines read: "Sometime Man Ray sometime. Sometime Man Ray sometime. Sometime Man Ray sometime. Sometime sometime."

▲ **FEBRUARY** The European edition of the *American Review* proclaims Paris to be the "capital of America."

● The Murphys make 23 quai des Grands-Augustins, their winter quarters and summer at the Hôtel du Cap d'Antibes.

● **FEBRUARY 9–MARCH 12** Murphy exhibits *Boat-Deck* [sic] (no. 2225) at the Salon des Indépendants. Because of its large size, employees try to hang it in the hallway, but Murphy, wanting to be displayed alongside his compatriots, creates a scandal. "If they think my picture is too big, I think the other paintings are too small." Matulka exhibits two *Peintures* (nos. 2080–2081). André Dunoyer Segonzac, a member of the jury, objects to exhibiting works by Bruce.

● **MARCH 22–APRIL 30** Storrs presents his first abstract skyscrapers at an exhibit called *L'Architecture et les arts qui s'y rattachent* hosted by the École Spéciale d'Architecture de Paris.

▲ **SPRING** Scott and Zelda Fitzgerald arrive in France.

■ **JULY 28** Quinn dies of cancer, aged 54. Except for Seurat's *Cirque*, which he donated to the Louvre, the rest of his collection is sold and dispersed.

● **SUMMER** Dreier visits Léger's studio.

● **OCTOBER 11** The "Bureau des Recherches Surréalistes" opens at 15 rue de Grenelle.

● **OCTOBER 15** Breton publishes the *Manifeste du surréalisme* (Éditions Kra).

● **NOVEMBER 1–DECEMBER 14** Mauny exhibits two paintings at the Salon d'Automne, *Transatlantique* (no. 1283) and *Portrait* (no. 1284, [Portrait of Gerald Murphy]).

● **DECEMBER 1** Man Ray publishes seven photos in the first issue of *La Révolution surréaliste,* founded by Breton as a successor to *Littérature* and edited by Pierre Naville and Benjamin Péret. Three of his portraits of the surrealist group appear on the cover.

1 9 2 5

● Paul Outerbridge travels to Europe. In Paris, he meets Abbott, Man Ray, and Steichen.

● Man Ray introduces Abbott to Atget.

● Léger contracts pneumonia and goes to stay with the Murphys in Antibes. During his absence, Ozenfant substitutes him at the Académie Moderne. Henceforth the two artists share the teaching load until the end of academic year 1928 or 1929.

● Le Corbusier and Ozenfant have a falling out.

■ Mauny makes his first trip to the United States.

● **JANUARY** De Maré returns from the United States with the Revue Nègre, introducing France to Joséphine Baker, who becomes a star attraction.

● **JANUARY 19–FEBRUARY 19** Storrs and Jules Pascin participate in the Briant-Robert Gallery exhibit *Exposition de 6 Peintres Américains – 2 Sculpteurs Américains.*

● **MARCH 21–MAY 3** Murphy exhibits *Montre* (no. 2424) and Lazzell (21 rue Bréa) *Étude* (no. 1977) at the Salon des Indépendants held in the Palais de Bois at Porte Maillot.

● **MAY 30** Lee Miller sails for Nice, then heads for Paris.

▲ **SUMMER** Murphy and family move into "Villa America," the home they built in Antibes.

● **SEPTEMBER 26–NOVEMBER 2** At the Salon d'Automne in the Tuileries, Lazzell exhibits two engravings titled *Paysage* (nos. 798–799), Mauny exhibits two paintings: *New York: Down Town* (no. 955) and *New York: Giants* (no. 956).

● **NOVEMBER** The *Exposition Internationale L'Art d'Aujourd'hui* (see p. 46), organized by Polish artist Victor J. Poznanski is held in the Syndicat des Antiquaires (18 rue de la Ville-l'Évêque). Exhibitors include Bruce (*Nature morte*, nos. 13–16), Lazzell (*Tableau*, no. 112), and Murphy (*Montre* and *Nature morte* [*Razor*], nos. 152 and 153).

● **NOVEMBER 14–25** *La Peinture Surréaliste*, the first group exhibit of surrealist painters, is held at the Galerie Pierre (13 rue Bonaparte). It includes works by Arp, de Chirico, Ernst, Paul Klee, André Masson, Joan Miró, Pierre Roy, and Man Ray, the sole American, who exhibits *La Marquise, 6.396.78, La Volière,* and some drawings.

■ **NOVEMBER 16–28** Léger's first solo exhibit in the United States is organized by the Société Anonyme and held at the Anderson Galleries. Works include *The City* (1919), *Three Women* (1921), and *Disks* (1918). The exhibition is a critical success but only four watercolors are purchased by Dreier. Stuart Davis, who first saw Léger's work at the Armory Show in 1913, attends the exhibit.

1 9 2 6

- Berenice Abbott leaves Man Ray to open her own photo studio on 44 rue du Bac. She makes portraits of Cocteau, Marie Laurencin, Max Ernst, Leo Stein, James Joyce, and Peggy Guggenheim.

- Thanks to Man Ray, Eugène Atget's photos are published in an issue of *La Révolution surréaliste* 7 (June 15). Man Ray acquires the photographs, keeping them in his personal collection until 1952, when they are bought by the George Eastman House.

- At the Galerie Druet, Gallatin discovers the work of Maury, which he admires (see p. 98). The two men become friends. Gallatin begins to paint, as a self-taught artist—only three of his works from this period have survived.

- Christian Zervos begins publishing *Cahiers d'Art*, from an office later located at 14 rue du Dragon. The magazine runs until 1960.

- ▲ JANUARY Lee Miller returns to the United States.

- ● MARCH Katherine Dreier travels to Paris. She and Duchamp visit artists' studios to choose works for an upcoming exhibit at the Société Anonyme. She commissions Man Ray to do a portrait of Mondrian in his studio at 26 rue du Départ.

- ● MARCH 20–MAY 2 At the Salon des Indépendants, held in the Palais de Bois at Porte Maillot, Murphy exhibits *Laboratoire* (no. 2635 b) and *Nature morte* (no. 2635 c, [Razor]); Lazzell exhibits *Peinture* (no. 2070) and *Trees* (engraving, no. 2071) and Mauny, *New York* (no. 2460 b) and *USA* (no. 2460 c).

- ● MARCH 26–APRIL The Galerie Surréaliste run by Jean Tual and coordinated by André Breton, opens at 16 rue Jacques-Callot, with an exhibition titled *Tableaux de Man Ray et Objets des Îles*. The gallery closes in 1928.

- ▲ JUNE The Hemingways, Fitzgeralds, and MacLeishes spend the summer in Antibes with the Murphys.

- ● JUNE 8–20 Abbott has her first solo exhibit, *Bérénice* [*sic*] *Abbott: Portraits Photographiques,* at the gallery Au Sacre du Printemps, run by Jan Slivinsky (5 rue du Cherche-Midi). The show features portraits of Cocteau, André Gide, Sylvia Beach, Marie Laurencin, and Joyce.

- ▲ SUMMER Man Ray spends the summer in Biarritz and Antibes, where Picasso introduces him to the Murphys, who commission him to make family portraits. Man Ray shoots the film, *Emak Bakia*, at the summer home of Arthur and Rose Wheeler (the film is named after the Wheeler's rented villa, which means "Leave me alone" in Basque).

- ● JULY 20 Alexander Calder arrives first in London then, four days later, in Paris, where he stays at the Hôtel de Versailles (60 boulevard du Montparnasse). He begins work on his miniature circus.

- ● AUGUST 26 Calder sets up a studio at 22 rue Daguerre.

- ● AUGUST 30 A private screening is held of *Anémic Cinéma* at 63 avenue des Champs-Élysées, a film by Duchamp with the help of Marc Allégret and Man Ray (who dubs it *Obscenema*).

- ● AUTUMN Michel Seuphor is introduced to Bruce by Robert Delaunay. Calder attends to the Académie de la Grande-Chaumière where he meets painter Arthur Frank and English engraver Stanley William Hayter, who introduces him to sculptor José de Creeft.

- ■ OCTOBER 13 Duchamp accompanies the works by Brancusi for the Brummer Gallery exhibit. Duchamp meets art dealer Julien Levy.

- ● OCTOBER 25–NOVEMBER 14 Storrs participates in an exhibit called *Artistes Américains de France*, held at the Galerie Jean Charpentier and organized by the Association Française d'Expansion et des Échanges Artistiques.

- ● NOVEMBER Publication of Man Ray's *Revolving Doors* at the Éditions Surréalistes (cats. 102 and 103).

- ■ *Anémic Cinéma* is screened at the Fifth Avenue Theater.

- ● NOVEMBER 2–26 Storrs is included in *Groupe de Peintres et Sculpteurs Américains de Paris*, organized by the American Art Association at the Galerie Durand-Ruel.

- ■ NOVEMBER 17–DECEMBER 25 Brancusi exhibition, organized by Duchamp, on view at the Brummer Gallery. Isamu Noguchi is strongly influenced by the abstract sculptures.

- ■ NOVEMBER 19–JANUARY 1, 1927 *International Exhibition of Modern Art Assembled by Société Anonyme* is held at the Brooklyn Museum of Art. Artists exhibited include Duchamp (no. 34 , *Disturbed Balance* and no. 35, *Glass*), Léger (no. 41, *Abstraction, Circus* and nos. 42–43, *Abstraction*), Demuth (no. 236, *Modern Conveniences*; no. 237, *Pacquet Boat, Paris* [*sic*]; no. 238, *Nospmas Megiap Nospmas*), Davis (no. 235, *Still Life*), Man Ray (no. 274, *Arc de Triomphe, Paris*; no. 275, *Rayographs*) and Storrs (no. 288, *Stone Study in Form I*; no. 289, *Stone Study in Form II*; no. 290, *Stone Study in Form III*). Storrs's *New York* (no. 291) is featured on the cover of the exhibition catalogue, which also includes Man Ray's portrait of Mondrian in his studio. In 1927, an abridged version of the exhibit travels to the Anderson Galleries, the Albright Art Gallery in Buffalo, and the Toronto Art Gallery. Duchamp, Vassily Kandinsky, Mondrian, Kurt Schwitters, and Léger are members of the selection committee.

- ● NOVEMBER 23 A private screening of Man Ray's *Emak Bakia* is held at the Vieux Colombier Theater, run by Jean Tedesco.

- ■ 8–22 DECEMBER *Retrospective Exhibition of Paintings by Stuart Davis,* his first, is held at the Whitney Studio Club.

- ● WINTER Seuphor pays a second visit to Bruce.

1 9 2 7

- ● William Einstein arrives in Paris, where he begins to study under Ozenfant and Léger at the Académie Moderne.

- ● Jean Xceron arrives in Paris.

- ● Jean Hélion meets the Uruguayan painter Joaquín Torres-García, with whom he visits exhibitions on rue de Seine and rue de la Boétie, and who introduces him to Theo Van Doesburg.

- ▲ Man Ray begins making numerous trips to the United States to attend exhibitions of his work.

- ● Levy spends time in Paris and marries Joella Loy, daughter of artist and poet Mina Loy. The couple is invited to dinners organized by Brancusi, also attended by Gertrude Stein and Sylvia Beach. Man Ray introduces Levy to Atget, while Duchamp introduces him to Peggy Guggenheim.

- ● Hayter opens Atelier 17 (see p. 154).

- ● FEBRUARY 27 Duchamp returns to Paris, where he rents a studio apartment at 11 rue Larrey, which he keeps until 1943.

- ■ MARCH 6 Man Ray goes to New York for the United States premiere of *Emak Bakia* at the Film Guild, then returns to Paris in early May.

- ● MARCH 6–MAY 1 Calder participates in a collective exhibit at Galerie La Boétie called *Salon des Humoristes*.

● **MARCH 30** Funded by a Guggenheim fellowship, Noguchi arrives in Paris. For five months he works as a studio assistant for Brancusi, whom he met through writer Robert McAlmon. Noguchi he also studies at la Grande-Chaumière and the Académie Colarossi, and meets Calder, Morris Kantor, and Davis. With help from his friend and fellow Japanese artist Foujita, Noguchi moves into 7 rue Belloni (now rue d'Arsonval).

● **APRIL** Launch of the English-language monthly magazine *transition*, edited in Paris by Eugène Jolas (see p. 208).

■ **10 APRIL** George Antheil presents his composition *Ballet Mécanique* at Carnegie Hall (see p. 64).

■ **MAY 16–28** Jane Heap, editor of *The Little Review*, organizes the *Machine-Age* exhibit at the Little Review Gallery. It features Demuth, Duchamp, and Sheeler, who are also part of the selection committee, along with Louis Lozowick. The exhibition drew inspiration from the Esprit Nouveau pavilion at the 1925 Art Déco exhibition in Paris. Léger is chosen to design the cover of the catalogue.

● **SUMMER** Mauny enables Gallatin to meet Picasso and Kahnweiler.

● George L. K. Morris registers at the École de Fontainebleau, headed by Russian philosopher George Ivanovich Gurdjieff. There Morris runs into Gallatin again, who encourages him to study with Léger at the Académie Moderne.

● **AUGUST** Calder has his first solo exhibit in Paris at the Galerie Jacques Seligmann.

● Berenice Abbott makes three photographic portraits of Atget in her studio, shortly before his death (cats. 138 and 139).

■ **AUTUMN** Calder returns to New York. By winter he is renting a room at 46 Charles Street where he presents performances of his circus.

■ **OCTOBER** Brancusi files a lawsuit against the United States Customs to have *Bird in Space* (1926) recognized as an artwork.

■ **NOVEMBER** Storrs arrives in New York, then heads to Chicago in December.

● **FROM NOVEMBER TO JANUARY 1928** The film *Emak Bakia* plays at the Studio des Ursulines.

■ **NOVEMBER 19–JANUARY 9, 1928** The *International Exhibition of Modern Art,* organized by the Société Anonyme, presents Duchamp's *Large Glass* to the public for the first time.

■ **DECEMBER 12** Gallatin's collection is opened to the public at New York University. Initially called the Gallery of Living Art, it is renamed in 1936 the Museum of Living Art.

■ **DECEMBER 13–JANUARY 25, 1928** The inaugural exhibition of the Gallery of Living Art presents 43 works by 24 artists from the school of Paris, in addition to 13 Americans. The European works in the collection are complemented by loans of American art by the likes of Charles Burchfield, Demuth, Sheeler, and Marin. After the museum closed in early 1943, much of the collection is donated to the Philadelphia Museum of Art.

1928

▲ Charles Shaw travels to Europe and divides his time between Paris and London during the next four years.

● Frederick Kann sojourns in Paris.

● Storrs acquires Léger's *Composition in Blue* (1921–27) on behalf of the Art Institute of Chicago. He is commissioned to sculpt *Ceres* (cat. 31) for the Board of Trade Building in Chicago.

● Calder meets Miró. The two men become friends.

● Noguchi works on a series of abstract gouaches (cats. 116–123) and sculptures (cats. 113–115), and moves his studio to 11 rue Dedouvre in Gentilly.

● The Galerie Georges Bernheim (109 rue du Faubourg-Saint-Honoré) organizes a solo exhibit devoted to Murphy.

■ Katherine Dreier acquires Bruce's *Composition III, IV,* and *V.*

● **JANUARY 20–FEBRUARY 29** At the Salon des Indépendants held in the Grand Palais des Champs-Élysées, Calder (9 East 8th Street, New York) exhibited *La Famille bourgeoise* (no. 678 b), Hélion (1 rue Marcel-Sembat) exhibited two paintings (nos. 1994 and 1995), and Lazzell (chez Lucien Lefebvre-Foinet, 19 rue Vavin) an engraving titled *La Tour de l'église* (no. 2461).

■ **FEBRUARY 20–MARCH 3** *Wire Sculpture by Alexander Calder* is organized by critic Carl Zigrosser at the Weyhe Gallery.

■ **MARCH 9–APRIL 1** Calder exhibits wire sculptures at the New York Society of Independent Artists exhibition in the Waldorf-Astoria Hotel, including a colossal *Romulus and Remus* and *Spring.*

■ **MAY** Julianna Force from the Whitney Studio Club acquires several paintings from Davis, enabling him to travel to Paris.

● **MAY 13** The Studio des Ursulines hosts the first private screening of Man Ray's film *L'Étoile de Mer* based on a poem by Robert Desnos. It is followed by several public screenings in May, then a run from October to January 1929.

● **MAY 24–JUNE 7** The *Premier Salon Indépendant de la Photographie,* better known as the "Salon de l'Escalier" (see p. 209), is held in the Comédie des Champs-Élysées (15 avenue Montaigne). Berenice Abbott, Outerbridge, and Man Ray notably participate, and Atget is given a retrospective.

● **MAY 25** *Nadja* by André Breton and illustrated by Man Ray, is published by Nouvelle Revue Française.

● **MID-JUNE** Davis arrives in Paris, bringing several paintings including the *Eggbeater* series (cat. 10), which he shows to Léger and Gertrude Stein. He sublets Matulka's studio, whom he had met at the Art Students League in New York.

● **JULY 2–13** *The Salon of American Artists,* a group exhibit including Calder, is held at the Galerie Jacques Seligmann, in the former Hôtel de Sagan.

● **MID-SEPTEMBER** Elliot Paul accompanies Davis to see the studio of Léger, who returns the visit. Léger is very impressed by the *Eggbeater* series.

● **AUTUMN** At the Café du Dome, Calder meets artist Jules Pascin, who soon began promoting his work.

● **OCTOBER** Berenice Abbott, thanks to help from Levy, acquires part of the Eugène Atget collection from André Calmettes, a close friend of Atget's who was then director of the Théâtre Municipal de Strasbourg. In 1929, when Abbott left France definitely, she took this collection to the United States.

● Elliot Paul writes an article on Davis for the October issue of *transition*. The article is illustrated with four paintings done in Paris, while the cover features *Hôtel de France* (see p. 208).

■ **OCTOBER 7–28** The Downtown Gallery, run by Edith Halpert, presents *Paintings by Americans: Exhibition of Works by Americans in Paris*. Works by Davis are included.

▲ **23 OCTOBER** Murphy returns to the United States, then to Hollywood, where he stays until January 1929.

● **NOVEMBER** Gertrude Stein, who met Davis through Elliot Paul, goes to his studio to see his recent work.

● **EARLY NOVEMBER** Calder rents a studio at 7 rue de Cels.

● **NOVEMBER 4–DECEMBER 16** At the Salon d'Automne held in the Grand Palais des Champs-Élysées, Bruce shows two *Peintures* (nos. 285 and 286), while Mauny (29 boulevard d'Ormesson, Enghien) exhibits a canvas titled *La Marine* (no. 1370).

■ **LATE 1928** Noguchi returns to New York.

● **WINTER** Abbott moves her photo studio to 18 rue Servandoni.

1929

▲ John Ferren travels to Europe.

■ The Murphys leave Paris definitely.

● Publication of the last issue of *La Révolution surréaliste,* which opens with the "Second Surrealist Manifesto."

● Works by John Graham are exhibited at the Galerie Zborowski (26 rue de Seine).

▲ **EARLY JANUARY** Man Ray begins shooting *Les Mystères du Château du Dé,* a film commissioned by vicomte Charles de Noailles, featuring his Villa Saint-Bernard in Hyères, built by architect Robert Mallet-Stevens. The film contains an implicit reference to Mallarmé's poem, *Un coup de dés jamais n'abolira le hasard.*

● **JANUARY 15–30** Galerie Georges Bernheim organizes a collective exhibition including six works by Murphy. The exhibition is mentioned in *L'Intransigeant* ("Quarante Tableaux de Guillaumin, œuvres de Morphy [*sic*]," January 14). *Cocktail* is reproduced in *Excelsior* (January 16) and in the *Journal des débats* (January 29).

● **JANUARY 18–FEBRUARY 28** At the Salon des Indépendants, Einstein exhibits two paintings and Calder his sculpture *Romulus and Remus* and *Spring*. Pascin puts Calder in contact with the Galerie Billiet.

● **JANUARY 25–FEBRUARY 7** *Sculptures, Bois et Fil de Fer de Alexander Calder* is hosted by the Galerie Billiet–Pierre Vorms (30 rue de la Boétie). Pascin writes the foreword to the catalogue. Davis is present at the opening, and the exhibition wins praise from critics.

▲ **FEBRUARY** Storrs meets Noguchi in Chicago.

■ Berenice Abbott takes a short trip to the United States and decides to return there to work. She opens a portrait studio at the Hôtel des Artistes near Central Park.

■ **FEBRUARY 4–23** *Wood Carvings by Alexander Calder* is on view at the Weyhe Gallery.

● **EARLY MARCH** American artist Niles Spencer introduces Davis to Hilaire Hiler, who goes to Davis's studio to see recent work.

■ **APRIL** Noguchi's abstract works from Paris are shown at the Eugene Schoen Gallery.

● **SPRING** Morris takes classes at Léger's Académie Moderne.

● **MAY** At the Salon des Tuileries, held in the Palais des Expositions (148 rue de l'Université), Calder is one of 23 Americans to participate exhibiting *Le Numéro* (no. 209).

● The last issue of *The Little Review* is published.

● **MAY 1** The Paris residence of the vicomte de Noailles is the scene of the first private screening for the crew of Man Ray's *Les Mystères du Château du Dé.*

● **MAY 22–JUNE 22** *Œuvres Anciennes et Nouvelles,* an exhibit of work by Storrs, is held at the Galerie l'Effort Moderne.

● **JUNE 12** A private screening of *Les Mystères du Château du Dé* is held at the Studio des Ursulines; also on the bill is *Un Chien Andalou* by Luis Buñuel and Salvador Dalí.

● **EARLY SUMMER** Lee Miller goes to Paris to meet Man Ray, bearing a letter of introduction from Steichen. She becomes Man Ray's model, assistant, and companion until 1932. Together they master the solarization technique.

▲ **AUGUST** Davis returns permanently to the United States.

▲ **OCTOBER** The Building Committee of the Board of Trade in Chicago approves the model of *Ceres* that Storrs had sent from France. His work is set atop the building.

● **NOVEMBER 2–14** An exhibit of Man Ray's *Tableaux et Dernières Rayographies* is held at the Galerie des Quatre Chemins.

● **NOVEMBER 3–DECEMBER 22** Bruce exhibits two *Natures mortes* (nos. 197 and 198) at the Salon d'Automne.

■ **NOVEMBER 8** Inauguration of the Museum of Modern Art (MoMA), founded by Lillie Bliss, Mary Sullivan, and Abby Aldrich Rockefeller. Alfred H. Barr Jr. is appointed director.

■ **NOVEMBER 27–DECEMBER 7** *Watercolors by Stuart Davis* is on view at the Whitney Studio Club.

■ **DECEMBER 15** Stieglitz opens his gallery, An American Place (509 Madison Avenue) where it continues to operate until his death in 1946.

1930

● Carl Holty, in Europe since 1926, moves to Paris.

● Arp introduces Hélion to Mondrian.

● Seuphor and Torres-García found the group called Cercle et Carré, notably joined by Arp, Kandinsky, Le Corbusier, Léger, Mondrian, and Ozenfant. A review of the same name is edited by Seuphor. In reaction, Van Doesburg, Hélion, Otto Carlsund, Léon-Arthur Tutundjian, and Marcel Wantz found a rival group and review, *Art Concret*.

● Éditions Kra publishes Breton's *Second Manifeste du surréalisme.*

● *Atget: photographe de Paris* is published simultaneously in Paris by Éditions Henri Jonquières and in New York by E. Weyhe.

■ Gallatin publishes the Gallery of Living Art's first catalogue, for which Mauny writes the foreword.

● The Galerie Van Leer exhibits work by Graham.

▲ Picasso is awarded the Carnegie Prize.

● **JANUARY–FEBRUARY** Calder participates in the 11th Salon de l'Araignée at the Galerie G. L. Manuel Frères.

● Storrs spends time in Paris.

● **JANUARY 17–MARCH 2** Calder exhibits two canvases, each titled *Composition* (nos. 640–641) at the Salon des Indépendants.

■ **JANUARY 19–FEBRUARY 16** MoMA organizes *Painting in Paris from American Collections* which includes works by Braque, Delaunay, Othon Friesz, Léger, Miró (no. 62, *Dog Barking at the Moon*), and Picasso.

■ **JANUARY 21–FEBRUARY 10** *Stuart Davis Hotels and Cafés,* an exhibit of his Paris work, is on view at the Downtown Gallery.

● **JANUARY 30** Léger visits Storrs in his studio. Storrs, in his diary, records Léger's surprise on seeing his abstract work (Washington, Smithsonian Institution, Archives of American Art, John Storrs Papers, I, Journal, January 30, 1930).

■ **MARCH** Storrs goes to New York, where he visits Stieglitz at his gallery, An American Place.

● **SPRING** Morris takes classes at Léger's Académie Moderne.

● **APRIL** Noguchi returns to his Gertilly studio for two months.

● **APRIL 18–MAY 1** Galerie 23 (23 rue de la Boétie), hosts the *Première Exposition Internationale du Groupe Cercle et Carré,* which notably includes Florence Henri, Torres-García, Mondrian, Arp, Sophie Taeuber-Arp, Nina Kandinsky, Kandinsky, Georges Vantongerloo, Jean Gorin, and Seuphor. The exhibit is advertised as the "first international exhibition of abstract art."

● **APRIL–SEPTEMBER** Lee Miller plays a part in Cocteau's film, *Le Sang d'un poète.*

● **JUNE** In the sixth issue of *Formes,* Gallatin publishes an article in which he criticizes the concept behind the founding of the Whitney Museum of American Art, namely the notion of a specifically American art.

● **OCTOBER** Calder's visit to Mondrian's studio provokes a crucial shift in his oeuvre. Fascinated by three squares of primary colors pinned to the walls, Calder suggests to Mondrian that these shapes be allowed to swing freely. Mondrian is not at all favorable to the suggestion, but Calder then begins to produce abstract compositions and soon imbues these neo-plastic forms with movement in the form of mobiles, some of which are motorized.

● **OCTOBER 14** Prompted by Viennese architect Frederick Kiesler, Calder invites Léger, Mondrian, and Le Corbusier to attend a performance of his miniature circus in his studio. Kiesler suggests that Calder invite Van Doesburg to the following evening's performance.

● **OCTOBER 25–NOVEMBER 24** Calder participates in the group exhibit organized by the Surindépendants at the Parc des Expositions (Porte de Versailles). He exhibits three wire sculptures, *Homme* (no. 54), *Femme* (no. 55), and *Composition* (no. 56), in addition to a sculpture in wood, *Femme couchée dans la forêt* (no. 57), and five drawings (nos. 58–62). Other participants include Einstein (7 villa Brune), who shows *Sadie Stix* (nos. 1–5), (nos. 141–145), Graham (chez J. Xceron, 86 rue Lepic), represented by a *Nature morte* (no. 197), *Composition* (no. 198), and *Peinture* (no. 199), and Frederick Kann (59 rue Froidevaux), who exhibits two sculptures, *Plaque* (nos. 255–256) and *Sculpture* (no. 257), as well as *Peinture* (no. 258) and *Dessin* (no. 259).

● **NOVEMBER 1–DECEMBER 14** Bruce shows a painting at the Salon d'Automne (no. 352 *Peinture*). It is the last work he ever exhibits.

1931

● After having visited Paris in 1926, Balcomb and Gertrude Greene decide to spend a year living on rue Bardinet.

● Holty meets Mondrian, with whom he would establish a friendship in the 1940s in the United States.

▲ Einstein and Hélion travel to the Soviet Union together.

● Morris meets Henri Matisse, who mentions the work of one of his students, Bruce.

● The Compagnie de Distribution de l'Électricité publishes a book, titled *Électricité,* which includes ten commissioned rayographs by Man Ray.

■ Abbott organizes an exhibit of Atget's photographs at the Weyhe Gallery, including six portraits of her by Atget.

● **LATE JANUARY** Calder returns to his residence at 7 villa Brune. He soon meets Hélion and Arp, and befriends both of them.

● **FEBRUARY 15** Hélion, Kandinsky, Arp and Van Doesburg found the Abstraction-Création group, in addition to a publication of the same name.

■ **MARCH 31–APRIL 19** Stuart Davis has a solo exhibit at the Downtown Gallery.

● **APRIL 27–MAY 9** *Alexander Calder: Volumes–Vecteurs–Densités. Dessins–Portraits* is on view at the Galerie Percier, (38 rue de la Boétie). It features Calder's wire portraits and his first abstract sculptures. Picasso meets Calder at the opening.

● **MAY 2** Calder and his wife, Louisa James, move to 14 rue de la Colonie.

■ **MAY 12–JUNE 11** *Alexander Calder: Mobiles* is held at the Julien Levy Gallery.

● **JUNE** Calder is invited to join the Abstraction-Création group.

▲ **AUGUST** Shortly after having begun a series called *New York–Paris* (cat. 16), Davis publishes a "Self-Interview" in *Creative Arts*, which describes his Paris experience (September 1931, p. 208–211). Illustrating the article is a photograph of Davis with *Place Pasdeloup* (cat. 13).

● **AUTUMN** Duchamp visits Calder in his studio.

■ **SEPTEMBER** Léger visits New York and Chicago, financed by Gerald and Sara Murphy. An exhibition of his drawings is organized by the John Becker Gallery (October 1–23). Upon his return to Paris, Léger publishes "NEW YORK vu par F. LÉGER, À Sara Murphy" in *Cahiers d'Art* 9–10 (1931).

■ **SEPTEMBER 26–OCTOBER 15** *Photographs by Berenice Abbott* is on view at the Julien Levy Gallery.

● **OCTOBER 23–NOVEMBER 22** Calder participates in the group show organized by the Surindépendants at the Parc des Expositions (Porte de Versailles), exhibiting two sculptures (nos. 51–52) and two paintings titled *Espaces vecteurs densités* (nos. 53–54). Xceron (15 rue Cauchois) also includes two *Peintures* (nos. 411–412).

■ **OCTOBER 31** Duchamp returns to New York, where he remains until January 20, 1934.

■ **NOVEMBER** Inauguration of the Whitney Museum of American Art, founded by Gertrude Vanderbilt Whitney after the Metropolitan Museum of Art refused to accept her collection of modern American art.

■ **NOVEMBER 2** Levy opens a gallery at 602 Madison Avenue, where he exhibits old and new photographs, followed by surrealist art.

■ **NOVEMBER 4** Gallatin organizes a reception to honor Léger at the Gallery of Living Art.

▲ **NOVEMBER 16** Inauguration of *Newer Super-Realism,* the first surrealist exhibition in the United States, at the Wadsworth Atheneum (Hartford, Connecticut). It is organized by A. Everett ("Chick") Austin, Jr., with the help of Levy, and features works by de Chirico, Dalí, Ernst, Masson, Miró, Picasso, Pierre Roy, and Léopold Survage.

● **DECEMBER 1–18** The Galerie de France hosts a solo show of work by Xceron in partnership with *Cahiers d'Art.* The exhibition is attended by Mondrian, Arp, Léger, Hélion, Van Doesburg, and Masson.

● **LATE 1931** Duchamp meets Hélion.

Ferren moves to Paris, where he stays until 1938. He learns engraving technique at Atelier 17.

Balcomb Greene devotes himself entirely to painting, attending sessions at the Académie de la Grande-Chaumière without following the formal courses taught there.

1 9 3 2

- During a trip across Europe, Ilya Bolotowsky stays briefly in Paris, where he admires works by de Chirico, Picasso, and Braque.

- Hélion edits the first issue of a review devoted to the Abstraction-Création group. He travels to the United States, and from this date onward, makes regular trips to New York.

- Delaunay invites Holty to join the Abstraction-Création group, making Holty one of the group's first American members (along with Calder).

- Roché meets Bruce for the last time.

- Léger opens L'Académie de l'Art Contemporain, a painting workshop on rue de la Sablière, and later located on rue du Moulin-Vert.

- The last issue of *transition* is published.

- The Galerie Vignon exhibits Man Ray's photographs.

- ■ JANUARY 9–29 Based on the Wadsworth Atheneum exhibit, Levy hosts *Surrealist Paintings, Drawings and Photographs*, which also includes American artists such as Herbert Bayer, Joseph Cornell (montages and *Bell Jar Object*), and Charles Howard. Cornell designs the invitation. As part of the show, the Julien Levy Gallery organizes "An Evening of Avant-Garde Film" that includes Léger and Murphy's *Ballet Mécanique*, Jay Leyda's *A Bronx Morning*, and Man Ray's *L'Étoile de Mer*.

- ● JANUARY 15–28 The Galerie Vignon organizes a group exhibit of drawings that includes work by Calder.

- ● JANUARY 15–FEBRUARY 1 Calder participates in the group exhibit organized by the Surindépendants at the Parc des Expositions (Porte de Versailles).

- ● JANUARY 18–FEBRUARY 6 *Artistes Américains de Paris* is organized by Chil Aronson at the Galerie de la Renaissance (11 rue Royale). It includes three paintings by Holty (216 boulevard Raspail), two by Graham, three compositions and a sculpture (*Abstraction*) by Kann, and three compositions by Xceron.

- ● FEBRUARY 12–29 *Calder: Ses Mobiles,* showing Calder's early motorized constructions, is held at the Galerie Vignon. Duchamp helps to design the exhibit. After having visited Calder's studio, Duchamp had described his recent works as "mobiles." Arp, on seeing this exhibit, then gives the name "stabiles" to Calder's non-motorized sculptures (seen at the Galerie Percier in 1931).

  APRIL Gallatin meets Delaunay, who encourages him to found a museum devoted to abstract art and its history. Delaunay puts Gallatin in touch with Hélion. Delaunay now succeeds Mauny as Gallatin's main artistic adviser, only to be replaced later that year by Hélion (until 1936).

- ■ APRIL 9–MAY 30 *Photographs by Man Ray,* the artist's first solo photography exhibit in New York, is on view at the Julien Levy Gallery.

- ■ MAY 12–JUNE 11 *Calder: Mobiles, Abstract Sculptures,* an exhibition of Calder's motorized sculptures, is held at the Julien Levy Gallery. Léger writes the foreword to the catalogue.

- ■ SEPTEMBER 26–OCTOBER 15 *Photographs by Berenice Abbott,* her first solo exhibit in New York, is held at the Julien Levy Gallery.

- ■ OCTOBER Lee Miller opens a photography studio at 8 East 48th Street.

- ■ OCTOBER 16 The Murphys return permanently to the United States, and Murphy slowly takes over his father's business, the Mark Cross company.

- ■ NOVEMBER 5–DECEMBER 3 The Julien Levy Gallery organizes Max Ernst's first solo exhibit in the United States, *Exhibition Surréaliste by Max Ernst*. Ernst designs the invitation.

- ● NOVEMBER 7 Calder, wanting to meet Storrs, invites him to come see his circus, representing the earliest known correspondence between the two artists.

- ■ NOVEMBER 26–DECEMBER 30 The Julien Levy Gallery presents Cornell's first solo exhibit (*Objects by Joseph Cornell: Minutiae, Glass Bells, Shadow Boxes, Coups d'Œil, Jouets Surréalistes*) along with *Etchings by Pablo Picasso: Illustrations for the Unknown Masterpiece*.

- ■ DECEMBER 30–JANUARY 25 *Lee Miller: Exhibition of Photographs,* her only solo exhibit during her lifetime, is presented at the Julien Levy Gallery.

1 9 3 3

- ■ Einstein returns to New York to work for his uncle Stieglitz at An American Place.

- ■ Around 1933, Bolotowsky first sees Miró's work at the Galerie Pierre Matisse, and also discovers Mondrian in the Gallatin collection.

- ● Gallatin meets Calder.

- ▲ Calder returns to the United States. Starting the following year, he spends summers in Roxbury, Connecticut, and winters in New York.

- ▲ Shaw returns to the United States.

- ■ Cornell and Lee Miller become friends. She photographs his work and takes several portraits of him (cat. 172).

- ■ Morris has his first solo exhibit at the Valentine Dudensing Gallery.

- ● JANUARY 19–31 Calder participates in a group exhibit organized by Abstraction-Création.

- ● MAY Through Hélion, Gallatin visits Mondrian and Arp in their studios.

- ● Bruce leaves Paris and moves to 18 rue de la Bonne-Aventure in Versailles.

- ● MAY 11–25 The Galerie Percier devotes a solo exhibit to the work of Xceron.

- ● MAY 16–18 *Présentation des Œuvres Récentes de Calder,* an exhibit of Calder's recent work, is on view at the Galerie Pierre Colle (29 rue Cambacérès).

- ■ JUNE Hélion returns with Calder to the United States, where he remains for several months. Hélion's first solo exhibit is organized by the John Becker Gallery.

- ● JUNE 7–18 *Exposition Surréaliste: Sculptures, Objets, Peintures, Dessins* is held at the Galerie Pierre Colle.

- ● JUNE 9–24 Galerie Pierre Loeb (2 rue des Beaux-Arts) organizes an exhibit of work by Arp, Calder, Hélion, Miró, Pevsner, and Seligmann, where Calder meets art critic James Johnson Sweeney.

- ● JULY 3 Bruce writes to Roché, announcing that he has destroyed most of the works remaining in his studio, except for twenty-one still lifes done between 1917 and 1930, stored in a shed on quai Malaquais. He offers them to Roché and Helen Hessel.

- ● JULY 30 Roché takes possession of Bruce's paintings.
- ■ NOVEMBER 9 Cornell sends Breton a photo by Lee Miller of one of his bell jar objects.
- ■ NOVEMBER 17–JANUARY 13, 1934 Duchamp organizes a second Brancusi exhibition at the Brummer Gallery. On this occasion, he meets Cornell.
- ■ DECEMBER 9 Gallatin commissions Hélion to present a lecture-tour at the Gallery of Living Art. Duchamp, Calder, and Morris attend the lecture, published in the collection's catalogue under the title, "The Evolution of Abstract Art as Shown in the Gallery of Living Art."
- ■ DECEMBER 12–JANUARY 3, 1934 The Julien Levy Gallery hosts a collective exhibit: *Objects by Joseph Cornell, Posters by Toulouse-Lautrec, Watercolors by Perkins Harnley, Montages by Harry Brown*.

1 9 3 4

- ● Kay Sage makes regular trips to Paris.
- ● Ferren befriends Hélion and joins the Abstraction-Création group, along with Kann.
- ■ Group A is founded in New York. Its members include Albers, Burgoyne Diller, Dreier, Gorky, and Graham.
- ● Les Éditions Rrose Sélavy produce the first copies of Duchamp's *Green Box*, containing 93 facsimiles of notes and documents related to the *Large Glass*.
- ■ JANUARY Harry Holtzman and Diller first see Mondrian's work at the Gallery of Living Art.
- ■ MARCH 6–APRIL 30 MoMA hosts the *Machine Art* exhibit.
- ● MAY Gallatin visits Léger's studio on several occasions.
- ● JUNE 13 Through Hélion, Gallatin meets César Domela, Wolfgang Paalen, and Hans Erni.
- ▲ JULY Léger stays once again with the Murphys at their "Villa America."
- ● JULY 2–10 *Xceron* exhibit is on view at the Galerie Pierre.
- ■ SEPTEMBER Charles Biederman moves to New York, where he meets Gallatin, Léger, Morris, Alfred Barr, Sweeney, and gallery owners Pierre Matisse and Charles Ratton.
- ■ OCTOBER *Photographs by Berenice Abbott* is held at the Museum of the City of New York.
- ▲ A book titled *Man Ray Photographies 1920–1934 Paris*, published by James Thrall Soby in Hartford (Conn.), features texts by Breton, Eluard, Rrose Sélavy, Tzara, and Man Ray.
- ● LATE OCTOBER Sweeney visits Léger in Paris to offer him an exhibit at the Renaissance Society in Chicago.
- ● DECEMBER Holtzman leaves for Paris with the intention of meeting Mondrian. He remains there for four months, and also meets Hélion.

1 9 3 5

- ■ Morris marries Suzy Frelinghuysen.
- ● Gallatin co-finances with Morris in France, the publication of a review titled *Plastique*. Morris, Calder, Holtzman, Césa Domela, and Arp participate in the project (five issues).
- ● Man Ray publishes photographs of Nusch, Paul Eluard's companion, accompanied by Eluard's poetry, in an anthology titled *Facile* (Éditions GLM).

- ▲ The Works Projects Administration (WPA) launches the Federal Arts Project (FAP) to support artists during the Great Depression. The program survives until 1943.
- ▲ Roy Stryker at the Federal Farm Security Administration (FSA) commissions photographers to produce visual records of the Depression.
- ■ FEBRUARY 12–MARCH 22 The Whitney Museum of American Art presents *Abstract Painting in America*, which includes works by Davis (no. 23, *Cask*, painting, 1934; no. 24, *Egg Beater No. 2*, painting, 1928; no. 25, *Egg Beater No. 3*, painting, 1928; no. 26, *Radio Tubes*, painting, 1931; no. 27, *Salt Shaker*, painting, 1932; no. 28, *Percolator*, gouache, 1921), Demuth (no. 29, *After All*, painting, n.d.; no. 30, *I Saw the Figure Five in Gold*, painting, n.d.; no. 31, *My Egypt*, painting, n.d.; no. 32, gouache, 1919; no. 33, *In the Province*, gouache, 1919; no. 34, *Province Town*, watercolor, 1918), Balcomb Green (no. 51, *3438*, painting, 1934), Matulka (no. 77, *Composition*, painting, n.d.; no. 8, *Interior*, painting, n.d.; no. 79, *Studio*, painting, n.d.), Storrs (no. 112, *Composition No. 1*, painting, 1932; no. 113, *Composition No. 4*, painting, n.d.), Graham (no. 50, *Family Group*, painting, 1932). Davis writes the introduction to the catalogue, and one of his drawings is featured on the cover.
- ■ MARCH 22–MAY 1 Xceron returns to the United States for his first New York exhibit at the Garland Gallery. He meets Sweeney and David Smith.
- ■ APRIL Morris helps Gallatin to select abstract paintings by Shaw for a solo exhibition held at the Gallery of Living Art from May to October.
- ● MAY Hélion arranges for Gallatin to meet Ferren.
- ■ MAY–OCTOBER Gallatin presents Shaw's first solo exhibit at the Gallery of Living Art.
- ● SUMMER Gallatin visits Arp, accompanied by Shaw. Shaw meets Hélion and Ferren.
- ■ SEPTEMBER 25 Léger heads for New York and Chicago, following a retrospective exhibit organized by the Renaissance Society of the University of Chicago, held first at MoMA (September 30 to October 24), and then at the Art Institute of Chicago (December 19 to January 19, 1936). On October 18, Léger gives a lecture, in French, on painting and avant-garde film (partly translated and published as "The New Realism" in *Art Front* (New York) 2, no. 8 (December 1935); the lecture includes a screening of his film *Ballet Mécanique* as well as *Entr'acte* by René Clair, accompanied with music by Erik Satie, adapted for piano by Darius Milhaud and performed by Antheil and Henry Brant.
- ▲ OCTOBER 25 Demuth dies in Lancaster.
- ● NOVEMBER Yvonne Zervos organizes a retrospective of Man Ray's paintings on the premises of the *Cahiers d'Art* gallery.
- ■ Gallatin, accompanied by Shaw, visits Biederman in his studio.

1 9 3 6

- ■ Holty returns to the United States; he befriends Davis and Graham in New York.
- ▲ Léger visits the United States and works with Willem de Kooning on a mural project for the WPA.
- ■ Harry Holtzman founds the American Abstract Artists association to promote geometric abstract art through meetings, lectures, and annual exhibitions. Members include artists such as Bolotowsky, Morris, and Biederman.

● Through Paul Rosenberg, Gallatin acquires the second version of Picasso's *Three Musicians* (1921), a canvas formerly in the Reber collection in Lausanne.

▲ Duchamp becomes Peggy Guggenheim's artistic advisor.

● A group exhibit of works by Arp, Ferren, Giacometti, Kandinsky, Hélion, Paalen, and Sophie Taeuber-Arp is held at the Galerie Pierre.

■ Ferren has a solo exhibit at Galerie Pierre Matisse
● in New York and at Galerie Pierre Loeb in Paris.

▲ WINTER Storrs spends the winter in Orléans with his family. The French government awards him the title of Chevalier de la Légion d'Honneur.

■ FEBRUARY After a ten-year hiatus, Gallatin takes up painting again.

● MARCH Léger returns to Paris.

■ MARCH 2–APRIL 19 At MoMA, Alfred Barr organizes *Cubism and Abstract Art*. Calder, Man Ray, and Edward McKnight-Kauffer are the only Americans included. Léger exhibits four paintings, including *Le [Grand] Déjeuner* [*Three Women*] The exhibit then travels to the San Francisco Museum of Art, the Cincinnati Art Museum, and the Minneapolis Institute of Arts, and in 1937, to the Cleveland Museum of Art, the Baltimore Museum of Art, the Rhode Island School of Design Museum of Art, and the Grand Rapids Art Gallery in Michigan.

■ MARCH 9–31 *Five Contemporary American Concretionists: Biederman, Calder, Ferren, Morris and Shaw*, organized by Gallatin, is held at the Paul Reinhardt Galleries. The exhibit functions as a kind of "Salon des Refusés" vis-à-vis the *Cubism and Abstract Art* exhibition. In modified form (with Gallatin replacing Calder), the show is hosted by the Galerie Pierre in Paris in June and by the Mayor Gallery in London in July (*Abstract Paintings by American Artists*).

■ APRIL 6–25 The Valentine gallery exhibits *Peintures Abstraites* by Hélion (presented again from December 1937 to January 15, 1938, and at the Arts Club of Chicago, February 4–18, 1938).

● MAY 22–29 *Exposition Surréaliste d'Objets*, organized by Breton, is held at the Galerie Charles Ratton (14 rue Marignan). Man Ray exhibits *Lanterne sourde et muette* (cat 90), *Boardwalk*, *Ce qui nous manque à tous*, *L'Orateur* and *Mon Rêve*; Duchamp, *La Bagarre d'Austerlitz*, *Porte-Bouteilles*, *Why Not Sneeze?*; Calder, *Mobile*.

■ MAY 25 Duchamp arrives in New York to restore and slightly modify his *Large Glass*, cracked during shipping from New York to West Redding, Connecticut, early in 1931.

● JUNE 15–29 *Cinq Peintres Américains: Biederman, Calder, Ferren, Morris et Shaw* is on view at the Galerie Pierre Loeb where Gallatin makes a photographic portrait of Miró.

■ JULY Hélion moves to New York for a year.

■ JULY 29 Bruce leaves Paris permanently, taking some twenty geometric paintings done between 1933 and 1936. He arrives in New York on August 3, and moves in with one of his sisters, Mary Bruce Payne.

● SEPTEMBER 7 Duchamp returns to Paris.

■ AUTUMN Levy publishes *Surrealism* (Black Sun Press) with a cover by Cornell. The book includes a screenplay by Cornell, *Monsieur Phot*.

● OCTOBER Biederman moves to Paris, where he meets the avant-garde abstractionists: Arp, Brancusi, Domela, Miró, Mondrian (through Sweeney), Anton Pevsner, and Vantongerloo.

▲ Duchamp organizes an exhibit of *Abstractions* by Hélion at the College Art Association (also presented at the Howard Putzel Gallery in Hollywood in February 1937).

■ NOVEMBER 12 Bruce commits suicide.

■ DECEMBER 7–JANUARY 17, 1937 Alfred Barr organizes *Fantastic Art, Dada, Surrealism* at MoMA. Calder, Cornell, and Duchamp are included. Man Ray is in New York for the opening. In 1937, the exhibit travels to the following venues: the Pennsylvania Museum of Art in Philadelphia, the Institute of Modern Art in Boston, the Museum of Fine Arts in Springfield, Mass., the Milwaukee Art Institute, the University Gallery of the University of Minnesota in Minneapolis, and the San Francisco Museum of Art.

1 9 3 7

● Kay Sage moves to Paris, and meets Yves Tanguy the following year.

▲ Storrs executes a monument in Brest, commemorating the role of the United States Navy during the World War I (destroyed July 4, 1941).

● Man Ray publishes twelve photographs in *La Photographie n'est pas l'art* (Éditions GLM).

■ Einstein's first solo exhibit in New York is held at An American Place.

■ The Julien Levy Gallery moves to 15 East 57th Street.

▲ FEBRUARY 5–27 Duchamp's first solo exhibition is held at the Arts Club of Chicago.

● MARCH The first issue of *Plastique* is published.

■ APRIL Gallatin joins the association of American Abstract Artists.

● SPRING Christian Zervos visits Biederman in his studio.

● LATE APRIL–EARLY MAY Calder returns to Paris, moving to 80 boulevard Arago.

● MAY 20–JUNE 2 *Peintures et Sculptures de John Storrs* is held at the Galerie Jeanne Bucher-Myrbor (9ter boulevard du Montparnasse). The opening is attended by Ozenfant, Jean Lurçat, Lipchitz, Léger, Louis Marcoussis, Zervos, Man Ray, Jacques Villon, Ernst, Miró, Arp, and Jean Chauvin.

● MAY 24–NOVEMBER 26 Calder executes his *Mercury Fountain* for the pavilion of the Spanish Republic at the Exposition Internationale des Arts et Techniques.

▲ MID-JUNE Biederman returns to the United States.

● JUNE 24 Gallatin and Domela visit the Arps in Meudon-Val-Fleury (Clamart) to discuss the preparation of their review, *Plastique*.

▲ SUMMER Hélion moves to Rockbridge Baths, Virginia, where he builds a studio and where he lives until 1939.

● Lee Miller travels to Paris, where she meets Roland Penrose.

● JULY 30–OCTOBER 31 On the occasion of the Universal Exposition, the Jeu de Paume hosts an exhibit titled *Origines et Développement de l'Art International Indépendant*. American artists are not very well represented, but include Benjamin G. Benno (*Deux Femmes*, 1937), Biederman (*Peinture*, 1935), Calder (a sculpture, 1937), Ferren (*Peinture*, 1937), Storrs, and Man Ray. Braque, Léger, Picasso, and Zervos are members of the selection committee.

● NOVEMBER 5–20 Galerie Jeanne Bucher exhibits drawings by Man Ray and publishes a book of his drawings with poetry by Paul Eluard, titled *Les Mains Libres, Dessins illustrés par les poèmes de Paul Eluard*.

- **DECEMBER 15–JANUARY 16, 1938** The *Charles Demuth Memorial Exhibition* is held at the Whitney Museum of American Art.
- **END OF 1937** Xceron leaves Paris for New York, where he helps Hilla Rebay to organize the Museum of Non-Objective Painting.

1938

- L'Académie de l'Art Contemporain moves into premises on Square Henry-Delormel.
- Sweeney publishes an article titled "L'Art contemporain aux États-Unis" in *Cahiers d'Art* (1–2), notably illustrating the work of Calder, Davis, Demuth, and Noguchi.
- **JANUARY–FEBRUARY** The Galerie des Beaux-Arts (140 rue du Faubourg-Saint-Honoré) hosts the *Exposition Internationale du Surréalisme*, organized by Breton and Eluard (see p. 155). Duchamp is credited as the exhibit's "begetter/umpire," Man Ray as its "master of lighting," Dalí and Ernst as "special advisers," Paalen as "superintendent of brushwood." The exhibit includes work by Cornell and Man Ray. Breton and Eluard publish *Le Dictionnaire abrégé du surréalisme* for the occasion.
- **APRIL 13** *Xceron: Recent Paintings,* organized by Sweeney, opens at the Nierendorf Gallery. Xceron meets Rebay.
- **SPRING** The issue of *Plastique* entirely devoted to American abstract art includes an article by Gallatin ("Abstract Painting and The Museum of Living Art") and contributions from members of the American Abstract Artists group such as Shaw, Balcomb Greene, and Morris.
- **MAY 24–JULY 31** In conjunction with MoMA, the Jeu de Paume organizes an exhibit titled *Trois Siècles d'Art aux États-Unis*. Calder is represented by a *Mobile* (no. 64, 1931, James Johnson Sweeney Collection) and Demuth by *Marins au bal* (no. 30, Albert Rothbart Collection, Ridgefield, Conn.).
- **JUNE 15–30** A group exhibit organized by Gallatin for the Galerie Pierre includes abstract paintings by the collector as well as Shaw's first *Plastic Polygons,* and paintings and sculptures by Morris.
- **AUGUST** Peggy Guggenheim visits Paris where, on the advice of Herbert Read, Duchamp and Van Doesburg, she acquires work by avant-garde artists with the idea of founding a museum of modern art in London.
- ▲ **SEPTEMBER** Léger travels to the United States. At Yale, he gives eight lectures with Alvar Aalto and Ozenfant on "Color in Architecture." He visits Calder at his Roxbury studio.
- ▲ **SEPTEMBER 21** Mondrian leaves for London.
- **OCTOBER 8–NOVEMBER 13** Kay Sage exhibits six compositions at the Salon des Surindépendants, including *An Important Event, A Little Later,* and *The World is Blue* (cat. 136).
- ▲ **NOVEMBER 8–27** Opening of the *Calder: Mobiles* exhibit at the George Walter Vincent Smith Gallery in Springfield, Massachusetts. Present at the opening are Alvar Aalto, Léger, Siegfried Giedion, and Katherine Dreier.

1939

- Kay Sage leaves France definitely. She helps many European artists to settle in the United States, first among them Tanguy, her future husband, who sets up his studio on Washington Square South.
- ▲ Storrs makes his last trip to the United States, returning to France in May.
- Abbott and Elizabeth MacCausland publish *Changing New York* (E. P. Dutton).
- **JANUARY 16–FEBRUARY 8** *Recent Paintings by Gallatin, Morris, Shaw* is held at the Galerie Jacques Seligmann.
- **MARCH** Léger returns from his third trip to the United States.
- **LATE MAY** Inauguration of the Museum of Non-Objective Painting, with Hilla Rebay as its director. After the death of founder Solomon Guggenheim in 1949, it became known as the Solomon R. Guggenheim Museum.
- **JUNE 1** *Art of Tomorrow* exhibit opens at the Museum of Non-Objective Painting, and includes work by Xceron.
- **AUTUMN** Clement Greenberg publishes an essay titled "Avant-Garde and Kitsch" in the *Partisan Review*.
- **DECEMBER 6–JANUARY 9, 1940** An *Exhibition of Objects by Joseph Cornell* is held at the Julien Levy Gallery.

SELECTED BIBLIOGRAPHY

I. BOOKS

Adamowicz, Elza. *Surrealist Collage in the Text and Image: Dissection of the Exquisite Corpse.* Cambridge: Cambridge University Press, 1998.

Alexandrian, Sarane. *Surrealist Art.* New York: Praeger Publishers, 1970.

Les Américains à Paris, 1917–1947. Engagement et représentation. Paris: Maisonneuve et Larose, 1989.

Anderson, Margaret. *My Thirty Years' War: The Autobiography Beginnings and Battles to 1930.* New York: Horizon Press, 1969.

Bailey, William G., ed. *Americans in Paris, 1900–1930. A Selected Annotated Bibliography.* New York: Greenwood Press, 1989.

Beach, Sylvia. *Shakespeare & Company.* Lincoln: University of Nebraska Press, 1991 [1959].

Bearden, Romare, and Harry Herderson. *A History of African-American Artists from 1792 to the Present.* New York: Pantheon Books, 1993.

Berger, John. "The Changing View of Man in the Portrait." In *The Moment of Cubism and Other Essays.* New York: Pantheon-Random House, 1969.

Brandon, Ruth. *Surreal Lives: The Surrealists 1917–1945.* New York: Grover Press, 1999.

Breton, André. *Œuvres complètes.* Paris: Gallimard, 1988.

Brilliant, Richard. *Portraiture.* Cambridge, Mass.: Harvard University Press, 1991.

Brown, Milton W. *American Painting from the Armory Show to the Depression.* Princeton: Princeton University Press, 1970.

Caws, Mary Ann, Rudolf Kuenzli, and Gwen Raaberg. *Surrealism and Women.* Cambridge, Mass.: MIT Press, 1991.

Chadwick, Whitney, ed. *Mirror Images: Women, Surrealism and Self-Representation.* Cambridge, Mass.: MIT Press, 1998.

Charters, James. *This Must Be the Place: Memoirs of Montparnasse.* London: Herbert Joseph Ltd., 1934.

Chassey, Éric de. *La Peinture efficace, une histoire de l'abstraction aux États-Unis, 1910–1960.* Paris: Gallimard, 2001.

Clarke, Graham, ed. *The Portrait in Photography.* London: Reaktion Books, 1992.

Cohen, Jean-Louis, and Hubert Damisch. *Américanisme et Modernité. L'idéal américain dans l'architecture.* Paris: Flammarion, 1993.

Colville, Georgiana, and Katharine Conley, eds. *La femme s'entête: la part du féminin dans le surréalisme.* Paris: Lachenel & Ritter, 1998.

Corn, Wanda. *The Great American Thing: Modern Art and National Identity, 1915–1935.* Berkeley: University of California Press, 1999.

Davidson, Abraham A. *Early American Modernist Painting, 1910–1935.* New York: Harper & Row, 1981.

Davidson, Jo. *Between Sittings.* New York: Dial Press, 1951.

Douglas, Ann. *Terrible Honesty: Mongrel Manhattan in the 1920s.* New York: Farrar, Straus & Giroux, 1995.

Fisher, Philip. *Making and Effacing Art: Modern American Art in a Culture of Museums.* Cambridge, Mass.: Harvard University Press, 1991.

Ford, Hugh. *Published in Paris: American and British Writers, Printers and Publishers in Paris, 1920–1939.* New York: MacMillan, 1975.

___. *Four Lives in Paris.* San Francisco: North Point Press, 1987.

Foster, Hal. *Compulsive Beauty.* Cambridge, Mass.: MIT Press, 1993.

Gee, Malcolm. *Dealers, Critics, and Collectors of Modern Painting: Aspects of the Parisian Art Market Between 1910 and 1930.* New York and London: Garland Publishing, 1981.

Golan, Romy. *Modernity and Nostalgia: Art and Politics in France between the Wars.* New Haven: Yale University Press, 1995.

Green, Christopher. *Cubism and Its Enemies: Modern Movements and Reaction in French Art, 1916–1928.* New Haven: Yale University Press, 1987.

Hambourg, Maria Morris. *Photographers & Authors: A Collection of Portraits of Twentieth-Century Writers.* Northfield, Minn.: Carleton College, 1984.

Hansen, Arlen J. *Expatriate Paris: A Cultural and Literary Guide to Paris of the 1920s.* New York: Arcade Publishing, 1990.

Hemingway, Ernest. *A Moveable Feast.* New York: Charles Scribner's Sons, 1964.

Herbert, James D. *Paris 1937: Worlds on Exhibition.* Ithaca, N.Y.: Cornell University Press, 1998.

Herbert, Robert L., ed. *Modern Artists on Art.* Englewood Cliffs, N.J.: Prentice-Hall, 1964.

Jacobs, Julia. *Julien Levy: Portrait of an Art Gallery.* Cambridge, Mass.: MIT Press, 1998.

Kaplan, Patricia Ender. "Geometric Abstraction in Paris in the 1930s." Ph.D. diss., City University of New York, 1978.

Klüver, Billy, and Julie Martin. *Kiki's Paris: Artists and Lovers, 1900–1930.* New York: Harry N. Abrams, 1989.

Krauss, Rosalind. *The Originality of the Avant-Garde and Other Modernist Myths.* Cambridge, Mass.: MIT Press, 1986.

___. *La Photographique: pour une théorie des écarts.* Translated by Marc Bloch and Jean Kempf. Paris: Éditions Macula, 1990.

___. *The Optical Unconscious.* Cambridge, Mass.: MIT Press, 1993.

Larsen, Susan C. "The American Abstract Artists Group: A History and Evolution of Its Impact Upon American Art." Ph.D. diss., Evanston, Ill.: Northwestern University, 1975.

Leininger-Miller, Theresa A. *New Negro Artists in Paris: African American Painters and Sculptors in the City of Light, 1922–1934.* New Brunswick, N.J.: Rutgers University Press, 2001.

Levy, Julien. *Memoir of an Art Gallery.* New York: G. P. Putnam and Sons, 1977.

___. *Surrealism.* New York: Da Capo Press, 1995 [1936].

Levy, Silvio, ed. *Surrealism: Surrealist Visuality.* Keele: Keele University Press, 1996.

MacLeish, Archibald. *Collected Poems, 1917–1952.* Boston: Houghton Mifflin Company, 1952.

Marquis, Alice Goldfarb. *Alfred H. Barr, Jr. Missionary for the Modern.* Chicago: Contemporary Books, 1989.

Miller, Henry. *Tropic of Cancer.* New York: Modern Library, 1983.

Miller, Tyrus. *Late Modernism, Politics, Fiction, and the Arts between the World Wars.* Berkeley: University of California Press, 1999.

Platt, Susan Nayes. *Modernism in the 1920s: Interpretations of Modern Art in New York from Expressionnism to Constructivism.* Ann Arbor, Mich.: University of Michigan Research Press, 1981.

Rich, Daniel Catton, ed. *The Flow of Art: Essays and Criticism of Henry McBride.* New York: Atheneum, 1975.

Rose, Barbara. *American Art since 1900.* London: Thames and Hudson, 1967.

___. *Readings in American Art, 1900–1975.* New York: Praeger Publishers, 1977.

Rosenfeld, Paul. *Port of New York: Essays on Fourteen American Moderns*. Urbana, Ill.: University of Illinois Press, 1966 [1924].

Rotily, Jocelyne. *Artistes américains à Paris,1914–1939: des artistes en quête d'identité dans le contexte franco-américain d'une époque entre guerres et paix*. Paris: L'Harmattan, 1998.

Sawin, Martica. *Surrealism in Exile and the Beginning of the New York School*. Cambridge, Mass.: MIT Press, 1995.

Schaffner, Ingrid, and Lisa Jacobs, eds. *Julien Levy: Portrait of an Art Gallery*. Cambridge, Mass.: MIT Press, 1998.

Schleier, Merrill. *The Skyscraper in American Art, 1890–1931*. Ann Arbor, Mich.: University of Michigan Research Press, 1986.

Silver, Kenneth E. *Esprit de Corps: The Art of the Parisian Avant-Garde and the First World War, 1914–1925*. Princeton: Princeton University Press, 1989.

Tashjian, Dickran. *A Boatload of Madmen: Surrealism and the American Avant-Garde, 1920–1950*. New York: Thames & Hudson, 1995.

Tissot, Roland. *Peinture et sculpture aux USA*. Paris: Armand Colin, 1973.

———. *L'Amérique et ses peintres*. Lyon: Presses Universitaires, 1980.

Tomkins, Calvin. *Living Well Is the Best Revenge*. New York: The Viking Press, 1971.

Tritschler, Thomas Candor. *American Abstract Artists, 1937–1941*. Ph.D. diss., Philadelphia: University of Pennsylvania, 1974.

Turner, Elizabeth Hutton. *American Artists in Paris, 1919–1929*. Ann Arbor, Mich.: University of Michigan Research Press, 1988.

Wasserman, Emily. *La Pittura Americana tra le Due Guerre: dal 1910 al 1940*. Milan: Fratelli Fabbri, 1970.

Watson, Steven. *Strange Bedfellows: The First American Avant-Garde*. New York: Abbeville Press, 1993.

Weber, Nicholas Fox. *Patron Saints: Five Rebels Who Opened America to a New Art, 1928–1943*. New York: Alfred A. Knopf, 1992.

Woodall, Joanna, ed. *Portraiture: Facing the Subject*. Manchester and New York: Manchester University Press, 1997.

II. EXHIBITION CATALOGUES

Exposition d'artistes de l'école américaine. Paris: Musée National du Luxembourg, Oct.–Nov. 1919.

Paris by Americans: Exhibition of Work by Americans in Paris. New York: Downtown Gallery, Oct. 7–28, 1928.

Artistes américains de Paris. Aronson, Chil. Paris: Galerie de la Renaissance, Le Triangle, 1932.

Trois Siècles d'art aux États-Unis. Peinture, sculpture, architecture, art populaire, photographie, cinéma. Paris: Musée du Jeu de Paume, Éditions des Musées Nationaux, May 24–July 31, 1938.

Abstract Painting and Sculpture in America. New York: The Museum of Modern Art, 1951.

États-Unis. Sculpture du xxᵉ siècle. Paris: Musée Rodin, 1965.

Four Americans in Paris: The Collections of Gertrude Stein and her Family. Hightower, J.-B., and Margaret Potter. New York: The Museum of Modern Art, 1970.

The Thirties Decade: American Artists and their European Contemporaries. Omaha, Neb.: Joslyn Art Museum, 1971.

Geometric Abstraction, 1926–1942. Elderfield, John. Dallas: Dallas Museum of Fine Arts, 1972.

Post-Mondrian Abstraction in America. Pincus-Witten, Robert. Chicago: Museum of Contemporary Art, 1973.

Avant-Garde Painting and Sculpture in America 1910–1925. Wilmington, Del: Delaware Art Museum, 1975.

Modern Portraits. The Self & Others. Varnedoe, Kirk, ed. New York: Wildenstein & Co., Department of Art History and Archaeology of Columbia University, 1976.

Two Hundred Years of American Sculpture. New York: Whitney Museum of American Art, 1976.

American Abstract Artists. Tritschler, Thomas Candor. Albuquerque: Art Museum, University of New Mexico, 1977.

Modern American Painting, 1910–1940: Toward a New Perspective. Agee, William C. Houston: Museum of Fine Arts, 1977.

Paris–New York. Paris: Musée National d'Art Moderne – Centre Georges Pompidou, 1977.

Surrealism and American Art, 1931–1947. Wechsler, Jeffrey. New Brunswick, N.J.: Rutgers University Art Gallery, 1977.

Abstraction–Création, 1931–1936. Münster: Westfalisches Landesmuseum für Kunst und Kulturgeschichte, Landschaftsverban Westfalen-Lippe, 1978.

John Quinn: Patron of the Avant-Garde. Zilczer, Judith. Washington D.C.: Hirshhorn Museum, 1978.

L'Aventure de Pierre Loeb. La Galerie Pierre, 1924–1964. Paris: Musée d'Art Moderne de la Ville de Paris, 1979.

Geometric Abstraction. Van Wagner, Judith K. Lincoln, Neb.: Sheldon Art Gallery, 1979.

American Abstract Artists: The Early Years. Rose, Barbara. New York: Sid Deutsch Gallery, 1980.

Les Américains de Paris, Arnaud, Jean-Robert, and Ante Glibota. Paris: Paris Art Center, 1982.

American Artists Abroad, 1900–1950. New York: Washburn Galleries, 1982.

Abstract Painting and Sculpture in America, 1927–1944. Lane, John R., and Susan C. Larsen. Pittsburgh: Museum of Art, Carnegie Institute, 1983.

L'Amour fou: Photography and Surrealism, Krauss, Rosalind, and Jane Livingston. Washington D.C.: Corcoran Gallery, 1985.

The Circle of Montparnasse: Jewish Artists in Paris, 1905–1945. Klüver, Billy, and Julie Martin. New York: The Jewish Museum, Universe Books, 1985.

Contrasts of Forms: Geometric Abstract Art, 1910–1980. Dabrowski, Magdalena. New York: Guggenheim Museum, 1985.

Identités de Disderi au Photomaton. Paris: Centre national de la photographie, 1985.

Purism and the Spirit of Synthesis. New York: Barbara Mathes Gallery, 1986.

Staging the Self: Self-Portrait Photography, 1840s–1980s. Lingwood, James, ed. London: National Portrait Gallery, 1986.

Arp 1886–1966. Minneapolis: The Minneapolis Institute of Arts, 1987.

Domela 65 ans d'abstraction. Paris: Musée d'Art Moderne de la Ville de Paris, 1987.

L'Esprit Nouveau: Le Corbusier et l'industrie, 1920–1925. Moos, Stanislaus von. Zurich: Museum für Gestaltung; Berlin: Ernst und Sohn, 1987.

Progressive Geometric Abstraction in America, 1934–1955: Selections from the Peter B. Fischer Collection. Clinton, N.Y.: Fred. L. Emerson Gallery, Hamilton College; Chicago: Terra Museum of American Art, 1987.

New York Cubists: Works by A. E. Gallatin, George L. K. Morris, and Charles G. Shaw from the Thirties and Forties. New York: Hirschl and Adler Galleries, 1988.

Afro-American Artists in Paris. New York: Bertha and Karl Leubsdorf Art Gallery, Hunter College of the City of New York, 1989.

Over Here: Modernism, The First Exile, 1909–1919. Providence, R.I.: Bell Gallery, Brown University, 1989.

Photography in the Modern Era: European Documents and Critical Writings, 1913–1940. New York: The Metropolitan Museum of Art, 1989.

Duncan Phillips Collects: Paris between the Wars. Turner, Elizabeth Hutton. Washington D.C.: The Phillips Collection, 1991.

The Modernist Tradition in American Watercolors, 1911–1939. Kushner, Marilyn. Evanston, Ill.: Mary and Leigh Block Gallery, Northwestern University, 1991.

Paris Connections: African American Artists in Paris. San Francisco: Bomani Gallery, 1992.

The Second Wave: American Abstraction of the 1930s and 1940s, Selections from the Penny and Elton Yasuna Collection. Strickler, Susan E., and Elaine Gustafson. Worcester, Mass.: Worcester Art Museum, 1992.

Crosscurrents: Americans in Paris 1900–1940. New York: Hirschl and Adler Galleries, 1993.

Precisionism in America, 1915–1941: Reordering Reality. Stavitsky, Gail. Montclair, N.J.: The Montclair Art Museum, 1994.

Abstract Painting and Sculpture in America. New York: The Museum of Modern Art, 1995.

Face Value: American Portraits. De Salvo, Donna. Southampton, New York: The Parrish Art Museum; Paris: Flammarion, 1995.

Americans in Paris, 1921–1931: Man Ray, Gerald Murphy, Stuart Davis, Alexander Calder. Turner, Elizabeth Hutton, Elizabeth Garrity Ellis, and Guy Davenport. Washington D.C.: The Phillips Collection, 1996.

Amérique de la Dépression. Artistes engagés dans l'Amérique des années trente. Paris: Galerie-Musée de la Seita, 1996.

Les Années trente en Europe. Paris: Musée d'Art Moderne de la Ville de Paris, 1997.

Exiles <and> Emigrés, The Flight of European Artists from Hitler. Barron, Stephanie. Los Angeles: Los Angeles, County Museum of Art, 1997.

Surrealism and American Art, 1932–1949. Boca Raton, Fl.: Boca Raton Museum of Art, 1997.

The American Century: Art and Culture, 1900–1950. Haskell, Barbara. New York: Whitney Museum of American Art, W. W. Norton Press, 1999.

Ghost in the Shell: Photography and the Human Soul, 1850–2000. Cambridge, Mass.: MIT Press, Los Angeles, County Museum of Art, 1999.

Surrealism: Two Private Eyes: The Nesuhi Ertegun and Daniel Filipacchi Collections. New York: Guggenheim Museum, 1999.

L'Amérique et les Modernes. Giverny: Musée d'Art Américain Giverny, 2000.

L'École de Paris, 1904–1929, La Part de l'autre. Paris: Musée d'Art Moderne de la Ville de Paris, 2000.

L'Esprit nouveau. Paris: Réunion des Musées Nationaux, 2001.

Surrealism: Desire Unbound. Mundy, Jennifer. London: Tate Modern, Tate Publishing, 2001.

Made in USA. Chassey, Éric de, ed. Bordeaux: Musée des Beaux-Arts, Rennes: Musée des Beaux-Arts; Bordeaux: Musée des Beaux-Arts; Paris: Réunion des Musées Nationaux, 2002.

Paris, Capital of the Arts 1900–1938. London: Royal Academy of Art, 2002.

The Park Avenue Cubists: Gallatin, Morris, Frelinghuysen, and Shaw. New York: Grey Art Gallery, New York University, Ashgate Publishing, 2002.

La Révolution Surréaliste. Paris: Musée National d'Art Moderne – Centre Georges Pompidou, 2002.

III. ARTISTS AND COLLECTORS

Berenice Abbott

Abbott, Berenice. *New York in the Thirties*. New York: Dover Publications, 1939.

Berman, Avis. "The Unflinching Eye of Berenice Abbott," *Art News* 80, no. 1 (January 1981): 89.

O'Neal, Hank. *Berenice Abbott: American Photographer*. New York: McGraw-Hill Book Company, 1982.

Worswick, Clark. *Berenice Abbott, Eugene Atget*. Santa Fe, NM.: Arena Editions, 2002.

Exh. cat. *Berenice Abbott Photographer: A Modern Vision*. Van Haaften, Julia. New York: The New York Public Library, 1989.

Exh. cat. *Berenice Abbott, photographies*. Paris: Centre National de la Photographie, 1995.

Eugène Atget

Abbott, Berenice. *Eugène Atget*. Praha: SNKLU, 1963.

Atget: photographe de Paris. Paris: Henri Jonquières; New York: E. Weyhe, 1930.

Lemagny, Jean-Claude, Sylvie Aubenas, and Pierre Borhan. *Atget, le pionnier*. Paris: Marval. 2000.

Szarowski, John. *Atget*. New York: Museum of Modern Art, 2000.

Szarkowski, Otto. "Atget en Amérique." In *Photographies*, 1986, 82–86.

Exh. cat. *Eugène Atget: 1857–1927*. Borcoman, James. Ottawa: Galerie Nationale du Canada, 1984.

Exh. cat. *Eugène Atget, itinéraires parisiens*. Paris: Musée Carnavalet, Paris Musées, 1999.

Charles Biederman

Bann, Stephen. "The Centrality of Charles Biederman." *Studio International* 178 (Sept. 1969): 71–74.

Biederman, Charles. *Art as the Evolution of Visual Knowledge*. Red Wing, Minn.: Art History Publishers, 1948.

Denny, Robin. "Charles Biederman: From the Actual to the Sublime." *Studio International* 178 (Sept. 1969): 65–67.

Hedberg, Gregory. "Two Biedermans for Minneapolis." *Minneapolis Institute of Arts Bulletin* 61 (1974): 52–53.

Hill, Anthony. "The Climate of Biederman." *Studio International* 178 (Sept. 1969): 68–70.

Kuspit, Donald B. "Charles Biederman's Abstract Analogues for Nature." *Art in America* 65 (May–June 1977): 80–83.

Lynton, Norbert. "Biederman." *Chroniques de l'Art vivant* 8 (February 1970): 15.

Martin, Kenneth. "Notes on Biederman." *Studio International* 178 (Sept. 1969): 60–65.

Sjöberg, Leif. "Biederman Structurism: Its Influences." *Art International* 10 (1966): 32–35.

Exh. cat. *Charles Biederman*. Thompson, Orrel. Rochester: Minnesota Art Center, 1967.

Exh. cat. *Charles Biederman: A Retrospective with Special Emphasis on the Structurist Works of 1936–1969*. Denny, Robyn, and Jan Van der Marck. London: Hayward Gallery, 1969.

Exh. cat. *Charles Biederman: A Retrospective*. Sjöberg, Leif, and Gregory Hedberg, eds. Minneapolis: Minneapolis Institute of Arts, 1976.

Exh. cat. *Charles Biederman: Selected Works, 1936–1984*. New York: Grace Borgenicht Gallery, 1985.

Ilya Bolotowsky

Larsen, Susan C. "Going Abstract in the Thirties: An Interview with Ilya Bolotowsky." *Art in America* 64 (Sept.–Oct. 1976): 70–79.

Rosenthal, Deborah. *Ilya Bolotowsky.* New York: Harry N. Abrams, 1985.

Rosenthal, Deborah. "Ilya Bolotowsky." *Arts* 52 (March 1978): 2.

Exh. cat. *Ilya Bolotowsky.* New York: Guggenheim Museum, 1974.

Exh. cat. *Bolotowsky: Paintings & Comments.* New York: Grace Borgenicht Gallery, 1974.

Patrick Henry Bruce

"Early American Modern: Patrick Henry Bruce." *Apollo* 110, no. 209 (July 1979): 68–69.

"Peinture/Nature Morte." *Carnegie Magazine* 54, pt. 8 (Oct. 1980): 2–3.

Agee, William C. "Patrick Henry Bruce: A Major American Artist of Early Modernism." *Arts in Virginia* 17, pt. 3 (spring 1977): 12–32.

Agee, William C. and Barbara Rose. "The Search for Patrick Henry Bruce." *Artnews* 78, pt. 6 (summer 1979): 72–75.

Seckel, H. "La Donation Seuphor." *Cahiers du MNAM* 1 (July–Sept. 1979): 136–159.

Exh. cat. *Patrick Henry Bruce: American Modernist. A Catalogue Raisonné.* Agee, William C., and Barbara Rose. New York: Museum of Modern Art, 1979.

Alexander Calder

Calder, Alexander. "Comment réaliser l'art?" *Abstraction-Création* 1 (1931): 6.

___. "Un Mobile." *Abstraction-Création* 2 (1933).

___. *An Autobiography with Pictures.* New York: Pantheon Books, 1966.

Jakovsky, Anatole. "Alexandre Calder." *Cahiers d'Art* 3, no. 5–6 (1933): 244–246.

Marter, Joan M. *Alexander Calder.* Cambridge: Cambridge University Press, 1991.

___. "Alexander Calder: Ambitious Young Sculptor of the 1930s." *Archives of American Art Journal* 16, no. 1 (1976): 2–8.

___. "Alexander Calder: Cosmic Imagery and the Use of Scientific Instruments." *Arts Magazine* 53, no. 2 (Oct. 1978): 108–113.

Masson, André. "L'atelier de Calder." *Cahiers d'Art* 24, no. 2 (1949): 274–275.

Pierre, Arnauld. "Motion and Reality in Calder's Work." *Louisiana Review* 36, no. 1 (Sept. 1995): 15.

___. "Mouvement et réalité dans l'œuvre de Calder: une interprétation." *Cahiers du MNAM* 47 (spring 1994): 56–75.

Sperling, L. Joy. "Calder in Paris: *The Circus* and Surrealism." *Archives of American Art Journal* 28, no. 2 (1988): 16–29.

Exh. cat. *Alexander Calder, Fernand Léger.* Amsterdam: Stedelijk Museum, July–August 1947.

Exh. cat. *Alexander Calder: Sculpture of the Nineteen Thirties.* Marshall, Richard. New York: Whitney Museum of American Art, 1987.

Exh. cat. *Alexander Calder, 1898–1976.* July 10–Oct. 6, 1996. Musée d'Art Moderne de la Ville de Paris, 1996.

Exh. cat. *Alexander Calder 1898–1976.* Prather, Marla, ed. Washington D.C.: National Gallery of Art, 1998.

Joseph Cornell

Cornell, Joseph. *Joseph Cornell's Theater of the Mind: Selected Diaries, Letters, and Files.* New York: Thames and Hudson, 1993.

Disjkra, Tashjian. *Joseph Cornell's Gifts of Desire.* Miami Beach: Grassfield Press, 1992.

Hauptman, Jodi. *Joseph Cornell: Stargazing in the Cinema.* New Haven: Yale University Press, 1999.

Waldman, Diane. *Joseph Cornell: Master of Dreams.* New York: Harry N. Abrams, 2002.

Exh. cat. *Joseph Cornell-Marcel Duchamp . . . in Resonance.* Houston: The Menil Collection; Philadelphia: Philadelphia Museum of Art, 1998.

Stuart Davis

Hills, Patricia. *Stuart Davis.* New York: Harry N. Abrams, 1996.

Kashur, Lewis. *Stuart Davis: An American in Paris.* New York: Whitney Museum of American Art at Philip Morris, 1987.

Kelder, Diane, ed. *Stuart Davis.* New York: Praeger Publishers, 1971.

Wilkin, Karen. *Stuart Davis.* New York: Abbeville Press, 1987.

Exh. cat. *Stuart Davis.* Villefosse, René Héron de. Paris: Musée d'Art Moderne de la Ville de Paris, 1966.

Exh. cat. *Stuart Davis: Art and Art Theory.* Lane, John R. Brooklyn: Brooklyn Museum, 1978.

Exh. cat. *Stuart Davis: Graphic Work and Related Paintings with a Catalogue Raisonné of the Prints.* Myers, Jane, ed. Fort Worth, Texas: Amon Carter Museum, 1986.

Exh. cat. *Stuart Davis: American Painter.* Sims, Lowery Stokes. New York: Metropolitan Museum, 1991.

Exh. cat. *Stuart Davis,* Rylands, Philip, ed. Venice: Collection Peggy Guggenheim; Milan: Electa, 1997.

Exh. cat. *Stuart Davis: Art and Theory, 1920–31.* Kelder, Diane. New York: Pierpont Morgan Library, 2002.

Charles Demuth

Allara, Pamela E. "Charles Demuth: Always a Seeker." *Arts Magazine* 50 (June 1976): 86–89.

Breslin, James E. " William Carlos Williams and Charles Demuth: Cross-Fertilization in the Arts." *Journal of Modern Literature* 6 (April 1977): 248–63.

Davidson, Abraham A. "Charles Demuth: Stylistic Developments." *Bulletin of Rhode Island School of Design* 54 (March 1968): 9–16.

___. "Demuth's Poster Portraits." *Artforum* 17 (Nov. 1978): 54–57.

Demuth, Charles. *Letters of Charles Demuth: American Artist, 1883–1935.* Philadelphia: Temple University Press, 2000.

Eiseman, Alvord L. *Charles Demuth.* New York: Watson-Guptill, 1982.

___. "Charles Demuth's Paintings of Lancaster Architecture: New Discoveries and Observations." *American Magazine* 61 (1987): 24–29.

Farnham, Emily E. *Charles Demuth: Behind the Laughing Mask.* Norman, Oklahoma: University of Oklahoma Press, 1971.

Gallatin, A. E. *Charles Demuth.* New York: William Edwin Rudge, 1927.

Koskovich, Gerard. "A Gay American Modernist: Homosexuality in the Life and Art of Charles Demuth." *The Advocate* (June 25, 1985).

Marling, K. A. "*My Egypt:* The Irony of the American Dream." *Winterthur Port* 15 (1980): 25–39.

Plous, Phyllis. "Charles Demuth and the Twenties." In *Charles Demuth: The Mechanical Encrusted on the Living.* Santa Barbara and Berkeley: University of California, 1971.

Weinberg, Jonathan. "Demuth and Difference." *Art in America* 76, no. 4 (April 1988): 188–95, 221, 223.

Weinberg, Jonathan. *Speaking for Vice: Homosexuality in the Art of Charles Demuth, Marsden Hartley and the First American Avant-Garde*. New Haven: Yale University Press, 1993.

Exh. cat. *Charles Demuth of Lancaster*. Fahlman, Betsy. Philadelphia: Philadelphia Museum of Art, 1983.

Exh. cat. *Charles Demuth*. Haskell, Barbara. New York: Whitney Museum of American Art with Abrams, 1987.

Exh. cat. *Charles Demuth: Poster Portraits, 1923–1929*. Frank, Robin Jaffee. New Haven: Yale University Art Gallery, 1994.

Marcel Duchamp

Bonk, Ecke. *Marcel Duchamp: The Box in a Valise*. New York: Rizzoli, 1989.

Buskirk, Martha, and Nixon Mignon. *The Duchamp Effect*. Cambridge: MIT Press, 1996.

Camfield, William A. *Marcel Duchamp: Fountain*. Houston: The Menil Collection, 1989.

Duchamp, Marcel. *Affectionately, Marcel: The Selected Correspondence of Marcel Duchamp*. New York: Art Publishers, 2000.

Fleuriet, Isabelle. "Marcel Duchamp aux États-Unis, Comment Jasper Johns a redécouvert Marcel Duchamp." Ph.D. diss., Paris: Université de Paris 1.

Gough-Cooper, Jennifer, and Jacques Caumont. *Ephemerides on and about Marcel Duchamp and Rrose Sélavy*. Cambridge, Mass: MIT Press.

Hulten, Pontus. *Marcel Duchamp: Work and Life*. Cambridge, Mass.: MIT Press, 1993.

Joselit, David. *Infinite Regress: Marcel Duchamp, 1910–1941*. Cambridge, Mass.: MIT Press, 1998.

Masheck, Joseph. *Marcel Duchamp in Perspective*. Cambridge, Mass.: Da Capo Press, 2002.

Mileaf, Janine A. "From Fountain to Fetish: Duchamp, Man Ray, Breton and Objects, 1917–1936." Ph.D. diss., Philadelphia: University of Pennsylvania, 1999.

Roché, Henri-Pierre. *Victor: Marcel Duchamp*. Paris: Musée National d'Art Moderne – Centre Georges Pompidou, 1977.

Sanouillet, Michel. *Duchamp du signe, écrits*. Paris: Flammarion, 1994.

Tomkins, Calvin. *Duchamp: A Biography*. New York: Henry Holt and Co., 1996.

Exh. cat. *Joseph Cornell-Marcel Duchamp . . . in Resonance*. Houston: The Menil Collection. Philadelphia: Philadelphia Museum of Art, 1998.

William Einstein

William Einstein, dessins, gouaches, pastels, peintures. Auction. Paris: Hôtel Drouot. May 19, 1970. Paris: J.-C. Bellier, 1970.

Exh. cat. *William Einstein: Picardie Venise*. Paris: Galerie Barbizon, 1958.

Exh. cat. *William Einstein*. Amiens: Maison de la Culture, 1972.

John Ferren

Gibson, Ann, and Irving Sandler. *The Abstract Spirit John Ferren, 1905–1970*. East Hampton, N.Y.: Pollock Krasner Home and Study Center, 1993.

Exh. cat. *Ferren: A Retrospective*. Bailey, Craig. New York: The Graduate School and University Center of the City University of New York, 1979.

Exh. cat. *John Ferren, 1905–1970: Paintings, Watercolors and Engravings of the 1930s*. New York: Am. Sachs, 1982.

Exh. cat. *John Ferren, The Formative Years: The 1930's in Paris and Spain*. Gibson, Ann, and Irving Sandler. East Hampton, N.Y.: Pollock-Krasner Home and Study Center; SUNY at Stony Brook; The Godwin-Ternbach Museum; Queens College, City University of New York, 1993.

Albert Eugene Gallatin

"The A. E. Gallatin Collection: An Early Adventure in Modern Art." *Philadelphia Museum of Art Bulletin* 89, no. 379–80 (winter–spring 1994): 3–47.

Gallatin, Albert Eugene. "Introduction." *American Abstract Artists* (March 1938): n.p.

Gallatin, Albert Eugene. "Abstract Painting and the Museum of Living Art." *Plastique* 3 (spring 1938). In *Plastique no 1–5 1937–1939*. New York: Arno Press, 1969, 6–11.

Harnoncourt, Anne d'. "A. E. Gallatin and the Arensbergs." *Apollo* 149 (July 1974): 52–61.

Larsen, Susan C. "Albert Gallatin: The Park Avenue Cubist Who Went Downtown." *Artnews* 77 (December 1978): 80–82.

Lederman, Mildred E. "Albert Eugene Gallatin and his Contributions to American Twentieth-Century Art." Ph.D. diss., New York: New York University, 1976.

Rosenthal, Deborah. "What Gallatin Collected." *Arts Magazine* 53, pt. 4 (December 1978): 120–121.

Shaw, Charles G. "Albert Eugene Gallatin: A Reminiscence." *Princeton University Library Chronicle* 14 (spring 1953): 135–140.

Stavitsky, Gail. "New York Cubists: Works by A. E. Gallatin, George L. K. Morris, and Charles Shaw." *Arts Magazine* 62 (April 1988).

Stavitsky, Gail. "The Development, Institutionalization and Impact of the A. E. Gallatin Collection of Modern Art." Ph.D. diss., New York: New York University, 1990.

———. "A. E. Gallatin and Robert Delaunay." *Sources: Notes in the History of Art* 11, pt. 3–4 (spring–summer 1992).

———. "A Landmark Exhibition: Five Contemporary American Concretionists, March 1936." *Archives of American Art Journal* 33, pt. 2 (1993): 2–10.

———. "A. E. Gallatin's Gallery and Museum of Living Art, 1927–1943." *American Art* 7, pt. 2 (spring 1993): 47–63.

———. "The A. E. Gallatin Collection: An Early Adventure in Modern Art." *Philadelphia Museum Art Bulletin* 89, no. 379–380 (winter–spring 1994): 3–47.

Exh. cat. Gallatin, Albert Eugene. *Gallery of Living Art: A. E. Gallatin Collection*. New York: New York University, 1933.

Exh. cat. *Paintings by Gallatin*. New York: Wittenborn, Schultz, 1948.

Exh. cat. *A. E. Gallatin Collection*. Philadelphia: Philadelphia Museum of Art, 1954.

Exh. cat. *American Artists in the A. E. Gallatin Collection*. New York: Washburn Gallery, 1981.

Exh. cat. *Albert Eugene Gallatin and His Circle*. Balken, Debra Bricker. University of Miami, The Lowe Art Museum; Pittsfield, Mass.: The Berkshire Museum, 1986.

Exh. cat. *New York Cubists: Works by A. E. Gallatin, George L. K. Morris, and Charles G. Shaw from the Thirties and Forties*. Dreishspoon, Douglas. New York: Hirschl & Adler Galleries, 1988.

Exh. cat. *The Park Avenue Cubists: Gallatin, Morris, Frelinghuysen and Shaw*. Balken, Debra Bricker, and Robert S. Lubar. New York: Grey Art Gallery, New York University, 2002.

Fritz Glarner

Ashton, Dore. "Fritz Glarner." *Art International* 7 (January 25, 1963) 48–54.

Krasne, Belle. "Fifty-Seventh Street in Review: Fritz Glarner." *Art Digest* 25 (February 15, 1951): 20.

Weinberg-Staber, Margit. *Fritz Glarner*. Zurich: ABC Verlag, 1976.

Exh. cat. *Fritz Glarner*. Berne: Kunsthalle, 1972.

Exh. cat. *Fritz Glarner*. Weinberg-Staber, Margit. Lugano: Museo Cantonale d'Arte, 1993.

John Graham

Graham, John D. *System and Dialectics of Art*. Baltimore: Books on Demand, 1971.

Herrera, Hayden. "Le Feu ardent: John Graham's Journal." *Archives of American Art Journal* 14, no. 2 (1974): 6–17.

Exh. cat. *John Graham: Artist and Avatar*. Johnson, Linda L. Washington D.C.: The Phillips Collection, 1987.

Balcomb Greene

Hale, Robert Beverley. *The Art of Balcomb Greene*. New York: Horizon Press, 1977.

Exh. cat. Baur, John I. H. *Balcomb Greene*. New York: American Federation of the Arts, 1961.

Exh. cat. *Balcomb Greene: A Retrospective 1937–1978*. East Hampton, N.Y.: Guild Hall, 1978.

Gertrude Greene

Moss, Jacqueline. "The Constructions of Gertrude Greene: The 1930s and 1940s." Master's thesis, New York: Queens College, City University of New York, 1980.

___. "Gertrude Greene: Constructions of the 1930s and 1940s." *Arts* 55 (April 1981): 120–127.

Exh. cat. *Gertrude Greene: Constructions, Collages, Paintings*. Hyman, Linda. New York: ACA Galleries, 1981.

Peggy Guggenheim

Gill, Anton. *Peggy Guggenheim: The Life of an Art Addict*. London: Harper Collins, 2001.

Guggenheim, Peggy. *Confessions of an Art Addict*. Hopewell, NJ: Ecco Press, 1997.

___. *Out of this Century: The Informal Memoirs of Peggy Guggenheim*. New York: Dial Press, 1946.

Weld, Jacqueline Bograd. *Peggy, the Wayward Guggenheim*. New York: Dutton, 1986.

Exh. cat. *Peggy Guggenheim: A Celebration*. Vail, Karole P. B. New York: Guggenheim Museum, 1998.

Stanley William Hayter

Exh. cat. *Atelier 17. 1927 Paris New-York 1950*. Reynolds, Graham. Paris: Galerie de Seine, 1981.

Exh. cat. *Hayter e l'Atelier 17*. Trassari, Filippetto Giuseppe, and Carlo Esposito, Carlo, eds. Rome: Calcographie nationale; Milan: Electa, 1990.

Exh. cat. *Hayter et l'atelier 17*. Gravelines: Musée du Dessin et de l'estampe, 1993.

Jean Hélion

Cousseau, Henry Claude. *Hélion*. Paris: Éditions du Regard, 1992.

Hélion, Jean. *Journal d'un peintre*. Paris: Éditions Maeght, 1992.

___. *Mémoires de la chambre jaune*. Paris: École Nationale Supérieure des Beaux-Arts, 1994.

___. *À perte de vue* suivie *Des choses revues*. Paris: IMEC, 1996.

___. *Lettres d'Amérique*. Correspondence with Raymond Queneau 1934–1967. Paris: IMEC, 1996.

Schipper, Merle. "Jean Hélion: The Abstract Years, 1929–1939." Ph.D. diss., Los Angeles: University of California, 1974.

Exh. cat. *Jean Hélion*. Ottinger, Didier. Paris: Centre Georges Pompidou, 1992.

Carl Holty

Holty, Carl. "Mondrian in New York: A Memoir." *Arts* 31 (Sept. 1957): 17–21.

"The Mechanics of Creativity of a Painter: A Memoir." *Leonardo* 1 (July 1968): 243–252.

Rembert, Virginia Pitts. "Carl Holty." *Arts* 55 (Dec. 1980): 11.

Exh. cat. Kaplan, Patricia. *Carl Holty/Fifty Years: A Retrospective Exhibition*. New York: The City University of New York, 1972.

Exh. cat. *Carl Holty*. New York: Andrew Crispo Gallery, 1974.

Exh. cat. *Carl Holty: The World Seen and Sensed*. Danoff, I. Michael. Milwaukee: Milwaukee Art Museum, 1980.

Le Corbusier, Charles-Édouard Jeanneret

Curtis, William J. R. *Le Corbusier: Ideas and Forms*. New York: Rizzoli, 1986.

Frampton, Kenneth. "Le Corbusier and *L'Esprit Nouveau*." *Oppositions* 15–16 (winter–spring 1979): 13–58.

Jeanneret, Charles-Édouard, and Amédée Ozenfant. *Après le cubisme*. Paris: Éditions des Commentaires, 1918.

Joly, Pierre. *Le Corbusier à Paris*. Lyon: La Manufacture; Paris: Délégation à l'Action Artistique de la Ville de Paris, 1987.

Turner, Paul Venable. *La Formation de Le Corbusier, idéalisme et mouvement moderne*. Paris: Macula, 1987.

Fernand Léger

Derouet, Christian, ed. *Fernand Léger, une correspondance poste restante, Lettres à Simone, 1931–1941, Les Cahiers du MNAM*. Hors-série/Archives, Paris: Musée National d'Art Moderne – Centre Georges Pompidou, 1997.

___. *Léger*. Collection Le Cabinet des dessins. Paris: Flammarion, 1997.

Fry, Edward F., ed. *Functions of Painting by Fernand Léger*. New York: The Viking Press, 1973.

Green, Christopher. *Léger and the Avant-Garde*. New Haven: Yale University Press, 1976.

Léger, Fernand. *Fonctions de la peinture*. Paris: Gallimard, 1997.

Léger, Fernand. *Mes voyages*. Paris: L'École des Loisirs, 1997 [1960].

Exh. cat. *Léger and Purist Paris*. Golding, John, and Christopher Green. London: Tate Gallery, 1970.

Exh. cat. *Fernand Léger: la poésie de l'objet*. Paris: Musée National d'Art Moderne – Centre Georges Pompidou, 1981.

Exh. cat. *Fernand Léger et l'esprit moderne: une alternative d'avant-garde à l'art non-objectif*. Fabre, Gladys, ed. Paris: Musée d'Art Moderne de la Ville de Paris, 1982.

Exh. cat. *Fernand Léger: le rythme de la vie moderne, 1911–1924*. Kosinski, Dorothy, ed. Translated from the German. Basel: Kunstmuseum; Paris: Flammarion, 1994.

Exh. cat. *Fernand Léger*. Derouet, Christian, and Claude Laugier. Paris: Musée National d'Art Moderne – Centre Georges Pompidou, 1997.

Exh. cat. *Fernand Léger*. Lanchner, Carolyn, ed. New York: Museum of Modern Art, 1998.

Man Ray

Amaya, Mario. "My Man Ray: Interview with Lee Miller." *Art in America* 63, no. 3 (May–June 1975): 57.

Baldwin, Neil. *Man Ray, American Artist.* New York: Clarkson N. Potter, 1988.

Baum, Timothy. *Man Ray's Paris Portraits, 1921–39.* Washington D.C.: Middendorf Gallery, 1989.

Bouhours, Jean-Michel, and Patrick de Haas. *Man Ray, directeur du mauvais movies.* Paris: Musée National d'Art Moderne – Centre Georges Pompidou, 1997.

Foresta, Merry, ed. *Perpetual Motif: The Art of Man Ray.* New York: Abbeville Press, 1988.

Gruber, Fritz L.. *Man Ray Portraits.* Gütersloh: Sigbert Mohn Verlag, 1963.

Gunther, Thomas Michael. "Man Ray and Co.: la fabrication d'un buste." *Colloque Atget: Actes du colloque.* June 14–15, 1985.

Hopkins, David. "Men Before the Mirror: Duchamp, Man Ray and Masculinity." *Art History* 21, no. 3 (Sept. 1998): 303–323.

Janus. *Man Ray: The Photographic Image.* Woodbury, New York: Barron's, 1980.

Klüver, Billy, and Julie Martin. *Man Ray.* Paris: Gallimard, 1989.

Man Ray, André Breton, Marcel Duchamp, *et al. Man Ray Photographies 1920–1934 Paris.* Hartford, Conn.: James Thrall Soby, 1934.

Man Ray, and Paul Eluard. *Les Mains libres, dessins illustrés par les poèmes de Paul Eluard.* Paris: Éditions Jeanne Bucher, 1937.

Man Ray. *Self Portrait.* Boston: Little, Brown, and Co., 1988 [1963].

Man Ray. Paris: Gallimard, 1989.

Miller, Lee. "I Worked with Man Ray." *Lilliput* 9 (Oct. 1941): 315.

Ribemont-Dessaignes, George. *Man Ray.* Collection Peintres Nouveaux. Paris: Gallimard, 1924.

Exh. cat. *Exposition Dada Man Ray.* Dec. 3–31, 1921. Paris: Librairie Six, 1921.

Exh. cat. *Man Ray, rétrospective 1912–1976.* Perlein, Gilbert, and Daniela Palazzoli. Nice: Musée d'Art moderne et d'art contemporain, 1997.

Exh. cat. *Man Ray, la photographie à l'envers.* Alain Sayag, ed., and Emmanuelle de l'Écotais. Paris: Galeries nationales du Grand Palais; Paris: Seuil, Paris: Musée National d'Art Moderne – Centre Georges Pompidou, 1998.

Exh. cat. *Paris as Gameboard: Man Ray's Atgets.* Laxton, Susan. New York: Miriam and Ira D. Wallach Art Gallery, Columbia University, 2002.

Jan Matulka

Clark, Carroll S., and Heskett, Louis, eds. *Jan Matulka 1890–1972.* Washington D.C.: Smithsonian Institution Press, 1980.

Thistlethwaite, Mark. "Forum: Jan Matulka's Cubist Abstraction." *Drawing* 14, pt. 4 (Nov.–Dec. 1992): 80–81.

Exh. cat. *Jan Matulka 1890–1972.* Foresta, Merry, and Patterson Sims. New York: Whitney Museum of American Art, Washington D.C., Smithsonian Institution Press, 1980.

Exh. cat. *Jan Matulka: Paintings of the 1920s and 1930s.* New York: Robert Schoelkopf Gallery, 1988.

Jacques Mauny

Derouet, Christian. "Vue de New York par Jacques Mauny." *Revue du Louvre* 4 (1987): 297–300.

Gallatin, Albert Eugene. *Jacques Mauny.* Paris: Éditions ces Quatre-Chemins, 1928.

___. "Jacques Mauny." *La Renaissance de l'art français* 9 (Sept. 1927): 412–416.

Gimpel, René. *Journal d'un collectionneur, marchand de tableaux.* Paris: Calmann-Lévy, 1963.

Giraudoux, Jean. *Amica America.* Paris: Éditions Paul-Émile-Frères, 1928.

Mauny, Jacques. "New York 1926." *L'Art vivant* 26 (Jan. 15, 1926): 53–58.

___. "Paris-New-York 1927." *L'Art vivant* 64 (Aug. 15, 1927): 636–639.

Exh. cat. *Réalistes des années 20, peintures de Yves Alix, Alfred Courmes, Jean Fautrier, Édouard Goerg, Marcel Gromaire, Jean Lurçat, Jacques Mauny.* Lefèvre, Sophie, and Derouet, Christian. Paris: Musée-Galerie de la Seita, 1998.

Lee Miller

Calvocoressi, Richard. *Lee Miller: portraits d'une vie.* Paris: La Martinière, 2002.

Roland Penrose. *Lee Miller: The Surrealist and the Photographer.* Edinburgh: Trustees of the National Galleries of Scotland, 2001.

Penrose, Roland. *The Lives of Lee Miller.* New York: Holt. Rinehart and Winston, 1985.

Exh. cat. *Lee Miller Photographer.* Livingstone, Jane. New York: Thames and Hudson, 1989.

Piet Mondrian

Cooper, Harry. *Mondrian: The Transatlantic Paintings.* New Haven: Yale University Press, 2001.

Joosten, Joop M. *Piet Mondrian, catalogue raisonné.* Paris: Éditions Cercle d'Art, 1998.

Mondrian, Piet. *Le Néo-plasticisme.* Paris: Éditions L'Effort Moderne, 1920.

Postma, Frans, and Cees Boekraad. *26, rue du Départ: Mondrian's Studio in Paris, 1921–1936.* Berlin: Ernst und Sohn, 1995.

Rembert, Virginia Pitts. "Mondrian: America and American Painting." Ph.D. diss., New York: Columbia University, 1970.

Schapiro, Meyer. *Mondrian: On the Humanity of Abstract Painting.* New York: George Braziller, 1995.

Exh. cat. *Mondrian, De Stijl and Their Impact.* Hammacher, A. M. New York: Marlborough-Gerson Gallery, 1964.

Exh. cat. *Mondrian and Neo-Plasticism in America.* Troy, Nancy J. New Haven: Yale University Art Gallery, 1979.

George L. K. Morris

Cikovski, Nicolai. "Notes and Footnotes on a Painting by George L. K. Morris." *University of New Mexico Art Museum Bulletin* 10 (1976–1977): 3–10.

Jackson, Ward. "George L. K. Morris: Forty Years of Abstract Art." *Art Journal* 32 (winter 1972–1973): 150–156.

Langhorne, Elizabeth. "George L. K. Morris: Critic." *Art Criticism* 1, no. 4 (1981): 20–39.

Lorenz, Melinda A. *George L. K. Morris: Artist and Critic.* Ann Arbor, Mich.: University of Michigan Research Press, 1982.

Stross, Dorian H. "George L. K. Morris, Artist and Advocate of Abstract Art or How an American Millionaire Found Meaning Through Modern Art." Master's thesis, Detroit, Mich.: Wayne State University, 1976.

Exh. cat. *George L. K. Morris: A Retrospective Exhibition of Paintings and Sculpture.* Washington D.C.: The Corcoran Gallery of Art, 1965.

Exh. cat. *George L. K. Morris: Abstract Art of the 1930s.* Ashton, Dore. New York: Hirschl and Adler Galleries, 1974.

Exh. cat. *Suzy Frelinghuysen & George L. K. Morris: American Abstract Artists Aspects of Their Work and Collection.* Balken, Deborah Bricker, and Deborah Menaker Rothschild. Williamstown, Mass.: Williams College Museum of Art, 1992.

Gerald Murphy

Agee, W. C. "Gerald Murphy Painter: Recent Discoveries, New Observations." *Arts Magazine* 59, no. 9 (May 1985): 78–80.

Conrad, B. "A Legend and an Eye." *Horizon* 26, pt. 4 (June 1983): 13–20.

Donnelly, Honoria Murphy, and Richard N. Billings. *Sara and Gerald: Villa America and After*. New York: Times Books, 1982.

Dos Passos, John. *The Best Times: An Informal Memoir*. New York: New American Library, 1966.

Herrara, Hayden. "Gerald Murphy: An Amurikin in Paris." *Art in America* 62, no. 5 (Sept.–Oct. 1974): 76–79.

Miller, Linda Patterson. *Letters from the Lost Generation: Gerald and Sara Murphy and Friends*. New Brunswick, N.J., 1991.

Pennington, Ellis Curtis. *Gerald Murphy: Toward an Understanding of His Art and Inspiration*. Washington D.C.: Board of Governors of the Federal Reserve System, 1983.

Tomkins, Calvin. *Living Well is the Best Revenge*. New York: The Modern Library, 1998.

Vaill, Amanda. *Everybody Was So Young: Gerald and Sara Murphy, A Lost Generation Love Story*. Boston: Houghton Mifflin, 1998.

Winkfield, Trevor. "From a Friend of Gerald Murphy." *Modern Painters* 11, no. 1 (spring 1998).

Exh. cat. *The Paintings of Gerald Murphy*. MacLeish, Archibald, and William Rubin. New York: Museum of Modern Art, 1974.

Exh. cat. *The Paintings of Gerald Murphy*. Rubin, William. New York: The Museum of Modern Art, 1979.

Exh. cat. *An American Painter in Paris: Gerald Murphy*. Stewart, Rick. Dallas Museum of Fine Arts, 1986.

Isamu Noguchi

Altshuler, Bruce. *Isamu Noguchi*. New York: Abbeville Press, 1994.

___. "Isamu Noguchi: Early Drawings from Paris and Beijing." *Drawing* 16, pt. 4 (Nov.–Dec. 1994): 73–77.

Apostolos-Cappadona, Diane, and Bruce Altshuler, eds. *Isamu Noguchi: Essays and Conversations*. New York: Harry N. Abrams, 1994.

Grove, Nancy, and Diane Botnick. *The Sculpture of Noguchi, 1924–1979*. New York: Garland Press, 1982.

Exh. cat. *Isamu Noguchi*. Tokyo: The National Museum of Modern Art, 1992.

Exh. cat. *Isamu Noguchi: Early Abstraction*. New York: Whitney Museum of American Art; Portland, Maine: Portland Museum of Art, 1994.

Exh. cat. *Isamu Noguchi: Sculptural Design*. Weil am Rhein: Vitra Design Museum, 2002.

Amédée Ozenfant

Ball, Susan L. *Ozenfant and Purism: The Evolution of a Style, 1915–1930*. Ann Arbor, Mich.: University of Michigan Research Press, 1981.

Ducros, Françoise. *Amédée Ozenfant*. Paris: Éditions du Cercle d'Art, 2002.

Golding, John. *Ozenfant*. New York: Knoedler & Co., 1973.

Ozenfant, Amédée. *Mémoires 1886–1962*. Paris: Seghers, 1968.

___. *Après le cubisme*. Paris: Altamira, 1999.

Ozenfant, Amédée and Charles-Édouard Jeanneret. *Après le cubisme*. Paris: Éditions des Commentaires, 1918.

Exh. cat. *Amédée Ozenfant*. Lemoine, Serge. Edited by Françoise Ducros. Saint-Quentin: Musée Antoine Lécuyer, 1985.

Exh. cat. *L'Esprit nouveau: Purism in Paris, 1918–1925*. Eliel, Carol S. Los Angeles: Los Angeles County Museum of Art; New York: Harry N. Abrams, 2001.

Mary Reynolds

Godlewski, Susan Glover. "Warm Ashes: The Life and Career of Mary Reynolds." In *Mary Reynolds and the Spirit of Surrealism*. The Art Institute of Chicago Museum Studies 22, 2, 1996: 102–115.

Exh. cat. *Surrealism and Its Affinities: The Mary Reynolds Collection*. Edwards, Hugh, ed. Chicago: Art Institute of Chicago, 1956.

Henri-Pierre Roché

Bonduelle Reliquet, Scarlett. *Henri-Pierre Roché collectionneur*. Master's thesis, Université Paris IV, 1997.

Kay Sage

Miller, Stephen R. "The Surrealist Imagery of Kay Sage." *Art International* 26 (Sept.–Oct. 1983): 32–47, 54–56.

Suther, Judith D. *A House of Her Own: Kay Sage, Solitary Surrealist*. Lincoln, Neb.: University of Nebraska Press, 1997.

Vieulle, Chantal. *Kay Sage ou le surréalisme américain, biographie 1898–1963*. Paris: Complicités, 1995.

Exh. cat. *Kay Sage, 1898–1963*. Ithaca, N.Y.: Herbert F. Johnson Museum of Art, Cornell University, 1977.

Charles G. Shaw

Larsen, Susan C. "Through the Looking Glass with Charles Shaw." *Arts Magazine* 51 (Dec. 1976): 80–82.

Pennington, Buck. "The 'Floating World' in the Twenties: The Jazz Age and Charles Green Shaw." *Archives of American Art Journal* 20 no. 4, (1980): 17–24.

Exh. cat. *Charles Shaw: Works from 1935 to 1942*. New York: Washburn Gallery, 1976.

Exh. cat. *Charles G. Shaw, 1892–1974*. New York: Washburn Gallery, 1982.

Exh. cat. *Montages by Charles Shaw*. New York: Washburn Gallery, 1983.

Exh. cat. *Charles G. Shaw, 1892–1974: Abstractions of the Thirties*. New York: Richard York Gallery, 1987.

Edward Steichen

Homer, William Inness. "Edward Steichen as Painter and Photographer, 1897–1908." *American Art Journal* 6 (Nov. 1974): 45–55.

Niven, Penelope. *Steichen: A Biography*. New York: Clarkson Potter, 1997.

Steichen's Legacy: Photographs, 1895–1973. New York: Alfred A. Knopf, 2000.

Exh. cat. *Edward Steichen: The Portraits*. Peterson, Christian A. San Francisco: Art Museum Association of America, 1984.

Exh. cat. *The Paintings of Edward Steichen*. Cohen di Pietro, Anne. Huntington, N.Y.: The Heckscher Museum, 1985.

Exh. cat. *From Tonalism to Modernism: The Paintings of Edward J. Steichen*. Goley, Mary Anne. Washington D.C.: Federal Reserve System, 1988.

Gertrude Stein

Bridgman, Richard. *Gertrude Stein in Pieces*. New York: Oxford University Press, 1970.

Burns, Edward. *The Letters of Gertrude Stein and Carl Van Vechten 1913–1946*. New York: Columbia University Press, 1986.

Mellow, James R. *Charmed Circle: Gertrude Stein and Company*. New York: Praeger Publishers, 1974.

Stein, Gertrude. *America and Alfred Stieglitz, A Collective Portrait*. New York: Literary Guild, 1934.

___. *Gertrude Stein: Portraits and Prayers*. New York: Random House, 1934.

___. *Everybody's Autobiography*. New York: Random House, 1937.

___. *Personal Recollections*. London: Peter Owen, 1971.

___. *The Making of Americans: Being a History of a Family's Progress*. Dalkey Archive Press, 1995 [1925].

Steiner, Wendy. *Exact Resemblance to Exact Resemblance: The Literary Portraiture of Gertrude Stein*. New Haven and London: Yale University Press, 1978.

White, R. L. *Gertrude Stein and Alice B. Toklas: A Reference Guide*. Boston: G. K. Hall, 1984.

Exh. cat. *Gertrude Stein: The American Connection*. Stavitsky, Gail. New York: Sid Deutsch Gallery, 1990.

John Storrs

Andre, Michael. "John Storrs." *Art News* 74 (May 1975): 94.

Bryant, Edward. "Rediscovery: John Storrs." *Art in America* 57 (May 1969): 66–71.

Davidson, Abraham. "John Storrs: Early Sculpture of the Machine Age." *Artforum* 13, pt. 3 (Nov. 1974): 41–45.

Dinin, Kenneth. "John Storrs: Organic Functionalism in a Modern Idiom." *Journal of Decorative and Propaganda Arts* 6 (fall 1987): 48–73.

Frackman, Noel Stern. "John Storrs and the Origins of Art Deco." Master's thesis, New York: New York University, 1975.

___. "The Art of John Storrs." Ph.D. diss., New York: New York University, 1987.

Pincus-Witten, Robert. "John Storrs." *Artforum* 9 (Feb. 1971): 76.

Tarbell, Roberta K. *John Storrs and Max Weber: Early Life and Work*. Dover: Faculty of the University of Delaware, 1968.

Teilman, Herdis Bull. "Three Early 20th Century American Sculptors." *Carnegie Magazine* 51, pt. 3 (March 1977): 112–118.

Zabel, B. "John Storrs." *Arts Magazine* 57, pt. 9 (May 1983): 21.

Exh. cat. *John Storrs*. Washington D.C.: The Corcoran Gallery of Art, 1969.

Exh. cat. *John Storrs: A Retrospective Exhibition of Sculpture*. Kirshner, Judith Russi. Chicago: Museum of Contemporary Art, 1976.

Exh. cat. *John Storrs and John Flanagan: Sculpture & Works on Paper*. Gordon, Jennifer. Williamstown, Mass.: Sterling and Francine Clark Art Institute, 1980.

Exh. cat. *John Storrs*. Frackman, Noel Stern. New York: Whitney Museum of American Art, 1987.

Carl Van Vechten

Burns, Edward. *The Letters of Gertrude Stein and Carl Van Vechten, 1913–1946*. New York: Columbia University Press, 1986.

Byrd, Rudolph P., ed. *Generations in Black and White: Photographs by Carl Van Vechten*. Athens, Ga.: University of Georgia Press, 1993.

Davis, Keith F. *Passionate Observer. Photographs by Carl Van Vechten*. Kansas City, Mo: Hallmark Cards, 1993.

Gardner, Paul. "Carl Van Vechten, Culture Connoisseur." *On Paper* 2, no. 5 (May–June 1998): 13–19.

Kellner, Bruce, ed. *Letters of Carl Van Vechten*. New Haven: Yale University Press, 1987.

Jean Xceron

Exh. cat. *Xceron, Selected Paintings 1929–1962*. New York: Rose Fried Gallery, 1962.

Exh. cat. *Jean Xceron*. New York: Solomon Guggenheim Museum, 1965.

CHECKLIST
OF EXHIBITED WORKS
NOT ILLUSTRATED
IN THE CATALOGUE

BERENICE ABBOTT
PORTRAIT OF ATGET, 1927
(LATER PRINT)
GELATIN SILVER-BROMIDE PRINT,
33.6 X 25.9 CM
MUSÉE CARNAVALET, PARIS
MAAG

EUGÈNE ATGET
AVENUE DES GOBELINS, 1925
GELATIN SILVER PRINTING-CUT
PAPER PRINT FROM DRY PLATE
NEGATIVE, 22.5 X 17.8 CM
THE ART INSTITUTE OF
CHICAGO.
JULIEN LEVY COLLECTION,
GIFT OF JEAN AND JULIEN LEVY,
1978.1039
TMAA

EUGÈNE ATGET
*UN COIN DU MARCHÉ DES
CARMES*, 1910–11
ALBUMEN PRINT, 21.8 X 17.6 CM
PARIS, MUSÉE CARNAVALET,
PH 3716
MAAG, TAM

MARCEL DUCHAMP
ELEMENTS OF A *BOÎTE-EN-VALISE*,
1935–41
MIXED MEDIAS
PRIVATE COLLECTION
MAAG

MAN RAY
[UNTITLED], 1923
GELATIN SILVER PRINT
(RAYOGRAPH), 29.6 X 23.8 CM
THE ART INSTITUTE OF
CHICAGO.
JULIEN LEVY COLLECTION,
SPECIAL PHOTOGRAPHY
ACQUISITION FUND, 1979.99
TMAA

PIET MONDRIAN
*LOZENGE COMPOSITION
WITH YELLOW, BLACK, BLUE, RED,
AND GRAY*, 1921
OIL ON CANVAS, 60 X 60 CM
THE ART INSTITUTE OF
CHICAGO.
GIFT OF EDGAR KAUFMANN, JR.,
1957.307
TMAA

KAY SAGE
THE MINUTES NO. 1, 1937, 1943
CHARCOAL ON PAPER, 26.7 X 19 CM
MATTATUCK MUSEUM,
WATERBURY, CONN., KSCX68.42.01
MAAG, TAM, TMAA

KAY SAGE
THE MINUTES NO. 2, 1937
CHARCOAL ON PAPER, 26.7 X 19 CM
MATTATUCK MUSEUM,
WATERBURY, CONN., KSCX68.42.02
MAAG, TAM, TMAA

CHARLES SHAW
INTERSECTING TRAPEZOIDS, 1936
OIL WITH SAND ON CANVAS,
87.6 X 72.4 CM
J. DONALD NICHOLS
COLLECTION.
COURTESY GARY SNYDER FINE ART,
NEW YORK
MAAG, TAM, TMAA

JOHN STORRS
ARCHITECTURAL STUDY, C. 1927
PLASTER, H. 160 CM
MUSÉE DE MER.
COLLECTION JOHN STORRS
MAAG, TAM, TMAA

INDEX

The index covers all parts of the book except such supplementary apparatus as the preface, notes and selected bibliography. Page numbers in *italics* refer to illustrations and page numbers in **bold type** to catalogue plates.